# PERSONAL RELATIONS THERAPY

# PERSONAL RELATIONS THERAPY:
# THE COLLECTED PAPERS
# OF H. J. S. GUNTRIP

Edited by

JEREMY HAZELL

JASON ARONSON INC.
*Northvale, New Jersey*
*London*

This book was set in 10 point Goudy by Lind Graphics of Upper Saddle River, New Jersey, and printed and bound by Haddon Craftsmen of Scranton, Pennsylvania.

**Library of Congress Cataloging-in-Publication Data**

Guntrip, Harry.
  Personal relations therapy : the collected papers of H.J.S.
  Guntrip / edited by Jeremy Hazell.
      p.   cm. – (Library of object relations)
  Includes bibliographical references and index.
  ISBN 1-56821-164-3
    1. Object relations (Psychoanalysis).   2. Psychoanalysis.
  3. Psychodynamic psychotherapy.   4. Psychoanalysis–History.
    I.   Hazell, Jeremy. II. Title. III. Series.
    [DNLM:   1. Psychoanalytic Therapy–collected works.
  2. Psychoanalysis–collected works.   3. Psychoanalytic Theory–
  collected works.   WM  460  G977pa 1994]
  RC455.4.023G86   1994
  616.89'17–dc20
  DNLM/DLC
  for Library of Congress                                      93-33868

Manufactured in the United States of America. Jason Aronson Inc. offers books and cassettes. For information and catalog write to Jason Aronson Inc., 230 Livingston Street, Northvale, New Jersey 07647.

# THE LIBRARY OF OBJECT RELATIONS

## A SERIES OF BOOKS EDITED BY
## DAVID E. SCHARFF AND JILL SAVEGE SCHARFF

Object relations theories of human interaction and development provide an expanding, increasingly useful body of theory for the understanding of individual development and pathology, for generating theories of human interaction, and for offering new avenues of treatment. They apply across the realms of human experience from the internal world of the individual to the human community, and from the clinical situation to everyday life. They inform clinical technique in every format from individual psychoanalysis and psychotherapy, through group therapy, to couple and family therapy.

**The Library of Object Relations** aims to introduce works that approach psychodynamic theory and therapy from an object relations point of view. It includes works from established and new writers who employ diverse aspects of British, American, and international object relations theory in helping individuals, families, couples, and groups. It features books that stress integration of psychoanalytic approaches with marital and family therapy, as well as those centered on individual psychotherapy and psychoanalysis.

To Bertha

# CONTENTS

# FOREWORD

THIS BOOK GIVES US THE broad sweep of work of a remarkable psychoanalytic writer, one whose place is at the forefront of our efforts to explain the role
of an emergent and resilient self in the organization and maintenance of human
relations. I believe that a substantial part of Guntrip's discovery, his work on a
painful and bleak frontier that was simultaneously within himself and in the realm
of the science of psychoanalysis, has been absorbed into the sensibility of the field
with far less attribution and direct appreciation than is warranted.

In drawing together these papers Jeremy Hazell has offered us far more than if
they were ancillary documents. Guntrip's books are synthesized documents, each
with a purpose and organic whole of its own. To a considerable degree, that
synthetic achievement obscures the humbler path of theoretical and personal
growth in Guntrip's thinking, therapeutic work, and theoretical contribution.
Here, however, as we follow the individual documents through the span of
Guntrip's productive psychoanalytic life, we can see the unfolding and change, the
review and reworking of old themes undisguised by the need to produce coherent
texts with each book. It is here that we can trace Guntrip's personal and theoretical
struggle, his questioning pastoral and scientific mind, his ardent dedication to
personal growth for himself and for his patients.

There are few scientific or even therapeutic writers known for their passion.
Guntrip is such a person. Urgently personal, assiduously critical of friends and foes,
of his own analysts, and of himself, he cares deeply, on every page. Jeremy Hazell
has documented in his account of therapy with Guntrip the deep and pervasive
sense of caring in Guntrip's clinical work that also emerges on these pages.

The publication of this work is an event that has a personal importance to many.
Jason Aronson tried to get Guntrip to publish a book made up of these collected
papers during his own lifetime. Jock Sutherland hoped to bring Guntrip's achievement more into the light. I had the privilege of hearing Guntrip give the landmark
paper on his analyses with Fairbairn and Winnicott in 1973 at the Tavistock Clinic,

and have been haunted by the experience of hearing him ever since. Guntrip brought a unique intensity to the examination of personal experience in constructing and validating psychoanalytic meaning. His heritage draws directly on the tradition of Freud, whose personal struggles formed the raw data for *The Interpretation of Dreams*. There are few works of such stature in the annals of our work, few examples of the blending of life and art, life and science.

Guntrip's work, his life exemplified through his work, is one of them. In this volume, Jeremy Hazell has done far more than simply collect the record. He has done that, and he has allowed it to stand for itself. But he has done so through his own lens, through a depth of understanding and valuing that shines through. His introduction is a record of the interweaving of Guntrip's personal growth with his psychoanalytic understanding. It is a Baedeker of Guntrip's travels, a rich appreciation, a tribute, and a fine work in its own right.

Guntrip's work is important to us, perhaps now more than ever. The issues with which he grappled have come to haunt us in a time of ever more consciousness of the toll of social and personal deprivation, and of a growing awareness that our work is not concerned with egos — with the mechanisms of an autonomous mind — as much as it is with selves in relation to others. Taking from his teachers and colleagues, from Fairbairn, Winnicott, and Sutherland, Guntrip worked tirelessly to teach that it is in the depth of personal relations that we find ourselves, and that dedication to this process offers us what we have to give to our patients.

Jeremy Hazell has drawn together the record of this personal journey. He has understood it, absorbed its meaning, and given it to us that we may use it and expand its reach. I am grateful to him for his dedication, and for the appearance of this collection at long last, a work that will illuminate paths of new exploration in psychoanalysis for many years to come.

David E. Scharff, M.D.
Co-editor, Library of Object Relations

# ACKNOWLEDGMENTS

I AM PARTICULARLY GRATEFUL TO Dr. Jason Aronson, the publisher of this volume, and Drs. David and Jill Scharff, the series editors, for making this book possible; to Maurice Kidd, for his friendship, for first introducing me to Guntrip's writings; to Murray Leishman, chairman of the Harry Guntrip Memorial Trust, for his active encouragement of this project; to Molly Sutherland for entrusting to me Guntrip's biographical material, together with his correspondence with W.R.D. Fairbairn and her late husband, Dr. J. D. Sutherland; to Gwen and Denis Greenald for their unhesitating support of the work, and their kind provision of private correspondence and memorabilia; to Bertha Guntrip for her generosity and warm-hearted encouragement at every stage; and especially to my wife, Valerie Hazell, for her constant and indispensable assistance in the organisation and production of this book.

The thought of our past years in me doth breed
Perpetual benediction: not indeed
For that which is most worthy to be blest . . . ;
But for those obstinate questionings
Of sense and outward things,
Fallings from us, vanishings;
Blank misgivings of a Creature
Moving about in worlds not realised. . . .

> —William Wordsworth
> "Intimations of Immortality from
> Recollections of Early Childhood"

# INTRODUCTION

IN 1975, IN A PAPER PUBLISHED posthumously, (Chapter 16) Harry Guntrip recorded his experience of analysis with Fairbairn and Winnicott, the details of which put the whole range of his earlier writings into intriguing perspective. That paper was a greatly condensed account of a projected "psychoanalytic autobiography," for which Guntrip accumulated a great deal of material toward the end of his life. His purpose was to make psychoanalytic theory live by reference to personal experience.

By way of introduction to this volume, therefore, it seems appropriate to set the collected papers in the context of Guntrip's own search for understanding, which was so closely related to the course of his professional development. His theory always closely followed his personal experience, both his subjective experience in his own analyses with Fairbairn and Winnicott and his "emotional perception" of the experiences of his schizoid patients. Thus Guntrip (1975) wrote:

> [O]n the difficult question of the sources of theory, it seems that our theory must be rooted in our psychopathology. That was implied in Freud's courageous self-analysis at a time when all was obscure. . . . If our theory is too rigid it is likely to conceptualise our ego-defences. If it is flexible and progressive, it is possible for it to conceptualise our ongoing growth processes, and throw light on others' problems and on therapeutic possibilities. [p. 156]

It is not surprising, therefore, that Guntrip's collected papers reflect the progress of his own search for understanding. The earlier papers are the formal presentation of a determined struggle on the part of a man of exceptional intelligence to achieve relief from mental pain by means of psychoanalytic understanding, a process which, from the start, he felt to be inseparable from empathic personal relationship. His later writings reflect a growing sense of personal fulfil-

1

ment. For example, Guntrip's concept of a regressed libidinal ego, withdrawn in fear and repressed—clearly a defensive structure—came also to represent the individual's dissociated "unevoked psychic potential," his "latent natural health." Correspondingly, Guntrip (1968) came to feel that Fairbairn's "pristine unitary ego," which implied "a whole individual at birth," should be understood to mean "pristine unitary psyche with latent ego-quality" waiting to relate and grow in a good relationship, for he came to believe that "although the human psyche does not always develop a very definite ego," an innate potentiality for ego development is never entirely lost (pp. 249–250). In addition to Guntrip's major papers, reference will be made here to a number of less formal writings, which show the astonishing range and vigour with which he pursued any task that he felt should be done, especially where the inherent value of the individual or the reality of his subjective experience was in danger of being discredited.

Guntrip's own background as a Congregational minister had closely acquainted him with all sorts and conditions of men, women, and children on the level of everyday living, and his earliest writings exude a passionate desire to make psychological understanding available to them. Moreover, he had about him a rugged individualism. He was always questioning received wisdom and gave the strong impression that he would have been uneasy to find himself in the majority. His first psychological book, *Psychology for Ministers and Social Workers*, was published in 1949, following his resignation from the full-time pastorate, in order to take the post of long-term research worker in psychotherapy in the psychiatry department at Leeds University and to develop his fast-growing psychotherapy practice. In the preface to that early book, which he wrote at the request of the Yorkshire Congregational moderator, Guntrip set forth a definition of psychotherapy that he never saw reason to change:

> Psychotherapy is a cooperative effort of two people, in the dynamic personal relationship of the analytical situation, to solve the problems of one of them. In the end, medical, religious and social work is the recreative power of knowledge applied in and through personal relationships. [p. 11]

Guntrip began his psychotherapy practice in 1938 when his general practitioner asked him to take on one of the physician's female patients. Guntrip agreed, on the understanding that he should receive supervision from Dr. H. Crichton-Miller of the Tavistock Clinic, London, with whom he had been in analysis, rather sporadically, for the preceding two years. The practice grew steadily with the onset of the Second World War, and in 1943 Guntrip's work became recognised by Dr. W. Macadam, a professor of medicine at Leeds University, who referred to him a steady stream of patients. Macadam also invited Guntrip to lecture to the Leeds medical students, as a "Temporary Lecturer in Psychology in Relation to Medicine." Thus Guntrip was well placed to augment the new psychiatry department that was set up after the war, with H. V. Dicks as professor and it was here that he undertook the research work in psychotherapy that continued for the rest of his life. In his review of this period, Guntrip (personal communication, 1973) noted that the problems he encountered were those of

> increasingly ill people who did not respond, as less ill people did, to the interpretation of their problems in Freudian terms of the Oedipus Complex . . . [which] seemed often to explain satisfactorily the conflicts of later childhood, but the more ill patients seemed to present problems of a much more obscure and profound origin, the nature of which I did not then understand.

These proved to be "schizoid problems of failure of the very beginnings of ego or self-development in the earliest infancy period," before oedipal rivalries could have developed.

## GUNTRIP'S SYMPTOMATOLOGY

Through his attempts to understand these seriously disturbed patients, Guntrip was coming ever closer to the roots of his own problem. This was chiefly of two kinds: a profoundly debilitating sense of weakness ("ego-weakness"), almost of nonexistence ("ego-loss"), at the heart of his personality, and a "manic defence" of extreme cerebral and general physical restlessness by which he strove to maintain a "viable ego" in consciousness, often at the expense of severe psychosomatic symptoms and sleeplessness. He knew from family lore that the problem of weakness was likely to be associated with the death of his baby brother, which he was said to have witnessed at the age of 3½ years and after which he collapsed and was thought to be dying. Although he had an amnesia for that event, he could recall that after a short convalescence with a motherly aunt he developed a series of psychosomatic illnesses for the next eighteen months, compelling his mother to attend to him. These consisted of fevers, stomachaches, heat spots, constipation, loss of appetite, and refusal to eat. There is evidence that his mother responded to him during that period, making him a "tent-bed" and coming in to see him from the shop she ran in the front of the house, but a further change occurred when, at the age of 5, Guntrip was circumcised, without explanation, on the table in the parlour where his brother had died. The physical disturbances stopped and he became markedly passive and submissive. Perhaps provoked by his nonresponsiveness, his mother beat him cruelly, until improved financial circumstances enabled her to sponsor his growing interest in sports, music, and carpentry as he entered puberty.

Throughout adolescence Guntrip was aware of strong schizoid tendencies. In his adopted family, the Salvation Army, he was continually preoccupied by a strong need to be apart, and despite a dauntingly exacting workrate, expressed by ministering to others, by his late teens he was disturbed by "experiences of apartness, of not understanding people, and of being somehow 'out of touch' " (Guntrip's "devotional diary," 1918).

As he proceeded through New College and University College, London and into the Congregational ministry, Guntrip was assailed recurrently by severe states of exhaustion whenever he was obliged to be in his mother's presence. During the vacation before his final year at the university, when the departure of a close friend, Leslie Tizard, coincided with "being at home with mother again," his symptoms of "lack of energy, tight head and extreme photophobia" lasted for the entire vacation of sixteen weeks, completely debilitating him. The combination of his mother's negativity—for she was consistently hostile to his relationship with his wife-to-be—and the departure of a brother-figure would appear to have rearoused the earlier "tent-bed" illnesses though without the feverish temperatures.

These were the bases of Guntrip's symptomatology. His father, though he possessed a quiet, supportive integrity that Guntrip always deeply appreciated, was quite unable to constitute a strong personal presence for him either to identify with or to contest. That his father did represent some underlying hope or respite for Guntrip is suggested by the latter's feeling that it was only his marriage to Bertha Kind in the year that his father died that saved him from a full-scale breakdown into the "exhaustion illness."

With his father gone, however, the new marriage was more than ever exposed to his mother's consistently destructive presence. As Guntrip began his new pastorate at Salem Congregational Church in Leeds, his symptoms worsened to include sleeplessness and acute sinusitis, as well as two further exhaustion illnesses associated with the departure of professional colleagues. Some indication of the severity of these states may be gathered from the fact that Guntrip's period of analysis with Crichton-Miller was arranged at the urgent instigation of the surgeon who operated (ineffectually) on his left sinus, so that Guntrip and his wife felt it appropriate to take rooms in London for the first six weeks of sessions.

Crichton-Miller's analysis, along classical Freudian lines, did little to alleviate Guntrip's problem, despite the latter's strenuous attempts to conform to the diagnosis that he was a "mother-fixated narcissan," defending himself against an unconscious identification with his father's passivity. His symptoms of insomnia and sinusitis were diagnosed as a reaction to the continual effort to avoid his father's passivity by maintaining his personality on the level of his mother's success in dominating everyone, which he was assumed to admire. No account was taken of his need to be or to have a self of his own, or of the complex family situation of his early years, which had prevented such a development. It was a moralistic diagnosis that sidetracked Guntrip's self-analysis for many years into a spate of self-criticism for any sign of self-assertiveness, rivalry, or jealousy of others' success. It was clear to Guntrip that his own problem, as well as those of schizoid patients, called for a deeper understanding than this character trait analysis. When he came to reread his sessional notes forty years later, he was astonished at how assiduously he had accepted and applied to himself, in the therapeutic situation, interpretations based on instinct theory with which he was in fundamental disagreement.

In time, it was not only Guntrip's symptoms but his dreams (of which he kept a meticulous record) that called for deeper analysis, in terms not of an Oedipus complex but of a profound fear that if he once let up on his struggle to keep going, he would collapse as he did after his brother's death, alone with a nonrelating mother. What haunted him was not the threat of his father's passivity, but of a relapse into his own unmothered state of breakdown. It was not until many years, and two analyses, later that Guntrip came to accept and integrate that deeply regressed heart of his personality.

## THE FAIRBAIRN PERIOD

Guntrip was much relieved when, in 1948, a new professor of psychiatry, Professor D. R. McCalman of Aberdeen, was appointed at Leeds. In his first address to the staff, McCalman lectured on Fairbairn's object-relations theory of psychoanalysis. At the time, Guntrip described how the lecture came as a revelation to him: "It was exactly what I had been trying to reach in my theoretical studies without the equipment to achieve it" (personal communication, 1973). At McCalman's prompting, Guntrip wrote to Fairbairn, who sent him copies of all the papers he had written. In the following year Fairbairn accepted him into a training analysis, for which Guntrip traveled from Leeds to Edinburgh for two days and four sessions each week. Guntrip wrote: "Fairbairn saved the situation for me as a psychotherapist . . . [for] without that deeper knowledge I could not have gone on" (personal communication, 1973).

Guntrip's own flair for writing resulted in the publication in 1951 of *You and Your Nerves*, which was based on a series of radio broadcast talks. He next turned his literary attention to Fairbairn's work. In the course of the next eighteen months he sent the manuscripts of two papers to Fairbairn for his consideration. They were the manuscripts of the first two papers in the present collection "A Study of Fairbairn's Theory of Schizoid Reactions" and "The Therapeutic Factor in Psychotherapy." In the first paper Guntrip gave vivid descriptions of the schizoid state that were effectively based on his own experience as well as that of his schizoid patients. Many years later the American analyst Bernard Landis described how, when he remarked that these descriptions were "graphic," Guntrip replied, "Well, it's all firsthand. I know what it is," and went on to describe "an acute sense of feeling shut in, trapped and lifeless that it was imperative to rectify" (Landis 1981, p. 112). In this paper the depressed state was contrasted with the earlier schizoid state against which it represents a defensive struggle to maintain a sense of relationship and spurious ego-strength by hating, thus warding off a deeper sense of depersonalisation and ego-loss at the expense of pathological guilt. The states were due, respectively, to exaggerated anger ("love made angry") at the oral biting stage and exaggerated hunger ("love made hungry") at the oral sucking stage. Both states were ego-reactions to unsatisfying objects, and the solution to the earlier schizoid problem was seen as a gradual dissolution of the identification of the weak ego with its bad object by the steady maturing of the personality toward differentiation and emotional equality with the analyst.

In the second paper Guntrip described the therapist's intervention along the lines of a good parent. Avoiding the extremes of erotic mothering on the one hand and impersonal technique on the other, the good parent acts as a savior, freeing the libidinal ego from his internal bad objects who are "dissipated" by his love and justice, both saving him from gross anxiety and, most importantly, supporting his development from infantile dependence to mature dependence.

The effect of the manuscripts on Fairbairn was mixed. His response shows a certain ambivalence. For one thing, Guntrip's first paper covered much of the ground that he himself had prepared for the first chapter of his own book (Fairbairn 1952). Although Guntrip's manuscript impressed him as "extremely good," Fairbairn made it clear that his own material, which he had already presented in a paper to the Scottish branch of the British Psychological Society but which he had temporarily mislaid, was crucial to his book and that he intended to use it. In fact, he wished that he had taken it into account before writing his *Revised Psychopathology of the Psychoneuroses and Psychoses*, so that he should have "avoided some of the inaccuracies [that] crept into the later papers" (personal communication, August 1951). It would seem that Guntrip's paper was, to some extent, viewed as an example of the very identification to which it draws attention. Guntrip's second paper evoked a sharper response. While Fairbairn (personal communication, 1957) paid tribute to the paper's undoubted quality, he wrote: "There are passages in which you give expression to ideas [that] are derived from me, without due acknowledgement of the source, when such an acknowledgement would be appropriate," and he proceeded to list them. Regarding the transference issues, he was equally unequivocal. Pointing out that they would have to be dealt with in sessions, he wrote, "Whilst it would not be a good thing for me to play the role of 'castrating father' in reality, it would be no better for you to implement in reality the stealing of your father's penis" (personal communication, May 1952).

It is interesting that Guntrip comments upon this kind of oedipal interpretation in the paper about his analyses (Chapter 16). He had never felt helped by such interpretations, because they were above the level of his deepest trauma and need. His identification with Fairbairn and his ideas, rather, was evidence of his profound need to make good the weakness resulting from early environmental failure. To some extent he was experiencing in analysis with Fairbairn the same oedipal interpretations that his own patients could not use, and that thus not only prevented him from reaching and resolving his deepest problem, but also ensured the perpetuation of infantile dependence and identification.

Fairbairn was not disposed to look a gift horse in the mouth. Guntrip's writing was more fluid and readable than his own, and his intellectual energy, though driven, was formidable. Thus Fairbairn finally acknowledged the value of Guntrip's active support for his views and offered constructive criticism, adding that Sutherland, at that time the editor of the *British Journal of Medical Psychology*, was also favourably impressed. It was in that journal that the papers duly appeared.

All Guntrip's papers at this time were written during the long train journeys between Leeds and Edinburgh and were typed by his wife, who backed him in his long search. Guntrip himself was clear that he could not have received the same benefit from his analyses without Bertha's support, for which he was profoundly grateful.

The formality of the analytical relationship with Fairbairn gradually softened as time went on. Correspondence was frequent, and when Fairbairn's (1952) book aroused a storm of criticism from orthodox analysts, Winnicott and Masud Khan among them, Guntrip was strong in defence of his mentor. Fairbairn was isolated in Edinburgh and suffered attacks from within his own psychiatric and academic community there (see Sutherland 1989). It is not surprising, therefore, that when formal sessions were over, Fairbairn discussed theoretical issues with Guntrip. However, although Guntrip later stated to Winnicott that he knew Fairbairn best in his letters and these discussions, he was never able to achieve with Fairbairn the deep, therapeutic intimacy that he needed. Fairbairn had worked effectively with children and psychotic patients earlier in his career (see Guntrip 1975, p. 146), but by 1954 he had come to distrust regression as a form of treatment and repeatedly warned Guntrip of its dangers.

Perhaps characteristically, it was to therapeutic regression that Guntrip now turned his attention, and it says much for Fairbairn's generosity of spirit that he himself wrote to Winnicott asking him to send Guntrip a copy of his "Metapsychological and Clinical Aspects of Regression within the Psychoanalytical Set-up" (Winnicott 1954 in Winnicott 1958), a paper that was to have a far-reaching and decisive effect upon Guntrip. Characteristically again, Guntrip, while he was increasingly certain of the need for therapeutic regression both for himself and his patients, took Winnicott to task for his poor theorising, especially regarding his rather indiscriminate use of the Freudian id when referring to the basis of the personality.

What preoccupied Guntrip was the increasing weakness of the lost heart of the self that lay beneath the level of the exaggerated hunger and anger aroused by unsatisfying personal relations. It seemed to him that unless the schizoid patient could regress to infantile dependence in the security of the therapist's understanding, his weakness could not be redressed. Moreover, he felt that the problem of depression could only be resolved if it were acknowledged that the anger and guilt involved represented a desperate attempt on the part of a weak ego to negotiate from strength rather than from weakness. This acknowledgement could not be made if the basis of the personality was held to be an impersonal id as a source of innately destructive aggression. Guntrip himself regarded aggression as a constructive, energetic striving aspect of the primary libidinal energy of the unified psyche-soma for object-relating, with a capacity to intensify, potentially destructively, when influenced by anxiety, especially separation anxiety. Although separation anxiety could begin very early, he believed aggression to be a capacity of the psyche-soma for object-seeking, not a biologically innate destructive drive (Guntrip 1971a, pp. 133–139).

Despite their differences, Winnicott was able to encourage Guntrip's attempts to implement therapeutic regression with his own schizoid patients, notably, a case described in *Personality Structure and Human Interaction* (Guntrip 1961, pp. 416–417). Winnicott confirmed that Guntrip was justified in moving beyond interpretive technique to a nurturant holding of the more severely ill patient: "In more severe cases this probably becomes the main thing over a phase. Some people think analysis has been abandoned when the analyst acts so, but I am sure that these people fail with analyses that could have succeeded" (personal communication, August 1954). From these and similar deliberations Guntrip produced the 1956 paper "Recent Developments in Psychoanalytic Theory" (Chapter 3) in which he drew together Fairbairn's theory of "dynamic structure" and Winnicott's views on therapeutic regression, suggesting that "the patient may have a genuine need for a therapeutic regression in order to recover his 'true self,' " and observing,

> we are very far here from the Freudian concepts of the id and ego, but we are much nearer psychological realities. Winnicott has not suggested that his views imply a revision of Freud's scheme of psychic structure. But clearly the psyche-soma is not an impersonal id, but the primary, natural self, the libidinal psyche, and it is the "true self" with which the patient must recover contact. [p. 90]

The paper forms the basis of his first major psychoanalytical book (1961) mentioned above, with the proposal that "the elaboration in Great Britain of a different theoretical orientation" (i.e., object-relations theory) forms a synthesis of the Freudian "psychobiological" thesis, and the American "culture pattern" antithesis, by developing concepts of the internal world "as parallel to external objects in the outer world, and so comes to correlate the internal and the external object relationships in which the personality is involved" (p. 83).

The year 1956 was a productive one for Guntrip. As the analysis developed with Fairbairn, he sought to bring together the new orientation with his religious experience in a new book, *Mental Pain and the Cure of Souls* (1956). He and Fairbairn found themselves in agreement that psychotherapy was sterile unless conducted from a point of view that makes the value of the person central, and moreover that those who had been accustomed to regard life from a religious standpoint were more likely to take this view than those whose outlook led them to approach the individual as an organism. In psychotherapeutic terms this distinction was represented by the comparison between object-relations theory and process theory, respectively.

The same year marked the centenary of the birth of Sigmund Freud. Guntrip was ineligible to attend the centenary celebrations, since he was not a member of the British Psychoanalytic Society. But with typical crusading spirit, he published "Centenary Reflections on the Work of Freud" (Chapter 4) in the Leeds University medical journal of that year, drawing attention, among other things, to the fact that Freud's greatness as a scientist was enhanced by his "human neuroses" and his use of self-knowledge for the advancement of science. The parallel with Guntrip himself is clear. The research psychotherapist was finding that his true field of research lay principally within himself. Not only was this the only field of which he had direct experience, but he believed that it was the indispensable basis for understanding others – all within the setting of a therapeutic relationship, the only "laboratory" in which repression could be eased and insight introjected.

In this same paper Guntrip continued his argument against the depersonalising methods of Eysenck and the behaviourists, who, in their desire for scientific status, showed a tendency to reduce the patient to an oversimplified mechanism. By contrast, Guntrip noted true science is never static and accepts the psychic reality of each patient in its own terms as a challenge to further understanding. In this quest, he argued, the real issue was not the battle between instincts and cultural pressures, as Freud maintained, but "how can we best secure the growth of human personality to full maturity" (p. 166), an endeavour that was ultimately of greater importance for humanity than the study of nuclear physics. One can perhaps detect in these arguments the struggles of a nonmedical psychoanalytic psychotherapist working daily in academic departments of psychiatry and psychology, with their strongly organic and behavioural influence.

Guntrip's own perception of what constituted the best conditions for the growth of the human personality to full maturity emerged clearly in a bout of correspondence in the pages of the *British Weekly* (1958) with J. C. McKenzie, professor of theology at Nottingham University. The argument centred upon the ability, or inability, of the psychotherapist to love the patient. McKenzie, while affirming his faith in love as the therapeutic factor, maintained that, since the psychotherapist could not love his patient, psychotherapy could not be therapeutic; only the love of God in Christ could set the patient free from his guilt. Guntrip detected in this attitude the same avoidance of the patient's need that he had encountered in classical Freudianism. He wrote:

> I have had to treat two patients who had previously been treated by psychotherapists who were cold, detached and intellectually remote, believing that to be, as Professor McKenzie apparently holds, the proper attitude for the therapist. The results were disastrous. In both cases, the patients became steadily more and more frustrated and disturbed until at length they could not stand the situation any longer and left the therapist, the one in a despairing, depressed condition and the other afraid of an accumulation of pent-up frustration-rage which was becoming incredibly difficult to manage. [See Appendix One, p. 400]

Stating his view that the psychotherapist's attitude should be "a maturely parental one," which one of his patients had described as a "cherishing" of her, he added,

> It is the psychotherapist's responsibility to discover what kind of parental relationship the patient needs in order to get better. . . . The child grows up to be a disturbed person because he is not loved for his own sake as a person in his own right, and as an ill adult he comes to the psychotherapist convinced beforehand that this "professional man" has no real interest or concern for him. The kind of love the patient needs is the kind of love that he may well feel in due course that the psychotherapist is the first person ever to give him. It involves taking him seriously as a person in his difficulties, respecting him as an individual in his own right even in his anxieties, treating him as someone with the right to be understood and not merely blamed, put-off, pressed and moulded to suit other people's convenience, re-garding him as a valuable human being with a nature of his own that needs a good human environment to grow in, showing him genuine human contact, real sympathy, believing in him so that in the course of time he can become capable of believing in himself. All these are ingredients of true parental love (agape not eros), and if the psychiatrist

[sic] cannot love his patients in that way, he had better give up psychotherapy. . . . Very slowly, perhaps over a period of years, as patient and psychotherapist work together, the patient grows little by little out of the legacy of an unhappy childhood, in and through the medium of his relationship with the therapist until at last the mature human being can emerge into healthy and active self-expression and self-fulfilment. . . . Moreover, as the patient gets better, he or she usually feels perfectly genuine emotions of gratitude and regard for the psychotherapist [that] represent an important aspect of the "cure": the patient, whose capacity to love has hitherto been choked by hates and fears, is now becoming free to feel in more natural ways. If the therapist were to reject the patient's love at that point he would inflict most serious damage to growing normality and confidence. [See Appendix One]

Guntrip's true feelings were often more vividly expressed in less formal publications. The vital heart of his therapy was his profound concern for the patient as a person, and all his interpretations were guided by that principle. He believed that such an approach to the schizoid patient is likely to involve him in a therapeutic regression to a state of "primary identification" with the therapist, in the medium of which he may outgrow the original identification with a maladaptive parent and so be enabled to proceed with his hitherto arrested development. In correspondence with Guntrip, Fairbairn made clear that despite his belief that identification was the original infantile form of relation to, and dependence on, objects, he remained extremely cautious regarding the regression involved, having himself suffered from the destructive pressure of a regressing patient. Moreover, it is not certain that Guntrip himself could have undergone a therapeutic regression with Fairbairn even if the latter had been more encouraging. In his very first psychoanalytical paper on schizoid reactions, Guntrip (1952) had described one of the anxieties involved in dissolving identification as the fear "that separation is felt to involve, not natural growth and development, but a violent, angry, destructive break-away, as if a baby, in being born, were bound to leave a dying mother behind" (p. 98). At the time, Fairbairn's health was deteriorating and he was recently bereft of his first wife. Thus Guntrip's feeling of a need to protect Fairbairn in his bereavement and illness would surely have hindered his own differentiation, by making him acutely concerned about its effects upon his ailing analyst (see Guntrip 1975, p. 151).

Guntrip, however, stated that he did derive considerable benefit from his analysis with Fairbairn. Not only had Fairbairn's analysis of the negative transference revealed the "complex structure" of Guntrip's internalised struggle to compel his mother to mother him from ages 3½ to 5, with "all the fears, rages and guilts" involved (Guntrip 1975, p. 150), but it had clearly shown how the internalised conflict had been reproduced in Guntrip's sinusitis, to the latter's very great, though sadly temporary, relief.

Indeed, Fairbairn himself described how he linked Guntrip's sinusitis to his anal-retentiveness in childhood. In his valuable paper "Observations on the Nature of Hysterical States" (1954), using the pseudonym Jack for Guntrip, Fairbairn wrote:

> [B]oth these bodily manifestations of an emotional blockage were found to represent dramatisations of an internal situation in which his relationship to a dominating, possessive and frustrating mother was crystallised and perpetuated; and, when, at a favourable opportunity, I pointed out to him that he was dramatising a state of imprisonment by his mother in his sinusitis, the symptom underwent a remarkable and almost immediate improvement. [p. 118]

It was also part of Fairbairn's thesis in the paper that "the development of hysterical symptoms depends upon the simultaneous experience of excitement, on the one hand, and frustration or rejection, on the other, all in the setting of object-relationships" (p. 113). Accordingly, he sought to demonstrate, by reference to two of Guntrip's dreams in which carnivorous animals were being suppressed (by a mother-figure and Guntrip, respectively) that both an oral-sadistic and a genital component were involved in the conflict. However, Guntrip, while he experienced little difficulty in recognising the oral component, was inclined to associate a sprawling leopard with the suppression of a vital energetic side of his personality when his brother was born, rather than a specifically genital component. In fact, although Fairbairn claimed to have brought home to Guntrip the existence of the genital component, it would appear that the latter had no serious problems in that area, apart from a short period of sexual impotence after his mother first moved permanently into his home. Fairbairn added a footnote to the effect that, whereas he regarded hysterical problems as essentially personal, he did not intend to minimise the importance of the specific field within which these problems are staged. Guntrip, however, felt that, far from minimising the genital field, Fairbairn was unable to move beyond oedipal analysis, where he kept him "marking time on the same spot," analysing "internalised libidinised and anti-libidinised bad object-relations," thereby keeping them operative in Guntrip's inner world, "as a defence against the deeper schizoid problem" (1975, p. 147) of ego weakness or loss in a relational vacuum.

Thus, despite its very considerable benefits, Fairbairn's analysis failed to deal with Guntrip's "withdrawnness"—his feeling of being out of touch and cut off from other people—which Guntrip increasingly felt to be "a problem in its own right, not just a defence against [Fairbairn's] closed system 'internal world of bad object-relations' " (Guntrip 1975, p. 147). He came to believe that there could be little therapeutic gain from an analysis that identifies sadistic or masochistic love-needs on the infantile or any other level, "unless these are shown to be expressions of ego-weakness, the desperate struggle of the infant-person to remain viable" (sessional record of Winnicott analysis). It is probably not without significance that Fairbairn's disguised account of the progress of Guntrip's analysis appeared in print in the same year (1954) as Winnicott's paper on regression, in which he addressed the very problem that Fairbairn at that time could not deal with.

Guntrip gradually ceased bringing his "real experiences" to Fairbairn, but his gradual running down of the analysis was balanced by increasingly mutually beneficial discussion of psychoanalytical issues, both in correspondence and in visits whenever his wife and he visited Scotland to see her mother in Perthshire. The correspondence testifies to the fact that Fairbairn was much helped and cheered by this, and there is no doubt that Guntrip sharpened his own intellectual capacities in these debates, as the opportunity for the working through of emotional issues diminished. In a letter to Sutherland years later, Guntrip recorded his pleasure that he had helped to keep "Fairbairn, the thinking analyst, alive to the end" (personal communication, September 1974).

A further fact that drew Guntrip's attention to his increasing need for therapeutic regression was the death of his friend Leslie Tizard, the effect of which was a reemergence of the exhaustion illness. This happened shortly before Fairbairn himself almost died from a severe attack of viral influenza, necessitating a break of six months in the analysis and making his retirement a serious possibility. Guntrip, despite a heavy workload and increasing weariness, paid tribute to Tizard by editing and completing two books on which they had collaborated, *Middle Age* and *Facing Life and Death*, both published in 1959. These events impressed upon him the idea that the core problem for psychotherapy was the weakness of the ego, against which the sadomasochistic inner world of bad-object relations was employed as a defence, bad relations being preferred to none. The threatened loss of the ego in a vacuum of relatedness was, for Guntrip, the heart of the problem, and as his analysis with Fairbairn was finally terminated in 1960, he produced "Ego-Weakness and the Hard Core of the Problem of Psychotherapy" (Chapter 5). In this and the next two papers in Section 2 of this book, he tried to work out intellectually what he could not experience emotionally with Fairbairn. It was not only an intellectualisation of his state, however, for "spontaneous insights kept welling up at all sorts of times," and he "jotted them down as they flowed with compelling intensity" (Guntrip 1975, p. 151).

## SCHIZOID COMPROMISE

The exhilaration of these outpourings was considerably offset by what was surely a manically excessive rate of clinical work. During the period of Fairbairn's illness

Guntrip was seeing twelve patients a day, five days a week, and writing on the other two days. He recalled in 1973, when he reviewed his analysis with Fairbairn, that he had never felt so ill as he did during this period, except in 1971 when Winnicott's death triggered off the final work-out of his childhood trauma (see Guntrip 1975, p. 154). One can sense his illness in the 1960 paper on ego weakness as he asks, "What is it that leads to the perpetuation of a weak, undeveloped, fearful and therefore 'infantile dependent' ego? . . . It remains buried in the unconscious and makes no progress to maturity" (p. 170).

In considering the various levels of internalised bad-object situations, into which the psychotherapist must prevent himself from being fitted by the patient in order to "outflank them by his genuine regard for him," Guntrip arrives at "the problems of regression . . . the most difficult problems of all for psychotherapy" (pp. 176–181). Although he saw regression as forced upon the child by impingement (Winnicott) or "needs of destructive intensity" (Fairbairn), he was also aware of "purposiveness" in regression as a search for womb-security and "a revival of identification." Thus he came to formulate his extension of Fairbairn's theory of endopsychic structure, proposing "the deepest split of all, of the Libidinal Ego into an active, masochistic, oral (anal and immature genital) Libidinal Ego, and a passive, Regressed Libidinal Ego . . . of profound schizoid, fear-ridden retreat from life with its threats of depersonalisation" (p. 183). Although he later became dissatisfied with "regressed" and "passive" as descriptive terms (Guntrip 1968, pp. 215–216), his retention of "libidinal" for the regressed ego carries the implication that, however devitalised it may become, the regressed ego never loses its libidinal (i.e., person-seeking) quality — a point that some writers have apparently failed to appreciate.[1] The paper ends with a note of cautious optimism and a reference to Winnicott: the "closed system" (Fairbairn) of internal self-persecution can yield to "an open system in touch with outer reality, an opportunity to grow out of deep-down fears in a good-object relationship with the therapist," if the latter "can reach the profoundly withdrawn Regressed Ego, relieve its fears and start it on the road to regrowth and rebirth, the discovery and development of all its latent potentialities. This is what Winnicott speaks of as a 'therapeutic regression'" (p. 184). Winnicott published his own paper "Ego Distortion in Terms of True and False Self" (1965) in the same year. He wrote to Guntrip to ask, "Is your Regressed Ego withdrawn or repressed?" Guntrip (1975) replied, "Both. First withdrawn and then kept repressed" (p. 147).

---

1. For example, in *Object Relations in Psychoanalytic Theory*, Greenberg and Mitchell (1983) state that Guntrip makes "flight the predominant motivation in human experience" (p. 215) this despite his clear statement in *Schizoid Phenomena, Object Relations and the Self* (1968) (from which they apparently derive this view) that "the ego is always a latent potentiality in . . . the *human* psyche" and "*the human psyche is an incipient ego* . . ." (pp. 249–250).

However reserved he may have been in the analytic situation, Fairbairn, who read the paper in manuscript, was unreserved in his approval of it. He responded to it in detail and concluded,

> I consider your concept of the splitting of the Libidinal Ego into two parts—an oral, needy libidinal ego, and a regressed libidinal ego—an original contribution of considerable explanatory value. It solves a problem which I had not hitherto succeeded in solving. Your emphasis on the "purposiveness" of regression is, if not entirely original in view of Winnicott's work, at any rate extremely good. [personal communication, January 1960.]

In the same letter, however, Fairbairn once again made clear his reservations concerning the implications of therapeutic regression, for both patient and therapist, adding,

> Don't forget that these difficulties in the case of one patient gave Winnicott a coronary thrombosis. I think it is worth considering whether such cases should only be treated under hospital conditions, and whether responsibility for the regressed patient should be shared by the nursing staff. If these patients need an "environment," why not provide them with one?

With canny Scottish practicality he proceeded to wonder who, if the regressed patient had "to abandon all effort," would pay the analyst's fees.

In 1961 Guntrip published his first major psychoanalytic book, *Personality Structure and Human Interaction*, to be accompanied in the same year by a second seminal paper, published in the *British Journal of Medical Psychology*, "The Schizoid Problem, Regression and the Struggle to Preserve an Ego (Chapter 6). In that paper Guntrip stated that he was concerned "with diagnosis, not treatment," and he showed a caution that suggests he had taken Fairbairn's warning to heart. He confronted the problem that if therapeutic regression was specific for the cure of profound ego-weakness, it could result in the loss of the conscious, familiar functioning ego. The patient, having regressed, "faces the appalling risk of the loss of definite selfhood," so that "regression and schizoid withdrawal are one and the same thing" (1961, p. 227). Guntrip concluded that unless skilled help were available to enable the person to grow out of his fears of a good relationship as engulfing, a "compromise situation" (i.e., Guntrip's own position at that time) "is often the best remedy" (p. 230). As he wondered once more about the causes of schizoid withdrawal, he again regarded Winnicott's "impingement" as "more primitive" than "deprivation of needs," though both play a part in provoking withdrawal. He concluded that "probably deprivation in the sense of 'tantalising refusal' leads to active oral phenomena, while impingement and deprivation as 'desertion' lead to shrinking away inside into a passive state" (p. 235). Guntrip was surely trying to discern, for his patients and for himself, the precise nature of the bad-object who provokes withdrawal of the regressed libidinal ego, and to distinguish it from the type of bad-object who activates the active oral phenomena (i.e., oral sadism) in the active libidinal ego.

In a moving description of his own handling of two seriously schizoid patients, Guntrip moves closer to the origin of his own deepest problem, the loss of the ego in a sheer vacuum of personal relations, and to what he feels is needed from the therapist. In both cases it was the sheer warmth of his feeling with and for the patients, experienced in their dreams and in the external reality of the sessions, that forestalled the emptying or fading away into unconsciousness of the ego. Clearly Guntrip's feelings for his patients stemmed from his own experience of similar states and his sense of what was needed. Thus he ends the paper with a plea for a patient to receive "an object relation of understanding acceptance and safeguarding his rights with a therapist who does not seek to force on the patient his preconceived views of what must be done; but who realises that deep down the patient knows his own business best if we can understand his language" (pp. 239–240). He does not hesitate to cite some encouraging examples from his own practice of patients who were able to unlearn, and to grow out of, their ruthless antilibidinal self-driving, while simultaneously gradually developing

> a constructive faith that if the needs of the Regressed Ego are met, first in relation to the therapist who protects it in its need for an initial passive dependence, this will not mean collapse and the loss of active powers for good and all, but a steady recuperation from deep strain, diminishing of deep fears, revitalising of the personality, and rebirth of an active ego that is spontaneous and does not have to be forced and driven; what Balint calls "the new beginning." [p. 244]

It seems probable that Guntrip was aware in the early 1960s of a growing ferment of ideas about the therapeutic effects of regression, of which Balint (1952, 1959) and Winnicott were prime exponents. Thus in this paper he suggested that his regressed ego was "identical" with Winnicott's "true self in cold storage"—though he wondered if its "storage" may, in the case of some patients, be warm rather than cold, since they were so reluctant to leave it.

Guntrip's next paper, "The Manic Depressive Problem in the Light of the Schizoid Process" (1962) (Chapter 7) together with the two preceding papers, formed the basis of his second major book, *Schizoid Phenomena, Object Relations and the Self* (1968). The paper was regarded by Fairbairn as Guntrip's profoundest yet.

He wrote,

> I congratulate you wholeheartedly. . . . Your idea of a split in the Libidinal Ego has proved very fruitful; as I have already indicated, it is quite original. It is your idea, not mine. . . . I think your idea of depression being the result of a failure to put up a defence against regression extremely . . . well worked out. The same applies to your conception of the role played by the manic defence. I also like your 'Fight or Flight' idea, and your contrast between love and fear of relationships – also your description of the Oedipus Complex in terms of a defence against regression. Then I like your thesis that depression arises out of an attempt to fend off depersonalisation by internalisation of the lost object as an accusing object. Altogether I think your paper is magnificent. [personal communication, July 1961]

After this article appeared in the *International Journal of Psycho-Analysis*, Fairbairn noted two further marks of originality and difference from himself; namely, that Guntrip, in proposing that depression was bound up with a defence against schizoid withdrawal, had concluded that there was only one ultimate psychopathological state, schizophrenia. Guntrip had also defined mania as a defence against schizoid withdrawal, rather than as a defence against depression. These were strong signs that his identification with Fairbairn was now well advanced in the process of dissolution – at any rate, at an intellectual level – and Fairbairn observed benignly: "You may well be right," and pointed out that "many of the phenomena described in cases of depression are really schizoid – apathy being one." He added, "You are certainly right in regarding hyperactivity as a characteristic manic symptom" (personal communication, June 1962). Maybe significantly, Fairbairn did not comment on the clinical section of the paper that contained a case description involving a successful controlled regression of a patient who had been diagnosed as constitutionally manic-depressive and beyond psychotherapeutic help. The patient's condition closely resembled Guntrip's own state, as exemplified by his manic work rate at that time. However that may be, one can only admire Fairbairn's acceptance of the limitations of his own theorising and his generous support of Guntrip's advance.

Their correspondence continued warmly through the publication in the *British Journal of Medical Psychology* of another paper by Guntrip in 1962, "The Schizoid Compromise and the Psychotherapeutic Stalemate" (Chapter 8). The title accurately and implicitly describes Guntrip's position at that time, and for a good time before that, of which he wrote: "I have come to regard a prolonged therapeutic stalemate . . . as a very important indication of the severity of the deepest level anxieties the patient will have to face if he ventures further. . . . He dare not give up and he dare not let go . . ." (p. 277). He went on to describe the patient as experiencing the "most intense fear as the Regressed Ego draws near to consciousness," both "utter and hopeless aloneness and yet also fear of the good object as smothering. . . . In truth the need to regress cannot be taken lightly." Yet, "given time and favourable circumstances, this problem can be resolved in psychoanalytical therapy" (pp. 285–286).

In a sense, the paper conveys an accurate impression of this highly independent man contemplating the increasing need for, and the possible consequences of, analysis with a therapist who took regressive needs seriously. On January 17, 1962, Guntrip wrote to Winnicott describing his problem, his early history, and his experience with Fairbairn, whose serious illness in 1958 had presaged the gradual ending of the analysis. He enclosed his paper on manic depression for Winnicott's interest and wrote, "I have one further paper on the stocks and perhaps it is significant that the subject is 'The Schizoid Compromise and the Therapeutic Stalemate' . . . beyond this point I don't at present see particularly clearly and I feel that some sessions with you will set things moving again, to the benefit of both myself and my work." Winnicott responded warmly, and the analysis for which Guntrip travelled from Leeds to London for two sessions each month began on March 6, 1962.

## THE WINNICOTT PERIOD

By the spring of 1963 Fairbairn's health had begun to deteriorate again, and he felt moved to express his appreciation of Guntrip's efforts to promote his work. He wrote: "I am deeply indebted to you for your furtherance of my work. I feel I have passed the ball to you now; and I feel I could not do better" (personal communication, 27th March 1963). On December 31, 1964, Fairbairn died. His last letter to Guntrip was an invitation to stay at his home while visiting Edinburgh to lecture at the Davidson Clinic.

In his 1963 paper "Psychodynamic Theory and the Problem of Psychotherapy" (Chapter 9) Guntrip pays considerable tribute to the work of Fairbairn, who remained "the only analyst who has taken up the task of the *overall* revision of theory" from the point of view of the ego as *"a unique centre of meaningful experience growing in the medium of personal relationships,"* which, as he states, represents "an impressive intellectual achievement" (pp. 166–167). In the section entitled "Psychotherapy," he complements Winnicott's description of a patient who, after a successful oedipal analysis, requested "therapeutic regression aiming at the rebirth of the true self," with some further encouraging results of his own use of controlled therapeutic regression with his schizoid patients, who had "never grown an adequate feeling of a real self" (p. 170). Guntrip was fortunate at that time to have the cooperation of the medical superintendent of Scalebor Park Psychiatric Hospital at Leeds, who supported him in his treatment there of regressed patients, despite considerable criticism from the staff. As he knew all too well, "There is an infant in the patient who actually *needs* to be accepted for what he is, by being helped to whatever degree of therapeutic regression proves to be necessary . . . to nullify the results of early environmental failure" (p. 172). In a letter to his daughter, Guntrip described how one of his clinic patients had, "after a long difficult analysis, broken down into a regressed state and entered Scalebor like a panicky, sobbing tiny child. Now she's out and I'm seeing her every day, and she's reliving in a fantastic way a grossly insecure childhood in a bad, drunken slum home" (personal communication, February 1962).

The feelings that Guntrip was now taking to Winnicott were of a similar intensity. At his first session, after Winnicott had drawn his attention to the absence of a "true meeting" between them, Guntrip replied, "I feel there is a part of me that withdrew and regressed, though I don't really know what that involves, but I need to get that part of me accepted." At their second session the next day he said, "I realise I did ask the date of a paper of yours because I needed to hear your voice and place you." Winnicott replied, "You know about me but I'm not a person to you yet, and you may go away feeling alone and that I'm not real" (sessional record, 1962). This must indeed have come as a revelation to a man who hitherto had only seen and heard these feelings reflected in his patients' needs of and feelings for himself as therapist, yet which he strove to conceptualise and to meet by his own analytically guided "sympathetic identification" with them (see Guntrip 1968, p. 349 ff). Nevertheless, he believed that this matching of his patient's experience to be the only basis on which genuine psychodynamic research could be carried out. In the gap between the two analyses he had conceptualised the problem; now he was gathering the clinical material in his own and his patients' experience to test, confirm, falsify, or amend the concepts, the ultimate results of which were to be reviewed in his paper on his experience of analysis with Fairbairn and Winnicott (Guntrip 1975). Meanwhile, some of the material was included in a new book, *Healing the Sick Mind* (1964), an extremely useful and readable summary of the new perspective, upon which Winnicott wrote to congratulate Guntrip.

The analysis had moved on to a point at which Winnicott observed: "In some sense a part of you did die. You had an experience of death, and need to find out that there is a way out with me, from having to be one of mother's dead objects" (sessional record, 1963). In the silences of their sessions Guntrip was encountering the fear of "absolute ultimate isolation," which he knew presaged the emergence into consciousness of the regressed ego.

Winnicott was careful not to avoid his patient's need by offering reassurance.

He said,

> That illness is there, and in a way always will be. You can't be as though
> it had never happened. When it stirs, you can feel as ill as ever. But you
> can grow strong enough to live with it. . . . Patients regress with the
> analyst to find security and become strong enough to re-encounter the
> illness, the original illness, and get over it. Patients suffer acute pain in
> regression. You want to know if I can help you with your illness, and
> not just make you push it away. You may fear I might need to make a
> success of your treatment instead of helping you to be ill and get over it.
> [sessional record, 1963]

One can imagine that such a fearless confrontation of the problems of
therapeutic regression had a releasing effect on Guntrip despite the acute pain
involved. The compelling intensity of his writing eased, and Guntrip began to
engage more publicly in person in the psychoanalytic world. In August 1964 he
gave a paper in response to R. D. Laing's presentation on psychotherapy at the
Sixth International Congress of Psychotherapy, and he told Winnicott, "I feel I was
there by right of my work. My paper was well received." It is no surprise that the
paper, which was eventually revised to become part of Chapter 13 in Guntrip's
*Schizoid Phenomena, Object Relations and the Self* (1968), emphasised the need for
therapist and patient to meet. He wrote,

> It is not easy for two people to meet. The clearing out of the 'carryover
> from the past, transference and counter-transference' clears the ground
> for therapist and patient to meet 'mentally face to face', and at long last
> *know* that they *know each other* as two real human beings. Most
> therapeutic sessions are experiences of transient reality amidst a lot of
> unreality. Real psychotherapy does as much for the therapist as for the
> patient, because he cannot pretend to himself or play roles in it. If he
> does, his patient cannot find him and nothing happens. [Guntrip 1968,
> p. 354]

The influence of Guntrip's analysis with Winnicott is clear, for in his session at the
end of July, just before he gave the above paper, he said to Winnicott, "I feel now
I've got my central self in touch with you. You've understood and accepted, and no
need to talk now. I can relax and be quiet" (sessional record, 1964).

Guntrip wrote no major psychoanalytic papers between 1963 and 1967, when
the fruits of the Winnicott analysis began to become manifest, though a number of
minor papers show evidence of the gains he was making during that period. The
present writer has recorded his experience of an extremely positive change in
Guntrip at this time, during the course of analysis with him (Hazell 1991). In 1967
Guntrip had been able to recover an experience of "the basic good" in his family,

represented by his father's reliable integrity and some original maternal feeling in his mother, the feeling of which he found reflected in his growing sense of security in the psychotherapeutic relationship. Thus he was able to say to Winnicott: "Now in silence with you I find my faith in the indestructibility of my internal good objects, and can relax and feel safe" (sessional record, February 1967). A decisive stage had been reached, for it was shortly after this that Winnicott made "a striking observation" in which he confirmed Guntrip's value to him: "You too have a good breast. I'm good for you, but you're good for me. Doing your analysis is the most reassuring thing that happens to me. . . . I don't need it and can cope without it, but in fact you are good for me." Guntrip (1975) commented, "Here at last I had a mother who could value her child . . ." (p. 153).

It is not surprising, therefore, that Guntrip in his next paper, "The Concept of Psychodynamic Science" (1967) (Chapter 10), emphasised the immediacy of our subjective experience of ourselves. He called for a language specific for emotional experience and the building up of a clinically tested body of reliable knowledge to form psychodynamic science, which is every bit as real as physical science, when considered in terms of the new philosophy of science described by Karl Popper in *The Logic of Scientific Discovery* (1959).

In the paper Guntrip emphasised that not only does our direct knowledge of ourselves as subjects enable us to know others by identification, but also that this knowing of each other in an atmosphere of mutual significance constitutes the next great challenge to conceptualisation:

> Psychodynamics is the study of that type of experience in which there is *reciprocity* between subject and object, and of the experience of ego-emptying and ego-loss when relationship and reciprocity fail. . . .
> Object relations theory has not come sufficiently to grips with conceptualising this . . . the complex fact of the personal relationship itself between two egos . . . two persons being both ego and object to one another at the same time, and in such a way that their reality as persons becomes, as it develops in the relationship, what neither of them would have become apart from the relationship. This is what happens in good marriages and friendships. It is what psychotherapy seeks to make possible for the patient who cannot achieve it in normal living. [pp. 42–43]

It was also what was happening to Guntrip in his analysis with Winnicott, and as Bacal and Newman (1990) have pointed out, Guntrip's view of the self as a function of mutually satisfactory relations constitutes an effective bridge between object relations theory and the self psychology of Heinz Kohut (1971, 1977). From this point, Guntrip's theoretical writings begin to express, with increasing confidence, his "ongoing growth processes . . . and the therapeutic possibilities" (Guntrip 1975, p. 156).

In the following year, Guntrip's major book, *Schizoid Phenomena, Object Relations and the Self* (1968), was published to favourable reviews. It contained much of the foregoing material, illustrating the plight of the schizoid sufferer. However in two chapters, 9 and 13, on the "Ultimate Foundations of Ego-Identity" and the "Psychotherapeutic Relationship," respectively, one can sense the writer's own feeling of relief as the stranglehold of the deathly feeling within him began to ease and a feeling of genuine life began to flow through the aching channels of his "static internal closed system," as his driven serviceableness gave way to what Winnicott has described as a "capacity for play" (1971, p. 38). Guntrip wrote:

> The ego in its earliest beginnings is the psychic subject experiencing itself as "satisfactorily in being". . . . It starts at some point in the feeling of security and the enjoyment of it, as part of the overall experience of "being with mother" prior to differentiation of subject and object. *The ego is the psyche growing to self-realisation and identity, in the initial experience of identification and shared emotional experience with the mother.* [p. 250]

It would be hard to find a clearer description in formal terms of Guntrip's own experience with Winnicott. Perhaps the most striking positive gain from the analysis was Guntrip's recovery of his lost vitality, expressed in "being creative . . . producing something rich in content . . . using the object and finding you don't destroy it" (Guntrip, 1975, p. 153)—an example perhaps of pure aggressive energy, flowing creatively in the service of the libidinal psyche, free from fear and the need to react.

## THE POSTANALYTIC PERIOD

One effect of his analysis with Winnicott was that Guntrip was moved to reevaluate themes he had discussed in earlier papers. Thus, in "The Concept of Psychodynamic Science" (1967) he returned to the theme of his 1956 paper on Freud, where he first considered the place of psychodynamic phenomena in scientific thought. In his next paper, "Religion in Relation to Personal Integration" (1969a) (Chapter 11) he applied his new insights to his views on religion, some of which he had discussed in his 1953 paper "The Therapeutic Factor in Psychotherapy." Then he spoke of the analyst as an "exorcist" dissipating the influence of the patients' internalised bad objects by love and justice. Sixteen years later he was drawing attention to the need of the patient to discover with his psychotherapist a new quality of experience based on

> a different kind of knowing, like the mother's intuitive, non-intellectual, emotional understanding of her baby through personal relating. . . . This kind of knowing, which is more than utilitarian, involves experiences which cannot be *known* unless they are *shared*: experiences of beauty, of love, and of the religious or personal way of feeling our one-ness with the totality of the "real." *To be whole human beings, we must be both poets and scientists, both lovers and technicians.* [p. 329]

One feels that Guntrip's reaffirmation of his religious faith at this point was no accident, for what he experienced and thought of as "the final tragedy"—"the emptying or loss of the ego in a vacuum of experience"—was at last being dissipated by the reality of the therapeutic relationship and by the discovery within himself of the regenerative powers of the human psyche, the "incipient ego."

Around the time that the paper was first delivered at the Seventh International Congress of Mental Health in London, Guntrip had had a remarkable dream, which he told to Winnicott: "I was with you for a session. I sat on the end of the couch, and you sat on it and put your feet up naturally, relaxed, very at ease. You gave me a kiss, as a father would kiss a son with straightforward affection and I returned it" (sessional record 1968). This was surely a development of the positive transference, for Guntrip's father characteristically relaxed on a couch at home after his day's work. Guntrip felt that the dream experience represented an entirely natural relationship and, as he (1975) later wrote, he could hardly convey "the powerful impression it made . . . to find Winnicott coming right into the emptiness of [my] object-relations situation in infancy with a non-relating mother" (p. 301).

Guntrip produced a number of minor works on the theme of religion around this period in which his views were more directly expressed. For example, in *Psychology and Spirituality* (1967a) he gave an example of a patient who said, "I have two problems, first religion and my position as a clergyman. I feel I have lost my faith. Second, from my earliest years I have had feelings of insecurity, and of being unwanted and uncared for, so that it is difficult to have normal relations with other people." Guntrip continued,

> These are not two problems, but two aspects of one . . . problem. . . .
> The first revelation of God to a human being is not in Christ, but in the love of the mother before the baby is old enough to know anything about God and Christ. If the mother evokes the infant's capacity for loving, then he will be able to return love for love, and will grow up

capable of knowing what "Christ" means, of seeing in this human life a
manifestation of the indefinable things we mean by the word
"God." . . . God is met with by us in a human life, for "God is love" and
love is of God, even the unborn capacity for loving in the psychopath.
[pp. 99–100]

In another paper, "The Interpretation of Fear and Guilt" (1967b), Guntrip
described the difficulty of meeting a severely emotionally deprived person, who is
often "even more afraid of love than of hate," feeling that "in the end, loving
involves such intense, starved, hungry, greedy needs, that love is a devouring and
stifling thing." He continued,

Therapeutic or healing love holds back, without deserting those it seeks
to help, only approaches slowly, step by step, as the anxious person is
able to accept help. . . . If our love can win through to reach the
frightened heart of the shut-in individual, then . . . you may say that a
therapeutic success has been achieved, or a soul has been reborn, but
these are only two ways of saying the same thing in the end . . . when
scientific understanding and religious faith in the absolute value of
every individual human person are welded together, then religion will
not be the obsessional neurosis of humanity as Freud said, but one of
the foundations of mental health. [p. 47]

In his early years Guntrip had found sanctuary from the deadly atmosphere of his
home with the good-hearted members of the Salvation Army, whose generosity
transcended their fundamentalism. He never forgot them.

In 1968 and 1969 Guntrip was invited to lecture at psychoanalytic centers in
New York and Los Angeles. He found the experiences stimulating, though he
encountered some criticism from the more orthodox analysts. On his return to
Britain, he found that his reputation had attracted a great deal of attention, both
in his own department at Leeds and in London, where the Institute of Psychoanalysis (of which he never became a member) expressed interest. He was also in
demand for public debate with opponents of psychoanalysis. In the first of these he
responded vigorously to a talk on the BBC by Max Hammerton of Cambridge
(Guntrip's notes for his reply, "What Did Freud Really Do?," are reproduced in
Appendix Two). The debate raged for some months, with notable figures lining up
on both sides. In August 1969 Guntrip wrote to Sutherland, "I may be prejudiced,
but I think I had the best of both rounds!" Another public debate occupied the
pages of the magazine *New Society*, whose editor called upon Guntrip to reply to an
article by Eysenck (Guntrip's response (1969b) appears in Appendix Three), whose

reductionism was the antithesis of Guntrip's belief in the inherent value of the individual as a person.

These activities, in addition to increased lecturing commitments and the two overseas visits, eventually took their toll on Guntrip. He had concluded his analysis with Winnicott on July 16, 1969, and by autumn 1970, a year after his return from Los Angeles, he had contracted pneumonia, having failed to comply with a warning from his doctor in February. One of the precipitating factors was his determination to respond to an invitation to lecture at the University of Aberdeen to mark the inauguration of the Psychotherapy and Social Psychology Section of the Royal Medical-Psychological Association. The lecture, which formed the substance of his 1971 paper, "The Ego-Psychology of Freud and Adler Re-examined in the 1970s" (Chapter 12) took place in the month before he was hospitalized for five weeks. In that same year Guntrip published his final book, *Psychoanalytic Theory, Therapy and the Self* which was a written record of two seminars—one on theory, the other on clinical material—that Guntrip had conducted at the Alanson White Institute in New York.

The Aberdeen lecture, which also marked the centenary of Adler's birth, conveys a developing sense of personal freedom despite Guntrip's physical exhaustion at the time. The sense of the indomitable spirit of human beings, so evident in the papers on religion, is recognisable again in his reference to "*the other aspect of our existence* (i.e., other than 'behavioral') *our subjective personal experiencing mental selves, with our purposes and values, loves and hates [which] persisted in being there to challenge understanding*, and did not go unnoticed" (pp. 306–307). The tone of this and subsequent papers bears witness to his own experience of the rediscovery of his "lost vital heart" with Winnicott, which many years earlier had been depicted by a "tomb-man" dream (Guntrip 1975, p. 150), concerning which he said to Winnicott in the last stages of his analysis, "He remained alive and you have let him out!" (sessional record 1968). Winnicott had helped him find a dissociated aspect of himself, a latent psychic potentiality for living and loving that his mother had been unable to evoke. Whereas Fairbairn had postulated the existence of a pristine unitary ego as the core of the personality, with a more or less developed capacity to relate to the therapist as a good object, Guntrip (1968), in *Schizoid Phenomena, Object-Relations and the Self*, proposed a "pristine unitary psyche with latent ego quality" waiting to develop to whatever degree the environment is experienced as facilitating. He continued,

> [A]lthough all psychic experience, however unintegrated or disintegrated, must have some degree of ego-quality as the experience of a "subject" . . . the human psyche does not always develop a very definite ego . . . if no very specific ego forms, the human being struggles along

"in existence" feeling that his experience has no proper centre and no coherent ground . . . in the worst case he may be psychotic. . . . [p. 250]

Accordingly, in the Freud and Adler paper, Guntrip (1971b) made the point that the

psychotic [who] has been frightened off into a drastic withdrawal by seriously bad relationships, or even definitely shut out of all relationship by parents who simply did not want him and did not relate at all to him . . . [is by no means] incapable of transference as Freud thought. What he is transferring to us is his basic conviction that no relationship is possible; he comes to us "out of touch" and lets us see it and hopes we will understand, for as Winnicott (1965) says, in the very last resort there is always a "true self" deeply hidden away in cold storage hoping for a chance of rebirth into a more accepting world. [p. 314]

The paper made an immediate impression, and to his very considerable satisfaction, Guntrip was asked to repeat it, just over a year later, as the first lecture to the Specialist Psychotherapists' Section of the newly established Royal College of Psychiatrists, London, where it was enthusiastically received.

By 1972 Guntrip had recovered considerably. He was in demand as a lecturer both at the Tavistock Institute of Human Relations and at the Institute of Psychoanalysis, where he addressed the Independent Middle Group. While in his writings and lectures he was confidently asserting the factual nature of psychic phenomena ("phenomenological reality"), he was still concerned that their factual nature was not generally accepted at the academic and clinical psychological level. Thus in 1972 he published "Orthodoxy and Revolution in Psychology" (Chapter 13) in the Bulletin of the British Psychological Society, in which he called for an integration of an introspectionist study of behaviour patterns with a more personalistic study of behaviour patterns interwoven with spontaneous and creative functioning, which in turn should be linked with a psychodynamic psychoanalytic psychology of psychopathological phenomena, to form a unified approach to the person as a whole individual, with the mixture of relatively normal and varyingly pathological experience.

A further sign of Guntrip's returning vitality was his untiring effort to secure republication of Fairbairn's book to include his unpublished papers. However, the publishers would neither alter the original format nor release the copyright, and so this attempt failed. Guntrip, until the end of his life, was intent on representing Fairbairn's views together with those of Winnicott, and he pressed Sutherland to write a biographical introduction to his own account (sadly unfinished), which later formed the basis for Sutherland's own book *Fairbairn's Journey into the Interior* (1989).

As a result of the impact of his American lecture tours, Guntrip published two papers in U.S. journals, both in 1973. In the first of these, "Sigmund Freud and Bertrand Russell" (1973a) (Chapter 14) taking Russell as his 'soul-brother' so to speak, he muses upon the therapeutic possibilities, had Russell been possessed of Freud's psychological motivation and opportunities. Citing A. Ayer (1972), Guntrip notes that Russell, like himself, had had "a sudden revelation of the loneliness of the human soul" and had realised that "nothing can penetrate it except the highest intensity of the sort of love that religious teachers have preached," concluding that "one should penetrate to the core of loneliness in each person and speak to that" (p. 278). It is surely also significant that Russell, like Guntrip himself, spent the last years of his life writing autobiographical material "in a last attempt to understand and make sense of his life" (see Guntrip 1975, p. 153). Guntrip also speculated that, had Freud had Russell's bleak childhood, he would have progressed beyond the Oedipus complex and transference analysis. The paper created a sensation in the United States, especially in New York, and there were many requests for reprints from many other parts of the world.

In his second American paper, "Science, Psychodynamic Reality, and Autistic Thinking" (1973b) (Chapter 15), Guntrip again confronted critics of psychoanalysis with the factual, incontestable nature of psychic experience, drawing on the work of Harold Searles (1959, 1971) with schizophrenic patients in support of his argument. The paper ends with a most moving account, though regrettably condensed, of Guntrip's own work, over twenty years, with a man who was "exhausted, having screaming nightmares, severe chest pains, and fears of attacking his wife" (p. 21). The account carries the unmistakable ring of truth. Much of Guntrip's therapeutic work was at this level. It was small wonder that he felt an urgent need to draw attention to "psychodynamic reality" and that he reacted sharply to suggestions by physical scientists such as Sir Peter Medawar (1969) that psychotherapy was a comforting surrender "to a professional and stipendiary God" (p. 7). Such a view had no place in the psychotherapy of Guntrip, who early in his analysis with Fairbairn had to be persuaded by the latter to charge "realistic fees." But, with characteristic astuteness, he reminds Medawar that the terrifying confusion of the schizophrenic causes him to find himself confused by "a whole Olympic Pantheon of professional, stipendiary and often very bad Gods," so that he was not "psychically free to conform to Medawar's theories" (p. 20).

There is no doubt that as his own physical health began to decline, Guntrip's motivational energy was optimal. In the autumn of 1973 he wrote to his daughter Gwen, "I have enough publishing work on the stocks to last several years—possibly four books: Fairbairn's Collected Papers, my own Collected Papers—which New York Science House [has] invited me to send them—and two new studies of

Fairbairn and Winnicott, based on fascinating material from my own analyses."
The reference to Science House was made with regard to an invitation to Guntrip
by Jason Aronson, the publisher of this present volume, to submit his collected
papers for publication. Guntrip was keen to respond, wishing especially "to
preserve the Aberdeen paper and the American papers," but was prevented by ill
health. The present writer discovered the correspondence while researching Guntrip's autobiographical writings and renewed the contact with Jason Aronson, who
responded warmly after twenty years. The present volume is the result.

In the last full year of his life it was the reevaluation of Fairbairn's work that
most preoccupied Guntrip. Not only did he wish to draw attention to Fairbairn's
"rejection of 'psychobiology' and his changing of the entire philosophical basis of
psychoanalysis, as the most important post-Freudian event in its history," but he
also wanted to show "signs of gradual change" that led to Fairbairn's acceptance of
his own extension of his theory and to carry out "a study of limitations of the kind
that necessitates Winnicott's work as the real post-Fairbairn development of
'Personal Object Relations Theory' " (personal communication, November 1974).
In fact, Guntrip had covered much of this ground by reference to his own
experience of analysis in an address to the Institute of Psychoanalysis in London,
and, realising that time was against his desire to complete his "psychoanalytic
autobiography" he now decided to develop his address as a paper. It was this paper,
published posthumously in 1975, that set in perspective all the earlier papers
collected in this volume, which, however much they may be seen as the development of a man's thought, could now also be understood as a record of a man's
striving for understanding of himself and his experience through two analyses.
Guntrip often observed that analysis characteristically moved through three stages:
(1) oedipal analysis, (2) schizoid compromise, and (3) regression and regrowth. It is
plausible to consider these stages as corresponding to (1) his analysis with Fairbairn,
(2) the interval between analyses when he produced his "theoretical advance," and
(3) the analysis with Winnicott. It is into these three sections that his collected
papers seem to me most naturally to fall, together with a final section containing
the post-Winnicott papers.

In a sense, Guntrip stands as representative for all those whose early
experience was of overwhelming instability, weakness, and fear; who cannot
experience themselves as "pristine unitary egos" in relation to their objects; whose
feeling of weakness overrides their capacity to claim what they lack; and whose
sense of relationship, and therefore of self, is always tentative and vacillating. They
are not psychically free to conform to theories and therapies that assume an intact
ego in a relationship with the therapist. Because of the combination of a cruel but
indomitable mother and a father who, though largely passive after marriage, had a
quiet integrity, and because of his own inherited gifts, Guntrip found it within
himself both to stand up to those who sought to confine psychoanalysis to those in

whom good enough mothering had given rise to a unitary ego and to stand up for and understand the many who had not.

In "My Experience of Analysis with Fairbairn and Winnicott" (1975) (Chapter 16) he describes how the amnesia of his baby brother's death was in fact the touchstone for an earlier problem. In noting the absence of a genuine meeting, Winnicott was also in a position to introduce Guntrip to a deeper perception of the origin of his problem, which he had hitherto associated with the first exhaustion illness after finding his brother dead. Winnicott maintained that the origin lay deeper: in an earlier experience of maternal neglect. He said, "You must have had an earlier illness before Percy was born and felt mother left you to look after yourself" (in Guntrip 1975, p. 152). Winnicott went on to suggest that Percy's arrival had enabled Guntrip to project his need onto the new baby and to look after it in him; hence his collapse when the baby died. In effect the amnesia had served as a mask, not for rage at the birth of a rival sibling, as some have suggested (Eigen 1981, Padel 1991), but for the deadly feeling of the loss of the emergent ego in a vacuum, of extreme ego-weakness or loss with a nonrelating mother. In the gaps of silence with Winnicott, Guntrip experienced in the transference that original abandonment by his mother, and Winnicott, noticing his discomfiture pointed out that the gaps were caused by his mother's forgetting him, not by any lapse of his, adding, "You're finding an earlier trauma which you might never recover without the help of the Percy trauma repeating it. You have to remember mother abandoning you by transference to me" (Guntrip 1975, p. 153).

This interpretation threw an entirely new light on Guntrip's manic defence. His driven intellectual energy, which Fairbairn had interpreted as "trying to steal father's penis" (p. 152) by taking over the analysis, was seen by Winnicott as Guntrip having to work hard to keep himself "in existence"—in effect, fighting for his very life, as it must have seemed to him, since in his very deepest experience he felt no life-sustaining relationship, only an indefinite gap. As Landis (1981) has stated, Guntrip "just did not believe that an analysis of the vicissitudes of sadism and anger was vital for his cure . . . not the experiencing of an alleged infantile rage nor subsequent vindictiveness but the incorporating of an affirming analytic relationship was the heart and means of cure" (pp. 114–115). Winnicott had searched in vain for Guntrip's "sadism," perhaps because the latter's early experience had been too barren for him to be able to consolidate sufficient ego-structure to support overt sadistic reactions. Instead, his experience was dominated by that other ego-reaction to threat, namely, fear.

Ultimately, the crucial difference between Guntrip's two analytical experiences was that, whereas Fairbairn took the existence of the ego for granted, Winnicott recognised the possibility of its nonexistence in a nonrelating environment. Thus Guntrip, like another of Winnicott's patients, came to feel fully communicated with for the first time when his feeling of nonexistence was recognised (Winnicott 1965, p. 151). Winnicott had written about this early state of privation in the paper on regression that he had sent to Guntrip in 1954 (in Winnicott 1958) and in which he emphasised that if the need for regression is not met, "the result is not anger, only a reproduction of the environmental failure situation that stopped the processes of self-growth. The individual's capacity to 'wish' has become interfered with, and we witness the re-appearance of the original cause of a sense of futility" (p. 288). Masud Khan (1975), in his introduction to Winnicott's collected papers, explains Winnicott's belief that

> a person on the point of the need to regress can never *manage* it on his own, or ask for it, unless someone can sense this need in him and reach out and meet it. . . . [T]here are persons whose primary care-taking environment has been so deficient that what they *need* to tell happened when they had not the necessary ego-capacities to cope with or cognise it. They could only *register* it. Hence the responsibility of the analyst to reach out, *read* and meet their *need*. [pp. xxiii–xxiv]

So it was in the case of Guntrip. Articulate, intelligent, and determined as he was, the heart of his nature was held in check and he could only put himself in the presence of someone who seemed both to promise the warmth of relation and to understand his fear of it, and wait—as Guntrip (1968) himself wrote, "a potential self awaiting a chance to be reborn into an environment in which it is possible to live and grow" (p. 405).

In the 1954 paper on regression Winnicott had noted "the way in which the individual stores up memories and ideas and potentialities . . . as if there is an expectation that favourable conditions may arise justifying regression and offering a new chance for forward development, which was rendered impossible or difficult initially by environmental failure" (p. 281). It would be difficult to find a truer description of Guntrip, with his photographic memory and compulsive thinking and conceptualising of his state and needs, possessing all the equipment for personal living, yet always in the background the drag of unrealised personal potential. The fact that he was able to describe so exactly what he needed of Fairbairn (see Hughes 1989) does not imply arrogance on his part, but only the laborious rationalised articulation of an unmet and fundamental longing for personal recognition. It was ultimately the reliving of that earlier trauma with Winnicott that enabled Guntrip to learn that, despite her "paralysing schizoid aloofness," his mother had almost certainly had a period of initial maternalism with him and to find her re-created in Winnicott in the transference (1975 p. 152).

Guntrip has recorded his view that "the ego potential at birth must be given something, however small, to begin to live by or it will die" (personal communication, November 1971). It was Winnicott's ability to facilitate the growth of this early potential that enabled Guntrip finally, after Winnicott had died, to integrate the extreme and desolate experience of a mother "who had no face, arms or breasts. She was merely a lap to sit on, not a person" (1975 p. 154). Unmothered herself, and forced to act as mother to younger siblings, four of whom died in childhood, she had entered marriage almost devoid of maternalism and determined to make her way in business. Later in Guntrip's childhood she was able to sponsor financially his hobbies and interests, and one might reasonably argue that she "transmitted" to him also a certain determination to keep going at all costs.

Guntrip (1975) records "a mood of sadness for my mother who was so damaged in childhood that she could neither be, nor enable me to be, our 'true selves' " (p. 155). He also makes clear that without his wife's understanding and support, he "could not have had those analyses or reached this result" (p. 155). The degree of disturbance that Guntrip experienced would surely have tried, very severely, even the strongest of marriage relationships, unsupported by psychotherapy. He himself certainly felt that the function of therapy (at every level, but most vitally at the schizoid level) was to

> provide a reliable and understanding human relationship of a kind that makes contact with the deeply repressed traumatised child in a way that enables one to become steadily more able to live, in the security of a new real relationship, with the traumatic legacy of the earliest formative years, as it seeps through or erupts into consciousness. [p. 155]

The subtitle of Guntrip's (1975) paper raises this question: How complete a result does psychoanalytic therapy achieve? The tone of the paper is very much one of the recovery of a basic vitality and the development of ego-strength as a function of growth in personal relationships. At the same time, Guntrip points out that one "cannot have a different set of memories" and quotes Fairbairn's view that, although "emotion can be drained out of the old patterns by new experience . . . water can always flow again in the old dried up water courses" (p. 145). Moreover, "Psychoanalytic therapy is not . . . an objective 'thing in itself' working automatically. It is a process of interaction, a function of two variables, the personalities of two people working together towards spontaneous growth" (p. 155). He is surely correct in stating, "There must be something wrong if an analyst is static when he deals with such dynamic experiences" (p. 155).

But there are signs that Guntrip may not have fully appreciated the need for "phase-appropriate responses from selfobjects throughout life" (Bacal and Newman 1990, p. 170), for he does give an impression of an indissoluble ego-relatedness once it is adequately laid down and experienced so that it becomes "an established property of the psyche" (1971a, p. 117). Certainly, in 1972, when the American analyst Bernard Landis visited him, Guntrip was still exposed to "the dread of aloneness" with which he had had a lifelong struggle and which he described by reference to a recent dream: "I was floating in dark space, attached by a long ectoplasmic cord, reaching from my naval to a shadowy feminine figure. The cord became thinner and thinner and snapped, leaving me falling in space in sheer panic" (Landis 1981, p. 115). Perhaps the point is made that the greatest sign of therapeutic effectiveness lies in the growing capacity of the patient to believe in the possibility of personal revival in mutually satisfying relations with another person, and thus to see how it is possible to live with the disturbed experience to whatever extent it recurs.

Toward the end of his life Guntrip corresponded more and more frequently with Sutherland. Although they differed on some points of theory, Guntrip valued their friendship, seeing Sutherland as a surviving younger brother. Their correspondence was at times spirited, as, for example, when Guntrip was frankly critical of Fairbairn's structural scheme for sticking too closely to Freud's tripartite pattern. He wrote: "The Anti-Libidinal Ego/Rejecting Object only accounts for aggression as *identification* with the Rejecting Object, against the Libidinal Ego, but not for *direct aggression*, anger against the Rejecting Object. [Fairbairn's] Central Ego is left to be simply Winnicott's 'False Self on a conformity basis,' which is a very incomplete analysis" (personal communication, October 4, 1973).

It was certainly a feature of Guntrip that his capacity for forthright, hard-hitting argument carried all the marks of true, unrestrained conviction. He was extremely vigorous and unfailingly just in all his debates at the professional level, and never patronising. He never retired from lecturing at Leeds University, and, as a colleague remarked, he was always in demand since he was "clear pointed and compelling because, above all, he had a message to convey" (Markillie 1975).

Guntrip died on February 18, 1975, at the age of 73. It was agreed that Sutherland should collate Guntrip's writing on science and psychoanalysis, which he had intended to include in his Fairbairn book. Sutherland did so, with characteristic care and respect.

"Psychoanalysis and Some Scientific and Philosophical Critics" (Chapter 17) was published in the *British Journal of Medical Psychology* in 1978. The final section especially makes compelling reading, containing further examples of Guntrip's devotion to his patients' needs, which was always his first priority, and by which he sought to demonstrate before the scientific world the indelible reality of subjective inner experience as it was gradually tested and validated in the medium of the therapeutic relationship. However important he believed it to be to confront with psychic reality those who were "imprisoned in physicalism," Guntrip's main concern was with the emotional maturity of the psychotherapist as a person. The following lines from his reply in *The Listener* magazine (1968) to a broadcast talk by Max Hammerton form a fitting summary of his views:

> The problem of psychotherapy is not that it is not scientific; it has its own kind of science. The difficulty is that we ourselves may not be equal to its demands. We may not have the depth of understanding, sympathy, tolerance, and capacity to take the strain that is required to help a suffering human being to drop his defences and lay bare his crippling fears, in the confidence that we can understand and stand by him till he has grown out of them. [See Appendix Two p. 411]

## REFERENCES

Ayer, A. (1972). *Russell*. London: Fontana Collins.

Bacal, H. A. and Newman, K. M. (1990). *Theories of Object Relations, Bridges to Self-Psychology*. New York: Columbia University Press.

Balint, M. (1952). *Primary Love and Psycho-Analytic Technique* (1st ed.). London: Hogarth.

———— (1959). *Thrills and Regressions*. London: Hogarth.

Eigen, M. (1981). Guntrip's analysis with Winnicott. *Contemporary Psychoanalysis* 17 (1):103–111.

Fairbairn, W. R. D. (1952). *Psychoanalytic Studies of the Personality*. London: Tavistock.

———— (1954). Observations on the nature of hysterical states. *British Journal of Medical Psychology* 27:105–125.

Greenberg, J. R. and Mitchell, S. A. (1983). *Object Relations in Psychoanalytic Theory*. Cambridge, MA: Harvard University Press.

Guntrip, H. (1949). *Psychology for Ministers and Social Workers*. London: Independent Press.

———— (1951). *You and Your Nerves* (rep. 1970 and retitled *Your Mind and Your Health*. London: Allen and Unwin.

———— (1952). A study of Fairbairn's theory of schizoid reactions. *British Journal of Medical Psychology* 25 (parts 2 and 3): 86–103.

———— (1953). The therapeutic factor in psychotherapy. *British Journal of Medical Psychology* 26 (part 2): 112–132.

———— (1956a). Recent developments in psychoanalytic theory. *British Journal of Medical Psychology* 29 (part 2): 82–99.

———— (1956b). Centenary reflections on the work of Freud. *Leeds University Medical Journal* 5 (3).

———— (1956c). *Mental Pain and the Cure of Souls*. London: Independent Press.

———— (1958). Reply to J. C. McKenzie's article "Limitations of Psychotherapy." *British Weekly* #6, March.

———— (1960). Ego-weakness and the hard core of the problem of psychotherapy. *British Journal of Medical Psychology* 33 (part 3): 163–184.

_____ (1961a). *Personality Structure and Human Interaction.* London: Hogarth.

_____ (1961b). The schizoid problem, regression and the struggle to preserve an ego. *British Journal of Medical Psychology* 34: 223–244.

_____ (1962a). The manic-depressive problem in the light of the schizoid process. *International Journal of Psycho-Analysis* 43: 98–112

_____ (1962b). The schizoid compromise and psychotherapeutic stalemate. *British Journal of Medical Psychology* 35: 273–287.

_____ (1963). Psychodynamic theory and the problem of psychotherapy. *British Journal of Medical Psychology* 36: 161–173.

_____ (1964). *Healing the Sick Mind.* London: Allen and Unwin.

_____ (1967a). The concept of psychodynamic science. *International Journal of Psycho-Analysis* 48: 32– 43.

_____ (1967b). "Psychology and spirituality" in *Spirituality for Today*, ed. E. James. London: S. C. M. Press.

_____ (1967c). The interpretation of guilt and fear. In *The Role of Religion in Mental Health*, pp. 41–49. London: National Association for Mental Health.

_____ (1968a). *Schizoid Phenomena, Object Relations and the Self.* London: Hogarth.

_____ (1968b). What did Freud really do? *The Listener* August 29th.

_____ (1969a). Religion in relation to personal integration. *British Journal of Medical Psychology* 42: 322–333.

_____ (1969b). Response to Eysenck's paper "Behaviour Therapy Versus Psychotherapy." *New Society.*

_____ (1971a). *Psychoanalytic Theory, Therapy and the Self.* London: Hogarth.

_____ (1971b). The ego psychology of Freud and Adler re-examined in the 1970s. *British Journal of Medical Psychology* 44:305–318.

_____ (1972). Orthodoxy and revolution in psychology. *Bulletin of the British Psychological Society* 25:275–280.

_____ (1973a). Sigmund Freud and Bertrand Russell. *Journal of Contemporary Psychoanalysis* 9:(3): XX–X.

_____ (1973b). Science, psychodynamic reality and autistic thinking. *Journal of the American Academy of Psychoanalysis* 1(1): 3–22.

_____ (1975). My experience of analysis with Fairbairn and Winnicott. *International Review of Psychoanalysis* 2:145–156.

_____ (1978). Psychoanalysis and some scientific and philosophical critics. *British Journal of Medical Psychology* 51:207–224.

Hazell, J. (1991). Reflections on my experience of psychoanalysis with Guntrip. *Contemporary Psychoanalysis* 27 (1):148–166.

Hughes, J. (1989). *Reshaping the Psychoanalytic Domain.* University of California Press.

Khan, M. (1975). Introduction. In D. W. Winnicott, *Through Paediatrics to Psychoanalysis*, pp. xi–xlix. London: Hogarth.

Kohut, H. (1971). *The Analysis of the Self.* New York: International Universities Press.

_____ (1977). *The Restoration of the Self.* New York: International Universities Press.

Landis, B. (1981). Discussions with Harry Guntrip. *Contemporary Psychoanalysis* 17(1):112–117.

Markillie, R. (1975). Obituary. *Leeds University Journal*, February.

Medawar, P. (1969). *Induction and Intuition in Scientific Thought*. London: Methuen.

Padel, J. (1991). Fairbairn's thought on the relationship of inner and outer worlds. *Free Association* 2(24):589–615.

Popper, K. (1959). *The Logic of Scientific Discovery*. London: Hutchinson.

Searles, H. (1959). Integration and differentiation in schizophremia. *British Journal of Medical Psychology* 32: 261–281.

_____ (1971). Pathologic symbiosis and autism. In *The Name of Life*, ed. B. Landis and Tauber. New York: Holt, Rinehart and Winston.

Sutherland, J. D. (1989). *Fairbairn's Journey into the Interior*. London: Free Association Books.

Tizard, L. (1959). *Facing Life and Death*. London: Allen and Unwin.

Tizard, L. and Guntrip, H. (1959). *Middle Age*. London: Allen and Unwin.

Winnicott, D. W. (1958). *Through Paediatrics to Psychoanalysis*. London: Hogarth.

_____ (1965). *The Maturational Processes and the Facilitating Environment*. London: Hogarth.

_____ (1971). *Playing and Reality*. London: Tavistock.

# Section I

## 1952–1958
# THE FAIRBAIRN PERIOD OF "BROADLY OEDIPAL" ANALYSIS

# 1

# EARLY PERCEPTIONS OF THE SCHIZOID PROBLEM[1]

## THE SCHIZOID CONDITION

The psychotherapist must be greatly concerned with those states of mind in which patients become inaccessible emotionally, when the patient seems to be bodily present but mentally absent. A patient, A, recently said 'I don't seem to come here' as if she came in body but did not bring herself with her. She found herself in the same state of mind when she asked the young man next door to go for a walk with her. He did and she became tired, dull, unable to talk; she commented: 'It was the same as when I come here: I don't seem to be present.' Her reactions to food were similar. She would long for a nice meal and sit down to it and find her appetite gone, as if she had nothing to do with eating. One patient, B, dreamed: 'My husband and I came to see you and he explained that I wasn't here because I'd gone to hospital.' Complaints of feeling cut off, shut off, out of touch, feeling apart or strange, of things being out of focus or unreal, of not feeling one with people, or of the point having gone out of life, interest flagging, things seeming futile and meaningless, all describe in various ways this state of mind. Patients often call it 'depression', but it lacks the heavy, black, inner sense of brooding, of anger and of guilt, which are not difficult to discover in depression. Depression is really a more extraverted state of mind, in which the patient is struggling not to break out into angry and aggressive behavior. The states described above are rather the 'schizoid states'. They are definitely introverted.

External relationships seem to have been emptied by a massive withdrawal of the real libidinal self. Effective mental activity has disappeared into a hidden inner world; the patient's conscious ego is emptied of vital feeling and action, and seems

---

1. Expanded from a paper read at the Clinical Discussion Group, Leeds Department of Psychiatry, June 16, 1951.

to have become unreal. You may catch glimpses of intense activity going on in the inner world through dreams and phantasies, but the patient's conscious ego merely reports these as if it were a neutral observer not personally involved in the inner drama of which it is a detached spectator. The attitude to the outer world is the same; *non-involvement and observation at a distance without any feeling*, like that of a press reporter describing a social gathering of which he is not a part, in which he has no personal interest, and by which he is bored. When a schizoid state supervenes, the conscious ego appears to be in a state of suspended animation in between two worlds, internal and external and having no real relationships with either of them. It has decreed an emotional and impulsive standstill, on the basis of keeping out of affective range and being unmoved.

These schizoid states may alternate with depression, and at times seem to be rather confusingly mixed with it so that both schizoid and depressive signs appear. They are of all degrees of intensity ranging from transient moods that come and go during a session, to states that persist over a long period, when they show very clearly and distinctly the specific schizoid traits.

An example of a patient, C, describing herself as depressed when she is really schizoid may be useful at this point. She opened the session by saying: 'I'm very depressed. I've been just sitting and couldn't get out of the chair. There seemed no purpose anywhere, the future blank. I'm very bored and want a big change. I feel hopeless, resigned, no way out, stuck. I'm wondering how I can manage somehow just to get around and put up with it.' (Analyst: 'Your solution is to damp everything down, don't feel anything, give up all real relationship to people on an emotional level, and just "do things" in a mechanical way, be a robot.') Her reaction brought out clearly the schizoid trait: 'Yes, I felt I didn't care, didn't register anything. Then I felt alarmed, felt this was dangerous. If I hadn't made myself do something I'd have just sat, not bothered, not interested.' (Analyst: 'That's your reaction in analysis to me: don't be influenced, don't be moved, don't be lured into reacting to me.') Her reply was: 'If I were moved at all, I'd feel very annoyed with you. I hate and detest you for making me feel like this. The more I'm inclined to be drawn towards you, the more I feel a fool, undermined.'

The mere fact of the analyst's presence as another human being with whom she needed to be emotionally real, i.e. express what she was actually feeling, created an emotional crisis in her with which she could only deal by abolishing the relationship. So her major defence against her anxieties is to keep herself emotionally out of reach, inaccessible, and keep everyone at arm's length. She once said: 'I'd rather hate you than love you', but this goes even further. She will neither love nor hate, she won't feel anything at all, and outwardly in sessions often appears lazy, bored at coming, and with a 'laissez faire' attitude. This then is the problem we seek to understand. What is really happening to these patients and why?

## FAIRBAIRN'S THEORY OF SCHIZOID REACTIONS

The purpose of this paper is to state Fairbairn's theory of schizoid reactions and to illustrate it by clinical material. His revolutionary rethinking of psycho-analytical theory was first presented as a recasting of the classic libido theory and as a revised psychopathology of the psychoses and psycho-neuroses. Only two points in his theory need to be mentioned here.

1. First he laid it down that the goal of the individual's libido is not pleasure, or merely subjective gratification, but the object itself. He says: 'Pleasure is the sign-post to the object' (1941, p. 255). The fundamental fact about human nature is our libidinal drive towards good object-relationships. The key biological formula is the adaptation of the organism to the environment. The key psychological formula is the relationship of the person to the human environment. The significance of human living lies in object-relationships, and only in such terms can our life be said to have a meaning.

Quite specially in this region lie the schizoid's problems. He is driven by anxiety to cut off all object-relations. Our needs, fears, frustrations, resentments and anxieties in our inevitable quest for good objects are the real problem in psychopathology, because they are the real problem in life itself. When difficulties in achieving and maintaining good object-relations are too pronounced, and human relations are attended with too great anxiety and conflict, desperate efforts are often made to deny and eliminate this basic need. People go into their shell, bury themselves in work of an impersonal nature, abolish relations with actual people so far as they can and devote themselves to abstractions, ideals, theories, organizations,[2] and so on. In the nature of the case these manoeuvres cannot succeed and always end disastrously, since they are an attempt to deny our very nature itself. Clearly we cannot do that and remain healthy.

The more people cut themselves off from human relations in the outer world, the more they are driven back on object-relations in their inner mental world, till the psychotic lives only in his inner world. But it is still a world of object-relations. We are constitutionally incapable of living as isolated units. The real loss of all objects would be equivalent to psychic death. Karen Horney (1946) says: 'Neuroses are generated by disturbances in human relationships.' But Horney thinks only in terms of relations to external objects at the conscious level. The real heart of the matter is a far less obvious danger, a repressed world of internalized psychic objects, bad objects, and 'bad-object situations'. What is new in all this is the theory of

---

2. This does not imply that such activities are necessarily always schizoid. That depends on how much personal feeling enters into the activity.

internal objects as developed in more elaborate form by Melanie Klein and Fairbairn, and the fact that Fairbairn makes object-relations, not instinctual impulses, the prior and important thing. It is the object that is the real goal of the libidinal drive. We seek persons not pleasures. Impulses are not psychic entities but reactions of an ego to objects.

What is meant by a world of internal objects may be expressed as follows: in some sense we retain all our experience in life and 'carry things in our minds'. If we did not, we would lose all continuity with our past, would only be able to live from moment to moment like butterflies alighting and flitting away, and no relationships or experiences could have any permanent values for us. Thus in some sense everything is mentally internalized, retained and inwardly possessed; that is our only defence against complete discontinuity in living, a distressing example of which we see in the man who loses his memory, and is consciously uprooted.

But things are mentally internalized and retained in two different ways which we call respectively *memory* and *internal objects*. Good objects are, in the first place, mentally internalized and retained only as memories. They are enjoyed at the time, the experience is satisfying and leaves no problems, and can later on be looked back to and reflected on with pleasure. In the case of a continuing good-object relationship of major importance as with a parent or marriage partner, we have a combination of memories of the happy past and confidence in the continuing possession of the good object in an externally real sense in the present and future. There is no reason here for setting up internalized objects. Outer experience suffices to meet our needs. On this point Fairbairn differs from Melanie Klein.

Objects are only internalized in a more radical way when the relationship turns into a bad-object situation through, say, the object changing or dying. When someone we need and love ceases to love us, or behaves in such a way that we interpret it as cessation of love, that person becomes, in an emotional, libidinal sense, a bad object. This happens to a child when his mother refuses the breast, weans the baby, or is cross, impatient and punitive, or is absent temporarily or for a longer period through illness, or permanently through death: it also happens when the person we need is emotionally detached and aloof and unresponsive. All that is experienced as frustration of the most important of all needs, as rejection and desertion or else as persecution and attack. Then the lost object, now become a bad object, is mentally internalized in a much more vital and fundamental sense than memory. Bereaved people dream vividly of the lost loved one, even years afterwards, as still actually alive. A patient, beset by a life-long fear of dying, was found under analysis, to be persistently dreaming of dead men in coffins. In one dream, the coffined figure was behind a curtain and his mind was on it all the time while he was busy in the dream with cheerful social activities. A fatal inner attraction to, and attachment to, the dead man threatened him and set up an actual fear of dying. The dead man was his father as he had seen him actually in his coffin. Another patient had a nightmare of his mother violently losing her temper with him, after she had been dead twelve years. *An inner psychic world* (see Riviere 1952) *has been set up duplicating the original situation, but it is an unhappy world in which one is tied to bad objects and feeling therefore always frustrated, hungry, angry, and guilty, and profoundly anxious.*

It is bad-objects which are internalized, because we cannot accept their badness and yet cannot give them up, cannot leave them alone, cannot master and control them in outer reality and so keep on struggling to possess them, alter them and compel them to change into good objects, in our inner psychic world. They never do change. In our inner unconscious world where we repress and lock away very early in life our original bad objects, they remain always rejecting, indifferent or hostile to us according to our actual outer experience. It must be emphasized that these internalized objects are not just phantasies. The child is emotionally identified with his objects, and when he mentally incorporates them he remains identified with them and they become part and parcel of the very psychic structure of his personality. The phantasies in which internal objects reveal their existence to consciousness are activities of the structures which constitute the internal objects. Objects are only internalized later in life in this radical way by fusion with already existing internal-object structures. In adult life situations in outer reality are unconsciously interpreted in the light of these situations persisting in unconscious, inner, and purely psychic reality. We live in the outer world with the emotions generated in the inner one. The fundamental psychopathological problem is: how do people deal with their internalized bad objects, to what extent do they feel identified with them, and how do they complicate relations with external objects. It is the object all the time that matters, whether external or internal, not pleasure.

2. From this point of view Fairbairn constructed a revised theory of the psychoses and psychoneuroses, the second point relevant for our purpose. In the orthodox Freud-Abraham view, these illnesses were due to arrests of libidinal development at fixation points in the first five years: schizophrenia at the oral sucking stage, manic-depression at the oral biting stage, paranoia at the early anal; obsessions at the late anal; and hysteria at the phallic or early genital stages. Fairbairn proposed a totally different view, based not on the fate of libidinal impulses, but on the nature of relationships with internal bad objects. For him, *the schizoid and depressive states are the two fundamental types of reaction in bad-object relationships, the two basic or ultimate dangers to be escaped from.* They originate in the difficulties experienced in object-relationships in the oral stage of absolute infantile dependence and he treats of paranoia, obsessions, hysteria and phobias as four different defensive techniques for dealing with internal bad objects so as to master them and ward off a relapse into the depressed or schizoid states of mind. This makes intelligible the fact that patients ring the changes actually on paranoid, obsessional, hysteric and phobic reactions even if any particular patient predomi-

nantly favours one technique most of the time. The psychoneuroses are, basically, defences against internal bad-object situations which would otherwise set up depressive or schizoid states; though these situations are usually re-activated by a bad external situation.

Thus what has to be done in deep treatment is to help the patient to drop these unsatisfactory techniques which never solve the problem, and find courage to become conscious of what lies behind these symptom-producing struggles with internal bad objects; in other words, to risk going back into the basic bad-object situations in which they feel they are succumbing to one or other of the two ultimate psychic dangers, depression or schizoid loss of affect. Naturally depressive and schizoid reactions constantly break through into consciousness, in varying degrees of severity, in spite of defences.

3. The nature of the two ultimately dangerous situations may be simply described. When you want love from a person who will not give it and so becomes a bad object to you, you can react in either or both of two ways. You may become angry and enraged at the frustration and want to make an aggressive attack on the bad object to force it to become good and stop frustrating you: like a small child who cannot get what it wants from the mother and who flies into a temper-tantrum and hammers on her with his little fists. This is the problem of hate or love made angry. It is an attack on a hostile, rejecting, actively refusing bad-object. It leads to *depression* for it rouses the fear that one's hate will destroy the very person one needs and loves.

But there is an earlier and more basic reaction. When you cannot get what you want from the person you need, instead of getting angry you may simply go on getting more and more hungry, and full of a sense of painful craving, and a longing to get total and complete possession of your love-object so that you cannot be left to starve. *Love made hungry* is the *schizoid* problem and it rouses the terrible fear that one's love has become so devouring and incorporative that love itself has become destructive. Depression is the fear of loving lest one's hate should destroy. Schizoid aloofness is the fear of loving lest one's love should destroy, which is far worse.

This difference of the two attitudes goes along with a difference in appearance, so to speak, of the object. The schizoid sees the object as a desirable deserter, or as Fairbairn calls it, an exciting *needed object*[3] whom he must go after hungrily but then draw back from lest he should devour and destroy it in his desperately intense need to get total possession of it. The depressive sees the object as a hateful denier, or in Fairbairn's term a *rejecting object* to be destroyed out of the way to make room for a good-object. Thus one patient constantly dreams of wanting a woman who goes away and leaves him, while another dreams of furious, murderous anger against a sinister person who robs him or gets between him and what he

---

3. Fairbairn now prefers simply the term 'Exciting Object' (E.O.).

wants. The schizoid is hungry for a desirable deserter, the depressive is murderous against a hateful robber.

Thus the two fundamental forms of internal bad objects are, in Fairbairn's terminology, the needed object and the rejecting object. In the course of years many externally real figures of both sexes may be absorbed, by layering and fusion, into these two internal bad objects, but at bottom they remain always two aspects of the breast-mother. They are always there, and parts of the ego (split off, disowned, secondary or subsidiary 'selves') are always having disturbing relationships with them, so that the depressive is always being goaded to anger, and the schizoid always being tantalized and made hungry.

The depressive position is later and more developed than the schizoid, for it is ambivalent. The hateful robber is really an aspect of the same person who is needed and desired, as if the mother excites the child's longing for her, gives him just enough to tantalize and inflame his appetite, and then robs him by taking herself away. This was neatly expressed in patient C's dream. 'I was enjoying my favourite meal and saved the nicest bit to the end, and then mother snatched it (the breast, herself) away under my nose. I was furious but when I protested she said "Don't be a baby".' There is the guilt reaction, agreeing with the denier against oneself and giving up one's own needs. Fairbairn holds that depression has occupied too exclusively the centre of the picture of psychopathological states as a result of Freud's concentration on obsessions with their ambivalence, guilt and super-ego problems. He believes the schizoid condition is the fundamental problem and is preambivalent.

Melanie Klein (1932, 1948) stressed how ambivalence rises to its maximum over the weaning crisis at a time when the infant has learned to bite and can react sadistically. Love and hate block each other. The infant attacks and also feels identified with, the object of his aggression, and so feels guilty and involves himself in the fate, factual or phantasied, of the object. Hate of the object involves hate of oneself, you suffer with the object you attack because you cannot give up the object and feel one with it. Hence the familiar guilt and depression after a bereavement: you feel guilty as if you have killed the lost person and depressed as if you were dying with him or her. Three patients who all suffered marked guilt and depression recovered repressed and internalized death-bed scenes of a parent.

What is the meaning of hate? It is not the absolute opposite of love; that would be indifference, having no interest in a person, not wanting a relationship and so having no reason for either loving or hating, feeling nothing. Hate is love grown angry because of rejection. We can only really hate a person if we want their love. Hate is an expression of frustrated love needs, an attempt to destroy the bad rejecting side of a person in the hope of leaving their good responsive side available, a struggle to alter them. The anxiety is over the danger of hate destroying both sides, and the easiest way out is to find two objects and love one and hate the other.

But as we have seen, the individual can adopt an earlier simpler reaction. Instead of reacting with anger, he can react with an enormously exaggerated sense of need. Desire becomes hunger and hunger becomes greed which is hunger grown frightened of losing what it wants. He feels so uncertain about possessing his love-object that he feels a desperate craving to make sure of it by getting it inside him, swallowing it and incorporating it. This is illustrated by patient B, who phantasied standing with a vacuum cleaner (herself, empty and hungry), and everyone who came near she sucked them into it. At a more normal and ordinarily conscious level this is expressed by patient C thus: 'I'm afraid I couldn't make moderate demands on people, so I don't make any demands at all.' Many people show openly this devouring possessiveness towards those they love. Many more repress it and keep out of real relations.

This dream brings out the schizoid situation. So much fear is felt of devouring everyone and so losing everyone in the process, that a general withdrawal from all external relationships is embarked on. Retreat into indifference, the true opposite of the love which is felt to be too dangerous to express. Want no one, make no demands, abolish all external relationships, and be aloof, cold, without any feeling, do not be moved by anything. The withdrawn libido is turned inwards, introverted. The patient goes into his shell and is busy only with internal objects, towards whom he feels the same devouring attitude. Outwardly everything seems futile and meaningless. Fairbairn considers that a sense of 'futility' is the specific schizoid affect. Just as the depressive is identified with the one he attacks and so hurts himself, so the schizoid is identified with the object he devours and loses, and so loses himself; e.g. the snake eating its own tail. The depressive fears loss of his object. The schizoid, in addition, fears loss of his ego, of himself.

## THE SCHIZOID'S RELATION TO OBJECTS (NEED AND FEAR OF OBJECT-RELATIONS)

### Active: Fear of Loss of the Object

*The Object as a Desired Deserter or 'Needed Object'*

Theory only lives when it is seen as describing the actual reactions of real people, though the material revealing the schizoid position only becomes undisguisedly accessible at deep levels of analysis, and is often not reached when defences are reasonably effective. In the very unstable schizoid it breaks through with disconcerting ease, a bad sign.

A headmaster, D, described himself as depressed, and went on to say, 'I don't feel so worried about the school or hopeless about the future.' He had said the same things the week before and regarded it as a sign of improvement, but the real meaning emerged when he remarked 'Perhaps my interest in school has flagged' and it appeared that his loss of the sense of hopelessness about the future was due simply to his not thinking about the future. He had cut it off. He then reported a dream of visiting a camp school. 'The resident head walked away when I arrived and left me to fend for myself and there was no meal ready for me.' He remarked: 'I'm preoccupied with what I'm going to eat and when, yet I don't eat a lot. Also I want to get away from people and am more comfortable when eating alone. I'm concerned at my loss of interest in school. I don't feel comfortable with father and prefer to be in another room. I'm very introverted; I feel totally cut off.'

Here is a gradually emerging description, not of depression but of a schizoid state, loss of interest in present and future, loss of appetite for food, getting away from people, introverted, totally cut off. The situation that calls out the reaction is that of being faced with a desired but deserting object, the head in the dream who prepares no meal for him, and leaves him to fend for himself when he is hungry. The head is the father, of whom he complains that he can never get near him: also the analyst to whom he says: 'you remain the analyst, you won't indulge me in a warm personal relationship, you won't be my friend. I want something more personal than analysis.' The schizoid is very sensitive and quickly feels unwanted, because he is always being deserted in his inner world.

Faced with these desired deserters he first feels exaggeratedly hungry, and then denies his hunger, eats little and turns away from people till he feels introverted and totally cut off. He has withdrawn his libido from the objects he cannot possess, and feels loss of interest and loss of appetite. There is little evidence of anger and guilt as there would be in depression; his attitude is more that of fear and retreat.

*The Object as Being Devoured*

The entire problem is frequently worked out over food. The above patient is hungry but rejects both food and people. He can only eat alone. The patient C says that whenever her husband comes in she at once feels hungry and must eat. Really she is hungry for him but dare not show it. The same turning away from what one feels too greedily and devouringly hungry for is shown very clearly by this same patient in other ways. Visiting friends she was handed a glass of sherry, took a quick sip and put it down and did not touch it again. She had felt she wanted to swallow it at one gulp. Her general attitude to food was one of rejection. Appetite would disappear at the sight of food, she would nibble at a dish and push it away, or force it down and feel sick. But what lay behind this rejecting attitude was expressed in a dream in which she was eating an enormous meal and just went on and on and on endlessly. She is getting as much as she can inside her before it is taken away as in the dream where her mother whipped it away under her nose. Her attitude is incorporative, to get it inside where she cannot be robbed of it, because she has no confidence about being given enough. The breast one is sure of can be sucked at contentedly and let go when one feels satisfied: one knows it will be available when needed again. The breast that does not come when wanted, is not satisfying when one has it because it might be snatched away before need is met. It rouses a desperate hungry urge to make sure of it, not by merely sucking at it but by swallowing it, getting it inside one altogether. The impulse changes from 'taking in from the breast' into an omnivorous urge to 'take in the whole breast itself'. The object is incorporated. The contented baby sucks, the angry and potentially depressive baby bites, the hungry and potentially schizoid baby wants to swallow, as in the case of the vacuum cleaner phantasy. A patient who at first made sucking noises in sessions, then changed to compulsive gulping and swallowing and nausea.

Fairbairn (1941, p. 252) writes: 'The paranoid, obsessional, and hysterical states—to which may be added the phobic state—essentially represent, not products of fixations at specific libidinal phases, but simply a variety of techniques employed to defend the ego against the effects of conflicts of oral origin.'

Now, as Fairbairn says: 'You can't eat your cake and have it.' This hungry, greedy, devouring, swallowing up, incorporating attitude leads to deep fears lest the real external object be lost. This anxiety about destroying and losing the love-object through being so devouringly hungry is terribly real. Thus the patient C, who has become more conscious of her love-hunger with the result that on the one hand her appetite for food has increased enormously, and on the other her anxious attitude to her husband has become more acute, says: 'When he comes in I feel ravenously hungry, and eat, but towards him I'm afraid I'm a nuisance. If I make advances to him I keep saying "I'm not a nuisance am I, you don't 'not want me' do you?" I'm terribly anxious about it all, it's an appalling situation, I'm scared stiff, it's all so violent. I've an urge to get hold of him and hold him so tight that he can't breathe, shut him off from everything but me.' She has the same transference reaction to the analyst. She dreamed that 'I came for treatment and you were going off to America with a lot of people. Someone dropped out so I went and you weren't pleased.' Her comment was 'you didn't want me but I wasn't going to be thrown off. I was thinking to-day of your getting ill, suppose you died. Then I got in a furious temper. I'd like to strangle you, kill you.' That is, get a strangle-hold on the analyst so that he could not leave her, but then he might be killed. The schizoid person is afraid of wearing out, of draining, or exhausting and ultimately losing love-objects. As Fairbairn says, the terrible dilemma of the schizoid is that love itself is destructive, and he dare not love. Hence he withdraws into detachment and aloofness. All intimate relationships are felt in terms of eating, swallowing up, and are too dangerous to be risked. The above patient says: 'I lay half awake looking at my husband and thinking, "What a pity he's going to die." It seemed fixed. Then I felt lonely, no point of relationship with all I could see. I love him so much but I seem to have no choice about destroying him. I want something badly and then daren't move a finger to get it. I'm paralysed.'

## Schizoid Reactions to Food and Eating

From the foregoing we may summarize the schizoid's reactions to food and eating, for since his basic problems in relation to objects derive from his reactions to the breast, food and eating naturally play a large part in his struggles to solve these problems. His reactions to people and to food are basically the same. Thus patient C says: 'Two men friends make me excited but it's not even a taste, only a smell of a good meal. I'm always feeling I want to be with one or the other of them, but I can't do it or I'll lose them both. One of them kissed me and I gave him a hug and a kiss and enjoyed it and wanted more. Ought I? I've sought desperately for so long and now I feel I must run away from it. I don't want to eat these days. I couldn't sleep. I felt I'd lost him: what if he or I had an accident and got killed. It's ridiculous but I'm in a constant furore of anxiety, I must see him: nothing else matters. I knew I'd be like this if I didn't see him but I didn't go. It's funny, I don't think I'm in love with him, yet I need him desperately. I can't engage in any other activity. I felt the same with a fellow ten years ago. He went away for a day and I was in an agony of fear; what if he were killed, an awful dread. It feels it must happen. I don't even like mentioning it in case this present friend gets killed, and I feel I'll have an accident, too. I get desperately tired, and feel empty inside and have to buy sweet biscuits and gobble them up.'

Thus she has the kind of relation with this man (and with all objects) that compromises her stable existence as a separate person when she is not with him: she goes to bits. She wants to eat him up as it were, and feels swallowed up in her relation to him, and feels the destruction of both is inevitable whether she is with him or apart from him.

The patient B, before she started analysis, was having visual hallucinations of leopards leaping across in front of her with their mouths wide open. At an advanced stage of treatment these faded into phantasies and she had a phantasy of two leopards trying to swallow each other's head. She would enjoy a hearty meal and then promptly be sick and reject it. *There is a constant oscillation between hungry eating and refusal to eat, longing for people and rejecting them.*

## The Transference Situation

The necessary and inevitable frustration of a patient's libidinal needs in the analytical situation is peculiarly well adapted to bring out schizoid reactions, as we have already noted. The patient longs for the analyst's love, may recognize intellectually that a steady, consistent, genuine, concern for the patient's well-being is a true form of love, yet, because it is not love in a full libidinal sense (Fairbairn reminds us that it is *agape*, not *eros*), the patient does not 'feel' it as love. He feels rather that the analyst is cold, indifferent, bored, not interested, not listening, busy with something else while the patient talks, rejective. Patients will react to the analyst's silence by stopping talking to make him say something. The analyst excites by his presence but does not libidinally satisfy, and so constantly arouses a hungry craving.

The patient will then begin to feel he is bad for the analyst, that he is wasting his time, depressing him by pouring out a long story of troubles. He will want, and fear, to make requests lest he is imposing on the analyst and making illegitimate demands. He may say 'How on earth can you stand this constant strain of listening to this sort of thing day after day?' and in general feels he is draining and exhausting, i.e. devouring, the analyst.

He will oscillate between expressing his need and feeling guilty about it. The patient A says: 'I felt I must get possession of something of yours. I thought I'd come early and enjoy your arm chair and read your books in the waiting room.' But then she switches over to: 'You can't possibly want to let me take up your time week after week.' Guilt and anxiety then dictate a reversal of the original relationship. The patient must now be passive and begins to see the analyst as the active devourer. He drains the patient of resources by charging fees, he wants to dominate and subjugate the patient, he will rob him of his personality. A patient, after along silence, says: 'I'm thinking I must be careful, you're going to get something out of me.' The analyst will absorb or rob the patient.

This terrible oscillation may make a patient feel confused and not know where he is. Thus a patient, E, says: 'I've been thinking I might lose your help, you'll make an excuse to get rid of me. I want more analysis but you don't bother with me. Analysis is only a very small part of a week. You don't understand me. There's a part of me I don't bring into analysis. I might be swallowed up in your personality and lose my individuality, so I adopt a condescending attitude to you. What you say isn't important, you're only a bourgeois therapist and don't understand the conditions of my life, your focus of analytical capacity is tiny, you're cabined within bourgeois ideas. But if I said what I felt, I'd make you depressed and lose your support. You ought to be able to give me specific advice to help me when I feel helpless and imprisoned. I feel much the same with my girl. In analysis I feel I should get out, and away from it I feel I should be in. This week I feel in a "no man's land".'

Here the whole dilemma of 'craving for' yet 'not being able to accept' the needed person, comes out in transference on the analyst. The swing over in transference to the opposite, from 'devouring' to 'being devoured', leads to the specific consideration of the passive aspect of the schizoid's relation to objects.

## Passive: Fear of the Loss of Independence

*The Object as Devouring the Ego*

The patients' fears of a devouring sense of need towards objects is paralleled by the fear that others have the same 'swallowing up' attitude to them. Thus patient C says: 'I can't stand crowds, they swallow me up. With you I feel if I accept your help I'll be subjugated, lose my personality, be smothered. Now I feel withdrawn like a snail, but now you can't swallow me up. I get a "shutting myself off" attitude which lessens my anxiety.'

The patient B, a very schizoid married woman of 30, has for a long time been talking out devouring phantasies of all kinds, and slowly emerging from her schizoid condition. She was thin, white, cold, aloof, frigid: often it was some time before she could start talking in session, and would arrive terrified but hiding it under an automatic laugh or bored expression. When she did start talking she would begin to look tense, and tears would roll silently down and she would say she felt frightened. Gradually she has begun to talk more freely and put on weight and colour and be capable of sexual relationships with her husband. Her phantasies included those of his penis eating her and of her vagina biting off his penis. On one occasion she said: 'Last night I felt excited at coming here to-day, and then terrified and confused. I couldn't sleep for thinking of you. I felt drawn towards you and then shot back. Then I felt I was one big mouth all over and just wanting to get you inside. But sometimes I feel you'll eat me.'

A male patient, F, of 40, living in a hostel reported that he had begun to get friendly with another very decent type of man there, and commented: 'I've begun to get frightened. I don't know why but I feel it's dangerous and I just cut myself off. When I see him coming I shoot off up to my bedroom.' Then he reported a nightmare from which he had awakened in great fear. A monster was coming after him and its huge mouth closed over him like a trap and he was engulfed. Then he burst out of its head and killed it. So the schizoid not only fears devouring and losing the love-object, but also that the other person will devour him. Then he becomes claustrophobic, and expresses this in such familiar ways as feeling restricted, tied, imprisoned, trapped, smothered, and must break away to be free and recover and safeguard his independence: so he retreats from object-relations. With people, he feels either bursting (if he is getting them into himself) or smothered (if he feels he is being absorbed and losing his personality in them). These anxieties are often expressed by starting up in the night feeling choking, and is one reason for fear of going to sleep.

*Relationships as a Mutual Devouring*

We are now in a position to appreciate the terrible dilemma in which the schizoid person is caught in object-relations. Owing to his intensely hungry and unsatisfied need for love, and his consequent incorporating and monopolizing attitude towards those he needs, he cannot help seeing his objects in the light of his own desires towards them. The result is that any relationship into which some genuine feeling goes, immediately comes to be felt deep down, and unconsciously experienced, as a mutual devouring. Such intense anxiety results that there seems to be no alternative but to withdraw from relationships altogether, to prevent the loss of his independence. Relationships are felt to be too dangerous to enter into.

## THE SCHIZOID RETREAT FROM OBJECTS

### The 'In and Out' Programme

The chronic dilemma in which the schizoid individual is placed, namely that he can neither be in a relationship with another person nor out of it, without in various ways risking the loss of both his object and himself, is due to the fact that he has not yet outgrown the particular kind of dependence on love-objects that is character-istic of infancy: namely identification in an emotional sense, and the wish to incorporate in a conative, active sense. He and those he loves feel to be part and parcel of one another, so that when separated he feels utterly insecure and lost, but when reunited he feels swallowed, absorbed, and loses his separate individuality by regression to infantile dependence. Thus he must always be rushing into a relationship for security and at once breaking out again for freedom and indepen-dence: an alternation between regression to the womb and the struggle to be born, between the merging of his ego in, and the differentiation of it from, the person he loves. The schizoid cannot stand alone, yet is always fighting desperately to defend his independence: like those film stars who spend their best years rushing into and out of one marriage after another.

This 'in and out' programme, always breaking away from what one is at the same time holding on to, is perhaps the most characteristic behavioural expression of the schizoid conflict. Thus a young man engaged to be married says: 'When I'm with Dorothy I'm quiet, I think "I can't afford to let myself go and let her see that I want her. I must let her see I can get on without her." So I keep away from her and appear indifferent.' He experienced the same conflict about jobs. He phantasied getting a job in South America or China, but in fact turned down every job that would take him away from home. A girl in the twenties says: 'When I'm at home I want to get away and when I'm away I want to get back home.' Patient A, who is a nurse residing in a hostel, says: 'The other night I decided I wanted to stay in the hostel and not go home, then I felt the hostel was a prison and I went home. As soon as I got there I wanted to go out again. Yesterday I rang mother to say I was coming home, and then immediately I felt exhausted and rang her again to say I was too tired to come. I'm always switching about, as soon as I'm with the person I want I feel they restrict me. I have wondered if I did get one of my two men friends would I then want to be free again.' The patient F, a bachelor of 40 who is engaged, says: 'If I kiss Mary my heart isn't in it. I hold my breath and count. I can only hug and kiss a dog because it doesn't want anything from me, there are no strings attached. I've always been like that, so I've got lots of acquaintances but no real close friends. I feel I want to stay in and go out, to read and not to read, to go to Church and not to go. I've actually gone into a Church and immediately come out again and then wanted to return in.'

So people find their lives slipping away changing houses, clothes, jobs, hobbies, friends, engagements and marriages, and unable to commit themselves to any one relationship in a stable and permanent way: always needing love yet always dreading being tied. This same conflict accounts for the tendency of engaged or married couples to phantasy about or feel attracted to someone else: as if they must preserve freedom of attachment at least in imagination. One patient remarked: 'I want to be loved but I mustn't be possessed.'

*Giving up Emotional Relations to External Objects*

The oscillation of 'in and out', 'rushing to and from', holding on and breaking away' is naturally profoundly disturbing and disruptive of all continuity in living, and at some point the anxiety aroused becomes so great that it cannot be sustained. It is then that a complete retreat from object-relations is embarked on, and the person becomes overtly schizoid, emotionally inaccessible, cut off.

This state of emotional apathy, of not suffering any feeling, excitement or enthusiasm, not experiencing either affection or anger, can be very successfully masked. If feeling is repressed, it is often possible to build up a kind of mechanized, robot personality. The ego that operates consciously becomes more a system than a person, a trained and disciplined instrument for 'doing the right and necessary thing' without any real feeling entering in. Fairbairn makes the highly important distinction between 'helping people without feeling' and 'loving'. Duty rather than affection becomes the key word. Patient A sought temporary relief from her disruptive conflict over her man friend by putting it away and making a list of all the things she ought to do, and systematically going through them one by one, routinizing her whole life — and that had been a life-long tendency. She had always had to 'do things in order'; even as a child she made a note-book list of games and had to play them in order.

The patient F, a man with strongly, in fact exclusively, religious interests, showed markedly this characteristic of helping people without really feeling for them. He said: 'I've no real emotional relations with people. I can't reciprocate tenderness. I can cry and suffer with people. I can help people, but when they stop suffering I'm finished. I can't enter into folks' joys and laughter. I can do things for people but shrink from them if they start thanking me.' His suffering with people was in fact his identifying himself as a suffering person with anyone else who suffered. Apart from that he allowed no emotional relationship to arise.

It is even possible to mask more effectively the real nature of the compulsive, unfeeling zeal in good works, by simulating a feeling of concern for others. Some shallow affect is helped out by behaviour expressive of deep care and consideration for other people; nevertheless, genuine feeling for other people is not really there. Such behaviour is not, of course, consciously insincere. It is a genuine effort to do the best that one can do in the absence of a capacity to release true feeling. What looks deceptively like genuine feeling for another person may break into consciousness, when in fact it is based on identification with the other person and is mainly a feeling of anxiety and pity for oneself.

Many practically useful types of personality are basically schizoid. Hard workers, compulsively unselfish folk, efficient organizers, highly intellectual people, may all accomplish valuable results, but it is often possible to detect an unfeeling callousness behind their good works, and a lack of sensitiveness to other people's feelings, in the way they will over-ride individuals in their devotion to causes.

The schizoid repression of feeling, and retreat from emotional relationships, may however go much further and produce a serious breakdown of constructive effort. Then the unhappy sufferer from incapacitating conflicts will succumb to real futility: nothing seems worth doing, interest dies, the world seems unreal, the ego feels depersonalized. Suicide may be attempted in a cold, calculated way to the accompaniment of such thoughts as 'I am useless, bad for everybody, I'll be best out of the way.' The patient F had never reached that point, but he said: 'I feel I love people in an impersonal way; it seems a false position; hypocritical. Perhaps I don't do any loving. I'm terrified when I see young people go off and being successful and I'm at a dead bottom, absolute dereliction, excommunicate.'

## THE FUNDAMENTAL PROBLEM: IDENTIFICATION

*Identification and Infantile Dependence*

It has already been mentioned that schizoid problems arise out of identification, which Fairbairn holds to be the original infantile form of relation to, and dependence on, objects. The criticism is sometimes made that psycho-analysis invents a strange terminology that the layman cannot apply to real life. We may therefore illustrate the state of identification with the love-object in the words of Ngaio Marsh (1935), a successful writer of detective fiction. In *Enter a Murderer* she creates the character of Surbonadier, a bad actor who expresses his immaturity by being a drug addict and blackmailer. Stephanie Vaughan, the leading lady, says: 'He was passionately in love with me. That doesn't begin to express it. He was completely and utterly absorbed as though apart from me he had no reality.' In other words, the man was swallowed up in his love-object, had no true individuality of his own, and could not exist in a state of separation from her. He had never become born out of his mother's psyche and differentiated as a separate and real person in his own right, and identification with another person remained at bottom the basis of all his personal relationships.

The patient E said: 'If I go away from home I feel I've lost something, but when I'm there I feel imprisoned. I feel my destiny is bound up with theirs and I can't get away, yet I feel they imprison me and ruin my life.' The patient A dreamed of being 'grafted on to another person'. The patient F said: 'Why should I be on bad terms with my sister? After all I am my sister', and then started in some surprise at what he had heard himself say. The patient B, struggling to master a blind compulsive longing for a male relative she played with as a child, said: 'I've always felt he's me and I'm him. I felt a terrible need to fuss around him and do everything for him. I want him to be touching me all the time. I feel there is no difference between him and me.' Fairbairn holds that identification is the cause of the compulsiveness of such feelings as infatuation. Identification is betrayed in a variety of curious ways, such as the fear of being buried alive, i.e. absorbed into another person, a return to the womb; also expressed in the suicidal urge to put one's head in a gas oven: or again in dressing in the clothes of another person. Patient C, feeling in a state of panic one night when her husband was away, felt safe when she slept in his pyjamas.

*Dissolving Identification: Separation-Anxiety, and Psychic Birth*

The regressive urge to remain identified for the sake of comfort and security conflicts with the developmental need to dissolve identification and differentiate oneself as a separate personality. This conflict, as it sways back and forth, sets up the 'in and out' programme. Identification, naturally, varies in degree, but the markedly schizoid person, in whom it plays such a fundamental part, begins to lose all true independence of feeling, thought and action as soon as a relationship with another person attains any degree of emotional reality. A single illuminating example will suffice.

The patient C says: 'I feel I lack the capacity to go out. I can never leave the people I love. If I go out I'm emptied, I lose myself. I can't get beyond that. If I become dependent on you, I'd enjoy my dependence on you too much and want to prolong babyhood. Being shut in means being warm, safe, and not confronted with unforeseen events.' But this kind of security is also a prison, so the patient goes on to say: 'I feel I'm walking up and down inside an enclosed space. I dreamed of a baby being born out of a gas oven (i.e. reversal of the suicide idea). I was struck with the danger of coming out, it was a long drop from the oven to the floor. I feel I'm disintegrating if I go out. The only feeling of being real comes with getting back in and being with someone. I don't feel alone inside even if there's no-one there. Sometimes I feel like someone falling out of an aeroplane, or falling through water and expecting to hit the bottom and there isn't one. I have strong impulses to throw myself out of the window.' This 'birth symbolism' shows that suicidal impulses may have opposite meanings. The gas oven means a return to the womb, a surrender to identification with mother. Falling out of the window means a struggle to separate and be born (and also casting out the person with whom one is identified). The struggle to dissolve identification is long and severe, and in analysis it recapitulates the whole process of growing up to the normal mixture of voluntary dependence and independence characteristic of the mature adult person. One of the major causes of anxiety is that separation is felt to involve, not natural growth and development, but a violent, angry, destructive break-away, as if a baby, in being born, were bound to leave a dying mother behind.

## SCHIZOID CHARACTERISTICS

There are various characteristics which specifically mark the schizoid personality, and the most general and all-embracing is:

*Introversion.* By the very meaning of the term, the schizoid is described as cut off from the world of outer reality in an emotional sense. All his libidinal desire and striving is directed inwards towards internal objects and he lives an intense inner life, often revealed in an astonishing wealth and richness of phantasy and imaginative life whenever that becomes accessible to observation; though mostly this varied phantasy life is carried on in secret, hidden away often even from the schizoid's own conscious self. His ego is split. But the barrier between the conscious and the unconscious self may be very thin in a deeply schizoid person and the world of internal objects and relationships may flood into and dominate consciousness very easily.

*Narcissism* is a schizoid characteristic that arises out of the predominantly interior life he lives. His love-objects are all inside him, and moreover he is greatly identified with them, so that his libidinal attachments appear to be to himself. This subtly deceptive situation was not recognized by Freud when he propounded his theory of autoeroticism and narcissism, and ego-libido as distinct from object-libido. The schizoid's physically incorporative feeling towards his love-objects is the bodily counterpart, or rather foundation, of the mentally incorporative attitude which leads to mental internalization of objects and the setting up of a world of internal psychic objects. But these mentally internalized objects, especially when the patient feels strongly identified with them, can be discovered, contacted and enjoyed, or even attacked, in his own body, when the external object is not there. One patient, who cannot be directly angry with another person, always goes away alone when her temper is roused and punches herself. She is identified with the object of her aggression which leads to a depressive state, though, of course, it is a libidinal attachment at bottom. The normally so-called autoerotic and narcissistic phenomena of thumb-sucking, masturbation, hugging oneself and so on are based on identification. Autoerotic phenomena are only secondarily autoerotic; autoerotism is a relationship with an external object who is identified with oneself, the baby's thumb deputizes for the mother's breast. Narcissism is a disguised object-relation. Thus the patient B felt depressed while bathing and cried silently, and then felt a strong urge to snuggle her head down on to her own shoulder, i.e. mother's shoulder in herself, and at once she felt better. Again sitting with her husband one evening reading, she became aware that she was thinking of an intimate relation with him and found she had slipped her hand inside her frock and was caressing her own breast. These phenomena lead to a third schizoid characteristic:

*Self-sufficiency.* The above patient was actually taking no notice of her husband as an external person: her relation with him was all going on inside herself and she felt contented. This introverted, narcissistic self-sufficiency which does without real external relationships while all emotional relations are carried on in the inner world, is a safeguard against anxiety breaking out in dealings with actual people. Self-sufficiency, or the attempt to get on without external relationships, comes out clearly in the case of patient C. She had been talking of wanting a baby, and then dreamed that she had a baby by her mother. It was suggested that having a baby meant getting something of her husband inside her, and deep down that felt to be getting something of mother inside her. But since she had often shown that she identified herself very much with babies, it would also represent being the baby inside the mother. She was wanting to set up a self-sufficiency situation in which she was both the mother and the baby. She replied: 'Yes, I always think of it as a girl. It gives me a feeling of security. I've got it all here under control, there's no uncertainty.' In such a position she could do without her husband and be all-sufficient within herself.

A *sense of superiority* naturally goes with self-sufficiency. One has no need of other people, they can be dispensed with. This over-compensates the deep-seated dependence on people which leads to feelings of inferiority, smallness and weakness. But there often goes with it a feeling of being different from other people. Thus a very obsessional patient reveals the schizoid background of her symptoms when she says: 'I'm always dissatisfied. As a child I would cry with boredom at the silly games the children played. It got worse in my teens, terrible boredom, futility, lack of interest. I would look at people and see them interested in things I thought silly. I felt I was different and had more brains. I was thinking deeply about the purpose of life.' She could think about life in the abstract but couldn't live it in real relationships with other people.

*Loss of affect* in external situations is an inevitable part of the total picture. A man in the late forties says: 'I find it difficult to be with mother. I ought to be more sympathetic to her than I can be. I always feel I'm not paying attention to what she says. I don't feel terribly drawn to anyone. I can feel cold about all the people who are near and dear to me. When my wife and I were having sexual relations she would say: "Do you love me?" I would answer: "Of course I do, but sex isn't love, it's only an experience." I could never see why that upset her.' Feeling was excluded even from sexual activity which was reduced to what one patient called 'an intermittent biological urge which seemed to have little connexion with "me" '.

*Loneliness* is an inescapable result of schizoid introversion and abolition of external relationships. It reveals itself in the intense longing for friendships and love which repeatedly break through. Loneliness in the midst of a crowd is the experience of the schizoid cut off from affective rapport.

*Depersonalization,* loss of the sense of identity and individuality, loss of oneself, brings out clearly the serious dangers of the schizoid state. Derealization of the outer world is involved as well. Thus the patient C maintains that the worst fright she ever had was a petrifying experience at the age of two years. 'I couldn't get hold of the idea that I was me. I lost the sense for a little while of being a separate entity. I was afraid to look at anything; and afraid to touch anything as if I didn't register touch. I couldn't believe I was doing things except mechanically. I saw everything in an unrealistic way. Everything seemed highly dangerous. I was terrified while it lasted. All my life since I've been saying to myself at intervals "I am me".'

## FAIRBAIRN AND FREUD

When one surveys the material here set out, it becomes apparent that Fairbairn's theory of the schizoid problem represents a radical revision in psycho-analytical thinking. Freud rested his theory of development and of the psychoneuroses on the centrality of the Oedipus situation in the last phase of infancy. Failure to solve the Oedipus conflict of incestuous love and jealous hate of the parent of the same sex led to regression to pregenital levels of sexual and emotional life and a lasting burden of guilt. This now looks rather like a pioneer's rough sketch-map of an uncharted territory by comparison with Fairbairn's detailed ordnance survey map of infantile development which is based on, but goes a long way beyond, Melanie Klein's discoveries about internal objects and the depressive position. The Oedipus problem as Freud saw it was, in fact, no more than the gateway opening into the area of the psychopathology of infancy. Yet Fairbairn's position is essentially simple. Once stated it should be apparent that man's need of a love-relationship is the fundamental thing in his life, and that the love-hunger and anger set up by frustration of this basic need must constitute the two primary problems of personality on the emotional level. Freud's 'guilt over the incestuous tie to the mother' now resolves itself into the primary necessity of overcoming infantile dependence on the parents, and on the mother in particular, in order to grow up to mature adulthood. The Oedipus conflict theory in a purely biological and sexual sense is seen to have misrepresented and distorted the real problem, and side-tracked inquiry. The fundamental emotional attitude of the child to both parents is the same and is determined, not by the sex of the parent but by the child's need for libidinal satisfaction and protective love, and a stable environment, and by the fact that all its relationships start off on the basis of identification. In its quest for a libidinally good object the child will turn from the mother to the father, and go back and forth between them many times. The less satisfactory the object-relationships with his parents prove to be in the course of development, the more the child remains embedded in relationships by identification, and the more it creates, the remains tied to, an inner world of bad internal objects who will thereafter dwell in its unconscious as an abiding fifth column of secret persecutors, at once exciting desire and denying satisfaction. A deep-seated ever unsatisfied hunger will be the foundation of the personality, creating the fundamental danger of the schizoid state.


## CULTURAL EXPRESSIONS OF SCHIZOID FEARS


Academic psychologists are fond of accusing psycho-analysts of dealing with abnormal minds and drawing from them unjustified conclusions about normal minds. In fact psycho-analysis shows conclusively that this is an entirely misleading distinction. It would be easy to demonstrate every psycho-pathological process from the study of so-called normal minds alone. Nowadays many people seek analysis not for specific neurotic breakdowns but for character and personality problems, and many of them are people who continue to hold effectively positions of responsibility and who are judged by the world at large to be 'normal' people. Thus psychopathology should be capable of throwing an important light on many aspects of ordinary social and cultural life. This is far too large a theme to be more than touched on here. A few hints must suffice.

*Common mild schizoid traits.*   One has only to collect up some of the common phrases that describe an introvert reaction in human relationships to realize how common the 'schizoid type' of personality is. One constantly hears in the social intercourse of daily life, such comments as 'he's gone into his shell', 'he only half listens to what you say', 'he's always preoccupied', or 'absent-minded', 'he lives in a world of ideas', 'he's an unpractical type', 'he's difficult to get to know', 'he couldn't enthuse about anything', 'he's a cold fish', 'he's very efficient but rather inhuman', and one could multiply the list. All these comments may well describe people whose general stability in any reasonable environment is quite adequate, but who clearly lack the capacity for simple, spontaneous, warm and friendly responsiveness to their human kind. Not infrequently they are more emotionally expressive towards animals than towards the human beings with whom they live or work. They are undemonstrative: it is not merely that they are the opposite of emotionally effervescent, but rather that their relationships with people are actually emotionally shallow. It is as well to recognize, from these schizoid types, that psycho-pathological phenomena cannot be set apart from the so-called 'normal'.

*Politics.*   All through the ages politics has rung the changes, with monotonous regularity, on the themes of 'freedom' and 'authority'. Men have fought passionately for liberty and independence; freedom from foreign domination, freedom from state paternalism and bureaucratic control, freedom from social and economic class oppression, freedom from the shackles of an imposed religious orthodoxy. Yet at other times men have proved to be just as willing, and indeed eager, to be embraced in, and supported and directed by, some totalitarian organization of state or church. No doubt urgent practical necessity often drives men one way or the other at different periods of history and in different phases of social change. But if we seek the ultimate motivations of human action, it is impossible not to link up this social and political oscillation of aim, with the 'in and out' programme of the schizoid person. Man's deepest needs make him dependent on others, but there is nothing more productive of the feeling of being tied or restricted than being overdependent through basic emotional immaturity. Certainly human beings in the mass are far less emotionally mature than they suppose themselves to be, and this accounts for much of the aggressiveness, the oppositionism, and the compulsive assertion of a false, forced, independence that are such obvious social behaviour trends. The schizoid person frequently 'has a bee in his bonnet' about freedom. The love of liberty has been for so long the keynote of British national life that what Erich Fromm (1942) calls 'the fear of freedom' found in totalitarianism, and in political as well as religious authoritarianism seems to us a strange aberration. It is well to realize that both motives are deeply rooted in the psychic structure of human personality.

*Ideology*. Much has been said of 'depressed eras' in history, but when one considers the cold, calculating, mechanical, ruthless, and unfeeling nature of the planned cruelty of political intellectuals and ideologists, we may well think this to be a 'schizoid era'. The cold and inscrutable Himmler showed all the marks of a deeply schizoid personality and his suicide was consistent. The schizoid intellectual wielding unlimited political power is perhaps the most dangerous type of leader. He is a devourer of the human rights of all whom he can rule. The way some of the most ruthless Nazis could turn to the study of theology was significant of a schizoid splitting of personality. But if we turn to the purely intellectual and cultural sphere it is not difficult to recognize the impersonal atmosphere of schizoid thinking in Hegelianism. Its dialectic of thesis breeding antithesis seems an intellectual version of the schizoid need for unity which in turn breeds the need for separation. Still more apparent is the schizoid sense of futility, disillusionment, and underlying anxiety in Existentialism. These thinkers, from Kierkegaard to Heidegger and Sartre, find human existence to be rooted in anxiety and insecurity, a fundamental dread that ultimately we have no certainties and the only thing we can affirm is 'nothingness', 'unreality', a final sense of triviality and meaninglessness. This surely is schizoid despair and loss of contact with the verities of emotional reality, rationalized into a philosophy; yet Existentialist thinkers, unlike the Logical Positivists, are calling us to face and deal with these real problems of our human situation. It is a sign of the mental state of our age.

## SUMMARY

We may finally summarize the emotional dilemma of the schizoid thus: he feels a deep dread of entering into a real personal relationship, i.e. one into which genuine feeling enters, because, though his need for a love-object is so great, yet he can only sustain a relationship at a deep emotional level, on the basis of infantile and absolute dependence. To the love-hungry schizoid faced internally with an exciting but deserting object all relationships are felt to be 'swallowing-up things' which trap and imprison and destroy. If your hate is destructive you are still free to love because you can find someone else to hate. But if you feel your love is destructive the situation is terrifying. You are always *impelled into* a relationship by your needs and at once *driven out* again by the fear either of exhausting your love-object by the demands you want to make or else losing your own individuality by over-dependence and identification. This 'in and out' oscillation is *the typical schizoid behaviour*, and to escape from it into detachment and loss of feeling is *the typical schizoid state*.

The schizoid feels faced with utter loss, and the destruction of both ego and object, whether in a relationship or out of it. In a relationship, identification involves loss of the ego, and incorporation involves a hungry devouring and losing of the object. In breaking away to independence, the object is destroyed as you fight a way out to freedom, or lost by separation, and the ego is destroyed or emptied by the loss of the object with whom it is identified. The only real solution is the dissolving of identification and the maturing of the personality: the differentiation of ego and object and the growth of a capacity for co-operative independence and mutuality.

## REFERENCES

Fairbairn, W. R. D. (1941). A revised psychopathology of the psychoses and psychoneuroses. *International Journal of Psycho-Analysis* 22:250.

———— (1944). Endopsychic structure considered in the light of object-relationships. *International Journal of Psycho-Analysis* 25:70.

Fromm, E. (1942). *The Fear of Freedom*. London: Kegan Paul.

Horney, K. (1946). *Our Inner Conflicts*. London: Kegan Paul.

Klein, M. (1932). *The Psycho-analysis of Children*. London: Hogarth Press.

———— (1948). *Contributions to Psycho-analysis*. London: Hogarth Press.

Marsh, N. (1935). *Enter a Murderer*. London: Penguin Books.

Riviere, J. (1952). The unconscious phantasy of an inner world. *International Journal of Psycho-Analysis* 33:160.

# 2

# THE PSYCHOTHERAPIST AS PARENT AND EXORCIST[1]

It IS WELL KNOWN THAT AS FREUD grew older he grew more cautious in his estimate of the therapeutic value of psycho-analysis, though he retained an undiminished regard for it as instrument of scientific research on mental life. His judgement may have been due to some undetected preconceptions in his own view of psychotherapy, or to the limiting effects on therapy of deficiencies in his theory which time and further research could remedy. It is now apparent that in practice psycho-analysis only has value as an instrument of scientific research into the painful areas of unconscious feeling and impulse because the patient believes that the method has therapeutic value and will relieve him of his disabilities. Even then his co-operation is opposed by tremendous inner resistance. If faith in the therapeutic value of psycho-analysis proves unwarranted, it will have no more value as a scientific method than have the laboratory methods of academic psychology. The person investigated just does not allow these to touch painful areas of his inner life. If ever we are to gain scientific understanding of the dynamic development and functioning of human personality we must learn to combine investigation and therapy. That is what psycho-analysis claims to do, and it is our only hope of entering this closely guarded, tenaciously defended area. This makes Freud's cautious estimate of the possibility of psychotherapy all the more challenging. Therapeutic optimism and pessimism have alternated in the history of the psycho-analytic movement. On the one hand there are blocked analyses, negative therapeutic reactions, the gaining of intellectual insight without accompanying emotional change and the fact that distortion and embitterment of human personality can go so far and be so deep-seated that the individual seems to be virtually inaccessible to healing influences. On the other hand, there is the undoubted fact that many patients do actually show great changes in personality, lose symptoms

---

1. Expanded from a paper read on May 8, 1952 at the Clinical Discussion Group, Department of Psychiatry, Leeds University.

63

and become happier and more effective people as a result of this form of treatment. The problem of the possibility and nature of psychotherapy calls for urgent and continuous investigation.

It may make for clarity of exposition if I first state simply my conclusions before elaborating the clinical material and reasoning that sustains them.

In conformity with 'object-relations' theory the therapeutic factor is to be found in the object-relations of patient and psychotherapist. Here, as in all other matters, 'object-relationships' are the fundamental thing in human living and in the functioning of personality, whether maladjusted or mature. A maladjusted person is 'cured' by the development that becomes possible in a relationship with a mature person. Thus the therapeutic situation makes a big demand on the psychotherapist, one that may well daunt his moral courage and make him approach his task with befitting humility.

This therapeutic factor is primarily in an object-relationship of a parental order. The patient grew maladjusted in bad-object relationships with parents and/or parent-substitutes. He can only develop in a good-object relationship. But he is, at bottom, a frightened child, and as such needs a parent-figure. In the psychothera-peutic, as in the family situation, the chances of the child growing to maturity depend on the extent to which the parent or parent-substitute can offer the possibility of a mature relationship. That is the reason why the real training for psycho-analytical therapy is to undergo a personal analysis. It is only secondarily to learn the technique, though that is important. It is primarily to increase the maturity of the psychotherapist. Similarly, the real meaning of a 'cure' for the patient is not removal of symptoms, or any degree of social and vocational rehabilitation, but the achievement of reasonable or optimum maturity as a person. The other welcome results follow from that. The child grows up without guilt and anxiety and becomes capable of living without parental (or analytical) support.

The fundamental therapeutic factor in psychotherapy is more akin to religion than to science since it is a matter of personal relationship rather than of the application of impersonal knowledge and technique. Bertrand Russell (1925, p. 28) once defined the good life as 'the life inspired by love and guided by knowledge', which provides a neat formula for relating the scientific and religious factor in psychotherapy and in human life generally. Religion has always stood for the saving power of the good-object relationship. *Religion is distinguished from science as the historical form under which the therapeutic factor for personality ills has been recognized and cultivated.* Unfortunately, it has so often lacked the accurate knowl-edge which science could supply of the nature of the problems and how best to apply the remedy. *Science* stands for the discovery of the necessary knowledge without which love may be ineffective.

## DIFFICULTIES IN ASSESSING PSYCHOTHERAPEUTIC RESULTS

The difficulties of promoting and assessing constructive changes in personality have sometimes led to a hasty scepticism about psychotherapy in general. A recent example is provided by Eysenck's estimate of the effects of psychotherapy.

> It is often assumed that psychotherapy, whether Freudian or eclectic, tends to alleviate or cure neurotic disorders. A search was made for follow up studies in this field. . . . It would appear that two out of every three severely ill neurotics are cured or at best improve very much within a period of two years *without benefit of psychotherapy*; a similar proportion show evidence of cure or improvement after eclectic psychotherapy. After psycho-analysis results are somewhat less propitious than after eclectic treatment, or after no treatment at all. The data fail to confirm the hypothesis that psychotherapy alleviates or cures mental illness. (1952a, p. 41)

The superficiality of this statistical approach is shown by the fact that it permits the assumption that after two years the 'cured' patient is in exactly the same state of mind whether he has received psychotherapeutic treatment or not. It would require a far more subtle method of investigation either to prove or to disprove this assumption.

It is stated that two out of three neurotics are cured or improve within two years without psychotherapy. This is a quite inadequate statement of the case. In 1950 the writer broadcast some short talks on 'Nerves' which brought in over 1500 letters from radio listeners. One of the outstanding facts in this correspondence was the large number of elderly people who reported that they had suffered their first nervous breakdown in the late teens or early twenties and that since then they had experienced severe and repeated relapses at intervals of four, five or so years up to the fifties or sixties (their age at the time of writing). All these would come within the category of 'cured or improved within two years', a result that is of little significance in any deeper sense. It is not surprising that remissions of overt neurosis should occur, since a neurotic illness is an emotional crisis, and emotion inevitably ebbs and flows in intensity. Anxieties of even deep origin are greatly affected, either stimulated or damped down, by every unfavourable or favourable change in circumstances. Emotional crises are reactions to changing situations both within the mind and in the outer world, and the natural and automatic defence of repression is not a fixed and constant factor: it is constantly being weakened or reinforced by the ever-changing life-situation. Disappearance of symptoms is not 'cure' in the psycho-analytical sense. The criteria for 'cure' can only be satisfied where there is evidence of some important and stabilizing change of personality.

In the second place, Eysenck states that 'a similar proportion (two-thirds) show evidence of cure or improvement after eclectic psychotherapy'. The implication, presumably, is that the same remission of neurosis would have taken place without psychotherapy. We have, however, seen that this has little real significance. It would be necessary to ascertain, first whether and how often relapses occurred after psychotherapy at intervals greater than two years; secondly how far psychotherapy *in each particular case* had led to some decisive personality change and what bearing that had on liability to relapse; and thirdly, if there was relapse, was it over the same conflict that the psychological treatment had dealt with. Psychotherapy cannot deal with everything at once.

In the third place, a statistical summary giving the numbers or proportions of patients who do or do not recover, with or without psychotherapy, has little meaning since it takes no account of the motives patients may have for recovery or non-recovery. Many patients feel guilty about taking treatment because of the opposition of disapproving relatives, or because they feel involved in talking about parents and relatives 'behind their backs' and feel they ought not to do that even in order to get well. Some types of patient, who are aggressive and wish always to be master of other people, or to be independent at all costs, find extreme difficulty in accepting psychotherapeutic treatment at all. They are always secretly wanting to frustrate and defeat their analyst even at the price of remaining ill. They dread admitting any kind of dependence on an analyst or on anyone. Again, other patients are genuinely terrified of the emotional upheaval they must face in psycho-analysis; they are perhaps constitutionally deficient in 'tension capacity' or ability to stand up to anxiety. Sometimes a patient's human environment is so frustrating that it offers no better alternative than illness and he has no real incentive to get well. Yet again some patients enter on psychotherapeutic treatment not because they themselves really want it or have arrived at their own conclusion that they need it, but because some other person, doctor or relative, has persuaded them to it. There is always an underlying resistance in such cases, which may not be surrendered.

Finally, there is a fundamental factor which is mentioned last because it opens up our main line of inquiry. The schizoid patient whose basic strategy in life is to keep outside of all real personal relationships and not allow any feeling to be evoked in him, may be unable to form any sufficiently real relationship with the psychotherapist for therapy to proceed. There is a real dilemma here. Until psychotherapy has helped him to effect some measure of genuine relationship with the analyst he cannot make much use of the treatment, yet, while he cannot effect this relationship spontaneously because of his anxieties, the treatment cannot get under way to help him. The problem is not insoluble in practice but constitutes probably the major difficulty in treatment.

This brings us to the most serious omission in any statistical analysis of therapeutic results. It fails to take into consideration the nature of the relationship between psychotherapist and patient, but treats of psychotherapy as if it were a fixed and known entity, the same thing in every case. The patient reacts at once, unconsciously if not consciously, to the person of the psychotherapist or analyst. If therapy were a purely objective, scientific procedure or 'method' this would not matter. The patient's reaction to the doctor in purely organic disease is not primarily important though this ceases to be true as one gets into the realm of psychosomatic illness. The therapeutic powers of the old family doctor rested to an incalculable extent on his personality and the personal relationship between doctor and patient. In the sphere of psychological healing this becomes the all-important factor which no statistical analysis of results can record or evaluate. No doubt analysts as individuals do better with some types of patient than with others. Patient and analyst need to be 'matched' to secure the best results. Dr George Groddeck would refuse to treat a patient if he did not take to him. It is certain that 'choice of analyst' is highly important from a patient's point of view. Such highly relevant factors are too subtle to be weighed in merely statistical scales. Eysenck's sweeping conclusion, 'the data fail to confirm the hypothesis that psychotherapy alleviates or cures neurotic mental illness', appears as a hasty unscientific generalization based on inadequate methods of investigation. It may be that some early distortions of personality become irreversible. But we do not need to prove that psychotherapy must be 100% effective in *every* case, to show that it is a real and valuable possibility.

## THE PERSONAL RELATION OF ANALYST AND PATIENT: TRANSFERENCE

The factor of personal relationship between analyst and patient was quickly recognized by Freud and incorporated into the body of psycho-analytical teaching under the term 'transference'. He saw how large a part the patient's emotional reactions to the analyst played in treatment. Usually patients very largely repress what they are feeling about their analyst and strive to maintain a consciously good relationship with him on the moral level of winning and keeping his approval. The repression of their actual feelings is, needless to say, like all repression, unconscious and automatic. Often they are quite unaware that they are feeling anything directly about their analyst, and are mostly very resistant to any interpretation of their behaviour designed to help them to become conscious of their feelings. Freud recognized that the patient 'transfers' on to the analyst repressed and forbidden infantile reactions to parents, both of love and hate. He held that the original neurosis must be replaced by a transference neurosis if a cure is to be achieved. It seems doubtful, however, whether the basic implication of this transference problem was realized. Though it was Freud who seized on the importance of this personal relationship factor in treatment, there is justification for thinking that he looked at it more from the point of view of the patient's reactions to the analyst than from the point of view of what the analyst was *in reality* to the patient.

It has become customary to speak of analysts' 'counter-transferences' to their patients, and these, presumably, should likewise be analysed. The writer once said to Fairbairn 'counter-transference must be harmful to a patient'. He replied: 'You may do more harm to a patient if you are too afraid of counter-transference.' The reason no doubt is that if the analyst eliminates all personal feeling for a patient in the interests of pure scientific objectivity, the patient will be too justified in feeling that he is dealing with someone who has no genuine interest in *him* as a person. Patients feel that anyway. They say: 'You can't be really concerned about me, I'm only one of a crowd of patients to you, I'm only a "case" to you: I need something more personal, more human than analysis. I want to feel you care for me, that you are my friend.' There is, naturally, a great deal of transference in this. It conceals sexual phantasies of intimate relationships with the analyst, which reproduce old, unsatisfied wishes towards parents. These can be made conscious if the patient feels safe, as in two cases of more innocent transference reactions which, however, greatly embarrassed two of my own patients. One, a married woman in the thirties with three children, suddenly felt she wanted to run over to me, climb on my lap and curl up and go to sleep, as she used to do with her father. The other, a headmaster in the forties, felt a strong wish to lay his head on my shoulder and have my arms round him, and recalled being held in his father's arms and laying his head on his father's shoulders. It was so real to him that he could smell the tobacco of father's pipe. These early erotic wishes must become conscious before they can be outgrown.

## THE ANALYST AS PROJECTION SCREEN AND AS REAL OBJECT

But the patient's *personal* needs towards the analyst are not exhausted by the transfer of infantile eroticism. *The patient has genuinely realistic emotional needs towards the analyst, and psychotherapy depends, it seems, almost entirely on their satisfaction.* If the analyst persists in being, in reality, a merely objective scientific intelligence with no personal feeling for the patient, he will repeat on the patient the original emotional trauma which laid the foundations of the illness. Those who were one of a sibling group are apt to say 'I'm no more than one of a crowd of patients to you', while those who were 'only children' will say: 'You ought not to have any other patients but me.' They are seeking a parent-child relationship. They unconsciously want it in the erotic form characteristic of infancy and, if they got it, it would keep them in an emotionally immature state. Yet if the patient were 'merely one of a crowd of patients' to the therapist, how could he be helped to develop a sense of his own reality and worth as a person. What the patient *needs* as a basis for recovery must be described in two stages. First he needs a parent-figure as a protector against gross anxiety. He feels like a drowning man with no lifebelt. The psychotherapist is first and foremost a 'saviour' to him: he will often say, if a good 'rapport' is established fairly soon: 'I feel you are the first person who has ever understood me, or taken the trouble to understand me': or, as one patient put it, 'An analyst is better than prayers.' But such frank dependence is equivalent to one aspect of the infantile parent-child relationship: it is the child's need for a purely supportive, protective, reassuring love. Cure depends on getting beyond that to the second stage. Here the patient begins dimly to feel that what, to some not very enlightened extent, he consciously desires and seeks, and *what he really needs, as distinct from what he unconsciously wants, is the later form of non-erotic parental love which is the real condition of the child's ability to grow up. The analyst or psychotherapist must do for the patient what his parents failed to do.* He must help him to give up his infantile erotic wishes towards parents by giving him a love that approves and supports his desire to be independent, and his developmental urge to become a person in his own right and to be himself. This releases him to take his erotic needs to a non-parental equal partner and to enter into new, extra-familial relationships. The analyst cannot do that unless he has got genuine feeling for the patient, and is not himself afraid of the emotional relationship or of the role the patient needs him to fill. But it takes a patient a long time to accept the analyst as a liberating parent. All the fears, distrusts and resentments he feels towards his own parents rise up again, and all their restrictive and rejective attitudes to him are projected on to the analyst. This is where psycho-analytical or psychotherapeutic techniques come in. The analyst's insight must detect the problems as they emerge, and his skill and technique must enable him to help the patient to uncover them.

Yet all that is of little avail unless there is the basis of a 'real' good relation over and above the 'transference disturbances'. These can go on more openly on the basis of a steadily deepening realistic confidence in the analyst, without which the patient will let out very little, however skilful the technique. He must have some firm standing ground in present-day reality if he is to revive, recognize and work through problems originating in the past. Even then there is no automatic guarantee that a patient will use analysis to be cured. After all he is still a person who can harbour and pursue purposes of his own. The psychotherapist has no power, nor should he have, to force a patient to get better against his will. He may have what are to him, on balance, more important purposes to serve than getting cured. He may be determined to revenge himself on the family, or by transference, on the psychotherapist. In that case he will use the analysis to get worse, not better, and will accuse the analyst of destroying everything he had to cling to, his beliefs, duties, ideals, hopes, illusions or what not. Thus he can finally say to the analyst: 'Look at the mess you've made of my life, look what you've done to me.' A negative therapeutic reaction enables him to 'expose' the bad parent or even the whole family, and the bad analyst all in one. Hate has its satisfactions in destructiveness even at the price of self-destruction. These may under certain circumstances appeal to a person more than the constructive satisfactions of love.

The final result a patient achieves in analysis may well be the result he sets out to achieve, in the sense of having unconsciously aimed at all along. If his aim is constructive he will respond to the analyst but he must have a real 'person' to respond to. No one will be saved from anxiety by talking to an impersonal 'projection screen'.

## OBSTACLES TO PSYCHOTHERAPY

Before we deal further with the analyst's significance for the patient, let us consider three basic obstacles to successful psychotherapy.

1. Physical pain often covers over, and defends against, mental pain, and the mental pain will emerge if the physical pain is lost. That is the situation in hysteria and psychosomatic illness. In that case, unless one can alleviate the mental pain, the patient dare not give up the physical pain which is easier to bear. Prof. Bonamy Dobree, in a Third Programme broadcast on Kipling, spoke of the poet's interest in mental breakdown and his knowledge of inner mental hells and horrors which have 'to be experienced to be appreciated'. 'In his younger days, he was eager only to tell the stories as part of the enthralling, darkly striated, pageant of life; later he became interested in the causes, and finally he was absorbed in the healing of the horror.' Dobree refers to the charge that Kipling was 'callous about physical pain' but replies that he knew 'it was as nothing compared with spiritual agony. This he states unequivocally in the *Hymn to Physical Pain* (1952, p. 967):

> Dread Mother of Forgetfulness
>     Who, when Thy reign begins,
> Wipest away the Soul's distress,
>     And memory of her sins. . . .

> Wherefore we praise Thee in the deep,
> And on our beds we pray
> For Thy return, that Thou may'st keep
> The Pains of Hell at bay!'

That is the situation the psychotherapist faces.

An elderly woman known to the writer lost her husband and, left alone, developed eczema all over her body. For more than a year medical treatment secured no more than improvements followed always by relapse. She was then cured by a kindly elderly woman herbalist who personally massaged a wonderful ointment into her for an hour twice a week. She was cured, no doubt, not by the ointment but by the 'mothering', albeit of an infantile erotic order. *Evidently in many cases a patient cannot give up an illness unless something better can be put in its place* as a defence, in the case of this woman against separation anxiety and depression. What kind of 'something better' can the psychotherapist give? Not infantile erotic mothering, but also certainly not a cold impersonal scientific technique of investigation. That has its place but it is not the therapeutic factor.

2. The second and fundamental obstacle to therapy, though in fact it is the same obstacle viewed in a deeper way, is what Fairbairn calls 'the libidinal cathexis of bad objects' (1943, p. 334). This is one of his most original and radical contributions. In the paper on 'Analysis Terminable and Interminable', Freud (1937, p. 332) describes psychotherapy as supporting the patient's ego against the quantitative strength of his innate instincts. He says: 'The quantitative factor of instinctual strength in the past opposed the efforts of the patient's ego to defend itself, and now that analysis has been called in to help, that same factor sets a limit to the efficiency of this new attempt. If the instincts are excessively strong the ego fails in its task. . . . The power of analysis is not infinite, it is limited. . . . We shall achieve our therapeutic purpose only when we can give a greater measure of analytical help to the patient's ego.' This instinct theory may well make us pessimistic about therapy. If the illness is due to innate biological drives which are too strong for the patient to master, then our chance of curing him seems very limited.

However, the biological concept of instinct is to-day under drastic criticism by psychologists. On the academic side Allport (1949), in America, and Vernon (1942) and Pear (1942) in this country, reject the concept, while Burt, (1941, 1943) Myers (1942) and Thouless (1951) reduce it to 'innate directional determining tendency' which clearly needs some actual object or situation for its evocation. Freud's concept of instinct, on a psychological level, is to-day increasingly regarded as a relic of faculty psychology. Horney (1939), Fromm (1942) and Sullivan (1947) in America have discarded instinct theory and Fairbairn in this country regards the term 'instinct' as only useful in an adjectival sense. These views are representative of a widespread movement of thought which either rejects altogether the utility and relevance of the concept of 'instinct' for human psychology, or drastically limits it to 'innate potentialities for reaction' which underlie developmental processes. The actual impulses and emotions with which we deal in patients are not in themselves fixed innate biological factors: they are reactions of the ego to persons and situations encountered in the active process of living. They are appropriate to the way the ego perceives the object, and express the ego's relation to the object. Change the object either in reality or in perception and the impulse and emotion change. In this sense the cure for troublesome emotions and impulses is simple in theory, if not in practice, i.e. change the human environment. As adults we can sometimes do that, as children practically never. A child's only way of escaping from the bad object aspect of family figures is by a kind of mental trick. The real object is split in the child's mind into two objects, one ideally good and one totally bad. The image of the good parent is projected, i.e. the real parent is idealized. The image of the bad parent is repressed and forms a highly disturbing 'mental object' inhabiting, and reacted to, in an unconscious inner world. A whole secret world of bad figures is internalized and embedded in the unconscious structure of the personality. *It is these 'internal bad objects' as they are now called, and not instincts, which cause the trouble. The turbulent emotions and impulses of the neurotic are not fixed inborn instincts; they are personal reactions to these frightening and frustrating figures in the unconscious, and they would die down if these internal persecutors were got rid of.*

Psycho-analysis is not the reinforcement of instinct-control, it is exorcism (Fairbairn 1943, pp. 333, 336), casting out the devils that haunt people in the unconscious inner world, devils who can be seen clearly enough in patients' dreams. Where then lies the difficulty? One would think patients would be only too glad to let go their devils but nothing could be further from the truth. One of my patients, a woman in the fifties, is still dreaming of her father thrashing her and she said: 'If that were happening at least I wouldn't be an ageing woman and living alone.' Another, a man of thirty who in real life cannot bring himself to leave a home in which he is violently unhappy, dreams of being on a muck heap frantically raking to find something valuable. A cyclist goes by and calls to him to come and join him, but he stays on the muck heap. 'Mucky' is one of his epithets for his mother. He won't give up his muck heap that he is still trying to get something out of. A third patient says: 'My husband and father are devils, but I never let go my devils.' Patients cling tenaciously to their *external* bad objects because they are indispensable persons. If they give them up in the outer world, they cling to them all the more inside as *internal* mental objects in the unconscious. To part with them sets up the fear of death. Bad parents are better than none. *The major source of resistance to psychotherapy is the extreme tenacity of our libidinal attachments to parents whatever they were like. This state of affairs is perpetuated, by repression, in the unconscious inner world where, at the deepest level, they are always bad figures. The analyst is regarded as someone who is going to rob the patient of his parents. It takes the patient a very long time to feel deep down that the analyst is in fact a better parent. Even accepting his help feels like a fundamental disloyalty to the patient's own parents and arouses guilt.* Family loyalty dictates the defence and justification of parents against all outsiders. One of my patients said: 'Sometimes I feel that this business is against my parents, that they haven't brought me up properly which I deny, and secondly that it's pulling me away from them which I don't want.' Fairbairn says:

> The resistance can only really be overcome when the transference situation has developed to a point at which the analyst has become such a good object to the patient that the latter is prepared to risk the release of bad objects from the unconscious. [1943, p. 332]

And again,

> It is only through the appeal of a good object that the libido can be induced to surrender its bad objects . . . it may well be that a conviction of the analyst's 'love' (in the sense of Agape and not Eros) on the part of the patient is no unimportant factor in promoting a successful therapeutic result. At any rate, such a result would appear to be compromised unless the analyst proves himself an unfailingly good object (in reality) to his patients. [1943, p. 336; also cf. sections 6 and 8]

Flügel (1945, p. 176 n) endorses Fairbairn's view. Giving up parents, even in the form of internal bad objects, arouses guilt and fears of punishment, fears of isolation and death, and fears of injuring and killing parents by leaving them. *The difficulty of emotional detachment from parents in the unconscious is the real reason why neurosis is so hard to cure.*

The view of psychotherapy here maintained is that the patient cannot be weaned from, and become independent of, internalized bad parental-objects, and so cannot become healthy and mature, unless he can consolidate a good relationship to his analyst as a real good-object. At this point we come upon a third fundamental obstacle to psychotherapy, namely the severe difficulties patients have about entering into any relationships at all with real human beings in their outer world, even though such relationships are what they most deeply need. Thus they both seek and resist a real good-object relationship with the analyst. In the depressive position their trouble is the ambivalence of their reactions. They cannot love him without finding that aggression and hate surge up as well. But the deeper and much more difficult problem is their reactions in the schizoid position. Here their need of love-objects is so starved and exaggerated, their basic attitude to people is so greedy, hungry and devouring, and thus they feel so destructive, that they are afraid to need, want and love anyone. They retreat into a cold, aloof, unfeeling detachment, sometimes masked by intellectual interest and a superficially friendly, co-operative attitude. Genuine 'rapport' is not there.

This difficulty is well illustrated by the headmaster already referred to (p. 118). The proof that he needed and sought a personal relationship with his analyst was indirectly provided by the way he resisted it. As he came into one session he observed: 'I feel an uprising of tension but the thought occurs that I'm old and you're older.' That thought embarrassed him, he did not know why. He went on to say:

> No one loves me because I'm old, but you're older still. One becomes less physically attractive as one grows older, and less likely to be loved. As I grow older there are fewer people by whom I can be loved in a paternal way. One's props get less. I feel angry but if I were aggressive you'd resent it; it would become a personal matter between us. It's only because as analyst and patient there's no personal relationship that I can let things out.

It was explained that he wanted, but was afraid, to see his analyst as a real human being who could have real feelings about him, afraid to allow the analytical relationship to become emotionally alive and personal, and that that was an effective defence which halted real progress in treatment. He was remaining detached from the analyst and keeping the analyst remote from himself. In that situation nothing of any emotional significance was likely to emerge and he would be safe from outbursts of anxiety. He was afraid of the very relationship he desired, that being his general problem in life. He replied: 'I find any personal relationship with anyone impossible. I don't really know what it means. I want a personal relationship but am too proud to ask for it, too independent.'

## THE ANALYST AS A REAL GOOD OBJECT

If the patient cannot, and dare not, part with his bad psychic objects in his inner world until the analyst has become for him a sufficiently good real object in his outer world, in what sense must the analyst become a good object whose 'love' cures the patient? Maxwell Gitelson (1952, p. 1) has recently written about 'The Emotional Position of the Analyst in the Psycho-Analytical Situation', and says that 'recent developments in the psychotherapeutic functions of psycho-analysis . . . have pointed to the importance of the analyst as a real object'. His paper, however, is confined to dealing largely with countertransferences, with the fact that 'the analyst may bring into the analytical situation interfering emotional factors' (p. 3). To off-set these he holds that the qualified analyst brings to the patient 'intellectually sublimated curiosity. . . . Object-attitudes including emphatic compassion . . . and helpfulness' and finally an emotionally 'open' and flexible personality 'in a spontaneous state of continuing self-analysis' (pp. 3–4). This does not carry us far enough. Gitelson rightly says that: 'the analyst as a mere screen does not exist in life. He cannot deny his personality nor its operation in the analytical situation as a significant factor' (p. 7). But he seems to draw back from the goal towards which his argument moves when he writes: 'This is far from saying, however, that his personality is the chief instrument of the therapy which we call psycho-analysis . . . It is of primary importance for the analyst to conduct himself so that the analytical process proceeds on the basis of what the patient brings to it' (p. 7). Surely what the patient brings to analysis represents at bottom a need which must be met by what the analyst brings to it. Gitelson concludes that: 'the sustaining psychotherapeutic factor in the conduct of an analysis, the real ego support that the patient needs, resides in the actuality of the analyst's own reality-testing attitudes' (p. 8). 'One can reveal as much of oneself as is needed to foster and support the patient's discovery of the reality of the actual interpersonal situation' (p. 7). This, however, still falls short of giving a definite statement of the nature of the specific element in 'the reality of the actual interpersonal situation' which meets the patient's need for a good-object who will enable him to give up his internal bad objects.

The urgency and reality of the need felt by one of my patients in this matter is vividly expressed in the following dream:

> I'm looking for Christ on the seashore. He rose up as if out of the sea
> and I admired His tall magnificent figure. Then I went with Him into a
> cave and became conscious of ghosts there and fled in stark terror. But
> He stayed there and I mustered up courage and went back in with
> Christ. Then the cave was a house and as He and I went upstairs He
> said 'You proved to have greater courage than I had' and I felt I detected
> some weakness in Him.

The patient associated the admired tall figure of Christ with that of his athletic father, and then remarked to the analyst

> I associate Him somehow with you, I've got the idea you may inveigle
> me into courage to face the ghosts and then let me down. Mother was
> the menacing figure. Father was weak, mute before her onslaughts. He
> once said it wasn't a good thing to have one parent constantly
> dominating another in front of a child, but he never showed any anger
> at all.

Here is the patient oscillating between the old fear that father lets him down if he tries to stand up to the violent-tempered mother, and the new wavering hope that the analyst will not let him down in facing up to the 'ghost' of the angry mother within. In a later dream he encountered the ghost of mother coming out of a room while a figure representing myself stood by. Such dreams give sharp point to Fairbairn's view that the analyst is an exorcist who helps the patient to cast out the ghosts or devils who haunt his inner world.

The analyst naturally does not seek to play the role of a Christ or Saviour, but it is clear that the patient needs to regard him in this light, as one without whose help he can neither face nor give up his internal bad objects. Only by working through that phase can he later give up his need for the analyst in the role of one who 'saves' him from bad objects. By then the analyst will have become a non-possessive good object, with whom the patient has out-grown the dependencies of childhood, and achieved the kind of satisfactory, mature relationship which is not lost or damaged by his going away ('leaving home') to live his own proper life.

Before, however, we seek to develop the point of view involved in this religious analogy, let us approach the problem from another angle. *The analyst is not a good object merely by virtue of being a good technician.* The technique of psycho-analysis *as such* does not cure. It is not endowed with any mystic healing power. It is simply a scientific method of investigating the unconscious, an instrument of research. It plays an essential part in psychotherapy but is not itself the therapeutic factor. It is a way of making unconscious mental contents conscious, though 'contents' is too mechanical a term. It means providing a patient with an opportunity to talk to someone with complete freedom to say anything and everything without encountering disapproval or retaliation, so that he can bring the unconscious operations of his personality to conscious awareness, and discover himself to himself in the act of self-expression.

But what is to be done with what becomes conscious? The technique of psycho-analysis provides both the therapist and patient with information. Certainly a problem cannot be solved until a patient has become consciously aware of it. Abreaction or 'talking out' (like 'acting out') further gives temporary relief to pent-up feeling, and temporary security is experienced in an ad hoc good relationship, but this does not of itself lead to permanent changes. Thus the analytical technique *as such* is more an instrument of research and of temporary relief than of radical therapy: at best it involves a transient therapeutic factor in that one cannot unburden oneself to any helpful listener without feeling less anxious and alone. If that were all, the results would be mainly intellectual, and would lead to no deep permanent emotional change.

*It is the continuing relationship of analyst and patient on an emotional level that enables the patient to deal with what is made conscious.* The writer (1948, p. 11) defined psychotherapy as

a co-operative effort of two people, in the dynamic personal relationship of the analytical situation, to solve the problems of one of them. In
the end, medical, religious and social work is the creative power of
knowledge applied in and through good personal relationships. The
need to understand this is bringing together workers in all these fields.

It seems necessary now to make the matter clearer by saying that it is only the kind
of knowledge that is arrived at as a living insight, which is felt, experienced, in the
medium of a good personal relationship, that has therapeutic value.

In the book quoted the writer developed the theme that integration, individuation and personal relationships were but distinguishable aspects of one and the
same thing which might be called 'mental health' from the psychiatric point of view
or 'peace' and 'salvation' from the religious point of view. Thus:

> The total self is always tending one way or the other, and it is in good
> or bad personal relationships that the personality grows morally and
> spiritually healthy or diseased. . . . The ethical choice in favour of love
> can only be actualized in and through the processes of development
> which are described from the psychological point of view as integration
> and individuation, the process of becoming a true, whole and harmo-
> nious self. That is what creates the state of mind called 'peace'; and
> there is an important link between the psychological idea of integration
> and the religious conception of peace. . . . As soon as we realize that in
> the large sense neurosis is simply the drama of human life, the struggle
> of fear, hate and love for mastery in the soul of man, we must see that
> what the psychologist describes as the integration process is the gradual
> harmonization of the personality in the course of its transition from
> hate to love; looked at psychiatrically that is identical with the transi-
> tion from disease to health, and from conflict to integration. Looked at
> religiously it is surely the same thing as that redemption from sin, from
> pride, hate, lovelessness and selfishness which is called 'salvation.'
> [1948, pp. 201–202]

Whatever terminology different interests may use to describe the change, the
important point is that *this therapeutic change can only come about in, and as a direct
result of, a good-object relationship.* That has been clearly understood by religious
thinkers. In terms of Fairbairn's view that object-relations have priority over
instinctive impulses and are the key to every psychological or personal process, *we
must regard the good-object relationship of the analyst to the patient as the therapeutic or
'saving' factor in psychotherapy.* In the terms of the dream quoted, the patient feels

that that is what saves him from his desperate plight in the power of his internal bad objects.

This is, of course, true in real life. The bad objects internalized and repressed in infancy can be progressively modified if the child experiences an increasingly good relationship to parents in the post-infancy period. That is the cue for psychotherapy. The maturing of personality takes place by natural growth and development on the basis of the right kind of parental love. In infancy, parental love has an erotic element and is expressed in physical handling of all kinds, in bodily contact and care. As the child grows up parental love must lose this erotic component, or rather the erotic component must be reduced to minor proportions, if the child is to become capable of marriage. Parental love should turn into a non-erotic, non-possessive, non-dominating, affection which supports the child in his development of separate and independent individuality. He is backed up and encouraged to think and act for himself, to explore, experiment, take risks, use and develop his own powers and in short helped to be 'himself'. This is the kind of parental love appropriate to latency and adolescence, and it leads finally to a replacing of the early erotic attachments which are dependent in the child and supporting in the parent, by mature relationships of mutual respect, equality, and the affection of friendship. Then the grown-up child is free without anxiety or guilt to enter an erotic relationship with an extra-familial partner, and to exercise an active and spontaneous personality free from inhibiting fears. This kind of parental love is what the Greeks called *agape*, not *eros*, and it is the kind of love the psycho-analyst and psychotherapist must give the patient because he did not get it from his parents in sufficient measure or in a satisfactory form. Parents and analysts can only approximate to this ideal of agape, or spiritual love, but only in so far as this is done can patients be helped to a cure.

For the achieving of the more permanent therapeutic results, something depends on how bad the internal bad objects are: they may be too terrifying for the patient to release them, even with the analyst's help. Much also depends on the general calibre of the patient. But perhaps most depends on the maturity of the analyst, on his capacity to give the patient the right kind of love (which carries with it the ability to avoid making technical mistakes in dealing with the patient) and on analysis lasting long enough for the patient really to grow in a consolidated good relationship. A famous Scottish preacher, Dr Chalmers, once described how a converted drunkard threw his bottles of beer out of the window when the love of God came into his heart. That showed, he said, 'the expulsive power of a new affection'. Likewise the patient gives up his attachment to his early frustrating love objects, and casts out his internal bad objects, only through 'the expulsive power of the new affection' that he gets from, and feels for, the parental analyst. He is able to grow to adult stature emotionally because it is the kind of love that approves of his doing so and helps the process. But there is a parable of Jesus which psychotherapists would do well to ponder. The devil was cast out of a man and the house of his soul left swept and garnished but empty, with the result that seven other devils came and took possession of him. If we could succeed in ridding patients of their symptoms without giving them a constructive relationship with ourselves to build on, we would do them more harm than good in the end. They never will give up their devils inside if they are given nothing in their place. Psychotherapy is more like exorcism than a purely scientific technique of treatment. It is a good-object relation that cures people by weaning them from bad objects who make them ill. It is not a fixed uniform procedure or method the results of which could be statistically estimated.

It should now be clear that it is the dynamic, personal factors which are the crux of the matter in psychotherapy, and that these are altogether too subtle to be taken account of by statistical study of the results of samples of psychotherapy. Such investigations do not envisage the *necessity* of studying the personalities and the developing relationship of patient and psychotherapist *in every case* before it would be possible to assess the nature of the 'cure' or the reasons for therapeutic failure. Eysenck speaks of cure or improvement 'without benefit of psychotherapy', but he makes no attempt to give meaning to the phrase by studying the life-situation and the personal relationships in the midst of which the patients did or did not recover. There is no such thing as improvement 'without benefit of psychotherapy' for life itself has its psychotherapeutic factors, of which professional psychotherapy is a scientifically specialized development. The meshes of the statistical scientific fish-net (*vide* Eddington) are too large to catch these 'facts' of interpersonal relations. We cannot, therefore, conclude that they are not 'facts' and infer that psychotherapy is to be scientifically debunked.

In a letter to the Editor of the *Quarterly Bulletin of the British Psychological Society*, Eysenck (1952b) compares 'papers devoted to scientific (experimental and statistical) studies in abnormal psychology' with 'papers dealing with ideographic, psycho-analytic and other "dynamic" topics'. The first he calls 'factual' and the second 'speculative'. But the fallacy of refusing the status of 'fact' to what one's own particular method is incapable of taking account of, has always been one of the most dangerous blind-spots of investigators; Eysenck has clearly fallen into that trap. Psychotherapy is not a purely scientific procedure since it involves the art of sustaining an actual kind of personal relationship. But a supposedly scientific study of psychotherapy by methods which fail to take into account the all-important personal factors of motivation and relationship, is not truly scientific.

Two psychotherapists may be treating two patients, using the same kind of technique and interpretations, and yet what really goes on in the two treatments may be utterly different, leading in one case to a blockage and in the other to a cure. That may be due partly to the patient, partly to the psychotherapist, and partly to whether they are or are not 'well matched', or to all three causes. But we shall certainly be led astray if we attribute therapeutic results purely to our technique of investigation. *The technique makes problems accessible to treatment. It is the relationship with the therapist that enables the problem to be solved.* Freud discovered that, at the very beginning. He wrote of his decision to drop hypnosis and the abreactive, cathartic technique, as follows:

> It was true that the disappearance of the symptoms went hand in hand with the catharsis, but total success turned out to be entirely dependent upon the patient's relation to the physician. . . . If that relation was disturbed, all the symptoms reappeared, just as though they had never been cleared up. [1922, p. 110]

Apparently Kipling also recognized this. Dobree writes:

> If, then, the world includes hells for men and women so intolerable that the strain actually breaks them, what is the cure? Kipling had all sorts of mechanism for healing, varieties of psycho-analysis which clear up complexes. But these are merely mechanisms, and the driving force, the virtue without which no cure can be effected is—I state this quite boldly—compassion. [1952, p. 963]

We must observe that the hells which finally break people are not those in the outer world. It is astonishing what human beings can stand if they are at peace within themselves. It is the hells hidden within the mind itself which are reactivated by the outer hells, that break our resistance. Furthermore, 'compassion' is not fully adequate as a description of the healing factor, though it is an essential element in it. But the distinction between 'mechanisms' and the 'therapeutic factor' is central to our theme.

## THE ANALOGY BETWEEN PSYCHOTHERAPY AND RELIGION

It is not suggested that the personal relation alone is important in psychotherapy and the technique irrelevant. The technique is necessary in order to make unconscious problems accessible once more to a new solution. Nor is it suggested that any kind of good-object relationship is therapeutic in the radical psycho-analytical sense. If it were, then a good marriage or a powerful religious experience could be relied on to cure neurosis and thoroughly mature the personality; whereas in fact the therapeutic effects they do often have are usually more due to their being a powerful support and defence against internal bad objects, than to their bringing about an exorcism of bad objects and a radical maturing of the self. It is maintained rather that *the special kind of good object that the patient needs to find in the analyst is best defined as the mature, non-possessive, non-dominating parent who approves and helps the child's development towards adult independence, self-reliance, and libidinal spontaneity, free from anxiety and guilt. The child can then grow up to the parent's level of maturity and become capable of adult love, friendship and creativity.*

It is time, however, that we now investigated the relationship which evidently exists between psychotherapy and religion. The subject has always intrigued psycho-analysts. Freud bestowed much thought upon it, though he was least objective and most obviously influenced by emotional bias when he wrote about religion and philosophy. The writer in the passages quoted (1948), pursued the link between religion and psychotherapy, not however in terms of detailed psychopathology and the problems of internal objects. Money-Kyrle (1951, p. 84 n) defines religion as 'a form of psychotherapy which promotes a belief in the existence of idealized good objects as a defence against persecutory and depressive guilt'. We must not pause here to discuss the metaphysical and theological, i.e. extra-psycho-analytical, questions that raises, except perhaps to say that the motive and the truth of a belief are not identical problems, and that a psycho-analytical definition does not settle *all* issues. We quote the definition rather as a clear acknowledgement of common ground which exists for religion and psychotherapy. That being so, there should be much to be learned from the study of religion as throwing light on the patient's psychotherapeutic needs, since it is the age-old form of psycho-therapy that man has always resorted to.

Fairbairn's article on 'The Repression and The Return of Bad Objects' is crucial for the nature of psychotherapy and he there utilizes religious concepts at a number of points in an illuminating way. Thus, in dealing with the 'moral defence' against repressed bad objects, he states that: 'Religious terms . . . provide the best representation for the adult mind of the situation as it presents itself to the child' (1943, p. 331). He describes the situation of the individual at the level of the super-ego or 'moral defence' organization, in religious terms, thus:

> It is better to be a sinner in a world ruled by God than to live in a world ruled by the Devil. A sinner in a world ruled by God may be bad: but there is always a certain sense of security to be derived from the fact that the world around is good—'God's in His heaven—All's right with the world!': and in any case there is always a hope of redemption. In a world ruled by the Devil the individual may escape the badness of being a sinner: but he is bad because the world around him is bad. Further, he can have no sense of security and no hope of redemption. The only prospect is one of death and destruction. [1943, pp. 331–332]

As we have seen, the unconscious is precisely the world ruled by the Devil, the cave of the patient's dream (p. 123) where dwell the terrifying ghosts whom he felt unable to face alone unless he could find a Christ, a Saviour, to go along with him. Jung, though he did not express it in psycho-analytical terms, sensed the patient's dilemma. He writes:

> The psychotherapist . . . must decide in every single case whether or not he is willing to stand by a human being with counsel and help upon what may be a daring misadventure . . . *man has never yet been able single handed to hold his own against the powers of darkness—that is of the unconscious. Man has always stood in need of the spiritual help that each individual's own religion held out to him.* [1933, p. 277]

Jung's conception of analytical treatment is not the same, in technique and method, as Fairbairn's fundamentally Freudian practice. The word 'counsel' belongs more to conscious re-education than to analysis. But Jung had realized both that the relationship of the patient and the analyst is the vital therapeutic factor and that it has a very close relationship to religious experience, as the words italicized in the quotation show. The matter, however, becomes far more clear when we think in terms of internal bad objects, than when we think in terms of archetypes. Fairbairn says:

> It is to the realm of these bad objects, I feel convinced, and not to the realm of the super-ego that the origin of all psychopathological developments is to be traced: for it may be said of all psychoneurotic and psychotic patients that, if a True Mass is being celebrated in the chancel, a Black Mass is being celebrated in the crypt. It becomes evident, accordingly, that the psychotherapist is the true successor to the exorcist. [1943, p. 333]

But how are these internal bad objects, these ghosts or devils, to be cast out? Or how can the patient become able to give them up? In discussing the case of Christoph Haitzmann, the subject of Freud's paper 'A Neurosis of Demoniacal Possession in the Seventeenth Century' (1923, p. 436), Fairbairn observes:

> It was only after his pact with the Devil was replaced by a pact with God that his freedom from symptoms was finally established. The moral would seem to be that it is only through the appeal of a good object that the libido can be induced to surrender its bad objects: and, if Christoph was relieved of his symptoms by a conviction of the love of God, it may well be that a conviction of the analyst's 'love' (in the sense of Agape and not Eros) on the part of the patient is no unimportant factor in promoting a successful therapeutic result. [1943, p. 336]

It would appear that patients, at different times, tend to seek in the analyst a good object of two different kinds. These correspond to the Christian conceptions of God and of Christ, personified justice and personified love. The patient will repeatedly seek to make the analyst the head and representative of his super-ego or moral defence and become convinced that the analyst must pass stern moral judgement on him. In fact a patient would become more, not less, anxious, if an analyst were to try to relieve guilt by undermining the patient's proper moral sense. The patient seeks to be saved from his unconscious *devils viewed as morally bad objects* by clinging to the analyst as a stern judge, even exalting him to the position of God the Father. One of my patients woke dreaming and thought he saw me standing in the corner of the room; then I changed into God, and the patient was afraid but stretched out his arms towards me in an appeal for help. Perhaps only a very naïve patient would express this tendency so frankly but since Freud says that God is the projected father image, we would expect patients at times to feel that the paternal analyst is God.

But another patient, who is a deeply religious man, says frankly that he does not like God the Father, a stern punishing figure; he fears and obeys Him but all his religious devotion is directed towards Christ. As a lonely and anxious little boy he would go to sleep phantasying himself comforted and loved on the bosom of Jesus, the Great Lover. *Christ is clearly a libidinally good object to offset the Devil as a libidinally bad object: while God the Father is a morally good object to offset the Devil as a morally bad object.* The patient certainly longs for the analyst to love and comfort him and so reassure and save him from his haunting inner fears, and frequently asks outright for such support.

It is tempting to suggest that since the internal bad objects frequently haunt the individual (in dreams) as ghosts, unseen sinister influences, an immaterial menace, they are offset in that respect by the third Christian conception of God as the Holy Ghost who 'fills', 'inspires', and pervades the soul as a good influence. The final place of the analyst in the life of a matured patient would not be ill represented as a pervading and inspiring influence for good, for love and creative activity. In Christian theology it is to be noted that the orthodox belief most emphatically insists on the unity of this triune God in three modes, a welcome insistence which points the way to the integration of all good objects, and therefore of the individual ego in relation to good objects. The splitting asunder of love and justice could only maintain disintegration in the ego. So far Christian theology has not been able to deal with the Devil in any other terms than total rejection, and certainly patients can only be cured by such a consolidated relationship to the analyst as a good-object in reality that they are able to relinquish their phantasied devils, who have no other existence than that with which they are endowed in being internally and psychically maintained. Thus as it were, they vanish as illusions. It is true there are objectively real counterparts of these devils in the form of bad human beings, of whom the political life as well as the criminal records of our generation give ample illustration. Yet these 'bad men' are bad because they are so dominated by, and identified with, their own inner devils, who likewise could, in theory at any rate, be dissipated into unreality. It seems a not unjustified inference to hold that devils *as such* are not integrated but evaporated and lost as psychic illusions at last. Thus good, not evil, is the basic, enduring reality of life. We should perhaps add that this psychological analysis is made without prejudice to the interest that other, philosophical and theological, disciplines have in the question. It is designed to show, first, that the evolution of the complex Christian doctrine of God meets point by point the needs for psychotherapy of the devil-haunted soul of man; and secondly that it does throw a highly illuminating light on what the psychoneurotic patient feels he needs to find in the psychotherapist. If we now say that devils and ghosts are internalized phantasied bad parents and God is the saving good parent sought in the healing, parental analyst, that is not necessarily all that is to be said on the subject. Man still faces, and feels he needs an adjustment to, an all embracing universal reality which he is as likely as ever to conceive in terms of religion in a larger sense, which raises issues with which psycho-analysis has no special competence to deal. So far as psychotherapy is concerned, the cured, matured patient has outgrown the need to find a Saviour in his analyst.

Returning to the narrower questions of psychotherapy, we may say that religion has always understood and used the true therapeutic factor of personal relationship without, however, possessing an accurate scientific understanding of the problems to which it needed to be applied. On the other hand, a purely scientifically orientated psychotherapy which imagines that the technique of treatment itself 'does the trick', may gather a lot of information about human nature and its troubles but lack the therapeutic factor to apply to them: and it will probably grow sceptical about psychotherapy. A true psychotherapy must be a combination of scientific technique for opening up the unconscious, and the parental factor of healing love. Prof. J. MacMurray holds that science concerns the relation of persons to things in terms of utility values, whilst religion concerns the relation of persons to persons in terms of intrinsic values. He writes: 'The field of religion is the whole field of common experience organized in relation to the central fact of personal relationship . . . the field of religion is the field of personal relations, and the datum from which religious reflection starts is the reciprocity or mutuality of these. Its problem is the problem of communion or community. Religion is about fellowship and community' (1936, p. 43). Thus the therapeutic factor may be properly described as religious.

The hell of suffering from which people need to be saved is the hell of love-starvation at bottom, for which the only cure is a good-object relationship in which personality can be reconstructed and matured free from anxiety and guilt. So fundamental is this factor of a saving personal relationship that the scientific technique of psycho-analysis cannot even be operated successfully without it. The patient lets nothing out of the unconscious except in proportion as he feels safe with the analyst. If repressed material is prematurely forced into consciousness by other methods, the patient will repress or forget it again, unless he has been able to grow a sufficiently deep trust in, and reliance on, his psychotherapist to be able to cope, on the basis of that relationship, with the problems which have emerged. Dr Clara Thompson has recently strongly emphasized this factor of personal relationship in psychotherapy. 'Around 1920 there was a growing feeling of pessimism about psychoanalysis as a method of therapy' (1952, p. 230). 'Around 1925 there was evidence that the goal of therapy was changing' (1952, p. 236). In discussing the analytical experience as 'an interpersonal situation' she says that in spite of the different theoretical orientations of different analysts, the patient achieves a cure 'if in the interpersonal experience with the analyst the patient's genuine problems of living have been explored' (1952, pp. 242–243).

## THE TECHNIQUE OF THE GOOD OBJECT

One further word must be said about the *technique* of 'being a real good object' to the patient. This cannot be accomplished, naturally, by direct intentional effort. It would be worse than useless to try to impress the patient with one's friendliness and one's concern for his welfare, or to try to persuade him into trust and reliance on oneself. Some patients would react erotically to such advances, others would react with fears of being influenced, possessed, tied, dominated. Even, at the best, if a patient were helped, he would only be consciously supported; at unconscious levels he would react with all the conflicts he always experiences in human relationships and would be less able to bring them out as reactions to his analyst for fear of disturbing the good relationship. Patients are patients because their fears are as strong as their needs with respect to good-object relations.

There is only one way for the patient to become convinced that the analyst is a good object for him, and that is to discover it for himself. This he can only do by working through his positive and negative transferences and finding out that what the analyst withholds (the erotic love and comforting support his infantile self craves for) is withheld for his real good; and that the analyst's apparent bad-object aspects are due to the projection of internal bad-object phantasies. Slowly he becomes ever more free to experience directly and in more mature ways the reality of the analyst as a mature helper who is enabling him to grow into a mature adult person. He 'discovers' that the analyst does 'love' him in the mature adult sense which releases him from his attachment to his infantile objects in his inner world, and helps him to venture into new and more satisfactory object-relationships in his outer world. At this point, maybe, one final comment calls to be made. For a 'perfect' therapeutic result, it is necessary that it should be open to the patient to establish basic good-object relationships in real life. For this reason, other things being equal, a better therapeutic result may be expected with a married man or woman in the thirties where the marriage contains genuine sound elements and possibilities of further development, than in the case of a spinster in the forties for whom the chances of a satisfying marriage are fast receding, or in the case of an elderly person most of whose life has been ruined by early difficulties and later neurosis, and who cannot now retrieve the position, having little active life to look forward to. There is not only the difficulty of helping the patient to accept a therapeutic relation to the analyst, but there is also the further difficulty of helping him to wean himself from too long-continuing dependence on the analyst, which would be equivalent to the grown-up child not being able to leave home. Just as a child would not leave his parents unless he had the prospect, in growing up, of a fuller life to enter into, so the patient cannot easily leave the analyst without relapse unless he has the chance of a real life of love and creative activity within his own measure to enter into. There must be a realistic incentive for therapeutic success. That enables the relationship between the matured patient and the analyst, after the close of treatment, finally to become something analogous to that of a child who has grown up, developed his own proper personality, left home to marry and run his own life and affairs, but whose affection for his parents, respect for their experience and good qualities, and pleasure in their interest and goodwill remains on an adult level.

## REFERENCES

Allport, G. W. (1949). *Personality*. London: Constable and Co.

Burt, C. (1941). Is the doctrine of instincts dead? A symposium. I. The case for human instincts. *British Journal of Educational Psychology* 11:155–172.

———— (1943). Is the doctrine of instincts dead? A symposium. VII. Conclusion. *British Journal of Educational Psychology* 13:1–15.

Dobree, B. (1952). *The Listener*, 12 June.

Eysenck, H. J. (1952a). *Quarterly Bulletin of the British Psychological Society* 3, no. 16 (April).

———— (1952b). 3, no. 17 (July).

Fairbairn, W. R. D. (1943). The repression and the return of bad objects. *British Journal of Educational Psychology* 19. (Reprinted as chapter 3 in *Psychoanalytic Studies of the Personality* (1952). London: Tavistock Publications Ltd.)

Flügel, J. C. (1945). *Man, Morals and Society*. London: Duckworth.

Freud, S. (1922). Psycho-analysis. *Collected Papers*, vol. 5. London: Hogarth Press.

———— (1923). A neurosis of demoniacal possession in the seventeenth century. *Collected Papers*, vol. 4. London: Hogarth Press.

———— (1937). Analysis terminable and interminable. *Collected Papers*, vol. 5. London: Hogarth Press.

Fromm, E. (1942). *The Fear of Freedom.* London: Kegan Paul.

Gitelson, M. (1952). The emotional position of the analyst in the psycho-analytic situation. *International Journal of Psycho-Analysis* 33.

Guntrip, H. (1948). *Psychology for Ministers and Social Workers.* London: Independent Press.

Horney, K. (1939). *New Ways in Psycho-Analysis.* London: Kegan Paul.

Jung, C. G. (1933). *Modern Man in Search of a Soul.* London: Kegan Paul.

MacMurray, J. (1936). *The Structure of Religious Experience.* London: Faber.

Money-Kyrle, R. (1951). *Psycho-Analysis and Politics.* London: Duckworth.

Myers, C. S. (1942). Is the doctrine of instincts dead? A symposium. VI. Retrospect and prospect. *British Journal of Educational Psychology* 12:148–155.

Pear, T. H. (1942). Is the doctrine of instincts dead? A symposium. V. Not dead, but obsolescent? *British Journal of Educational Psychology* 12:139–147.

Russell, B. (1925). *What I Believe.* London: Kegan Paul.

Sullivan, H. S. (1947). *Conception of Modern Psychiatry.* Washington, DC: William Alanson White Psychiatric Foundation.

Thompson, C. (1952). *Psycho-Analysis: Its Evolution and Development.* London: Allen and Unwin.

Thouless, R. H. (1951). *Social and General Psychology,* 3rd ed. London: University Tutorial Press.

Vernon, P. E. (1942). *British Journal of Educational Psychology* 12:1.

# 3

# OBJECT RELATIONS THEORY AS A SYNTHESIS OF THE INTRAPSYCHIC AND THE INTERPERSONAL

PSYCHOANALYTICAL THEORY HAS been in a state of continuous development from the beginning. The genius of its creator, Sigmund Freud, so dominated this process that, during his lifetime, theoretical developments were almost if not quite wholly determined by himself. Here and there in his writings he adopts suggestions from some fellow workers, while their contributions were in the main elaborations and developments of new theories which he himself propounded. In sober truth all the fundamental new ideas *did* come from Freud himself.

Though we await the judgement of an impartial historian of psychoanalysis (if such there can be in matters so closely touching human emotions) it is probably not unfair to state that the works of men like Jung, W. Reich and Rank, each in different ways, exhibited ultimately a speculative bent rather than the predominantly scientific, analytical, clinical line of Freud, while Adler may be said to have raised the problem of ego-analysis prematurely, and too superficially. But it must be admitted that Freud's own speculative bent broke out in his theory of the death instinct. He himself wrote: 'What follows is speculation, often far-fetched speculation, which the reader will consider or dismiss according to his individual predilection' (1920, p. 27). Nevertheless, he thereafter refers to the conclusions of this book as if they were now established facts. His speculations in the realm of the application of psychoanalysis to sociology have less bearing on basic matters of theory than have those in the book just quoted.

It was, however, indisputably Freud's own work that established psychoanalysis as a coherent and closely knit system. Perhaps it was inevitable that in the first phase of psychodynamic investigation schools formed in isolation from one another, and an unscientific atmosphere of 'orthodoxy versus heresy and deviation' arose. At least this protected the distinctive features of Freud's own work, which could have been obscured and lost, to the great disadvantage of future workers. Development has gone on within the psychoanalytic movement more narrowly defined, and it has been felt necessary to state that theoretical progress cannot be halted with the death of Freud. Brierley writes:

> As knowledge grows, older hypotheses become inadequate and have to be revised, expanded, or reformulated to contain newer facts. Freud did this himself, time after time, and if psycho-analysis is to continue to develop as a living science this process of recasting hypotheses and expanding theory must also continue. . . . To expect to conserve the letter of all Freud's statements, as a kind of 'Bible of Psycho-analysis' is to condemn psycho-analytic enquiry to stasis and, therefore, psycho-analysis as a science to death. [1951, p. 89]

But it is not insignificant that such words needed to be written. *In a broad sense an unconscious pattern of development as a process of a dialectical type can now be discerned.* Recent developments have not been haphazard and purely individualistic contributions. They have rather been determined by, and have arisen out of, that larger and all-embracing milieu of cultural change within which psychoanalysts like all other investigators must do their thinking. For example the influence of sociology (a science much less developed in Freud's creative period than now), on American psychoanalytic thought is recognized. Fairbairn has referred to the influence of a changing scientific and cultural orientation in calling for a revision of basic psychoanalytical theory at those points where it was determined by the atomistic scientific outlook of Helmholtz, a view that now no longer dominates physics or science in general. Furthermore, in Freud's day, the concept of the 'person' and of 'personality' had not assumed the importance in philosophical thinking that it came to do later, with far-reaching effects on all the human sciences. Culturally and conceptually, to-day is the era of human personal relationships rather than of instincts; the problem is, given innate endowment, how is that shaped by what goes on between people?

In tracing out the broadly dialectical pattern of development in psychoanalytical theory, we find some help (again, only in a broad way) in taking note of the differences between psychoanalytical thinking in different geographical areas. Balint, in 1937, referred to different emphases in London, Vienna and Budapest. We can recognize the same phenomenon on a larger scale affecting total theoretical orientation. A useful way of correlating recent developments is the following dialectical scheme, which, however, is not intended to be pressed rigidly or regarded as a strictly chronological development, but used only as a guiding idea:

**Thesis.** The original *European* psychobiology of Freud and his early co-workers from 1890 onwards, an 'instinct-theory' which was not modified by the later development in the 1920's of a more purely psychological ego-analysis. This may be referred to as the classic psychoanalytical teaching.

*Antithesis.* The rise of psychosociology in *America*, in the 'culture-pattern' and 'character-analysis' theories of writers like Karen Horney, Erich Fromm, and H. S. Sullivan, from the 1930's.

*Synthesis.* The elaboration in *Great Britain* of a different theoretical orientation which, while not indifferent to sociological and biological consider-ations, developed the concepts of the 'internal object' and the 'inner psychic world' as parallel to external objects and the outer world, and so comes to correlate the internal and the external object-relationships in which the personality is involved. This development arises out of the work of Melanie Klein and others, and is worked out in a systematic and comprehensive way by Fairbairn. It too dates from the 1930's.

Clara Thompson, in her recent book (1952), unfortunately only deals with phases one and two and quite ignores the British contribution which is in truth an exceedingly radical and important one.

## THESIS: THE CLASSIC FREUDIAN THEORY

In order to make clear where and why development was needed, we must consider certain aspects of the theory of psychoanalysis as laid down by Freud. Considered developmentally his work falls into two parts. The instinct theory (1890 to 1920) culminated in the monograph *Beyond the Pleasure Principle* where he outlined his final view of a dualism of instinctive equipment, libido and aggression, the life and death instincts. After that Freud produced a considerable reorientation in his thinking, with the development of ego-analysis and the scheme of psychic struc-ture, namely the id, ego and super-ego. Hartmann, Kris & Loewenstein write:

> Since a structural viewpoint was introduced into psychoanalytic think-ing, hypotheses previously established must be reintegrated. The task of synchronization is larger than it might seem at first. [1946, p. 12]

We have then to consider what criticisms of instinct theory in general, and of Freud's instinct theory in particular, and also what criticisms of his scheme of psychic structure, have arisen; and what is the relationship between these two parts of Freud's theory. To consider only criticisms, which is our business here, may seem an unduly negative approach to Freud's work, so we should remember that the most constructive critics themselves rest on a firm basis of Freud's discoveries, and their criticism is evidence of the vitality of his achievement.

## Freud's Instinct Theory

The concept of instinct was borrowed by Freud as a working concept to start with. It was already current in the biological and general thought of his day and was much used by academic psychologists. Freud and W. McDougall made instinct the basis of their psychological theories. Broadly speaking the concept has proved of more use in animal than in human psychology. Animal behavior is largely based on specific instincts resting on a definite neurological structure. The nest-building instinct of birds, the web-spinning instinct of spiders, the pecking instinct of the newly hatched chick, are cases in point; though as one comes higher up in the scale of complexity of animal life, intelligence becomes an increasingly obvious factor in modifying pure instinctive reaction. McDougall ultimately replaced the concept of instinct by that of 'propensity', a more vague and general term, in the case of human beings. Any simple instinct theory is now viewed with disfavour by academic psychologists, though the existence of innate motivational factors is accepted. Thouless sums up his discussion as follows:

> There seems to be no reason for denying the existence of human instincts or propensities if these are defined as innate forces behind behaviour. It seems better to avoid the word 'instinct' in connection with human behaviour, since this word may lead to misunderstanding. On the other hand, it is doubtful whether the conception of human instincts or propensities is of much service in explaining differences between societies or between individuals, since it is not possible to determine how far these differences are innate and how far they are acquired. There seem to be strong reasons for rejecting the doctrine that the driving forces behind human behavior are entirely derived from innate propensities. [1951, p. 41]

Allport states his views in the following words:

> The instinct theory asserts that there are . . . propensities operating 'prior to experience and independent of training'. . . . In recent years it has become common to reject this somewhat extravagant portrayal of human purposes. . . . The doctrine of drive is a rather crude biological conception. . . . The personality itself supplies many of the forces to which it must adjust. [1949, p. 119]

The psychology of personality must be a psychology of post-instinctive behavior. . . . Whatever the original drives or 'irritabilities' of the infant are, they become completely transformed in the course of growth into contemporaneous systems of motives. [1949, pp. 194–195]

Thus the sucking reflex in the newborn infant is instinctive like the innate specific behavior patterns of more primitive forms of life, but the 'sucking need and the sucking attitude to life' of the adult neurotic is certainly no simple instinctive phenomenon. The general innate factors in man are better described in the term of C. S. Myers as 'innate directional determining tendencies' to react in certain ways when certain types of situation call for appropriate response. In particular, it is not held that specific impulses exist prior to experience. Rather an innate tendency is a precondition of a specific impulse arising in response to a specific environmental object or situation. Thus the 'instinct' of aggression would not mean that we are permanently charged with an aggressive drive, always straining at the leash and seeking an outlet, whether there be good cause for anger and attack or not. Anger and aggression form an innate potentiality for reaction when we meet with frustration or danger.

This general position of academic psychology with respect to the theory of instinct is of great interest when we consider the views that Freud propounded. The general development of his instinct theory is well known. It passed through three stages. First, instincts of self-preservation and race preservation, of hunger and sex, were suggested, the former being regarded as ego-instincts and the latter as belonging to the primary unconscious. With the theory of narcissism, Freud recognized libidinal or sexual instincts in the ego; and he finally determined on the dualism of libido and aggression in the form of life instincts and death instincts. These libidinal and destructive drives were both innate and operated prior to experience, and were at perpetual warfare in the organism. Aggression had nothing originally to do with frustration and operated primarily within the organism, working towards its destruction. What we know practically and clinically as aggression was the extraversion of this original self-destructive innate drive, its turning outwards against objects in the interests of self-preservation. This theory means that the basic conflict within human nature is ultimately irreducible and its final outcome in the victory of the destructive drive is only staved off for a time by compromises in which the two opposite drives coalesce, as in sadism and masochism, or else are both turned upon objects as in ambivalence, a problem which is then practically solved for the time being through keeping the two drives apart by choosing different objects for love and hate.

Freud's early paper, 'Civilized sexual morality and modern nervousness' (1908), illustrates a view of instinct from which he never really departed. The impulses of sex and aggression are dangerous innate forces which operate without regard to social necessities and moral values. The ego must defend itself against them at all costs, but is shut up to three possibilities. It can repress them and become neurotic, or express them and become criminal, or (and this is a possibility open only to the favored few) sublimate them into socially acceptable activities that have cultural value. On this view psychotherapy is limited to (a) strengthening the ego against the force of the innate drives, and (b) persuading society to lower its cultural demands to the absolute capacity of human beings. In the paper referred to, Freud writes:

> Our civilization is, generally speaking, founded on the suppression of instincts. Each individual has contributed some renunciation of his sense of dominating power, and the aggressive and vindictive tendency of his personality. From these sources the common stock of the material and ideal wealth of civilization has been accumulated. [1908, p. 82]

> The task of mastering such a mighty impulse as the sexual instinct is one which may well absorb all the energies of a human being. Mastery through sublimation, diverting the sexual energy away from its sexual goal to higher cultural aims, succeeds with a minority, and with them only intermittently . . . of the others, most become neurotic or other-wise come to grief. [1908, p. 88]

Granting the correctness of this theory of biochemically determined instinc-tive drives existing prior to experience and possessing a fixed and absolute quantity of energy, Freud's conclusions follow quite logically. His dilemma is that the denial of instinct is necessary for culture and civilization, whilst the gratification of instinct and the relaxation of culture is necessary for health. This pessimistic conclusion may well arouse our suspicions, which find support in the criticism of instinct theory by academic psychologists, for whom instinct has more and more fallen into the background, as a primary potentiality for reaction which is shaped to specific modes of behavior only by post-natal experience. This in fact was what Freud himself came to understand when he undertook his analysis of the ego, and created his theory of psychic structure, which allows for motivational forces which were not originally present in the psyche but come into existence as a result of internalizing external, parental and social, demands. But Freud did not recognize that this necessitated a revision of his original theory of instincts.

It is, of course, true that human beings present all the appearance of being possessed of dangerous and socially recalcitrant sexual and aggressive drives, but psychoanalytic study of these phenomena has itself made it clear that they are not in that form innate and essentially unmodifiable impulses. They are, in fact, neurotic phenomena, and when the innate potentialities of human beings operate in a mature and mentally healthy person they do not take this form of dangerous anti-social drives calling for mastery by repression or sublimation. It seems that Freud early confused 'instinctual' and 'neurotic' and created a theory of instincts which implies that our fundamental drive to activity, our 'life-force', is simply the energy of physical appetite and not a function of the 'total personality'. Sexual difficulties are now seen as due not to the constitutional strength of the sexual instinct, but to the developmental immaturity of the whole personality, and more specifically to the internal and unconscious perpetuation in the psyche of the frustrating object-relationships of early life. The same applies to compulsive aggressive tendencies. *Neurotic suffering is not due to the repression of strong and healthy constitutional sexuality and aggression, but to the struggle to master infantile and immature impulses which are continually evoked in the unconscious inner world.* The important issue at stake, theoretically, is that if Freud's instinct theory were correct, the problem could only be solved by repression or cultural regression, except for a favoured minority. The diagnosis now available at least opens the possibility of solving the problem by promoting conditions that aid the emotional maturing of the individual without necessitating the sacrifice of cultural aims.

Freud's theory involves a negative theory of culture, as existing to enforce and reconcile men to renunciation of instincts. His view of culture arose from his theory that aggressive and libidinal impulses are essentially nonaltruistic and represent a basic biologically determined instinctive endowment, which lies behind even their aggravated and frustrated forms, and which cannot be changed. Thus human nature is innately unfitted for, and hostile to, good personal relationships. It is only fitted for the exploitation of objects in the interests of biological, appetitive needs. Freud's picture of the 'state of nature' in *The Future of an Illusion* (1927, p. 25) outdoes Hobbes's picture of it as 'nasty, brutish and short'. There is no room here for such a conception as that of the realization of a man's true nature and individuality in development towards maturity.

It will be convenient to include at this point the criticism of Freud's theory of instinct put forward by the American 'culture-pattern' school, and, from a different point of view, by Fairbairn, leaving their positive contributions for later consideration. Clara Thompson has summarized the criticisms made by such writers as Karen Horney, Erich Fromm and H. S. Sullivan in her book. She writes:

> The emphasis on constitution turned attention away from what we would now call the cultural orientation. . . . The impression grew on Freud that the patient fell ill primarily because of the strength of his own constitutional drives. . . . It tended to close his mind to the significance of environment and led him to pay too little attention to the role of the emotional problems of parents in contributing to the difficulties of their children. . . . Freud did not envision people in terms

of developing powers and total personalities. He thought of them much more mechanistically – as victims of the search for the release of tension. [1952, pp. 9–10, 42–43]

These writers maintain that the neurotic sexuality of oral, anal and genital kinds, and the manner of sexual development through oral, anal and genital phases, which Freud took to be a basic biological phenomenon, is highly culturally conditioned. Customs of breast-feeding, and of cleanliness training, and tolerance or intolerance of the child's early masturbatory activities, are the main determining factors in the patterning of sexuality around these functions. Similarly, the degree of intensity of the Oedipus conflict is determined by the extent to which neurotic parents force this situation upon the child, so that it is not to be regarded as mainly an inevitable biological phenomenon. Differing cultural patterns play a large part in determining the kind of pressures parents put upon their children, often leading to the gross inhibition of any kind of natural and spontaneous behaviour on the part of the child. Karen Horney regarded what Freud called instincts as largely 'neurotic personality trends'.

Freud's theory of a death instinct has met with much criticism. Otto Fenichel cites a number of objections of which the chief are as follows:

There is no proof that (aggressive drives) always and necessarily came into being by a turning outwards of more primary self-destructive drives. . . . It seems rather as if aggressiveness were originally . . . a mode in which instinctual aims are sometimes striven for, in response to frustrations or even spontaneously. . . . A death instinct would not be compatible with the approved biological concept of instinct. The clinical facts of self-destruction likewise do not necessitate the assumption of a genuine self-destructive instinct. [1945, p. 60]

Thompson writes:

[Freud] assumes that suicide and destructiveness towards other are products of the death instinct. More recent observations by others, however, suggest that they have much more to do with the feeling of being thwarted in living. . . . Aggression normally appears in response to frustration. It represents a distortion of the attempt to master life, but cruelty for its own sake probably only occurs as a result of having experienced it from others. Far from being a product of the death instinct, it is an expression of the organism's attempt to live. [1952, pp. 52–54]

Fairbairn's criticism of Freud's instinct theory is based on fundamental theoretical considerations which go beyond clinical observation. It is bound up with the problem of psychic structure and the question of general cultural orientation already mentioned. Fairbairn writes:

> If 'impulses' cannot be considered apart from objects, whether external or internal, it is equally impossible to consider them apart from ego structures. . . . 'Impulses' are but the dynamic aspects of endopsychic structures, and cannot be said to exist in the absence of such structures. . . . Ultimately, 'impulses' must be simply regarded as constituting the forms of activity in which the life of ego structures consists. [1952, p. 88]

Thus Fairbairn discards Freud's divorce of energy and structure, involved in differentiating an id and an ego. For Freud the id is the source of instinctive energies, id-impulses, while the ego is the organized structure of controls. He favours instead a theory of 'dynamic structure' in which energy and structure are not treated as separate factors, but 'instincts' are the 'forms of energy' and 'impulses' are the 'forms of activity' which 'constitute the dynamic of endopsychic structures'. This theory avoids the now outmoded 'atomistic' type of theory. He writes:

> Freud's divorce of energy from structure represents a limitation imposed upon his thought by the general scientific atmosphere of his day. The scientific atmosphere of Freud's day was largely dominated by the Helmholtzian conception that the universe consisted in a conglomeration of inert, immutable and indivisible particles to which motion was imparted by a fixed quantity of energy separate from these particles. However, modern atomic physics has changed all that. . . . So far as psychoanalysis is concerned, one of the unfortunate results of the divorce of energy from structure is that, in its dynamic aspects, psychoanalytical theory has been unduly permeated by conceptions of hypothetical 'impulses' and 'instincts' which bombard passive structures. . . . From the standpoint of dynamic structure, 'instinct' is *not the stimulus* to psychic activity, but itself consists in characteristic activity on the part of a psychical structure. Similarly, 'impulse' is not, so to speak, a kick in the pants administered out of the blue to a surprised, and perhaps somewhat pained, ego, but a psychical structure in action—a psychical structure doing something to something or somebody. [1952, p. 150]

Thus Fairbairn envisages:

A replacement of the outmoded impulse psychology, which, once
adopted, Freud had never seen fit to abandon, by a new psychology of
dynamic structure,

in which (and this conforms with the views of academic psychology on the
question) instincts as mental entities are discarded and

the instinctive endowment of mankind only assumes the form of
general trends which require experience to enable them to acquire a
more differentiated pattern. [1952, p. 157]

Nor are the structural units to be hypostatized either. He refers to

[t]he impossibility of regarding these functioning structural units as
*mental entities*. After all, the general tendency of modern science is to
throw suspicion upon entities; and it was under the influence of this
tendency that the old 'faculty psychology' perished. Perhaps the ar-
rangement of mental phenomena into functioning structural groups is
the most that can be attempted by psychological science. At any rate,
it would appear contrary to the spirit of modern science to confer the
status of entity upon 'instincts'; and in the light of modern knowledge
an instinct seems best regarded as a characteristic dynamic pattern of
behavior. [1952, p. 218]

Fairbairn has undoubtedly raised, in this discussion of the concept of
'instinct', the fundamental issue for psychoanalytical theory. The publication of E.
Jones's *Sigmund Freud: Life and Work*, vol 1, and of Freud's letters to Fleiss (1954) has
confirmed in the clearest possible way the tremendous extent to which Freud's
thinking was dominated by the scientific outlook of his time, and in particular by
the concepts of Helmholtzian physical and physiological atomistic views. It is
established that Freud to the end regarded psychological, and psychoanalytical,
theories as a stop-gap mode of thinking to be used consistently and exhaustively,
but only until such time as the phenomena can be explained in physical terms. In
fact the theorizing of Freud is to a large extent the transference into the psychological sphere of the broad pattern of 'thought-forms' characteristic of physical
science. It is this, in the end, that makes necessary the radical re-thinking of the
theories by means of which he explained the far-reaching discoveries he made
concerning mental functioning. Freud's thought-forms are revealed in such terms
as 'mental apparatus', 'defence mechanism', the impersonality of the biological id,
etc., and this type of theory needs to be recast into terms suitable to the study of
personal phenomena. M. Brierley's consideration of psychoanalysis from the point

of view of personology points this way, though her treatment of it as process theory perpetuates the earlier point of view of reducing personal to impersonal phenomena.

## Freud's Ego-Psychology and Structural Concepts

In his early studies of hysteria Freud was naturally preoccupied with dissociation phenomena, and therefore with the differentiation of the psyche into conscious and unconscious, and with the reformulation of dissociation into dynamic repression. He then became concerned with the study of what was repressed and created his instinct and libido theory. His later study of depression and of obsessional neurosis turned his attention to the factor producing repression. This he regarded as a moral factor, conscience reinforcing the controlling ego, and so he came to plan out the organizational pattern of the total psyche in structural terms. The result looks very much like a scientific description of the traditional tripartite division of personality into body, mind and spirit; i.e. instincts, the self of everyday life, and conscience; the id, ego and super-ego. Nevertheless, this was a tremendously significant theoretical advance. Psychic conflict had hitherto been understood in terms of the controlling ego mastering instinct-derivatives, isolated impulses, in deference to outer reality. Now the problem of conflict between the ego and the super-ego arises and this is a problem of conflict between psychic structures as theoretical wholes within the larger whole of the total psyche. This ought naturally to have led to a reformulation of the earlier view of repression of isolated impulses, by way of a structural definition of that aspect of personality represented by the basic, natural, instinctive needs. Instead the two different views were allowed to continue side by side. As Hartmann, Kris and Loewenstein say:

> Functions of the id center around the basic needs of man . . . rooted in instinctual drives. . . . Functions of the ego center around the relation to reality . . . we speak of the ego as of a specific organ of adjustment. . . . Functions of the super-ego center around moral demands. Self-criticism . . . self-punishment and the formation of ideals. [1946, p. 15]

This Freudian scheme of psychic structure laid the foundations for all subsequent study of the internal dynamics of personality in terms of a properly psychological and *psycho*-dynamic theory, even though it does not prove immune from criticism, and, as Fairbairn puts it, 'a developing psychology of the ego came to be superimposed upon an already established psychology of instinct' (1952, p. 59). Critical examination of this scheme has mainly come from orthodox Freudians and from Fairbairn. The culture-pattern writers have little to say about this problem.

## The Id and the Ego

It is at once apparent that 'id' is a biological concept, while 'ego' and 'super-ego' are psychological concepts, so that the scheme rests on mixed principles of classification. The id is natural energy, which is conceived as separate from ego and super-ego which are structural developments. Alexander writes:

> The notion of the id, as originally defined, is problematical. Strictly speaking, a completely unorganized, inherited mass of instinctual urges is not found even at birth. Learning starts immediately at birth, and it is therefore difficult to see at what period the sharp distinction between an unorganized id and an organized ego obtains. [1949, p. 83]

Hartmann et al. deal with this problem:

> Freud speaks of a gradual differentiation of the ego from the id; and as an end result of this process of differentiation the ego, as a highly structured organization, is opposed to the id. Freud's formulation has obvious disadvantages. It implies that the infant's equipment at birth is part of the id. It seems, however, that the innate apparatus and reflexes cannot all be part of the id, in the sense generally accepted in psychoanalysis. We suggest a different assumption; namely, that of an undifferentiated phase during which both the id and the ego are formed. . . . To the degree to which differentiation takes place man is equipped with a special organ of adaptation, i.e. with the ego. . . . The differentiation accounts for the nature of the instinctual drives of man, sharply distinguished as they are from animal instincts. . . . Many manifestations of the id are farther removed from reality than any comparable behaviour of animals. [1946, p. 19]

Thus we have the id and ego as parallel differentiations within the primary and at first undifferentiated total psychic self, while the id is no longer simply instinct such as is found in animals. They further describe the differentiation of ego and id as brought about by the infant's mixed experience of part deprivation and part gratification. The ego is evidently the primary self in so far as it adjusts itself to reality by reconciling itself to deprivation or postponement of satisfaction, while the id is plainly that same primary self in so far as it goes on demanding gratification. *All justification for the continued use of the impersonal term 'id' has thus* gone. We must anticipate by observing that so far apparently only Fairbairn has recognized this and discarded the unsatisfactory term 'id' in favour of the term 'libidinal ego', the primary natural self with its libidinal needs. It is in no sense a mere impersonal biological energy. In Freud's sense the id is not a structure properly speaking, and what it represents can only be included in a structural scheme if its proper 'ego' or 'personal self' quality is recognized.

*The Ego*

The Freudian ego is that part of the primary self which is modified to conform to the demands of the environment, becoming an organ of *adaptation*. This raises acute problems. Hartmann et al. observe that 'Freud's use of the word [ego] is ambiguous. He uses ego in reference to a psychical organization and to the whole person' (1946, p. 16). Prior to the publication of *Beyond the Pleasure Principle* (1920), psychoanalysis 'had first come to know [the ego] only as a repressive, censoring agency' (p. 69). With the development of the theory of narcissism the ego expanded into 'the true and original reservoir of libido and it is only from that reservoir that libido is extended on to objects' (p. 70). He considered further that the ego contained destructive instincts as well. Just as object-libido was the extraversion of narcissistic ego-libido, so aggression against objects was the extraversion of self-destructive ego trends. The ego had swallowed up everything and become in effect the primary, unitary total psychic self, i.e. the whole person, the primary reservoir of all instinctual energies, libidinal and aggressive. In *Group Psychology and the Analysis of the Ego* Freud wrote (1921) 'the ego's nucleus, which comprises the "archaic inheritance" of the human mind, is unconscious' (p. 10, footnote). This is really the concept of the primary psychic self of the undifferentiated phase of Hartmann, Kris and Loewenstein, out of which the Freudian conforming, adaptive, ego is differentiated from the natural libidinal self (the Freudian id).

With *The Ego and the Id* (1923), however, Freud explicitly repudiated that view. 'Some earlier suggestions about a "nucleus of the ego", never very definitely formulated, require to be put right, since the system Pcpt-cs (perceptual consciousness) alone can be regarded as the nucleus of the ego' (pp. 34–35, footnote 2). He here swings back to restricting the term ego to the superficial phenomenon of anxiety-motivated adaptation to outer reality, while the rest of the total self is relegated to an impersonal id. This gives us little help in dealing with the statement of one of my patients: 'I have grown up to be an outer shell of conformities and I've lost touch with any real "me" inside.' The problem may be expressed as by Karen Horney in her criticism that Freud's ego is a neurotic phenomenon. It emerges in a much more profound way in the views of Winnicott. We have already observed that Freud's scheme is clearly linked to the traditional tripartite division of body, mind and spirit, i.e. id, ego and super-ego. The equating of body and id, mind and ego is implied in Winnicott's paper, 'Mind and its relation to the psyche-soma' (1954, pp. 201–209). Thus he writes:

> The mind of an individual . . . specializes out from the psyche-soma. The mind does not exist as an entity in the individual's scheme of things provided the individual psyche-soma or body scheme has come satisfactorily through the very early developmental stages; mind is then no more than a special case of the functioning of the psyche-soma. In the study of a developing individual the mind will often be found to be developing a *false entity*, and a false localization. [p. 201]

> Certain kinds of failure on the part of the mother, especially erratic behaviour, produce over-anxiety of the mental functioning. Here, in the overgrowth of the mental function reactive to erratic mothering, we see that there can develop an opposition between the mind and the psyche-soma. . . . Clinically this can go along with . . . a false personal growth on a compliance basis. . . . The psyche of the individual gets 'seduced' away into this mind from the intimate relationship which the psyche originally had with the soma. The result is a mind-psyche, which is pathological. [p. 203]

The mind is located then in the head while the psyche-soma is left to reside in the body. This is, in fact, a description of Freud's view of the differentiation of the ego, as an adaptive, conforming function, from the id which it is supposed to control. But like Horney, Winnicott recognizes that this ego is a pathological, false growth. He also clearly implies that the id, or better psyche-soma, is the primary, natural self, and is by no means impersonal.

In his paper on 'Metapsychological and clinical aspects of regression within the psychoanalytical set-up' (Winnicott 1955, pp. 16–26) the psyche-soma becomes the 'true self' and the 'mind' becomes the 'false self'. The patient may have a genuine need for a therapeutic regression in order to recover his 'true self', while the 'false self' acts meanwhile as a 'caretaker self' in its adaptation to the outer world, until the 'true self' develops and the 'false self' can be surrendered to the analyst. We are very far here from the Freudian concepts of the id and ego, but we are much nearer to psychological realities. Winnicott has not suggested that his views imply a revision of Freud's scheme of psychic structure. But clearly the psyche-soma is not an impersonal id, but the primary, natural self, the libidinal psyche, and it is the 'true self' with which the patient must recover contact. There is no place, however, in Freud's scheme for the concept of a 'true self' for it is certainly neither id nor ego in Freud's sense. Similarly, the 'mind' or 'false self' represents the adaptive, conforming aspect of the psyche as a pathological ego-growth in so far as it is split off from and opposed to the id, psyche-soma, or true primary self. This important clinical fact is not provided for in Freud's concept of the ego, and it is clear that his 'differentiation of the ego from the id' in fact conceals the fundamental splitting of the originally unitary psychic self which is the basis of all psychosis and psychoneurosis. We may observe that the terms 'true' and 'false' self are not strictly scientific terms but rather descriptive and evaluatory, and a new terminology is required to replace the id and ego of Freud's scheme.

*The Super-ego*

Here again Freud's striking term has proved to be only the first step towards the analysis of the clinical facts. Alexander made sometimes a more and at other times a less rigid distinction between an unconscious super-ego and a conscious ego-ideal, though he did not take up Melanie Klein's distinction between persecutory and depressive anxiety. He treats the super-ego as a moral phenomenon throughout. Melanie Klein treats a very early and purely sadistic super-ego as a bad internal object. In general, orthodox writers provide no solution to the problem of the relationship between this very early sadistic internal persecutor as, properly speaking, a premoral or non-moral function, and the later developed moral conscience with which it can fuse in varying degrees. Hartmann, Kris and Loewenstein (1946) also regard the super-ego as complex, though in a somewhat different way. They adhere to Freud's view that the super-ego is a creation of the oedipal conflict; it is a castrator and a phallic phase phenomenon. On the other hand, they regard morality as having its origins in the pre-oedipal period. The super-ego functions have 'precursors' (p. 33) which, like the super-ego, develop on the basis of identifications with parents, compliance with their demands, guilt over rebellion and the turning of aggression against the self (p. 32). Thus the super-ego appears now to be, not the origin of morality, but only one, though a very special one, of its later developments in the particular critical oedipal phase. In opposition to the general trend of the views of Alexander and Melanie Klein, their view is that the origins of the 'ego-ideal' are earlier than the formation of the cruel, sadistic, castrating super-ego. Thus of the three terms, id, ego and super-ego, the term super-ego seems in the end to be the most unsatisfactory by reason of its confusing complexity and it stands in need of closer analysis on the basis of clinical material.

# THE 'CULTURE-PATTERN' THEORY:
## A SOCIOLOGICAL ANTITHESIS

The work of Karen Horney and Erich Fromm, and in a remoter sense H. S. Sullivan, may be considered as a development of Adler's early attempt to analyse the ego in terms of inferiority feelings and compensatory power-drives, though their analysis is far more extensive and benefits from the impact of detailed cultural and sociological studies. Like Adler, they sit lightly to the Freudian concept of the deep unconscious and, for that reason, their illuminating studies of the importance of 'culture-patterns' in neurosis have more descriptive importance in extension than explanatory value in etiological depth.

## Fromm and Horney

*Erich Fromm* is more the analytically orientated social psychologist dealing with politics, morality and religion, and relating psychological to economic factors. He regards human problems as arising, not out of the need to satisfy instincts, but out of 'the specific kind of relatedness of the individual towards the world and to himself' (Mullahy 1948, p. 241). The basic concept of all these writers is that our specific ways of dealing with our human environment are cultural, not instinctual, phenomena. Fromm and Horney both came finally to stress an idea that Freud made no use of, but which appears in Jung as 'individuation', and recently in Winnicott's concept of 'the true self', namely, that individuals under the stress of anxiety create a false, socially conformist, superficial self beneath which their true nature and potentialities fail to be realized.

*Karen Horney* analysed conscious and preconscious motivations, especially the more deeply unrecognized character traits manifested by an individual in his human relationships in the present day. Unlike Reich (1934) these writers do not recognize this as the analysis of a defensive character-armour that bars the way to the deep unconscious. Thus their work is condemned to an ultimate superficiality from the point of view of psychodynamic theory. They provide a dynamic account of the conscious and preconscious ego (the Freudian 'conforming' or 'adaptive' or 'reality-ego' or Winnicott's 'false self') in its inter-personal relationships in the external 'here and now'. For Karen Horney, neurosis was constituted by compulsive, anxiety-motivated character-trends. These originate in childhood in parent-child relationships and develop under social pressures. She does not, however, explain by what means their original infantile hard core is perpetuated in the psyche throughout life. Having discarded instinct theory, she has nothing to put in its place as a means of giving a structural view of the deep unconscious as a region of psychic life outside the socially adapted ego. To use Allport's term, Horney's is a theory of the 'functional autonomy' of character-trends formed in early life. The unconscious is for her no longer the deep unconscious of fixation to childhood love-objects in Freud's sense. It is rather simply the unrecognized aspects of contemporary character-structure. She therefore underestimates how literally early object-relationships can be reproduced in transference, both in analysis and in real life.

The truth is rather that while culture-patterns and culturally imposed conflicts determine the outbreak and form of neuroses, they do not account for their deep unconscious etiology, except in so far as they play a large part in determining the kind of impact the parents make on the infant and growing child. Horney has only a functional, not a structural, view of the unconscious in terms of the ordinary social self. She has lost touch with the clinically observed fact that early bad-object relationships become encapsulated in the unconscious, and that the neurotic constantly moulds later situations and experiences to fit the internally preserved pattern of early ones. She has allowed sociology to influence her psychopathology, but has not produced a psychopathology which could have a profound influence on sociology.

Psychotherapy, with Horney and Fromm, tends to have a moralistic flavour. It is a matter of the individual discovering his unsuspected anti-social trends so that he can correct them. But since the persistence of the character-formation of which they are a part is assumed rather than explained, it is not clear how it can be changed. The patient may well feel more guilty than ever over his lack of success. Horney rendered an important service in shifting the emphasis from instincts to human relationships, and in analysing compulsive sexual and aggressive trends as themselves neurotic needs for love and power, not natural manifestations of instincts. But these 'neurotic character-trends' still remain inexplicable solely in terms of culture patterns and external social pressures. Her emphasis on true self-realization is of extreme importance but it is weakened by the absence of a sound theory of psychic structure.

## H. S. Sullivan

Sullivan was an independent psychiatrist, influenced by psychoanalysis, but working out a theory of his own which he called 'The Theory of Interpersonal Relations.' Nevertheless, reference must be made to him, since he illustrates so clearly the reaction from a biological to a psychosocial point of view. He held that 'man is not a creature of instinct' (1947, p. 14). In the words of Clara Thompson: 'He holds that, given a biological substrate, the human is the product of interaction with other human beings, that it is out of the personal and social forces acting upon one from the day of birth that the personality emerges' (1952, p. 211).

Unlike Horney and Fromm, and the emphasis developing in British psycho-analysis, he regards the unique individuality of the patients as outside the scope of science and so confines himself solely to what goes on between people, especially between the observed patient and the psychotherapist as a *participant observer*. The individual is under pressure from his own needs and from those significant persons around him whose approval he must have. His personality develops as a 'self-system' or a 'self-dynamism', which only includes what does not incur parental disapproval. Anxiety excludes all else. Human needs fall into two groups, 'satisfactions' and 'security'. Needs for satisfactions arise out of the biological substrate, such as needs for food, water, sleep, sex, etc., while needs for security are predominantly cultural needs. 'There is continuity between the biological and the cultural. A human being is an acculturated biological organism' (Mullahy 1947, p. 122). It is in this process of acculturation that our *actual* impulses and drives are shaped.

> Pre-existing fixed drives do not explain an interpersonal situation. . . . [Human behaviour] is malleable, fluid, changeable to an almost incalculable degree. . . . Interpersonal behaviour does not occur, obviously, in a mechanical, rigidly stereotyped manner. . . . It is, then, a-person-integrated-in-a-situation-with-another-person-to-persons, an inter-personal situation, which one studies. . . . It is inaccurate to speak of a-person-in-isolation-manifesting-this-or-that-tendency-or-drive. [Mullahy 1947, p. 123]

This view, that impulses are functions of object-relationship situations, is one aspect of the view that Fairbairn puts forth. How near to the British theory of 'internal objects' and 'internal object-relationships' Sullivan and his school came is clear when they point out that some of the 'persons' with whom one can have interpersonal relations are 'illusory' or 'fantastic personifications', and also that 'impulses and drives cohere in "dynamisms", relatively enduring configurations of energy' (Mullahy 1947, p. 123). If the 'fantastic personifications' were recognized more fundamentally as Melanie Klein's 'internal psychic objects' and as Fairbairn's 'dynamic object-structures'; and the 'dynamisms' as Fairbairn's 'ego-structures', then Sullivan would have transcended the 'culture-pattern theory'. But he proceeded no further on that line, and gives us instead a study of the process of acculturation of the 'self-dynamism' or conscious ego only. Perhaps because his interest in schizophrenia did not force on him problems of conscience and guilt as distinct from anxiety, he provides no theory of psychic structure beyond the 'self-dynamism' as an anxiety-product, which also gives us no clue to the problem of the realization of the true or natural self. 'The self may be said to be made up of reflected appraisals' (Sullivan 1947, p. 10). Thus, as Horney said of the Freudian ego, it is a neurotic phenomenon and not a healthy development.

Sullivan's theory of the 'self-dynamism', Horney's 'idealized image of the self', and Fromm's theory of 'automaton conformity', all in different ways constitute a detailed study of the results of family, social and cultural pressure on ego development, and serve as an investigation into Freud's 'reality-ego', to the neglect, however, of the Freudian deep unconscious against which it is to so great an extent a defensive barrier.

# BRITISH DEVELOPMENTS. INTERNAL OBJECTS AND THE INNER WORLD. SYNTHESIS

The sociological reaction of the 'culture-pattern' school served to bring human relations rather than instincts to the forefront as the vital determining factors in psychological development. However, their neglect of the unconscious confined them to the study of the ordinary ego of everyday life. The great achievement of the British psychoanalysts may be said to consist in carrying the concept of object-relationships into the investigation of the total psyche, making possible an account of the 'unconscious' parts of the psyche as well in terms of object-relationships.

## Melanie Klein

The all-important first step was taken when Melanie Klein developed Freud's concept of the super-ego into a thorough-going investigation of all the ways in which infants internalize their emotionally significant (primarily parental) objects, good and bad. Freud created the concept of an internal psychic object without specifically using that term, when he represented conscience as functioning in the form of a separate ego, a super-ego, over against the ego and described it as a mentally internalized image of parents in their disciplinarian, authoritarian, moral and ideal aspect. From the point of view of the ego, however, the super-ego is not an ego but an object in the first place, an internal object to which the ego is tied in varying relationships of fear, resentment, submission, obedience, anxious admiration, love and longing for approval. The ego's identification with this internal object creates the ego-ideal and this obscured the primary 'object' aspect of the super-ego. But Klein discovered other internal psychic objects corresponding to other aspects of parents; some of these, of very early origin, were part-objects, a breast, a penis, often symbolized in dreams as an animal of frightening aspect; others were whole objects dating from a time when the infant became able to perceive people in increasingly complete ways. The earlier the formation of these internal objects occurred, the more they were apt to be cruel persecutors, sadistic precursors of the later moral 'super-ego'. When this inner world of mental 'objects' is emotionally activated it may break into consciousness as phantasy or dream and we can then witness its powerful psychic reality.

Melanie Klein developed a valuable distinction between persecutory and depressive anxiety, the former arising as a result of internal attack by bad objects, the latter being due to phantasied internal loss of good objects. She came thus to view the unconscious as an *inner world*, in which complex relationships of the ego with objects are being actively lived, a psychic world in which the patient lives a life bound to the past, wherein much of his emotional experience is out of touch with the present-day reality, a mental world in which the past remains alive as a psychic present. All human beings, therefore, live in two worlds at once, an inner psychic world representing past experience and for the most part repressed and unconscious, and the outer material world of the present day which is dealt with in consciousness. Evidently our life in both can only be understood in terms of object-relationships, so that it is possible to explain our psychic life in completely *personal* terms throughout. Melanie Klein did not proceed to this revision of Freud's psychodynamic theory. Yet her work points in this direction, since it carries object-relationships first of all back into earliest infancy, so casting doubt on the Freudian primary autoerotic, objectless stage, and presenting the infant as a whole true self from the start; and in the second place it carries object-relationships down into the unconscious, making possible a structural view of the unconscious, which is a properly psychological one. If Melanie Klein had gone beyond the description of internalized object-relations in the unconscious in terms of phantasy, and had represented the phantasies as the activities of psychic structures, she would have been compelled to embark on an extensive rethinking of theory. Instead, phantasies are simply taken as representatives of instinct (Isaacs 1948). Thus her endopsychic discoveries are only added on to the pre-existing psychobiology, including her acceptance of the death instinct, and fitted to the orthodox 'id, ego, super-ego' analysis of structure. Nevertheless, it is her work that has made possible a consistently *psycho*dynamic theory of human development. Her work has stood the test of much adverse criticism, most of which has been about terminology (Bibring, Glover) and has not shaken her basic clinical findings.

These appear to the present writer to constitute the outstanding turning-point in later psychoanalytical development since they give us the kind of approach and concepts which alone make possible a genuine synthesis of the 'internal depth psychology' of Freud and the 'external human relations psychology' of the sociologically orientated writers. Here we see how ego and object mutually interpenetrate one another in human experience, and how the environment enters into the constitution of the psychic individual even while he himself is acting upon and moulding the environment. Ego and object are mutually constitutive. This is what Sullivan means by the integration of an interpersonal situation, but he did not carry this as deep into the analysis of psychic life as the work of Klein does. In popular terms, the world and the soul are linked in indissoluble unity so that we must understand both or neither. All one-sided approaches are rendered null and void.

A further highly important aspect of her work is her detailed investigation of the enormous part played by aggression, infantile sadism, in the early development of the personality. Though she accepts the speculative idea of a death instinct, she really replaces it by an exhaustive clinical analysis of aggression in terms of projection, introjection, the formation of internal bad objects, and the creation of persecutory and depressive anxiety. Her work, not appreciated in America, and not yet adequately appreciated by all British analysts, has increasing influence beyond the Kleinian school in the narrower sense. It is marked in the work of Winnicott already quoted. The work of Balint, while not specifically Kleinian, is closely sympathetic, and brings the Ferenczi tradition out into the open and into contact with recent developments. A primary emphasis on object-relations, and especially on the influence of parents in shaping the psychogenesis of the child's personality, was always central with Ferenczi, carrying with it an emphasis on an active analyst-patient relationship in psychotherapy that went beyond the classic conception of the impersonal analyst as mainly a projection-screen for transference phantasies and an interpreter of them.

## W. R. D. Fairbairn

Fairbairn has made the work of Melanie Klein on 'internal objects' and 'internal object-relations', the basis of a thorough rethinking of psychodynamic theory. This has already been outlined so far as it concerns the change of emphasis from instincts to the priority of object-relations as the determining factors in development; and the adoption of a theory of dynamic structure. He defines psychology as a 'study of the relationships of the individual to his objects, whilst, in similar terms, psychopathology may be said to resolve itself more specifically into a study of the relationships of the ego to its internalized objects' (1952, p. 60). We shall conclude, therefore, with a mention of Fairbairn's theory of endopsychic structure. With his work the term *endopsychic structure* becomes for the first time fully appropriate. The theory is based on the object-relations principle throughout. He regards libidinal needs not as a search for the pleasure of psychic and physical detensioning (a deteriorated form of behaviour arising out of despair of the possibility of good object-relationships), but as a quest for the necessary and intrinsic satisfactions of a good relationship with a satisfying personal object. When that need is not met, aggression arises as a reaction to libidinal frustration and deprivation. Aggression is thus secondary to libidinal needs, but is also fundamental to the creation of psychopathological states.

'The pristine personality of the child consists of a unitary dynamic ego' (1955, p. 107) and, in proportion as the child encounters satisfying objects-relationships from the start, i.e. good mothering, so that he is loved as a real person in his own right, then good and satisfactory ego development results. In so far as he encounters unsatisfying object-relationships his pristine psychic wholeness and integrity is lost. Melanie Klein holds that the infant inevitably internalizes his objects because he is oral, as if mental internalization were the counterpart of eating or taking in. Fairbairn holds that there is no motive for internalizing a satisfying object; it is simply enjoyed and good ego development results. The infant in the pre-ambivalent stage mentally internalizes the unsatisfying object in an effort to solve the problem it presents, and therewith structural differentiation in the ego begins: i.e. the ego becomes functionally and structurally split. This is the ultimate cause of all psychopathological phenomena since the ego becomes divided against itself.

Ambivalence arises with the internalization of the unsatisfying object. Since the object is not wholly bad, the infant feels both love and hate towards it, and 'splitting' develops to deal with this intolerable situation. The object has an exciting aspect and a rejecting aspect, both of which are emotionally bad to the child, and these are split off as separate internal objects and repressed. The tolerable re-mainder then appears as an *ideal* object, i.e. it is not now identical with the *real* object since it has no upsetting aspects and appears as perfect or in no way emotionally disturbing.

As a result of this splitting of the object, the ego is split functionally and structurally, because of persisting cathexis of three different types of object. The *libidinally exciting* but unsatisfying object arouses and maintains in the infant a state of unrelieved need and craving. This intolerable aspect of experience is repressed in the form of an internal bad-object relationship between an intensely needy and never satisfied *libidinal ego* and an intensely stimulating but unsatisfying *exciting object*. This level of sheer libidinal deprivation gives rise to schizoid phenomena, for the infant becomes afraid of his own violently hungry love needs, becomes afraid to love lest he should devour and destroy his needed love-objects, and so cuts himself off from object-relationships in any vital emotional sense. Melanie Klein has recognized the importance of Fairbairn's work on schizoid states (1952, pp. 198 and 293 ff).

The *libidinally rejecting* object, whether passively rejective, indifferent, ne-glectful, or actively rejective, angry, aggressive, arouses fear and anger in the child. This intolerable aspect of experience is repressed in the form of an internal bad-object relationship between a *rejecting object* which presents itself as a persecu-tor, and an ego that escapes persecution by abandoning the position of libidinal need and demand, and finding safety in identification with the rejecting object. The rejecting object becomes endowed through this identification with the infant's own anger and aggression, and develops into an internal persecutor of fantastic sadism, while the ego that is identified with it becomes itself increasingly sadistic, a vicious circle of mounting aggression all of which is directed against the libidinal ego and the exciting object. Fairbairn at first called this sadistic ego the 'internal saboteur' since it operates within the personality as an active opponent and inhibitor of all libidinal needs and strivings. He now, however, calls this the *anti-libidinal ego* a more exact scientific term which covers all the phenomena of the turning of aggression against the self. Here arise depressive phenomena.

With the repression of the 'libidinal ego-exciting object' and the 'anti-libidinal ego-rejecting object', aspects of experience, a consciously functioning ego is left, the *central ego* striving to please, appease, obey, conform to and love the external real object which is cathected, however unrealistically, in terms of the *ideal object*, the tolerable remainder of the internalized object after its exciting and rejective aspects have been subtracted. At this level moral functions develop in course of time as the ideal object becomes the basis of the child's ego-ideal, a central ego possession. Thus ego and objects are split together in a tripartite way and a complete endopsychic situation is set up, describable only in object-relationship terms, the pattern of which is fundamental for all human beings, however varied the individual differences comprised within it may be. The central ego functions consciously while its two basic emotional functions, libidinal and aggressive, are considerably lost to it by the splitting off and repressing of two subsidiary egos, the libidinal ego and the anti-libidinal ego, in an infantile state. This central ego, being itself only a partial and therefore inadequate ego, seeks to retain external good-object relations by idealizing its objects, ignoring their libidinally exciting aspect, and avoiding arousing their rejective aspect, both of which are dealt with at the unconscious level as internalized bad objects, the exciting object and the rejecting object.

This threefold analysis of endopsychic structure appears to meet all the difficulties examined earlier that have been raised concerning the 'id, ego, super-ego' scheme. *The id* can now be viewed personally as the primary libidinal ego. The ego of Freud, a conforming and adaptive ego, is an aspect of the more important concept of the central ego of our conscious living. The complexity of the super-ego can now be resolved into its components. Fairbairn seeks to meet the difficulty appreciated by Alexander, when he pointed out that the super-ego operates on two different levels, the primitive sadistic super-ego and the moral conscience. The primitive sadistic super-ego is the alliance between the rejecting object and the anti-libidinal ego, so that clinically we find patients oscillating between feeling menaced by some persecuting figure and feeling that they persecute themselves. This level of experience is pre-moral or amoral and merely persecutory. The rejecting object and the anti-libidinal ego maintain a constant attack on the libidinal ego and the exciting object, thus forming the hard core of the anti-libidinal factor in the personality, and supporting 'the [direct] repression exercised against it [the libidinal ego] by the central ego, which it thus seems appropriate to describe as a process of *indirect repression*' (1955, p. 108). This indirect repression is responsible for Melanie Klein's 'persecutory anxiety'.

What develops into the moral component of the super-ego is the ideal object. In neurosis, this seeks to control and dominate the central ego, thus supporting its repression of both the libidinal ego and the anti-libidinal ego. The central ego, being in fact the remainder of the original primary self, is, of course, the agent of primary repression by aggressive rejection of the internal exciting object and the internal rejecting object in the first place, a procedure which involved it in the loss by repression of the parts of itself cathecting those internal objects. The central ego, however, remains also in touch with the outer world and is open to continuing educative influences, which is not true of the repressed parts of the personality. This leads to the evolution of two different types of guilt and morality, the one morbid and the other increasingly realistic and mature. Under the attack of the anti-libidinal ego, the libidinal ego develops not only *persecutory anxiety* but, at a slightly later stage, *persecutory guilt*, which is Melanie Klein's 'depressive anxiety'. The morbid guilt of depression is so persecutory in nature that it is clear that the anti-libidinal ego plays the dominant part in its creation. It contains a large amount of what Freud called 'borrowed guilt' (1949, p. 72), and it leads to the development of a pathological morality of an ultra-authoritarian kind: i.e. in Christian terms, a harsh Calvinistic morality of law rather than love. If the central ego has to do with parents who are, even as idealized outer figures, too intolerant of the child's libido and aggression, the 'super-ego conscience' will develop little beyond the level of the sadistic, persecuting, rejecting object and anti-libidinal ego.

We may comment at this point on the familiar psychoanalytical idea that 'super-ego morality' needs to be replaced by a rational morality. This is better expressed as the replacement of persecutory morality by the morality of love. 'Super-ego morality' is psychopathological since it rests on splitting phenomena. It involves, as Fairbairn's analysis shows, both the sadistic persecution of the libidinal ego by the anti-libidinal ego, and an attempt to control the psyche as a whole by a central ego morality based on the ideal object and so likely to be perfectionist and unrealistic. But since the central ego is the part of the ego which retains the capacity to deal with outer reality it will do this in ever more realistic ways as infantile ego splitting is outgrown. 'The super-ego conscience' involves the attack of one ego upon another. A mature conscience is a function of genuine *self*-judgement on the part of the central ego by virtue of its possession of an ego ideal which becomes progressively more realistic as re-integration proceeds and as external objects are perceived in their own true nature and not in the light of the projection of an internal ideal object.

Fairbairn's scheme has the advantage of being consistently psychological throughout, of answering to clinically observed facts more closely than the original scheme, and of clarifying the two outstanding anomalies in human nature; i.e. the co-existence of a primitive non- or pre-moral level of psychic life with the civilized moral level on the one hand, and on the other the fact that the individual functions as a self-frustrating entity by reason of his being radically divided between libidinal and anti-libidinal factors in his organization. The bare bones of conceptual analysis come to life when clothed with the flesh and blood of clinical facts. A male patient reports that his relationship with is wife is one of constant rows and antagonism, while he finds another woman at work sexually exciting; but neither of them are his ideal woman for a wife. His ideal wife is clearly described in terms of the internal ideal object who is perfectly supporting but in no way emotionally disturbing. His actual wife is the rejecting object and the other woman is the exciting object. Hereby he reveals the tripartite split in his own ego setting up needs for three quite different types of women. Fairbairn writes:

> The conception of this basic endopsychic situation provides an alternative, couched in terms of personal relationships and dynamic structure, to Freud's description of the psyche in terms of id, ego and super-ego, based as this is upon a Helmholtzian divorce of energy from structure no longer accepted in physics, and combined as it is, albeit at the expense of no little inconsistency, with a non-personal psychology conceived in terms of biological instincts and erotogenic zones. [1955, p. 109]

In conclusion, the most urgent task now confronting psychoanalysis would seem to be that of re-investigating the whole problem of psychotherapy in terms of 'object-relations theory', particularly with a view to the question of the part played by the relationship of analyst and patient as the really therapeutic factor. This is a larger question than that of transference, and the work of Melanie Klein, Fairbairn, Winnicott, and the Ferenczi tradition all bear together on this, the ultimate, practical problem, to which Sullivan's view of the therapist as a 'participant observer' is also relevant.

## REFERENCES

Alexander, F. (1949). *Fundamentals of Psycho-Analysis*. London: Allen and Unwin.

Allport, G. W. (1949). *Personality*. London: Constable.

Balint, M. (1939). Early developmental states of the ego and primary object love. *International Journal of Psycho-Analysis* 30:265–273.

Brierley, M. (1951). *Trends in Psycho-Analysis*. London: Hogarth Press.

Fairbairn, W. R. D. (1952). *Psychoanalytic Studies of the Personality*. London: Tavistock Publications Ltd.

_____ (1955). Observations on the nature of hysterical states. *British Journal of Medical Psychology* 21(2):105–125.

Fenichel, O. (1945). *The Psychoanalytic Theory of Neurosis*. London: Kegan Paul.

Freud, S. (1908). Civilized sexual morality and modern nervousness. *Collected Papers*, vol 2. London: Hogarth Press. (1949.)

_____ (1920). *Beyond the Pleasure Principle*. London: Hogarth Press (rep. 1950).

_____ (1921). *Group Psychology and the Analysis of the Ego*. London: Hogarth Press (rep. 1922).

_____ (1923). *The Ego and the Id*. London: Hogarth Press (rep. 1949).

_____ (1927). *The Future of an Illusion*. London: Hogarth Press (rep. 1928).

_____ (1954). *The Origins of Psycho-Analysis* (Fleiss Letters). London: Imago.

Fromm, E. (1942). *The Fear of Freedom*. London: Kegan Paul.

_____ (1949). *Man for Himself*. London: Kegan Paul.

_____ (1951). *Psycho-Analysis and Religion*. London: Gollancz.

Hartmann, H., Kris, E., and Loewenstein, R. M. (1946). Comments on the formation of psychic structure. *Psychoanalytic Study of the Child*, vol. 2. London: Imago.

Horney, K. (1937). *The Neurotic Personality of Our Time*. London: Kegan Paul.

_____ (1939). *New Ways in Psycho-Analysis*. London: Kegan Paul.

_____ (1951). *Neurosis and Human Growth*. London: Kegan Paul.

Isaacs, S. (1948). The nature and function of phantasy. *International Journal of Psycho-Analysis* 29 (2):73.

Jones, E. (1953). *Sigmund Freud: Life and Work*. London: Hogarth Press.

Klein, M. (1932). *The Psycho-Analysis of Children*. London: Hogarth Press.

_____ (1948). *Contributions to Psycho-Analysis*. London: Hogarth Press.

Klein, M., et al. (1952). *Developments in Psycho-Analysis*. London: Hogarth Press.

Mullahy, P. (1947). Appendix to *Conceptions of Modern Psychiatry* by H. S. Sullivan. New York: Norton, for William Alanson White Psychiatric Foundation.

_____ (1948). *Oedipus Myth and Complex*. New York: Hermitage Press.

Reich, W. (1934). *Character Analysis*. New York: Orgone Institute Press.

Sullivan, H. S. (1947). *Conceptions of Modern Psychiatry*. New York: Norton, for William Alanson White Psychiatric Foundation.

_____ (1953). *The Interpersonal Theory of Psychiatry*. New York: Norton, for William Alanson White Psychiatric Foundation.

_____ (1954). *The Psychiatric Interview*. New York: Norton, for William Alanson White Psychiatric Foundation.

Thompson, C. (1952). *Psychoanalysis: Evolution and Development*. London: Allen and Unwin.

Thouless, R. H. (1951). *General and Social Psychology*, 3rd ed. London: University Tutorial Press.

Winnicott, D. W. (1954). Mind and its relation to the psyche-soma. *British Journal of Medical Psychology* 27(4):201–9.

_____ (1955). Metapsychological and clinical aspects of regression within the psychoanalytical set-up. *International Journal of Psycho-Analysis* 36:1.

# 4

# MOVING BEYOND FREUD TO "A MORE ACTIVELY PERSONAL KIND OF TREATMENT"

T HE CENTENARY OF THE BIRTH of Freud was celebrated by psychoanalytical societies in many lands, and was widely commented on in the press and in B.B.C. programmes in this country. Dr. Ernest Jones, in a broadcast on 6th May, expressed the view that tributes to Freud's greatness were in no way exaggerated, but added: "I am much more diffident about similar laudatory eulogies concerning Freud's influence on the world . . . the better acquainted one is with Freud's work the more one realizes how little of it has been absorbed by the outside world" (Jones, 1956). While many have referred with appreciation to his contribution, there is often in references to Freud a cautious comment to the effect that not all of his teaching is now accepted. This caution is of dubious meaning. Freud's theoretical system has been under constant critical examination and revision, but that is no more than must be said of every scientific theory. Physics did not stand still with Newton or astronomy with Galileo; nor was it ever likely that psychodynamic theory, the scientific study of the emotional and impulsive basis of human personality, would stand still with Freud.

One suspects, however, that this is not what is meant by contemporary warnings that not all of Freud's theories are now accepted. Professor O. L. Zangwill recently wrote: "Broadly speaking, Freud's ideas have surprisingly often proved right. But in certain of his claims he has been decisively proved wrong. Although a final opinion cannot yet be given, it seems likely that Freud's system – when shorn of its extravagances – will earn a secure place in the history of medical endeavour" (Zangwill, 1956). One detects here the tone, so often adopted by those who write about Freud, of qualified approval, somewhat patronising agreement (cp. "Freud's ideas have *surprisingly* often proved right"), and depreciatory hints at "extravagances". This attitude of grudging admission that Freud really has done something lasting, together with signs of uneasiness about the acceptance of it, is now the fashion with many. We do not quite like Freud, but we cannot get rid of him, so he must be made safe.

Such critics are usually better at vague generalizations than at exact, carefully documented statements. Professor Zangwill does not say what claims Freud made which have been "decisively proved wrong", nor what aspects of his system are "extravagances". These so-called claims certainly cannot be therapeutic ones, for of all analysts Freud was the most cautious as to the possibility of psychotherapeutic results. He restricted psychoanalysis to certain types of neurosis and personality, had little belief in rapid-cure methods, stated explicitly that human nature only changes very slowly, and possibly valued psychoanalysis more for scientific research than for psychotherapy. As for Freud being "right", what is truly *surprising*, if we consider his clinical observations and insight as distinct from his theoretical concepts, is that Freud was so often and so searchingly right. By "extravagances" such critics usually mean Freud's alleged, though in fact non-existent, pan-sexualism. Dr. Jones (1956) wrote: "The still less informed are apt to assert that according to Freud everything has a sexual origin, forgetting thereby how much of his theory has to do with the conflict of sexual and moral impulses." We must in fact look behind these criticisms to factors that belong to more general and also more personal attitudes to the work of Freud, if we are to evaluate and understand them.

## THE IMPACT OF FREUD

Without deliberate intention, Freud broke upon the world as a disturber of the mental peace of those whose defence against anxiety was the ostrich policy of complacent, if vigorous, affirmation of traditional views of the functioning of human beings in their personal life and social behaviour. Socrates once observed that he was a gadfly. His awkward questions and persistent probing enquiries stung men into thinking afresh on matters that they would have preferred to take for granted. Freud made precisely that Socratic impact at the turn of last century. We see this in the way psychoanalysis has influenced the dissection of character in many a modern novel. Its subtle penetration is far greater than its official recognition.

The majority, not only in medicine but in religion, education and politics, preferred to go on blindly accepting traditional views in Freud's day, as indeed many still do. The problems and perversities of the personal life of human beings were held to be due either to organic defect or moral wilfulness. Neurosis, at that time chiefly thought of in terms of hysteria, and equated in the Middle Ages with witchcraft, was, in the 1880's, treated as delinquency, with the underlying reservation among medical men that in so far as that was not the case it had a purely physical cause. A dramatic reorientation of thought "happened" to Freud when, in 1885, he went to study under the famous French neurologist Charcot at the Salpêtrière. He found Charcot treating hysteria seriously as a genuine problem calling for exacting scientific research, and treating it as a disturbance of human personality occurring not on a purely physical level, nor on an exclusively moral level, but calling for a new and pioneer investigation of psychological cause and effect. Charcot's demonstration by hypnosis of the reality and power of *unconscious* mental factors to determine conscious mental reactions and behaviour opened a new field of research for Freud. It was one which he proceeded to make in a specially thorough way his own territory.

It was not long before Freud began to be made painfully aware of the fact that the unconscious *is* unconscious because we human beings want it to be unconscious. We do not like to discover parts of our personality that are less mature than we consciously believe ourselves to be. Furthermore, it is uncanny and wounding to our self-respect to have to realize that we are influenced by things in ourselves of which we are not consciously aware. The attempt to bring the hidden areas of personality to consciousness was met by fierce resistance, especially when Freud revealed them to consist of primitive and infantile components that we wish to believe we have outgrown. Not only did this resistance occur in patients who could only emerge from neurotic illness when its unconscious mental causes were brought to light, but also in thinkers and people in general whose mental security-systems were the product of a culture that rested on the denial of unconscious factors in human personality.

Freud broke into a region which had always been so utterly forbidden that both its existence and the taboo on its recognition were, in the ordinary sense, unknown. Just as the gadfly Socrates (in spite of the Delphic injunction, "Know thyself") was put to death for his temerity in disturbing men in their wish not to know themselves too well, so the modern gadfly Freud was greeted with howls of rage, recrimination and ridicule when he dared to seek to show us to ourselves. In truth, the work of Freud went far deeper than that of Socrates, who pursued his probing on a purely intellectual and philosophic level. Freud probed into the deeper and darker regions of our unconscious emotional life. Socrates forced men to recognize that *they did not know what they really meant* when they used words like "justice". Freud forced men to recognize that *they did not know what they were really feeling* underneath their conscious mask of accepted social and moral attitudes.

Thanks to the recently published life of Freud by Dr. Jones (1954, 1955) (the only surviving member of the early psycho-analytical "big-four", Freud, Ferenczi, Abraham and Jones) we know that long before Freud disturbed the world around him, he had to face, and did face with great courage, the fact that he was profoundly disturbing himself in his quest for the truth about men. As a result, Freud has now become to us a more human and sympathetic figure than he appeared to be when tardy recognition of his achievement had turned him into one of the Olympians. We can now see him in his human frailty, a man of like flesh and blood with ourselves, discovering first of all in himself the neurotic phenomena he was the first to begin to understand in other people, and ultimately to reveal as present in varying degrees in all human beings without exception. The more we know of the anxiety, depression, doubt and discouragement, and of some of the serious physical disturbances due to emotional conflict and tension, that Freud endured as he fought his way through in order to catch the first all-important glimpses of the truth, the more our respect for the man and our appreciation of his true greatness is enhanced. It is fair to say that not only his glib detractors, but many of his serious critics, have not themselves travelled first the hard road to self-knowledge that Freud travelled, a discipline which is essential to the proper evaluation of his findings. From this point of view psychoanalysis is a scientific experiment which has to be repeated in order to be re-examined.

## FREUD AS PIONEER

Naturally, not all Freud's theoretical formulations have stood the test of time. He himself did not expect it. In 1909 he wrote to Jung (Jones 1955):

> Your surmise that after my departure my errors might be adored as holy relics amused me enormously, but I don't believe it. On the contrary, I think my followers will hasten to demolish as swiftly as possible everything that is not safe and sound in what I leave behind.

In 1924, he wrote to Joan Riviere, who was translating *The Ego and the Id* : "The book will be obsolete in thirty years" (Klein et al. 1952).

Freud began to research and write before the modern development of sociology had arisen, and before the modern emphasis on "personality" and the "person" as distinct from the "organism" had become so fundamental. He himself only began his psychological investigations at the age of forty, and against the background of his natural science education in the Helmholtzian atomic theory of the "billiard ball universe" type. Solid matter moving in empty space was supposed to account for everything, and "mind" was, as T. H. Huxley said, only an "epiphenomenon", like the steam whistle on the train that had no effect on its motion. It cost Freud much agony of mind, in face of the disbelief and ostracism of his scientific colleagues, to win his way to a clear perception of psychological phenomena as facts in their own right, calling for investigation in their own appropriate terms and not in terms borrowed from physics, physiology and biology.

In a sense Freud never was able completely to outgrow his own early scientific education. Much of the recent development of psychoanalytical theory beyond Freud is concerned with correcting his excessively biological orientation by a more properly psychological theory of our psychic life, though Freud himself paved the way for this. Thus, the concept of "instinct" today falls steadily into the background, while that of "human and personal relations" takes its place as the basic explanatory concept. It is not so much innate endowment as what goes on between human beings that accounts for the development of character and personality and its manifestations in social (or anti-social) behaviour and psychoneurotic illness. Yet the greatness of Freud can be seen in the fact that he himself provided the starting-points for all the present-day theoretical developments beyond his own position.

It was Freud who first compelled us to see that it is what goes on between the child and his parents from the moment of birth and throughout the first five years, that is the true "cause" of that first and profoundest shaping of the psychic self for good or ill, the pattern of which underlies all later development and forms the *unconscious* and deeply repressed basic structure of the personality. He made it clear that adolescence offers the last chance for spontaneous modification of this pattern, and that thereafter its alteration in any radical way is a task of the utmost difficulty. It can only be partially accomplished by deep psycho-analytic treatment in favourable cases, though it is certainly possible to do that for a number of people to a sufficient degree to release them from the crippling effects of nervous illness. When psycho-analytical treatment is not suitable for the individual case or not likely to succeed, Freud's work throws much light on why that is so. His discoveries have dominated the development of psychotherapy, and led to the far-flung Child Guidance movement, since it has come to be appreciated that in these matters prevention is better than cure.

## WELCOME HOSTILITY

The position now is that so much of Freud's work has been permanently absorbed (not always with fair acknowledgement) into psychiatric and psychotherapeutic theory, and has greatly influenced educational, social and even religious thinking, that Freud has begun to be respectable. The gadfly we need to save us from complacency is likely thus to be neutralized. What happened to Christianity could equally well happen to psychoanalysis: it can be intellectually accepted, given formal recognition, and neatly shelved, so that it loses its capacity to disturb us into a realistic facing of ourselves. Conventional acceptance is ever the best defence against awkward truth. Fortunately signs are not wanting that psychoanalysis still has power to disturb and provoke opposition. The relatives of most patients are usually automatically against it even when they profess some belief in it. So long as it is still thought necessary to warn us that "not everything in Freud is now accepted", those who think for themselves will be stimulated to make their own independent study of him. A recent 600-page textbook of "Clinical Psychiatry" by Mayer-Gross, Slater and Roth (1954) provides further welcome reassurance that psychoanalysis has not yet lost its power to arouse emotional opposition; for though the authors in the first chapter explicitly accept at least fifty per cent of Freud's basic teaching, they cannot refrain from thereafter launching into a highly unscientific and emotionally biassed tirade aimed at discouraging any further attempts to take Freud seriously. Professor Eysenck, writing as a psychologist, as distinct from a psychotherapist or analyst, loses no opportunity of attacking psychoanalysis and psychotherapy. The work of Freud will never be safer than when it evokes hostility. Opponents are usually the best advertisers of what is important.

## DANGERS OF PSYCHOLOGICAL SCIENCE

There are many who, like Eysenck, prefer a purely descriptive psychology based on "objective tests" (the objectivity of which, however, is subject to much doubt even among psychologists). It is much less disturbing to its practitioners and to the public than is direct dealing with the anxiety-ridden psychodynamic aspects of our personality in an intimate psychotherapeutic relationship. There must always be a grave danger of wanting to limit our knowledge of human beings to what can be discovered by techniques of scientific detachment. In fact the role and influence of science in its study of human nature raises altogether disturbing questions. Purely objective scientific investigation by an emotionally neutral investigator depersonalizes the subject of the investigation. He becomes an object of scientific curiosity, a specimen. Ways of manipulating him can be discovered which ignore his sensitiveness as a suffering human person. The subject will, naturally, never be able personally to reveal his deepest problems to such investigators. He finds it hard enough to reveal them even to the sympathetic investigator who comes to help and heal.

But methods of scientific re-conditioning by impersonal techniques could be discovered which, though ostensibly aiming at therapy (at least in the sense of being symptom-relieving) could well be used by political dictators for other purposes. This is no bogey but a grim fact that has already arisen in the practises of state trials in totalitarian countries. In favour of Freud's psychoanalysis it must be said that it depends entirely on personal co-operation between patient and analyst and never achieves, or tries to achieve, its therapeutic aim except in proportion as the patient becomes convinced that he is respected and helped in his own right and for his own sake as a person. Yet even Freudian psychoanalysis may not be immune from this danger, for Freud sought to make it a purely scientific method in the operation of which the analyst was to remain a quite detached and impersonal figure. Fortunately this method of pursuing psychoanalysis is usually found to end in blocking all progress. Another recent development concerns the recognition of the need of the more seriously ill patient for a more actively personal type of treatment, which can still be psychoanalytical in its radical methods of getting to the bottom of the patient's emotional conflicts. But if psychoanalysis as a purely impersonal scientific technique of investigation is of dubious value for setting patients free from anxieties and liberating them for the development of healthy spontaneity and individuality, it may yet discover facts about the way the human mind develops from infancy onwards, that could be used for the shaping of psychological conditioning techniques of diabolical efficiency. The mobilization of childish guilt in political prisoners to "soften them up" before trial, is a case in point.

We have real enough cause for fear lest the knowledge accumulated by natural science should be used to destroy mankind. It would be a far more ghastly fate for the knowledge accumulated by psychological science to be used to enslave mankind, by careful conditioning from birth onwards. There are already plenty of people to be found whose personality is so grossly inhibited, who are so internally crushed by a ruthless, authoritarian "super-ego" or fiercely dictatorial conscience, that every spontaneous feeling, original thought or challenging impulse is at once met inside them by a storm of anxiety and guilt which crushes the "bad, rebellious child" into subservience again. They have often grown up like that under the influence of people who believed that they were doing their best for the child. Once we understand completely the psychodynamic processes that lead to such enslavement of human personality, what is to prevent interested parties who can remain in power long enough from using that knowledge to stamp out the very desire and will for freedom? This is in fact a process that has already been extensively developed in more superficial ways by means of intensive propagandist conditioning of whole populations carried down at least as far as the educational regimes of the school years; and the terrible thing is that human beings once enslaved can become attached to slavery. The destructive possibilities of A- and H-bombs may not prove to be the most fearsome of the evil possibilities of scientific knowledge applied to human life.

A lesser version of this same problem confronts us within the range of normal human living. The battle between coercion and freedom, authority and spontaneity, law and love, has raged all through history, and always hitherto with the same result. These are regarded as mutually exclusive opposites by different types of personality. Those who are in the seat of authority, whether they be parents, teachers, politicians or religious leaders, generally tend to assume that human beings are only capable of being civilized by pressure and discipline. In fact Freud himself believed that, as he made plain in *The Future of an Illusion* (1928). He regarded the general run of men as destructive by nature and disinclined to work, and as motivated only by a quest for sensuous pleasure; so that "culture" and civilization rested on the denial of "instincts". Either we had to relax or defy cultural standards in the interests of mental health, or else accept neurosis as the price to be paid for civilization. In that sense all authoritarians are Freudians in their basic assumptions about human nature, though whereas Freud used these assumptions as a plea for relaxation, the cultural rulers always use them as an argument for discipline, control and "conditioning", thus breeding rebels whom they then regard as proofs of the truth of their beliefs. Even Freud held that only a select minority are capable of escaping from this dilemma by resort to what he called "sublimation" — surely a psychological counterpart of the religious doctrine of "election" which will hardly commend itself to us.


## CONCLUSION


In fact, however, these ideas of Freud arose out of his theory that human motivation was fixed by "instincts" that are antisocial and recalcitrant to altruistic purposes. We must now, however, restate the problem. It is not really a battle between innate instincts and the cultural pressures of civilized society (a view unfortunately implied in the traditional Christian doctrine of "original sin"). The real issue is, how can we best secure the growth of human personality to full maturity? In practice, the problem is that those who operate regimes of discipline and control, whether in the home or in society at large, are usually motivated mainly by the love of power and the need to vent their own hate and aggression on those over whom they have charge. We need to solve the problem of the wise balance between freedom for self-discovery by self-expression, and control that takes the form of loving and supporting guidance of the child who otherwise could become a prey to anxiety if left too much to his own devices. The main obstacle is that we ourselves need to be very mature to be able to deal with either children or subordinates in that manner. Thus the work of Freudian psychoanalysis leads us deeper than ever into the heart of this perennial and most difficult and urgent of all human problems. Certainly its best established result is that suppression if it begins early enough leads to paralysis of personality in a more profound way than has ever hitherto been understood, and that only loving regimes offer any real chance for healthy human development. Those who regard a human personality as a more significant form of existence than an atom must regard the discoveries of Freud as opening up a field of knowledge that must ultimately out-weigh in importance that explored by the nuclear physicists.

## REFERENCES

Freud, S. (1928). *The Future of an Illusion*. London: Hogarth Press.

Jones, E. (1954, 1955). *Sigmund Freud: Life and Work* (2 vols.). London: Hogarth Press.

———— (1956). *The Listener*, May 10, p. 589.

Klein, M., Heimann, P., Isaacs, S., and Rivière. J. (1952) "Developments in psychoanalysis." London: Hogarth Press. p. 1.

Mayer-Gross, W., Slater, E. T. O., and Roth. M. (1954) "Clinical psychiatry." London: Cassell.

Zangwill, O. L. (1956) *Radio Times*, May 4, p. 4.

# Section II

# 1960–1962
# THE SCHIZOID
# COMPROMISE:
# THE NEED AND FEAR
# OF REGRESSION

# 5

# DEEPER PERCEPTION OF THE SCHIZOID PROBLEM

## EGO-PSYCHOLOGY

In 1913 Freud wrote: 'The shortening of the analytic treatment remains a reasonable wish, the realization of which . . . is being sought after in various ways. Unfortunately it is opposed by a very important element in the situation – namely, the slowness with which profound changes in the mind bring themselves about.' Nothing has happened since those words were written to modify that judgement. Psychotherapy remains a slow and difficult process. Nevertheless, we cannot scientifically remain content with a statement to the effect that mental change of a profound order is difficult. Even if it can never be any other than slow and difficult, we want to know why this is so, and there is always the chance that greater understanding may enable us to make psychotherapy more effective. If change were too easy and mental structure too fluid, the result would not be quicker psychotherapy but general instability. Relative stability at any point of the scale between immaturity and maturity involves that once an individual has developed a certain organizational pattern of personality he is able to retain it with a high degree of persistence. Disturbed patterns persist as stubbornly as more harmonious ones. Yet, some personality patterns are so disadvantageous to their owners that we would gladly know whether and how they can be changed quickly enough to give the person a chance to live normally. The whole situation is a challenge to deeper investigation, and perhaps also to the rethinking of things that we are familiar with. It could be that the slowness of psychotherapy is not only due to the inherent difficulty of the problem, but also to the possibility that our psychodynamic interpretations are still in some vital sense missing the mark. Everything in a given field cannot be seen from one point of view, and often a change of viewpoint brings unexpected disclosures.

Psychoanalytic therapy was at first based on interpretations designed to uncover repressed libidinal needs and aggressive impulses. The phrases 'releasing the patient's libido' and 'releasing the patient's aggression' were characteristic of that approach. It led to the creation of a popular ideal of 'the uninhibited person'. But it was found that in so far as this was achieved, it made only a very doubtful contribution to the deep maturing of the personality as a whole. It may relieve the patient of some practical disabilities that spring from inhibitions. He may be better able to ask for what he wants and better able to stand up for himself. Yet, when he has done so, he all too often recognizes that the impulses he has released are very immature ones, and he is liable to incur social criticism and an increase of guilt in self-condemnation. In fact, if he does not, he will not progress any further. To aim simply at the release of repressed immature and anxiety-driven impulses as if that were equivalent to the freeing of the healthy instinctive drives of a mature person, was seen to be naïve and a therapeutic delusion. Neither do impulses automatically mature by becoming conscious and being expressed. It is useless releasing impulses unless they are considered all the time as expressions of an *ego*, and indicative of the state in which that ego exists. For these, among other reasons, Fairbairn abandoned 'impulse psychology' in favour of more radical ego-analysis.

The striking feature of the development of psychodynamic theory in the last thirty or so years is that, through the work of Melanie Klein in which emphasis was shifting from the impulse to the object, there has now begun to emerge a steady trend towards concentration on the ego. The re-orientation of psychodynamic theory from the point of view of the ego is certain to bring new insights as old facts are looked at in a new way. Adler raised the problem of the ego in his theory of the inferiority complex and the will-to-power; but he raised it superficially, prematurely and mostly at the social level. It was from Freud himself that the real impetus to ego-analysis came in the 1920's. His structural scheme, id, ego and super-ego, in spite of its inadequacies, was a tremendous first step towards *putting the ego in the centre of the picture* where hitherto psychobiological impulse had reigned supreme. This is clear from the statement of Anna Freud: 'There have been periods in the development of psychoanalytical science when the theoretical study of the individual ego was distinctly unpopular. . . . Whenever interest was transferred from the deeper to the more superficial strata—whenever, that is to say, research was deflected from the id to the ego—it was felt that here was the beginning of apostasy' (1936). However, it is also clear from this that the dynamic depths of the psyche were still regarded as an impersonal 'id' while the ego belonged to the 'more superficial strata'. So long as that relic of the earlier 'impulse psychology' remained, no satisfactory ego-theory could develop.

Freud stated clearly that: 'We shall achieve our therapeutic purpose only when we give a greater measure of analytic help to the patient's ego' (1937). Earlier he had written concerning 'the therapeutic efforts of psychoanalysis' that: *Their object is to strengthen the ego, to make it more independent of the super-ego,* (present writer's italics) to widen its field of vision, and so to extend its organization that it can take over more portions of the id' (1933).

With some re-interpretation of terms, nothing could be nearer the truth about psychotherapy. It is our psychotherapeutic charter. Its great importance, however, was obscured by the fact that the Freudian theory of an ego limited to the 'superficial strata' could give no meaning to 'ego' adequate to the implications of this statement. Freud's theory remained one of ego and super-ego control of psychobiological impulse. The ego remained a superficially developed control-apparatus 'on the surface of the id' and not a true self, not the real core of the personality. It becomes ever more clear to-day that *we require the term 'ego' to stand for the core of the individual's nature and self-knowledge as a 'person', and 'I' in personal relationships with other 'I's.* Fairbairn has recently written: 'All inner problems resolve themselves ultimately into ego-problems' (1958). Winnicott speaks of 'therapeutic regression' in search of the 'true self' which has early been repressed and lies hidden behind a 'false self' which functions socially, a point of view which classic psychoanalytical theory cannot explain intelligibly. In fact, psychodynamic theory is changing its orientation from 'the release and/or control of instinctive impulses' to the 'maturing of the ego into an adult personality'. Perhaps we should put it in an even more elementary way, 'the individual's struggle to achieve and preserve a stable ego', and we must rethink all the familiar problems from this point of view.

Moreover, this is really the patient's point of view. A patient of mine once said: 'I have grown up an outer shell of conformities inside which I have lost touch with the real "me".' She felt she had not got a proper ego. In developing 'Object-Relations Theory' Fairbairn presented the view that we must go beyond the repression of memories, emotions and impulses and consider the repression of the object, making use of Melanie Klein's theory of 'internal objects' (Fairbairn 1952). His work, however, has gone on to direct attention to the other half of the object-relationship, namely the ego. It is clear that our need for object-relationships lies in the fact that without them it is impossible to develop an ego that is sound, strong and stable: and that is what all human beings fundamentally need. Fairbairn quoted a patient as saying: 'You're always talking about my wanting this and that desire satisfied; but what I really want is a father' (1952). Now, however, we have to go one step beyond that and say the reason why the patient wants a father (and needs an analyst) is that without a satisfactory relationship with another person he cannot become a developing ego, he cannot find himself. That is why patients are so often found complaining 'I don't know who or what I am, I don't seem to have a mind of my own, I don't feel to be a real person at all.' Their early object-relationships were such that they were unable to 'find themselves' in any definite way.

The nature of the problem involved seems to me to be this: the primary drive in every human being is to become a 'person', to achieve a solid ego-formation, to develop a personality, in order to live. This, however, can only be done in the medium of personal object-relationships. If these are good, the infant undergoes a natural and unselfconscious good ego-development. If these are bad, ego-development is seriously compromised from the start; and there are no fears worse or deeper than those which arise out of having to cope with life when one feels that one is just not a real person, that one's ego is basically weak, perhaps that one has hardly got an ego at all. These are the ultimate fears in our patients. Thus one patient, who was often driven to make the kind of complaints cited in the previous paragraph, once burst out with: 'I'm afraid of life, of everything. Fear's the key.' Psychotherapy as a process whereby the patient is helped to achieve a mature ego and overcome his deep fear of life is the logical goal of Fairbairn's revision of theory and of Winnicott's work in the clinical and therapeutic field. It is the overcoming of 'infantile dependence' which Fairbairn regards as the root cause of psychoneurosis (the Oedipus Complex being simply one example of this infantile dependence), and it is the discovery of the 'true self' which Winnicott regards as buried behind the defensive operations of the years. These two points of view appear to me to be the starting-points of research on psychotherapy to-day. 'Infantile dependence' could not be more clearly illustrated as the cause of trouble than in the remark of a patient, himself a doctor: 'I'm sick to death of dragging round with me wherever I go a timid small child inside me.' That child was the weak, overburdened basic ego that just could not stand up to life. The fact that this 'baby' has then to be repudiated, at the demand of the outer world, later internalized as an inner demand, appears in a patient's dream. 'I was eating my favourite meal when my mother came into the room and snatched it away from me. As I went to protest she said "Don't be a baby".' These two instances define for us, in the patient's own terms the nature of the problem they bring to us. *An infantile ego has been rejected and repressed. ('Don't be a baby.') It remains, therefore, undeveloped and weak, and natural growth of personality comes to a standstill.*

## THE FEAR OF EGO-WEAKNESS

If we may now, for a moment, forget all the complex theories of psychiatric, psychoanalytical and psychological learning, and watch human beings at first hand as they struggle with life in and through their dealings with the people round them, we may ask ourselves the simple question, 'What are people most afraid of?' The multifarious ways in which people are on the defensive against one another, in business, social life, marriage and parenthood, and even leisure activities, suggests that the one omnipresent fear is the fear of appearing weak, inadequate, less of a person than others or less than equal to the demands of the situation, a failure: the fear of letting oneself down and looking a fool in face of an unsupportive and even hostile world. This fear lies behind all the rationalized self-assertiveness and aggressiveness, the subtle exhibitionism, the disguised boasting, the competitiveness or avoidance of competition, the need of praise, reassurance, and approval, the safety-first tactics and security seeking, and a multitude of other defensive reactions to life that lie open and on the surface for all to see.

If we now turn back to our patients with this in mind, we find the same fear of appearing weak, often in the manifest form of a sense of shame and humiliation in having to seek this sort of treatment at all. In this context, fear of the hostile world appears as fear of being despised if it is known that they have such treatment. But behind this fear, without exception, we come upon the fact that patients suffer from very serious feelings of actual weakness and inadequacy as a result of which they are in a state of perpetual anxiety. Their fear of appearing weak has a foundation in fact, and likewise their fear of a hostile world also, in early life, had a foundation in fact. It is true that feelings of weakness have no direct relationship to the patient's actual ability. They are found in the most able people, professional folk with good qualifications, men successfully running their own businesses and so on. One of the most undermined personalities I have ever come across, so far as basic lack of self-confidence was concerned, was a surgeon who had practised excellently for twenty years. But he said that no one knew the torture it had been. Every time the telephone rang he was in a state of utter anxiety, feeling certain that he was going to be asked to perform an operation that he could not do, or that he would fail in it. The feeling of weakness arises out of the lack of a reliable feeling of one's own reality and identity as an ego. Patients will say 'I'm not sure of myself, sometimes I don't feel like a real person at all'.

With many patients, however, this deep down fundamental weakness of the ego is not obvious to them. We may be able to recognize its signs, but the patient's energies are strenuously devoted to hiding, denying, disproving, disguising, or mastering and crushing out if possible whatever degree of these feelings of weakness, fear, timidity and inability to cope with life that they find in them. The famous 'resistance' to psychotherapy which was one of Freud's most important discoveries is, in the first instance, mainly an attempt to deny the need for treatment. Patients will either play down their problems, minimize their symptoms, state frankly that they feel psychotherapy is humiliating and that they ought to be able to manage these difficulties themselves, resent the most carefully and tactfully made interpretations as criticism, and are very anxious that no one should know that they are consulting a psychotherapist; or else they will set forth their problems as unfair or inexplicable inflictions, with an attitude implying 'There's nothing really wrong with me but somehow these misfortunes have befallen me' and they feel they can rightly claim help for such things (a claim in which, in fact, they are justified in the end). Most patients, apart from the few who have had the opportunity of gaining some insight, seek the removal of their symptoms without realizing the necessity of undergoing some basic changes in themselves, for they do not recognize their symptoms as evidences of basic weakness in their personality. If they do, they all the more regard treatment as a humiliation, and are on the defensive from the start. These patients are often right in fearing that they will be looked down upon, judging by the rather thinly veiled contempt with which hysterics are sometimes referred to, even by some psychiatrists. In any case, the patients look down upon themselves. One of my patients dreamed that she went past my rooms on top of a tram, but looking down she also saw herself entering in, and thought 'Look at that silly creature going in there'.

The more one reflects on things from this point of view, the more impressive do the facts become. The resistance to psychotherapy is strictly on a par with the defensiveness of people against one another in everyday life. If we study this question in the light of the mass of psychopathological data at our disposal to-day (which did not yet exist in the early days of psychoanalysis), we shall come near the heart of the matter. There is a greater or lesser degree of immaturity in the personality-structure of most human beings, and this immaturity is experienced as definite weakness and inadequacy of the ego in face of the adult tasks of life. The unremitting and strenuous efforts to overcome or hide this weakness, which they do not know how, genuinely, to grow out of, constitutes, together with the weakness itself, the mass of psychopathological experience and behaviour, as seen not only in patients but also in the general low level of mental health in the community. The struggle to force a weak ego to face life, or, even more fundamentally, the struggle to preserve an ego at all, is the cause of psychosomatic tensions and illness.

There are important reasons why so many human beings are in a state of constant anxiety because they feel weak and inadequate at the very core of their inner self. Maybe we are barely emerging from the psychological Dark Ages so far as the great mass of the population is concerned, in the matter of bringing up children. Possibly also there are one or two primitive tribes whose simple culture is totally ignorant of our so-called scientific civilization, yet its pattern of 'permissive- ness' embodied far more psychological wisdom than any forms of capitalist or communist society known to our anxiety-ridden world. Some other primitive tribes have been described as having a paranoid culture pattern, but certainly throughout our modern civilization East and West, right and left wing, religious and scientific, there goes on a mass production of basically insecure and psychologically weakened human beings faster than any method has yet been found to cope with them. Masses of children grow up frightened at heart. Moreover, our patients constantly meet a critical and unsympathetic reaction from friends. 'Oh, we could all give in like that if we let ourselves, you must pull yourself together. You should think less of yourself and more of other people.' So the cultural attitudes drive them to feel ashamed of weakness and to simulate strength. Ian Suttie, many years ago now, spoke of the 'taboo on tenderness' in our culture. But the matter goes deeper. The reason why there is a taboo on tenderness is that tenderness is regarded as weakness in all but the most private relations of life, and many people regard it as weakness even there and introduce patterns of domination into the love-life itself. The real taboo is on weakness, the one great crime is to be weak, the thing that none dare confess to is feeling weak, however much the real weakness was brought into being when they were so young that they knew nothing of the import of what was happening to them. You cannot afford to be weak in a competitive world which you feel is mostly hostile to you, and if anyone is so unfortunate as to discover that his infancy has left him with too great a measure of arrested emotional development and a failure of ego-growth in the important early stages, then he soon learns to bend all his energies to hiding or mastering the infant within.

## THE BASIC EMOTIONAL PREDICAMENT

The problem of ego-weakness has been slowly thrusting itself to the forefront of psychodynamic research. Perhaps the terrific resistance to admitting and facing 'basic ego-weakness rooted in fear' that all human beings show both in social life and as patients, is reflected in the slowness with which psychiatric and psychoanalytic research has come to face this problem. It may be that we ourselves would rather not be forced to see it too clearly lest we should find a text-book in our own hearts. It is less disturbing even to theorists to think in terms of mastering instinctive drives rather than of helping a frightened infant inside to grow up. It is more comfortable to think of ourselves as endowed with powerful libidinal and aggressive instincts, than to recognize that unmanageable libidinal and aggressive impulses are reactions to and defences against fear. If one has a 'mighty sexual instinct' (Freud, 1908) and a mighty aggressive instinct, one does not feel *weak*, but only *bad*. The history of psychodynamic theory can be seen as the story of our long struggle to overcome our scientifically rationalized resistance to the truth. A survey of the titles of articles in the *International Journal of Psycho-Analysis* and the *British Journal of Medical Psychology* suggests that we are becoming overweighted with complex analyses and, nowadays, statistical studies of secondary phenomena, of interesting organic and psychodynamic morbidities, and all the while 'The Basic Human Dilemma' in which our patients are caught is being missed; namely that they were born into a situation in which they were unable to lay the foundations of a strong ego-development, and have grown up feeling at bottom inadequate to the demands of living, even though they may not be conscious of this, full of fear and struggling with considerable though varying degrees of success to keep going and shoulder their responsibilities. This fact of basic ego-weakness is the hard core of all personality disturbance and of the problem of psychotherapy. The one line of research that would seem to be most urgent and relevant to all forms of mental illness, other than the purely organic in origin, is that which goes to the tap root, the failure or inability of the child in the environment it is born into, to lay the foundations of an adequate strong, well-developed, self-confident and capable personality equal to the adult tasks in life.

From the point of view of psychotherapy the problem is why and how this early arrest of ego-development persists? Once an initial failure has occurred in laying the foundations of a non-anxious and active self in infancy, a mental organization evidently comes into being of a kind which effectively blocks the possibility of any further deep-level emotional growth. Life then turns into an unceasing fight to force oneself to be equal to adult living without ever feeling that one is so in any fundamental way. One very able graduate professional man said: 'It's hell having to go through life screwing yourself up to face everything, although you know you can do it.' It is this psychic situation on its inner side that proliferates into all the psychiatric disorders. The one fact which overrides everything else is that society demands that the baby must grow up to become a capable adult, an internally strong enough and self-confident enough person to be able to look after himself and make his own contribution to life among other people. He must achieve a personality, an ego, adequate to the situation of grown-up existence if he is to live without internally caused fears and breakdown. Yet the plain fact is that probably a majority of human beings never do feel adequate to living and are involved in this process of 'screwing themselves up'. Freud pictured this state of things when, in his own terms, he spoke of the poor ego being so hard pressed by three taskmasters, the id, the super-ego and the outer world. Fears of ego-breakdown and ego-loss within come to be even greater than the original fears of outer reality. Freud's 'ego' as we have seen is only the 'ego of everyday life' in a purely controlling sense, and not the real dynamic source or centre of the personality. Freud called it the Reality Ego, the ego in touch with the outer world, what Fairbairn calls the Central Ego, and it is not of this familiar ego, not of this part of the total psychic self, that basic ego-weakness is a characteristic. It is true that a profound sense of weakness and inadequacy may and does break through into the familiar conscious ego of everyday life, but it does not originate there. When this breakthrough does occur, it is because the normal Central-Ego defences have cracked. Usually the Central-Ego functions as a defence against this devastating sense of weakness, seeking to prevent its invasion of everyday living. The Obsessional Character, for instance, gives us a striking example of a Central Ego organized on a rigid and unyielding pattern of absolute self-control with no weakness shown: though in fact the Central Ego may here be said to have been captured by the Freudian sadistic 'super-ego'.

Ego-weakness in the ultimate sense in which it is basic and causal for all kinds of personality disorder is a property of the infantile part of the psyche which Fairbairn calls the Libidinal Ego and which Freud called the 'id'. 'Id' is, strictly speaking, a psychologically useless term. It is not capable of standing for anything meaningful except the bare notion of impersonal biological instinctive energy, and that is something that we never meet with in clinical experience. We meet only with energies that represent the functioning of a personal aspect or part of the total personal psychic self, mature or immature. The term 'id' can convey nothing more than the idea that the energies used by the Libidinal Ego have a biological source. Fairbairn's term has a more significant connotation. The primary nature of the infant is endowed with natural libidinal needs and energies in virtue of which, in a good environment, it will grow into a strong, active and definitely individual personality. But, where personality disorder exists, that did not happen. The Libidinal Ego represents the structural differentiation of that aspect of the total psyche in a state of deprivation, frustration and distress, and hence of impotent rage, fear and knowledge of its own weakness. It is the infantile and fear-ridden Libidinal Ego (for which 'id' is an inadequate term) that is the seat of 'basic ego-weakness', and this is a deeper problem than that portion of the feeling of weakness that seeps through at various times into the ego of everyday consciousness. Here is an ego-weakness, the greater part of which is kept hidden and repressed, dammed in behind all the defences that enable the Central Ego to function even if with anxiety on the adult plane. My experience is that resistance in analysis is directed with terrific determination to the task of keeping this weak infantile ego under heavy repression. Ego-weakness consists not in lack of energy or innate ability, but in this unremitting state of basic fear and lack of self-confidence of which the individual feels ashamed.

The most obvious ways in which the person with a basically weak and immature ego seeks to protect himself in face of outer world pressures and inner world fears is to hide the part of himself that is a child facing a life that feels too big for him, behind Central Ego detachment, or aggressiveness, or conversion of tensions into bodily illnesses, or obsessional self-mastery, sheltering from realities behind technical professional knowledge, compulsive addiction to duty and un- selfish serviceableness to others, and so on. All the psychoneurotic defences come into play. The more serious pathological states of depression and schizoid apathy, depersonalization, suicidal trends and schizophrenic disintegration of the ego, undoubtedly represent complex conditions in which the infantile Libidinal Ego feels driven towards the ultimate psychic dangers. The defensive states represent rather the attempt to force a pseudo-adult pattern which masks the frightened child inside. This frightened child inside, the basically weak infantile Libidinal Ego, has, as it were, been split off and repudiated in an attempt to live without fears. This represents the hate and fear of weakness of which we have spoken. Our fear and intolerance of weakness is naturally great, and is so embedded in our culture-pattern and is so additionally stimulated in the infant by the adults who handle him, that he is driven to a premature repudiation of his weak infantile ego and to an attempt to force an equally premature pseudo-adult self. In seeking to overcome his weakness, the child employs a method which ensures its perpetuation, creating an endopsychic situation in which natural development is impossible. We must, in a moment, set this forth in more scientific terms, but it represents what we may well call the 'Basic Emotional Predicament' for human beings in growing up, the human dilemma: though I believe there have existed a few simple cultures in which this dilemma did not necessarily arise.

It appears to me that we are in danger of being so overloaded with medical and psychological learning concerning the ramifications of the disease-process once it is in being in the personality, that the tap-root is not recognized with sufficient clarity. We may miss the overall shape and meaning of the illness in studying the variety of its manifestations. Human infants, so long biologically and psychologically dependent on their parents, are not in the mass very successful in growing up to mature adulthood. What keeps the child alive inside so long? Why is he not normally and naturally outgrown as the years go by, along with increasing physical and intellectual maturity? A person in a good state of mental health as a result of a good early emotional development does not feel to be an inadequate and frightened child inside. One does not have to have outstanding powers or exceptional endowments to feel quite sufficiently self-confident for normal purposes. It is much more a matter of the emotional attitude in which one lives with oneself in one's inner mental make-up. An enormous number of people are unable to achieve an emotional development to mature, unafraid, self-reliant and affectionate adulthood. Why, however, is it not easier for human beings to make a belated growth in ego-strength after childhood is left behind? On a purely conscious Central-Ego level many people, in fact, do. But it is startling to find through deep analysis, how little this has affected the situation in the profoundly repressed unconscious. We may, therefore, state in this way the problem of the psychodynamic hard core of resistance to psychotherapy: when once the infantile ego has become disturbed and arrested in its development in the earliest stages, so that it comes to feel its weakness and to exist in a state of fear, what is it that keeps it thereafter fixed so stubbornly in that position of basic ego-weakness? What is it that leads to the perpetuation of a weak, undeveloped, fearful and therefore 'infantile dependent' ego (in Fairbairn's sense). It remains buried in the deep unconscious and makes no progress to maturity, in spite of the strenuous efforts of the 'self of everyday life' (Fairbairn's Central Ego) to grow and function as an adult. Why is this endopsychic situation so hard to change? And in what form does it persist so statically? Here is the basic emotional predicament.

## ANTILIBIDINAL RESISTANCE TO PSYCHOTHERAPY

We are now so used to saying that the causes lie back in childhood that we may miss the vital point of this problem. It is true that the origins or starting-point of the trouble lie back in childhood, but the actual emotional cause of instability and weakness in the personality in later life is something different, something that is going on in the personality right here and now. It is a peculiar feature of the mental organization of the individual (his endopsychic structure) which keeps him in that original state of basic fear and weakness, and perpetuates it and even intensifies it as time goes on. We have stated this in non-technical language as the fear and hate of weakness in the face of the necessities of living, and in comparison with other people. But we have to be able to show how this fear and hate come to be permanently embodied in the organizational structure of the psyche.

The situation must arise in this way: a disturbing or as Winnicott (1954) calls it 'impinging' environment in infancy and childhood makes the infant aware of his smallness, weakness and helplessness, and at the same time makes him feel very frightened. The specific feeling of being little, helpless and frightened can emerge with great definiteness in deep analyses. Gradually the child must become convinced that, if he could put it into such words, it is too frightening to be weak in an unfriendly and menacing world, and also that one cannot afford to have needs that one cannot get satisfied. They make you dependent and, if you cannot change your world, you must change yourself. Thus he comes to fear and hate his own weakness and his own neediness; and now he faces the task of growing up with an intolerance of his immaturity. This is very much bound up with and reflects the impatience and intolerance that grown-ups have of the dependence of the infant and the childishness of the child. One patient described how his crying as a child drew on him such contempt and ragging that he managed suddenly to suppress it, only to find the crying fits replaced by temper attacks. Another patient described how his attitude to his small son changed during the course of his analysis. At first when the boy cried, the father would feel in an absolute fury of intolerance and shout at the boy to stop it at once, which only made him worse. Then later on he managed to moderate this and would say: 'Come on now, stop this crying, you're a big boy now.' The patient explained that as a boy he was himself often very frightened of his father but never dared to cry though he often felt like it. But his son was not a 'big boy now' and the father was trying to force him to a premature assumption of an attitude older than his years, because this was what had happened in his own case. Finally, however, he worked through to a third position, and he says: 'Now, when the lad cries I don't feel that old fury. I can accept his childishness better and I say "I'm sorry old chap you're so upset. I know how you feel, but never mind. You have your cry and you'll feel a lot better soon".' That, he says, works far better, and in a short time the tears are dried and the boy has forgotten it all. But all too often the child is educated into the same intolerance of his childishness that the parents felt towards their own. A self-frustrating situation of deep internal self-hate arises, along with a concentrated attempt to drive and force oneself to the conscious feeling and behaviour that is regarded as adult, in the light of the pseudo-mature patterns of the grown-ups around. This pseudo-adult pattern may be conventional, practical, moral, critical, intellectual or even aggressive, angry, cruel, but it always masks an inward self-hate and self-persecution. The child models his own fear and hate of his immaturity on the parental attitudes of intolerance and rejection of it, so that he comes to treat his primary needy dependent but now disturbed self as if it were a part of his whole self that he could disown, split off, hide and repress and even crush out of existence, while his 'ego of everyday life' is compelled to develop tougher or at least more socially approved characteristics. The child's ego has now, as Fairbairn shows, been disrupted and falls into three parts or aspects. The original needy and now frightened and persecuted infant (the Libidinal Ego), a newly developed persecuting ego that bends all its energies to hating the weak infant (an Anti-libidinal Ego), and the conscious self of everyday living that seeks security by adopting approved standards (the Central Ego). The Central Ego is in principle conscious; the conflict between the Antilibidinal Ego and the Libidinal Ego is driven down by repression and kept unconscious for the most part, though its effects can and do seep through into consciousness as immature needs, fears, loves and hates. In the hysteric, the Central Ego is much influenced by the suffering Libidinal Ego. In depressed and obsessional persons the central ego may be all but captured by the Antilibidinal Ego. In these patients hostile self-attack and punishing self-mastery are quite visible. All sado-masochistic phenomena are expressions of the deep-down persecution of the Libidinal Ego by the Antilibidinal Ego. I have adopted Fairbairn's structural terminology because, so far as I can see, it gives a much more accurate analysis and description of the facts than do Freud's terms, id, ego and super-ego. But just as we have seen that the weak infantile Libidinal Ego covers in part what Freud referred to as the id, so now we note that the harsh and persecuting Antilibidinal Ego covers what Freud meant by the sadistic part of the Super-ego. I can see no good reason now for continuing to use the terms id and super-ego in view of their lack of precise obvious meaning, the unpsychological nature of the term id, and the confusing mixture of primitive sadistic self-persecution and moral conscience in the term super-ego. We have now an accurate analysis of the fact that Freud made quite explicit, namely that very early in life a human being tends to become cruelly divided against himself and becomes a self-frustrating and even at times a self-destroying creature. Such an individual falls ill eventually because his secret, sadistic attack upon himself, his despising of his immaturity, his hating of his weakness, and his attempts to crush out his unsatisfied libidinal needs, become a much greater danger and menace to him than the outer world normally and usually is. The Libidinal Ego's fear of the Antilibidinal Ego comes to be even greater than the fear of the external world which often reflects it. Difficulties in real life that could actually be met and coped with are repeatedly felt to be intolerable because of the weakening effect of the self-persecution and the incessant fear and hate kept going inside: the basis on which later morbid guilt is developed.

The hard core of personality illness then is this persisting structuralized version of intolerance and rejection, through fear and later on guilt, of the originally disturbed child, now existing as the deepest repressed, immature level of the personality, a source of internal weakness; a situation compensated for by the forcing of a pseudo-patterned adult ego on the level of everyday consciousness, an artifact not a natural growth from the depths of the primary nature. The degree of self-hate and self-persecution going on in the unconscious determines the degree of the illness, and in severe cases a person can become panic-stricken and go to pieces under the virulence of this internal self-attack on the primary child self. An accurate estimate of the nature and intensity of this can usually be got from a patient's reactions to actual difficult children or to immaturity in grown-ups, and also from their sado-masochistic fantasies or dreams, and the painfulness of their physical psychogenic symptoms. The Central Ego is partly a struggle to cope with the outer world and partly a defensive system against the dangers of the inner world. It deserves a better label than Winnicott's 'false self' though there is truth in that. It is not really the patient's full and proper self, but it does contain very much that can and should be taken up into his true self as integration proceeds. 'False Self' would more truly describe the Antilibidinal Ego. The sado-masochistic deadlock between the cruel Antilibidinal Ego attacking the weak and suffering Libidinal Ego in the deep unconscious is the hard core of the illness against which the Central Ego is the defence. That Ego-weakness is not due to lack of energy is evident from the tremendous energy shown by the Antilibidinal Ego in psychic self-attack. The Libidinal Ego feels weak because energy is made over to its persecutor. Ego-weakness can exist along with psychic strength.

One patient, a single woman in the late thirties, in whom 'the illness' so seriously sabotaged her capacity to carry on normal relationships with people that it was with great difficulty that she was able to keep a job, revealed this internal self-persecutory situation naïvely and without disguise. She would rave against girl children and in fantasy describe how she would crush a girl child if she had one, and would then fall to punching herself (which perpetuated the beatings her mother gave her.) One day I said to her: 'You must feel terrified being hit like that'. She said: 'I'm not being hit. I'm the one that's doing the hitting.' Another patient, much older, exhibited the same self-persecutory set-up verbally. Whenever she made any slight mistake, she would begin shouting at herself at the top of her voice:

'You stupid thing, why don't you think, you ought to have known better' and so on, which were in fact the very words her mother used against her in daily nagging. We can see here in an unmistakable way the Antilibidinal Ego identified with the angry parent in a vicious attack on the Libidinal Ego which is treated as a bad selfish child, but even more deeply feared and hated as a weak child. The first of these patients says she was always crying as a child, and despised herself for it. Ultimately she managed to suppress this symptom of childhood depression and its place was taken by these furious outbursts of self-hate.

In these two examples, the Central Ego has been captured by the Antilibidinal Ego, which is openly and undisguisedly a self-hater. In the following example the whole pattern of threefold splitting is revealed, though the Antilibidinal Ego is kept under strong, controlling repression. The patient, a male in the forties, had a most unhappy early home life and was a badly depressed child. He grew to despise himself as a 'cry-baby' and a 'little worm'; he repressed this tearful little boy and built up a rigidly controlled, capable, unemotional and aloof Central Ego to deal with the outer world. But he suffered from recurring bouts of depression and his emotional life in the inner world was expressed in violent sado-masochistic fantasies and dreams. After a long analysis during which his depressed childhood self was drawn nearer to consciousness in recognizable form, he came to session one day saying: 'Just before I set out I felt apprehensive and as if I could burst into tears; a reaction I suppose to coming here.' I asked him why he should feel depressed on coming to see me.

He replied: 'I see a picture of a little boy shut up alone in a room crying. If one were in a house where there was such a child, it would depend on how interesting one's work was whether you were aware of him. Sometimes I become aware of him and at other times when very busy I can forget him.' I said: 'Your fantasy is really that you as a grown-up person are working in one room and wanting to forget a crying little boy shut up in another room. What about that?' He answered: 'The obvious thing is to go to the child and find out why he's crying and comfort him. Why didn't I think of that at first? That strikes me as very odd.' My reply was to ask who shut the little boy in that room and why, and he said: 'He's a nuisance. You can't get on with your work with a crying child around.' That answered his question. He did not think of going to help the child because he regarded him as a nuisance, and he was the person who had shut him away there so as to forget him, or some part of him that did not appear in the fantasy had shut the child away. I suggested that a part of him that aggressively hated the child was being kept hidden, itself repressed, but that it guarded the door and tried not to let the child out or let me in to help. He replied that he saw that that must be true but that he was not conscious of feeling any such self-hate. I was able to remind him that in the previous session he had said: 'I like to think that I can be tolerant to a problem child and to the problem child in myself, but I can't. I am intolerant and aggressive to myself, and though I disagree with the way my parents brought me up, I operate en bloc all their standards against myself.' (Transference implications in this material have not been touched on, as it is used specifically to cast light on endopsychic structure.)

Here is a clear picture of the threefold differentiation of the ego; the Central Ego of everyday life working in one room and wanting to forget what is going on elsewhere, the distressed, weak and helpless child shut away in the unconscious as a disowned and hated Libidinal Ego in an immature state, and the implied if repressed Antilibidinal Ego hating the child and regarding him as a nuisance to be got rid of. It is as if once the child is badly disturbed and realizes he is too weak to alter his environment, he feels driven to attempt the only other thing possible, namely to alter himself in such a way that he no longer feels so frightened and weak, or at least seeks to prevent himself being conscious of it. He develops an intense dislike of himself in the state he is in and, so to speak, detaches this hostile part of himself and sends it on a mission to crush out the frightened, needy and therefore dependent child, so as to leave the rest of himself free to cope with the outer world with something more of the feeling of being a personality. It is the struggle for an ego all the time. The more successful this trick is (and parents so often help and educate the child to perform it) the more self-destructive it becomes, because the crushed child is the primary self and its repression progressively leads to self-exhaustion. We have to think of this threefold splitting of the ego as the pattern of a total strategy for facing life in an attempt to 'negotiate from strength, not weakness'. The one thing that the child cannot do for himself is to give himself a basic sense of security since that is a function of object-relationship. All that can be done is for the Central Ego to seek to become independent of needs for other people. The patient can become self-blinded, deluded, into believing that hate is the only way to carry on, including hate of himself in so far as he wants something different; and some aspects of the outer world support his view. In fact, justice must be done to the Antilibidinal Ego because it is the child's struggle to keep himself going when he feels afraid and has no real help.

We may now refer back to Freud's statement about psychotherapy as aiming to 'strengthen the ego and make it more independent of the super-ego'. This statement embodied prophetic insight and gives us a basic truth about psychotherapy, but the terms now need reinterpretation. The ego that needs to be strengthened is not just the Central Ego or 'outer-reality ego' of everyday consciousness, but the patient's primary nature which is repressed and arrested in development in a state of frustrated, weak, frightened and suffering immaturity. We can hardly call this without qualification the 'true self' as Winnicott does (1954, 1955) but it does contain all the individual's true potentialities. If it can be reached, protected, supported and freed from the internal persecutor, it is capable of rapid development and integration with all that is valuable and realistic in the Central Ego. Psychotherapy must aim at the maturing of the infantile Libidinal Ego (which represents in however limited a way the primary nature) and its integration with the Central Ego to which it will restore full emotional capacity, spontaneity and creativeness. This aim is bitterly opposed by another part of the personality, the Antilibidinal Ego, which has long dedicated all the patient's anger, hate and aggression to crushing his needs and fears. The Antilibidinal Ego is not re-integrated *qua* antilibidinal. Its aggression is taken back into the service of the Libidinal Ego and matured. The patient, in the Antilibidinal Ego, to quote Fairbairn, uses 'a maximum of his aggression to subdue a maximum of his libidinal need' (1952). The reason apparently is that libidinal need is held to be the main characteristic of the dependent infant, and all dependence is hated as weakness. It seeks to maintain a 'personality without needs for other people', self-sufficient, ultra-independent, hard and rejective. It always fails to recognize that its patterning by identification with the rejective parent and its 'power cult' in relationships of domination over others are actually but thinly disguised dependence. That is why persons of this type of conscious personality so usually break down when they lose those they have tyrannized over.

The hostility, however, of the Antilibidinal Ego to direct dependence on anyone for help, and its hatred of the admission of needs, is the real source of all 'resistance' to psychotherapy, and of resistance to the psychotherapist. It hates the needy child inside and it hates the therapist to whom he desires to turn for help. Its opposition is so unyielding that there can be no doubt that this is the very centre of the problem of psychotherapy. It is the Antilibidinal Ego that keeps the basic self weak by active persecution and by denying it any relationship in which it could grow strong, and thus makes 'cure' such a slow and difficult process. This is the field of detailed psychopathology where close psychodynamic analysis is so necessary if one is to find out exactly what is happening in the patient. I have had a number of dreams from a variety of patients in which one or other of their parents sought to interfere with and stop the analysis. One woman dreamed that her mother followed her to my room and tried to shoot her as she was entering. Another woman patient felt that her mother was hovering outside the window trying to get in and break up the session. A male patient dreamed that his mother burst into the room during a session and planted herself between him and me, saying to him 'What have you been saying about me?' and to me 'What ideas have you been putting into my son's head?' Such dreams and fantasies represent a process of opposition that is developing in the patient's mind against the analyst and hostile to treatment, and the process belongs to the Antilibidinal Ego with its identifications with rejective parents. The identification is not usually so obvious and undisguised as in these instances.

Moreover, it is not by any means clear to the patient that rejection and hate of the analyst and of his own infantile libidinal self go together. He may voice one or the other, but only rarely both together. One patient expressed a serious degree of ego-weakness followed by equally virulent self-rejection, thus: 'I feel inferior, I'm not sure of my identity, I've made a mess of life, I'm feeble, poor and don't feel worth anything. Away from mother it all feels messy inside me, not solid, like a jelly fish. I'm nothing definite and substantial, only frightened, woffling and clinging to anything for safety, it's an indescribable feeling.' Then she goes on: 'I hate myself, I wish I wasn't me, I'd like to get rid of myself.' Here is her self-rejection, her antilibidinal concentration on running herself down, but on another occasion her antilibidinal reaction turns to rob her of my help. She says: 'I've felt very small all this week and dependent on you. Then I felt I ought to be more independent of you and stop coming to you. Mother thinks I ought to be able to do without treatment now. I feel guilty about it. But I'm not strong enough yet not to have your support'. Often the antilibidinal reaction against the analyst is more serious. One patient, at a time of great strain over an event which profoundly disturbed her, oscillated between an intensified sense of need for my help, and, on one occasion, an outburst, motivated by very serious fear of her panicky feelings of weakness, in which she said with great tension 'You want me to come creeping and crawling to you but I'll show you.' Nevertheless, the more difficult antilibidinal reactions of resistance to treatment are those which are subtly disguised, and only develop slowly in the unconscious. It is certain that whenever a patient begins to turn to the analyst with any deeper and more genuine measure of trust and dependence and acceptance of help, at once a hidden process of opposition starts up and will sooner or later gather strength and lead to a subtle change of mood that makes the patient no longer able to co-operate as fully as he consciously wishes to do. These antilibidinal reactions to anyone from whom help or affection is needed and sought are not confined to analysis, and they conspicuously sabotage marital and sexual relationships. In fact, the patient's mood can change and turn against anything and everything that is proving good and valuable and helpful in life, as if in secret he were playing to himself the part of the mother in the dream of that patient who was eating her favourite meal: the mother snatched it away and said 'Don't be a baby.' The Antilibidinal Ego will snatch everything away if it can, not only analysis but friends, religious comforts, creative activities, marriage, and we need to be able to determine the exact source of its power as carefully as we are able, remembering that it is not an entity per se, but one aspect of the patient's total, if divided self; and, withal, to be respected as his genuine struggle to keep his ego in being.

## THE STATIC INTERNAL CLOSED SYSTEM

We may now recognize the antilibidinal factor in the personality, which is the source of resistance to psychotherapy, as the same factor that has all along obstructed any natural basic maturing of the ego, once it had become disturbed. This antilibidinal factor arises out of the child's necessity, as it seems to him, to make himself independent of all help since the kind of help he requires does not seem obtainable. He must make his own internal arrangements to maintain his personality and stand by them. These arrangements consist of his own version of an Antilibidinal Ego sadistically mastering the frightened and weak infantile Libidinal Ego. Bound up with this is the world of internal objects which Kleinian analysis has laid bare. With regard to this set-up in its entirety, Fairbairn has recently spoken of: 'A further defensive aim which I have now come to regard as the greatest of all sources of resistance – viz. the maintenance of the patient's internal world as a closed system' (1958). He describes the dreams of one patient as reflecting: 'A movement in the direction of maintaining relationships with objects in the inner world at the expense of a realistic and therapeutic relationship with the analyst, viz. a movement having the aim of preserving inner reality as a closed system. Such an aim on the patient's part seems to me to constitute the most formidable resistance encountered in psychoanalytical treatment' (1958). He also regards this 'closed system' as a 'static internal situation' (1958). Thus one of my patients, writing to me from a residential Conference, explained why she had not written earlier although she had felt extremely anxious, saying: 'It was important to me to be able at least to *contain it* without having to come flying to you for help. I would just be too humiliated.' The same patient once said: 'Sometimes I feel I can only keep myself going by hating. I can't stop fighting. I won't give it up, I can't give in. I feel I'll lose everything if I do': a desperate antilibidinal struggle for an ego by means of independence. This desperate state of mind had come into being because she had had to fight all through her childhood to maintain a personality of her own in face of an over-powering father who frightened her. But to resist his domination she had to fight not only against him but against her fear of him. The frightened child had to force herself to defy the angry father even though that could only mean increasing fear and emotional exhaustion. In having to fight father with his own weapons, she reproduced some of his attitudes, such as the view that all human beings are selfish and only fight for their own ends, and that love is weakness, a truly 'antilibidinal' attitude embodied in a cynical view of life. This cynical Antilibidinal Ego was a mental reproduction of her father set up inside her, so far as her attitude to her needy and frightened child-self was concerned. That had to be crushed out for the purposes of 'the fight', so that her Libidinal Ego was in the terrifying position of being faced with an internal version of the intolerant father as another part of herself from which, therefore, there was no escape. This situation can drive a personality to a state of terror.

The Antilibidinal Ego, being considerably based on identification with the external bad object, involves resisting that bad object by a method that opens the gates of the fortress and lets him inside. By the time this patient had left home, she was more persecuted by her paternal Antilibidinal Ego inside than by her actual difficult father outside. Yet in this predicament, every patient agrees in saying: 'I can't change, I feel hopeless.' Whatever his more realistic Central Ego desires, the closed self-persecutory system of his inner world will only admit the analyst if it can fit him into its own pattern. It will not admit him as someone seeking to change the state of affairs and rescue the suffering Libidinal Ego from its plight. This 'closed system' situation is illustrated by a painting of the above quoted patient. It was a closed picture frame, the inside edge of which was an unbroken array of sharp teeth all pointing in at the patient. She lay as a helpless, masochistic figure in the bottom right-hand corner, faced with two menacing swords and a great hammer crashing down on her. Detached, but also inside the frame, were two praying hands stretched out appealing for help, but in vain because there was no one inside that set-up who represented a helper; the hands could not get outside to make their appeal, and no one could get in to bring aid. This is how the unconscious inner sado-masochistic world, inside which the distressed child is imprisoned, is felt by the patient, and it will not surprise us that this patient had suffered a paranoid-schizophrenic breakdown. I have found this inner prison often dreamed of under the symbol of the Concentration Camp. So the patient feels it is hopeless to change and he will never get better. The Antilibidinal Ego stands across the path of psychotherapy and blocks it, shutting the Libidinal Ego in the torture house and shutting the helpful analyst out.

The problem of the analyst is, on the one hand, how to prevent himself from being merely fitted into the pattern of this inner world as either the persecutor or the libidinal object who is hated in company with the Libidinal Ego (negative transference) and, on the other hand, how to break into this closed system as a helper able to initiate change. The Antilibidinal Ego will resist such a development to the bitter end. The system cannot be absolutely closed or no progress would ever be made at all, but every little breach that is made in it, at once evokes a powerful antilibidinal reaction aimed at closing it up again. Every time the patient seeks help and protection through reliance on the analyst in a positive transference, a negative transference immediately begins to develop unconsciously and will assuredly presently break out. Thus a naïve enthusiasm on the part of the analyst in taking sides with the Libidinal Ego, and an over-anxious pressing desire to 'save' the patient can only provoke sooner or later a fierce antilibidinal reaction and is self-defeating.

Freud (1923) wrote concerning the 'negative therapeutic reaction':

There is something in these people that sets itself against their recovery and dreads its approach as though it were a danger. . . . In the end we come to see that we are dealing with what may be called a 'moral' factor, a sense of guilt, which is finding atonement in the illness and is refusing to give up the penalty of suffering. We are justified in regarding this rather disheartening explanation as conclusive. But as far as the patient is concerned this sense of guilt is dumb; it does not tell him he is guilty; he does not feel guilty, he simply feels ill. This sense of guilt expresses itself only as a resistance to recovery which it is extremely difficult to overcome. It is also particularly difficult to convince the patient that this motive lies behind his continuing to be ill; he holds fast to the more obvious explanation that treatment by analysis is not the right remedy for his case.

This fundamental resistance to treatment which Freud ascribes to unconscious guilt may now be explained in a broader way. It is the antilibidinal refusal to admit any need in the patient or allow any help from anyone. Pathological guilt is only one of the various aspects of a complex effort to crush out the weak and needy child. Moreover, maintaining a guilt-relation to an internalized harsh parent is itself a defence against more primitive terrors. Freud added a footnote to this passage in which he says:

The battle with the obstacle of an unconscious sense of guilt is not made easy for the analyst. Nothing can be done against it directly, and nothing indirectly but the slow procedure of unmasking its unconscious repressed roots, and of thus gradually changing it into a conscious sense of guilt.

He is here calling us to the need for more rigorous analysis and the making conscious of all the motives that sustain what we must now see as the closed system of the inner world of internal bad objects and the Antilibidinal Ego, in which is concentrated all the patient's secret and repressed hatred of his infantile dependent Libidinal Ego, the source of his basic weakness. If direct assault on this inner redoubt only intensifies resistance, perhaps an analysis that goes deep enough can get behind it.

## ANALYSIS OF MOTIVES SUSTAINING THE ANTILIBIDINAL EGO

We seek to know how a patient can escape from his destructive relationship to internalized bad objects so as to enter into a constructive therapeutic relationship with the analyst. The closed system itself must have constructive implications or the patient would not maintain it with such desperate determination. The factors that sustain it are certainly complex.

## The Antilibidinal Ego Represents an Object-Relationship to Parents

Whether we view the Libidinal Ego as in the bondage of fear or guilt, that is imposed by an Antilibidinal Ego which in part represents the frightening or accusing parents. Fear and guilt are both object-relationships, and undoubtedly in the end human beings prefer bad relationships to none at all. The infant in the first place was in distress because he was unable to get a good relationship and so his need of and attachment to his parents had to be met by both suffering under them and identifying with them as bad objects. It is a long-standing psychoanalytical view that identification is a substitute for a lost object-relation. The infant comes to possess his disturbing parents in himself, in his developing Antilibidinal Ego, and its dissolution, therefore, will feel to him equivalent to the loss of parents. An inability to separate from parents with whom the relationship is mainly bad is illustrated by a patient sent for treatment during the war. She stated that she knew what was the matter with her. She had to live with her parents and they hated her and she hated them, but she could not get away. It was wartime and she could not get another job with as good a wage, and digs were hard to get. But it emerged that a few weeks before coming to me she had been offered promotion with an increased wage and with accommodation provided in another town, and she had refused it. She was too insecure to venture and therefore too attached to break away. The same kind of emotional relationship exists in the inner world. Though the internal bad-object relationship is felt to be persecution and a prison, the infantile Libidinal Ego is afraid to leave it. Thus a male patient dreamed of wondering why he did not try to escape from a Concentration Camp; but thought that though it was a bad place to be in, yet it was probably worse outside, and he was used to the camp, familiar with its life, and knew how to 'get by', and he decided to stay in.

This clinging to the closed inner world seems from this point of view to be based on the fear that, since one must have parents at all costs, bad parents are better than none, and if you break away you will only be out of the frying pan into the fire. But that attachment is also at work is shown in the patient who operated all his parents standards against himself even though he disagreed with them. There is deep loyalty to the parental mores. The Antilibidinal Ego goes on 'bringing the patient up' in the same way as did the parents. Furthermore, the disturbed child feels a need to be controlled, even though it be by the very parents who upset him.

Out of this, a clash in the patient's mind often becomes visible in dreams between parents and analyst. Thus a female patient who had had actually cruel treatment as a child, dreamed that she was being hurried along a road by her father who was cross and nagging her, when she saw me on the other side of the street, pulled her hand out of his and dashed across to me, refusing to return when he shouted at her. On another occasion she reported a dream that her mother had been beating her when I arrived and drove the mother away. Then later I had to go off on business (i.e. the end of a session) and she burst in tears and ran after her mother who began beating her again. A bad object is better than none, she could not be alone and her relation to a cruel mother was her most deeply rooted object-relationship. A striking dream of a female patient was to the effect that she met a terrifying lion and lioness and fled up a nearby tree for safety. But the tree was a young one and bent under her weight, putting her nearly but not quite back within reach of the animals. She said: 'Of course, the lion and lioness are my parents, and I think you are the young tree. I've known them all my life but I've only known you a year or two, and that's too young a relationship to protect me from their influence. When I'm here I'm sure you know best but when I'm at home I feel they must be right.' One sees here the little-developed Libidinal Ego which has no convictions of its own.

Patients, however, easily escape from seeing the real implication of these dreams, and discuss them as if it were now still a question of relationships with their actual parents. They do not easily grasp the fact that the parents in their dreams are parts of themselves, processes going on in their own minds, and represent now not so much their real parents as their own parent-influenced self, the Antilibidinal Ego in which they possess their parents by identifying themselves with them. It is necessary to make this clear, not only in the interests of solving their internal problems, but also in the interests of allowing for improved realistic relations with the actual parents where they are still alive.

## The Antilibidinal Ego Further Represents the Struggle to Possess an Ego

The more ill a patient is, the more certain it is that deep analysis will in the end bring to light extremely frightening feelings that he has no proper or satisfactory ego of his own. Here is the basic ego-weakness of which we have spoken. We have seen how, in the struggle to achieve an ego strong enough to live by, the child turns against his own actual ego as infantile, weak, and all too prone to betray him into the power of the adults through his dependent needs. The ferocity with which this internal 'turning against the self' can persist for years into subsequent adult life is seen in this dream of a man of forty. 'I dreamed that I saw a small dog in the house. It looked weak and was falling over on its side and lay there as if injured. I tried to shoo it away but it did not move. I suddenly felt an intense fury against it and wanted to kick it out. I felt I shouldn't treat it like that, but if I pushed it with my hands even that little dog might bite. Then it wasn't there, then it was there again.' The little dog, like the fantasy of the crying little boy quoted earlier, was the infantile Libidinal Ego, the small hurt little child of years ago still alive within, hated, ignored but thrusting itself again into notice. In proportion as this repression of the original libidinally needy self is successful, it leaves the child with little ego of his own; or, perhaps we should say that in order to achieve this repression of his original self, the child must borrow an ego from elsewhere to do it with. However we put it, an identification is made with parents and this comes to take the place of any further natural development in the child of an ego that is genuinely his own. The identification with bad objects serves as a substitute for proper ego-growth. Thus the dissolving of this identification is likely to be felt by the patient as the loss of his own personality. Since he has not been able to grow a mature ego of his own with deep roots in his primary nature, if he gives up the Antilibidinal Ego he has nothing to fall back on but his infantile dependent self, and he feels threatened with a regression the extent of which he cannot foresee. We must remind ourselves that the Antilibidinal Ego represents the patient's struggle to retain an active ego to live by in spite of his fears. Thus, since it represents both an object-relationship and an ego, in a situation where the patient does not possess either in a satisfactory form, it is apparent that he will have the greatest difficulty in growing out of this unnatural growth in his personality structure.

## The Antilibidinal Ego Confers a Sense of Power, Even If Only over the Self

This is involved in the two previous situations. The child feels weak because he cannot master his environment to better his position. If he identifies with the persecutory adults in order to repress his infantile self, he is taking on the personality of those who appear as the powerful figures in his little world. Undoubtedly, patients experience a sinister sense of power and satisfaction in exercising a cruel and destructive repression on their own anxious child self. This is apparent when a patient will fantasy scenes of angry and aggressive treatment of a child. 'Wouldn't I love to make it squirm' or 'I'd break every bone in its vile little body, I'd crush it.' This cruelty to the child within is the root of all cruel treatment of real children, and one regularly finds patients who are parents dreaming of their inward treatment of their own immature ego under the symbol of similar treatment of their own children. One such dream is particularly clear. The patient, a male, says: 'I dreamed that I and my father and my little boy were walking in the park by the lake, and suddenly my son broke away, dashed to the rowing boats, jumped into one and pulled off. He wanted to do things on his own. My father and I looked at each other. The lad had to be taught a lesson and I got in a boat and rowed after him, tipped him into the water to teach him and then pulled him out and brought him back to where my father was.' Here is the original father–son relationship repeating itself, by means of an obvious identification, in the next generation. But the sense of power over the child is itself an ego-booster. The child whose self-confidence has been undermined seeks to restore it by the exercise of power over himself, a dangerous antilibidinal situation that effectively puts an end to all normal development, especially of the power to love. Enjoying a feeling of power in self-hate easily alternates with feeling a sense of power over others by hating them. The cultivation of a fictitious sense of strength in the hating, Antilibidinal Ego, i.e. an embittered personality, has to substitute for genuine ego-strength.

Thus, in and through his Antilibidinal Ego the patient enjoys a feeling of object-relationship and the security of being under control, the sense of the possession of an ego, and the sense of power, even though it is all in a fundamentally self-destructive way. He is not likely to be able to sacrifice all this easily unless he feels very sure of getting something far better in exchange. His problem is that he must risk dropping all pretences with himself that he is more adult and tough than he really feels to be deep down, in order that he may come back to the anxious child that he once was and still feels to be inside; and begin again from there to treat this injured part of himself in a more constructive manner that promotes genuine growth instead of an artificial toughness as a mask for hidden fear.

## ANALYTICAL OUTFLANKING OF THE INTERNAL CLOSED SYSTEM

We have seen that Freud, faced with the 'negative therapeutic reaction' came to the conclusion that nothing could be done against it directly. In fact, the analysis of the antilibidinal resistance to psychotherapy in terms of the motives described in the last section, true though they no doubt are, does not by any means dissolve this resistance away. If it did, analytical psychotherapy would be a speedier process. Dissatisfaction with therapeutic results ought to act as a spur to deeper investigation. My impression is that unless we can go deeper still at this point, continued analysis of the internal bad-objects world in terms of its contents only, perpetuates anxiety and confirms the patient in its maintenance. He can become bogged down in an 'interminable analysis' of what is actually a 'security system' in spite of its psychopathological effects. If we cannot break up the closed system by a direct attack, perhaps we can outflank it by discovering what it is a defence against. If laying bare its motivations piece-meal, motivations of both object-relations and ego-maintenance, does not break it up, then we must take it as a whole and seek to discover what lies behind its existence as a total structure. Why do human beings maintain an internal object-relations world at all, especially when it is necessarily predominantly an internal bad-objects world. What greater danger is being avoided in electing to face the dangers of the internal bad-object world, which in the extreme go as far as schizophrenic terror of disintegration and depressive paralysis.

The answer to this question would provide a still deeper analysis of the basic ego-weakness that is the tap-root of all later problems. So far we have only considered the *repression* of the weak though still active Libidinal Ego in the interests of the Central Ego of outer-world life. There is another range of phenomena of a quite different kind consisting of *withdrawal*. What is repressed is thrust down into unconsciousness because it is felt to be a danger to our conscious life and activity in the social world. But withdrawal is a retreat from dangers which in the first place come from the outer world. The schizoid retreat from the outer to the inner world has of recent years attracted increasing attention. Fairbairn in 1941 regarded it as due to the fear that the outer world will arouse needs of destructive intensity, so that the fear of destroying love-objects precipitates a breaking off of object-relationships (1952). Winnicott stresses impingement (1954) or pressure of an intolerable kind by external reality on the tender infantile psyche, causing it to shrink back into itself out of reach of harm. In both cases fear is the motivating force behind withdrawal of an essential part of the whole self from object-relations in real life.

Both repression of, and withdrawal by, the infantile Libidinal Ego prevent further normal development of the basic natural self. But schizoid withdrawal into an inner world seems ultimately a more important cause of ego-weakness than repression, especially when we consider how far it may go. It is a more radical process than repression, which I suggest is a secondary phenomenon arising when attempts to counteract withdrawal lead to the generation of dangerous anti-social impulses. These arise out of the maintenance of an internal world of bad-object relations which suggests that the function of this world as a whole is to prevent a too drastic schizoid withdrawal from the condition of an active ego in object-relationships. It halts the retreat from reality half-way and saves the ego from total breaking off of object-relations. The destructive love-needs which Fairbairn describes call for both repression of antisocial impulse (oral sadism) and the withdrawal of the oral-sadistic Libidinal Ego from the outer world to operate only in an internal fantasy world. The fear-dictated retreat from impingement of which Winnicott speaks involves escape even from *internal* bad objects, withdrawal of a more radical kind such as constitutes regression. Much clinical material seems to me to demonstrate that we are here dealing with two different levels of inner reality. Only when we reach and deal with the patient's deepest withdrawnness, are we getting at the real root of his troubles. Here all the difficult problems of regression will be encountered, the most difficult problems of all for psychotherapy. Regression has never yet been fully conceptualized and fitted into its place in the general scheme.

Some degree of 'withdrawnness' from full contact with outer reality can be found in the background of all psychopathological phenomena and it is the result of fear. Thus a patient in the forties recovered sufficiently under psychoanalytic treatment to be able not only to resume work, but to pass some accountancy examinations he had never before been able to study for effectively. At that stage he said: 'I find I don't take much notice of the weather. I'm too busy inside watching myself and I don't take a lot of notice of what goes on outside me. Mother said I used to "swoon" and I'm afraid of fainting. Its like losing myself, it feels like going down inside myself and losing consciousness. At times I've been afraid to go to sleep. As a boy I was afraid to lie down in bed in case I got smothered, and could only sleep propped up on pillows. I remember when small thinking "I wonder who I am? Why am I here?" I suspected I didn't belong to the family and would feel thousands of miles away.' Here are the marks of an early schizoid withdrawal into himself, carrying with it the threat of depersonalization of the conscious self. He then dreamed 'I suddenly found I still had the little dog I possessed as a boy. I'd had it shut up in a box and forgotten all these years and thought "Why is it in there? Its time I let it out." To my surprise it wasn't angry at being shut in but pleased now to be let out.' The dog represented a specifically withdrawn 'ego of childhood' recognizable as structurally distinct. Only now could he feel that it might come out again. This appears to be what Winnicott means by a 'true self' put in cold storage and awaiting a chance of rebirth.

The difference between repression and withdrawal was brought home to me forcibly by a patient who worked through an hysteric phase to reveal a basic schizoid condition. In the hysteric phase she dreamed of being undermined in her adult life by a hungry baby whom she kept under her apron hidden, and who needed feeding though she could not attend to it. Here is her needy, demanding, internally active oral Libidinal Ego, and energy has to be drawn off from her outer world life to keep it repressed. Gradually she worked through the hysteric phase and lost her physical symptoms, only to find herself frighteningly detached and out of touch with everything, living in a mechanical way and markedly schizoid. Her hysteria had proved to be what Fairbairn calls a psychoneurotic defence against a primary psychic danger. She would begin every session with the quiet remark, 'You're miles away, you've gone away from me', thus projecting on to me her own withdrawnness. She then reported a lump in her tummy. She was sure it was in her womb and was terrified that if she told the doctor he would 'take it away' and that would be the end of her; she would be only an empty shell. She thought of it as a baby but never as an active hungry baby, only as a dead baby, or buried alive, lying still, never moving, growing bigger perhaps but it could never come out. She would say 'I can't come out. I'll only be rejected.' She had been an unwanted baby, parked out on her mother's sister who did not want to be burdened with her. Faced with her frightening withdrawnness, she had reverted again to the defence of an hysteric conversion symptom, but now the bodily substitute represented not a hungry oral ego but a withdrawn frightened ego regressed into the womb of the Unconscious. In this part of the personality one finds that the important thing is not sex or aggression but simply fear. Thus an elderly spinster lost by death a valued friend, and felt empty, lifeless, and would wake at night with 'airy fairy feelings, like a little nothing floating in the void'. This depersonalization by loss of a good object she began to counteract by taking refuge in bad-object relations, in the form of quarrelling with neighbours. Then insomnia developed as a defence against losing herself in sleep and she lay awake 'thinking'. She said 'It doesn't matter what I think about so long as I keep thinking about something or somebody', a struggle to keep her adult ego in being. One is reminded of Descartes dictum 'Cogito, ergo sum' ['I think, therefore I am']. She became exhausted and could hardly drag herself out of bed in the morning. I suggested to her that she was afraid of facing the world without her friend, and felt an intense need to withdraw and bury herself in bed for safety, and yet she was fighting against that. She replied 'I've got a peculiar thought. When you said that, I associated myself with an egg-cell in a womb. Yesterday I listened to a wireless talk on that and it fascinated me. The man said the fertilized egg finds a soft place in the lining of the uterus and hides away there and grows. I got a mental picture of it and its come back now.' Then after a pause she became tense and said 'Oh! a terror of adults has suddenly welled up in me. I feel overwhelmed by the feeling of grown-up people who are so masterful and overbearing. Its awful, they grip the life out of me. (That was an accurate picture of both her parents.) I couldn't tell this fear to neighbours or friends, only you would understand.' The bereavement had laid bare her withdrawn Libidinal Ego of an infancy in a hard home. It was no longer either sexual or aggressive, but afraid and longing to remain shut in. Its exposure rearoused her old intense fear of the adult world, and she was only reassured by feeling safe with me.

The deepest root of psychopathological phenomena, then, is not a sexual instinct or an aggressive instinct. These instinctive impulses belong to the struggle to stay in object-relationships, and are mobilized in an attempt to counteract a too drastic retreat from reality. They flourish most of all in the inner world of dreams and fantasies, where internal object-relations are maintained to serve a double purpose. They satisfy the need to remain withdrawn from the outer world, while they halt the headlong retreat inside, short of complete regression to a womb-like state. For regressive trends always tend to fantasies of a return to the womb, intensified needs for bed and sleep, inability to get up in the morning, longings to escape from responsibility and activity, to retire and to feel exhausted, rather than to feel impulse-tension except in the form of flight to some 'safe inside' position.

The more specific is the regressed ego in the personality, the more deep dreamless sleep seems to be equated with re-entry into the safety of the womb, or, from the Central Ego point of view, profound regression, and the dream world is a defence against it. It is intensely desired by one part of the personality and intensely feared by another. The dream world is half-way between the womb and the outer world. Dreams allow of the simultaneous withdrawal from outer reality and maintenance of an active ego. Daydreams show the withdrawnness from external reality. Nightdreams show as resistance to passive dependence in deep sleep.

Insomnia, or refusal to quit the Central Ego level, is an even more drastic attempted defence against regression. All this is part of the struggle to maintain an active ego in face of a powerful, fear-driven urge to withdraw, the struggle to counter-act the 'shut in' self. When this state of being 'locked up inside' is converted into physical symptoms, we are then confronted with constipation, retention of urine, sexual impotence, sinus blocking, the tight band round the head, and the patient's secondary fears of not being able to escape from this self-imprisonment, a claustro-phobic reaction, lead to the use of 'opening medicine', nasal inhalers and sprays, and the development of diarrhoea and frequency of micturition. The real trouble is that the patient cannot respond to the outer world with any true feeling except fear. One male patient who gave all the signs of being a hearty extravert, a successful, energetic business man, complained of being 'stopped up' physically and reported all the above symptoms. In fact he was a bad relaxer, and hard-driven activity betrayed a characteristic drive to maintain perpetual motion. He had to 'keep going'. At his second session he reported a simple vivid dream which had startled him. 'I walked out of my business and left my home, wife and family. I just went away, I don't know where', a revelation of the regression and withdrawnness against which he was putting up such a fight. In the deepest withdrawn Regressed Libidinal Ego we do not find active sexual and aggressive impulses, but fear and the desperate need to be quiet, still, warm, safe, and protected while recovery takes place. If we are to speak of instincts, then the deepest cause of psychopathological phenomena is not sex or aggression but fear and the instinctive reaction of flight from the outer world of real bad objects in infancy. Everything else is defence and the struggle to counteract and over-compensate the retreat of the withdrawn Regressed Ego.

It will be seen that I have come to draw a sharp distinction between the Oral active Libidinal Ego and the passive Regressed Libidinal Ego. In fact, to carry the analysis of ego-weakness to the deepest level, I believe we must recognize one further step in the process of ego-splitting as analysed by Fairbairn, namely a split in the Libidinal Ego itself. His scheme of endopsychic structure conceptualizes the first stage of the schizoid withdrawal from the outer world by the differentiation between the Central Ego of outer reality and the repressed partial egos operating in the world of internal object relations. The splitting of the ego in the inner world into a Libidinal Ego and an Antilibidinal Ego conceptualizes the struggle carried on by the child to master and subdue his weakness by turning his aggression against his own libidinal needs. This forms the 'closed system' of mostly bad internal object-relationships, the sado-masochistic inner world of psychoneurosis and psychosis, in which we find our patients so fast imprisoned. I believe that a further split must be admitted. The persecuted Libidinal Ego finds itself in no better case in this world of internal bad objects than it was originally in outer reality, and it repeats the same manoeuvre again. It leaves part of itself as it were to carry on the struggle with bad objects in this world of dream and symptom-formation, while in part it withdraws still deeper into the unconscious, breaking off all object-relations except the most elementary one of a return to the womb and a revival of identification. This represents the deepest split of all, of the Libidinal Ego into an active, masochistic, oral (anal and immature genital) Libidinal Ego and a passive Regressed Libidinal Ego. The masochistic Libidinal Ego is the ego of psychosis and psychoneurosis, the Regressed Libidinal Ego is the ego of profound schizoid, fear-driven retreat from life with its threats of depersonalization.

We may now see why the 'closed system' of internal bad-object relations and of antilibidinal self-persecution is such a 'static internal situation' and so hard to change. In its entirety it represents a desperate attempt to fend off regression and depersonalization in any degree. Its method for the most part is to use fantasies and at times 'acted-out' bad-object relationships to keep the distinct and separate identity of the ego in being. Bad relationships are often better than good relationships in the short run for that purpose, since good relationships are so often felt to be smothering, especially when there is present a still deeper flight back into the womb. *Psychotherapy and the internal bad-object world represent rival policies for the saving of the ego.* The antilibidinal policy is to maintain unchanged the internal closed system of self-persecution of the traumatized child within, in an attempt to force an adult ego in consciousness. Psychotherapy by the psychoanalytical method is really an invitation into an open system in touch with outer reality, an opportunity to grow out of deep-down fears in a good-object relationship with the therapist. But this will only succeed in a radical way if the therapist can reach the profoundly withdrawn Regressed Ego, relieve its fears and start it on the road to regrowth and rebirth and the discovery and development of all its latent potentialities. This is what Winnicott speaks of as 'therapeutic regression' (1955). Whether the recognition of this makes psychotherapy any easier is quite another matter. Here lies our greatest need for research, but at least it is better to know what we have to deal with, and to deal with the primary factor in illness rather than treat secondary and defensive factors as the causes.

## REFERENCES

Fairbairn, W. R. D. (1952). *Psycho-analytical Studies of the Personality*. London: Tavistock Publications.
———— (1958). On the nature and aims of psycho-analytical treatment. *International Journal of Psycho-Analysis* 39:374.
Freud, A. (1936). *The Ego and the Mechanisms of Defence*. London: Hogarth.
Freud, S. (1908). 'Civilized' sexual morality and modern nervousness. In *Collected Papers*, 2. London: Hogarth Press (rep. 1950).

_____ (1913). Further recommendations in the technique of psychoanalysis. In *Collected Papers*, 2. London: Hogarth Press (rep. 1950).

_____ (1923). *The Ego and the Id*. London: Hogarth. 1949.

_____ (1933). *New Introductory Lectures*. London: Hogarth. 1946.

_____ (1937). Analysis, terminable and interminable. In *Collected Papers*, 5. London: Hogarth Press (rep. 1950).

Winnicott, D. W. (1954). Mind and its relation to the psyche-soma. *British Journal of Medical Psychology* 27:201.

_____ (1955). Metapsychological and clinical aspects of regression within the psychoanalytical set-up. *International Journal of Psycho-Analysis* 36:16.

# 6

# THE APPALLING RISK OF THE LOSS OF DEFINITE SELFHOOD AND THE STRUGGLE TO RETAIN A "FAMILIAR SELF"

## REGRESSIVE PHENOMENA

A number of years ago I had a patient, a professional man in the forties, who in his own view presented only one symptom. He was embarrassingly preoccupied with breasts and felt compelled to look at every woman he passed. He regarded his shy and introverted make-up as simply natural. 'I'm not naturally a good mixer, not one of the sociable sort.' He felt that his preoccupation had something to do with the fact that his wife was an extremely cold and unresponsive woman, as also had been his mother, whom he always thought of as 'buttoned up tight to the neck'. This preoccupation with breasts appeared to be a regressive symptom and went along with a number of childish feelings which he intensely disliked admitting. As analysis proceeded his dwelling on breasts diminished markedly, but its place was taken by a spate of phantasies, all of the same type, in which his interest was intense. They went on for a number of weeks, gathering force and competing seriously with his professional work in the daytime. The general theme, embroidered by endless variations, was that he would retire to an isolated part of the country on the sea coast, and there build a strong house and wall it off from the busy inland life. No one was allowed to enter his domain and those who tried to break in by force were miraculously kept at bay. As contrasted with his professional and social life, his inner mental life constituted a house of that kind inside which he lived apart, and into which no one from the outside was ever genuinely admitted.

The series came to a head with a tremendous phantasy of building an impregnable castle on top of a breast-shaped mountain, walling it round with impassable defences, and taking up residence inside. The authorities camped round about and tried to storm his citadel but were quite unable to break in. He clearly felt some uneasiness about this 'safe inside' position, did not wish to be a totally self-made prisoner, and arranged to emerge at times in disguise to inspect the outer world, but no one could get in to contact him. Finally he saw me coming up the mountain side, hurled great boulders at me and drove me off. The phantasy shows some evidence of a wish for a position of security at the breast, in conformity with his symptom, but, like the phantasies that preceded it, the real theme is retreat to a 'safe inside' situation. In this phantasy he oscillates between a breast he can leave and return to, and a womb he can get safe inside. A week or two later he suddenly broke off analysis, using a passing illness of his wife as a reason. The phantasies and the analysis had revealed the powerful regressive drive that underlay his general character of schizoid detachment and withdrawal from real personal relationships. At that time I regarded the phantasies as all of a piece with the interest in breasts, and as a further extension of regression into the depths of infantile experience, beyond the breast into the womb where he would be 'safe inside'. I have now come to regard that as an incomplete interpretation.

I am inclined to think that interpreting his preoccupation with breasts simply as regression broke down what was in fact a defence against the final regression, and led him back into the ultimate regressive impulse to return to the safety of the womb. Breasts are the concern of the baby who has been born and is staying in and reacting to the world outside the womb. His compulsion to cling desperately to breasts and not give them up, was a constructive and forward-looking struggle to defeat his powerful longing to take flight from the post-natal world, return to the womb and be safe inside. Perhaps if, at that time, I had credited his presenting symptom with this constructive motivation, we might both have uncovered his deep regressive drive back to a protected passive state, and also supported in the analysis his struggle to preserve an active, even if on that deep level, as yet only an infantile, breast-seeking ego. Perhaps he withdrew from analysis through fear that it was betraying him into the power of his regressive flight from active living.

I did not at that time recognize the element of determined defence against schizoid withdrawal and regression which I now feel to be the essential purpose of a good many reactions which, considered from the adult point of view only, present the appearance of merely infantile phenomena. All post-natal phenomena, however infantile in themselves, as oral, anal and some genital phenomena are, belong to the sphere of active 'object-relations' of a differentiated kind, and so can serve as a defence against the impulse to withdraw into passive ante-natal security. This is a clue of far-reaching importance for the understanding of the whole range of psychopathological experiences. The facts about regression and phantasies of a return to the womb have long been familiar to analysts. Nevertheless, they have never been securely placed in the theoretical structure of psycho-analysis. Schizophrenic and depressive states were linked by Abraham to the oral-sucking and oral-biting phases of infancy, but phantasies of a return to the womb have simply been taken as part of the phantasy material of regression in general. *The withdrawn schizoid states* have been loosely linked with schizophrenia in much the same way as the 'depressive character' is related to 'depressive psychosis'. Much clinical material makes me feel that they have a more definite significance.

## EXISTING THEORETICAL CONCEPTS

The history of psychoanalysis records one major attempt to take account of ante-natal life in a psychologically meaningful way, namely Otto Rank's 'Birth Trauma' theory of neurosis. This misfired because he founded it on the assumption that a physical trauma at birth was the origin of all anxiety. He sought a psychoanalytic means of securing a quick unmasking and reliving of this birth-trauma in the fond hope that neurosis would then prove amenable to rapid cure. Treatment and cure appeared as a process of 'rebirth', implying that in some sense the neurotic personality was still 'in the womb'. Freud exposed the fallacy of this theory as a whole. In a letter to Abraham in February 1924, he wrote:

> I do not hesitate to say that I regard this work [of Rank] as highly significant, that it has given me much to think about, and that I have not yet come to a definite judgement about it. . . . We have long been familiar with womb phantasies and recognized their importance, but in ⸺ the prominence which Rank has given them they achieve a far higher significance and reveal in a flash the biological background of the Oedipus complex. To repeat it in my own language: some instinct must be associated with the birth trauma which aims at restoring the previous existence, one might call it the urge for happiness, under-standing there that the concept 'happiness' is mostly used in an erotic meaning. Rank now goes further than psychopathology, and shows how men alter the outer world in the service of this instinct, whereas neurotics save themselves this trouble by taking the short cut of phantasying a return to the womb. [Jones 1957]

Freud regarded this phantasy of a return to the womb as an erotic wish all of a piece with the Oedipal incestuous desire for the mother, and as opposed by the father's prohibition arousing guilt. In March 1924 he wrote again to Abraham:

> Let us take the most extreme case, that Ferenczi and Rank make a direct assertion that we have been wrong in pausing at the Oedipus complex. The real decision is to be found in the birth trauma, and whoever had not overcome that would come to shipwreck in the Oedipus situation. Then, instead of our actual aetiology of the neuro-

ses, we should have one conditioned by physiological accidents, since those who became neurotic would be either the children who had suffered a specially severe birth trauma or had brought to the world an organization specially sensitive to trauma. [Jones 1957]

Freud rejected Rank's views on two grounds principally, that he found the cause of neurosis in a physical accident (thus failing to give a true psychodynamic aetiology) and even then there was no evidence that a quick unmasking of a birth trauma could produce a rapid cure. Freud's criticism was decisive and yet we are no nearer to seeing the true significance of these womb phantasies and of regressive phenomena in general. After the publication in 1926 of Freud's *Inhibitions, Symptoms and Anxiety*, Jones wrote to him: 'You were wise enough to do what none of us others could do: namely to learn something from it all by allowing Rank's views to work on you in a stimulating and fruitful way' (Jones 1957). We must continue to do that ourselves for the solution of the problem has not yet been arrived at.

Freud regarded phantasies of a return to the womb as having the same basic significance as the Oedipal desire for the mother. The maternal genital, breast and womb were all to be held as alike objects of the incest wish. Wishes for them, when activated in adult life, constitute a progressive return to ever earlier stages of the positive, active, infantile sexual drive. This, I now feel, overlooks an important fact. Further, Freud regards the 'instinctive drive' active in these regressions to 'restore the previous existence' as 'the urge for (erotic) happiness'. This also, I believe, misses the real point, and in such a way as to hide the motivational difference between phantasies of a return to the womb, and breast and incest phantasies. Womb phantasies cancel post-natal object-relations, breast and incest phantasies do not. This fact makes an enormous difference to the ego, which is quite peculiarly dependent on object-relationships for its strength and its sense of its own reality.

The situation revealed by the case material with which I began shows that the patient felt quite simply that the entire external world into which he had emerged at birth was hostile and dangerous and he was afraid of it. If we are to use 'instinct' terminology, then his regressive longing to get back inside the safe place was caused, not by incestuous longing for erotic happiness with the mother, but by *fear*. It is true fear dictates a return to the mother, but for safety rather than for pleasure. He felt he had been born into a menacing outer world and fear stimulated the instinctive reaction of *flight*, escape, withdrawal back into the secure fortress from which he had emerged. From this point of view it would appear that phantasies of the breast, and of anal and incestuous genital relations with the mother of post-natal existence, are expressions of a struggle by a different part of the personality to 'stay born' and function in the world of differentiated object-relations as a separate ego. They are a defence against the danger of being drawn down into another part of the personality which has 'gone back inside' to save itself from being overwhelmed; for this 'going back inside' does very peculiar and frightening things to the ego. What seems to promise security in one sense is feared as annihilating in another. That was why my patient provided for his emergence in disguise, at least to inspect, to keep up some contact with, the outer world. Rank was close to the ultimate problem in psychodynamics but hit on the wrong solution, in repudiating which Freud, in turn, failed to hit on the right one. The point of view from which the problem could be solved, a point of view arising out of the study of schizoid phenomena, had not then emerged.

Since 1924 much work has been done on the early years of infancy. Melanie Klein has carried intensive analytical investigations back into Freud's pre-Oedipal period. She showed that 'persecutory anxiety' antedates 'depressive anxiety', and that the infant of the first few months is capable of *fear* so intense that it can amount to fear of death in the absolute sense of annihilation. It is true that Mrs Klein regarded this fear of destruction as due ultimately to fear of the internal working of the hypothetical death instinct and therefore as an almost wholly endopsychic phenomenon. However, Freud's speculative theory of a death instinct met with little acceptance among analysts, and was rendered unnecessary by the genuinely new development of Mrs Klein's 'internal objects theory'. This, and her view of the intense fear that can dominate the infant in the earliest period are indispensable for solving the problem of the profoundest regression underlying schizoid states.

Three other contributions bear vitally on our problem, those of Winnicott and Balint from the clinical, and Fairbairn from the theoretical point of view. In this section we are concerned with theory and Fairbairn's revision of psycho-analytical theory appears to me to be the necessary framework within which this problem can be understood. He transferred emphasis from instincts to the self or ego which owns them, and from impulses to the object-relationships within which they become active. He did this under pressure from his clinical work with schizoid patients, and was led beyond Depression to the Schizoid state as the basis of all psychopathological developments. A 'personal' rather than a 'psychobiological' theory eventuated. Freud's analysis of the ego is a conceptualization of depression — a theory of endopsychic structure as essentially a matter of ego and super-ego control and/or repression of raw id-impulses of an anti-social order. Guilt, ulti-mately in an unconscious form, is the dynamic of the process and the real source of resistance to psychotherapy (Freud 1923). By contrast, Fairbairn's analysis of the ego is a conceptualization of the schizoid process, and meets the demand that process makes for a theory of endopsychic structure which makes intelligible the 'ego-splitting' that schizoid withdrawal involves. Here the dynamic is not guilt but simple fear. Since schizoid withdrawal is, in the first place, from a bad frightening outer world, Fairbairn does not regard the infant's psychic life as almost wholly endopsychically determined in the way Mrs Klein did.

He regards the infant as from the start a whole, unitary, dynamic ego, however primitive, reacting to his object-world, development being determined by the kind of reception he meets. External object-relations determine the start and future course of endopsychic development in the structural sense. The pristine psyche of the infant is not an unintegrated collection of ego-nuclei, nor is it objectless and purely autoerotic. The work of Mrs Klein in fact outmoded both those elements of the original psychoanalytic theory, though she wavered on the first point. Fairbairn is explicit that the infant from the start is a whole, if primitive, dynamic ego with a unitary striving, at first dim and blind, towards the object-relationships he needs for further ego-development. It is an infantile ego of this kind, already a 'person' in essence in however elementary a way, that we must conceive of as capable of experiencing the intense 'persecutory anxiety', the sheer fear, that Mrs Klein found could characterize the very first few months of life. E. Jones wrote: 'Dr Fairbairn starts at the centre of the personality, the ego, and depicts its strivings and difficulties in its endeavour to reach an object where it may find support . . . a fresh approach in psycho-analysis' (Fairbairn 1952).

Fairbairn's theory of endopsychic structure enables us to conceptualize regression as withdrawal from a bad external world, in search of security in an inner world. His conviction that the schizoid problem is the ultimate basis of all psychopathological developments is of major importance. He points out that the problem of the schizoid individual is that his withdrawal in fear results in an inability to effect genuine relationships with personal objects; a fear which is so great, and which leads to a consequent isolation which tends to become so absolute, that in the end he risks the total loss of all objects and therewith the loss of his own ego as well. His attempt to save his ego from persecution by a flight inside to safety creates an even more serious danger of losing it in another way. This is the indispensable starting-point for the study of regression. It is illustrated with startling clarity by the dream of a University lecturer of a marked schizoid intellectual type. He reported 'I dreamed that I took off from the earth in a space ship. Floating about in empty space I at first thought it was marvellous. I thought "There's not a single person here to interfere with me". Then suddenly I panicked at the thought "Suppose I can't get back".'

The schizoid person can withdraw so thoroughly into himself that he fears losing touch altogether with his external object world. A young wife, who had become deeply schizoid in early childhood through sheer maternal neglect, was faced with the coming into the home of a loud voiced and domineering mother-in-law. She said simply: 'She scares me. I feel I am just going miles away. Its frightening. I fear I'll get so far away I can't get back. I fear I'll go insane.' She had to ring me several nights in succession to keep touch and allay fear.

It is at that point that the schizoid person begins to face the danger of the depersonalization of his ego-of-everyday-life, along with the de-realization of his environment, and he faces the appalling risk of the loss of definite self-hood. The patient first cited had good reason to provide for his emergence in disguise to contact reality outside his castle. Yet this was not 'contact' but only 'observing from a detached standpoint'. He had no real relationship because he was afraid to let the outer world get in, to contact him. Regression and schizoid withdrawal are one and the same thing. Mrs Klein was influenced by Fairbairn's work on the schizoid problem and adopted his term 'schizoid' as an addition to her own term 'paranoid' to describe the earliest developmental 'position', antedating the later 'depressive' position. The combined term 'paranoid-schizoid' position is not, however, strictly accurate. Just as the 'depressive position' is guilt-burdened, so the 'paranoid position' is fear-ridden. The 'schizoid position' is still deeper, for an infantile ego has withdrawn to safety inside away from persecution, or is resolutely seeking to do so.

'Paranoid' and 'schizoid' represent 'danger' and 'flight' respectively. Mrs Klein holds that failure to work through this total situation renders the child unable later to solve the problems of the depressive position, so that he may regress to and reactivate the earlier problems, as a defence against the pain of unresolvable depression. Mrs Klein regarded the 'depressive position' as the central one for development, the stage at which what Winnicott (1955b) calls 'ruth' or 'concern' for others arises, and the development of moral feeling in the civilized person. The earlier paranoid and schizoid or persecuted and withdrawn positions are pre-moral and allow of no concern for others. The question of defence, however, can work the other way round. The paranoid individual faces physical persecution (as in terrors of being torn to pieces) and the depressed individual faces moral persecution (as, for example, in feeling surrounded by accusing eyes and pointing fingers), so that Mrs Klein regards both positions as setting up a primary form of anxiety. In fact, most individuals prefer to face either depressive anxiety (guilt) or persecutory anxiety, or an oscillation between them, rather than face the extreme schizoid loss of every-thing, both objects and ego. Both persecutory anxiety and depressive anxiety are object-relations experiences, while the schizoid position cancels object-relations in the attempt to escape from anxiety of all kinds.

Though schizoid withdrawal and regression are fundamentally the same phenomenon, they have different meanings for different parts of the total self. From the point of view of the Central Ego, i.e. the conscious self of everyday living, withdrawal means total loss. From the point of view of the part of the self that has withdrawn, it is not 'loss' but 'regression' or retreat backwards inside the small safe place, as represented in the extreme by the phantasy of a return to the womb. We must therefore allow for three basic developmental positions, schizoid (or re-gressed), paranoid (or persecuted) and depressed (or guilt-burdened); and the paranoid and depressed positions can both be used as a defence against the schizoid position. When an individual is inwardly menaced by an involuntary schizoid flight from reality and depersonalization (as when too deep fear is too intensely aroused) he will fight to preserve his ego by taking refuge in internal bad-object phantasies of a persecutory or accusatory kind. Then, unwittingly projecting these on to outer reality he maintains touch with the world by feeling that people are either plotting his ruin or criticizing and blaming him for everything he does. Fairbairn classes the paranoid reaction with the psychoneurotic reactions as techniques for the manipulation of internal objects as a defence against the primary dangers of schizoid apathy and depressions, and places the main emphasis on the underlying 'schizoid position' as determinative of all subsequent development. We may agree that the 'depressive position' is decisive for the moral, social and civilized development of the infant, but the clinical material I present appears to me to confirm Fairbairn's view that schizoid phenomena, and the flight from object-relations, are more widespread than depression, are more frequently presented clinically, and that the schizoid position is the vital one for development and for psychopathology.

## CLINICAL DESCRIPTION OF THE SCHIZOID PERSONALITY

Womb phantasies represent the extreme schizoid reaction, the ultimate regression, and we shall begin with the more common, mild characteristics which show the extraordinary prevalence of schizoid, i.e. detached or withdrawn, states of mind. In an earlier study of schizoid states (1952) I used the term 'the In and Out Programme' to describe the dilemma in which schizoid people find themselves with respect to object-relationships. They are caught in a conflict between equally strong needs for and fears of close good personal contacts, and in practice often find themselves alternatively driven *into* a relationship by their needs and then driven *out* again by their fears. The schizoid person, because of his fears, cannot *give himself* fully or permanently to anyone or anything with feeling. His most persisting object-relationships are emotionally neutral, often simply intellectual. This plays havoc with consistency in living. He tends to be unreliable and changeable. He wants what he hasn't got, and begins to lose interest and want to get away from it when he has it. This particularly undermines friendships and love relationships but can become a general discontent with most things. 'Absence makes the heart grow fonder' is true of schizoid people unless too much fear is roused, and then it turns love to hate. The schizoid individual can often feel strong longings for another person so long as he or she is not there, but the actual presence of the other person causes an emotional withdrawal which may range from coldness, loss of interest and inability to find anything to say, to hostility and revulsion. 'Presence makes the heart grow less fond.' Many a patient complains that he carries on long conversations with the therapist 'in his head' but his mind goes blank when in session. So the schizoid person is liable to be constantly 'in and out' of any and every kind of situation.

He usually has a rich and active phantasy life, but in real life is often tepid and weak in enthusiasm, is apt to suffer from inexplicable losses of interest and feels little zest in living. Yet deep inside he has particularly intense needs. He can live in imagination but not in the world of material reality from which he is primarily withdrawn into himself. He wants to realize his dreams in real life but if he finds a dream coming true externally he seems to be unaccountably unable to accept and enjoy it, especially if it concerns a personal relationship. One spinster patient had longed for years to marry and at the age of forty was able to develop her first serious friendship with a male. He was an excellent man in general but a rather reserved bachelor and not very forthcoming as a lover. As long as she was not sure how much he cared for her, she impatiently and often angrily desired him to be more demonstrative. In fact she did draw him out and then it suddenly dawned on her that he really did want her, and she at once took fright, lost interest, and became critical and off-putting. A crisis developed in her which exploded in one session the moment she entered the consulting room. She stood in the middle of the floor and said in a tense voice: 'I can't come near you. Don't come near me. I'll have to go away, miles away, and live all alone.' I asked her what she was afraid of and she replied: 'If you get close to people, you get swallowed up, you go inside.'

Here was a striking expression of the claustrophobic reaction to close relations that the schizoid person experiences, and which had kept her lonely all her life. She had earlier speculated as to which of two male acquaintances she would like to marry if she had the chance, and said: 'Whichever one I chose, I would immediately feel it ought to be the other one.' The schizoid person dreads that a close relationship will involve loss of freedom and independence. This predicament leads to many variations of reaction. To be 'in' with one person, it may be necessary to have someone else to keep at a distance. To remain 'in' with the marriage partner, may necessitate being 'out' with the children or parents; or to be 'in' with one child may involve being 'out' with another one. Sometimes it leads to deep-seated fluctuations of moods with the same person, varying from periods of warm emotion to other periods of coldness and distance. No consistent full free warmth of affection can be achieved.

This claustrophobic reaction to any genuine close relationship is seen in the dream of a female patient that her sister was being very loving and affectionate to her and she was enjoying it; then suddenly she felt panicky and thought 'We're getting too close, its dangerous, something dreadful will happen', and she broke away. This 'in and out' policy, alternately dictated by needs and fears, has serious effects on sexual relationships in marriage so that a man may only be able to risk sexual relationships with a woman he is not 'tied' to and does not really love, while he is unconsciously inhibited by deep fears of too close a bodily relationship to the woman he does love. He splits himself into a mental self and a bodily self, and if he is 'in' with the mind he must be 'out' with the body and vice versa. He cannot commit the whole of himself to one person.

Schizoid persons are extremely liable to fear good and loving relationships more than bad and hostile ones, the reason why they face such exceptional difficulties in personal relationships. As soon as they feel they are getting close to someone they experience an automatic and sometimes catastrophically uncontrollable withdrawal of all positive feeling accompanied by great fear. This more commonly appears in the milder form of unaccountable loss of interest. Thus two male patients revealed a history of broken engagements. The engagements were made on the crest of a wave of strong emotion and almost immediately a state of panic and alarm supervened to make them rush to break it off. Their reaction was: 'I feel trapped, doomed.'

This fundamental schizoid fear, which is expressed by patients with monotonous regularity by the use of the words: dread of being smothered, stifled, suffocated, possessed, tied, imprisoned, swallowed up, dominated, absorbed, if a close relationship is risked, is often experienced in vaguer general forms. Thus the safeguarding of independence, even to being unable to accept any suggestion or tolerate any advice, becomes quite an obsession. It begets a fear of committing oneself to anyone or anything in any way. People will change clothes, houses, jobs, interests, as well as chopping and changing in friendships and marriage. *Indecision* is a typical result. Sudden enthusiasms are followed by loss of interest. One patient reported what is in fact quite a common symptom. He said 'I can't really settle myself to read a book. I think "I'd like to read that" and I start it and just when I begin to enjoy it I lose interest and think "Oh! I don't want to go on with this. I'd rather read that other book." I've got six books all on the go together just now, and can't give myself properly to any one of them to finish it.' The bibliophilic Don Juan is likely to collect and possess books without reading them. This schizoid fear of full self-committal accounts for much inability to concentrate attention in study.

This 'in and out' policy makes life extremely difficult, so we find that a marked schizoid tendency is to effect a compromise in a half-way house position, neither in nor out. The famous Schopenhauer parable, adopted by Freud, of the porcupines, illustrates the position accurately even if its account of the motivation is too limited. A number of porcupines huddled together because they were cold, but found that they pricked each other with their quills and so drew apart again. They went on in this 'in and out' fashion till ultimately they established a mean distance where they were not quite so cold but also did not prick each other. One patient says: 'I live on the edge of life all the time, in a state of muted feelings, neither very miserable nor really happy. I don't enter into anything enough to enjoy it.' Another patient says: 'I'm a chronic non-joiner. I go to the meetings or lectures of some society and quite like them up to a point, but as soon as someone asks me to join

I never go again.' A third patient, of extensive philosophical interests, says: 'I'm an adept at the art of brinkmanship. In group discussion I don't put forward a view of my own. I wait to hear what someone else will say and then I remark "Yes, I rather think something like that" but I'm thinking "I don't really agree with him". I won't belong to a recognized school of thought yet I have a dread of going out into the wilderness and standing alone on some definite views of my own. I hover half way. It has stopped me doing any creative work.'

Thus, the schizoid person's needs plus fears of good relationships drive him to ring the changes on being in and out with the same person or thing, being in with one and out with another, or compromising in a half-way position, neither in nor out. Unless skilled help is available to enable the person to grow out of his fears of good relationships, the compromise position is often the best remedy for it is more practically workable than disruptive oscillations. During the course of treatment the patient may have to fall back on this compromise, as it were for a breathing space, from time to time while the anxieties of close relationships are being faced. Yet in this compromise position people live far below their real potentialities and life seems dull and unsatisfying. If we could pursue this problem into a mass study of human beings in their everyday existence, we would probably be shocked at the enormous number of people who cannot live life to the full, and not through any lack of means or opportunity, but through lack of emotional capacity to give themselves to anything fully. Here is a cause of boredoms, discontents, dissatisfactions, which are often disguised as economic and social but which no economic or political means can cure. The person with schizoid tendencies so usually feels that he is 'missing the bus' and life is passing him by, and it eases his mind superficially if he can find a scapegoat. One patient who lived an unnecessarily restricted life, partly because his withdrawnness involved him in travel phobias, phantasied that he was living at a small wayside country station on the moors, on the side of a main railway line, and all the mainline traffic rushed through and past but never stopped there.

It is far more common to find people exhibiting mild traits of introversion, and poor affective contact with their outer world, than exhibiting signs of true depression, and as Fairbairn has pointed out (1952) most people, when they say they are depressed, really mean that they are apathetic and feel life to be futile, the schizoid state. The poor mixer, the poor conversationalist, the strong silent man, people who live in a narrow world of their own and fear all new ideas and ways, the diffident and shrinking and shy folk, the mildly apathetic who are not particularly interested in anything, the person of dull mechanical routine and robot-like activity into which little feeling enters, who never ventures on anything unfamiliar, are all in various degrees withdrawn and out of the full main stream of living. One patient dreamed that he was in a small boat in a backwater off a main rushing river. It was choked with weeds and he was struggling to get his boat out into the current and could not. Such people have but little effective emotional rapport with their world. They are in the grip of fear deep down and remain drawn back out of reach of being hurt.

On the other hand, this fundamental detachment is often masked and hidden under a façade of compulsive sociability, incessant talking, and hectic activity. One gets the feeling that such people are acting a somewhat exhausting part. Patients will say 'I feel vaguely that I'm play-acting and that my life isn't real'. The jester or comedian or the person who is 'the life and soul of the party' in public is often 'depressed' in private. Schizoid shallowness of feeling in the part of the personality that deals with the outer world in everyday life is the cause of inability to find much real satisfaction in living. The emotional core of the personality is withdrawn from the self that lives in the external world. The outer self, like a skilled actor, can act even an emotional part mechanically while thinking of other things. A middle-aged woman patient discovered in the course of analysis that she did not need the spectacles she was wearing and discarded them. She said: 'I realize I've only worn them because I felt safer behind that screen. I could look through it at the world.' A somewhat common schizoid symptom is the feeling of a plateglass wall between the patient and the world. Another patient says: 'I feel I'm safe inside my body looking out at the world through my eyes.' One is reminded of the Greek idea of the body as the prisonhouse of the soul, one of many marks of a schizoid mentality in the Greek intellectualist view of life. Winnicott's account of the split between the psyche and the soma throws much light on this. The healthy personality does not feel to be in two parts, one hiding from the world within the other, but whole and all of a piece and active as a unity.

Both the part of the personality which is deeply withdrawn and out of touch, and the part of the personality left to maintain some shallow and precarious contact with the outer world, depleted of emotional vitality, are withdrawn, but the former more profoundly so. The deeply withdrawn part of the whole self is profoundly 'schizoid', extensively 'cut off'. The ego of everyday life is not so fully cut off. It maintains a mechanical rather than an emotional contact, and tends to feel affectively devitalized, emptied even to the risk of depersonalization. Dreams in which the patient is only an observer of the activities of others are fairly common. An unmarried woman in the thirties dreamed that she stood at a little distance and watched a man and woman kiss, became terrified, and ran away and hid. In her first position she was considerably withdrawn but not entirely out of touch. In her second position she was completely cut off. In fact, patients maintain both positions at the same time in different parts of their total self, and the process of withdrawal in successive stages through fear emerges as a major cause of what we have come to call 'ego-splitting', the loss of unity of the self.

This state of affairs creates two problems. The part of the self that struggles to keep touch with life feels intense fear of the deeper and more secret, withdrawn self, which appears to be endowed with a great capacity to attract and draw down more and more of the rest of the personality into itself. Hence extensive defences are operated against it. If those defences fail, the ego of everyday consciousness experiences a progressively terrifying loss of interest, energy, zest, verging towards exhaustion, apathy, derealization of the environment and depersonalization of the conscious ego. It becomes like an empty shell out of which the living individual has departed to some safer retreat. If that goes too far, the Central Ego, the ordinary outer world self, becomes incapable of carrying on its normal life, and the whole personality succumbs to a full scale 'regressive breakdown'.

Fortunately, there are several ways in which life in the outer world can be kept going in spite of a considerable measure of withdrawal of the vital feeling-self. Ways of living can be devised which do not depend on immediate vitality of 'feeling for' the object-world. Three such ways are common. The schizoid intellectual lives on the basis of 'thinking', the obsessional moralist on the basis of 'duty' and the 'organization-man' on the basis of carrying on automatically in a fixed routine. If the emotionally withdrawn person can by such means ward off a great deal of the impact of real life, and prevent its pressures from playing on the secret inner fear-ridden feeling-life, then a relatively stabilized schizoid character may result; a human being who functions as an efficient robot within a restricted and safe conception of how life is to be lived. Life is the pursuit of truth, not love; the thinking out of an ideology, and ideas become more important than people. It tends to the Greek rather than the Christian view of life, and the scientific rather than the religious view. In religion it exalts theology above love of one's neighbour. In politics, it exalts a party creed above humane feeling, so that people have to be 'done good to' and forced to accept the right kind of social order for their own interest even if you have to kill many of them in cold blood to make the rest accept this nostrum.

This outlook can easily slip over into the unswerving performance of 'duty' in a rigidly conceived way, doing the 'right thing' according to one's own fixed conception without regard to human realities, or concern for the feelings of others; much as Graham Greene's 'Quiet American' created havoc everywhere by the way he 'acted on principle'. Or again life may be reduced to simply carrying on the usual routine, doing the obvious thing, in a mechanical manner, seeking not even to think, in a cold neutral state of mind that freezes everyone around but is safe for the person concerned. All degrees of this kind of stabilization of the schizoid personality occur, from mild tendency to fixed type.

The schizoid intellectual is a particularly important type, for he can become a serious social menace especially if he comes to political power. Highly abstract philosophy seems unwittingly designed to prove Descartes' dictum, 'Cogito, ergo sum', 'I think, therefore I am', the perfect formula for the schizoid intellectual's struggle to possess an ego. A natural human being would be more likely to start from 'I feel, therefore I am'. Even the schizoid person can become rapidly convinced of his own reality for the time being by feeling angry, whereas his thinking is usually a not very convincing struggle to hold on to a somewhat desiccated personal reality. This happens when a person cannot go to sleep but lies awake 'thinking'. Thus a patient suffering from a very traumatic bereavement felt 'emptied' and would ward off attacks of depersonalization in the night by lying awake for hours just thinking. She said it did not seem to matter what she thought about so long as she continued to think. When an elaborate ideology is fanatically defended it is usually a substitute for a true self.

Behind all these methods by which the schizoid person struggles to save himself from too far-reaching a withdrawal from outer reality with its consequences of loss of the ego, lies the hidden danger of a secret part of the personality which is devoted to a fixed attitude of retreat from life in the outer world. It is the part of the total self that most needs help and healing. Its two most extreme expressions are regressive breakdown and phantasies of a return to the womb. In face of this internal threat, the business of maintaining an ego is fraught with unceasing anxiety. The schizoid problem is an 'Ego' problem. Like the British Army at Dunkirk, the too hard-pressed child retreats to save himself from annihilating defeat, so that back in a protected security he may recover strength; an analogy which suggests that the schizoid withdrawal, if we understand it aright, is a healthy phenomenon in the circumstances which initiate it. By retreating back 'inside the safe place', the British Army gained the chance to recover and lived to fight another day. Winnicott holds that under stress the infant withdraws his real self from the fray to await a better chance of rebirth later on (1955a). Yet this retreat to save a 'hidden ego' also goes a long way to undermine the 'manifest ego'. This is the problem presented for solution by schizoid data.

## CAUSES AND STAGES OF SCHIZOID WITHDRAWAL

### Fear and Flight from External Reality

The most pathological schizoid withdrawal takes place astonishingly early, in the first year of life. It can, of course, occur at any time of life as a generalized reaction, but the more it is found to be structurally embedded in the personality the earlier it originally occurred. It can then, certainly, be intensified and consolidated all through later childhood and evoked by pressures in real life at any time, but there is little doubt that in the beginning it is associated with what Melanie Klein called 'persecutory anxiety' and 'the infantile anxiety situations'. It is a 'fear and flight' reaction in the face of danger. The view of the later Freud and of Mrs Klein that the *ultimate* source of the danger is wholly internal, a 'Death Instinct', innate active aggression working inwardly, threatening destruction against the primary psyche, has found no general acceptance. It would be unscientific to fall back on such a speculative idea when satisfactory clinical analysis is available. The view of the earlier Freud that psychopathological development began, not with innate aggression but with the libidinal drives of the sexual instinct aiming at erotic pleasure and proving to be incompatible with social reality, at least implied that the source of the trouble was more in the environment than in the infant. The world into which the infant was born could not tolerate his nature and his needs and he came up against painful frustrations. However, this view does not cover all the facts.

Fairbairn takes a wider view of libidinal need as not limited to the sexual but embracing all that is involved in the need for personal relationships, on however simple and primitive a level at the beginning: the goal of libidinal need is not pleasure but the object (at first the breast and the mother). The frustration of libidinal need for good object-relations both arouses aggression and intensifies libidinal needs till the infant fears his love-needs as destructive towards his objects. In the later 'depressive position' which Winnicott calls the stage of 'ruth' or 'concern for the object' this would lead to guilt. But at this earliest stage it leads to the schizoid withdrawal, a simple fear reaction, away from the danger of devouring and therefore losing the love-object. Schizoid persons have given up the outward expression of needs, while also being haunted by the fear of losing love-objects. One patient says: 'I can't make moderate demands so I don't make any at all', and another insists 'I lose everyone I love'. Yet the schizoid fear is not so much on behalf of the object as on behalf of the ego and the consequences to it of losing the object. Here lies the difference between the moral and the pre-moral level of development. The schizoid personality is basically on a pre-moral level; hence the horrifying callousness schizoid people can manifest. It is not in accordance with Fairbairn's psychodynamic outlook to treat these libidinal needs as discrete entities demanding satisfaction in and for themselves. They are the needs of an ego. Since the need for an object arises from the fact that without object-relations no strong ego-development is possible, we must conclude that the satisfaction of libidinal needs is not an end in itself but is an experience of good-object relationships in which the infant discovers himself as a person, and his ego-development proceeds firmly and self-confidently. Fairbairn's view brings out the question of ego-growth in weakness or in strength as the background of all problems arising out of fears, conflicts and withdrawals over frustrated needs.

Deprivation of needs is, however, not the only cause of schizoid withdrawal, and Winnicott emphasizes what seems to be an even more primitive situation. Not only must the mother meet the infant's needs when he feels them, but she must not force herself on him in ways and at times that he does not want. That constitutes 'impingement' on the as yet weak, immature and sensitive ego of the infant. He cannot stand this and shrinks away into himself. There are many other sources of 'impingement' in loveless, authoritarian and quarrelsome families and often sheer fear is aroused in the tiny child. Fairbairn has also recently stressed in private conversation that trouble arises not only over the child's needs for the parents, but also over the parents' pressures on the child who is often exploited in the interests of the parents' needs, not the baby's. The startle-reaction to sudden loud noise is perhaps the simplest case of fear at impingement, and such impingement experiences, particularly at the hands of parents, begin the building up of basic impressions that the whole outer world is not supporting but hostile.

Judging by the reflexion of these early events in the psychopathology of adults, this factor of impingement and pressure of a hostile environment, bearing to an intolerable degree on the tender infant mind, is the true source of 'persecutory anxiety', of fear of annihilation, and of flight back inside, of withdrawal of the emotionally traumatized infant Libidinal Ego into itself out of reach of the dangerous outer world. What an adult may do consciously, as in the case of a wife who felt that her husband was inconsiderate and said 'I built a wall round myself so that I should not be hurt', the infant does instinctively. He takes flight inwards from the outer world. Fear of deprived and therefore dangerous active oral-sadistic libidinal needs belongs to a higher level, that of the struggle to remain in object-relationships. It precipitates withdrawal in two ways, however, through fear of devouring and losing the object, and through fear of retaliation and of being devoured by the object. This latter fear may develop into guilt and the fear of punishment. Withdrawal from direct frightening impingement by the object in the first place is more primitive. Deep fear-enforced withdrawal from object-relations is then to a regressed passive level of a womb-like state inside. Severe schizoid states disclose a total fear of the entire outer world, and deprivation and impingement combine. The world is a frightening emptiness when it does not respond and meet the infant's needs, and a frightening persecutor when it actively and hurtfully impinges. The infant cannot develop a secure and strong ego-sense either in a vacuum or under intolerable pressure and he seeks to return to a vaguely remembered earlier safe place, even though in fact he can only withdraw into isolation within himself.

With one patient, a doctor, suffering from apparent 'depression' which was really apathy, indifference, and loss of zest for work, the analytical uncovering of a clear-cut castration fear, led to an outbreak of apathy, loss of interest and energy so serious that for a time he could hardly carry on his daily work. It was a herculean effort to get himself out of bed and one day he was quite unable to get up. He lay in bed all day, curled up and covered over with bed-clothes, refusing food and conversation and requiring only to be left alone in absolute peace. That night he dreamed that he went to a confinement case and found the baby sitting on the edge of the vagina wondering whether to come out or go back in, and could not decide whether to bring it out or put it back. He was experiencing the most deeply regressed part of his personality where he felt and phantasied a return to the womb, an escape from sheer fear of castration, not by father but by mother and aunt. The whole family life had been one of anxiety, a nagging mother, a drinking father, quarrelling parents, pressure on the child to be 'no trouble' from babyhood, and then as he grew older a mother and aunt who made actual and literal castration threats, sometimes as a joke, sometimes semi-seriously. 'If you're not a good boy I'll cut it off', accompanied by half gestures towards the little boy with knife or scissors which terrified him. But that well-founded castration complex, which brought back a wealth of detailed memories, was but the end-product of all the child's memories of a mother whose basic hostility to him he had always sensed. His serious schizoid-regressive illness was the result of a withdrawal into himself which must have taken place first at an extremely early age to escape intolerable impingement by his family life.

Deprivation of libidinal needs and separation anxiety play their part along with impingement in provoking withdrawal, not only by intensifying needs till they seem too dangerous to express, but also by the threat of emptying the ego. One very schizoid agoraphobic patient reacted primarily to gross neglect and rejection by her mother in the first year. Outwardly the position improved at about 1 year when a neighbour said 'Excuse me Mrs X but you only take notice of your older child, you never take any notice of the baby'. The mother's guilt then made her subject the baby to oppressive attention but the damage was done. Before the vacuum changed into a smothering environment the mother's emotional withdrawal from the child had been met by the child's emotional withdrawal from the mother. She developed so-called epileptic fits in the first year, which faded out into 'dizzy turns'. They must have represented the collapse of her conscious ego as what Winnicott would call her 'real self' took flight from a world in which she could find nothing by which she could live. In after years, when the patient's husband was called up for military service, this represented at bottom her mother's desertion of her and she broke down in acute anxiety, could not be left alone, and remained house-bound, withdrawn from life and 'safe inside'. Late in analysis, when she felt she had got back to the very beginning, she reported a dream. 'I was small and I pointed a brush at mother like a magnet to draw her to me. She came but said "I can't be bothered with you, I'm going to help Mrs So-and-So". I felt a terrible shock, like an electric shock, inside— "So you didn't want me"—as if the bottom dropped out of me, life seeped away and I felt emptied.' Did that 'shock' represent her original 'epileptic fits'? During that same night she dreamed that she 'just fell, collapsed', and in fact she did do that next day. The importance of an object-relationship for the maintenance of the ego, both in real life and in psychotherapy, is clear from the dream in which this patient fell. She dreamed that she met a woman and asked her the way; when the woman did not answer she 'just fell'. Then she was with me and

I took her hand 'to warm her up', i.e. bring her back to life. One seriously schizoid male patient who had to sit during sessions so that he could see me, at times would begin to fade away into unconsciousness, a process which was only arrested if I held his hand till he felt securely in touch again.

Impingement and rejection or deprivation of needs for object-relationships must be bracketed together as defining the traumatic situation which drives the infant into a retreat within himself in search of a return to the womb. Probably deprivation in the sense of 'tantalizing refusal' leads to *active* oral phenomena while impingement and deprivation as 'desertion' lead to shrinking away inside into a passive state.

## A Two-Stage Withdrawal from External and Internal Bad Objects

The previous section describes the origins of the first stage of what appears to be a two-stage retreat from bad-object relationships. This initial escape is from the outer material world into an inner mental one. But contact with the object-world cannot be given up, especially at this early age, without threatening to lead to loss or emptying of the ego. Thus part of the total self must be left to function on the conscious level and keep touch with the world of real external objects. If that were not done, and relationship with outer reality were wholly given up, the infant would presumably die. Thus a 'splitting' of the hitherto unitary, pristine ego occurs, into a part dealing with the outer world (Freud's 'reality-ego' and Fairbairn's 'Central Ego') and a part that has withdrawn into the inner mental world.

The withdrawn part of the total self must also, however, keep in object-relationships if it is to maintain its experience of itself as a definite ego. The 'mind', instead of being simply an active function dealing with the outer world, becomes a place to live in. As Melanie Klein has shown, the infant internalizes his objects and builds up an inner world of object-relations. Fairbairn regards the infant as internalizing his unsatisfying objects in an effort to master them in inner reality because he cannot master them in the outer world. In the result, however, they are felt to be as powerful and terrifying in inner reality as in outer, a 'fifth column' of internal persecutors or saboteurs who have infiltrated into the inner world where the infant has sought relief inside himself from pressure. A serious predicament has arisen. On the face of it no further retreat seems possible and a series of fresh manoeuvres are made. Fairbairn has described these in terms of 'object-splitting' and 'ego-splitting' processes, which build up the structure of the inner world in terms of endopsychic object-relations. The internal unsatisfying object is split into its three main aspects, libidinally exciting, libidinally rejective, and emotionally neutral or good and undisturbing. The last or Ideal Object is projected back into the real object and what has all the appearance of an external object-relationship is maintained with it by the Central Ego, the ordinary ego of everyday living. Nevertheless, this is not a properly objective relation, for the object is not fully realistically perceived but only experienced in the light of a partial image projected from inner reality. Thus, once some measure of schizoid withdrawal has been set up, such contact with the outer world as is maintained is defective and governed by the projection of partial and over-simplified images of the object: a fact constantly demonstrated by the poor judgement of others, the over- or under-estimation of either good or bad qualities, commonly displayed by people.

Then, while the real object (the actual parent) is unrealistically idealized, his or her exciting and rejective aspects remain as distinguishable and separated phantasied objects of the infant's need for relationships in the inner world. Thus, the unity of that part of the ego which has withdrawn inside away from outer reality becomes split into an ego attached to the Exciting Object and an ego attached to the Rejective Object. Just as the Exciting Object arouses libidinal needs while the Rejective Object denies them, so the attachment to the Exciting Object results in a *Libidinal Ego* characterized by ever-active and unsatisfied desires which come to be felt in angry and sadistic ways; and the attachment to the Rejective Object results in an *Antilibidinal Ego* based on an identification which reproduces the hostility of the Rejecting Object to libidinal needs. Inevitably the Libidinal Ego is hated and persecuted by the Antilibidinal Ego as well as by the Rejective Object, so that the infant has now become divided against himself. This is easy to recognize in the contempt and scorn shown by many patients of their own needs to depend for help on other people or on the analyst. It is seen also in the fear and hate of weakness that is embedded in our cultural attitudes. The internal persecution of the Libidinal Ego by the Antilibidinal Ego is vividly seen in the dream of a male patient. He was sitting in an armchair in my room wanting to relax, but at the same time he was also standing behind the chair looking down on the 'him' that was sitting in the chair, with an expression of hate and hostility and raising a dagger to kill the needy weak self.

At this stage, the part of the ego which has withdrawn from outer reality has now created for itself a complex inner world of objects both exciting and persecuting. The existence of these internal objects enables the parts of the ego which maintain relations with them to retain ego-sense. It seems evident that the real need which dictates the creation of Melanie Klein's world of internal objects, good and bad, and the processes of ego-splitting described by Fairbairn, is not simply the urge to master the object but the vital need of the psyche to retain an ego-sense. This can only be done by maintaining object-relations at least in the inner mental world, after withdrawing in that part of one's personal life from the outer material one. So long as a continuing phantasy life can be kept going by the Libidinal and Antilibidinal Egos, the ego is kept in being though cut off from outer reality. At one time the Libidinal Ego is sadistically phantasying the incorporation of its Exciting

Object in inner reality, at another the Antilibidinal Ego has possessed itself of the sadism and along with the Rejective Object phantasies crushing or slave-driving the masochistically suffering Libidinal Ego. (According to Fairbairn, internal objects are psychic structures just as much as partial egos are. The total psychic self 'impersonates' objects to itself in the inner world so as to retain ego-sense in phantasied relations.) Though this kind of inner life results in states of acute 'persecutory anxiety', the ego is still in being; it has not succumbed to depersonalization after breaking off emotional rapport with objects in real life. This is indeed the rationale of the creation and maintenance of the Kleinian Internal Objects world: it is a defence against ego-loss, which shows why it is so hard for the patient to give it up.

Yet the position of the withdrawn ego is little bettered, for its enemies have infiltrated into its safe retreat where they are even harder to get away from than before. Freud realized that when, in the early days of psychoanalysis, the sources of internal dangers were thought to be 'instinct-derivatives'. He stressed that the ego cannot escape from what is actually a part of internal reality. This, however, turns out not to be entirely true; or at least it is indubitably true that the ego makes one further attempt to escape from the intolerable internal pressures put upon it by its post-natal world of bad objects. It is the Libidinal Ego which is the part of the originally whole and now split ego in which the persecutory pressure is felt; and clinical facts have suggested to me that it repeats, in face of the *internal* bad-object world, the same manoeuvre that was made by the whole ego when it sought to withdraw from the *external* bad-object world. It leaves parts of itself to carry on such relations as are possible, in sado-masochistic terms, with the Exciting and Rejecting Objects of the internal phantasy world, while the traumatized, sensitive and exhausted heart of it withdraws deeper still. The evidence provided by regressive behaviour, regressive symptoms and regressive dreams and phantasies, shows that this most deeply withdrawn ego feels and phantasies a return to the womb, safe inside the 'fortress' from which it probably still has some dim memory of having emerged. Only thus can the clinical facts be conceptualized, facts of the distinct and separate functioning of an active oral infantile Libidinal Ego tied to a terrifying world of internal bad-object relations, and of a passive regressed Libidinal Ego concerned only with an imperative need to escape and be 'safe inside' and giving up all definite object-relations in favour of an enclosing protective environment. It is the irresistible pull of this Regressed Ego under certain circumstances that precipitates the schizoid breakdown in the most extreme cases, but its powerful pull manifested in the teeth of stubborn resistance and defence accounts for all the tensions and illnesses that arise out of this desperate struggle to possess and to retain an ego.

I first made this suggestion of a final split in the Libidinal Ego itself, in an article on 'Ego Weakness and the Hard Core of the Problem of Psychotherapy'

(1960) and traced out some of its consequences in the closing section of a book 'Personality Structure and Human Interaction' (1961). Here I have sought to give fuller clinical evidence for this view. In addition to the two levels of ego-splitting which Fairbairn describes, namely, first that between the Central Ego in touch with the outer world and a withdrawn ego in the inner world, and second the further splitting of this withdrawn ego into the Libidinal Ego and the Antilibidinal Ego, there is a third and ultimate split in the Libidinal Ego itself. It divides into an active sado-masochistic Oral ego which continues to maintain internal bad-object relations, and a passive Regressed Ego which seeks to return to the antenatal state of absolute passive dependent security; here in quietude, repose and immobility it may find the opportunity to recuperate and grow to a rebirth, as Winnicott holds (1955a.) I suggest that this Regressed Ego is identical with what Winnicott calls the 'true self' put into cold storage to await the chance of rebirth in better conditions. I do not, however, feel sure whether the Regressed Ego feels itself to be 'frozen in cold storage' (frozen in fear probably) or whether it feels hidden in the deepest unconscious in the warmth of an hallucinated intra-uterine condition. Some patients appear to feel one way and others the other.

The dream of a University Lecturer which shows how little his academic life had touched his deeper mentality, illustrates this two-stage retreat: 'I was on a tropical South Seas island and thought I was all alone. Then I found it was full of white people who were very hostile to me and surged at me. I found a little hut on the shore and rushed into it and barred the door and windows and got into bed.' He has retreated from civilization to his lonely island (his internal world) only to find that his bad objects, white people, are still with him. So he makes a second retreat which is a complete regression. In defence against this he had twice succumbed to a manic psychosis followed by a depressed, apathetic state. The fact that this manoeuvre involves a splitting of the withdrawn Libidinal Ego into two is seen in another dream in which the patient was in the consulting room of the analyst. There were two little boys in the room whom he wanted to send out, but the analyst was looking after them and wished them to remain. They sat together on chairs; one was unnaturally alert and watchful, keeping in touch with every-thing that went on, while the other had a dull expressionless face and took no notice of anything at all, but was completely withdrawn. Here are the active Oral Ego and the passive Regressed Ego, along with the Central Ego, i.e. the patient in his familiar everyday self, sitting apart in an armchair. But his Antilibidinal Ego was in concealed partnership with the Central Ego and hostile to the children.

## Regression to a Symbolic Womb

Since this Regressed Ego is the basis of the most dangerous and undermining psychopathological developments, it is as well to reflect on the fact that it is in itself a necessary, reasonable and healthy reaction to danger. Something is wrong primarily not with the infant but with the environment. The problems arise from the fact, not that what the frightened and regressed infant seeks is psychopathological in itself, but that it is something that, however realistically needed, it ought not to be driven to want, and in any case is exceedingly difficult to obtain in any substitute form once the actual womb has been left. The primitive wholeness of the ego is now lost in a fourfold split, a depleted Central Ego coping with the outer world; a demanding Libidinal Ego inside persecuted by an angry Antilibidinal Ego (the Kleinian internal world); and finally a Regressed Ego which knows and accepts the fact that it is overwhelmed by fear and in a state of exhaustion, and that it will never be in any fit state to live unless it can, so to speak, escape into a mental convalescence where it can lie quiet, protected, and be given a chance to recuperate.

I have heard Fairbairn's scheme of endopsychic structure criticized as too complicated (though we do not criticize physics on such grounds). The criticism is not valid. Of Freud's scheme Colby (1955) writes:

> There are . . . theoretical disadvantages to the id-ego-superego model. Today its simplicity makes it insufficient to conceptualize specifically enough the manifold functions of psychic activity. . . . In psychoanalysis our knowledge has increased in such a way that to subsume the complexities of psychic activity under three undivided categories is to stretch generalizations perhaps too far.

The complexity describes the terrible disintegration that can be forced on the tender and weak infantile ego if it is subjected to pressures it is too immature to bear. Freud (1938) wrote in his last book: 'The weak and immature ego of the first phase of childhood is permanently damaged by the strain put upon it in the effort to ward off the dangers that are peculiar to that period of life.' He further states: 'The view which postulates that in all psychoses there is a *split in the ego* could not demand so much notice, if it were not for the fact that it turns out to apply also to other conditions more like the neuroses and, finally, to the neuroses themselves.' Fairbairn's scheme reduces to order the tangled mass of self-contradictory reactions presented to us as clinical material, and reveals this permanent damage to the immature ego in the form of the 'ego-splitting' of which Freud speaks. The additional structural complexity that I have added is called for by clinical data that we have long failed to include properly in any structural scheme. It conceptualizes the ultimate desperate bid made by the overtaxed infant to save himself, a move which perpetuates thereafter what we may call a 'structural headquarters of fear' in the personality as a basis for the danger of regressive breakdown in later life.

The *Regressed Ego* denotes, not a freely available generalized 'fear and flight' reaction but the deepest structurally specific part of the complex personality, existing in a settled attitude of fear, weakness, withdrawal and absolute dependence not in the active post-natal infantile sense but in a passive ante-natal sense. It represents the most profoundly traumatized part of the personality and is the hidden cause of all regressive phenomena from conscious escapist phantasies to complete schizoid apathy, unless its need is understood and met; but there lies the greatest difficulty and challenge to therapy. In a letter to the writer dated 1 January 1960, Fairbairn accepted this extension of his structural theory. He wrote: 'I consider your concept of the splitting of the Libidinal Ego into two parts – an oral needy Libidinal Ego and a Regressed Libidinal Ego – as an original contribution of considerable explanatory value. It solves a problem which I had not hitherto succeeded in solving.' Winnicott wrote on 31 October, 1960: 'Your split in the Libidinal Ego seems to have a lot in common with my "hidden true self" and the "false self built upon a compliance basis" (a defence in illness, and in health simply the polite self that does not wear its heart on its sleeve). I do think that research can usefully be based on these ideas that are in the air and which you are developing in your own way.' It is a pleasure to quote these two writers to whose pioneering work in theory and therapy I owe most for stimulus. I would, however, think that Winnicott's 'false compliant self in health' corresponds to the Central Ego of Fairbairn and his 'False compliant self as a defence in illness' corresponds to Fairbairn's Antilibidinal Ego, especially in its function of hating weakness. This to me especially seems to warrant the term 'false self'.

How can the need of the exhausted Regressed Ego for recuperation in and rebirth from a reproduction of the womb-state be met at all, and how can it be met without the risk of undermining the Central Ego of everyday living? That seems to be the ultimate problem for psychotherapy. There is evidence that in some cases it can be done, though we have almost everything to learn about this process. At least it is safe to say that it cannot be done without the aid of a psychotherapist, i.e. the setting up of a therapeutic object-relationship. This is the significance of Winnicott's work on 'therapeutic regression'. The unsatisfactory results of psychotherapy hitherto must be the result of this problem not having been recognized earlier. When the individual is left to himself, he can only do what he was driven to do as a child, struggle to repress his regressive trends by developing a hard and hostile attitude to any 'weakness' in himself, i.e. develop an Antilibidinal Ego which is really the child's determined effort to keep himself going by being independent (Guntrip 1960). If his Regressed Ego becomes irresistible he can only provide for it by a regressive illness. Perhaps, if he did not give in to that in time and compel his environment to take responsibility for him, he would die of psychic self-exhaustion. The psychotherapist must help the patient to find a way of substituting a controlled and constructive regression for an uncontrolled and involuntary one in the form of an illness that might be an irretrievable disaster for the patient's real-life status. But

I believe that this also cannot be done, not only without the aid of a psychotherapist, but of a psychoanalytical psychotherapist; for the main obstacle to the patient's accepting a constructive regression in treatment is his own Antilibidinal Ego which needs the closest analytical uncovering. The final aim of this therapy is to convert regression into rebirth and regrowth. This must result from the Regressed Ego finding for the first time an object-relationship of understanding acceptance and safeguarding of its rights, with a therapist who does not seek to force on the patient his pre-conceived views of what must be done; but who realizes that deep down the patient knows his own business best, if we can understand his language. But before the problem of therapy can be solved we must understand how the patient's struggles to save himself form a resistance to the true therapy.


## THE FIGHT AGAINST REGRESSION


### The Determined Drive Backwards

We have stated that, left to himself, the individual can only either provide for his Regressed Ego in the extreme case by illness, owing to the practical difficulties of providing for it in any other way, or else seek to suppress it as an internal danger threatening to undermine his adjustment to real life in the outer world. The vague influence of a regressed part of the total self is easy to recognize in many people as an attitude of getting through life with as little trouble as possible, getting out of things if they can, and having to push themselves to do what they must. Generally a sustained if automatic effort is made over the years to stave off regression in any more definite sense, though many people have a history of periodic breakdowns say every four or five years, with minor signs of nervous strain and tension in between. In many cases, however, very vigorous defences of an antilibidinal nature (antilibidinal towards others) are built into the personality and direct very energetic if over-tense drives into real life.

The individual from the beginning has had to cope with the problem himself. No one has really known or understood what was going on in the child, and so far as his deeper life was concerned he had to bring himself up and manage himself in secret. Hence the self-centredness and introversion of schizoid persons. Life becomes a long, hidden, tension-filled struggle against regressive trends. Tremendous tension can be masked by a calm exterior, but is often not masked, breaking out physically if not in other ways. Melanie Klein and Fairbairn treat the psychoneurotic states as defences against the psychotic dangers of schizoid apathy and depression. If, however, the deepest danger is regression to passivity, we must regard all states, psychotic as well as neurotic, in which an 'active' ego struggles and suffers, as defences.

The ultimate characteristic of the Regressed Ego is dependent passivity, the vegetative passivity of the intra-uterine state which fostered original growth and can foster recuperation. Nature heals in a state of rest. That is the goal. Nevertheless, the Regressed Ego shows great energy and activity in pursuit of its goal, an activity in reverse that carries it not into life but out of it. There is a great deal of research to be done on various aspects of regression for, clinically, the picture presented is confusing. One comes across states which suggest that there is a Regressed Ego which feels to be already 'in the womb' and oblivious to all else, or if not in a warm safe hiding place then completely withdrawn, immobilized in fear, and having never emerged since the first drastic schizoid retreat in infancy. Some patients, after long analysis, can find themselves suddenly totally 'cut off' and living in the deepest, most hidden schizoid part of their total self which they have at last contacted and must live in and with till they regain emotional rapport with the outer world at that deep level. Again, a Regressed Ego, which in itself seems quite dissociated, exerts a powerful pull on the rest of the personality, drawing it down while it resists frantically. Yet again, at times the whole self seems to have become a Regressing Ego showing great energy in a drive backwards towards the goal not as yet reached; and sometimes the Regressed Ego is phantasied as in the womb and resisting every effort to force it to a premature rebirth.

Thus a male patient in the thirties dreamed that he was working, doing business correspondence at a table, when he suddenly felt an invisible and irresistible pull emanating from a pale passive invalid in the bedroom. Only after a tremendous struggle was he able to break the spell and save himself from being drawn in there. Here the Regressed Ego is 'pulling' the Central Ego down into itself and success would mean breakdown into illness such as this patient had already experienced once. But the other aspect of the situation was revealed in a dream of the same patient during his earlier illness. He dreamed that he was driving a peculiar car, which was closed in with no proper outlook on his side. In the passenger seat was another man with a definite personality who could see out more clearly. The dreamer who was 'driving blind' felt that they ought to have been somewhere else taking part in some activity that involved duties and responsibilities but he was gleeful that they were not and he was driving away taking the other man with him. Here the Regressing Ego is sweeping the Central Ego away out of the pressures of active life in a determined but blind drive into oblivion and passivity, i.e. breakdown. Just as the first dream represents a successful later effort to resist another breakdown into illness, the second one represents the original breakdown in full career.

Once the Regressed Ego feels to have reached its goal of retreat deep inside the hidden, womb-like state of the deepest unconscious, the Central Ego seems to have little success in drawing it out again. Thus an unmarried woman in middle life dreamed that she was watching a child-birth, but the baby could not be got out. Its head emerged but then it stuck fast, and even ropes tied on to it and passed through the window and fastened to horses who were driven to pull failed to drag it out. This patient was telling herself that she could not force her Regressed Ego to a rebirth. In this state some patients manage to carry on routine living in a de-emotionalized, cold, mechanical way. This patient felt exhausted with the fight to keep her Central Ego functioning. Some patients exhibit more the determined drive backwards into regression or the pull of their Regressed Ego on the rest of their personality, others give the impression that a part of their personality has for long been inaccessible and hidden away quite out of touch with outer life. I am inclined to feel that in every case there is a deepest part of the original ego split off and hidden in a state of regression, corresponding to what Winnicott calls the 'true self' hidden away in safe storage to await a favourable chance of rebirth. The more active phenomena of the 'pull and drive' to regression may represent the conflicts set up in the psyche over the effects on the whole, of the existence of a profound Regressed Ego originating in very early life. This creates, from the point of view of external living, a struggle between longings for, fears of, and resistances against breakdown. The 'struggle to preserve an ego' has two aspects: the struggle to preserve the Central Ego of everyday life from being undermined by regression, and the struggle to preserve the basic Libidinal Ego, the core of the personality, from being crushed by overpowering outer reality or lost irretrievably when it withdraws deep within out of reach of being hurt.

This latter aspect of the problem emerges in tragic self-contradictoriness in the problem of schizoid suicide. The longing to die represents the schizoid need to withdraw the ego from a world that is too much for it to cope with. Whereas depressive suicide is the result of an angry destructive impulse, schizoid suicide is the result of apathy towards real life which cannot be accepted any longer. All available energy goes into a quiet but tenacious determination to fade out into oblivion, by means of gas, hypnotic pills or drowning. One patient expressed the longing to die at a time of great stress and I suggested that what she wanted was not destruction, non-existence, but escape into warmth, comfort and being almost but not quite unconscious. She said 'That's it; just conscious enough to be aware of being warm and safe', like having gas at the dentist's to escape pain, which appeared to her 'like a very pleasant way of dying'. Unfortunately, in practice, more is achieved than is intended and the patient may die.

## The Need to Save the Ego by Internal Object-Relations

Once the fear-dictated retreat from outer reality has been set up, the schizoid individual has two opposed needs both of which must be met unless death is to supervene; the need to withdraw from intolerable reality and the need to remain in touch with it, to save the ego in both cases. This is what enforces the final ego-split into an active suffering and a passive regressed Libidinal Ego. The flight into regression begets a counter-flight back into object-relations again. But this return to objects must still compromise with fear and the need to remain withdrawn, and this leads to the creation of an object-world that enables the ego to be both withdrawn, yet not 'in the womb', the Kleinian world of 'internal objects,' dream and phantasy, a world of object-relationships which is also withdrawn 'inside' out of the external world. This par excellence is the world of psychoneurotic and psychotic experience. Sometimes the flight back from deep regression to objects in the sense of 'internal objects' appears to go further and become a return to the external world itself. But close inspection shows this to be illusory. It is not a return to the actual reality of external objects as such in their own right, but a projection on to them of the internal world of phantasy objects, which accounts for the unrealistic reactions of psychotic and psychoneurotic patients to real people. Living in the internal phantasy world and the projected phantasy world both constitute a defence against loss of the ego by too complete regression and depersonalization, while remaining in varying degrees withdrawn from external reality which is still felt to be hostile.

This type of defence, however, has its own dangers. Over and above the ultimate danger of ego-loss by schizoid depersonalization, there are three further dangers of ego-loss that arise in this mid-region of defensive activities. The flight back to objects is at first a return to the bad objects from whom escape was originally sought. Bad object-relations at first safeguard the separate identity of the ego by setting it in clear opposition to its object, a defence much used. The frightened person becomes quarrelsome, but this may go too far and get out of control, mounting up to persecutory anxiety in the inner world and the schizophrenic fear of being torn to pieces. There appear to be two ways of escape from this schizophrenic terror of disintegration of the ego under persecution by internal bad objects or under the pressures of real life experienced in the internal persecutory set-up. The flight to good objects gives rise to another perilous situation for the ego. The basic attitude to good objects is already fixed as a panic-stricken flight inside for safety. Even short of that, the relation to a good object is so much one of fear-enforced infantile dependence that it feels smothering, as already noted. Thus *claustrophobic* anxiety arises, to be distinguished from the schizoid fear of ego-loss by depersonalization, the typical state to which the Central Ego in touch with the outer world is reduced when all vitality has been drained out of it by too complete regression. This could lead to death and total ego-loss. The claustrophobic fear of being stifled by being shut in is the price to be paid for seeking safety through flight back inside. The active ego is in danger of being lost by reduction to a state of passivity in which no self-expression is now possible.

Thus *no objects* involve the fear of ego-loss by depersonalization, *bad objects* involve the fear of ego-loss by disintegration under destructive persecution, *good objects* involve the fear of the loss of the active ego by imprisonment in smothering passivity. One further possibility remains, a compromise between bad and good objects. If one hates good objects instead of bad ones, there will not be the same danger of retaliation by the object and also smothering is avoided. But now a fourth danger appears. If one hates a good object the ego feels fear, not primarily for itself but for the object. Guilt will arise and with it Mrs Klein's 'depressive anxiety' in place of the more primitive 'persecutory anxiety'. *Ambivalent object-relations* involve fear of loss of the ego for all practical purposes through the paralysis of depression, in which state the ego dare not do anything at all for fear of doing wrong. The good object becomes an accusatory object and the ego feels morally persecuted. We may thus grade the dangers to which the ego feels exposed. The ultimate and worst danger is that of total ego-loss, represented in consciousness by depersonalization, and by such profound apathy through schizoid withdrawal and regression that death would ensue. Against this danger the defence of resort to bad object-relations tends to over-develop, and leads either to schizophrenic terror of disintegration under violent persecution, or depressive paralysis under merciless accusation and pathological guilt. Nevertheless these two psychotic dangers arise out of the operation of the defence of bad object-relations against the ultimate schizoid danger.

With the claustrophobic anxiety of being shut in and stifled in good object-relations we ascend to the level of what Melanie Klein and Fairbairn agree to regard as the defence of psychoneurosis against psychosis. Thus the claustrophobic fear of being stifled is the least virulent danger to which the ego is exposed. Its overcoming, so that good object-relations can be accepted without fear, even when in order to secure the rebirth of the deepest Regressed Ego they must involve a measure of passive dependence at first, is the obvious line of advance to the psychotherapeutic goal. This complex situation in its entirety is illustrated in the early sessions of a patient who, prior to analysis, had suffered a paranoid-schizophrenic illness. During the opening sessions she oscillated violently between hopes and fears concerning myself. 'You'll let me down, you'll walk out on me, you don't feel any real concern about me, you'll tell me my attitudes are all wrong'; or else, in defence against her fears, 'I hate you, I feel furious with you, I could murder you', and then at other times 'When I come here I'm numb, I can't feel anything'. It was a sign of progress when, after two months, she could say: 'The other night I felt you did care about me and I was near to tears.' This was soon followed by 'I feel I hate you and myself when I think I creep and crawl to you and depend on you'. Here are the serious difficulties of an utterly insecure ego rushing from one kind of relationship (in the transference situation) to another more in the hope of escaping dangers than of finding security. The inner situation is brought out plainly in her dreams at this time.

*Dream 1.* 'People were pushing into my room and I was trying to keep them out. Then I rushed out into a church, flung myself at the feet of the Mother Superior and asked to enter a convent.' Here is a powerful regressive flight from bad objects (especially a persecuting father) into the maternal womb and the practical danger of an undermining flight from life. To counteract this she turns the good mother, who in being a refuge might swallow up her personality, into a bad object with whom, by antagonism, she can maintain her separateness. Thus in *Dream 2*: 'I was with mother in the bedroom and got furious. She said "You can go to bed". I said "I can do that any time". Then she was on a bike coming at me. I pulled her on the ground and said "There, enjoy your masochistic pleasures".' But this hate of her good object frightened her, for in *Dream 3* she excluded herself altogether from the good protective situation. 'There was a party at my Minister's house. I wanted to go but was not invited. I rushed in hoping not to be noticed but his wife saw me and said "You've not been invited. You can't stay." I was in despair.' But rather than have no objects at all, and having run into difficulties with both good and bad ones, she turned in *Dreams 4 and 5* to ambivalent morally persecutory situations. 'I was bending over waiting to be caned', and more explicitly 'Mother and father were smiling and arranging for me to be beaten. I felt "Oh! well, it's belonging to home anyway".' She mentioned that in a previous treatment with a psychiatrist she had attacked him to make him control her forcibly, 'like Daddy did'. This patient would say at various times: 'Whichever way I turn, I feel there's no way out.'

## THE PSYCHOTHERAPY OF THE REGRESSED EGO

This article deals with diagnosis, not treatment, and only a brief word can be said about psychotherapy. Usually, it is a very long time before the patient can consistently accept and bring to the analyst the regressed, passively dependent ego. The analysis of antilibidinal reactions against not so much active as passive libidinal needs, constitutes, I believe, the most important part of 'analysing'. I have seen real improvements appear and be retained when what Winnicott calls 'therapeutic regression' at last comes to be understood and accepted. I sought to explore the difficulties of arriving at that constructive stage in my paper *Ego-Weakness and the Hard Core of the Problem of Psychotherapy* (1960). This approach to therapeutic analysis shows that the cause of trouble is not to be found in the vicissitudes of separate instinctive drives which operate in antisocial ways, but in the basic weakness of the infantile ego perpetuated in a fear-ridden state. Infantile fear, regressive flight from reality and resulting ego-weakness in the face of the real outer world are at the bottom of all personality disorders. Our natural impulse-life is not normally antisocial but becomes such through the forced self-assertion and even violence of an antilibidinal attempt to over-compensate weakness. Our greatest need is to understand more about the earliest stages of strong ego-development and of the ways in which it can be prevented, or promoted.

The hope and possibility of the rebirth of the regressed ego is the obvious final problem raised in the interests of psychotherapy. I cannot see that we know very much about it as yet. Winnicott has opened a pathway that many research workers will tread before the problem is mastered. I hope to be able to report clinical data on this matter. At this stage I feel only able to say that I have found encouraging results with several patients who each in his or her own different way, have been able to find security for their Regressed Ego in the psychotherapeutic relationship. There appear to be two aspects of the problem. The first is the slow growth out of their antilibidinal (Freudian sadistic super-ego) persecution of themselves; they need to unlearn their ruthless driving of themselves by ceaseless inner mental pressure to keep going as 'forced pseudo-adults' and to acquire the courage to adopt more of the understanding attitude of the therapist to the hardpressed and frightened child within. Simultaneously with this there goes on a second process, the growth of a constructive faith that if the needs of the Regressed Ego are met, first in the relation to the therapist who protects it in its need for an initial passive dependence, this will mean not collapse and loss of active powers for good and all, but a steady recuperation from deep strain, diminishing of deep fears, revitalization of the personality, and rebirth of an active ego that is spontaneous and does not have to be forced and driven; what Balint calls 'the new beginning'.

## REFERENCES

Colby, K. M. (1955). *Energy and Structure in Psychoanalysis*. New York: Ronald Press.

Fairbairn, W. R. D. (1952). *Psychoanalytic Studies of the Personality*. London: Tavistock Publications.

Freud, S. (1923). *The Ego and the Id*. London: Hogarth Press (rep. 1949).

_____ (1926). *Inhibitions, Symptoms and Anxiety. Standard Edition* 20. London: Hogarth Press (rep. 1959).

_____ (1938). *An Outline of Psycho-Analysis*. London: Hogarth Press (rep. 1949).

Guntrip, H. (1952). A study of Fairbairn's theory of schizoid reactions. *British Journal of Medical Psychology* 25:86.

_____ (1960). Ego-weakness and the hard core of the problem of psychotherapy. *British Journal of Medical Psychology* 33:163.

_____ (1961). *Personality Structure and Human Interaction*. London: Hogarth Press.

Jones, E. (1957). *Sigmund Freud: Life and Work*, vol. 3. London: Hogarth Press.

Winnicott, D. W. (1954). Mind and its relation to the psyche-soma. *British Journal of Medical Psychology* 27:201.

_____ (1955a). Metapsychological and clinical aspects of regression within the psychoanalytical set-up. *International Journal of Psycho-Analysis* 36:16.

_____ (1955b). The depressive position in normal emotional development. *British Journal of Medical Psychology* 28:89.

# 7

# DEVITALISATION AND THE MANIC DEFENCE

## THE REORIENTATION OF PSYCHODYNAMIC THEORY

The increasing emphasis of recent years on the schizoid problem represents the emergence of a distinct point of view in psychodynamic studies; a point of view, moreover, which diverges markedly from the traditional centuries-old approach to human problems. Like all other phenomena, psychopathological phenomena disclose hitherto unrecognized aspects when looked at from a different viewpoint. Psycho-analysis began when Freud, after a prolonged struggle, changed his line of approach to psychoneurosis from the neuropathology in which he was trained to the psychopathology in which he was to prove the greatest of all pioneer investigators. For a long time, the priority was hardly the evolving of a theory but rather the 'seeing of what was there to be seen' and theorized about. So long as advance at first depended mainly on the accumulation of data, Freud could adopt and use the traditional theory of human problems as a sufficient basis or framework for his thinking: i.e. the theory of conflicts arising from the need to control bad impulses rooted in 'the flesh'. He could get on with the pressing task of observation and description of psychopathological phenomena, not so much from the outside like Kraepelin and Bleuler and psychiatrists in general, but from the inside as suggested by the work of Charcot on hypnotic experiences and the unconscious. From 1880 to somewhere between 1910 and 1920 that was his main work, and those who only read Freud's monographs on theory and not his clinical papers hardly know the real Freud.

So far as his results were conceptualized in theory in this first period, this did not affect the simple traditional framework or scheme, of natural instincts versus social controls. His great theoretical concepts evolved in this first stage were those of repression, resistance, the censor, transference, the meaning of dreams and symbolism, infantile sexuality, the 'family' or 'Oedipus complex', and so on. This work has gone on with the fuller investigation of schizoid data in the last twenty or so years, and the work of collecting data has become fairly complete.

By 1920, however, it was already apparent that the increasing range of facts pressing on Freud's notice was calling for examination from other points of view than that of the traditional theory of bad impulses rooted in the flesh and calling for drastic control. This was the view of the pre-scientific philosophical and religious psychology of Greece and Palestine, and had always been the universal common-sense view as indeed it is today. The ancient Persian Zoroastrians thought of a warfare between matter as evil and mind as good. Plato's famous picture of human nature as a chariot with two horses and a charioteer is described by Sir R. Livingstone (1935) thus:

> He describes human nature by a simile. On the outside men look like human beings, but under their skin three creatures are concealed: a monster with many heads, some wild, some tame, . . . the desires and passions: a lion—the spirited quality which will fight . . . ; and a human being—the rational element. . . . Plato urges us to make the man supreme and see that, helped by the lion, he controls the many-headed beast. [pp. 140–141]

St Paul's doctrine of unceasing warfare between the flesh and the spirit, the law of the members and the law of the mind, and the traditional trichotomy of body, mind, and spirit represent the same diagnosis of the human predicament. As a first hypothetical basis for his investigations Freud had adopted this 'theory' and given it a scientific dress. The 'many-headed beast of the desires and passions' and the 'law of the members' became the instincts of sex and aggression functioning anti-socially according to a 'pleasure principle' and leading to a Hobbesian world in which life would be 'nasty, brutish and short' (cp. *The Future of an Illusion*). The 'lion' becomes aggression taken up by the sadistic superego and turned against the id instinct-derivatives. The 'law of the mind' and the 'charioteer of reason' (on whom Freud, like Plato, pinned all his hopes, as he makes clear in the last chapter of *New Introductory Lectures*), becomes the ego seeking to operate by a 'reality principle'.

This basic way of looking at things Freud never changed, and indeed the kind of change called for is only slowly becoming apparent. But the terms id, ego, and superego in which he came to embody it stand also for something that was to prove of far greater importance than this traditional scheme. They represent the fact that Freud made a second reorientation in his thinking, from the psychobiological to the endo-psychic-structural point of view. Hartmann (1960) has stressed the tremendous importance of Freud's importation into psychodynamic science of the structural viewpoint. He has recently written: 'It was above all Freud's introduction of the structural point of view that made the psycho-analytic approach . . . more subtle and more conclusive' (p. 245, and elsewhere). In fact it gave ego-analysis priority over instincts in psycho-analytic thinking. Ego-splitting, a concept which Freud presents quite explicitly as fundamental in the last section of his unfinished, posthumous *Outline of Psycho-Analysis*, begins to take the place of impulse-control as the centre of interest. It is possible now to see that this actually implies a shift of emphasis from a *psychology of depression* to a *psychology of the schizoid process*. All psychopathological phenomena look different when viewed from the schizoid rather than the depressive point of view.

## THE 'DEPRESSIVE' AND THE 'SCHIZOID' STANDPOINTS

In a paper in 1961 I compared Freud's structural analysis of the personality, the id-ego-superego scheme, as a conceptualization of depression, with Fairbairn's revised theory of endopsychic structure as a conceptualization of the schizoid process. This difference in fact registers and consolidates the shift of viewpoint already referred to, and it enforces a reassessment of all phenomena. Fairbairn was the first, and is as yet the only analyst to attempt the systematic revision of theory on this basis. At the outset, after a searching study of 'Schizoid Factors in the Personality' in 1940 (Fairbairn 1952) (Ch. 1), he introduced his 'Revised Psychopathology of the Psychoses and Psychoneuroses' in 1941 with these words:

> Within recent years I have become increasingly interested in the problems presented by patients displaying schizoid tendencies. . . . The result has been the emergence of a point of view which, if it proves to be well-founded, must necessarily have far-reaching implications both for psychiatry in general and for psycho-analysis in particular. My various findings and the conclusions to which they lead involve not only a considerable revision of prevailing ideas regarding the nature and aetiology of schizoid conditions, but also a considerable revision of ideas regarding the prevalence of schizoid processes and a corresponding change in current clinical conceptions of the various psycho-neuroses and psychoses . . . a recasting and reorientation of the libido theory together with a modification of various classical psycho-analytical concepts. [Fairbairn 1952, p. 28]

It seems now, looking back over the twenty years since those words were written, a matter of considerable surprise that this prophecy has not stimulated a more explicit theoretical response, a realization that some fundamental change was in process of developing, and specific attempts to think it out in detail. What has happened is that *schizoid phenomena have been investigated while in the main a psychology of depression has been adhered to*. In truth, I believe that this change of standpoint from the depressive to the schizoid position in viewing human problems involves some quite special difficulties. It is so radical and ultimate that it encounters our deepest and most powerful resistances; and that here the patient's resistance against consciously experiencing what it is that needs to be cured, is supported by an unrealized resistance in the analyst against having to see it. I have been driven to conclude that the *age-old 'depressive diagnosis' involves man's greatest and most consistent self-deception.* We have all been in unconscious collusion, suffering individuals, religious philosophical and eductional thinkers, and now psychodynamic researchers, to keep attention diverted from the deepest and ultimate causal factors and concentrated on a middle region of defensive endopsychic activity mistakenly regarded as causal and ultimate. This, I believe, is the conclusion to which the investigation of schizoid phenomena is pushing us. It will suffice at this point to say that this tremendous resistance to the truth is based on *mankind's universal preference for feeling bad but strong, rather than feeling weak and afraid. The 'depressive' diagnosis fixes our attention on our badness, the 'schizoid' diagnosis fixes it on our weakness*; a frightening change of emphasis, and the more we explore it, the more far-reaching it appears to be.

Freud's id-ego-superego theory, we have seen, had two aspects; it was the first great step in the adoption of the structural viewpoint, but it was also an embodiment of the traditional theory, an analysis of human personality on the basis of depressive phenomena. The id was the psycho-biological source of innate and in the last analysis unsocializable instincts of sex and aggression. Culture has to be defended against nature. If the defence fails we get criminality, if it succeeds too drastically we get neurosis. As Freud (1937) stated in his essay 'Analysis, Terminable and Interminable' psychotherapy is helping the ego in its struggle against powerful antisocial instincts. The only way of avoiding either criminality or illness is to achieve maturity, not in the sense of basic socialization but in the sense of sublimation, a hypothetical process of detaching enough energy from the original instinctive aims to be redirected to valuable cultural goals. The original instinctive aims can, however, always be found still being energetically pursued under repression in the unconscious. I do not think there is any real difference in principle here between Plato, St. Paul, and Freud. For all three, human nature is the scene of an unending internal strife, and there is no real possibility of 'cure', only of 'compromise and relative stability' so long as man remains 'in the flesh'.

The classical psycho-analytical theory is that antisocial impulses, biologically determined, which certainly might be better tolerated socially than they usually are, must be controlled and in the process such intense guilt and repression are developed that the whole psyche is liable to fall into a state of illness and depressive paralysis. Unconscious guilt was for Freud (1923) the great source of resistance to psychotherapy (p. 72, note). The patient feels that he is bad and ought to accept the punishment of going on being ill. Official Christianity took the side of repression (though the Gospels, the later St Paul, and the Johannine tradition had wiser insights). Freud took the side of easing repression and showing more toleration of instincts while strengthening the ego for rational control. But both agree as to the basic nature of the problem.

This depressive pattern has always been the favoured diagnosis. It is expressed in psycho-analytical terms as the alliance of the superego and the ego to control the id, while psychotherapy seeks to moderate the harshness of the superego control and to strengthen the ego. The theory is simple, precise, understandable, and it implies the possibility of practical measures on the social level to deal with the situation. Police control, legal punishment, denunciatory public opinion, moral disapproval, religious preaching of 'sin', all conspire to discipline recalcitrant instincts. In *The Future of an Illusion* Freud (1927) wrote:

> Every individual is virtually an enemy of civilization, though civilization is supposed to be an object of universal human interest. It is remarkable that, little as men are able to exist in isolation, they should nevertheless feel as a heavy burden the sacrifices which civilization expects of them in order to make a communal life possible. Thus civilization has to be defended against the individual.
>
> One thus gets an impression that civilization is something which was imposed on a resisting majority by a minority which understood how to obtain possession of the means to power and coercion. [p. 6] It seems rather that every civilization must be built up on coercion and renunciation of instinct. . . . One has, I think, to reckon with the fact that there are present in all men destructive, and therefore anti-social and anti-cultural trends.
>
> It is just as impossible to do without control of the mass by a minority as it is to dispense with coercion in the work of civilization. For masses are lazy and unintelligent; they have no love for instinctual renunciation, and they are not to be convinced by argument of its inevitability; and the individuals composing them support one another in giving free rein to their indiscipline. [p. 7]

The only way to better this situation is

> to lessen the burden of the instinctual sacrifices imposed on men, to reconcile men to those which must necessarily remain and to provide a compensation for them' [p. 7]

The fact that psycho-analytical therapy, and every other kind of therapy, has always found this result so extremely difficult to secure with the individual is surely all of a piece with the catastrophic failures of practically all civilizations to maintain peace, security, and reasonable human happiness for more than short periods.

Nevertheless, though it seems to be proved beyond all doubt that we are very bad, since who dare gainsay such a trio as Plato, St Paul, and Freud, yet thank God we are not weak. We have *a mighty sexual instinct* and *a powerful destructive and aggressive instinct*, and if we are incapable of living together peaceably for long except as controlled subordinates (and always supposing that our powerful coercive controllers do not fall out among themselves and drag us into the fray), at least we can glorify aggression as heroism, and live like Sir Tristram and Sir Palomides and others of King Arthur's knights who idealized the role of picking quarrels with all and sundry to prove what 'mighty men of valour' they were (Malory 1470). The incompleteness of the 'depressive' diagnosis is seen the moment we realize that human beings always prefer to feel bad and strong rather than weak. *The diagnosis of 'antisocial instincts' has always been man's most convincing rationalization of his plight, a subtle defence against the alarming truth that the real trouble is fear, flight from life at deep levels, and the failure of basic strong ego-formation*, resulting in consequent inadequacy, both felt and factual, in coping with life.

The fact that human beings prefer feeling 'bad somebodies' rather than 'weak nonentities' emerges historically and socially. There is the story of the ancient Greek who burned down a temple because he could not gain recognition in any other way, and much crime and delinquency must be motivated by the quest for a sense of power and for notoriety for destructive behaviour, to cover the felt inability to achieve true value by constructive work. This comes out clearly in the following examples of clinical work.

> One patient, a married woman in the thirties who had been actually cruelly brought up and felt utterly useless and worthless, described how at her first school she felt a terrible need to be noticed by the teachers, and bent all her energies to pleasing them by good work and good behaviour. As a result she was simply taken for granted as a girl who would not cause any trouble. Being already a very schizoid personality, this made her feel depersonalized. She could not stand this, and when she changed schools she felt she must compel the teachers to take notice of her or she would feel just worth nothing at all. So she became a 'bad' girl and a ringleader in mischief. She got plenty of notice then and felt much safer and stronger that way.
>
> Another married woman, also in the thirties, had grown up to feel that she was regarded by her family as inferior. She hadn't got the good looks or lively talk of her sisters, was shy, and in fact experienced transient states of depersonalization at a very early age. She was ignored by a busy father and

was the perpetual butt of the criticisms of a very unstable mother. She would sit away in a corner when visitors came, feeling that it was hopeless for her to make any mark by good qualities. But in her late teens she suddenly developed a serious mental breakdown and her parents were alarmed. Her father became sympathetic and devoted to her, her mother said she was mad. She would say 'No, I'm not mad, I'm bad', because her most obvious symptom was a compulsion to curse God, her parents and sisters, and 'bad words and bad thoughts', aggressive, murderous and sexual (with a strong anal colouring) would be 'running in my head'. She insisted on telling her parents all these curses and bad thoughts, and quite consciously knew she was shocking them. She felt proud of herself for being so daring, though she felt she could not stop it. The reason was clear when she said: 'I felt strong, powerful, when I was cursing and swearing. If I wasn't being bad, I could only shrink away into a corner and feel I was nobody.'

A male patient, a large employer of labour, came to analysis because he was so aggressive with employees that he was always having labour troubles. He had been brought up on a regime of demand that he should not be a nuisance to his parents, and felt quite unwanted, unappreciated, and no good. If he was anything at all, he was 'just a rotter'. He began every session for a very long time by saying 'I'm cross as usual'. When gradually he arrived at some insight into this, he said: 'I know why I'm so aggressive with employees. I must get angry or I'm just scared stiff of them. When I can get angry I feel plenty of energy and I can do things; otherwise I'm nervous and always tired and feel I'm no good.'

Historically in ideology, and psychologically in the individual, the area of bad impulses, control, guilt, and depression lay right across the path of psychodynamic investigation and blocked the way backwards, as it was intended to do. Freud's great task was to analyse this area. That is the significance of his shift of interest from hysteria to obsessional neurosis, depression and 'superego' phenomena. So successful was his analysis that he opened the way to what lay deeper, and made a start with the structural analysis of the ego. Here lies the significance of Fairbairn's call 'Back to Hysteria' and his radical development of structural ego-analysis. Until the 'depressive' area was analysed, the 'schizoid' area could not properly be investigated. But it begins now to appear that only if the schizoid background is taken into account can the depressive foreground be thoroughly understood. The 'depressive' area of conflict over bad impulses comes into being when the individual exploits his active impulses in anti-social ways to counteract a deep compulsion to withdraw, break off object-relations and risk losing the ego. Moreover, it becomes clear that the deeper schizoid problem was always thrusting through the more obvious depressive one. This we must now examine.

## THE MANIC-DEPRESSIVE CONDITION AND ITS COMPLEXITY

Clinical depression needs now to be examined specifically from the point of view of the schizoid problem. Fairbairn states that in his experience true depression is more rare in the consulting room than schizoid phenomena, and that is also my experience. I do not know whether this may be due to the general decline in guilt-inducing forms of religion. We do not now have the 'Hell-fire' preaching and the violent denunciatory 'sin and repentance' sermons of an earlier age. The patients in whom I have most clearly found classic depression were all religious people who were driven to use and distort their religious beliefs as a defence in terms of guilt-inducement against a basic schizoid problem. It is perhaps more characteristic of this generation to adopt a superior attitude to morality and to reject guilt and depression in favour of the 'couldn't care less' attitude; a quite definite schizoid phenomenon in its detachment and irresponsibility towards other people.

The manic-depressive condition is, in all its varying degrees of severity, a mixed condition, and denotes a very complex state of mind in which a basic problem is countered by defences which in turn call for further defences. This becomes apparent in papers in the recent 'Symposium on "Depressive Illness"' (Klein 1960, 16–19) where the guilt factor seems to drop more and more into second place and the factor of regression comes more and more to the front. Guilt is the heart of the depressive problem proper in the classical usage in which this term came to be technically defined, whereas regression is a schizoid phenomenon (see Guntrip 1960, 1961a, 1961b). It seems that one can see the schizoid problem always pushing through the depressive mask. This would explain why patients say they are 'depressed' when they mean apathetic merely, irrespective of whether the apathy is associated with guilt feelings, conscious or unconscious.

### The Mixed Condition

In the Symposium referred to, the contribution of Nacht and Racamier presents the classic conception, while the developing change in the basic theoretical conception of this illness is most apparent in the contributions of Zetzel and Rosenfeld. But the earlier classic concept and the newly developing concepts are not yet clearly demarcated and related, so that the question 'What is the manic-depressive illness?' has a somewhat confused answer. Both Zetzel and Rosenfeld present clearly enough *the change of emphasis from guilt and repression of sadistic instincts to the problems of frustrated ego-development, resultant ego-splitting and ego-weakness, and the dangers of regression and ego loss. Yet these two quite different groups*

*of psychopathological phenomena are still confusingly held together under the term
'depression'.*

Rosenfeld (1960) states the classic diagnosis of depressive illness as 'precipitated by an object-loss' (pp. 512–13) in which 'the patients unconsciously believed
that their aggression had omnipotently produced the death or illness of the object'.
To clarify the complexity of this illness as it presents itself clinically, we must at this
stage limit the term 'depression' to this quite definite psychic state. Depression is
then, as it has been classically treated, a guilt illness, pathological mourning, the
paralysing effects of which are due to the repression of sadism and aggression. This
distinction is preserved when Scott (1960) writes: 'Our literature contains less about
the relationship of pathological mourning to more regressed states . . . than one
might expect with such a crucial metapsychological problem which stands midway
between the schizophrenias and the neuroses' (p. 497).

Thus Zetzel (1960) says: 'Abraham's original formulations with regard to
depressive illness appear to have become more rather than less compatible with the
general body of psycho-analytical knowledge over the passage of time. In particular,
the importance he attached to object-relations, aggression, and the mastery of
ambivalence have been confirmed by psycho-analysts of every school of thought.'
Of depression in this sense it is particularly true that there are 'infantile precursors'
of the illness in adult life. She points out that the work of Abraham, Jacobson,
Rado, Spitz, and particularly Klein are an 'attempt to understand adult depression
by reconstruction of its infantile prototypes'. 'The most far-reaching analogies
between adult depressive illness and early developmental phases have been proposed by Mrs Klein and the English school. A universal, infantile depressive
position has been postulated, the general characteristic of which determines
depressive responses in adult life.' In this connexion Zetzel mentions the 'primary
importance attached to early object-relations', and Rosenfeld writes: 'It is characteristic of such situations (i.e. object-loss) that all earlier experiences of object-loss
are mobilized leading back to the earliest anxieties of the infant mother relationship, a factor which might be regarded as a confirmation of the central importance
of the depressive position as outlined by Melanie Klein.' This conception links
depression particularly closely with the Oedipus stage, as Klein stresses, with its
ambivalence of love and hate and its guilt. We must return presently to this
question. This is the classic concept of depression and it makes depression clear,
specific and identifiable. It is of depression in this sense that Fairbairn said that it is
not presented clinically anything like as frequently as schizoid problems. Moreover
it becomes ever more clear that it does not by any means cover the whole clinical
picture of what has, evidently too loosely, been termed depression.

There is another group of phenomena which, as clinically presented, is
commonly to be found mixed up with depression as above defined whenever that
is present. These phenomena are not illuminated by the concepts of ambivalence,

repression, and guilt. These are the phenomena that led to increasing concentration on ego-psychology and the facts concerning ego-splitting and regression, i.e. the schizoid problem. The two sets of facts, depressive and regressive, come face to face with competing claims to priority when Rosenfeld writes: 'the psycho-analysis of ego disturbances, like the splitting of the ego, has an important contribution to make to the understanding of the depressive illness,' but then goes on to say that: 'The importance of the internal object-relations in depression has, however, still to be regarded as the most important aspect of the depressive illness.' Rosenfeld shows that, clinically, the classic view of depression does not cover all the facts presented in a very complicated illness and recognizes the different nature of the phenomena now more and more attracting attention, but he cannot say outright that the classic view of depression, if applied to the total illness, is inadequate. While it is no doubt true that ambivalent and guilt-burdened object-relations are the important element in classic depression, nevertheless depression proper in that narrowly defined sense is not the most important element in the actual total illness as we meet with it in the patient. I shall hope to show that *depression in the classic sense is set up by the failure of a certain type of defence against a powerful underlying compulsion to seek safety in a regressive withdrawal from object-relations. We have to turn our attention to ego-loss, ego-splitting, and regression.*

Rosenfeld puts alongside the classic concept of 'object-loss', as the precipitating factor in the depressive illness, the parallel concept of 'ego-loss'. He writes: 'We might ask if it is only a disturbance in an object-relation which may mobilize depression. Freud had raised the question early on whether an injury to the ego or to *narcissism* may alone precipitate depression. I found in some of the patients breaking down with acute depression that they were confronted with a situation which made them aware that they themselves or their lives had been incomplete in certain ways. The patients were overcome by an acute sense of failure. They felt they had not fulfilled the promise of their gifts or had not developed their personality sufficiently. They were suddenly overwhelmed by a conviction that it might now be too late for them to find themselves and their purpose in life. . . . This depression may be regarded as an awareness that certain parts of the patient's personality had been split off and denied. . . . These parts include not only aggressive features but are related to a capacity of the ego to bear depression, pain, and suffering.' Rosenfeld goes on to say that the problem of depression 'has to be understood not only from the point of view of object-relations but in terms of ego psychology.'

I would suggest that this fails to distinguish and properly to relate together two different levels of the complex whole of the illness, unless it is recognized that the importance of object-relations lies in the fact that without them the ego cannot maintain itself. It is not a question of object-loss and ego-loss being alternative precipitating factors, nor of the split-off and denied parts of the personality being either or both aggressive features and ego-capacity to bear pain. The situation I have found in patients is that in order to escape the terrors of ego-loss through schizoid withdrawal from object-relations (depersonalization) they have fled back into ambivalent object-relations only to find that their hate threatens them with object-loss and guilt and depression. The depression arises out of the failure of a defence against an *underlying* regression. I would rather say, therefore, that 'depression has to be understood . . . from the point of view of object relations', i.e. the need and struggle to retain object-relations, but that the deeper problem of regression which it masks has to be understood 'in terms of ego psychology'. In the long run it is only ego psychology that can supply the key to any and all psychological problems. Rosenfeld himself says: 'In such depressions there is a regression to the phase of infancy where the original splitting of the ego has taken place'. This is on a much deeper level than that of the repression of 'aggressive features' which plays so vital a part in depression proper. The repression of sadism is a relatively superficial 'splitting off or denial' of a part of the personality. I have suggested elsewhere (see Guntrip 1960, 1961a, 1961b) that the deepest ego-split is that which occurs under persecutory anxiety in what Fairbairn calls the infantile libidinal ego, a split into an *active oral ego* which remains in a sadomasochistic inner world, and a *passive regressed ego* which seeks a return to the womb for security away from all terrifying bad object relations. Winnicott agrees that this corresponds to what he calls the 'hidden true self' awaiting a chance of rebirth. I regard this as the basis of all *schizoid characteristics, the deep secret flight from life, in seeking a defence against which the rest of the personality lands itself in a variety of psychotic and psychoneurotic states*, among which one of the most important is depression. It would clear up much confusion to restrict the term depression to its narrow and classical definition and correlate depression with ambivalent and guilt-burdened object-loss, and to regard it as arising through the failure of one type of defence against the dangers of regression with ego-loss. We must then recognize two strata of the complex illness that has hitherto gone by the name of depression. Rosenfeld speaks of 'a progressive and reparative drive, namely an attempt to regain these lost parts of the self'. This will be the swing back from schizoid withdrawal to a recovery of object-relations, good, bad, or ambivalent according to the chosen strategy of the patient. Among other things, this will lead to the manic defence, which presumably can operate, if with different characteristics, against both the depressive and the schizoid regressive dangers. Against depression it will take the form of a repudiation of all moral feeling and guilt; against the dangers of regression to passivity and ego-breakdown of the type of basic withdrawal it will take the form of compulsive activity. This latter is in my experience much the commonest form of manic state, and exists more often than not in particularly secret and hidden mental forms as an inability to relax and stop thinking, and especially to sleep. The total illness is very inadequately called manic-depressive, and should at least be called manic-depressive-regressive, recognizing that the schizoid component is more dangerous and deeper than the depressive one.

We may here refer to the brief contribution to the symposium by Klein (1960) entitled 'A Note on Depression in the Schizophrenic'. She writes: 'The often-observed connection between the groups of schizophrenic and manic-depressive illnesses can in my view be explained by the developmental link existing in infancy between the paranoid-schizoid and depressive positions. The persecutory anxieties and splitting processes characteristic of the paranoid-schizoid position continue, though changed in strength and form, into the depressive position. . . . The link between these two positions—with all the changes in the ego which they imply—is that they are both the outcome of the struggle between the life and death instincts. In the earlier stage (extending over the first three or four months of life) the anxieties arising from this struggle take on a paranoid form and the still incoherent ego is driven to reinforce splitting processes. With the growing strength of the ego, the depressive position arises. During this stage paranoid anxieties and schizoid mechanisms diminish and depressive anxiety gains in strength. Here too, we can see the working of the conflict between life and death instincts. The changes which have taken place are the result of alterations in the states of fusion between the two instincts' (p. 509).

I take it that the statement 'The persecutory anxieties and splitting processes characteristic of the paranoid-schizoid position continue . . . into the depressive position' confirms my view that depression rests on a schizoid basis and that the schizoid trends can always be seen pushing through the depressive overlay. But I do not find that clinical evidence supports Klein's contention that 'paranoid anxieties and schizoid mechanisms diminish and depressive anxiety gains in strength'. I believe that to be a very deceptive appearance. Whenever I have treated depression as a struggle to keep in object-relationships, employing bad-object relations of an accusatory or morally persecutory form, as a defence against the dangers of schizoid withdrawal from all object relations, I have always found that with surprising rapidity the depressive reaction was pushed aside by a striking outbreak of markedly schizoid symptoms. These showed no sign of having been diminished by depression; rather it was clear that it was the hidden power of the schizoid flight from outer reality that was being counteracted by seeking refuge in ambivalent object-relations, only to find that these in turn led to depression.

The source of Klein's views on this matter seems to derive from the confusing use of the unscientific and unverified hypothesis, one ought perhaps to say the mythology, of life and death instincts, instead of abiding by purely factual clinical analysis. This hypothetical death instinct, of the reality of which hardly any analysts have ever been convinced, was assumed to be an innate destructive drive aimed primarily against the organism itself, and regarded by Klein as projected by the infant on to his environment. Persecutory anxiety is therefore self-manufactured and unrealistic in the last resort. So far as I can see clinical evidence establishes the exact opposite of this view. Fear, persecutory anxiety, arises in the first place as a result of an actually bad, persecutory environment. Anger and aggression arise as an attempt to master fear by removing its cause, but in the infant they only lead to the discovery of helplessness and therewith the inturning of aggression against his own weak ego. This powerfully reinforces the splitting process already set up by fear and flight from a bad outer world. This inturning of aggression does not, however, necessarily lead to fear of death, but more often to masochistic suffering in the inner world which the patient cannot easily be helped to give up. It is true that under certain circumstances this can mount up to schizophrenic terror of being torn to bits, but I have usually found that the fear of death related ultimately to an unconscious inner knowledge of the existence of an ego-undermining and powerful drive to a flight from life and reality, the dread of collapse into a depersonalized state of combined object-loss and ego-loss. If there is any meaning, then, to be found in the terms 'life and death instincts' it will refer to the conflict between active and passive trends, progressive and regressive drives, in the personality. This can mount in intensity to a veritable struggle between living and dying, but such imaginative and inexact terms are better not used.

To return to Zetzel, her position is the same as that of Rosenfeld. She observes that 'our concepts of anxiety and depression . . . have changed with the development of ego-psychology'. She quotes Bibring (1953) as saying: 'Anxiety and depression represent diametrically opposed basic ego responses. Anxiety as a reaction to danger indicates the ego's desire to survive. The ego challenged by the danger mobilizes the signal of anxiety and prepares for fight or flight. In depression the opposite takes place; the ego is paralysed because it finds itself incapable to meet the danger.' Zetzel comments: 'The key word, of course, in this more recent formulation is "ego".'

It seems to me, however, more useful to keep anxiety and depression closely associated by means of Klein's valuable formulation of two kinds of anxiety, persecutory and depressive. We can then use Bibring's reference to the fact that the endangered ego can react in either of two ways, by 'fight or flight'. If it reacts by flight, the infant ego can only fly in one way, inside itself. It is precipitated into schizoid withdrawal and ego-splitting. In fact, it usually does do this, and then as the 'outer-reality ego' (in contrast with the now withdrawn and passive ego) strengthens, it seeks to 'fight' its way back to object-relations. This it may do on two levels. Since the return of a frightened ego must be to bad-object relations, it is a decision to face danger rather than withdraw; i.e. to make use of bad-object relations to keep touch with the object world. On a more primitive level this leads to persecutory, paranoid anxieties which may mount to schizophrenic terrors. On a more developed level, it leads to guilt under moral persecution which may amount to depressive anxieties and even to the paralysis of severe depression. The opposite possibilities of flight and fight lead on the one hand to regression and on the other to psychotic conflict-states and further psychoneurotic defences, which are attempts to deal with internal bad-object relationships.

Zetzel confuses these different things when she says first that: 'Depression, like anxiety, is a subjective experience, integral to human development and mastery of conflict, frustration, disappointment and loss'; but then adds 'it is also the main presenting symptom of a regressive clinical syndrome'. The first statement applies to the results of the 'fight reaction', i.e. classic depression, while the second refers to the effects of the 'flight reaction', or regression. We are brought back to the necessity for distinguishing regression as a schizoid phenomenon, differing from and *underlying* depression as a guilt paralysis in ambivalent object-relationships. It is the difference between fear and anger, and between withdrawal and the repression of sadism. *Aggression is characteristic of the depressive setup, but fear and flight is the key to the regressive situation, against which the former is employed as a defence.*

Just as Rosenfeld contrasts depression as due to object-loss with another type of depression (really 'regression') involving ego-loss, so Zetzel regards disturbed infantile prototypical object-relations as repeated in classic depression but evidently correlates the regressive aspect of the illness with the propensity of early disturbances for causing developmental failure of the ego. In contrast with the previous group of writers mentioned, she says that Bowlby, Rank, Mahler, Rochlin, 'rather emphasize the primary importance of early experience in determining ego-development and the capacity for genuine object-relations' (pp. 477–8). From the point of view of ego-psychology we would say that biological events (such as childbirth, involution) are able to evoke 'depression-regression' because they play upon the basic ego-weakness and stimulate the fight or flight reaction, i.e. depression or regression. Zetzel says: 'It is essential to make a distinction between the total helplessness implied by Freud's definition of a traumatic situation and the relative helplessness implicit in Bibring's conception of loss of self-esteem.' This seems to be a matter of the depth to which any trauma penetrates in activating basic ego-weakness and consequent flight from life, or of the extent to which the deep down feeling of not having a proper ego breaks through into consciousness.

The fact is that in Zetzel's exposition, regression looms ever larger in the picture. 'The ego of the seriously depressed patient has undergone qualitative regressive alterations with associated intrapsychic changes of a widespread nature' (p. 479). Nevertheless she still holds fast to 'the significance of the aggressive instinct' and 'the crucial importance of unmastered aggression in the theory of depressive illness', and she quotes Bibring as saying 'The blow to self-esteem is due to the unexpected awareness of the existence of latent aggressive tendencies within the self.' This appears to be an attempt to keep the old garment while sewing on a new patch. Blows to self-esteem ultimately come from discovering that one feels weak. Zetzel, however, has to come back to 'the whole problem of the regressive implications. . . . It is here that current ego-analysis appears to differ most widely from the early formulations' (p. 480). The only way to clear up this confused oscillating is to separate classic depression as the defensive top-layer of aggression and guilt, from regression as the bottom layer of fear and flight.

The whole illness is a complex mixture of depression and schizoid factors. If the presenting picture is at first one of classic depression and guilt, it is best relieved by exposing it as a defence against a deeper schizoid withdrawal from any and all kinds of object relations. In my experience it is much more common to find the schizoid patient whose regressive trends become unconsciously active, and who then resorts intermittently to a flight forwards into guilt and depression. Classic depression is then revealed clearly as arising out of the failure of an attempted defence against ultimate regression by resort to 'fight' rather than 'flight'. Bad object relations are better than no objects at all, until they run away with the patient in his inner world, get out of hand, and produce their own insoluble problems. In passing, it may be said that unless we allow for a universal resistance to the proper recognition of our basic fear and weakness, it is hard to explain why an 'instinct of aggression' has been given such prominence in psycho-analytic theory, while the equally obvious phenomena of 'instinctive flight' have been so passed over. Classic psycho-analytic theory has always treated anxiety as secondary to the working of sexual and aggressive drives. We now have to recognize that *pathological* sexual and aggressive drives are not primary factors but are secondary to the working of elementary fear, anxiety, and flight.

## Abraham's Picture of Classical Depression

In their article on 'Depressive States' S. Nacht and P. C. Racamier (1960) say, 'We define depression as *a pathological state of conscious psychic suffering and guilt, accompanied by a marked reduction in the sense of personal values, and a diminution of mental, psycho-motor, and even organic activity, unrelated to actual deficiency.*' It may be said that the last half of the definition concerning the 'marked reduction' is just as true of plainly regressed states, though people suffering from guilt-depression usually show little diminution of mental activity so far as self-accusation is concerned. However, Nacht and Racamier's definition is based on the general theory of man that prevailed in classic psychoanalysis. They write:

> The study of depressive states leads the psycho-analyst to the centre of the fundamental drama that troubles the heart of man, for man is possessed by two apparently equal and contradictory powers, pulling him in opposite directions. Yet sometimes these forces may be inti-

mately blended and linked together, and even, occasionally, replace each other. Thus man is moved by an imperious need to love, to create and construct, and by an opposing and equally tyrannical desire to hate and destroy.

In the first two sections I have already shown reason for rejecting that view, as the psycho-analytical equivalent of the age-old doctrine of evil lusts and passions of the flesh opposed to the rational mind, and the doctrine of original sin. It appears to me that *the conflict of love and hate in human nature is secondary to the conflict of love and fear, or the need for human relationship versus the fear-ridden flight from all relationships.* This comes out clearly in Abraham's classic pioneer picture of depression in 1911, at a time long before any realistic ego-analysis had been initiated by the Freud of the 1920's; a time when the psyche could only be thought of in terms of an instinctive unconscious and a regulating ego of consciousness.

The case history Abraham (1911) describes as depressed is that of a basically schizoid personality struggling to keep a precarious contact with the object-relations world by means of hostility, hatred, and aggression in sporadic outbursts, countered by guilt. 'He had an indefinite feeling that his state of depression was a punishment' (p. 141). Certainly at that date the priority for analysis was this problem of guilt-depression. It was the success and thorough-going nature of the whole psycho-analytical exploration of the details and complexities of this area of the mental life that has led on to open up the deeper schizoid level. But we can also see that when Abraham wrote 'I do not wish to discuss states of depression occurring in dementia praecox' (p. 139) the sound policy of not seeking to analyse everything at once but taking problems one by one led in this case to a nonrecognition of the schizoid factors in the case he did describe. The patient as a child was depreciated in comparison with his older brother, while a delicate younger brother got most of the attention. He never felt satisfied at home, and got little with which to develop a soundly based ego. He grew up to hate both parents and brothers and feel jealousy to a degree that once led to a violent and injurious attack on the younger brother. That all this, bringing in its train feelings of moral unworthiness and guilt, was part of a desperate struggle to keep in effective relationship with his object world, is clear from the rest of the descriptive data.

Abraham observed that 'every neurotic state of depression . . . contains a tendency to deny life' (p. 138). This boy's denial of life took the form of a manifest schizoid withdrawal from human relationships. He 'never made any real companions, kept to himself. . . . He had no friends. He was quite aware of his lack of real energy when he compared himself with others' (p. 140). That this withdrawal from human contacts as emotionally hurtful was adequately motivated is clear. He had 'no encouragement at home. His father was contemptuous of him in his presence' (p. 140). His first attack of depression occurred in a specific way when his teacher once called him 'a physical and mental cripple' in front of the class (p. 140). The 'depression', it is to be noted, was not called out by the accusation of being 'bad' but of being 'weak'. 'Even later he made no companions. He kept away from them intentionally too, because he was afraid of being thought an inferior sort of person. . . . His life was a solitary one. He was positively afraid of women. . . . He showed little energy in practical life; it was always difficult for him to form a resolution or to come to a decision in difficult situations.' This is a picture not of a guilt-burdened but of a devitalized personality. Grief over the loss of a good object is normal. Depersonalization over the loss of a good object is schizoid. Guilt and depression (pathological mourning) arise out of an attempt to fend off depersonalization by internalization of the lost object as an accusing object, identification then leading to self-accusation.

The problem of devitalization is of crucial importance. In view of the chronic fatigue and exhaustion such patients frequently suffer, it is as important a descriptive term for this illness as depression and regression. Of the above-mentioned patient Abraham wrote: 'In every situation he suffers from feelings of inadequacy and stands helpless before the problems of life' (p. 139). 'In his depressive phase the patient's frame of mind was "depressed" or "apathetic" (I reproduce his own words) according to the severity of his condition. He was inhibited, had to force himself to do the simplest things, and spoke slowly and softly. He wished he was dead and entertained thoughts of suicide.' He would often say to himself 'I am an outcast' or 'I do not belong to the world.' 'He felt non-existent and would often imagine himself disappearing from the world without leaving a trace. During these states of mind he suffered from exhaustion' (p. 141). So far as my experience goes these are the characteristic ways in which the schizoid person describes his experience of feeling withdrawn and cut off from outer reality, and so losing 'self' also in a vacuum of experience, while his attenuated central ego trying to keep touch with the real world feels utterly deprived of all energy.

The classic theory as stated by Abraham was that this loss of energy was the result of the repression of the sexual and aggressive instincts. 'His sexual instinct, which at first had shown itself so strongly, had become paralysed through repression' (p. 140). 'He was weakened or deprived of his energy through the repression of his hatred or . . . of the originally overstrong sadistic component of his libido' (p. 139). I believe, however, that this puts the cart before the horse. *I see no reason to think that sexual and aggressive potentialities operate in disturbed and antisocial ways, except in the fear-ridden person, and then they represent the exploitation of two among other active capacities as a method of overcoming devitalization and passivity.* Abraham says: 'Depression sets in when (the neurotic) has given up his sexual aim.' It seems to me, however, that it is because regression and devitalization are already there that impotence supervenes and sexual and also aggressive outbursts reappear again as part of the manic defence.

A study of the manic defence should serve to complete the reorientation of theory concerning this illness, and the whole field of psychopathology. It is usually held that manic elation is essentially a moral revolt. The paralysing restraints of the sadistic superego are suddenly overthrown and the person feels omnipotently free to do as he likes. Such tendencies do appear, but I do not believe they are the essence of the manic defence, but secondary characteristics. Abraham wrote of his patient:

> [At 28 years] a condition of hypomania appeared and this now alter-nated with his depressive attacks. At the commencement of this manic phase he would be roused out of his apathy and would become mentally active and gradually even overactive. He used to do a great deal, knew no fatigue, woke early in the morning, and concerned himself with plans connected with his career. He became enterprising and believed himself capable of performing great things, was talkative and inclined to laugh and joke and make puns. . . . At the height of his manic phase his euphoria tended to pass over into irritability and impulsive vio-lence. . . . In the periods of depression he slept well but during the manic phase he was very restless, especially during the second half of the night. Nearly every night a sexual excitement used to overtake him with sudden violence. [p. 142]

It is clear from this that the basic characteristic of this state is not amoral violence but simply *over-activity*. The manic state is not a defence against the repression of *active* impulses, even though that at times enters into it, but a desperate attempt to force the whole psyche out of a state of devitalized *passivity* and regression. The harder the struggle to defeat the passive regressed ego, the more incapable of relaxation and rest the patient becomes. His mind must be kept going non-stop, night as well as day. Deep sleep is feared as regression and every effort is made either to prevent its occurrence by insomnia (which is therefore a manic symptom) or to keep up a constant interference with it by active dreaming, and repeated waking. When the battle becomes a losing one it may well happen that, as Abraham observed, euphoria turns into aggression and violent sexuality. The pathological forms of sexual and aggressive impulse are aspects of the struggle to defeat regression and flight from life on the part of a person who, at the deepest mental level, feels he hardly has an ego at all. But there are also other 'active capacities' which can be used for this purpose besides sex and aggression, such as thinking, overworking, the hectic social round and so on. Abraham writes: 'The affect of depression is as widely spread among all forms of neuroses and psychoses as is that of anxiety' (p. 137). That will not surprise us when we realize that the basic psychopathological problem is the struggle to keep active at all, with a basic ego that is fear-ridden and undeveloped, and a central ego that is devitalized.

## A CASE OF MANIC-DEPRESSION

The foregoing conclusions may, perhaps, best be summarized by presenting a brief account of an actual case.

A deeply religious man in the late forties, married, with one child, had been diagnosed twelve years earlier by a psychiatrist as constitutionally manic-depressive, and was told that there was nothing to be done but control the condition by means of drugs. This 'control' proved in practice to be of little use to him, and his life was a misery as he swung between periods of profound depression with sluggish inactivity and acute guilt over his uselessness, and periods of compulsive early rising and hectic overwork. He could at such times feel acute guilt over sexual fantasies and over aggressive outbursts in real life which he found hard to control, especially with his wife and child. Apart from these extremes in his general attitudes he was rigidly puritan, intolerant of many things 'on principle', a strict disciplinarian and extremely independent. He said 'I have St Augustine's "heart of steel towards myself".'

Analysis of his guilt brought out ever more clearly that it was aimed mainly against his feelings of weakness, and guilt was mixed with contempt of himself. It was weak to be 'depressed', to be inactive and unable to work, to indulge in sexual fantasies or to want sexual relationships. It was weak to be unable to control his temper and irritability, and also to need anyone's help. His 'ego-ideal' was that of the strong and rather silent man who had iron self-control, which he could relax at times for the child's amusement in nonsense talk and joking: behind this he remained a deadly serious person. With his University training and gifts of leadership he was, when at his best, a successful and valuable obsessional personality, but this was always breaking down into the manic-depressive mood swing.

It emerged that he could and did periodically use the defence of a conversion hysteria technique against his 'depression', and during one period of about eighteen months during his five years' analysis he had recurring bouts of four to five weeks of laryngitis or lumbago. Invariably as these faded out under analysis he would begin to feel consciously 'depressed' again.

These two physical conditions, however, so clearly symbolized a state of withdrawal from active life in weakness and incapacity, in which he could hardly talk or walk about and had to be off work, that they proved to be a valuable means of directing his attention away from his supposed bad impulses, sexual and aggressive, and towards the more unwelcome insight that he felt weak. His life had been one long struggle to keep going at all since he really felt and always had felt inadequate and apprehensive. He said: 'It's hell going through life having to screw yourself up all the time to face everything you have to do, even though you know you can do it.' Gradually analysis focused less and less on guilt over sex and aggression, and more and more on his fears, timidities, shrinking from life and the constant tension of forcing himself on in the teeth of these drawbacks. His manic-depressive cycle appeared to him now as an oscillation between ruthless overdriving of his secretly frightened inner self, leading on to collapse into physical and mental exhaustion. He could see clearly enough how his parents had completely undermined or prevented the development of any natural, spontaneous self-confidence in him, and how seriously beset he had been in his teens by a crippling feeling of inadequacy and inability to 'make good'.

For practical purposes his treatment began to focus more and more around his present inability to relax and rest. He was afraid to 'let go' into sleep and could not still his overactive mind. The analysis of his hidden inner manic drive in terms of his dread that if he once stopped he would never get started again, enabled him to see its real significance. It was a desperate struggle to overcome the emotionally crippled and fear-ridden child inside, and to force himself to be adult; a well-intentioned but self-defeating method of trying to become a real 'person' while a weak, infantile ego was hidden in the depths of his unconscious. My interpretation of his depressive guilt as all a part of his organized system of self-forcing, and as a defence against his secret and hidden 'frightened child' self who was in a state of constant retreat from life, led to the revelation of lifelong but hitherto undisclosed schizoid characteristics.

This occurred when, after three and a half years of treatment, he entered on a period of some five months which proved to be a fundamental 'working through' of the hard core of his self-frustrating personality make-up. Since then, with diminishing and minor ups and downs, he has shown a quiet and steady improvement. He has been able to feel much greater interest in his work, a marked betterment in his relations with his wife both emotionally and sexually, greater patience with his child, more tolerance with other people and with himself, much less fear of facing people, and a marked improvement in capacity for tactful handling of people, and a more simple and straightforward conflict-free relationship with me. I shall summarize briefly this critical therapeutic 'break-through' period. (The numbers represent the chronological order of the most important sessions during those five months.)

1. 'I get a picture of myself in the dark behind a door, banging on it. Ah! It's a memory. We were shut up in a dark cupboard when naughty . . . I shut myself in now and get panicky. I've got a fundamental fear. At times it gets near to undermining the adult and I fear collapse.'

2. His father had died a few months earlier at an advanced age, and he said: 'Consciously I don't bother about father's death. He's just gone. Its impersonal. But I want to get down to my real feelings.'

3. 'I never had a father who loved and cared for his children. I'm sensitive to the sufferings of children.' I commented: 'But you inflict suffering on your own child-self.' He replied: 'I'm tired and would like you to put me to sleep, and wake and find all my troubles solved.' That was one of the first signs of real dependence on my help.

4. 'It's warm and comfortable in your room but I feel I ought to be uncomfortable.' He reported a dream. 'I saw a coffin open and a man in it talking. I was very concerned because the lid was to be put on and he'd be buried alive. Then he folded his arms and said "Maybe now I'll be able to relax".' He added: 'I'm talking at a terrific rate now. I used to be terrified of being buried alive.' I pointed out that he was fighting against being buried alive inside himself; that a part of him had for long been so buried, and he feared relaxation, sleep, and any dependence on me or his wife because he felt it would mean losing his active self and slipping down into this regressed passive one. Until he got over that fear he could not begin to recuperate at a deep unconscious level. He said: 'I feel I ought not to want my wife's breast or any comfort. Sexual intercourse ought to be purely mechanical. I'm afraid to let go and let you help me.'

5. The basic problem, should the weak and frightened child in him be allowed to depend and be helped, or should he be ruthlessly driven on in a forced pseudo-adult way, now became focused in the transference. He had a long series of fantasies each week as he approached my rooms and saw my car outside. At first he would fantasy smashing it up, then later he would get in and drive it off. Again, I would be in it and he would get in and lean his head on my shoulder and put an arm round me but then suddenly attack me and take over the driving. Later still he fantasied my driving and himself being in the passenger seat, and finally he saw himself getting into my car, curling up on the back seat and going fast asleep, knowing that I would approve. His hostile resistances to me earlier were clearly a defence against his fear of helpless dependence on me, and masked a fantasy of a return to the womb.

6. This was the most critical session. He felt 'in a queer mood, can't concentrate. I just sit and stare and can't apply myself to the job in hand. I lose interest. I want to escape from all responsibility to people. I feel I haven't got a mind. I had to go to a business meeting and had no feeling, no interest, no anger, only sad. I had intercourse with my wife and had no particular feelings.' Here was a schizoid, detached, impersonal, apathetic state, something much deeper than his earlier depressive guilt. I interpreted this to him, and he said: 'I've always been a keen cricketer. In 1946-7 England were

touring Australia and I was apathetic and couldn't understand why men should bother to play cricket. It was when I was becoming friendly with the girl I married. I had months of this apathy. It was awful, empty, nothing to live for, everything futile.' I suggested that he had been withdrawing in deep fear from his growing disposition to trust and depend more frankly on both his wife and me. That session was a turning point.

7. At the next session he felt better and from then on he increasingly frequently reported improvement. He mentioned a dream. 'I went down into a tower and then had to go through a tunnel to get out. Though I had come in that way I was horrified.' A clear fantasy of a return to the womb, showing that he was in touch with his lost regressed ego in the deep unconscious, the cause of all his schizoid reactions. He said 'I wish you'd attack me and give me a chance to fight. A love-relationship is smothering. I used to have premature ejaculation but now I go on and on and can't react, holding back. I'll be swallowed up. It's equivalent to lying on this couch.' The couch had been for a few weeks the focus of his conflict between the dependent child and the compulsively independent adult. From the start he had compromised and never allowed the couch-problem to be analysed till now. He did not want to sit in the patient's armchair; that was exclusively adult. He did not want to lie on the couch; that was exclusively infantile. So he sat on the couch with his feet on the floor, for the first three and three quarter years of analysis. In this session for the first time he tentatively put one foot up on the couch, and at once began to say: 'Should I sit in the chair? Lying on this couch suggests going to sleep, surrender, losing independence of you. I've always been afraid of an anaesthetic. Now I sit on the couch with one foot on the ground, afraid to be absolutely in your power. I had a dream that you'd taken my penis off and I just put it back on and it stayed there.'

8. At the next session he lay down at once and said: 'Now I'm lying on the couch properly, much more comfortable. The last two nights I've had satisfying intercourse with my wife. I've always wanted to get away from the real world. I had very little happiness in life and marriage when I came to see you, and now I've got a lot, and am very grateful.' Then he suddenly added: 'Now I want to get off the couch. I'm afraid of any close relationship.'

9. He produced another fantasy of smashing my car and then said 'It would be so nice to give up the struggle and sink back into warm human flesh, surrender, letting go.' I said, 'You're frightened of that but you need it. If you can let your passive, exhausted self of early life recuperate here, you'll become better able to be active outside without driving yourself.' He replied, 'When you said that I felt a great sense of relief'

10. The four sessions 6–9 seemed to be the vital heart of the analysis. His old manic-depressive-guilt pattern had quite gone and did not return. It

had changed into the conflict over accepting his regressed ego in sessions so that he could maintain an active adult ego in his outer life without forcing and exhausting himself. But the problem was not easily solved. In this session he was tense. He said: 'I've been wanting to come and was all for lying on the couch and relaxing, but then I lashed myself, accused myself of being lazy and drove myself to work by discipline. The only way I've ever known how to solve my problems was to drive myself.' This is, in fact, what Fairbairn calls the antilibidinal ego, the struggling child crushing out his needs, and, I believe, particularly the passive ones.

Not long after this he came in to one session and said: 'I've only two things to say', and he said them and added 'Now I want to relax'. He lay back and sank into a deep doze for about forty minutes. At the next session he said: 'Last session has changed something in me. I feel somehow calmer, stronger.' Following that critical five months period he was able to make steady progress, his variations of mood bearing no resemblance to his original cyclothymia. Fifteen months later he reported in one session: 'Generally I feel very fit these days, a positive attitude to life, things are going well. I'm more in love with my wife and sex relations are enjoyable. There are still some problems but life has a different feel. It's a breaking free and getting out of prison.' One must admit that not all regressions can be contained within the analytic situation as this one was, but even then I believe them to be treatable by combined support and analysis, if one is prepared to do it.

## THE OEDIPUS COMPLEX, DEPRESSION AND REGRESSION

It remains briefly to relate this *manic-regressive* illness to the oedipal situation with which ambivalent manic-depressive illness has always been closely linked, especially by Klein. There are two aspects of the oedipal situation, its *infantile dependence* aspect and its *object-relations* aspect. Fairbairn regards the Oedipus complex as an end-product of infantile insecurity and not as the cause of psychoneurosis per se. The *cause* he regards as infantile dependence. There are, however, two forms of infantile dependence, passive and active. The passive form is, as we have seen, a regressive return to a womb-like state inside, a flight from life which cancels out object-relations in the post-natal sense. The active form is the struggle of the infant to hold on to object-relations in a bad-object environment, to fight for the satisfaction of needs, ending up usually in having to put up with bad objects rather than take flight and have none at all. The regressed schizoid ego is the basis of depersonalization states, and of what I would call the *passive neurosis*. The active struggling oral ego is the basis of masochistic suffering, while the antilibidinal ego which develops over against it is the source of sadistic phenomena. Together these two structures form the sado-masochistic internal world of neurotic dream-life and symptom formation, what Fairbairn (1958) calls the static internal closed system (p. 380) and this constitutes the *active neurosis*. In its entirety I believe it to be maintained as a defence against regression into the passive neurosis of flight from real life.

During the struggles of the transitional period in which the oral infant is trying to develop towards mature dependence and adulthood, infantile dependence of the active kind, which maintains object-relationship, will find expression in the so-called pre-oedipal stages. Oral and anal fantasies and conflicts will gradually develop to the full oedipal level of genital, incestuous, and guilt fantasies. These express not an inevitable biologically fixed instinctive reaction of the growing child to the needed parents, but a continuous anxious clinging to parents of the still infantile dependent child. Menaced within by early fears and a regressive drive, the child cannot develop adequate self-confidence and self-reliance in real-life activities, and must maintain his ego by fantasied object-relations with parent-figures in his inner world. They are of necessity basically bad-object relations, though unreal, idealized fantasied good-object relations to the exciting object are formed as a defence against unbearable insecurity. This is the Oedipus complex, and it represents not biological necessity but ego-weakness. The more pathological it is, the more its active dependence hides a deeper, rejected, passive regressed dependence.

As an internal-object relations phenomenon Fairbairn regards the Oedipus complex as set up by splitting the internalized unsatisfying parental objects into an exciting object and a rejecting object, differentiating and fusing the relevant aspects of both the mother and the father. In his inner fantasy world the male child (unless driven to develop homosexually) then takes the mother as the exciting object and the father as the rejecting object. His libidinal ego seeks the mother, his antilibidinal ego forms by identification with the father. As his libidinal ego seeks the exciting object in his fantasy, it is persecuted by his antilibidinal ego and rejecting object, giving rise to oedipal guilt. The fully developed Oedipus complex forms as the end-product of the sado-masochistic static internal closed system of the neurotic unconscious. This shows Freud's great insight, when he first came upon this phenomenon, in fastening on it as of crucial importance. It is, however, not so much the cause of the active neurosis as the substance of it. This internal bad-objects world comes into being as a result of the child's struggle to preserve an active ego when he is in a state of fear-dictated withdrawal from an outer reality (the home life) which is too difficult for him to cope with. The struggle is necessitated by the fact that the profoundest effect of infantile ego-weakness through fear is the longing to regress, to take flight from a menacing world which the infant is too small and weak to deal with. Desperate struggles are made to check and counteract this flight from life by exploiting any available *active* relationship that would ward off the attempted return to the womb-state. One patient, suffering from obsessive breast-fantasies, lost them under analysis only to find them replaced by frank regression fantasies of shutting himself away in safe strongholds. (See Guntrip 1961b). The patient whose case was presented in the last section, struggling at one point against a longing to lie back on the couch and sleep, counteracted that by fantasying himself sitting in the patient's arm-chair, which then turned into himself as a child sitting on the pot having a battle of wills with mother. It is in this light that we must view the Oedipus complex. It gathers up into itself earlier oral and anal fantasies, and its incestuous wishes, hate, and guilt are additional means of warding off regressive trends and retaining an active ego. As a highly developed form of inner world life it is both withdrawn and active. It stands midway between, and is a compromise between, infantile dependence in its ultimate form of regression and the maintenance of an active ego in real life. As an internal activity it betrays fear of the outer world, as a tie to parents it expresses infantile dependence, and yet as an object-relations phenomenon it shows the struggle to preserve an active ego and hold to a more developed if not genuinely adult position. Its ambivalence and guilt are the core of classic depression, which is the price paid for using the Oedipus complex as a defence against regression. If the Oedipus complex is analysed as if it were the ultimate and causal factor in neurosis, then we help the patient to maintain this defence and keep the deeper schizoid problem hidden. If it is analysed for what it really is, a defence against the deeper schizoid level, then we begin to bring out the regressed ego whose interests are not oedipal at all, but simply a desperate need for security and a chance to recuperate in a safe retreat until it can gather the strength to be reborn. Arthur Miller in the film *The Misfits*, I believe, makes one character say: 'Most of us are just looking for a place to hide and watch it all go by.' What to do about this regressed infant when we have uncovered him is the problem that holds the key to radical psychotherapy.

Meanwhile it must be said that the existence of a passive regressed ego or factor as *the ultimate underlying problem* in the personality does not lessen the importance of the classic problems of the more accessible sado-masochistic level already long familiar to analysts. They are still as real as ever, and we meet them in our patients and they require analysis. But our analysis of them will be greatly affected by whether we regard them as ultimate per se, or whether we see through them as defences against the deeper, really ultimate, schizoid level. It is from that point of view that I suggest we ought to speak of a *manic-regressive illness*, and recognize classic *depression* as the result of one important phase of the struggle against the devitalization and depersonalization with which regression finally threatens the ego of our outer-world living.

# REFERENCES

Abraham, K. (1911). 'Notes on the Psycho-Analytical Investigation and Treatment of Manic-Depressive Insanity.' *Selected Papers*. London: Hogarth Press (rep. 1927).

Fairbairn, W. R. D. (1952). *Psychoanalytic Studies of the Personality*. London: Tavistock.

_____ (1958). On the nature and aims of psycho-analytical treatment. *International Journal of Psycho-Analysis* 39.

Freud, S. (1908). "Civilized" sexual morality and modern nervous illness. *Standard Edition* 9.

_____ (1923). The ego and the id. *Standard Edition* 19.

_____ (1927). The future of an illusion. *Standard Edition* 21.

_____ (1933). *New Introductory Lectures*. London: Hogarth Press.

_____ (1937). Analysis terminable and interminable. *Collected Papers* 5.

Guntrip, H. (1960). Ego weakness and the hard core of the problem of psychotherapy. *British Journal of Medical Psychology* 33.

_____ (1961a). *Personality Structure and Human Interaction*. London: Hogarth Press.

_____ (1961b). The schizoid problem, regression and the struggle to preserve an ego. *British Journal of Medical Psychology* 34.

Hartmann, H. (1960). Towards a concept of mental health. *British Journal of Medical Psychology* 33.

Klein, M. (1960). A note on depression in the schizophrenic. *International Journal of Psycho-Analysis* 41.

Livingstone, Sir R. (1935). *Greek Ideals and Modern Life*. London: Oxford Univ. Press.

Malory, Sir T. (1470). *Morte d'Arthur*.

Nacht, S., and Racamier, P. C. (1960). Depressive states. *International Journal of Psycho-Analysis* 41.

Rosenfeld, H. (1960). A note on the precipitating factor in depressive illness. *International Journal of Psycho-Analysis* 41.

Scott, W. C. M. (1960). Depression, confusion and multivalence. *International Journal of Psycho-Analysis* 41.

Zetzel, E. (1960). Introduction on depressive illness. *International Journal of Psycho-Analysis* 41.

# Section III

## 1962–1969
## THE WINNICOTT PERIOD: REGRESSION AND REGROWTH

# 8

# "IN TRUTH THE NEED TO REGRESS CANNOT BE TAKEN LIGHTLY"[1]

## THE SCHIZOID COMPROMISE

Ostensibly, every patient wants to be cured of neurosis quickly, so that he can get on with living. Whatever 'resistances' the patient thereafter puts up, wittingly or unwittingly, to treatment, there is no doubt that his 'Reality-Ego' does want to be finished with the illness as such, and as soon as possible. The length of time involved in psychotherapy is a sore trial to him. He feels that his progress is too slow and too small, and that life will have gone by before he is capable of living it properly. It may be that better understanding of the problems involved will shorten treatment, though in the nature of the case a healing process which is a *regrowing process* just as much when it concerns the mental self as when it concerns the body, cannot be artificially hurried however much we may wish it. All that we can do is to discover the obstacles to regrowth, provide a relationship in which the patient can come to feel secure, and leave 'nature' to prosecute her healing work at her own pace. The time factor in psychotherapy can never be simply in the therapist's power to more than a small extent, and it is much easier for all concerned to hinder and lengthen treatment than to shorten it.

What is usually not realized at the outset, nor for a long time, by the patient is that he himself will play the largest part in hindering, that he will do so mostly unknowingly, and that this is inevitable because it is bound up with the very nature of this kind of illness. I did have one patient who, at the outset, said 'I'm very afraid I'll ruin this treatment in the end'. Most patients do not have so much insight. This bears vitally on the criticism often made that psychoanalysis in fact is an interminable process. The psychoanalytical researcher can only put aside impatient criticism and go on pondering the actual clinical data he meets. There is certainly

---

1. Read at meeting of Tavistock Clinic, London, 1962.

no quick and easy way of making a mature and stable adult personality out of the legacy of an undermined childhood. Moreover, the patient, however ill, is still a 'person in his own right'. He is ill because in some way he was not treated as one in childhood. He feels an urgent necessity to *defend* his own independence and freedom of self-determination as a person; and he feels this all the more, the less of a person deep down he feels to be. In a sense, he wants to be rid of the illness without changing his familiar self-identity, even when he has some insight into the fact that this kind of illness robs him of genuine freedom. Still, he cannot allow anything to be put across on him, even if it is supposed to be for his good. Because he feels menaced in the very essence of his selfhood, he is bound to be on the defensive against the very person whose help he seeks. All these difficulties have their roots in the schizoid problem, for the one thing above all others that is so hard as to seem at times almost impossible for the aloof schizoid personality, is to effect a genuine relationship with any other human being, including the psychotherapist. In proportion as a patient is schizoid he is afraid of people just as much as he needs them. This is a dilemma in which he cannot avoid seeking compromise solutions until such time as his fears diminish and allow his needs to be met. All through his treatment he will be tossed about between his fears of isolation and his fears of emotional proximity.

A male patient in the forties, married and with a family, who suffered exceptionally severe anxieties over every kind of family separation, summed up his position thus: 'I'm the prey of deep terrifying fundamental fears if I'm not in control of all our relationships with regard to separation. If my wife is away and is late returning or I don't know when she'll be back I panic. I feel I'm in control of the situation if I can be certain she'll be back at the stated time, or if I can go away and come back and know she'll be there. I don't mind her being away if I can get at her, and then I don't want to. I even feel relief at being alone, so long as I can have them all back the moment I need them. But I hate and fear and loathe this dependent weak part of me, and it makes me hate those I depend on.' Thus, this kind of insecurity makes it important to have an absolute guarantee of never being deserted and left really alone; yet it also carries with it a dread of weak over-dependence on the needed person, the fear of being betrayed into a subordinate, submissive clinging to one's protector in which one's own individual personality will be stifled. This patient had to have his wife always there so that he could both leave her and return to her at will. This kind of relationship, the 'in and out programme' (Guntrip 1952, 1961b) is not only typical of schizoid persons, but practically inevitable for them. It is the only way they can maintain a viable compromise between their equally intense, conflicting *needs* and *fears* of personal relationships. I naturally pointed out to this patient that he had exactly the same problem with me and that it was the major 'sticking-point' in psychotherapy. He could feel severe anxiety at the thought of not having me to come to, and yet when he came he found it extremely difficult to bring out frankly his 'weak and dependent self', the legacy of his insecure childhood. His compromise often was to come and discuss things on an intellectual level, being present physically and intellectually but, as it were, absent emotionally. I once had a patient who often said 'There's a part of me I never bring in here'.

Schizoid patients suffer from what Laing (1959) has called 'ontological insecurity', using the terminology of Existentialist philosophy. This philosophy regards human existence as fundamentally rooted in anxiety and insecurity, and, if one may judge from the clear signs of a schizoid mentality of aloofness and detachment in the writings of Jean Paul Sartre, this philosophy is an intellectual conceptualization of the fundamentally schizoid plight of practically all human beings. I have referred to 'schizoid patients' but what patients are not schizoid at bottom. As Fairbairn has pointed out, schizoid problems are far commoner in clinical practice than depression, and when patients say they are 'depressed' they nearly always mean not guilt-burdened but apathetic, devitalized and feeling that life is futile. 'Ontological insecurity' means insecurity as to one's essential being and existence as a person, insecurity about one's Ego-identity, the feeling of basic inadequacy in coping with life, and inability to maintain oneself as in any sense an equal in relationships with other people. It involves therefore urgent needs for support, but at the same time a great fear of too close relationships which feel to be a threat to one's own status as an individual. The schizoid person, to whatever degree he is schizoid, hovers between *two opposite fears, the fear of isolation in independence with loss of his ego in a vacuum of experience, and the fear of bondage to, of imprisonment or absorption in, the personality of whomsoever he rushes to for protection.* A patient once said to me 'I know that all my active feelings about you are only defences against the feeling of wanting to be safe inside you'. Fairbairn once said to me in conversation: 'The person one breaks away to, turns into the person one has to break away from again'. That is the schizoid dilemma, equal inability either to do with or without the needed protector, the parent-figure whom the insecure child inside must have, but whom the struggling adult conscious self cannot tolerate or admit. It clearly presents the greatest possible obstacle to psychotherapy.

This is strikingly illustrated in the case of a female patient who seemed, on the face of it, to be a gentle natured person who made no secret of her nervousness, timidity, fear of being alone and need for constant support. Nevertheless, in a quiet and rather secret, inward way, she revealed a most unyielding need to keep herself going without help, and found it exceptionally hard to put any real trust in and reliance on me. She wanted to but it 'did not happen'. She complained repeatedly that I was supportive during session time but she had to live her life when I was not there, so that I was not really of much use to her. She knew that she was free to ring me up when she was in a panic, but for the most part she would rush to a drug instead. It took her a very long time to admit that the trouble was not really that I was not physically present with her at her work and in her home life, but that the moment she got out of the consulting room she mentally dismissed me. 'Now I'll have to get on without help and do it myself.' Then she fell into the panics of isolation, would be driven in desperation to carry on long conversations with me in her head, and yet when she arrived for the next session would have nothing to say. Often the session began with her not even being able to sit down. She would stand, immobile and speechless, aloof and uncommunicative. As usually happens with such patients, as the end of the session began to draw near there would be so much to say that it was hard to get it all in. This constant oscillation between 'near and far', dependence and independence, trust and distrust, *acceptance of and resistance to treatment, the need of a security-giving relationship and fear of all relationships as a threat to one's separate existence as a proper person* presents itself for analysis under a thousand forms all the way through the process of psychotherapy. *When the patient can establish a persistent compromise halfway between the two extremes, the result is 'blocked analysis' and therapeutic stalemate.*

This is illustrated by two dreams of the above patient. 'I was having a meal with a friend alone, and suddenly my sister and her whole family came in and just sat down and began to eat. There wasn't enough food to go round and no one noticed that I was having to go without.' It did not occur to her that she herself had made up the dream that way and that was how she wanted it. It was far too much of an unreserved commitment to be alone with one friend in a cosy tête-à-tête. This had to be broken up, yet so as not to shut her out altogether. She was still there but not very deeply involved in what was happening. That was her basic attitude to sessions. She often dreamed of coming to see me and finding me busy with other patients, and would often express jealousy of my other patients and say that I ought to have only her. These complaints only faded away when I pointed out that this apparent jealousy masked her fear of any real relationship, and in fact the existence of my other patients reassured her. They were like the other members of her family she brought into the dream to dilute the personal relationship situation, and leave her free to maintain her 'half in and half out' position. She wanted some person all to herself, yet was secretly glad of the protection of rival claimants to that person's attention.

# PSYCHOANALYSIS AND THE THEORY OF THE SCHIZOID PROBLEM

Before we can uncover all the cleverly hidden forms of the schizoid compromise, it is necessary to clarify our theoretical approach. To possess an adequate psychodynamic theory does not automatically make us good therapists, but it does help us

not to misinterpret what we see, and an inadequate theory can block the development of insight in the analyst. Incidently, *theoretical* stalemate, the congealing of
theory into a rigid orthodoxy which does not admit of really fresh approaches, must
itself be a defence, of the nature of the schizoid compromise, against new and
disturbing truth. What we might call a shift of the centre of gravity in psychodynamic theory has been taking place ever since Freud, in the 1920's, turned his
attention from the problems of impulse-control to the more difficult and fundamental problems of ego-growth and distortion. This meant the analysis, not of
moral and pseudo-moral conflicts over so-called instinctive drives, but the analysis
of the structural development of the ego, with special reference to 'ego-splitting'. It
is significant that Freud's last, unfinished book (1938) *An Outline of Psycho-Analysis*,
stops short in the uncompleted Part 3 with the subjects of 'ego splitting' and 'the
internal world'. James Strachey tells us in his Preface that Freud broke off at that
point and did not return to the subject, turning instead to another piece of writing,
itself unfinished. Could it be that Freud knew that he had raised the vital problem
for future theoretical developments, but that the clinical data did not yet exist for
its satisfactory solution? In the quarter of a century that has elapsed since Freud
died, much psychoanalytical investigation of psychotic, and particularly schizophrenic, conditions has gone on, and the theoretical work of Melanie Klein and
Fairbairn has pushed far ahead along the path Freud opened up. It was the work of
Fairbairn on the revision of theory that in particular brought out clearly the shift
of interest from classical depressive to schizoid problems. In *Personality Structure and
Human Interaction* (1961a) I sought to trace in detail the development of this change
of viewpoint, and in the closing section of that book, and in a series of articles
(1960, 1961b, 1962) I sought to pursue its implications for the deeper understanding
and psychotherapeutic treatment of schizoid conditions. On close investigation the
manic-depressive problem resolves itself back into a manic-regressive problem, the
problem of the struggles of a profoundly withdrawn and schizoid personality to
overcome powerful underlying regressive trends and keep in effective touch with
the outer world (Guntrip 1962). Whatever clinical problem is dealt with, if analysis
goes far enough one finds oneself going behind the easily accessible conflicts over
sexual and aggressive drives, to the deeper conflicts over primary fears, and the
secret flight from life of the weak and undeveloped infantile ego, hidden deep in the
unconscious (Guntrip 1960, 1961b). In this present article it is my purpose rather to
see what light the study of schizoid problems throws on psychotherapy. But we
shall be concerned at this stage not so much with suggestions for psychotherapeutic
treatment as with the difficulties that stand in the way of treatment by psychoanalytical therapy, when neurosis is looked at from the schizoid point of view. In
other words, what light does the schizoid process throw on 'resistance'?

Freud made it clear that *every* patient *resists* treatment, no matter how much
he may also want it, and that the resistance can be so serious as to lead to a state of

'blocked analysis'. In a famous passage in *The Ego and The Id* (1923, p. 72 footnote) he attributed this to the operation of an unconscious sense of guilt, which makes the patient accept his illness as a punishment which he must not seek to evade. At that date schizoid processes were very little taken into account and were not recognized as the real basis of psychopathological developments. So long as the root causes of psychoneurosis were held to belong to the sadomasochistic fusions of sexual and aggressive drives, so that impulse-control was the major problem, this explanation by means of 'unconscious guilt' was the obviously correct one. The moment, however, we realize that these conflicts over anti-social impulses are defensive in nature, and arise out of the patient's frantic struggles to force his basically schizoid personality back into touch with outer reality, to put energy back into his detached and de-emotionalized self of everyday living, and to counteract his deep-seated regressive flight from life motivated by his earliest unmastered fears, it becomes necessary to seek a deeper explanation of 'blocked analysis'. Even if its cause is regarded as 'guilt', it soon becomes apparent that this guilt is felt not so much over sex and aggression, as over weakness and fear, and tends to take more and more the form, not of moral guilt, but of contempt and hatred of a part of the personality which the patient feels will 'let him down'.

A striking example of the fact that it is not 'guilt over bad impulses' but 'fear of weakness' that is the cause of 'resistance', is the following comment of a male patient: 'I play a "cat and mouse" game with myself. "Why can't you stop being a mouse?" Then I turn the tables and say "Why can't you leave me alone?" It's all very well coming here but at bottom I don't want to get better, or only part of me does.' I suggested that his 'cat and mouse' game with himself was a rival policy to psychotherapy, a struggle to solve the problem his own way. He was being a cat to himself to prove that he wasn't nothing but a mouse. He replied 'It's like putting your head in a gas oven to get your name in the papers. Do the stupid thing in a big way. I've had years of analysis and I'll go on for ever. I'm not going to be one of those people who can be cured in six months. One must have some distinction.'

The fundamental conflict in human personality is not that of a sadistic if 'moral' superego attacking cannibalistic or murderous incestuous impulses. It is the desperate struggle of a person who feels at bottom to be no more than a helpless and frightened infant, dependent on other people, to compel himself to keep going 'under his own steam' by hating and driving his basic infantile self, which is so deeply withdrawn from all real object-relationships. It is the struggle to master and defeat chronic infantile dependent needs by internal violence, and force the outer-world self to carry on in a state of maximum independence of other people. Herein lies the substance of the schizoid conflict between needs and fears of human relationships. It is a rival policy to that of psychotherapy for that involves acceptance of the therapist's help to get well. In a word, fear of weakness rather than guilt over bad impulses is the basic cause of resistance to treatment. So great is the human being's fear of appearing weak that he will rather be bad and suffer guilt; and he will also rather go on being ill and suffering the miseries of neurosis than admit the implication of weakness by the acceptance of the therapist's help. Yet the patient is in truth weak, through no fault of his own. He has been gravely damaged in infancy and childhood, he is deeply fear-ridden and his emotional ego-development has been arrested at the deepest levels, so that his inner self is in a state of chronically anxious infantile dependence and craves all the time for a good parent-figure with whom he can get a new start. Thus *he can neither fully accept nor fully reject the therapist, and most of the difficulties of treatment lie in his desperate need to set up and maintain some form of compromise relationship.*

## FORMS OF THE SCHIZOID COMPROMISE AS A DEFENCE AGAINST PSYCHOTHERAPY

### Blocked Analysis Itself as a Compromise

The essence of the schizoid compromise is to find a way of retaining a relationship in such a form that it shall not involve any full emotional response. It is quite easy to do this with psychoanalytical treatment. The patient keeps on coming but does not make any real progress. He exhibits recurring moods of restlessness, complains of feeling 'stuck', says 'We're getting nowhere with this' and toys with the idea of stopping treatment. But he does not stop. He keeps coming without opening out any real emotional issues for analysis. Some patients give the impression of being prepared to go on indefinitely like that, deriving some quite valuable support from sessions but not undergoing any real development of personality. I have come to regard a prolonged therapeutic stalemate of this kind as a very important indication of the severity of the deepest level anxieties the patient will have to face if he ventures farther. He dare not give up, or serious anxiety will break out, and he dare not 'let go' and take the plunge into genuine analysis, or just as serious anxiety will be released. I once had a patient who, instead of continuing analysis on a dead monotonous level of unbroken stalemate, kept breaking off and returning again. Once she dreamed that she was walking along a road and came up against an enormous blank wall which simply barred the way forward. I suggested that this was her way of saying that she knew that her progress in treatment was completely at a standstill. She was at a dead end. She replied 'I've got to go on, if you can stand it.' I said 'I can stand it if you can.' Finally, however, she revealed the plain fact that she could not stand that committal of herself to another person that a real therapeutic relationship would have implied, for she brought the following dream.

'I got on a tramcar and walked straight through to the driver's platform, turned the driver off and drove the car myself.' As we had only just begun one of her periods of return to analysis, I put it to her that the tram was the treatment and I was the driver, and she felt the situation to be one in which she was in my power which she could not tolerate. Only if she could take complete charge of the analysis and run it herself, could she go on with it: but in that case it would not be treatment and would do her no good. She did not come next time and finally ended her analysis at that point. Nevertheless she was not able quite to give me up, for much later on she sent me a copy of one of my own books, filled in all the margins with critical comments. She was still 'keeping going' by holding on to a now internalized struggle for power with the analyst, which never produced any constructive results because it kept her half in and half out of the relationship.

A blocked analysis is always liable sooner or later to break down in some such way as this. So long as it does not break down there is a chance of analysing the forms of compromise the patient sets up and promoting some progress. Yet there is no certainty about this. I had a male patient who persisted steadily in a long analysis. He was a very able man, running a skilled business of his own, a bachelor living alone, and a man of intellectual interests over and above his business. He had come to analysis for depressed moods, because he was well informed about analytical treatment and was convinced that it was the only way he could be helped. He had an extremely bleak childhood, and had repressed real terror of a psychotic father. His early analysis moved through the usual sexual and aggressive conflicts, sado-masochistic dreams and phantasies, guilt, and some punishing physical symptoms, to a point where his depression was markedly relieved. There he stuck fast. He said 'I feel that all the outlying areas of my neurosis have been cleared up and I have come up against a circular wall, too high to get over, and there are no doors or windows in it. I keep going round and round it and I don't know what is inside.' It became clear, at any rate in an intellectual way, that what lay behind it was the self of his childhood which he felt was 'a miserable little worm.' The only emotional indications of its presence deep inside were occasional feelings that it would do him good to have a good cry, and sudden attacks of exhaustion, when he would go home and go to bed and sleep it off. In general he was a tightly organized, obsessional hard worker, liked and respected by his employees to whom he was fair and just. He could not involve himself in any closer kind of human relationship, though he had always wanted to be married. After the 'circular wall' phantasy he would say 'I can't let anything disturbing out this session. I've got an important business meeting tomorrow,' and constantly commented 'There's something I'm doing that holds up the analysis. I wish I knew what it was.' This was analysed from many points of view, but he never succeeded in giving up this stalling reaction. Then one day he did not turn up and I learned that he had been found dead from a coronary thrombosis. That gives the measure of the severity of the internal tensions he locked up inside himself. If he could have risked a complete regressive illness (as he would have had to do, if it had been pneumonia) at an early enough period, he could no doubt have escaped the thrombosis and solved his psychic problems. But it is not easy to get a regressive illness accepted and understood: also he had a business to run. His steady and determined persistence in what came to be a blocked analysis was a schizoid compromise which probably he had no option but to maintain; and to support him in it was the only way of giving him such help as he could accept. Such a case makes it clear that *resistance* is not perverseness, or negative transference, or moral fault, but a defence of the patient's very existence as a person within the limits of what is possible to him. Such resistance and blocked analysis, in so far as it is successful, must seem practically preferable to opening up devastating conflicts in order to seek a real solution. I am confirmed in this view by the severity of the struggle to get the deep hidden schizoid ego reborn, in a number of patients who have been able to go beyond a purely defensive position. From one point of view, the schizoid compromise is a struggle to maintain stability, even though from another it is a resistance against psychotherapy, the kind of treatment that involves opening up disturbing inner problems to get a chance to solve them. In this sense, this kind of stability is an evasion of the real solution, but it is not for us to say lightly whether a patient should or even can lay himself open to the radical cure. That depends partly on whether he gets the support he needs from his therapist, but ultimately on the degree of severity of his deepest problems, especially in the light of his present day real-life situation. My impression is that if the patient can face it, he will, and if he cannot, no amount of analysis will make him do so.

## Compromise Techniques in the Patient's 'Management' of Analysis

These are much simpler matters and fairly easy to recognize, and need not detain us at length. They often take the form of trying to turn analysis into an intellectual discussion. One patient began by saying that he looked on the analysis as 'a valuable course in psychology.' Others will bring for discussion their intellectual problems about religion or morality or human relations in society, or their doubts about psychoanalysis. I do not think that this kind of material can be just rejected as a defensive manoeuvre. It can well be that the patient feels that his intellect is the one part of his personality that he can function with, and if he is just ruthlessly stopped from using it in sessions he may well feel 'castrated,' or as I would prefer to say, reduced to a nonentity, depersonalized. The grown-up self needs support and understanding in analysis as well as the child. For that reason, when treating patients who work in medical, psychological or social fields, I have never refused to co-operate when they have wished to discuss some of their own 'cases' in session. It is on a par with the parent-patient wishing at times to discuss the problems of his children. One can be too purist in this matter. The patient is very likely quite genuinely needing help, and does feel that his analyst is a person capable of giving it to him. It is all the more important, when afterwards he says 'I was never able to discuss anything frankly with my parents.' It is best to go through with this and use it to help the patient to see where his difficulties in dealing with others are bound up with his own problems. Then it can lead back into analysis proper. Only when too persistent a use is made of this kind of discussion must it be challenged as a schizoid compromise, an attempt to keep going in relationship with the therapist while keeping the inner self withdrawn.

One male patient proceeded with his defence against analysis by flooding every session with long recitals of endless dreams, simply recounting one after another without a stop. That this was quite a serious compulsion was evident from the fact that for a long time my assertion that these dreams were a waste of time since he never made any use of them, made no impression on him. By cramming the sessions with dreams he could prevent my saying anything that might stir up anxiety. When at last he did consent to have a look at a dream before hurrying on to the next, he would set about the intellectual analysis of its meaning (which he was able to do since he was well versed, professionally, in symbolism) or else keep on asking me questions as to what I thought this or that meant. I judged it inadvisable to let him come up against too blank a wall of non-response on my part, and carefully selected the points on which I did comment, to help him to become aware of his deeper anxieties. Gradually he became able to drop this compromise method of coming for analysis without having it, and then he began to 'feel' how much his very schizoid personality was out of real touch with his environment. The theme of loneliness took the place of somewhat excited dreamtelling.

This is a convenient place at which to stress the fact that *dreaming is itself the schizoid compromise par excellence, and, as such, dreaming is a rival policy to psychotherapy.* This is apparent, not only from the above case, but from those patients who will occasionally say 'I'm not going to tell you my dream, you'd only spoil it', or who even begin to tell a dream and suddenly forget it completely. One patient dreamed furiously every night, yet could never remember a thing in the morning. He then decided to take pencil and paper to bed and write down his dreams during the night, while he had them quite clearly in mind. To his surprise he just stopped dreaming and after a few nights he no longer troubled to take up his paper and pencil. At once he began dreaming furiously again. Dreaming is the maintenance of an internal life, withdrawn from the outer world, in which the outer world, including the analyst, is not to be allowed to share. It is essentially a schizoid phenomenon based on the fact that the over-anxious or insufficiently formed ego cannot maintain itself in existence without object-relationships. The loss of all objects simply leads to depersonalization. Therefore, when the infant makes a mental withdrawal from a too traumatic external world, he runs the grave risk of losing his own ego the deeper he takes flight into himself. I have had a number of patients who quite clearly remembered as tiny children having 'queer' states of mind in which they did not know who they were and felt everything to be unreal. Lord Tennyson as a boy must have withdrawn into himself from a very gloomily and bitterly depressed father, and was once found alone staring into space and mechanically repeating his name, 'Alfred, Alfred'. He grew up to be intensely shy and to suffer from sudden marked 'absences of mind'. This is the danger that the early schizoid flight from outer reality incurs, and the obvious way to counteract it is to set up an internal world of imaginary object-relationships in the mind, the world of dream and phantasy. Thus, young Anthony Trollope, ostracized by everyone at Winchester and Harrow Schools on account of his poverty, developed a persistent and elaborate phantasy world which he carried on from day to day and even from year to year, until at last he disciplined it into a gift for novel-writing.

The two indubitably real parts of the personality are the self of everyday conscious living, and the fear-ridden small child in a state of schizoid withdrawn-ness deep in the unconscious. The intermediate dream-world is an artefact, a defence against the dangers of withdrawal. As a wish-fulfilment, it is primarily an expression of the wish to remain in being, by having a world to live in when you have lost the real one. Wish-fulfilment would be better described as ego-maintenance. That is why dreaming is such a constant phenomenon in the night. In proportion as tendencies to feel depersonalized are strong, night and sleep are felt as a dangerous risk of ego-loss. Patients will say 'I fear I may never wake up again' or as one patient said 'I have to keep waking up at intervals to see how I'm getting on. It's so difficult going to sleep because it feels like going some place where there isn't anybody and you're really by yourself.' Then dreaming keeps the ego in being. If too much interest is allowed to become 'fixated' on dreams in analysis, it positively helps the patient to maintain his schizoid defence, and it may well be that much dream analysis which looks fairly convincing and useful is, from the patient's point of view, much more intellectual than emotional. I have been very impressed with the extent to which patients begin to live out emotionally in a genuine and consciously anxious way, states of mind that they expressed quite clearly in one or two notable dreams probably one or two years previously. Thus, if dreams are a 'royal road into the unconscious' in so far as it is a defensive inner world, they are also a rival policy to psychotherapy, the patient's struggle to solve his own problems in his own way. Most dreams belong to what Fairbairn has called 'the static internal closed system' (1958), the private world which is the patient's answer to the badness of his real world, and into which he does not want anyone else to intrude. Therefore, when we have learned all that may contribute in a dream to the patient's insight into himself, the dreaming-activity should itself be interpreted as his form of *resistance* to the whole outer world, including the analyst. Otherwise, the handling of dream material may give the patient an excellent chance of maintaining his schizoid compromise of being only half in touch with the analyst. I should, perhaps, say that I am speaking here of dreaming as we come upon it in patients. It cannot be said that *all* dreaming is schizoid and pathological of necessity, even though in actual fact most dreaming is. We may illustrate the problem by comparison with abstract thinking. When we are doing something that presents no difficulty, our thinking is tied to our immediate activity step by step, and is directly orientated to outer reality. The schizoid intellectual, on the other hand, has retreated from direct dealings with the outer world, makes thinking an end in itself, and is 'sicklied o'er with the pale cast of thought'. Thinking has become an interior life carried on in withdrawnness from real object-relations. Most dreaming, and certainly the dreaming of patients, is of that nature.

There is, however, another kind of abstract thinking in which the thinker, having come up against an unsolved problem which halts his activity, 'withdraws' or 'stops to think'. The construction of a scientific theory, or the planning of a battle by a general who is trying to see beforehand what his opponent's moves are likely to be, illustrates this. This is a kind of abstract thinking which is not aimed at 'withdrawal from reality' but at 'mental preparation for further action'. It does not belong to a self-contained 'static internal closed system', but is directed towards action in the real world all the time. There is no reason why a healthy-minded person should not at times do some of his deep inward 'preparation for future living' in dreams. Maybe Jung's view that some dreams have an outlook on the future comes in at this point. But such dreams will not be a disturbing compulsion like the dreams of pathological anxiety.

One patient said: 'I begin to see what you meant when you said dreaming is an alternative policy to psychotherapy. I'm not interested in anything real, because if you're interested in anything you come slap up against people. I can only live my dream and phantasy life. If I were interested in people I could be interested in lots of things. But I'm afraid of people. In my dream world I'm really all by myself and that's what I want to be, to get back to my dream world, a protected world. If I get too deep into it, I may not be able to get back from it, but what will I do if I stop dreaming. My real interests are so few, I've nothing to think or talk about.' I reminded him that he was too afraid of people to have any interests. He replied 'I'm cross with you now'. I said I thought that was because I am a real, not an imaginary person, and called him out of his dream world into the real one. He said 'I'm angry because I feel anything you say is interference in my private world. Dreaming is against psychotherapy and it's against life.'

Sometimes a patient's general behaviour expresses this compromise. One patient found great difficulty in deciding where to sit. She felt the couch was somehow unnatural and isolating, the patient's armchair seemed to be 'too adult' a position. Anywhere too near to me was she felt frightening. Finally she compromised by sitting on the floor fairly close to me but with her back to me, obviously at one and the same time seeking and yet rejecting any relationship with me. Another patient made use of a small stool which she could move closer to or farther away from me, according to which way her anxieties developed. One male patient lay on the couch and wanted me to place my armchair close to it where he could see me, which I did. But after a while he got anxious and needed me to take my chair away to the other side of the room. This 'to-ing and fro-ing' often has to be repeated and analysed many times till its significance really gets home to the patient. Some patients will keep their overcoat on, buttoned up tight, expressing their self-enclosure and withdrawnness from the therapist, and it is a good sign when of their own accord they begin to take it off in the natural way and leave it outside the room.

## Schizoid Compromise in Real Life Which is Not Brought into Analysis

Hold-ups in analysis are sometimes discovered to be related to a successful schizoid 'half in and half out' relationship which the patient is maintaining in real life, but is keeping hidden from the analyst. He fears, of course, that if it is analysed he will have to give it up and so lose the protection of relative stability it gives him. Sometimes one discovers that a patient's entire practical life is conducted in terms of 'brinkmanship' (Guntrip, 1961b). They do not properly 'belong' to anything. However interested they become in any organization, if they are asked to join they stop going. It is amazing how far systematic non-committal can be carried in relationships with friends, organizations, jobs, houses or what not, so that the patient is for ever on the move, like a butterfly alighting for a time and then flitting on. One patient mentioned casually, not thinking that it had any significance, that he never went to the same place twice for a holiday. That this has meaning is clear when it is compared with the opposite fact of the person who goes always to the same safe and familiar place, and would not dream of going anywhere else. The way ordinary life is conducted gives plentiful material for studying the conflicts that go on between needs and fears of close relationship. One female patient at once dislikes all the clothes she buys as soon as she has got them home, however much she felt 'I just must have that dress' so long as it was in the shop. Many patients will not think of mentioning such things as these, because they cannot risk seeing their inner meaning. They slip out 'by accident' as casual asides. One such observation may lead to the opening up of whole areas of successful compromise in which the patient is entrenched.

A not uncommon compromise that is kept out of analysis and operates as a successful defence against real progress is the secret sexual affair. One patient's regular sexual relationship with a married woman provided for the emotional support of his dependent infantile self in a way which saved him from the dangerous close involvement of marriage, but it also saved him from really bringing his fear-ridden infantile inner self into the treatment relationship. The position enabled him to maintain in real life a duplicate version of the schizoid split between the infant and the adult in himself. The infant was so to speak 'kept quiet' by a sexual affair which was completely cut off from all the rest of his life and left his adult hard-working self free to go its own way. Two parts of himself were kept out of relationship with each other. Prostitution and homosexuality are clear cases of schizoid compromise, evading full commitment to the real relationship of marriage. That is why they are hard to cure. Under these conditions clearly no progress is going to be made in analysis. An analogous situation is sometimes met with in the treatment of a medical man. He is always trying to do without the analyst by depending on his own self-prescribed drugs, and so long as any of these schizoid compromises in real life are kept out of analysis, the result is a serious blocking of progress.

## Classical Analysis Utilized as a Defensive Position to Mark Time In

This possibility has already been envisaged in dealing with dream-analysis, but it is a much more far-reaching danger than that. I have been driven to the conclusion that classical analysis, not being orientated to the uncovering of the schizoid problem, inadvertently helps the patient to maintain his defences against it. That is not to say that no benefit can be derived from classical analysis. By classical analysis I mean an analysis based on the theoretical position that the cause of neurosis is the Oedipus Complex, the conflicts over the patient's incestuous desires for the parent of the opposite sex, and fear, guilt and hate for the parent of the same sex. This is the theoretical position which results from the analysis of depression, and it must be regarded as Freud's first great pioneering contribution that he analysed depression and the area of moral and pseudo-moral conflict so exhaustively as to open the way for still deeper probing into the inner life of man. The measure of success which can be obtained by analysis on this basis of theory is illustrated by the example of the male patient who had the 'circular wall' phantasy. He came for treatment for an orthodox depression, a gloomy, angry, guilt bur- dened, resentful but paralysed state of mind. He presented Oedipal material in plenty, dreams of being in bed with mother, of fighting and castrating father, of being castrated himself, of being dragged before courts of justice and condemned for criminal activities. His conscious phantasy, both sexual and as it concerned motor car driving, was sado-masochistic in full detail. Anal material both in dreams and symptoms was plentiful. The analysis of all this did without doubt moderate his depression so that life became practically more comfortable for him, and his work was less interfered with by his moods. At his first session he said 'I feel that I've got a bag of dung inside me which I want to get rid of and can't'. Over a number of years of a long analysis he held to this idea and could not give it up. It stood for the notion that his trouble was something in his personality or make-up which was bad, unclean, which mother (who was a martinet in cleanliness training) would frown on and about which he felt guilty. He clung to this idea long after his depressive moods had faded. It is not, therefore, to be wondered at that he remained a very highly organized obsessional character. His was one of the cases that led me to feel that the results of classical analysis at best were an improvement of the patient's character-pattern in the form of either *a milder and more livable obsessional character*, in which very efficient self-control and self-management was maintained, or else *a milder and somewhat easier schizoid character*, in which the typical schizoid compromise between being in and out of relationships was managed in a sufficiently socialized form to make daily life more possible without risking any dangerously strong feeling being aroused.

This means that classical analysis does not get to the ultimate roots of the psychopathological problems. It treats sexual and aggressive problems as ultimate factors in their own right and does not seek to go behind them by seeing them as defences against the deeper problems of the most primitive fears. Of course, the primitive fears will break through, but it all depends on the interpretations put upon them, as to what will happen to them. If fears are regarded as secondary phenomena, anxiety reactions to bad impulses, then obsessional and schizoid defences will be strengthened and the primary fears buried. In considering the Oedipus Complex, we must note that an Oedipal phantasy is neither on the one hand an adult marriage with real life commitment, nor is it on the other hand frank pregenital infantile dependence. Oedipal phantasies are an end-product of infantile phantasy life and represent a child's struggle to overcome infantile dependence by disguising it in semi-adult form. But the hidden infantile dependence is but thinly disguised, as may be judged from Fairbairn's comment that hysteric genitality is so extremely oral (1954). The Oedipal phantasy life arises when an anxious child withdraws from his outer world, and seeks to compensate for his inability to make progress in dealing with real life, by setting up a schizoid substitute for it inside. We have already seen that this whole inner world phantasy life is basically a defence against the dangers of too drastic withdrawal. The Oedipus Complex always masks poor relationship with parents in reality, and should be analysed in such a way as to lead to the discovery of the hopeless, shut in, detached infantile ego which has given up real object-relations as unobtainable and sought safety in regression into the unconscious. In the case of one patient who had actually been seduced by her father, the physical relationship was certainly a schizoid compromise on his part between his inability to give her a genuinely personal relationship and his prevailing tendency to ignore her altogether. This Oedipal situation had been the patient's one anxiety-burdened hope as a child of meaning anything to her father, and therefore of feeling herself to be something of a person. In analysis she naturally produced a fully developed Oedipal transference, and clung to this stubbornly as a defence against a genuine therapeutic relationship; for this would have meant bringing her disillusioned, apathetic childhood self to a real person for real help. Sexual relationships, both in reality and phantasy, are a common substitute for real personal relations. One bachelor patient who was a quite remote personality with little feeling about anything, described his occasional sexual affairs as due to the need to discharge 'an intermittent biological urge which has nothing to do with me'.

The above example of Oedipal transference suggests that transference analysis on the basis of an impulse-psychology falls into the trap of being doubly schizoid. In the first place it treats the Oedipal phantasy, which is itself a schizoid compromise between real life and flight from reality, as if it were a matter of genuine natural instinctive feelings and desires which are ultimate factors in their own right. Then, having been encouraged to believe that his deceptive Oedipal feelings are genuine loves and hates, the patient is further helped to believe that his feelings for his analyst are not realistic but are transferred from his parents of long ago. In this situation the patient is helped to concentrate attention on the unreal as if it were real; and becomes unable to experience in a frank and undisguised way what his actual and quite realistic feelings for his analyst are. What he is really feeling, without being able to let it emerge plainly, is that he is a frightened, weak and helpless small child needing to depend on his analyst for protection and support, while at the same time he is afraid he will be ridiculed and rejected if he shows this openly, and is forestalling the rejection by rejecting himself. His attention is kept diverted from all this, if he is allowed to believe that his Oedipus Complex is the ultimate root of his neurosis. In that case a schizoid compromise is maintained by unwitting collusion of analyst and patient.

It must, however, be recognized that what I have spoken of as 'classical Oedipal analysis' is much less a specific entity in practice today, than it may appear to be in theory. The work of Mrs Klein has forced analysis ever deeper into the pre-Oedipal, pre-genital levels. It is true that she carried the term 'Oedipus Complex' back into far earlier periods than that covered by Freud's original use of the term. In practice, her work has taken clinical analysis deeper down than the classical Oedipal level, into the earliest paranoid and schizoid problems. Here we are not dealing with the child struggling with the problems of socialization in a multi-personal family group; but with the primary two-person mother-child relationship in which the earliest ego-splitting and creation of internal objects occurs.

The position, however, is still confused because, as Balint points out, theory lags behind practice. Mrs Klein imposed her new object-relations developments on the more or less unaltered classical psychobiology of Freud. She did not, as Fairbairn did, seek to revise basic theory adequately to take into account the shift from depressive to schizoid problems. Writing in 1949, some six years after Fairbairn's revisionary work, Balint still found theory tied to 'the physiological or biological bias' rather than 'the object-relation bias', and based on the data of depressions and obsessional neurosis rather than on hysteric-paranoid-schizoid phenomena (Balint 1952, pp. 226–231), and he was still calling for 'a transition between the old theories and the new ones' (p. 231). So far Fairbairn alone has attempted this in a full and systematic way. What I have said about the possibility of using analysis on the basis of the pure classical psychobiological Oedipal theory as an unwitting support for resistance, simply reemphasizes the need for theory to catch up with practice. It is an important sign of progress that practice is already so far ahead of theory in this matter. It is wise, however, to stress this, in view of Balint's reference to 'the unconscious gratification [that] lies hidden behind the undisturbed use of accustomed ways of thinking', which 'is best shown by the often quite irrational resistance that almost every analyst puts up at the suggestion that he might learn to use or even only to understand a frame of reference considerably different from his own' (p. 232). Such a state of affairs can hardly fail to be a drag on the wheels of therapeutic practice. It would appear to be time that resistance was overcome to considering the schizoid, as opposed to the depressive, 'frame of reference' in the construction of theory, so that theory can become a better support to therapy.

## THE NECESSITY OF THE SCHIZOID COMPROMISE AS AN INTERMEDIATE PHASE TO THE EMERGENCE OF THE REGRESSED EGO

Though I have sought to show how this need to set up a middle position, in which the patient is neither completely isolated nor yet fully committed to object-relationships, is the cause, in general, of psychotherapeutic stalemate and blocked analysis, it must also be added that this situation should not be too ruthlessly exposed. It is, in fact, often a necessary stage through which the patient has to pass on his way to facing at long last, first his frightening sense of fundamental isolation; and then the fears of the real good relationships which alone can heal his early hurt and liberate his devitalized infantile ego for healthy and vigorous growth. The emergence of the ultimate withdrawn infantile self is the hardest of all ordeals for the patient.

In previous papers (1960, 1961b, 1962) I have given reasons for the view that, in proportion to the severity of the patient's illness, a definite part of his total self is specifically withdrawn into the unconscious in a state of extreme infantile regression. This 'Regressed Ego' is the headquarters of all the most serious fears, and it feels a powerful need for complete protected passive dependence in which recuperation can take place and a rebirth of an active ego be achieved. Nevertheless, patients experience the most intense fear as this Regressed Ego draws near to consciousness. It brings with it a sense of utter and hopeless aloneness and yet also a fear of the good-object relationship as smothering. The patient feels that his need for some measure of regressed dependence on his therapist will involve him in the loss of self-determination, of independence and even of individuality itself. He cannot feel it as the starting-point of new growth in security. In truth, the need to regress cannot be taken lightly. In the most ill it may involve hospitalization. In others I find that sufficient regression can be experienced in sessions while the active self is kept going outside. In some other cases, it seems that specific regression is not needed, and 'withdrawing' tendencies can be reversed in a normal transference-analysis.

The schizoid problem and its compromise solutions show, however, where the ultimate difficulties of psychotherapy lie, and just how difficult it is and why. The patient *cannot* easily and quickly abandon his inadequate solutions or defences, for what he feels to be the uncertain promise of a real solution, bought at the price of encountering such severe anxieties. He can only do so by easy stages, and meanwhile must use whatever schizoid compromises between accepting and rejecting treatment as he can. In truth he endures other anxieties by holding on to his own attempts to carry on in his own way, which are as severe as the fears of over-dependence and far more destructive. But since the real 'cure' *seems* to involve sinking his own personality in passive dependence on that of another person, we must admit that the patient is confronted with a formidable prospect. Often, if he could not effect some compromise relationship, he would have to break off treatment. I once had a patient who had previously and consciously spent several years *using* psychiatrists as 'someone to argue with', giving them no chance to help her because she felt that the degree of dependence involved would be too humiliating. It would take a major cultural revolution to create an atmosphere in which patients might find it easier to accept psychotherapy; a cultural atmosphere from which not only Suttie's 'taboo on tenderness' had disappeared, but also its deeper implication, the 'taboo on weakness'. Then, perhaps, illness of the mind could be treated with the same acceptance of the need for 'healing in a state of passive recuperation' as is already accorded to illness of the body.

Yet the final difficulty is in the patient's own mental make-up. Two patients of mine needed to accept a regressive illness which involved hospitalization. One, with a gentler nature who made no difficulty about accepting help, 'gave in' to the situation thoroughly and made an excellent recovery. He came out to return to work straight away and, with diminishing frequency of analysis, maintained his improvement. The other, an obsessional, hard-driving and at times aggressive worker who could not be tolerant to himself, could not surrender his struggle to drive himself on. He came out of hospital, having got over the acute crisis, but still with a lot of tension and conflict. His own comment was: 'I couldn't make the best use of hospital. I couldn't give in. I felt I had to be adult and keep myself active.' If we turn from purely theoretical possibilities to simply practical ones, especially where it is not possible for the patient to have a very long analysis, we may have to accept a useful schizoid compromise. If the patient feels a very intense need to safeguard his independence and freedom for self-determination, which he feels to be compromised by accepting help, we must recognize that the solution of this problem will take a long time. If for any reasons the patient cannot go through with such a long analysis, it may well be that he needs to be helped to accept the fact that he cannot force himself beyond a certain point in making human relationships, and must find out what compromises between being too involved and too isolated work best for him. Yet I am sure that, given time and favourable circumstances, this problem can be resolved in psycho-analytical therapy.

We must certainly concentrate our best efforts in research to this end, for the feeling of angry frustration, of being caught in a trap which is their own mental make-up, of being entangled in a web of difficulties and only becoming more and more entangled the more they struggle to get free, is a very serious problem with some patients. The naturally active, energetic and capable persons who cannot succeed, or be contented, in becoming cold, emotionally neutralized intellectuals, and yet cannot effect stable and happy human relationships and get on with living, can reach a point of volcanic eruption. They cannot stand the utter frustration of their inability to escape from their own need for compromise, half in and half out, solutions. If such a person has no understanding and reliable therapist, the result can be tragedy for himself, for others, or for both. It is well for him if he has the safeguard of a genuine therapeutic relationship at such a time, which offers him a chance to grow some deep level security on the basis of which he can find a way out of his trap.

# REFERENCES

Balint, M. (1952). *Primary Love and Psycho-analytic Technique.* London: Hogarth Press.

Fairbairn, W. R. D. (1954). Obsevations on the nature of hysterical states. *British Journal of Medical Psychology* 27(3):105–125.

———— (1958). On the nature and aims of psycho-analytical treatment. *International Journal of Psycho-Analysis* 29(5):374–385.

Freud, S. (1923). *The Ego and the Id.* London: Hogarth Press. New York: Norton.

———— (1938). *Outline of Psycho-Analysis.* London: Hogarth Press.

Guntrip, H. (1952). A study of Fairbairn's theory of schizoid reactions. *British Journal of Medical Psychology* 25(2, 3):86–103.

_____ (1960). Ego-weakness and the hard core of the problem of psychotherapy. *British Journal of Medical Psychology* 33(3):163–184.

_____ (1961a). *Personality Structure and Human Interaction*. London: Hogarth Press.

_____ (1961b). The schizoid process, regression and the struggle to preserve an ego. *British Journal of Medical Psychology* 34(3, 4):223.

_____ (1962). Manic-depression in the light of the schizoid process. *International Journal of Psycho-Analysis* 43(2, 3).

Laing, R. D. (1959). *The Divided Self*. London: Tavistock Publications.

# 9

# THE INFANT IN THE PATIENT: A UNIQUE CENTRE OF MEANINGFUL EXPERIENCE[1]

THE TITLE OF THIS PAPER[2] may well appear pretentiously large in scope. It is best, therefore, to make it clear at the outset that I mean simply to convey the notion of tracing developments in psychodynamic theory to see how they bear on the only partially solved problem of psychotherapy. This became a particular interest of mine from about 1950 as my clinical concern came to centre specially in the study of schizoid problems. The results of this work began to emerge by 1960, and throughout I had found Fairbairn's formulations in the field of theory invaluable. Two concepts, the *Ego* and the *Schizoid Process*, came to dominate the enquiry. They at once suggest a contrast to a psychodynamic theory based on the very different concepts of *Instincts* and *Depression*, as in the classic Freudian theory. Nevertheless, the fact that in the 1920's Freud himself turned his interest from instincts to the analysis of the ego, shows that what we have to consider is not two opposed views, but a development which has been going on in psychodynamic research for some forty years. For this development Freud himself provided the initial impetus and it arose logically out of his own earlier work.

It may be well at this point to pause and reflect on the nature and place of theory in our work. All are agreed that we do not interpret to patients in theoretical terms, nor do we seek to fit the patient into a pre-determined theoretical scheme. Were we to do so, we would learn nothing new from our clinical work. This error in technique is, probably, not in fact always avoided. We must use our theoretical concepts to guide our thinking in trying to understand the patient, and therapists

---

1. This [chapter] is expanded from a paper read to the medical section, B. Ps. S., June 27, 1962, as a summary of my view of recent developments. It therefore, of necessity, refers to some already published clinical material which was important in shaping the point of view presented.

2. The paper's original title is "Psychodynamic Theory and the Problem of Psycho-therapy."

obviously do not find it easy to let what the patient presents modify the concepts they are used to and have acquired a vested emotional interest in. Nevertheless, human problems are still so far from solution that we cannot afford to become theoretically static. *Concepts* are most useful at the stage at which they are being formed. They represent the intellectual effort to clarify and formulate new insights which are emerging in the thick of the pressure of clinical work. For a time they act as signposts pointing the way in the right direction for the next advance: but concepts date. By the time further new experience has begun to gather, previous concepts have become stereotyped and too rigid, and they then act as a barrier to fresh thinking. This has been the fate of some of Freud's concepts, in particular those of instinct, libido, aggression (as an innate drive), the id, the super-ego, the Oedipus Complex. It is now becoming clear that they mark stages in an advancing psychodynamic enquiry. Freud opened the way to still deeper levels where new insights and new concepts are called for. To try to work on new material with nothing but the old conceptual tools retards deeper understanding.

Psychoanalysis has been carried, as Freud himself was, by clinical pressures to ever deeper levels of psychic life, so that it may be said in general that we have no choice now but to focus our thinking more on the problems of ego development in the first year than on the Oedipal problems, of later infancy. Mrs Klein's attempt to read back the three-person Oedipal problems, dated at 3–4 years in the classic theory, into the first-year two-person problems, was not generally accepted, but was eloquent proof that a change in basic theoretical standpoint was developing. The process of change has been at work ever since Freud turned definitely to ego analysis in the 1920's, but of all the analysts who have contributed to the slow furthering of this change, so far only one, Fairbairn, has made a specific attempt to think out the nature of the fundamental reorientation of theory that is going on. He would be the last person to wish that his contribution to theory should, in turn, become a fixed and stereotyped scheme blocking the way to further insight. Nevertheless, he has formulated certain basic concepts which appear to be as necessary for the intelligible ordering of our field of knowledge at this stage, as were Freud's Oedipal concepts and his structural terms at earlier stages. Fairbairn's work is no more a mere proposed change in terminology, as some critics suggest, than was Freud's.

I hold no particular brief for any conceptual terminology as final. Terms are only useful tools to be discarded when we find better ones. No doubt in fifty years time wholesale revision will have taken place. The term 'libidinal', though useful, is far from satisfactory as standing for the fundamental life-drive in the human being to become a 'person'. Its historical associations are too narrowing for it to be adequate to this new orientation that we have now to take into account. If the term 'libidinal' is revised, all Fairbairn's terms will have to be revised. Meanwhile, till someone suggests a better term than 'libidinal', I feel compelled to say that, once mastered, I have found Fairbairn's terminology closer to clinical realities than any other, and too valuable not to be used. Balint writes: 'How much unconscious gratification lies hidden behind the undisturbed use of accustomed ways of thinking . . . is best shown by the often quite irrational resistance that almost every analyst puts up at the suggestion that he might learn to use or even only to understand a frame of reference considerably different from his own' (1952, p. 232). I shall seek in what follows to place Fairbairn's work in what seems to me to be its proper position and context in the march of psychodynamic theory, to show in what way I found it invaluable in my own particular study of schizoid problems, and to present it as a challenge to willingness to think, where necessary, in new terms as new insights develop. At the International Congress of Psychoanalysis in Edinburgh in 1961, one speaker objected to Winnicott asking us to use 'new terms such as "impinge-ment", etc.'. But the time seems to have come when progress will be blocked if we persist in trying to pour supplies of new wine into old bottles that are too small.

My own interest in this whole matter was aroused when, around 1950, three patients, each in their own way presented the same problem.

The first was a middle-aged, unmarried engineer running his own business; well educated, who sought analysis of his own accord for attacks of guilt-burdened depression. He had some six years of orthodox analysis whose content would be familiar to every analyst. He talked out his early loveless family life, his submissive-ness to his egotistical mother and fear and hate of his violent father, sibling jealousies and adolescent rebellion. He produced Oedipal and Castration dreams, sado-masochistic fantasies, genital, anal and oral; guilt and punishment reactions. A classic psychoanalytic text-book could be written out of his material. Throughout he remained a conscientious hard-working obsessional personality, with all his emotions under tremendous internal control. His personality type did not change but he improved greatly as compared with his original crippling depressions. His ego defences, we may say, were modified and he felt more free to work. He summed up his position thus: 'I'm very much better. I feel I've cleared all the outlying areas of my neurosis, but I feel I've come up against a circular wall with no doors or windows and too high to see over. I go round and round it and have no idea what is inside. I know there's something I'm doing that blocks further analysis and I don't know what it is. It's difficult to let anything more out. I've got to keep fit to run my business.' Here, apparently, was *a closely guarded hurt and hidden part of his inner self into which neither I, nor even his own conscious self, was allowed to intrude.* He once dreamed of going down into an underground passage and coming to a halt at a locked door marked 'hidden treasure'.

The second patient, an older, very ill professional woman whose doctor said she would never work again, had a similar background and normal Oedipal analysis during which she returned to work, suffered no further breakdown, and was able to work till she qualified for a full pension. She then seemed to stick, and like the first patient held her gains but made no further progress. At that point she dreamed of walking along a road and coming up against a huge wall. There was no way of getting forward and she did not know what lay on the other side. Her comment was 'I've got to go on, if you can stand it'. She clearly felt that if she succeeded it would mean a difficult time for both of us. Here again was *this clear-cut unconscious knowledge of an inaccessible cut-off part of the inner personal life into which the patient seemed unable and afraid to penetrate*, but which had to be opened up to reach a real 'cure'.

The third patient, a medical man in middle life, presented the same theme in a different way. This was the case with which I opened my 1961 paper on 'The schizoid problem and regression'. His presenting symptom, an embarrassing and active preoccupation with breasts, faded out under analysis only to be replaced by powerful phantasies of retirement from active living into some impregnable stronghold isolated from the outer world. Like the other patients he carried on his active professional life. This then must have indicated *the drastic withdrawal from the outer world of a specialized part of his personality existing passively inside the fortress, the impassable wall*. These patients were markedly schizoid, detached, shut in, had great difficulty in human relationships, and would feel alone and out of touch in a group.

At this point I tried to write a paper on 'The Schizoid Citadel' but could not arrive at any satisfying conclusion. Therefore, as a starting point for enquiry, I made a clinical study of 'Fairbairn's theory of schizoid reactions' (Guntrip 1952) and set out, first, to gather fresh clinical material on schizoid problems, and secondly, to survey the development of psychodynamic theory from Freud to the American 'Culture Pattern' writers, and to Mrs Klein and Fairbairn, to see what pointers were emerging to the solution of this problem. The result of this historical study I presented in the book *Personality Structure and Human Interaction* (1961a). On the clinical side, I owe everything to a group of schizoid patients whose variety was fascinating: a biologist, a communist, a hospital sister, a university lecturer, a grandmother in her fifties, a young borderline schizophrenic wife, a social worker who had had a paranoid schizophrenic breakdown, a young middle-aged mother who was also a language teacher, an outstandingly successful but most unhappy business man, and so on. Their treatment always seemed to move ultimately beyond the range of the classic psychoanalytical phenomena, the conflicts over sex, aggression, guilt and depression. All patients began by producing this kind of material, which occupied analysis in the first few years. For what came after that I did not find much help, except in the interpretation of details, in the literature on schizoid problems. It seemed to lack intrinsic connexion with the existing psychoanalytical theory of Oedipal and depressive problems. I had to let impressions accumulate, and only in the last three years have these begun, as I feel, to disclose some definite pattern.

*One strongly emerging theoretical trend* provided the necessary standing-ground for thinking. In 1949 Balint called for a transition from a physiological and biological bias to an object-relations bias in theory (1952). That was exactly the major trend that stood out in the historical survey. It was visible in the work of Americans such as Horney, Fromm and Sullivan, though more from the social and 'culture-pattern' point of view. As early as 1942–44 Fairbairn made a fundamental revision of theory on exactly the lines Balint called for, from the endopsychic rather than the cultural viewpoint (1952). Here and elsewhere were the signs of a growing and widespread consensus of thought which can be expressed in several different but parallel and related ways. Theory has been moving from concentration on the parts to attention to the whole, from the biological to the properly psychological, from instinct vicissitudes to ego development, from instinct gratification to ego maintenance, and from the depressive level of impulse management to the deeper schizoid level where the foundations of a *whole* personality are, or are not, laid. Throughout, the concepts of *the Ego* and *the Schizoid Process* became ever more dominant.

*Classic psychoanalytical theory is a moral psychology* of the struggle to direct and control innate antisocial but discrete and separate instinctive drives of sex and aggression, by means of guilt. This, when it produces too drastic repression instead of 'sublimation', leads to the mental paralysis of internalized aggression, self-punishment and depression. When Freud turned to ego analysis, however, he started lines of enquiry which were destined to lead to a quite different orientation; for schizoid problems turn out to be, not problems of the gratification or control of instincts, but problems of ego splitting and the struggle to recover and preserve a whole adequate ego or self with which to face life. This newer type of theory had much to say about the problems of my patients who were unconsciously guarding their secret schizoid citadel in which some vital part of their total self apparently lay buried, hidden and lost to use. Impulse psychology had little enlightenment to offer on this.

Here I must record my agreement with Fairbairn that the term 'psychobiological' is an illegitimate hybrid which confuses two different disciplines. It is like that earlier hybrid 'physiological psychology' as set forth in McDougall's book (1905). It was just physiology and not psychology at all. We study the one whole of the human being on different levels of abstraction for scientific purposes. Biology is one level, psychology is another. Each deals with phenomena, organic or psychic, which the other cannot handle. When it comes to *therapy*, knowledge from *all* disciplines must be taken into account. We do not suppose ourselves to be dealing with two separate entities, one called body and the other mind, but neither can we study such a complex whole as if it were a kind of Irish stew in which everything is lumped together in one pot. We must abstract its main distinguishable aspects and stick consistently to what we select to study.

*The business of psychodynamic research is with that aspect of the whole man which we call the motivated and meaningful life of the growing 'person' and his difficulties and developments in object relationships with other persons.* A dynamic psychology of the 'person' is not an instinct theory but an ego theory in which instincts are not entities per se but functions of the ego. The way an instinctive capacity operates is an expression of the state of the ego. The trend of psychoanalytic theory moves steadily in that direction. Instinct theory per se becomes more and more useless in clinical work, and ego theory more and more relevant. Outside the sphere of pure psychodynamics, I would think that the philosopher J. MacMurray has given the coup de grâce to instinct theory in the study of human persons, in his *Gifford Lectures*, Vol. 2, 'Persons in relation'. The most important single subject of investigation on all sides is the earliest stages of ego growth, as in the work of the Kleinians, Fairbairn, Winnicott, and researches into the psychodynamics of schizophrenia. The classical Oedipal, social, sexual and aggressive conflicts are dropping into their place as aspects of the internal, sado-masochistic, self-exhausting struggle of *an already divided self* to maintain psychic defences against ego collapse.

I have thus come to feel that the first great task which confronted Freud in his pioneer exploration was that of analysing the area of moral and pseudo-moral conflict. This had hitherto comprised man's whole traditional account of his nature and troubles; and it blocked the way to more radical understanding. Freud did analyse it so exhaustively that he opened the way to the deeper level hidden beneath it. The result of Freud's work is that unrealistic traditional ideas about children have been replaced by an ever deeper knowledge of the very earliest infantile fears and ego weakness. Freud actually took over the traditional popular and philosophical psychology of Plato and St Paul as his starting point. St Paul was content with a dualism of the 'law of the mind' and the 'law of the members' in inevitable warfare. Plato gave us the trichotomy which the Western world has accepted right up to Freud and the present day. Human nature comprised a lustful beast, a spirited lion and a rational man, the id, the super-ego and the ego. Plato's many-headed beast of the lusts and passions of the flesh and St Paul's 'law of the members' became the powerful anti-social instincts of sex and aggression in the id. Plato's charioteer of reason and St Paul's 'law of the mind' became the controlling ego with its scientific reason. Just as Plato's 'reason' made an ally of the lion, the fighting principle, turning it against the beast to enforce control, so Freud envisaged the ego working with the sadistic super-ego to turn aggression inwards against the self, and showed how pathological guilt produced depression.

Freud used the traditional philosophical moral psychology of impulse control, but he used it in a wholly new way, to guide an original and factual clinical analysis of the detailed mental processes involved in man's experience of moral and pseudo-moral conflict. All this was analysed so exhaustively that it represents a reasonably completed scientific investigation of man's sado-masochistic struggle to civilize the recalcitrant impulse-life he finds within himself. Yet Freud failed to answer or even to ask the crucial question. Since man is without doubt social by nature, how does it come about that he feels such anti-social impulses so often? Why do men have anti-social impulses? Freud, like all his predecessors, simply assumed that they were innate, that in man's nature there was an unresolvable contradiction of good and evil. This is the traditional view of man in our culture.

However, Freud's analysis of moral conflict unwittingly revealed the fact that this is not the whole of, nor even the deepest element in, the psychic experience of human beings. In fact, man's age-old conviction that all his troubles come from his possession of mighty if nearly uncivilizable instincts of his animal nature, turns out to be our greatest rationalization and self-deception. We have preferred to boost our egos by the belief that even if we are *bad*, we are at any rate *strong* in the possession of 'mighty instincts'. Men have not wanted to see the truth that we distort our instincts into anti-social drives in our struggle to suppress the fact that deep within our make-up we are tied to a weak, fear-ridden infantile ego that we never completely outgrow. Thus Fairbairn regarded 'infantile dependence', not the 'Oedipus Complex' as the cause of neurosis. The Oedipus Complex is a problem of 'instincts'. Infantile dependence is a problem of 'ego weakness'. Depression is the psychology of badness. The schizoid problem opens up the psychology of our fundamental weakness, and human beings would rather be bad than weak. This shift in the centre of gravity in psychodynamic theory will enforce a radical reassessment of all philosophical, moral, educational and religious views of human nature.

Psychoanalytic practice seems to be in advance of psychoanalytic theory in this matter. In my paper on 'The manic-depressive problem in the light of the schizoid process' (1962) I traced how, in the 1960 'Symposium on depression' in the *International Journal of Psycho-Analysis*, the papers oscillated between two opposite poles of this complex illness. Viewed as *classic depression* it was explained by reference to ambivalent object relations and guilt over sexual and aggressive drives. Yet there appeared to be another aspect of it characterized as *regression*, which needed to be explained rather by ego splitting, arrested ego development, weakness, lack of self-fulfilment, and apathy. But depression and regression were not clearly related, though Zetzel remarked that in the modern view of depression the significant new concept was that of the 'ego'. It is, however, hopeless to deal with ego psychology in terms of instinct theory. The problems of ego psychology are those of loss of unity and ego weakness, depersonalization, the sense of unreality, lack of a proper sense of personal identity, of the terror some patients experience of feeling so 'far away' and 'shut in' that they feel they'll never get back in touch again. These phenomena can only be dealt with by a theory based firmly on the analysis of the schizoid processes of withdrawal to the inner world under the impact of primary fears. It is in this region that the uncertain beginnings of ego development are to be found.

So far only Fairbairn has sought systematically to re-orientate theory from a depressive to a schizoid foundation. Nevertheless, the whole drift of psychoanalysis today is in that direction. In a recent private communication Fairbairn stated that the internal situation described in terms of object splitting and ego splitting 'represents a basic schizoid position which is more fundamental than the depressive position described by Melanie Klein. . . . A theory of the personality conceived in terms of object-relations is in contrast to one conceived in terms of instincts and their vicissitudes.' Freud's structural terms, id, super-ego, ego, give an account of classic depression and moral conflict. Fairbairn's structural terms, libidinal ego, antilibidinal ego, central ego, give an account of the schizoid process and the loss of the primary unity of the self.

As I see it there have been four stages in the development of psychoanalytic theory: (1) *Freud's original instinct theory*, which enabled a penetrating analysis of moral and pseudomoral conflict to be made. This led to (2) *Freud's ego analysis.* Because this remained tied to instinct theory, it could not give more than a superficial account of the ego, as a utilitarian apparatus of impulse control, an instrument of adaptation to external reality, a means of perceptual consciousness, etc. Before an adequate theory of *the ego as a real personal self* could be worked out, a third stage had to come about. (3) *Mrs Klein had to explore the psychology of the object as psychically internalized to become a factor in ego development.* She explored the psychology of internal object relations as thoroughly as Freud had explored that of impulse management. Mrs Klein's work is 'an object-relations theory with emphasis on the object' and it led to a fourth stage, (4) *Fairbairn's 'object-relations theory with emphasis on the ego'*. Fairbairn's primary interest had always been in the ego, as seen in an early paper on a patient's dream-personifications of herself. But he made no progress with this till Mrs Klein's work made its impact on him, as he is the first to acknowledge. Now, his work brings out clearly that the importance of the object is not primarily that of being a 'means of instinctual gratification'; this gives only a psychology of instinct vicissitudes. The importance of the object lies in the fact that it is 'a necessity for ego development'; this gives us a psychology of ego vicissitudes, ego differentiations, splittings and what not. He brought Mrs Klein's 'object-relations theory' back full circle to ego theory again, but this time not to Freud's superficial ego theory, but to *a fundamental ego theory which makes psychodynamics a genuine theory of a real self or person, a unique centre of meaningful experience growing in the medium of personal relationships.* Fairbairn is, of course, far from being the only analyst to see the need to orientate theory and therapy afresh to the true selfhood of the whole person. Winnicott writes that the goal of therapy is: 'the shift of the operational centre from the false self to the true self. . . . That which proceeds from the true self feels real' (p. 292, 1958). Again: 'In favourable cases there follows at last a new sense of self in the patient and a sense of the progress that means true growth' (pp. 289–290). Winnicott's theory of the true and false self is likewise a theory of ego splitting and deals with phenomena that Freud's structural terms take no account of. Fairbairn, however, is the only analyst who has taken up the task of the *overall* revision of theory from this point of view. The result is an impressive intellectual achievement.

In the communication quoted Fairbairn regards separation anxiety as the earliest and original anxiety, and as the basic cause of the schizoid process of flight or withdrawal of part of the now split ego from contact with the outer world. There are several causes of separation anxiety. Fairbairn earlier stressed that unsatisfied love needs become dangerous and the infant draws back. Winnicott stresses the infant's direct fear of the 'impingement' of a bad object, and the infant finding himself simply deserted, neglected. However caused, the danger of separation is that the infant, starting life with a primitive and quite undeveloped ego, just cannot stand the loss of his object. He cannot retain his primitive wholeness and develop a sense of identity and selfhood without an object relation. *Separation anxiety then is a pointer to the last and worst fear, fear of loss of the ego itself, of depersonalization and the sense of unreality.* The reason why patients hold on with such tenacity to their Kleinian inner world of internal bad objects, and their Freudian inner world of Oedipal conflicts over sex and aggression, is that they have so weakened their *external* object relations by early schizoid withdrawal inside, that they are compelled to maintain a world of internal phantasied objects to keep their ego in being at all.

It seems to me that conflicts over sex, aggression and guilt are, in the last analysis, used as defences against depersonalization, and the patient is reluctant to give them up. Patients will try to go back to these classic conflicts unless we keep them well analysed, rather than face the terrors of realizing how small, weak and radically cut off, shut in and unreal they feel at bottom. A dream of a male patient of fifty illustrates this. 'I was engaged with someone (undoubtedly his tyrannical father) in a tremendous fight for life. I defended myself so vigorously that he suddenly stopped fighting altogether. I then immediately felt let down, disappointed and quite at a loss, and thought "Oh! I didn't bargain for this".' His real life was conducted very much in terms of rationalized aggression, opposing authority, attacking abuses, defending his independence, all really in the interests of keeping his insecure ego in being. He couldn't keep going without the help of a fight. Another patient said: 'If I don't get angry with my employees, I'm too timid to face them. I feel some energy when I'm angry, otherwise I feel just a nobody.' *That is the basic problem in psychopathology, the schizoid problem of feeling a nobody, of never having grown an adequate feeling of a real self.* If we go far enough it always emerges in some degree from behind the classic conflicts. I suspect this to be more true of all human beings than we like to know, and that the chronic aggression which seems to be the hallmark of 'man' is but a veneer over basic ego weakness.

## PSYCHOTHERAPY

When we turn from theory to consider its bearings on therapy, this conclusion hardly makes the task of psychotherapy look any easier. In my group of patients I began to observe the emergence of a fairly consistent pattern of three stages of treatment, which we may call the stages of (1) Oedipal Conflict, (2) Schizoid Compromise and (3) Regression and Regrowth.

*In the first stage* whatever diagnostic label might be stuck on the patient, hysteric, obsessional, anxiety state, etc., the first few years of analysis dealt with the problems of the child struggling to adapt and maintain himself in an unhelpful family situation widening out into the social environment. This is broadly the 'Classic Oedipal analysis' of defences and conflicts concerning ambivalent object relations of love and hate, primarily with parents and then transferred into wider areas of living. As symptoms faded, the underlying conflicts over sex, aggression and guilt would emerge and classic depression have to be dealt with. Such analysis would lead to marked improvements which were very welcome, yet left the feeling of something else unspecified still to be dealt with. The analysis produced valuable but not final results just because it dealt with defences, not causes. Thus ten years ago a man came to me very depressed after the death of his father. He said 'I can afford time and money for 100 sessions'. I advised him to spread them over two years since growth is a matter of time. In addition to his depression, he was in a rut in his work and his childless marriage was hardly happy. At the end of his 100 sessions he was definitely improved. He had got out of his rut at work, taken a better job and was doing well. He and his wife had faced their problem and adopted a child. I heard from him recently that he was carrying on well. I had told him that his whole problem could not be cleared up in 100 sessions and he accepted that. He said he still had occasional moods but felt he understood and could manage them, and his work and home life were satisfactory. That is a worthwhile result if not a complete one. In practice, the greater part, certainly of short-term psychotherapy, is on this level. In the early days of psychoanalysis a year was adequate for treatment. Fairbairn once said to me: 'The more we analyse the ego, the longer analyses become.' I found that the initial Oedipal analysis usually led on to:

*A second stage* of marking time on the ground gained, retaining improvements by effecting a more rational control, i.e. a modified and more reasonable obsessional or schizoid character. If maintained, this may well represent, for all practical purposes, a cure: in fact it is itself a schizoid compromise in varying degrees. The patient does not do without personal relations, yet cannot wholly do with them, or cannot stand their being too close and involving. He takes up a 'half in and half out' position in which he hopes to remain relatively undisturbed. Like the patient cited, he may leave analysis and with luck remain stable. There is no doubt that such relative stabilization is possible, and can and does work in a number of cases. If a patient *can* stabilize to that extent without going deeper, it is not good to probe deeper. Nevertheless, not all analyses can terminate at that stage. The patient may leave and later encounter too severe real-life stresses which break him down again and bring him back to treatment. Or he may stick at analysis without really making use of it, seeking to make analysis itself his compromise solution, gaining some support from sessions but not changing much. This may break down; the patient feels frustrated, leaves in a resentful mood, and finds that his resentment of the now absent analyst is quite a useful if hardly constructive motivation helping to keep his ego functioning. Lastly, the patient may stick at analysis and allow his compromises to be analysed till slowly he gets beneath them. Whether he has returned to analysis with a second breakdown or carried on doggedly till the deepest levels were reached, the result is much the same.

The way in which the schizoid compromise solution is attempted and is liable to break down is best illustrated by two actual cases. A male patient in the early fifties, who had decided to end a long analysis and move to another city to start life afresh said 'The height of my ambition now is to get through life without trouble. It's not that bad an aim, a bit negative; it has a certain vegetable feel about it, a kind of blankness. Under such circumstances you don't feel anything much at all. That's a preferable state to feeling awful. Big changes have gone on in me really. It's a tremendous relief not to feel so frightened, nor so excited in a bad way. Yet it feels also like losing something.' The last remark showed that he was aware that this was not a final, positive result, but a compromise solution aiming at maintaining improvements. It lacked the vital sense of reality in living.

How a well-established compromise solution can break down is seen in the case of a woman of 48 years. She had recovered complete physical health after a long analysis, and at a late age took a university course to qualify for a profession, established her independence of parents, got a flat and a car of her own and made all the progress it was possible to make along those lines. The fact that this welcome improvement and independence also included a schizoid compromise, protecting her from any real involvement in personal relations, became clear when she suddenly panicked at the prospect of marriage. In one session she said: 'I think I'll be best keeping my freedom and independence; my job and money, flat and car, and not feeling too deeply about anything. I don't want to feel love or hate. If I feel I become a baby. If I skate over the surface and don't feel much, I can be more grown up, and in a way I enjoy life better then, especially driving my car. Really I'm a child and don't want to do anything, I only want to go home to mother and father. I picture our family living on a desert island and never going out of it. I can't really face life. I never wanted to do a job, only stay at home and do housework with mother. But I know they can't live for ever and I've got to think out a different way of life. Perhaps really I'll drift into marriage, though with my eyes open, and make something of it.' The challenge of marriage, however, made it increasingly difficult for her to maintain her improvement based on schizoid compromise, and she was pushed beyond it.

*The third stage.* Here problems are now quite different, specifically schizoid rather than depressed. One begins to lay bare the terrified infant in retreat from life and hiding in his inner citadel, the problem of my three patients of twelve years ago. Fairbairn writes: 'Such an individual provides the most striking evidence of a conflict between an extreme reluctance to abandon infantile dependence and a desperate longing to renounce it; and it is at once fascinating and pathetic to watch the patient, like a timid mouse, alternately creeping out of the shelter of his hole to peep at the world of outer objects and then beating a hasty retreat' (1952, p. 39). Two more recent cases were decisive for me. (i) A married woman of fifty, during a prolonged hysteric phase, dreamed of a hungry, greedy, clamouring baby hidden under her apron, the symbolic representation of an active orally sadistic infant who had to be kept under control or none would like her. When she had worked through that level she became markedly schizoid, quiet, shut-in, silent, finding it hard to maintain any interest in life, beginning each session by saying 'You've gone miles away from me'. She now produced a phantasy of a dead, or else a sleeping baby buried alive, in her womb, and felt that she had a lump inside her tummy as if pregnant. (ii) The second patient was a male who had an earlier period of analysis of exceptionally sado-masochistic oral material and intense conflicts over both sexual and aggressive impulses which he controlled with great difficulty. He reached a stage where his original guilt-depression faded away and he could carry on as a successful if obsessionally hardworking professional man. Then an unusually severe run of family troubles broke him down again. When he returned to treatment he was plainly struggling against a powerful regressive drive, feeling exhausted, and having phantasies of an infant wrapped away in a warm and comfortable womb.

It was this material that first suggested to me that what Fairbairn calls the *libidinal ego*, corresponding to the libidinal aspect of the Freudian 'id', the dependent needy infant, itself undergoes a further and final split. It is already split off and isolated in the personality by repression, by the Freudian ego and super-ego, or what Fairbairn calls the central ego and antilibidinal ego. To this internal persecution the infantile ego produces a double reaction of 'anger and fight' and also 'fear and flight'. This leads to the deepest ego split of all, into an active oral ego and a helpless regressed ego as a final hidden danger. Psychoanalysis has taken full account of the 'ego vicissitudes' of anger and the aggressive or fighting impulses in face of threat. It has not taken the same full account of the 'ego vicissitudes' of fear and flight from life, and so has never satisfactorily fitted regression into the conceptual framework. In practice, regression is usually treated as a nuisance to be checked. I believe regressive trends are in fact derived from a structurally specific part of the total self which is deeply withdrawn, the schizoid ego par excellence, the hidden self in the schizoid citadel. It has undergone a two-stage withdrawal, first, from a persecutory outer world of external bad objects; and secondly, from a persecutory inner world of internal bad objects, and above all the antilibidinal ego (Guntrip 1961b).

Psychotherapy may produce valuable results *en route*, but it cannot be radical unless it reaches and releases this lost heart of the total self which is not only repressed, but also too terrified to re-emerge. So far as I can see, though our terminology is different, this is what Winnicott is saying when he describes a patient as having had a successful Oedipal analysis, and then later coming to him for a treatment which he calls 'therapeutic regression aiming at the rebirth of the true self' (1958, p. 249, 'Mind and its relation to the psyche-soma').

This problem justifies us in saying that what psychoanalysis has discovered so far is just how difficult radical psychotherapy is. It presents us with two final problems for analytic research.

First that of 'resistance to treatment', which now turns out to be due not simply to unconscious guilt, but to sheer fear of collapse into a self which is too weak and fear-ridden to face life. The infantile dependence which Fairbairn regards as the true cause of neurosis is something which the patient has been taught culturally to despise, and emotionally fears as undermining his efforts to carry his adult responsibilities. He fights against any real dependence on his therapist, believing that it will throw him back on the weakest part of his personality, rather than be a position of emotional security setting him free for regrowth. What Balint (1952) calls 'primary passive love' is the necessary starting point for his 'new beginning', when the basic ego has been too badly damaged in early childhood. But the patient has spent his life fighting against just this, and feels intense contempt and self-hate over it. This is more elementary than the moral super-ego; not fear of bad impulses but fear of weakness. This, I think, is the ultimate meaning of Fairbairn's antilibidinal ego. It enshrines the frightened child's fear of his own weakness, his desperate struggle to overcome it by self-forcing methods, and by the denial of all needs, especially passive ones.

Fairbairn's antilibidinal ego (the denial of needs) is thus the patient's main defence against the 'dangers' of regression, and is therefore the chief source of resistance to a good therapeutic relationship with the analyst by means of which a controlled constructive regression could be undergone to whatever extent it may be necessary to make possible regrowth. At the same time it illuminates Fairbairn's view that resistance is due to 'libidinal cathexis of the bad object' (1952, pp. 72 ff.), for if the patient cannot let himself have a good object, he must cling to bad objects, either in phantasy or fact, or risk the loss of his ego. One sees patients undergoing self-imposed tortures mentally which they do not seem able to give up. They cannot trust themselves to the therapist because, having been let down by their environment in infancy, they had to keep going by a fanatical internal cult of enforced independence which they are afraid to relax (Guntrip 1960). Hence Fairbairn's further view that the patient struggles to maintain his neurosis as an 'internal closed system' (1958).

If at last the patient can undergo and accept a therapeutically controlled regression, the second and worse problem emerges. He will experience terrifying states of despair, feeling utterly shut-in and hopeless about any rebirth. For a long time he oscillates between regression and resistance. The analysis of Oedipal conflicts seems to me relatively straightforward by comparison with the analysis of the complex infantile schizoid fears and persecutory anxieties which originally prevented the growth of a strong basic ego, and now bar the way to the rebirth of the lost heart of the self. One patient recently reported that while she was sitting in a bus she suddenly had a queer purely mental experience. 'I felt I was nobody, neither body, soul nor spirit. I felt that I, the real "I", was nothing at all.' Here is the patient's discovery of the basic need to find a real self.

The problem is constituted, not only by the existence of persecutory fears, but also by the persistence of an undeveloped, weak infantile ego state; a vicious circle in which the fears block ego development and the weak ego remains exposed to fears. Psychotherapy has to provide a new security in which a new growth can begin. Just how afraid the patient is, is shown in a letter from the woman of 48 years already referred to.

> I am consumed with fear. I have always been and still am terrified of everything and everybody. Terrified of doing things, too afraid to live at all. All my life I have been running away and trying to hide. That is what I am doing here in this job and this flat. I want to hide and be undisturbed by the world and other people. I want to sleep and let the world go by. Yet there is another side of me that longs to *live*, and wants to be able to do things and live an interesting life free from *fear*. But it is such a struggle always fighting *fears*. The prospect of marrying has brought this to the fore. I want love desperately yet I am afraid to accept it or even to believe in it. I have been trying to force myself to go the pace alone but I need help desperately.

So far as I can see the very real gains and developments in her 'ego of everyday life' as a result of the earlier orthodox analysis, enabled her to face the uncovering of a regressed infant in herself. But, until that was regrown, no therapy could be complete. Is it safe or possible to go so deep with everyone?

At this point three practical problems arise, two of them being related almost as mutually exclusive opposites. The question can be asked, on the one hand, whether increased knowledge of the regressed infantile ego in the schizoid citadel will enable us to uncover it more quickly and so shorten the ever-lengthening process of psychoanalytical treatment? In any absolute sense I cannot think this is practicable. Premature interpretation of the existence of the most withdrawn part of the complex ego will yield no better result than premature interpretation of any other problem. The patient will either not understand or else grasp the meaning only in an intellectual way. If the patient is nearer to the emergence in an emotional way of this basic withdrawnness, interpretation of it before he can stand it will only intensify his defences. There is no short cut. The patient's strongest defences are permanently mobilized to keep his regressed ego and his passive needs hidden, for when they begin to emerge he feels he is really 'breaking down'. All the Oedipal and compromise positions involved in his defensive system must be patiently worked through and in that process the patient comes to feel strong enough and well enough understood and supported to face the ultimate test of bringing the fear-ridden infant into the treatment relationship.

If we were to try at once to drive straight to the tap-root of all problems, the schizoid problem, we would not only risk fitting the patient into a theory, block him by trying to take up conflicts not in the natural order of their unfolding, and learn nothing new, but a problem of an opposite kind would arise; namely, granted that the schizoid problem is the ultimate one, if we insist with too narrow and rigid logic on this, we may fall into the trap of thinking that nothing else matters. This would lead to premature attempts at reduction of all problems to this one problem, in psychotherapy, much as Rank (1929) thought he could go straight to his 'birth trauma' and clear everything up quickly. That would be a delusion. The patient will dictate how fast the analysis can move by what and how much he can cope with as it goes along. One can only deal with what the patient presents and let the next phase grow out of that. I have never felt able to do more than keep a sharp lookout for any signs of 'withdrawnness' the patient actually does present, and take care not to hold up the analysis by treating conflicts over sex and aggression as ultimates when the patient is ready to go behind them.

We cannot afford to concentrate attention exclusively on any one thing, whether it be the Oedipal problem, the depressive position, or schizoid withdrawal and regression. We can only recognize that psychoanalytical investigation has discovered these problems in that order as it has worked deeper. We must use all concepts which are relevant to whatever the patient presents and keep an open mind for anything 'new' he discloses. Psychodynamic theory will not come to a final closure in our generation. Assuming that, so far as we can see at present, the schizoid problem is the basic one, certainly not all patients begin by presenting this kind of material. If they do, they are more than averagely ill, and even then its complexity is enormous and we know all too little about primary ego development as yet. So we must not allow theory to become dogma but use it as a signpost.

The third question that will very likely be raised is that the patient *wants* to be treated as a baby, with the implication that he should not be indulged in this. I believe that to be a grave misrepresentation of the case. There is an infant in the patient who actually *needs* to be accepted for what he is, by being helped to whatever degree of 'therapeutic regression' proves to be necessary. But there is also a 'forced antilibidinal adult' in the patient who hates this. If the patient senses that the therapist is on the defensive against his deepest needs, this will have the effect of forcing them to the front, and he may well be driven to become demanding and try to manipulate an analyst (parent) who basically rejects him. If, however, the patient slowly realizes the analyst will accept and help the baby in him, it has the effect of bringing his antilibidinal defences into the open, and we witness the intensity of the patient's resistance to treatment as a struggle *not* to depend on the analyst for help. This is a situation the analysis of which leads to far more real progress towards a more secure, relaxed, non-anxious and spontaneously loving personality. We need to know more about the processes of rebirth and regrowth of the profoundly withdrawn infant self hidden in the schizoid citadel, and what kind of relationship of the analyst with the patient is required to make that possible. One patient said simply: 'If I could feel loved, I'm sure I'd grow. Can I be sure you genuinely care for the baby in me?'—a statement which makes it clear that fundamentally what the patient is seeking and needing is a relationship of a parental order which is sufficiently reliable and understanding to nullify the results of early environmental failure.

## REFERENCES

Balint, M. (1952). *Primary Love and Psychoanalytic Technique*. London: Hogarth Press.

Fairbairn, W. R. D. (1952). *Psychoanalytic Studies of the Personality*. London: Tavistock Publications.

_____ (1958). On the nature and aims of psycho-analytical treatment. *International Journal of Psycho-Analysis* 39:374–385.

Guntrip, H. (1952). A study of Fairbairn's theory of schizoid reactions. *British Journal of Medical Psychology* 25: 86–103.

_____ (1960). Ego-weakness and the hard core of the problem of psychotherapy. *British Journal of Medical Psychology* 33: 163–184.

_____ (1961a). *Personality Structure and Human Interaction*. London: Hogarth Press.

_____ (1961b). The schizoid problem, regression and the struggle to preserve an ego. *British Journal of Medical Psychology*. 34: 223–244.

_____ (1962). The manic-depressive problem in the light of the schizoid process. *International Journal of Psycho-Analysis* 43: 98–113.

McDougall, W. (1905). *Physiological Psychology*. London: Dent.

Rank, O. (1929). *The Trauma of Birth*. London: Kegan Paul.

Winnicott, D. W. (1958). *Collected Papers: Through Paediatrics to Psycho-Analysis*. London: Tavistock Publications.

# 10

# THINKING WHAT WE FEEL; FEELING WHAT WE THINK

T HE PAPER ON "THE CONCEPT OF MIND" by H. J. Home (1966) re-aroused my interest in this subject which had concerned me closely in writing *Personality Structure and Human Interaction* in 1961. I give a brief indication of the position taken by Mr Home, as our starting point here. He defined "mind" as the meaning of "behaviour". We do not speak of the "behaviour" of *dead (inanimate) objects* but only of their activity, because it has no "meaning". "Meaning" only exists for *live objects* and constitutes their subjective experience of their own activities and those of other live objects, in terms of their aims and purposes. He regarded science (i.e. "natural" science) as the study of the activities of dead objects. The objective methods of such science are useless for dealing with the "meanings" of the subjective experience of live objects, but this is what psycho-analysis sets out to study. He concluded that psycho-analytic or psychodynamic thinking is not "scientific" but is "humanistic thinking", based on our knowledge of ourselves and our capacity to identify with (and therefore to know inwardly) other people.

The basic emerging problem is that of *the status and nature of specifically psychodynamic studies*. Home worked out thoroughly one of the two possible answers, namely that *psychodynamics* is not a scientific but a humanist study. The other possible answer is to expand the meaning of science. Like the philosopher Hume, he pursued an important line of argument to its logical bitter end and so highlighted all the problems involved. This present discussion of the concept of psychodynamic science falls into three parts: (1) a discussion of the terms "physical" and "mental" science, or the "natural" sciences and psychology, (2) the raising of the question "Have we really got a 'mental' science?", and (3) is "Object-Relations Theory" a true psychodynamic science?

## "PHYSICAL" AND "MENTAL" SCIENCE

We must at the start guard against befogging the theoretical issue by confusing it with a false antithesis between a scientific and a human approach. A surgeon can

251

be capable of sympathy with his patient however objectively and impersonally scientific he is in his medical theory and practice. It is true that a person who has, shall we say, a flair for personal relationships is likely to feel drawn to psychother-apy, while others are more at home in laboratory research. This does not bear on our problem, except when someone who cannot do or is antagonistic to psycho-therapy, prefers a definition of science which rules out a personal relationships approach. Thus, Eysenck says that psychologists explain but do not understand human beings.

What concerns us is *the theoretical question of the definition of science*. If psychodynamic studies are scientific, then there are two kinds or levels of science. There are fundamental differences between the methods and the type of concep-tualization employed in the physical sciences, and in the *psychodynamic* studies which are the theoretical basis of psychotherapy. I shall speak of "physical" or "material" science, not "natural" science, because psychic phenomena are as "nat-ural" as physical ones. The term is a relic of a time when scientists thought that psychic phenomena did not deserve to be given the status of reality, as in Huxley's view of mind as an epiphenomenon, related to the body like a whistle to a train, playing no part in its running. The train would "go" just as well without the whistle. Only physical phenomena were thought worthy of, or regarded as open to, scientific study. Many regard that stage as now over. In a more subtle sense I do not believe it is over. Home put the question "Is psychodynamics a science after all?" If it is, we have not yet really decided in what sense.

The classic view of science still holds in many minds. The extraordinary material and technological success of physical science compared with the extremely modest achievements of mental science support this. There is an emotional addiction to a view of science which is, in fact, being intellectually superseded. This seems to be strong in psychiatry, and to be subtly present in much psycho-analytical writing, because in this field we operate closest to our own psychological weaknesses; more so than in the physical sciences, which therefore provide us with an escape. Even Freud, when anxious, longed to get back to the physiological laboratory again, where he felt on safer ground. Astronomy, physics, and chem-istry provide the primary model, with mathematics, for what is entitled to be called science. They were the earliest sciences to arise, because they dealt with the kind of phenomena which were easiest to treat scientifically, and they did not encounter so much subjective emotional resistance in the investigator, as when we study human nature. Physiology, neurology and biochemistry were built up on the same scien-tific model. They dealt with "material" phenomena, and the pseudo-philosophy of scientific materialism classed mental phenomena with religion and fiction, as not only outside science but not really important, mere imagination.

I shall, however, refer here to "material" and "mental" science. This does not imply any definition of "matter" as opposed to "mind" as entities. I mean simply that material science studies those aspects of reality which we investigate by sensory perception and experimental methods based on it. One can study behaviour this way, and call it psychology, but it is not psychology. It is not about the psyche, but only about the outward expression of some aspects of it as behaviour, a most incomplete guide to the full nature of a "person" and the whole range of his subjective experience. To quote Dicks:

> While behaviour is subject to scientific observation of an objective kind, experience is not – it needs to be shared and understood.

Physical scientists do not usually regard psychic phenomena as having the same material trustworthiness for investigation as material facts. In whatever way we acquire our knowledge of our thoughts, feelings and volitions, we do not get to know them by seeing, hearing, touching, tasting or smelling them, but by a *wholly subjective inner process which we call recognition or realization of our immediate experience.* They are what Gellner (1959) calls "warm mental entities, introspectible mental experiences". Of course, sensory perception is also a subjective experience, but it has an objective reference which is entirely absent from our experiencing of ourselves.

We know our thoughts and feelings do not have any necessary objective counterpart in the outer world, but they have a reality of their own, *psychic reality.* This direct immediate knowledge of psychic reality is quite different from our sensory experience of the outer world. *Our knowledge of our thoughts and feelings is our experience of ourselves as "subjects".* We can mentally know ourselves in this manner without any intermediary method or technique of investigation. There is nothing else *at all* that we can know in this direct manner. We may, and often do for our own motives, deceive ourselves and distort our immediate experience of ourselves. In that case we directly experience the distortion. It is still true that when we realise that we are thinking this thought or feeling this emotion at this moment, that knowledge has an absoluteness about it which cannot be questioned. Free association rests on this. We never consciously know all that we experience, but whatever else a free-associating patient may or may not know about himself, he knows with certainty that he *is* thinking and feeling whatever associations occur to him as he talks, and that that knowledge is dependable. Psycho-analysis bases itself on this fact, the fact that, even if only slowly, *psychic reality reveals itself to us directly,* that *the analytic method frees more of it to do so and that it has to be taken seriously as a fact.* It is only *of our own experience* that this is true, and our capacity to know and understand other people's experience is based on our knowledge of our own. Our understanding of others is an inference based on our knowledge of ourselves, will not be more thorough than our knowledge of ourselves, and must be tested and justified by further experience. That is why a personal analysis is indispensable for a psycho-analyst. But we can know others "on the inside" by identification, as Home stressed, because we know ourselves directly "on the inside"; and *this is a phenomenon entirely absent from the physical sciences.* In this sense "material objects" have no subjective or "inside" aspects, and can be wholly satisfactorily studied objectively.

Possibly because of this difference, many scientifically trained people seem reluctant to recognize psychic reality as a fact. Mayer-Gross, Slater and Roth (1954) say that

> instability in the attitude of psychiatrists is made all the easier by the subjectivity and *the lack of precision of psychological data* [their italics]. Mental events can only be described in words that are themselves often open to varied interpretation. Many terms in psychiatry are taken from everyday language, and are not clearly defined. . . . Much psychiatric literature of today owes its existence to the possibility of playing with words and concepts; and the scientific worker in psychiatry must constantly bear in mind the risks of vagueness and verbosity.

Yet they are not complaining of carelessness in the precise use of terms, but of something deeper. They speak of the "instability of attitude" of students of psychiatric phenomena. "Attitude" to what? They mean instability of attitude to what is and is not science. They write:

> This book is based on the conviction of the authors that the foundations of psychiatry have to be laid *on the ground of the natural sciences* [their italics]. An attempt is made to apply the methods and resources of a scientific approach to the problems of clinical psychiatry.

They simply equate science with "natural" science, and reject any description of psychic reality that does not conform to natural science terminology, as "not clearly defined", "vague and verbose", and "playing with words". But it is not for a scientist to try to dictate to facts, but to try to understand what is there; and psychic reality is indisputably there, and moreover its study cannot be carried on "on the ground of the natural sciences". We need a "mental" or "*psychodynamic*" science, distinguished from "physical" science. This conclusion is supported by Taylor in *The Explanation of Behaviour* (1964). He writes:

> To assume from the superiority of Galileo's principles in the sciences of inanimate nature, that they *must* provide the model for the sciences of animate behaviour, is to make a speculative leap, not to enunciate a necessary conclusion (p. 25).

He concludes that "Behaviourist Psychology" shows the invalidity of one form of mechanistic explanation of behaviour, which can only be explained teleologically by reference to purpose; that Behaviourism is "non-psychological psychology".

## HAVE WE GOT A "MENTAL" SCIENCE?

It has been reserved for psycho-analysis to show respect for, and create the definite concept of, "psychic reality", denoting as stubborn a fact as can be found anywhere, in the sense that a fact is what is effective. Yet it is not a fact that can be studied by the same kind of methods used in physical science. We gain nothing by avoiding the use of the term "mental" even though we do not work with a dualistic philosophy or regard "mind" as a separate "thing". *"Matter" and "mind" are the age-old and honoured terms by means of which mankind has expressed its direct recognition of the fact that there are two quite different aspects of our existence.* This is a fact that it seems many people have not yet come to terms with on the level of scientific thinking. They still hanker after the false simplification of "scientific materialism". If we refuse to turn a blind eye to this ineradicable dualism in our experience of existence, then there are only two possible solutions:

1. To limit science to the study of material phenomena and agree with Home that mental phenomena call for a different kind of thinking.
2. To expand the meaning of science to include the study of "mental" phenomena in its own and not in physical terms.

Can we really do that? It is not satisfactorily done by the development of the social sciences. They look to us to supply a psychodynamic science for them to work with. Otherwise they can only deal with behaviour and study it objectively.

Nor do I think that biology provides the type of thinking required to do justice to mental or psychic phenomena. I agree with Home that biology comes under the heading of physical science. As I understood him he distinguished between studying live objects and dead objects, but there is an ambiguity in the word "object". It covers both personal and impersonal objects but the difference matters in psychodynamics. The objects we are interested in are capable of being, and in fact are, subjects of experience. The objects of natural science are either not capable of being subjects, or when they are it does not matter to science, which ignores that aspect of their reality. When live objects are studied as subjects, we have psychodynamic science. On the other hand when live subjects are studied as objects only, as is done by biology, neurology, behaviouristic psychology and sociology, then we have the classic model of "natural" science. There is an element of objectivity in every kind of study and every kind of relationship, but I would prefer to sum the matter up by saying that *psychodynamics studies its objects basically as "subjects", while traditional science studies whatever it does study as "objects only". It is this exclusively objective approach of classical science that fails to do justice to "persons" as "subjects of experience". Psychodynamic studies pose a genuinely new problem for science, which cannot be handled by the classic scientific modes of conceptualization.* Thus either science in the traditional sense will have its absolute limits revealed, or else it will undergo radical revision as to the meaning of science. This revision is actually already under way, for it is found that there is not the old-fashioned solidity and simplicity about matter, space, and time that used to be assumed.

There may, however, be more to be said for Home's view that science can only deal with "dead objects" or with live objects as if they were dead. There is an arresting passage in Bion's (1962) *Learning from Experience*, chapter 6. He calls sense-impressions $\beta$-elements, which a hypothetical $\alpha$-function works up into $\alpha$-elements, thoughts that can be used. He says of some patients that "evading the experience of contact with live objects by destroying $\alpha$-function" makes them unable to have a relationship with anything except as *an automaton*, i.e. a dead object. He then observes:

> The scientist whose investigations include the stuff of life finds himself in a situation that has a parallel in such patients. The breakdown in the patient's equipment for thinking leads to dominance by a mental life in which his universe is populated by inanimate objects. The inability of even the most advanced human beings to make use of their thoughts, because the capacity to think is rudimentary in all of us, means that the field for investigation, all investigation being ultimately scientific, is limited, by human inadequacy, to those phenomena that have the characteristics of the inanimate. We assume that the psychotic limitation is due to illness; but that that of the scientist is not. . . . It appears that our rudimentary equipment for "thinking" thoughts is adequate when the problems are associated with the inanimate, but not when the object for investigation is the phenomenon of life itself. Confronted with the complexities of the human mind the analyst must be circumspect in following even accepted scientific method; its weakness may be closer to the weakness of psychotic thinking than superficial scrutiny would admit.

Bion sees that traditional science would depersonalize man, or as Wordsworth said "We murder to dissect". The psychotic and the scientific limitations appear to meet in the schizoid intellectual (and there are many among scientists) who can only think about inanimate objects, not about live subjects, for he is too basically anxious to risk identification and the sharing and understanding of experience. For him, as for power politicians, persons are things. Home can claim Bion as a powerful ally. Science is limited to the investigation of inanimate objects, which seems to imply that some other kind of thinking must deal with live subjects.

Nevertheless, I would prefer to accept Bion's shrewd observation about the nature of most of what is called scientific or "natural" science thinking, and go on to explore whether the concept of science cannot still be expanded to take in the study of "live subjects". Bion provides a reason for science remaining for so long bound up with the ideology of scientific materialism, which Macmurray described as neither scientific nor philosophical, but only a popular prejudice based on the prestige of science. It may have deeper causes; partly emotional, in that people feel safer on what they *think* is the more solid ground of material facts, but more, according to Bion, because of the sheer limitations of our capacity to think beyond the range of inanimate facts. It is of a piece with this that many physical scientists regard the human sciences such as anthropology, sociology and psychology as either an inferior sort of science, or even not properly science at all. A reviewer of Teilhard de Chardin deprecated his claim to be regarded as a scientist because his anthropological pursuits did not have the exactness required by the real sciences with their mathematical tools. For this very reason psychology, in its fight for scientific status, has always had to encounter attempts to reduce it to something less than psychology, such as neurology, biology or physiology. We know what a terrific struggle Freud had to move in an opposite direction.

We cannot, however, reduce psychodynamics to psychobiology. This does not involve ignoring biology for its proper contributions, as for example in problems of heredity, but it avoids the confusion of thought arising from mixing two different levels of abstraction. For example, term like "meaning" and "experience" belong specifically to the psychological level. As I understand it, biology does not deal with a living creature as a "subject" whose experience and actions have meaning for himself and others, but as an objective phenomenon to be studied from the outside by experimental methods, rather than appreciated from the inside by identification, sympathy, empathy, or what-have-you. Biology for most scientists surely means biochemical, just as psychology for material scientists means psycho-physical. I fancy that in those compound terms the important components are "chemical" and "physical". "Bio" and "psycho" are added as consolation prizes. In spite of the powerful support of Bion's argument that the scientific intellect is too limited to deal with anything but the inanimate, I would rather not distinguish, as Home does, between the "live" and the "dead" as the fields of study respectively of psychodynamics and physical science, for this seems to me to indicate only the difference between biology and physics. We are more concerned with the difference between the merely animate and the personal, i.e. between the personal, and the subpersonal and impersonal: for there are forms of existence which are alive but of no interest to us in psycho-dynamics because they are not personal (such as fleas, bugs, mosquitos, plants). *We are concerned with the study of the "person", with that level of abstraction at which we speak of the human being as not a "thing" or an "organism" but a "unique individual".* We only talk significantly about persons when we talk of their experiencing their environment and themselves in a way that has meaning. The difference between these two levels of thinking is clear from the fact that a person has no meaning for his merely material environment, but that environment has meaning for him. I mean nothing to the mountains of Glencoe but they mean a great deal to me. *It is the "person", the unique and individual "subject" of meaningful experience that the methods of traditional science so fail to deal with. Psychodynamics is the science of the personal subject, not of mere objects. Psychodynamics is the touchstone of whether psychology in its own right has really been accepted as a science.*

Psychotherapists, whether psychiatric like Sullivan, or psycho-analytic like Szasz and Colby, have produced stout protests against the reduction of psychodynamics to something less than itself. Szasz (1956) wrote:

> Mathematics can function as a tool in physics and astronomy without the identity of those sciences suffering thereby. Psychology cannot so use mathematics without thereby altering its own identity. It appears that in psychology the very process of expressing experiences in highly abstract symbols—even if they pertain to phenomena which are ordinarily thought of as psychological—alters one's conception of the nature of the problem.

Sullivan and Colby are, however, somewhat equivocal.
Sullivan (1955) writes:

> Biological and neurological terms are utterly inadequate for studying everything in life. . . . I hope that you will not try to build up in your thinking correlations (i.e. of "somatic" organization with psychiatrically important phenomena) that are either purely imaginary or relatively unproven, which may give you the idea that you are in a solid reliable field in contrast to one which is curiously intangible. If a person really thinks that his thoughts about nerves and synapses and the rest have a higher order of merit than his thoughts about signs and symbols, all I can say is, Heaven help him.

So far so good, but then Sullivan rules out the study of the person's "unique individuality". He says it is a great thing in our wives and children but we are not concerned with it in science. But it is the very point in question when we ask what is the nature and status of psychodynamic studies. "Unique individuality" is just what we are concerned with, for in Sullivan's "interpersonal relationships", what we are and how we react is most closely bound up with what the other person is, and *vice versa*. Sullivan is saying that something knowable is outside science. After proclaiming the limitations of physical science, Sullivan fails to establish a psychodynamic science on its own proper level, which may warn us of the difficulties.

Colby (1955) also illustrates the failure of a thinker, who certainly understands the limitations of physical science, to establish psychodynamic science satisfactorily. He speaks of levels of integration in reality and of abstraction in thought, and writes:

> At each level of integration, characteristic and new properties emerge which are not entirely explainable in terms of levels below them. For these new properties, special methods of study and a special language are required. . . . At the psychic level of integration, between the neuronal and the social, we assume certain properties to be the consequence of what our language calls psychic functions. . . . The higher we go in theoretical abstraction, and the further away we get from material tangible substances, the more difficult it seems for some to grasp what it is that is being discussed. Many simply cannot understand what it means to theorise on a psychic level. We must now abandon them as ill-starred and continue on in a psychological language.

What then is Colby's psychological language? We find we are after all no further forward. He says:

> We consider psychic functions to be performed by a hypothetical psychic apparatus. It is an imaginary, postulated organization, a construct which aids our understanding of certain observable properties . . . But there is no point-to-point correspondence between the psychic apparatus and the brain.

He avoids the reduction of psychology to physiology but has not arrived at a true psychology. An "apparatus for studying observable properties" is a physical science concept, quite unsuitable for representing personality. At best it could only conceptualize the study of behaviour, not of the experience of a personal self which has unique individuality. "Meaning", which is so vital to the reality of psychic experience and everything that psycho-analysis studies, is not "an observable property". We can see or hear certain agreed ways we have of conveying our meanings to one another, but "meaning" in itself is not observable; it can only be subjectively realised, appreciated. So true is this that, when we have written or said something and believe we have made it crystal clear, we can be disconcerted to find that someone thinks we have written or said something entirely different from what we meant. Colby proceeds to elaborate a diagram of endopsychic structure which might well pass as a diagram of a computer or electronic brain, processing in-put and delivering out-put. Thus even those who see that psychodynamics call for a new or broader conception of science, do not yet see clearly what a truly "psychodynamic" science will be like.

The contribution of Hutten (1956) is important at this point. He writes:

> [In psychodynamics] we describe all happenings in terms of psychical reality, and so can dispense with the frame-work of physical space-time which does not apply to mental phenomena.

He accepts multiplicity of causes and over-determination as essential to psychological theory and in no way militating against its scientific status. It is heartening to find a professor of physics who does not use the term "cause" with its old scientific meaning in the realm of psychology. He says:

> Classical physics is taken as the standard when it is said that a scientific theory must explain a given phenomenon in one way only; but this is not really true even there, and certainly not in modern physics. Underneath this ideal is, I think, the metaphysical belief in the mechanical determinism of past centuries, according to which everything in the world is connected by the iron chain of necessity.

Hutten confirms my feeling that a view of science which is gradually becoming outdated intellectually, is still held for unconscious emotional reasons. Just as Freud said that the religious believer projected the father-image onto the universe for security reasons, so many a scientific believer projects onto the universe the "iron-chain-of-necessity" image, scientific materialism, also for security reasons. They feel on safer ground then. There is nothing like dealing at first hand with *psychic* reality, for encountering disturbance.

Psycho-analysis itself grew up so much under the sway of the classic scientific outlook, that Freud could not really escape that projection himself. Thus many attempts to make psycho-analysis scientific have in fact been unrecognised attempts after all to press it back into the mould of the material science type of theory. This becomes increasingly unsatisfactory as the modern philosophy of science makes it plain that physical science no longer sanctions the old solid reliable deterministic universe, a closed system in which we know to a certainty exactly what is what. Thus Popper in *The Logic of Scientific Discovery* (1959) writes:

The empirical basis of objective science has nothing absolute in it. Science does not rest upon rock bottom. The bold structure of its theories rises as it were above a swamp. It is like a building erected upon piles. The piles are driven down from above into a swamp, but not down to any natural or given base; and when we cease to drive our piles into the deeper layers, it is not because we have reached firm ground. We simply stop when we are satisfied that they are firm enough to carry the structure, at least for the time being.

By the "swamp" I take it Popper means the area of ultimate ignorance beyond our limited knowledge. Bertrand Russell's prophecy many years ago that one day science would have discovered everything and provided a gigantic card index in which we could look up the answers to every possible question, seems now unconvincing. Since the movement of science has been from the physical to the psychical, it is comforting, when we are puzzled by psychic reality, to remember that physical reality is part of the same swamp, and we are only trying to drive the piles a bit deeper. How are we doing this?

Hutten has thoroughly excluded physical models for psychic reality, but I do not feel he has yet arrived at a full *psycho*dynamic science. He says:

The usual cause-and-effect language breaks down when we want to treat processes in which we cannot immediately recognize some constant element. The language works only if the process is no more than the displacement of a permanent thing in space-time under the influence of a constant force. This is largely true for physics, but even there exist examples where this no longer holds. . . . A psycho-analytic explanation is about a conflict or a process. . . . The same set of data (may) lead to exactly opposite results . . . which shows that the processes underlying human behaviour are dynamical in the sense that they represent a conflict or tension between two opposite poles.

What this demonstrates is that psycho-analysis has a right to its own terminology and cannot be strictly modelled on physical science. Hutten looks in the right direction when he says that in psychodynamics we speak not about

causal laws but about the *aetiology* of an illness. Instead of description and prediction we have *diagnosis* and *prognosis*. . . . Unlike mass points human beings have a history and we cannot hope to predict their future from their present alone.

But neither can we hope to predict their future at all, even from their present plus their history. What Hutten is glimpsing is *the human personal subject of experience as the source of psychodynamic phenomena*. Unless we think of Hutten's "processes" and "tensions" and "opposite poles" as manifestations of the life of a personal subject, we shall find we have slipped back into some kind of physical science terminology, and are not on the proper level of psychodynamics. We seek a genuinely *psychodynamic* theory, not tied to the physical conception of science, yet not giving up the claim to be scientific. *Psychodynamics is called on to conceptualize what science has never hitherto regarded as coming within its purview, namely the human being as a unique centre of highly individual experience and responsibility.*

## IS "OBJECT-RELATIONS THEORY" A TRUE PSYCHODYNAMIC SCIENCE?

In what terms can we construct psychodynamic science? I have much sympathy with Home's view that some metapsychological statements *literally* do not mean anything, as for example when Segal (1964) tells us that "the infant projects the death instinct into the breast". This extraordinary statement is due both to careless use of words (if the infant has such a thing as a death instinct, it certainly cannot project it anywhere else), and a confused mixing of psychodynamic and biological concepts. "Projection" is a psychodynamic concept, "instinct" is a biological concept. An instinct cannot be projected. Moreover, though Freud said "Instincts are our mythology", and on its first introduction spoke of the "death instinct" as a speculation he, and certainly Melanie Klein, and Segal thereafter, treated it simply as an undisputed fact. Credible theory cannot be created in this way.

This difficulty of the confused mixing of psychodynamic and biological concepts is perhaps clarified indirectly by a statement of Foulkes (1965) on Group Therapy. He said:

> Psycho-analysis is a biological theory which has only very reluctantly been pushed into being a social theory by the pressure of psychotherapy. Group therapy is not psycho-analysis.

The first sentence is, I am sure, right. Psychotherapy is a social, personal relationship problem. This is obvious in group therapy but not really less so in individual analysis. Thus, psycho-analysis, which came into being as a result of a search for a method of, and a theoretical basis for, psychotherapy, did not, after all, *in its original form*, provide one. Psycho-analysis *began* as a biological theory, and has been very reluctant to be pushed into being more than that. But it has been so pushed by the pressures of psychotherapy, which needs a social and personal relations theory. Is that not the explanation of the great difference between the pre-1920 biological stage of Freud's work, and the post-1920 psychodynamic stage growing out of the theory of the superego, a concept which owed nothing at all to biology but is a pure psychodynamic concept? What Foulkes called "the pressure of psychotherapy" is the pressure of the facts about human beings as persons, demanding a theory which goes beyond both physiology and biology to the highest level of abstraction, where we study the unique individual. In this first period Freud struggled to transcend physiology and arrived at psychobiology. In his second period he began to transcend psychobiology and move on to a consistent *psycho-dynamic* theory of personal object-relations. With his concept of the super-ego, we begin to see, not an organism dominated by instincts, but an "ego which has instincts among its various properties", shaped as a whole in the matrix of human interaction. But the drag of biology and of the metapsychology built on it proved strong, and the result is seen in the work of Melanie Klein. She moved steadily towards a fully-developed object-relations theory while at the same time clinging all the more tightly to an instinct-theory metapsychology, giving us the unfortunate death instinct, constitutional envy and so on. Nevertheless, the direction that development was taking, was bound to demand a re-evaluation of the term "ego", as more than just a control-apparatus. In the work of Fairbairn it became what etymologically it really is, a term denoting the "I", the core of the personal self, the essence of the "whole human being".

The difficulties in psycho-analytic theory arise from its having remained too tied to classic "natural science" concepts, particularly in biological form. This could not have been avoided. Psycho-analysis arose in the natural science era. It was only Freud's work that forced recognition of psychic reality in a new way. Everything cannot be done at once. New insight grows gradually out of a period of confusion in which old and new overlap. But Foulkes was surely right when he said that the pressures of psychotherapy have forced theory to move on, I would say to a consistently psychodynamic theory of the unique individual in his personal relations. *This is what the emergence of "Object-Relations" theory is about.*

The argument so far can be brought to a head by a closer look at the work of Bion. He criticizes psycho-analytic theories for being "a compound of observed material and abstraction from it". He seeks a theory of "the practice of psycho-analysis" which uses only "pure scientific abstraction". What is meant by "pure scientific abstraction"? Abstract terms must be appropriate and relevant to the level of reality at which the abstraction is made. Is he making a psychodynamic theory of the person? His abstractness might seem a target for Szasz's criticism that in expressing psychological experiences in highly abstract symbols we alter our conception of the nature of the problem. Nevertheless Bion's concepts imply a dynamic experiencing person whose processes he symbolizes. He uses the symbols

$\alpha$ and $\beta$ to avoid prejudging issues by premature description. Thus he speaks of our capacity for thought-making as $\alpha$-function so as to avoid the risk of defining it concretely in advance of adequate knowledge. This is entirely legitimate. He postulates $\beta$-elements as experiences of, and $\alpha$-function as a dynamic activity of, an individual psyche. $\alpha$-function operates on two different sets of data, sense impressions and emotions. These are the $\beta$-elements which $\alpha$-function works up into thoughts usable for thinking. Wisdom points out[1] that the theory requires two levels of both consciousness and comprehension, a primitive consciousness and comprehension of $\beta$-elements or the raw materials of experiences, and then a more developed level of consciousness and comprehension on which $\alpha$-function does its work and produces "thoughts". If $\alpha$-function fails we cannot think, for we have no thoughts to think with. Here again we must distinguish two levels of thinking, thinking as a process that develops "thoughts" and thinking as a process that uses "thoughts". There seem then to be three levels of psychic activity, immediate experience (sense data and emotions), thought-production, and reflection on experience (science). These can only be theoretically distinguished in our actual experience, except where pathological states artificially isolate them. $\beta$-elements are the starting-point of all our experience, $\alpha$-function is our "digestion" of it, (Bion's term) and science is our reflection on it.

The immediate experience of sense impressions must be the raw material of physical science, from which our $\alpha$-function builds up such understanding as we can achieve, of the external world. But that cannot be the model for mental science, for the raw material of that is not sense impressions but emotions, i.e. our experience of ourselves as subjects in relation to objects. Our $\alpha$-function may well operate less adequately on emotions than on sense-impressions, so that we find thought-building easier about objects than about subjects. Here may lie the innate limits of our capacity for thinking that Bion refers to. One result is that it is difficult to talk about mental phenomena in any other than metaphorical language. Our language is based primarily on sensory experience. We apply the terminology of sense-perception to psychic phenomena when we speak of the unconscious as "deep down", or of the schizoid person as "shut in" and "out of touch with his world", or of the ego as "split". But patients themselves describe their experience that way and what other language would express it as accurately, for the purposes of primary description. This no doubt is what Home meant in a private communication when he said that he regarded the language of psychology as ordinary language. This is the criticism of Mayer-Gross and others (1954) that "terms in psychiatry are taken from everyday language" and that psychic phenomena "lack precision". But they do not lack precision if we look for the right kind of precision, precise expression of emotional, not sensory experience. "Shut in" does not express a spatial relation but a state of mind,

---

1. In a review-article (unpublished) on Bion's work.

a substitution of self-communing for object-relationship. The possibility of thought-building is easier for physical science, but cannot be an impossibility for mental science, for after all we are dealing with facts, the facts of psychic experience and reality.

Using Bion's ideas, physical science is the result of his hypothetical $\alpha$-function turning our immediate experience of sense impressions of objects into thoughts of objects, which are then developed through the levels of dream-thoughts, concepts, scientific systems and finally algebraic calculus. But this *physical science is simply an account of the easier half of our experience to think about and conceptualize. Mental science is about the more difficult half of our experience to conceptualize, not the objective world but ourselves as the subjects of experience. It must be thought of as $\alpha$-function turning the $\beta$-elements of our emotional experience of "ourselves in relation to others", into thoughts which can be developed into psychodynamic science.* This is the difference between the science of objects known from the outside, and of subjects known from the inside. We have made more headway with the first than the second. My own feeling is that "Object Relations" theory is the nearest we have got yet to a true psychodynamic science. It is not all the way there but it is on the way. It appears to me that Home's "humanistic thinking" is the description of our immediate experience of ourselves in ordinary everyday language. If that were substituted for "Psychodynamic Science" I think it would be open to Gellner's (1959) criticism of "ideographic science", as

> [a] study which claims to know individual things "in their full individuality" and without the intermediary of general terms or concepts.

*We must have general concepts, but derived from the study of experience, not of behaviour. There must be a further stage of reflection, or thinking about experience, which is psychodynamic science, working with general abstract ideas of personal, not impersonal, reality.*

Freud's work has developed into the exploration of the subjective personal life of man, the understanding of our inner experience, as distinct from the objective description of behaviour. Instincts are no longer all-important and the central place in the theory is now taken by the ego, the core of the personal self, in living relations with other persons or selves. Freud's supreme achievement was to rise superior to his scientific origins and challenge science to go beyond treating human beings as laboratory specimens to be investigated and manipulated, and see them as persons whose lives mean something to themselves and others; persons who can only really be known and helped by someone who does not just objectively diagnose their illness and prescribe treatment, but who knows and in a way shares their experience of suffering, goes along with them in seeking to understand it, and offers them a relationship in which they rediscover their lost capacity to trust and love. The analytic session and the therapeutic relationship is the laboratory in which psychodynamic science is formulated, and all the time it is a problem of understanding what is going on here and now between two persons, how their past experience contaminates their present meeting, how that can be eliminated and replaced by realistic mature relationship, i.e. how two "egos" can meet in a fully shared experience. This is what the "Object-Relations" theory, emerging from the work of Melanie Klein and Fairbairn is in process of exploring and formulating: what Martin Buber calls the "I-Thou" relation in contrast to the scientific "I-It" relation.

Before we look specifically at "Object-Relations" theory, it must be noted that so far use has been made of Bion's views only as they concern "thought-building", the development of the intellectual function with its ultimate consequence, the creation of science. This corresponds to Winnicott's use of the term "mind" as distinct from "psyche". Mind is not there at the beginning as psyche is. Later in the first year, brain maturation makes intellectual activity possible, and Winnicott then speaks of "mind" or the infant's "thinking" capacity as gradually becoming able to take over the care of the child from the mother. The primary psyche he regards as not simply a reflection of somatic experience, for it may be but loosely related to the body in the first months of life. Soma and psyche are distinguishable aspects of the whole "person". Winnicott (1958) writes:

> The psyche of a normal infant may lose touch with the body, and there may be phases in which it is not easy for the infant to come suddenly back into the body, for instance, when waking from deep sleep.

The psyche must learn to integrate somatic experience, and this it can only do if environmental adaptation to the infant's needs is adequate. The fact that the infant psyche can lose touch with the body and regain it frequently in the earliest months, emphasizes what psychoanalysis calls "psychic reality" as distinct from "material (somatic) reality". The psyche (Fairbairn's "pristine ego"), which Winnicott says is "from the beginning . . . already a human being, a unit", experiences the soma, and develops an inner relation to it, comes to "own it" or feels at one with it, and this is part of the integration of personality as experience develops.

In "object-relational" terms, the infant psyche is from the start potentially an ego, or as Fairbairn puts it a "pristine ego" as yet undifferentiated as to internal structure, and it needs a good enough human environment to make possible the actualization of the ego through a developing process in object-relations. Here we may return to Bion's "emotions" as "β-elements" and he includes in his list of basic "functions of the personality" the emotions of loving and hating. I do not understand why "fearing" is omitted. He includes in his basic functions "reaction between the paranoid-schizoid and depressive positions", and fear is the basis of the paranoid-schizoid position in exactly the same way as hate is the basis of depression. The omission of fear seems to be due to the persistence of the traditional psycho-analytical view that the fundamental conflict is that between love and hate. Freud held that hate is the primary human reaction to the environment and that fear is the secondary result of hate. The study of the schizoid position as antedating depression makes it clear that the very opposite is the truth. Human beings hate because they are afraid. If the weak and dependent infant finds his environment unsupporting and even hostile while he is as yet quite unable to defend and support himself, fear dictates withdrawal and the breaking off of relationships. It is fear that makes it impossible to love and the conflict between love and fear is the fundamental problem. In an intractable environment, it leaves the infant with only one choice, that between "flight" and "fight", between schizoid withdrawal or the development of hate, of fighting back at those who make it impossible to love, as the only means of maintaining object-relations. It takes a strong and stable person to love; hate is a defence of weakness and fear.

The simplest elements of our psychic experience in its emotional aspect are (1) a natural capacity to trust, depend on and *love* (at first unconsciously) the good object, and grow with it feeling secure; (2) *fear* of the bad object, precipitating schizoid withdrawal and the breakdown of object-relationships, which can only be maintained at the price of paranoid persecutory anxiety; (3) *hate* of the bad object in an attempt to retrieve the situation, force it to become helpful and restore object-relations. (This refers to pathological hate. There is a healthy hate which a mature person will feel as a response to, say, intentional evil such as deliberate cruelty); (4) *guilt*, insofar as, unlike fear, hate implies love and involves hurting love-objects, thus evoking the urge to reparation; and/or (5) *self-punishment*, self-suppression, the sadistic "superego" or "antilibidinal ego", with resulting loss of physical and emotional spontaneity, and the growth of rigidities of character and inhibition of functions. (6) Out of this inherently unstable and highly complex inner situation, having fear and the lost capacity to love at the bottom of it, personality illness arises. This is not the result of failure of mere gratification of instincts, but of the tension and conflict of the desperate struggle to achieve and maintain a viable ego, a self adequate to cope with living in the outer world. These are the emotional experiences which $\alpha$-function must "digest" (Bion) and turn into "thoughts" if we are to be able to understand them and build up a psychodynamic science. They are all object-relational experiences. We have to deal with the ego-growth in object-relations.

Laing (1965) has criticised Object-Relations Theory in a way which it seems pertinent at this point to examine. He said:

The object-relations theory attempts to achieve, as Guntrip has argued, a synthesis between the intra-and the inter-personal. Its concepts of

internal and external objects, of closed and open systems, go a considerable way. Yet it is still "objects" not "persons" that are written of.

In an earlier version of his paper he put this more strongly: "The objects, in
object-relations theory, are internal objects, not other persons." This latter criticism would appear to me to be true of Kleinian theory, where internal objects are
formed first of all, not by external experience, but by the internal operation of a
biological factor, the innate conflict of the life and death instincts, which is then
projected onto external objects. The internal life of the ego *could* be worked out as
a solipsistic affair and the external world need be no more than a blank projection
screen. So far as Fairbairn's object-relations theory is concerned internal objects
belong properly to the realms of the psychopathological, since they are internalized
in the first instance because they are bad objects. This, it seems, is supported by
Bion's view that good experience is digested and worked up by α-function into
thoughts. Bad experience remains undigested, a foreign body in the mind which
the psychic subject then seeks to project. In health, ideally, our objects are not
internal objects but real persons, even though in fact none of us can be as healthy
as that. But our internal objects are reflections of our experience of real persons
from earliest infancy. Psychotherapy aims at cure by real relationship between two
human beings as persons. In it, the psychopathological relationship of the ego to its
internal objects as revealed in the transference, steadily changes into the healthy
reality of objectively real personal, or ego to ego, relations, first achieved by the
patient with the therapist, and then becoming capable of extension to the rest of
life. The "ego" for Fairbairn was not an "apparatus" nor merely a structural part of
a psychic system. It is the personal self, so that when the primary ego is split in
experience of other real persons, each aspect of it retains "ego" quality as a
functioning aspect of the basic self.

    Should we speak of "Object-Relations" theory or of "Personal-" or "Ego-" or
"Subject-Relations" theory? In one way the term "object-relations" begins to date. It
reminds one of Freud's "sexual object" which was there to gratify an instinct, not to
provide a two-way relationship. On the other hand there is no intrinsic objection
to the use of the term "object" provided it is not held to imply an exclusively
impersonal object. Even then, a science of human experience must *include* Buber's
"I–It" relation, the ego-object relationship where the object is impersonal, since this
is a valid part of the experience of the ego, not solely in the sense of the scientific
investigation of material objects, but in the sense of say, the appreciation of beauty
in nature. Nevertheless what really concerns psychodynamic science is the ego-
object experience where the object is another ego. Only then do we have the full
reality of personal experience and personal relations. Psychodynamics is the study
of that type of experience in which there is *reciprocity* between subject and object,

and of the experience of ego-emptying and ego-loss when relationship and reciprocity fail.

I made my own view clear in Chapter 17 of *Personality Structure and Human Interaction* (1961). I described immature relations as essentially *unequal* and of the "one-up-and-the-other-down" type. This is natural in the case of parent and child but pathological as between adults, as for example in the sado-masochistic relationship. In a way each is "using" the other rather than "relating personally" to the other, and such relations tend towards the "I–It" pattern. Mature relations are two-way relations between emotional equals, characterized by mutuality, spontaneity, co-operation, appreciation, and the preservation of individuality in partnership. There can be no "turning of the tables" in this kind of relationship, for it is the same both ways. Each goes on being and becoming, because of what the other is being and becoming, in their personal interaction and mutual knowledge. Object-relations theory has not yet come sufficiently to grips with conceptualizing this. It does now possess a truly psychodynamic theory of the development of the individual ego in personal relationships; but not of the complex fact of the personal relationship itself between two egos. From Freud's ego and superego, through Melanie Klein's internal objects, projection and introjection, to Fairbairn's splitting of both ego and objects in relationship, and finally Winnicott's tracing of the absolute origin of the ego in the maternal relationship, we have a highly important view of what happens to the individual psyche under the impact of personal relations in real life. But the theory has not yet properly conceptualized Martin Buber's "I–Thou" relation, two persons being both ego and object to one another at the same time, and in such a way that their reality as persons becomes, as it develops in the relationship, what neither of them would have become apart from the relationship. This is what happens in a good marriage, and a good friendship. This is what psychotherapy seeks to make possible, for the patient who cannot, because of his inner problems, achieve it in normal living. This is what out theory has to deal with. This raises the fundamental question: how far can we know and be known by one another?

## REFERENCES

Bion, W. R. (1962). *Learning from Experience.* London: Heinemann.

Colby, K. (1955). *Energy and Structure in Psychoanalysis.* New York: Ronald.

Foulkes, S. (1965). Group psychotherapy: the group-analytic view. *Proceedings of the 6th International Congress of Psychotherapy*, ed. Pines and Spoerri. New York and Basle: Karger.

Gellner, E. (1959). *Words and Things.* London: Gollancz.

Guntrip, H. (1961). *Personality Structure and Human Interaction*. London: Hogarth Press.

Home, H. J. (1966). The concept of mind. *International Journal of Psycho-Analysis* 47.

Hutten, E. H. (1956). On explanation in psychology and physics. *British Journal of Philosophical Science* 7.

Laing, R. (1965). Practice and theory: the present situation. *Proceedings of the 6th International Congress of Psychotherapy*. (*see* Foulkes 1965).

Mayer-Gross, W., Slater, E, and Roth, M. (1954). *Clinical Psychiatry*, 1st ed. London: Cassell.

Popper, K. (1959). *The Logic of Scientific Discovery*. London: Hutchinson.

Segal, H. (1964). *Introduction to the Work of Melanie Klein*. London: Heinemann.

Sullivan, H. S. (1955). *Conceptions of Modern Psychiatry*. London: Tavistock Publications.

Szasz, T. (1956). Is the concept of entropy relevant to psychology and psychiatry? *Psychiatry* 19.

Taylor, C. (1964). *The Explanation of Behaviour*. London: Kegan Paul.

Winnicott, D. W. (1958). The first year of life: modern views on the emotional development. In *The Family and Individual Development*. London: Tavistock Publications, (rep. 1965).

# 11

# THE HEART OF THE PERSONAL[1]

THE THEME OF THIS MEMORIAL LECTURE to Mary Hemingway Rees, 'Religion in Relation to Personal Integration', indicates one of her special interests. It is a formidable task to try to 'think together' two great areas of human living in which I am deeply interested, psychotherapy and religion. But I must first rule out any misunderstanding of what I am going to talk about. I shall not discuss the Christian, Jewish, Hindu or Mohammedan religions, or any religious cults or creeds that arose in particular historical and cultural conditions. Today we can all share in the gifts to humanity of the great seers, Jesus, the Buddha, Socrates, Mohammed, Confucius, and many others, who saw beyond that obsession with purely material ends, described by Wordsworth as: 'Getting and spending, we lay waste our powers'. The world today is a much smaller place than it was 100 years ago, and it has become more possible for us to think in terms of our common shared humanity than it was in, say, A.D. 1800. Then, most individuals throughout the world hardly knew of the existence of any other culture than their own, and the religion in which they were brought up must have seemed the only religion. Today, radio, television and air travel have brought us all together from every part of the globe, and parochialism is impossible. We must learn to think in terms of the fundamental realities of experience in which we *all* share as human beings. By religion, then, I shall mean a basic human experience which, however differently it may be expressed in different times and places, is essentially the same for all men. 'Experience of what?' is the question we seek to answer. I want to explore the fundamental nature of the religious experience as such.

First we may note that if Freud did not contribute much to the question of the nature of religious experience per se, he did show that there are neurotic forms of religion which are an essentially infantile longing for a lost Mummy and Daddy. If,

---

1. Mary Hemingway Rees Memorial Lecture, given at the 7th International Congress of Mental Health, London, on August 12, 1968.

however, we dismiss all religion because there is such a thing as neurotic religion, we are on dangerous ground, for there are also neurotic forms of politics, of art, of marriage. Fairbairn once said to me: 'If we psychoanalyse everything, what will there be left?' We cannot dismiss anything because it *can* be neurotic, for neurosis is simply the disturbed and anxious expression of normal and ineradicable human needs, a distorted expression of human truth. It is the investigation of neurosis that has taught us so much about what is normal and basic for man. We cannot draw any hard and fast line between the normal and the neurotic; do not all of us partake to some extent in the fears, anxieties and insecurities that man is heir to. The chronic uncertainty of the very disturbed human being as to his viability as a 'person', itself throws a flood of light on the essential truth about human nature, and is one of the facts that can throw light on the nature of religious experience. Freud was precipitate in discarding religion because he found neurotic forms of it. But he did say definitely that his atheism was not part of psychoanalysis. If religion can express neurotic dependence, atheism can express equally neurotic independence. There is no easy negative solution of our problem along these lines.

However, a scientific education still tends to make people deny any kind of reality to religion; and to regard the human needs traditionally met by religion, as met now by political creeds, scientific knowledge or philosophical insights. I shall not spend long arguing this point, but be content with two references, the first to Bertrand Russell. This eminent philosopher proved to his own satisfaction that man is merely an insignificant accident in a purely mechanistic universe, knowable only by the methods of impersonal objective scientific experimentation. *Man* is wholly without any intrinsic meaning and value; indeed meaning and value are non-existent in the scientist's universe. But when Russell turned from scientific theory about the universe to the practical social, political and moral problems of our daily living, he found himself resolutely championing the rights of individual human beings to be valued, respected, left in undisputed possession of their intellectual and emotional liberty. According to the 'Rights of Man', no totalitarianism has any moral or any other kind of right to ride roughshod over the individual's need for freedom to be fully human. But this does not agree with the view that human beings are meaningless accidents of no value whatever. Russell could not have it both ways, and had the courage to say that *if we seek justification for believing in the sacred rights of human beings to be respected as persons having intrinsic value, we must seek it in the higher religions, for we cannot find it in science* (1944). There is no real difficulty in this. Science does not find meaning, value and purpose in the phenomena it studies, simply because it is not its concern to look for them. It does not investigate that side of existence. It gives us the tools and knowledge to manipulate our environment, including our own bodies. It cannot give us the values and meanings of our relating to one another as persons, which alone makes our existence significant. Physical science alone, uncontrolled by the imperative spiritual values of our personal living in human fellowship, is more likely to destroy us than save us, with its nuclear missiles and its horrific annihilating germ warfare weapons. What disturbs many scientists today is that their discoveries are so quickly harnessed to destructive ends. We have to consider seriously the possibility of some group of schizoid psychopaths, who can so easily seize power in the political field, recklessly unleashing destructive forces that could not be counteracted. There is no reason in science for this not to happen. It would merely be another meaningless event.

But it would be irrational to blame science for what is not the proper business of science. We have to move beyond science into the realm of moral and spiritual values to find the forces that can control science: and then we are in the field of both mental health and religion, and find the two cannot easily be separated. If we do not define mental health in a narrow medical way, nor religion in some particular sectarian sense but take it in its universal meaning, then we may consider whether mental health and religion are not two closely related ways of looking at the same thing. It is relevant here to define 'integration' and 'maturity'. The term 'integration' in our title is usually a synonym for mental health in the sense of outgrowing internal divisions and conflicts, split-ego states, and the achievement of a fully functioning 'whole' self. 'Maturity' is defined in dictionaries as 'fully developed', 'perfected by natural growth'. Psychologically I suggest it means *the realization of our full potentialities as persons in personal relationships*. None of us ever are integrated or mature in those full meanings, but they are important goals to have in mind. It may well be that integration, maturity, mental health and religious experience are all closely related.

I will illustrate this by a reference to an American psychoanalyst who paid me a visit. We discussed our analytical interests, and then he said: 'I am a Jew, brought up in the orthodox Jewish religion. When I trained as a doctor, I felt my scientific outlook made it impossible to believe the orthodox faith. I could not become an atheist, which is only being negatively dogmatic and is equally unprovable. I decided to call myself an agnostic, and suspend judgement till I gained further experience. Then I came across Fairbairn's book on psychoanalytic object-relations theory, and your expositions of it. A group of us studied this approach *which put the nature of personal relationships in the centre of the field of inquiry*. I then found that some of us were feeling that Freud's atheism was getting old-fashioned and out of date, and we began to rethink the whole subject. We started with the fact that all through human history there has been something called "religious experience", and we are trying to find out what it is. We feel this psychology of "personal relationships" is most likely to throw real light on the matter.'

That seems to me a valid approach. Our subject is 'Religion in Relation to Personal Integration'. The finding of present-day 'object-relations theory' is that personal integration is a function of growth in the medium of loving personal relationships. Since religion is pre-eminently an experience of personal relationship, which extends the 'personal' interpretation of experience to the nth degree, to embrace both man and his universe in one meaningful whole, the integrating nature of fully developed personal relationship experience, is our most solid clue to the nature of religious experience. It is not my business to deal with philosophical and metaphysical problems, but to examine whether psychology can throw any light on the nature of religion. In doing this I am not using a circular argument, defining integration as religious experience and then treating religious experience as integration. I see both of them as closely related manifestations of *the basic development-process of human living, which is a process of personal-relating at every stage.* A personality split by fears and hates cannot relate constructively to any environmental reality, human or universal. Fears and hates are only outgrown and a healthy 'wholeness' restored by the influence of a healing or therapeutic relationship. Personal integration and personal relationships are a beneficient circle in fact; just as deteriorating relationships and ego-disintegration form a vicious circle leading to catastrophic breakdown. The conflict-ridden ego struggling to relate may fall victim to illusory and regressive forms of both human love and religion. Someone must offer us the real thing before we can make use of it. *But integration is a product of personal relationship, and, as I see, human love and religious experience are two levels of this same basic phenomenon.*

Can there be integrated personalities not related to loving personal relationships? That needs study in depth. Integration is not an all or none matter. Mostly we are more or less integrated, achieving such partial degrees of integration as we can, using whatever supportive good relations come our way. Integration is not the same thing as a life unified on a conscious level by devotion to some exclusive interest or life-work. That is possible along with a lot of hidden tension. Psychological integration must include a sense of inward peace and poise, of wholeness in depth and the security of inward unity. We all dimly sense the possibility of this in our most self-fulfilling moments. In psychodynamic terms, this is our natural pathway of development, when we have the good fortune to grow in good personal relationships from infancy onwards. Is it not what religion describes as 'the peace that passes all understanding', an experience in which the individual and his environment cannot be separated, for it includes a marked sense of security, which can never be found in isolation.

*To discuss religion, we must establish some common ground as to what it is, not in terms of doctrines or organizations but of facts of experience.* We must isolate the essence of 'religious experience' as religious people describe it, and might take the mystics of all religions as our guide; and bring to bear on that, any relevant psychological knowledge. This will not be behavioural or experimental psychology, or psychobiology, but the psychology of 'personal relationships', which psychoanalytic 'object-relations theory' presents as the medium of ego-growth, beginning with the secure infant with the loving mother. It is an analysis of the same *kind* of experience as religious writers describe in not very different terms. Freud (1927) saw that when he described religion as a regression to infantile dependence, and the projection of the parent-image on to the universe. But that only describes neurotic religion. *It is more realistic to see this basically important 'personal relations factor' as not in itself infantile, but as the essential permanent factor in our existence at every stage of life, and as itself undergoing a process of maturing that is central to all our development as persons.* It is the core of all our experience in social life, friendship and marriage, in the ramifications of our cultural life and finally in our religion. For the purpose of this lecture I take *'religion'* not as theological doctrine, nor as an intellectual activity, or an organization; though people who have religious experience must think and theorize about it, and organize in relation to it. I take it as *an overall way of experiencing life, of experiencing ourselves and our relationships together; an experience of growing personal integration or self-realization through communion with all that is around us, and finally our way of relating to the universe, the total reality which has, after all, evolved us with the intelligence and motivation to explore this problem: all that is meant by 'experience of God'.*

Let us now turn to the other concept in our title, 'integration', the 'wholeness' or 'psychic unity' which results from growing out of inner conflicts and ego-splits. In the last 40 years, a great change has come over 'psychoanalytic studies of the personality', to use the title of Fairbairn's book. Psychoanalysis began as a psycho-biology, seeing us as victims of mighty, antisocial, turbulent instincts, sexual and aggressive. The poor little conscious ego was too weak to control what Rapaport called 'the seething cauldron, the battle of the Titans in the unconscious', the chaotic instincts with which our animal ancestry was held to have endowed us. Even Erikson, who really transcended this crude theory of the evolutionary past surviving in us unmodified, perpetuated the idea by suggesting the Centaur 'with its human top and its bestial under-pinnings' as the model of human nature. Freud was at least logical when he stated that on this view most of us are doomed to be either criminal or neurotically repressed. The Centaur model implies that evolution proceeds like the building of a brick wall, layer on unmodified layer, with no real unity as a living whole but only contiguity of parts. Surely evolution is a process which really modifies each stage as it becomes an appropriate constituent of a new and more developed whole. *A man is not a human top on an unchanged animal bottom half, but a new kind of total being. Humans do not have crude animal instincts left over from a primitive past.* Where basic organs and functions persist, they operate in a far more complex product of biological evolution. We have 'human energies' that do not conform to patterns of animal instinct. The concept of 'instinct' is now widely rejected as not useful in human psychology. Fairbairn only used the term adjectivally as indicating 'dynamic patterns of activity which characterize human ego structures'. While recognizing certain biologically innate behaviour patterns, psy-

choanalysis is outgrowing the theory of instincts as reservoirs of energy or motivating entities determining our whole psychic life.

*Emphasis has moved away from 'instinct entities' and their control, on to the vital
problem of how we begin to grow an ego, the core of a personal self, in infancy; and how
this growth in personal reality is rooted in the baby's environment of personal relations, first
with the mother, then the father, family, neighbours, school, and the ever-widening world
around.* Psychodynamic science is not now about 'mechanisms' for the control of
inherited biopsychic drives, thought of in terms of quantitative energy-concepts. It
is about the recovery of psychic wholeness when, in its pristine form, it is disrupted
by early bad experiences. These, as Melanie Klein showed, are mentally retained
and distort the growth of the ego or core of personal selfhood. This is known as
'object-relations theory' in Great Britain and 'interpersonal relations theory' in
America, and has grown out of the original classical instinct theory. This redirec-
tion of psychoanalytic thinking really began with Freud himself, when, after 1920,
he centred his concern more and more on group psychology, and the analysis of the
ego in the field of human relationships.

No one school of thought is responsible for this move from instincts to personal
relations. It belongs to the cultural tide flowing today as a reaction against the
depersonalizing type of thinking characteristic of physical science, as unsuitable for
studying 'man' as a 'person'. In America, Harry Stack Sullivan, as early as the 1920s,
rejected 'human instincts', worked with the concept of a biological (not an animal)
'substrate of personality', and then defined psychiatry as

> the study of processes that involve or go on between people . . . the
> field of interpersonal relations.

This led in America to a great flowering of social psychology. We do not, of course,
reject biology. What is rejected is 'organicism, mechanistic biopsychology' as an
explanatory theory. We reject the confusion of different disciplines. Physics must be
physics, and biology biology, and psychodynamics must be psychodynamics, the
study of the psychosomatic whole of human beings as 'persons', not just 'organisms'.

'Object-relations' thinkers in Great Britain, stimulated by Melanie Klein's
work, went deeper into our inner psychic make-up than American social psychology did, largely because Sullivan, in stressing the interpersonal, hardly explored the intrapsychic. He studied what went on between people, but not so
clearly what went on inside the individual. Melanie Klein achieved a new kind of
analysis of *the internal world of our unconscious*, not as a battle-ground where
primitive instincts fought to break out from ego and superego control, but as *an
internal world of ego-object relations*. We see it in our dreams and childhood fantasies,
where we live a highly personal subjective life of relating to either frightening bad
figures or supportive good ones; the child's fantasy of wicked witches or fairy

godmothers. Years later we find adult patients haunted in nightmares by images of persecuting parents many years after they have died, and see how dependent this makes them on protective relations with helpful people in real life. Only so can they survive the deep-seated depressions and despairs that arise because they feel tied in their deeper mind to bad unloving persecuting persons belonging to their child-hood.

This kind of psychology, developed by Klein and Fairbairn, is now taken back to the very beginnings of the growth of the personal ego by Winnicott. He describes how the mother's 'primary maternal preoccupation' with her baby enables her by profound identification with this little being who began life as part of her, to know intuitively, in a way that the scientifically trained doctor or psychologist cannot know, what her baby is feeling and needing. She provides for him a near-perfect environment of love, care, understanding and valuation. *Winnicott holds that the baby's ego is as weak or strong as the mother's ego-support is weak or strong. His work spotlights what the 'object-relations theory' clarifies, that a human infant cannot begin to be an ego, self or person, except in the medium of good personal relationship.* In a personal vacuum, an environment empty of genuine human rapport, the infant's potentiality for growth of personal selfhood is stunted, and may even be destroyed at the outset. The baby's predicament is expressed by very ill patients who will say: 'I feel quite cut off, unreal, paralysed, a nonentity.'

If the baby has to relate to a bad environment, he grows profoundly disturbed by fears, hates and guilts. If the human environment is not actively bad, persecut-ing, frightening, but simply lacking in true love, devaluing, ignoring, then the baby may suffer an even worse fate. He will feel *stranded in an impersonal milieu, a world empty of any capacity to relate to him and evoke his human potential. He can develop the worst of all psychopathological states, the schizoid condition of withdrawn isolation, fundamental loneliness, profoundly out of touch with his entire outer world*; so that people seem like 'things' and the material world around him seems like a flat unreal imitation. The depersonalized schizoid individual living in a derealized world is the ultimate tragedy, of lack of true personal relationships aborting the very beginnings of 'personal integration' and 'true selfhood'. In fact, we human beings cannot be human, cannot be 'persons' in an empty world. For good or ill, the universe has begotten us with an absolute need to be able to *relate* in fully *personal* terms to *an environment that we feel relates beneficiently to us.* As one little girl said: 'What's the use of being me, if nobody cares?' In fact, if nobody cares, we cannot even get a start in being a 'me'. Spitz demonstrated that if a baby is too seriously deprived of maternal handling, it can deteriorate and die. Bowlby has shown the enormous importance of 'attachments to the mother'. Winnicott regards the basic internal condition of mature, strong, integrated personality as 'basic ego-relatedness", a built-in experience of being in touch, a sense of belonging, of being understood and valued, that arises out of good mothering at the start and remains the inner core of our capacity to face adult life without feelings of isolation. One of the tragic moments in my experience of psychotherapy was when a young man said: 'I'm a non-person. I'm a good scientist but when my day's work is done, I don't know how to relate to people. I can't make friends. I'm a non-person.' *We have to go deeper than the ambivalent love-hate and guilt problems of depression to find the root cause of human distress. Fairbairn's work pointed to the schizoid state of depersonalization through lack of essential personal relations, the emptying or loss of the ego in a vacuum of personal experience, as the final tragedy.* This is the basic conclusion of psychodynamic research, that *human beings have an absolute need for a personal environment that values us as persons, if we are to be able to become and survive as persons.*

I return now to the American analyst who moved from the study of 'personal object-relations' to a rethinking of the nature of religious experience. He sensed that these two were closely related. Here we must not confuse two different things. One is *the relevance of the current forms of religious thought and worship.* These can cease to be helpful in changed cultural conditions, and new forms of religious expression and symbolism do repeatedly evolve. The other is *the reality of the religious experience as such,* which basically does not change. I suggest that *'religious experience' is the same kind of 'stuff' as human 'personal relations experience'.* They differ in 'range' but not in 'type', and both promote personal integration or 'wholeness' of personality in which a human being feels 'at home' in both the human and the universal milieu, experiencing a sense of kinship and belonging. I think it is not a natural or healthy state of mind to experience the universe as merely a stark soulless mechanism which degrades and depersonalizes us to the level of meaningless accidents in an impersonal cosmic process. How real is the experience of the universe as a living environment with which one's own life is bound up, was brought home to me recently by a patient, himself a scientist. He dreamed: 'I was manipulating a colour TV set. It kept fading into a dull grey. I did not want that and kept trying to get it back to colour. When I did it came alive and came out of the screen and was the real world.' He was dreaming of his own growth out of dull impersonal schizoid apathy into a live experience of a real world. He commented: 'I used to think my problem was sex but it isn't. My sex would be all right if I was all right. What I want is to feel like a real live person. I so often see the world as a screen image, no depth, not my world. But when I feel real, the world feels real, and I feel well.' To this man the world was an alien place, when he could not feel a real person himself, and relate to it on that basis of experience. When he felt real and in touch himself, his whole way of life and the world around him changed and 'came alive'. At the end of the session he said: 'I used to see you as an analyst. Now I see you as a person.' *The impersonal scientific approach to the universe is the proper one for the practical purposes of science. But it becomes essentially schizoid if it goes further and tries to dictate our whole philosophy of existence.*

Science is utilitarian knowledge of how to manage the universe as a machine.

It says nothing about the subjective personal meanings and values, the qualitative rather than quantitative aspects of reality for our human living. I am speaking now of physical science. It is not impossible to get scientific, objectively stated knowledge of our subjective personal experience, but that is the task of 'psychodynamic science'. That is a new departure for science and cannot be carried on in the traditional physical science thought-forms. Physical science has outside, not inside information about us as living persons. When Crick and Watson discovered the double helix structure of the DNA molecule, they did not discover what 'life' is, but only the physical structure of the complex molecule that carries 'life'. It may help to find a cancer-cure, and make possible dangerous experiments in modifying existing forms of life, with incalculable consequences. But it will shed no light at all on what we mean by 'love' as a meaningful experience. Science can tell us how our body functions sexually, but cannot explain the experience of two people who are genuinely in love. It cannot explain why a promiscuous man once said to me: 'Sex is a much over-rated pleasure. I'm bored with it'; nor why it seemed like a revelation of new truth to him when I commented: 'Of course; none of your women have ever meant a thing to you'.

These are the kinds of facts that the methods of physical science cannot deal with. They are outside the scope of traditional science; they are in the realm of personal, cultural and ultimately religious experience. They call for a different kind of knowing, like the mother's intuitive, non-intellectual, emotional understanding of her baby through personal relating. This kind of knowing is found in artistic, poetic and religious experience. To conceptualize it intellectually, we need a new approach and different terminology. Erikson (1950) writes of 'a new kind of intellectual process specific for psychoanalysis'. Scientific utilitarian knowledge is indispensable when we want to *manipulate* the universe, to make a computer or cure a disease, make an atom bomb or travel to the moon. Such knowledge is irrelevant when we want to *relate* to the universe as a living environment in which we can be 'persons'. Russell Davis, Professor of Mental Health, Bristol, writes that for *understanding* persons and personal relations the psychiatry of the text book appears to be capable of contributing little. Ibsen and Hamlet are of more interest than Mayer-Gross, Slater and Roth (Davis 1968). For that purpose poetry may be nearer to the truth than physical science. Wordsworth wrote of the beautiful Wye valley

> I have felt,
> A presence that disturbs me with the joy
> Of elevated thoughts, a sense sublime
> Of something far more deeply interfused
> Whose dwelling is the light of setting suns,
> And the round ocean and the living air,

> And the blue sky, and in the mind of man:
> A motion and a spirit that impels
> All thinking things, all objects of all thought,
> And rolls through all things. Therefore am I still
> A lover . . .

This kind of knowing, which is more than utilitarian, involves experiences which cannot *be known* unless they are *shared*: experiences of beauty, of love and of the religious or personal way of feeling our oneness with the totality of the 'real'. *To be whole human beings, we must be both poets and scientists, both lovers and technicians.* It has been suggested to me that mature human love can extinguish the need for religion. It can certainly extinguish, by transcending, a neurotic need for religion. The person finds stability in a real relationship instead of fantasy. If a person has expressed a *need* for religious experience through out-of-date dogmas or inadequate symbolisms of worship, he may lose interest in these when he finds real human love. But to the best of my knowledge, *'mature human love' makes a person more sensitive to his whole environment, and I think is actually one part of a full religious experience.* It is immature infatuations that shut two people up together and exclude them from healthy rapport with their environing world.

This something called 'religious experience' has always existed and achieved expression in artistic and poetic forms. It belongs to the 'personal' side of living, expressed not in mathematical formulae or intellectual theories, but in emotionally meaningful symbols. Psychoanalytic therapy also works by the interpretation of symbolized experiences of personal relationships, and healing has always been an essential part of religion, including its psychological factors, long before modern theories arose. The saying of Jesus 'Thy faith hath made thee whole' I am sure has parallels in all the great religions. Winnicott makes the striking suggestion that all culture is at heart the symbolic expression of our experience of personal relationships, and that the actual beginning of culture is the 'transitional object', the little child's cuddly toy which represents and is a symbol of mother when she is not to be seen. This is the first symbol or *'representation of relationship', the starting-point of our ever-elaborating cultural expression of our experience of our environing universe as not depersonalizing us, a world in which 'persons' can feel at home with a sense of belonging.* I suggest that the fullest personal integration and maturing, the profoundest sense of inner strength and meaningfulness in living, includes the religious way of experiencing our existence in this world. Then the values of our personal lives have more than mere transient reality and we as persons have firm standing ground. Another way of putting this is to say that, however varied the forms religion has taken, and however much religion, like all other human experiences, has been liable to extravagant and neurotic forms, *there has always been 'religious experience' as a fact, because it is a natural phenomenon.*

We are in a fundamental cultural dilemma today. The Ages of Faith were followed by the Age of Reason, of the Humes and Voltaires, with *a choice between religion and rationalistic philosophy*. Hume found in life no connecting principle, no purpose, and had come to regard it as a restless, aimless heaving up and down on a waste ocean of blind sensations. Last century the dilemma changed into *a choice between Religion and Science*, as many still see it. But this is already becoming a false antithesis philosophically. At the turn of the century science was thought to have no limitations. Years ago Bertrand Russell said that science would eventually compile a complete card-index of every fact in the universe and have the answer to every possible question. Today, Dr John Taylor, a London physicist, tells us, on the BBC Third Programme, that you cannot have a scientific theory that explains itself. It always rests on basic unexplained concepts, and in every direction scientific inquiry runs up against ultimate indefinable mysteries.

Yet the *antithesis persists as a choice between a personal and a non-personal or impersonal philosophy of living*. We have no time to trace this in the conflict between democracy and totalitarian ideologies in politics, but there is *a danger of an erosion of personal values even in democracy. Technology is the way material science is transformed into a social structure of living*. Fortunately there is a lot of sound criticism of the subtle ways of influencing people that our technological age has devised, using scientific discoveries. One way is the development of the mass media of communication, which are not so much means of communicating as means of creating a mass mind pushed down to its lowest common denominator, a morbid interest in sex and violence; even though that itself can be a blind protest against the mechanization of living and the denuding of truly personal values. Another way is the ransacking of the results of psychological research by advertising specialists, to find ways of irrational, emotional control of people's minds in the interests of salesmanship. I mention this to show how *our basic cultural dilemma has now emerged in the field of psychological science itself*. We have *non-dynamic behaviour theories* describing human beings as just repertoires of behaviour patterns to be treated by techniques of reconditioning to force their behaviour patterns to conform to the social norms: to quote Dr Dicks (1950) 'to mould them like lead pipes till they fit'. Such an impersonal approach is a clear threat to 'personal values'. Over and against this is the *dynamic psychology* of the psychoanalytic and psychotherapeutic schools, standing for man's basic freedom and right not to be manipulated, but to be supported till he can find his own proper mature selfhood. In contrast to the purely scientific approach, the *psychotherapist* does not set out to 'cure' a patient and expect him to get well in a given time. He seeks to create for a 'person' a situation of secure understanding relationship in which he can *grow* at his own pace, out of all that he is afraid of in his present day disturbed self. The emergence of psychotherapy out of the womb of a 'natural science culture' shows that the spirit of man cannot be suppressed. The reality of the 'person' with his right to be a 'unique' individual always reasserts itself. *There is no reason in science itself why its discoveries should not be used by technology in ways that threaten to impoverish the personal realities of living. But there is today a ground-swell of reaction against this trend. Many people are aware that we are far better at making efficient machines than at rearing happy human beings.*

The exact opposite of both 'personal integration' and 'religious experience' is seen in the way people realize the destructiveness of isolation when deprived of adequate personal relationships in a world that seems impersonal. One elderly woman said: 'I feel everything is quite unreal round me. I feel quite out of touch. I can't reach you. If you can't reach me, I'm lost.' A middle-aged mother put the same experience into a vivid dream. 'I was alone on an empty seashore and terrified. Then I saw your house up the beach, but the tide had come in round me and I was cut off, and panicked. But then I saw a boat tied to your gate and thought calmly "It's all right. I can't get to him but he can get to me!" ' They were convinced that they could not survive as 'persons' in a totally impersonal environment. The rage and hate one can feel of an impersonal loveless world is shown in a dream of a man with a psychotic mother. 'I was hiding in a dugout. There was a vast nuclear explosion. Later I crept out and found everything destroyed. I was utterly alone and frozen with fear.' Hate relations, however, lead back into isolation, so in a later dream he tried to cut *all* feeling out and have a *purely intellectual relationship with his world*; the most perfect schizoid dream I have encountered. He was back in the dugout, hiding from the outer world under a mechanical turret. It had two periscopes for eyes, two slits and a tape recorder for ears, and a hole for a mouth through which he transmitted messages to the world outside. Cut off from healthy emotional relations, a prisoner inside himself, his head functioned as a bit of machinery for purely intellectual communication through scientific instruments which protected him from living contacts. That is what happens if we try to substitute science for religion. *In fact, science and religion belong together as the body and soul of personal living.* Many of the greatest scientists have been deeply religious. To oppose science and religion is false. Science alone supplies our need for tools, and reveals the astonishing order and pattern of the material universe, and its extraordinary evolutionary drive to development. *In some incomprehensible way, the universe itself is not a static mechanism, but alive and growing. But science can tell us nothing about its meaning, value and purpose. Here we have only the quality of our experience as persons to guide us.* Today, psychodynamic science is showing us another kind of order, not material but personal, the way the human infant grows in the medium of intimate personal relationships, to develop stable, mature loving personhood. I suggest that this is the key to *that still wider-ranging experience that human history has called 'religion', a way of experiencing the universe that does not condemn us all to meaningless schizoid isolation*, but relates us to a personal heart of reality, that we refer to by the indefinable term 'God', experienced but not explained, the 'ultimate indefinable mystery' that Dr Taylor finds science always running up against.

We cannot escape experiencing what we may not be able to explain, and when we are thrown back on the genuineness of our experience, it is easy to deceive ourselves. Many under pressure of intense need have believed that they had genuinely fallen in love, only to find that it was a self-deluding infatuation. So in religion, deeply felt needs can persuade people that an intensely believed dogma or an assiduously practised form of worship *is* a real religious experience, when it may only be a substitute for 'real relatedness'. *Private experience has to be tested by comparisons and by the stress of life itself. But all through history human beings have felt this need to experience the universe as validating their reality as persons. I see this not as a speculative dogma but as a fact of human experience, the reason why the historical religions have arisen at all, and survived.* Today, three such different movements as Existentialism, Communist philosophy (as distinct from power politics) and psychoanalysis have all become preoccupied with the experience of 'alienation' as a widespread phenomenon in human lives. We can evade its experience by pressures of conscious activities, political, social, cultural and even formally religious. Fanaticism in any cause is a flight from frightening emptiness within. What I believe to be a psychological fact, and the one full answer to alienation, is the basic religious experience of the universe as not alien to our nature as 'persons', a sense of oneness with ultimate reality akin to the experience of human love, what Jung (1936) referred to when he wrote of 'what the living religions of every age have given to people'. My own 'depth psychology' study of human beings in distress, has led me to regard the assertion that science has made religion unnecessary, as a major example of wishful thinking, aimed at diverting attention from the frightening sense of alienation from which perhaps we all suffer to some degree.

It used to be argued that in pre-scientific times men invented religion because of their 'powerlessness' in the face of nature; and science has altered all that. But it is not 'powerlessness' that is the real problem, but isolation, loneliness, the sense of personal unreality, the answer to which is 'personal relationship', all the way from the infant's need of the mother to the adult's experience of this extraordinary universe in which our life is set. This experience achieves concrete expression in many different credal concepts and symbols, in different ages, cultures, races and nations. None of these forms in which religion finds 'a local habitation and a name' can be the final wholly true intellectual expression of the experience. The history of ideas and institutions never stands still, and they are only fully useful to the generation that makes them. If we forget that, the 'forms' of religious expression can become a dead hand stifling the growth of true religious experience, and an excuse for persecuting heretics who may well be seeing something more clearly than we do. Nevertheless, the cultural past has to be built on, not just rejected. *One remarkable fact is the large amount of common material in the symbols of all times. There is a continuity of insight in which all races and ages share, whether dimly or sophisticatedly, because at bottom the essential religious experience is the same for all men.* I feel a spontaneous sympathy for the extremely sensitive mythology of the African Bushman, as recounted by Laurens van der Post, in spite of my Western philosophical education. *The capacity to have this experience is intrinsically more important than computers, for personally satisfying and meaningful living.* Some of us do not have this experience, just as some of us do not have the experience of human love, and probably those who do, only have it imperfectly. We are all only partly free to have the full range of our possible human experience. I would not dare to claim that I possess any great depth of religious experience, but only to have sensed enough to be convinced that it is a reality. It is not the profession of a faith, but the possession of the experience that matters, and it is an integrating factor in life. I have not attempted any philosophical or metaphysical justification of religion. I have simply taken it as an historic fact of human experience and sought to show what light modern psychodynamic science throws on its nature as the culmination of the 'personal-relationship essence' of human living.

## REFERENCES

Bowlby, J. (1953). *Child Care and the Growth of Love.* Harmondsworth: Penguin Books.

Davis, D. R. (1968). Personal view. *British Medical Journal* 2: 555.

Dicks, H. V. (1950). In search of our proper ethic. *British Journal of Medical Psychology* 23:1–14.

Erikson, E. (1950). *Childhood and Society.* Harmondsworth: Penguin Books (rep. 1965).

Fairbairn, W. R. D. (1952). *Psychoanalytic Studies of the Personality.* London: Tavistock Publications.

Freud, S. (1927). The future of an illusion. *Standard Edition* 21.

Jung, C. G. (1936). *Modern Man in Search of a Soul.* London: Kegan Paul.

Post, L. Van Der (1961). *The Heart of the Hunter.* London: Hogarth Press.

Russell, B. (1944). *The Philosophy of Bertrand Russell.* Chicago: Northwestern University Press.

Sullivan, H. S. (1940). *Conceptions of Modern Psychiatry.* London: Tavistock Publications.

Winnicott, D. W. (1965a). *The Family and Individual Development,* ch. 2. London: Tavistock Publications.

———— (1965b). *The Maturational Processes and the Facilitating Environment.* London: Hogarth Press.

———— (1967). The location of cultural experience. *International Journal of Psycho-Analysis* 48: 368–372.

# Section IV

# 1971–1978
# "LIVING":
# THE POST-WINNICOTT
# PERIOD

# 12

# FREUD, ADLER AND DICKIE VALENTINE[1]

T HIS IS A DUAL-PURPOSE LECTURE, first to mark the centenary of the birth of Alfred Adler, who died of a heart attack in 1937 in Union Street, Aberdeen, on the last day of a course of lectures he gave at the University, one result of which was the setting up of a Professorial Chair in Psychiatry; secondly, to open a Conference on Psychotherapy, individual and social, in our present age, a Conference to inaugurate the Psychotherapy and Social Psychiatry Section of the Royal Medico-Psychological Association. In view of this dual purpose it would not be appropriate to deal only with past history. I shall seek to relate the ideas that originated up to 70 years ago to our contemporary knowledge and needs.

I preface this with a general observation. We can surely at this distance of time ignore the elements of temperamental clash and embittered controversy that marked the early days of psychoanalysis. It is more dignified now, as well as showing more intellectual common sense and scientific objectivity, to accept the fact that these frictions of personality are common to all and every aspect of human affairs, and the students of 'human psychology' cannot be exempt from their own human limitations and imperfections. Freud, Adler and Jung were, in this respect, no better and no worse than the rest of us, but being the first daring explorers of this highly dangerous explosive field of 'human subjectivity' and our 'personal psychic life', a field sown thick with hidden land-mines in the form of 'unconscious repressed conflicts', they were more exposed to unforeseen risks than they were in a position to recognize; just as much today, controversial argument, playing as it does on our individual differences, can generate tendencies to mutual excommunication. If our own 'psychodynamic discipline' has at all matured us, it is now time for us to rise above sectarianism, in the sense of ideologically rigid, closed 'schools of theory', to create an intellectually open-minded 'field of psychodynamic inquiry'

---

1. A slight amplification of a lecture given at Aberdeen University Medical School, September 18, 1970.

within which like-minded students could form 'groups' in stimulating intercourse with other 'groups', not as rival claimants to the possession of the whole truth. This would not preclude each group carrying out its own 'training programme', so long as 'training' does not amount to 'indoctrination'. The schismatic history of theological sectarianism, orthodoxy and heterodoxy has been all too closely paralleled in the history of psychological theory and therapy, and warns us that we all tend to have too much personal emotional investment in our theories for security sake, to be easily able to consider without prejudice the different ideas of other workers in our field.

There is, however, another quite practical problem that tends to keep us apart. Life is short and time is so fully occupied that we have little of it to spare for the detailed study of views other than those we are most used to. Few of us can aspire to be a Dieter Wyss, whose *Depth Psychology: A Critical History* (1966) covers every existing 'school' or 'trend of opinion' in the field of psychodynamic studies, an encyclopaedic volume which can do for us what we cannot do for ourselves: at least keep us open-mindedly informed of the possibilities of there being more than one serious point of view, theoretically, about psychotherapy. It is in this spirit that I shall set out to explore once again the theories of Freud and Adler. So much does space and time circumscribe us, that Jung must be omitted here.

Towards the end of last century, one of those great dramatic developments of the human mind, in its exploration of the mystery of existence, came about. These developments are never recognizable at the start. They begin with a few penetrating minds whose work expands slowly, until eventually history looks back and describes how in such and such an era a new religion arose, a new philosophy emerged, a new technology changed the lives of millions, a new science came to birth. All such movements come to be represented by a few great names, though many take part. Religions centre on such towering names as Moses, Christ, the Buddha, Mohammed, Confucius. We are in humbler but still exalted company with the philosophers, Socrates, Plato and Aristotle, and the more prosaic Descartes, Hume and Kant. In politics, the great creators were for centuries great conquerors, Alexander, Julius Caesar, Charlemagne, Napoleon. By the 18th century a new phenomenon appeared, the revolutionary political philosopher and a dictator ready to enforce his ideas in practice, Rousseau and Robespierre, and Marx and Lenin.

But already by the 19th and 20th centuries another mighty force had come into being in the form of 'physical science'. Even here some names acquired a symbolic significance, Galileo in astronomy, Darwin in biology, Newton in physics. They made a new kind of mental approach to the understanding of the material environment in which our life is set, a non-emotional, purely objective, factual and experimental one, laying bare the workings of the physical machine, from planets and chemical elements to organic bodies and micro-organisms which enable our speculative selves to exist. The material universe and everything in it has, so to speak, been taken apart into ever smaller and smaller particles, to see what they were made of and how we might control them, until now at last the ultimate particles, the proton and electron, have surprised everyone by the fact that when they collide, they do not break up into still smaller groups of 'things' but disappear into a wave of energy. No one knows what that is, but as Bertrand Russell (1946) said, at least it is not a 'thing'. I have reason for mentioning these matters, for the great intellectual and practical problem today is 'things and persons', and what is the difference between them. Physical science, or the pseudo-philosophy of 'scientific materialism' that was fathered on to it, has for a hundred years taken over the mantle of dogmatism that had previously been the property of theology. The physical scientists did not set out to be intellectual dictators, but to do an honest job of investigation, but 'materialism' became a dogma which invaded our own field of psychological interests; so that early in this century we had J. B. Watson denying the existence of 'consciousness'. One wonders how he could be 'consciously aware' of the non-existence of consciousness. His Pavlovian descendants, Skinner and Eysenck, try to forbid us to use any psychological terms at all. You must not say, 'The rat goes down path $L$ because he desires food' for 'desire' is that shocking thing, a teleological psychological term. It actually has 'meaning' and indicates 'purpose', while every good physiological psychologist knows that such mystic things do not exist. All you are permitted to say is that 'If path $A$ is blocked, the rat goes down path $L$'. You must not ask such an unrealistic, dangerous question as to 'why' he should want to go down either path; though as Professor Charles Taylor points out in *The Explanation of Behaviour* (1964), a satiated rat will not bother to go down any path. *If new eras of thinking had come to an end with the development of 'physical science', we would have been debarred from asking any intelligent questions about ourselves in our own private and deep inner experience, and the significance of our relations with one another.*

It is therefore appropriate at this point to say that *the other aspect of our existence, our subjective personal experiencing mental selves, with our purposes and values, loves and hates, persisted in being there to challenge understanding*, and did not go unnoticed. Around the turn of the century a new development arose, among a few people who dared to turn their minds back upon themselves and their fellows to seek deeper understanding. Foreshadowed by the medical hypnotists, it began quietly with one man, Sigmund Freud, working practically alone for ten years from 1890, but has now spread into a world-wide endeavour of what we have come to call psychodynamic inquiry and psychotherapeutic endeavour. Its 'Heroic Age' was from about 1890 to 1914, and three names have stood out to represent it, Freud, Adler and Jung. I think few would dispute Freud's claim to the first place, but it is not given to any one man to know everything. There is something to be learned from the study of all three of these innovators in the field of an entirely new type of study of 'man' in his private, personal and social living. How different were these three men. Freud the scientist, Adler the pragmatist, Jung the mystic. Yet they all three stood together as a developing influence to counteract the blatant 'materialistic psychology' that has had too long a reign this century; though on this matter Freud is the least clear of the three. Adler and Jung in their different ways were unmistakably 'on the side of the angels'. Adler held to the unique individuality of each human being, and created an unmistakable 'ego psychology'. Jung worked out a theory of 'individuation', of finding the true centre of the personal self. Neither of them would have acquiesced in behaviourism, or non-psychological psychology. Freud had a harder time over this problem. Jung's deep interest in religious mysticism protected him from a surrender to materialistic science. Adler's rugged individualism made him see the intensity of the individual's struggle to find and maintain a place for his own personal self in his social world, as more important than problems of neurophysiology. Adler would never have tried to write Freud's 'Psychology for Neurologists'. Adler's was a social psychology, not a psychobiology in the Freudian sense. Adler both gained and lost by this difference. He lost touch with Freud's 'depth psychology' which was the best thing the instinct theory did for Freud; it enabled him to create a psychology of the unconscious, the most important single item in psychodynamic theory from the practical point of view. But breaking with Freud enabled Adler to develop an 'ego psychology' long before Freud came up with this problem seriously, after the First World War. Winnicott has said that Jung early achieved particular insights that psychoanalysts are only just beginning to come up with, and they are inclined to feel that Jung jumped the gun. I think contemporary psychoanalytic 'object-relations theory' can now give a firmer basis to Jung's intuitive observations about 'individuation' than Jung himself could provide. I have not seen any similar recognition by a psychoanalyst that Adler also had insights that early anticipated later psychoanalytic developments, and in that he has been underestimated.

All three of these innovators are now dead, Freud and Adler over 30 years ago, and their basic ideas were developed from 50 to 70 years ago. Quoting them now is beginning to look rather like quoting Newton in physics. It is not easy for us always to remember how different was the intellectual climate of science in their heyday. If Freud could have grown up in the intellectual climate of the philosophy of science of Sir Karl Popper, he would have felt far freer to develop a properly psychodynamic science, instead of a psychobiology that is for ever struggling to transcend itself and grow into being a true psychology of the 'person-ego growing in personal relationships'. If Freud could have known of the pronouncement of one of our greatest neurophysiologists, Lord Adrian (1968), that while perhaps most of our everyday activity could be explained on behavioural lines, 'there is one thing that does not fit into this neat and tidy scheme, the "I" that does the thinking, feeling and willing', he would have felt free to cut loose from the ties of a dubious psychobiology and develop a genuine psychodynamic ego psychology, an insight into what is meant by our being 'persons' and not 'things' or 'machines'. With Bronowski's (1965) view that man is both a machine and a self, and that there are two qualitatively different kinds of knowledge, knowledge of the machine, the organism, which is physical science, and knowledge of the self, which is to us psychodynamic science, or Taylor's 'psychological psychology', he would not have remained tied to what is clearly an inconsistent and outmoded 'instinct theory'. He would, I believe, have developed an 'ego-psychology' far earlier, that would have made for easier cooperation between him and Adler, at least so far as theory is concerned.

It should be clear to us that sex and aggression are not instinctive 'drive-entities', as Fairbairn put it 'giving the ego a kick in the pants' from behind (1952). Sex clearly is one of the biochemically based 'appetites', which, like eating and drinking, excreting and even breathing, can be either over-stimulated, or partially or wholly inhibited, or left free to function normally, according to the state of the ego as a whole personal self. Sex is certainly not our major causal drive. Aggression is not a permanent destructive drive, or death instinct in us, in spite of Konrad Lorenz and Anthony Storr. Aggression is the natural parallel to anxiety. When Freud changed his theory of anxiety, and no longer regarded it as dammed up sexual tension but as 'an ego reaction to threat', he missed a golden opportunity to explain aggression in the same way. There are two ego reactions to threat, fight and flight, or aggression and anxiety leading to fear-dictated withdrawal. Freud's psychobiology is today an unnecessary encumbrance to a realistic ego-and-object-relations theory of our personal selves. Without it, I think that he would have developed, not a control-apparatus-ego, but a 'whole-person-ego' theory, and this would have put him in a position to have seen the importance of Adler's stress on the ego as the individual fighting to win and keep his place among his fellows. While Adler and Jung were wholly on the side of the 'personalists' as against the 'materialists', Freud was only about 50 per cent so, with his pessimistic view of human nature, and his late conclusion that psychoanalysis would probably turn out to be more important as an instrument of scientific research than as a psychotherapy. If it fails as therapy it will be useless as a research method. Adler, who was a brilliant psychotherapist, especially with children, would never have arrived at such a view.

Yet I think Freud would have been set free intellectually in the climate of our present-day 'anti-reductionist philosophy'. In 'Analysis, Terminable and Interminable' (1937) when he says 'where id was, let ego be', he was plainly asking for what was impossible on his own theory, for in classic Freudianism all the drive energy lies in the instincts and the ego is only a 'control-apparatus'. Bowlby (1969) rejects Freud's concept of 'psychic energy' on the ground that all energy is physical only; that I disagree with, and regard it, like Bowlby's obvious fear of 'teleological thinking', as a capitulation to scientific materialism. I reject Freud's concept of psychic energy for the opposite reason, that in fact it is not really psychic. Bowlby seems not to recognize that Freud's psychic energy was in fact simply 'physical energy' (biological drive) labelled as psychic; but it is testimony to the fact that Freud was wanting to find a way of escape from the bondage to physical science if he could, because his real genius was for truly psychological intuitive insights into human motivations. *Freud badly needed what was unobtainable in his time, intellectual freedom to develop a truly psychodynamic science, in which 'psychic energy' would really be psychic, i.e. it would be 'motivational energy'.* This is implied in Adler's view of the inferiority complex. Physical science has no right to a monopoly of the term energy, when a man's values and purposes and fundamental aims in life can be so powerful as to motivate a whole life-time of strenuous and self-sacrificial activity. 'Motivational energy', greatly influenced by internalized early parental object-relationships, is the core of Freud's theory of the unconscious, as is shown by the concept of the 'superego', but he never seemed clearly to recognize this. The whole idea of the ego having to borrow energy from the id and neutralize it, in order to control the id, as in Hartmann (1964), is mere playing with words. Adler accepted that the ego has its own teleological, motivational, purposive energies, which are psychic, not physical. The person-ego, or true self living through its bodily organism, is the driver, not the car. Adler did not have the same kind of intellectual scientific inhibitions as Freud had. He began his own independent psychological observations, as a general practitioner, by seeing that patients who had organic handicaps strove to compensate for their sense of inferiority, a true theory of motivation. He saw his patients as a good family doctor ought to see them, as real persons, individuals with an aim in life, and a sense of values, and a capacity for suffering if for any reason they felt inadequate and devalued. Adler simply accepted the reality of the patient as a 'person' who had a 'personal life' to live, and 'personal values', a personal 'life style' to motivate his strivings not to be left out of the race and tamely accept inferiority, if he could do anything to prevent it. Freud began to psychologize, not from the point of view of the general practitioner but of the scientific laboratory research worker, and for long wished to give up psychoanalysis and return to his neurology laboratory which did not pose such awkward 'unscientific' problems as psychopathology presented. Yet in fact Freud did not surrender, but went bravely on with his scientific conscience and his psychologically intuitive genius at war inside him. In spite of all, Freud along with Adler and Jung have been major influences helping to keep alive the possibility of a truly 'psychological psychology' in the era of scientific impersonalism: the reality of 'persons' as well as 'things'.

I referred just now to the growing 'anti-reductionist' philosophy of science, and will quote some examples. Dr Chance of Birmingham (1968), the ethologist, denies that 'behaviour' can be analysed into, or reduced to, 'atomic particles of behaviour' in the Eysenckian fashion and specifically rejects reductionism as out of date. He is concerned with the significance of the behavioural 'wholes' that are built up, not with what bits and pieces they could be taken apart into. Dr Bannister, a clinical psychologist, rejects behaviouristic reductionism, and writes:

> The chances of developing a science of physiological psychology are about as good (or as bad) as the chances of developing a chemical sociology or a biological astronomy. . . . The unquestioning acceptance of physiological psychology most often stems from a reductionist approach. Reductionism is a philosophic posture which assumes that physiology is somehow nearer to reality than psychology and therefore a more 'basic science'. [1968]
>
> The medical model for treating psychological disturbance has already shown itself to be inappropriate and must eventually be replaced by a psychological model. [1969]

Sir Denis Hill made that same point in his inaugural lecture at the London Institute of Psychiatry. But finally, a Director of Medical Research, Sir Peter Medawar (1969) (whose view is the more welcome as he is not exactly friendly to psychoanalysis) sets forth the 'hierarchical model of the structure of knowledge', that it is like a building with a ground floor which is physics and chemistry, and then rises tier by tier upwards, with physiology, biology, ethology, sociology, and finally psychology, first behaviouristic, and finally truly personal psychology. He does not enumerate the tiers or floors as exactly as I have done but that is what his theory involves, based, as he states, on the views of Popper. The important point is that he specifically insists that *the process of thought can only move forwards, and upwards, not backwards and downwards.* At each level on the way up, new phenomena arise which call for new concepts which cannot be explained in terms of the concepts used on the floor below. Such a theory of knowledge would have been a godsend to Freud and would have enabled him to use his psychological genius untrammelled. Both Adler and Jung could and would have made full use of it, and in spite of their different types of mind, all three might have found more to agree than to differ about in the end. I think that in the growing struggle against the materialistic impersonalism of physical science, the psychodynamic studies of Freud, Adler and Jung have played a larger part than can yet be estimated. It is their work that has kept alive the fully psychological personal approach of the psychotherapist, in spite of all its detractors. Adler's views must have their share of recognition in this matter. All three stood for a radically new way of studying human beings in their personal lives.

We need not concern ourselves with their temperamental clashes and schismatic differences of opinion; these are common to most human undertakings.

It would, I think, have been better if they had never met, but each developed his own ideas in his own circle of adherents apart. Then other independent minds could have assessed and related their views without controversy. Adler and Freud were such different types of personality. Adler was a social extravert, gregarious, and a second son frankly jealous of his model eldest brother. He once said to Phyllis Bottome (1939), his biographer: 'My eldest brother is still ahead of me and always will be.' Thus, having to strive to overcome a sense of inferiority was bound to be the starting-point of his psychology, a motivational ego problem. Freud was an eldest brother, used to the sense of authority that position gave him. It was reflected in his early theoretical blindness to the primary importance of mothers, and his automatic acceptance of the idea at first, that it is the father who is the dominant family head, the superego incarnate. On the theories of both of them, therefore, they were in an emotional relationship which gave them little chance of working together. We have to remember that the first analysts did not have the advantage of having a personal analysis. It will be useful to look at their differences.

Freud himself was a battle ground between a rigidly scientific training and a daring psychologically speculative intelligence, with unique intuitive gifts. It was certainly not his Helmholtzian science nor the influence of Brücke the physiologist that drove him into the exploration of psychic life and later to write about religion, civilization and its discontents, Leonardo da Vinci, and Moses and Monotheism. He was at once an austere intellectual with a deep if often hidden warmth of heart. He would write to Pfister as 'Dear Man of God'. His scientific systematizing intellect at first produced a clear-cut neurological theory which, only after a tremendous struggle did he accept, was unable to meet the need for psychological understanding. In view of his own and Hartmann's stress on psychoanalysis as a biological science, it is doubtful whether Freud ever was able to let himself see that psychological understanding goes right beyond physical science. Yet the other half of him, his genius for true psychological intuitive insight allied to his speculative intellect, kept his theories for ever on the move, and particularly after the 1914–18 war, he became ever more deeply concerned about 'ego' problems, and problems of civilization and religion; and he redefined anxiety as an 'ego-reaction to threat'. I think we may fairly say that 'ego-reaction to threat' exactly defines the point of view with which Adler started 20 years earlier. I do not see any evidence that the tragedy of the war forced Adler, as it did Freud, into a major new development of theory. Adler's theory was already an 'ego theory'. One great thing Freud had done, through his explorations of sexuality, taking him back into early childhood, was to establish, as demonstrable fact, the existence of an 'unconscious but enormously active area' in our personality, manifested in both conscious and dreaming fantasy and symptoms. He showed that this 'unconscious' was principally the all too active persisting legacy of our early childhood experiences. It remains that, whether we believe in instincts or not. He endowed us with a 'depth psychology' such as the world had never known before, which remains permanent even though Freud's-views of its contents and processes have undergone change. The Kleinian 'internal objects' theory, and the work of Fairbairn, Winnicott, Balint and others have established, not so much a double unconscious, a primary biological id, and a secondary repressed unconscious of forbidden impulses, but the fact that *we all live in two worlds at once, an inner world where the self of our early life is still bogged down in early traumatic life-situations, and an outer world of the present day where we live subject to interference from this inner world,* what Freud called transference and resistance. He once wrote most generously, in 'The History of the Psychoanalytic Movement' (1914):

> Any line of investigation, no matter what its direction, which recognizes transference and resistance as the starting-point of its work, may call itself psychoanalysis, though it arrives at results different from my own.

In the same work, Freud accused Adler of making psychoanalysis into a system, but I would think Freud was more of a system-maker than Adler, and many of his followers made 'classical Freudian oedipal theory' into a system that admitted of no real development. It would have been better if Hitler had not dispersed the original hard core of the Freudian circle, but had left mid-European psychoanalysis to grow and exercise its influence from there, and also left Adler's thirty child guidance clinics at schools untouched. Then, under the stimulus of their work, therapists in Britain and America and child guidance workers all over Europe could have been more free to develop their psychodynamic theory and therapy in their own very different atmospheres.

By comparison with Freud, Adler was a very different kind of man and was bound to produce a different type of theory, a less elaborately systematic and more fluid, but humanly realistic, set of ideas. Adler was essentially an individualist by temperament. I do not mean that as a criticism. I mean that he made a strong and therapeutic impact on his patients by his individuality, while Freud sat out of sight behind the patient's couch. He grew medically, not out of Freud's laboratory milieu, but out of general medical practice. His psychological interests began independently of Freud, with his observations of how his patients compensated for their organic inferiorities or handicaps in their personality development. This was not a starting-point that would naturally lead him to a 'depth psychology' in the sense in which that was the most important of Freud's contributions. That was something that Adler failed to take really into account. His own view of the unconscious was more superficial. On the other hand, his starting-point enabled him to create an ego psychology, and see the importance of ego problems long before Freud did, at a time when, as Anna Freud admitted (1936), it was heterodox to discuss the ego.

When, however, in course of time, Freud came up with this problem, he had laid deeper foundations for an ego psychology than Adler achieved, as may now be seen from the ego theories of Fairbairn, Winnicott and others. That does not mean that Adler's contributions to 'ego psychology' are not important. His actual analysis of patients' ego problems was always clinically extremely acute and insightful, but they needed to be integrated with deeper views of the total personality. Adler remained socially orientated and Freud remained scientifically (in the narrower sense) orientated. When Freud ventured into the social field, he showed himself to be a deeply convinced pessimist about human nature. He was an analyst of the impersonal universal constituents (as he saw them) of the human psyche. Adler analysed the struggling social individual.

At this point, we may look at Adler's chapter 19 in *Individual Psychology* (1929) on 'The Role of the Unconscious in Neurosis', dated 1913. After 11 years of friction, he had broken away from Freud in 1911 to develop his own theory of 'individual psychology'. Curiously, I find myself agreeing with Adler at many points as against the Freud of that period, and yet I still feel that these very points are more fundamentally explained today, not by Freud but by later developments that have arisen on the basis of Freud's work. Adler did not accept Freud's 'Oedipus complex', and substituted the valuable 'family constellation' concept; but contemporary psychoanalysis itself now holds a broader view of oedipal problems than the original over-simple classic theory, and also has gone much deeper down into the far more important pre-oedipal problems of the schizoid infantile level. Again, Adler rejected Freud's view of a sex instinct as the fundamental motivational drive, the causal force, in all human action, and he insisted that human character and action must be explained teleologically. I definitely agree with Adler. When we come, however, to the key concept of 'the unconscious', Adler's view seems to me too superficial. The unconscious calls for a far more profound understanding, of the kind that post-Freudian theory has today developed. Not that we could have expected either Freud or Adler to have achieved this more profound view at that time, 60 years ago. It is rather that it has developed on the basis of Freud's, not Adler's, starting-point.

Adler had recognized his patients' struggles to compensate for what he held to be organic inferiorities, and when he seized on this sense of 'inferiority' as the starting-point of the neurotic process, he had in fact made the first approach to what we now know as the 'schizoid problem'. Not that anyone could have recognized that then. Freud had accepted the general psychiatric view of an absolute division between neurosis and psychosis. Neurotics could be treated because they were capable of personal transference relations and could project their early oedipal relations with parents on to the analyst and work through them. Psychotics were thought to be incapable of transference and unreachable by psychoanalytic therapy, which called for an 'intact ego'. We now know that the idea of an 'intact ego' is a fiction. It is all a matter of degree. The neurotic has enough ego-sense to be struggling to relate, but his ego is weak, torn by conflicts rooted in early relations to parents and siblings just because these were unsatisfactory. Adler was more occupied with the position of siblings in the 'family constellation', Freud with the relations of children to parents, which the family constellation concept could include. The more clear-cut the oedipal problem, the more clear it is that neurotic parents forced it on the child. In fact, the patient's unconscious inner world, and therefore his external struggles to relate to people, are far more complex than either the oedipal or family constellation concepts account for. What emerges as you go ever deeper into the childhood of a very disturbed patient is that his problems in relating now in adult life are not simply due to his being tied to lusty powerful sexual and aggressive instincts and relations to parents, or simply to feeling an 'inferior' among siblings, but to the fact that *both oedipal relations and omnipotence fantasies are pathetic efforts to manufacture a pseudo-relationship out of sexual and aggressive emotions or the 'will to power', because genuine personal relations have been non-existent.* The quality of truly parental personal relationship was so poor that in the last resort, if he dared let himself know how he really felt, the child would feel that he was out of touch with everyone, living in an emotional vacuum in which he could find no one with whom he could experience himself as real. The schizoid patient at worst feels he has not got an ego, and while in part and at the level of consciousness he fights to make contacts of any kind, to feel some sort of self, at bottom he is in despair at his feeling of utter emptiness. The feelings of inferiority, Adler's starting-point, are betraying signs, according to their degree of severity, of an ultimate failure of genuine ego development at the very start. We could not expect either Freud or Adler to recognize what over half a century of research enabled a Fairbairn and a Winnicott to see and conceptualize. It was Fairbairn who was one of the first to say that the more severe hysterias have roots deep down in the schizoid, and schizophrenic problems. Freud's 'Oedipus complex' was the 'form' in which he discovered the intensity of his patients' struggles to hold on to *relationships* at all costs, and exploit sex and aggression for the purpose, thus exposing themselves to neurotic guilt. Adler's 'inferiority complex' theory was the 'form' in which he discovered the other half of the whole problem, the patients' struggles to find a *self* with which to relate to others. In this discovery he had touched the tip of an iceberg which had far more below the surface of consciousness than it was possible for anyone at that time to see. 'Inferiority feelings' were the betraying signs of a degree of ego weakness which could, at the worst, be total. Inferiority is a symptom, not a cause of problems, and to ascribe it simply to a need to overcome 'organic or other inferiorities' is to be misled as to its real nature. Serious actual physical handicaps are rare, differences of natural endowments are not interpreted as 'organic inferiorities' by a child who grows up securely mothered and valued for his own sake. In a broad sense all children are 'organically inferior' to older siblings and adults, simply because they are small and weak. But this does not start every child off on the road of neurotic over-compensation and the development of grandiose and omnipotent fantasies and wishes.

The origin of the problem is not in organic or real inferiorities but in the failure of parents to give basic emotional security to the child, so that he cannot grow an ego strong enough to cope with his real-life situation. He has not developed what Winnicott calls a built in 'basic ego-relatedness' (1965). My own experience is that patients who have this fundamental problem in very severe form feel, *not inferior, but different* in a way that puzzles and confuses them, and in the worst cases actually empty. They will say, 'I feel I haven't got a self. I'm a nobody, a non-person'. In conversation, Dr Weissman (Chairman, Adlerian Society of Great Britain) suggested that Adler's 'inferiority feeling' was the same thing as the 'schizoid state'. That, however, is not the case. If a person feels 'inferior' he is in a relationship to another person whom he feels is superior. The 'schizoid state' is caused by the 'emptying experience' of there being no one there to relate to in any way, living in a psychic vacuum in which both 'world' and 'self' feel unreal.

In one important matter Adler was nearer the truth than Freud, in that he did not draw the then accepted absolute distinction between psychosis and neurosis. If Phyllis Bottome (1939) is right, Adler held that the chief difference between the psychotic and the neurotic is that while

> the neurotic builds up an unreal world to live in, he can live in it or not as he chooses, and he more than suspects its unreality; whereas a psychotic is compelled to live in his unreal world, while he has ceased to doubt that it is unreal. Adler used to say, 'I always feel a cold sensation at the base of my spine when I find myself in the same room as a psychotic. *He is a man who has cut himself off* [my italics] from the rest of mankind'. Adler did not believe that psychotherapy in treating a psychotic is different in kind - but merely in degree - from that of the treatment of a neurotic, but always a far longer and slower process, with far more likelihood of serious relapses.

Adler was certainly right there, as contemporary psychoanalysis recognizes. Marion Milner's recent full length case-history of a 20 years' successful treatment of a schizophrenic girl entitled *The Hands of the Living God* (1969) is proof positive. But Adler could not make full use of that insight, nor do I think anyone else at that time could have done; the clinical evidence for a full 'depth psychology' was not then available.

There is, however, a particular reason why Adler did not probe deeper. He regarded both neurosis and psychosis as the patient's choice. The psychotic has 'cut

himself off from the rest of mankind'. Bottome (1939) writes that he would explain
to the neurotic

> how he exaggerated his difficulties, and how to tackle the real obstacle
> in a sensible way. He would say 'I believe that by changing our opinion
> of ourselves we can also change ourselves'.

I wish it were so easy, though I am sure that back in 1900–1914 we could not expect
anyone to have seen the bedrock truth. Adler's individual moral approach, not in
blaming the patient, but in making him responsible for resolving his problems by
an active conscious choice, did in fact blind him to the ultimate facts, while Freud's
theory of the 'depth psychology' of the unconscious made it possible later on to
arrive at the bedrock truth today, and that is that the neurotic has not simply
'chosen' to over-compensate for what he feels to be organic inferiorities, by
omnipotence fantasies; he is struggling to cope with life with an ego that has been
weakened, undermined, by unsupportive family relationships in the earliest impressionable and vulnerable years of infancy and through early childhood. The
psychotic has not 'cut himself off from the rest of mankind'. He has been frightened
off into a drastic withdrawal by seriously bad relationships, or even definitely shut
out of all relationship by parents who simply did not want him and did not relate
at all to him. He has been left to grow in a vacuum of personal relations. Nor is it
true that he is incapable of transference as Freud thought. What he is transferring
to us is his basic conviction that no relationship is possible; he comes to us 'out of
touch' and lets us see it and hopes we will understand, for as Winnicott (1965) says,
in the very last resort there is always a 'true self' deeply hidden away in cold storage
hoping for a chance of a rebirth into a more accepting world. One extremely
schizoid patient of mine would say, 'I feel when I come here I leave part of myself
outside', clearly hoping I could help him to link up with it again; or why tell me
about it? Another patient dreamed of being a little girl in a high chair in a gloomy
kitchen, staring at a man lying asleep or drunk, sprawled half on a sofa and half on
the floor. No mother was there; she was in fact working at a factory, and father, a
drunken sailor, presently disappeared for good and all. She later dreamed of a tiny
baby locked up in a steel drawer, staring with wide open expressionless eyes because
there was nothing to see, and she said, 'I can't get to you. If you can't get to me I'm
lost'. Later she had that 'gloomy kitchen' dream again, but this time I came in and
carried her out. I have described these phenomena in detail in *Schizoid Phenomena,
Object Relations and the Self*, Parts 1 and 3 (1968). This is how the schizoid and
schizophrenic has transference experiences. They communicate to us their cut-
offness, and if we cannot understand that and help them, by getting slowly into
touch with the lost heart of their innermost self, they are lost indeed. All that could
not have been seen as far back as the beginning of this century and was not seen by

either Adler or Freud, but Freud's depth psychology, in a way he hardly foresaw, going deeper than oedipal problems, has helped us most, at this vital point.

Adler's view, so far as I understand it, was that the child growing into adulthood, with a basic sense of inferiority, seeks through his 'will to power' to overcome or overcompensate for that 'inferiority' by creating a 'fictive goal of superiority', of omnipotence. As this becomes ever more unrealistic it must be shielded from the test of contact with reality. Adler (1929) wrote:

> The patient makes use of the unconscious in order to be able to follow the old goal of superiority. . . . One of his artifices is to transfer the goal into the realm of the unconscious . . . The frequent antithesis between the conscious and the unconscious impulses is only an antithesis of means. For the purpose of heightening the feeling of personality or the attainment of the goal of god-likeness, it is irrelevant.

In 1900–1913 that was shrewd and penetrating analysis, and we should judge a man's writings always in the light of the period when they were written. But we cannot now accept that as a correct analysis of the deep unconscious. It makes it little more than one aspect of neurotic choice or stratagem; to protect godlike fantasy from the disillusioning test of contact with conscious reality, it must be made and kept unconscious. Adler's unconscious is created by choice. He wrote:

> If this 'moral' goal is hidden away in some experience or fantasy, the patient may to such an extent fall a victim to amnesia . . . that the fictive goal become lost to view . . . When the neurotic life-plan might nullify itself by coming into direct opposition with the feeling of the community, then its life-plan is formed in the unconscious . . . Psychotherapy can begin here by bringing into consciousness the guiding ideas of greatness, thereby rendering their influence upon active life impossible. [1929, p. 230]

This is a good description of the early days of psychotherapy, when it was held that helping the patient to achieve conscious 'insight' was the curative factor. 'Insight therapy' is still a label much in use but it does not correspond to the realities of treatment. The development of 'insight' during psychotherapy is more the result than the cause of good progress; a sign that a 'growth process' is under way due to the efficacy of the therapeutic personal relationship of patient and analyst. Insight then stabilizes and helps on that process. I think that in this respect Adler stood where all the early psychotherapists stood. They put too much responsibility on the child and the patient for the existence of his weaknesses and his defences, and expected him to be able to alter himself, if he could be got to see what he was up to.

Phyllis Bottome (1939) includes in her biography of Adler, as an appendix, the Memorial Address given by Dr Lydia Sicher, and she makes the Adlerian position completely clear.

> Adler no longer regarded neurosis as a disease *sui generis*, but unmasked it as a social deviation, as the effect of imperfect 'cooperation' with the collective action of humanity. The neurotic is no longer to be treated as a sick person to be pitied, who by the ordinance of fate has become a victim of heredity, his environment or his instincts, but as a *person who has made a mistake, who has not learned to accommodate himself to the rules of the game of life* [my italics]. Perception, feeling, thinking and willing— all the bodily and mental situations of an individual—are actively directed by himself, and are employed unintentionally and unknowingly for the purpose of safeguarding his own personal ideal, which allows him to develop an activity centred solely on himself.

Hysterical behaviour certainly can look just like that at times, if we do not recognize the terrible fears that are hidden behind the exploitatory behaviour of the florid hysteric reaction. But to leave it at that superficial level of analysis does grave injustice to deeply disturbed people who are more like a person flung into the sea when he cannot swim, but only frantically clutch at anything that looks like a life-belt.

When we examine now those theoretical beginnings of psychodynamic research, we find pretty much what we would expect to find; valuable initial insights that opened up unsuspected depths. Looked at today, Adler offers a too simple theory of the self in his 'individual psychology', and Freud offered too simple a theory of 'personal relations' in his 'Oedipus complex' and 'instinct theory' but here were the two halves of the truth or the beginnings of them, the truth that a 'personal ego or self cannot be created or grow in a vacuum of personal relations, or in bad personal relations'. The unconscious is not a stratagem for hiding our neurotic choices or fictive goals; it is the accumulated experience of our entire infancy and early childhood at the hands of the all-powerful adults who formed us. We have no choice about its creation, and we can only acquire the possibility of a regrowth to normal stability and self-confidence after a bad start, if someone can give us the kind of reliable and understanding, valuing relationship that Balint called 'recognition', i.e. recognition by the therapist of the patient's actual reality as a person in his own right, in a way that slowly sinks in and sets going new growth processes leading to the rebirth of a genuine self. A human being is not born with a fully formed ego, however infantile. He is rather 'a psyche with human personal ego-potential', needing good human relations in which to grow. Professor Stoller (1968) of Los Angeles says that the formative factor for good or ill is the 'minute by minute, hour by hour, day by day, month by month, year by year impact of the atmosphere of the parents on the child', and that is what is built-in as we grow up, as the foundation of all later adult development. Our contemporary 'object-relations theory of the personality', that a true self can only grow in the soil of personal relations with other selves, beginning with the baby and the mother, settles once for all the question of the nature of the therapeutic factor, as not a 'technique of treatment' but a 'quality of relationship'. A patient who had a psychotic mother, and began therapy as an ill man, off work and stuck in a junior position, and who has progressed steadily through a long period of therapy to the very top of his professional tree, came in recently and sat down and said straight away, 'I feel relaxed now the moment I come in and sit down. It used to be half way through sessions before I could feel like that'. His capacity to do his work in a relaxed state of mind has developed *pari passu* with his capacity to relax in sessions. There has been plenty of dream analysis, and life-story telling, and frightened and angry transferences and all that one finds in the textbooks, but all the time there has been a slow growing process of feeling more and more like a real person in relation to me. That is what we have to make possible for our patients, most of all for the deeply schizoid ones. We are in luck if we find a simple case where a symptom can be cleared up in a few weeks or months by 'insight therapy'. That can and does happen, but they are not the cases we learn most from. The deeper we go, the more severely we ourselves are tested, till finally we might say, if I may venture to elaborate the words of St Paul:

> Though I speak with the tongues of men and angels, popes and cardinals, archbishops and theologians, philosophers and scientists, psychiatrists and psychotherapists, Freudians, Kleinians, Adlerians, and Jungians, and though I have the gift of prophecy (of interpretation and insight) and understand all mysteries and all knowledge (of all the psychodynamic theories) and have not love (therapeutic love, the kind of love a genuine parent can give to a child), I am a sounding brass and tinkling cymbal.

Where real therapy is going on, we and our patients are growing together at the same time, and neither of us can be the same afterwards. What Adler called 'the power to turn a minus into a plus' is in the end the 'power to grow from being an insecure child into being an adult', and mental processes are, as he said, not causal, not driven from behind by a force, but teleological, drawn forwards to the goal of our self-fulfilment in personal relationships.

The child's ego or self can be fragmented by multiple inconsistencies in the ways adults handle him. He needs a 'whole' therapist to grow whole with. At one extreme Freud was impersonal in treatment, the interpreting 'mirror' analyst, out of sight behind a couch. At the other extreme Adler was entirely personal, even to letting patients invade his private life and follow him on holidays, not I think the best way of helping the child in the patient to grow up and go his own way. But in those early pioneering days, all methods needed to be tried; yet in the end Freud grew pessimistic about therapy and Adler did not. Not that 'personal therapy' has to go to Adler's extreme. It is true, as St John wrote, that 'perfect love casteth out fear' but therapeutic love is not subjective involvement, but objective respect for, and understanding of, the other person's reality so that he can find himself. The one absolute, fundamental need is not for 'satisfaction' or 'gratification' of instincts, but for stable psychic 'existence' itself; not a need to be sexual or aggressive or superior or to be boss, but simply to 'be', to feel so sure you are a real person that you are hardly conscious of it as you enjoy living. The ultimate fear is not of sex deprivation or persecution or inferiority, but the terrible fear of just 'not being anything', of feeling empty, a nobody, a non-person. People will do anything to fill that gulf with compulsive repetitive thoughts or acts, anxieties, aggressions, obsessions, physical symptoms, anything, rather than be threatened by the fear of the loss of the self, of depersonalization. That is the depth to which Adler's inferiority complex and Freud's repetition compulsion pointed. Psychotherapists have no monopoly of this truth. For confirmation, may I appeal to an unexpected source. The title of a 'pop' song by Dickie Valentine is 'The Best Thing to Be Is a Person'.

Any discussion of psychotherapy, to be realistic, must admit that, while it can provide an answer to the individual problems of the lucky few who can get it (and however many therapists we train, their patients will still be the lucky few, especially when we remember the importance of matching patient and therapist), it cannot by itself be the answer to the massive problem of social or community mental disturbance or instabilities of personality. The work of the specialists provides the basis for the answer, but the total problem of mental disturbance is so vast as to be beyond the reach of individual therapy. Professor Sir Denis Hill has already warned us that the case load of deviant characters, drug addicts, alcoholics, sexual offenders, delinquents and so on, many of them not, properly speaking, medical cases at all, is more than the medical profession can possibly cope with, and he has called for the training of both medical and non-medical personnel in psychotherapy (1969).

But the full answer must be based on the principle that prevention is better than cure. The principles and conditions of stable, healthy personality develop-ment, as clarified by the specialists, have somehow to be brought home to teenagers, parents and teachers, and to social workers of all kinds, ministers and clergy, and even politicians and business executives. The stark truth about the causes of personality distress, and the rationalized disguises it assumes when not breaking out as illness (Freud pointed out that crime, i.e. anti-social behaviour, aggressiveness, is the other side of neurosis), and the basic necessities in the personal care of children at all age levels, beginning with mother and infant, must soak ever deeper into our culture. The process has already begun in the increasing education of all the social work professions in the principles of psychodynamics. We must give Adler his due as a pioneer of this movement, with his thirty child guidance clinics attached to schools, and lectures to teachers, and conferences with parents. The only danger here lies in its being done amateurishly. Expertly done it can nip in the bud a tremendous lot of trouble.

## REFERENCES

Adler, A. (1929). *Individual Psychology*, rev. ed. London: Kegan Paul.

Adrian, Lord (1968). Quoted by C. Burt (1968). Brain and consciousness. *British Journal of Psychology* 59:55–69.

Balint, M. (1968). *The Basic Fault*. London: Tavistock Publications.

Bannister, D. (1968). The myth of physiological psychology. *Bulletin of the British Psychological Society* 21:229–231.

_____ (1969). Clinical psychology and psychotherapy. *Bulletin of the British Psychological Society* 22:299–301.

Bottome, P. (1939). *Alfred Adler: Apostle of Freedom*. London: Faber.

Bowlby, J. (1969). *Attachment and Loss*, vol. 1. London: Hogarth Press.

Bronowski, J. (1965). *The Identity of Man*. Harmondsworth: Penguin Books.

Chance, M. R. A. (1968). Ethology and psychopharmacology. In *Psycho-pharmacology*, ed. C. R. B. Joyce. London: Tavistock Publications.

Fairbairn, W. R. D. (1952). *Psychoanalytic Studies of the Personality*. London: Routledge & Kegan Paul.

Freud, A. (1936). *The Ego and the Mechanisms of Defence*. London: Hogarth Press.

Freud, S. (1914). History of the psychoanalytic movement. *Standard Edition* 14.

_____ (1937). Analysis, terminable and interminable. *Standard Edition* 23.

Guntrip, H. (1968). *Schizoid Phenomena, Object Relations and the Self*. London: Hogarth Press.

Hartmann, H. (1964). *Essays on Ego Psychology*. London: Hogarth Press.

Hill, D. (1969). Psychiatric education during a period of social change. *British Medical Journal* 1:205– 209.

Medawar, P. (1969). *Induction and Intuition in Scientific Thought*. London: Methuen.

Milner, M. (1969). *The Hands of the Living God*. London: Hogarth Press.

Russell, B. (1946). *History of Western Philosophy*. London: Allen & Unwin.

Stoller, R. (1968). *Sex and Gender*. New York: Science House.

Taylor, C. (1964). *The Explanation of Behaviour*. London: Routledge & Kegan Paul.

Winnicott, D. (1965). *The Maturational Processes and the Facilitating Environment*. London: Hogarth Press.

Wyss, D. (1966). *Depth Psychology: A Critical History*. London: Allen & Unwin.

# 13

# PSYCHOLOGY AND COMMON SENSE

THE TERMS OF MY TITLE[1] ARE taken from the debate between Professor Kuhn and Sir Karl Popper on the nature of science, of which more anon. The title could as well be 'What is a "Scientific" Psychology?' A survey of British Psychological Society *Bulletins* over the last ten years shows a marked shift of opinion, gathering force, as to what constitutes 'psychology'. This coincides with far-reaching changes in the overall philosophy of science. The two cogent articles by Joynson (1970, 1972) summarize an incipient revolution in psychology. It may cause some surprise that as a psychoanalytical therapist I do not want to see too violent a pendulum swing of opinion, but an open-minded dialogue between psychoanalysis and some constructive contributions of behaviourism. Some bias on both sides is no obstacle. Sir Peter Medawar (1969) states: 'Innocent unbiased observation is a myth: "experience itself is a specimen of knowledge which involves understanding", said Kant'. I have never worried about criticisms that psychoanalysis is not science. Laboratory experimentalists do not have the 'experience that is a species of knowledge' of human beings, day in and day out suffering anxieties of often suicidal intensity. I always felt, what I think Joynson demonstrates, that psychologists were mostly more concerned to be 'scientific' than to be truly 'psychological'. I left University College, London, in the 1920s with a divided mind about both psychology and psychoanalysis. I felt that efforts to make psychology a physical science were a blind alley, ending in nothing but just physiology, valuable in its proper place but not psychology. Joynson substantiates this. At the same time I had misgivings about an inner contradiction within psychoanalysis, between its 'physicalistic' psychobiology of instincts and the intuitively accurate, personalistic or truly 'psychological' insights of Freud into the vicissitudes of the personal self growing in unfavourable environments of bad personal relations. As Joynson noted, Freud's early biological unconscious overshadowed the ego or personal self.

---

1. The paper's original title is "Orthodoxy and Revolution in Psychology."

Psychoanalysis could not make up its mind whether it was biology or psychology (which is still true of Hartmann's ego psychology and unnecessarily true of Kleinian psychoanalytic theory), and psychologists could not make up their minds whether their studies were physiology or psychology. For me, the question, regarded by many intellectuals as unreal, 'Is psychoanalysis a science?' was only part of the larger question, 'Is any kind of psychology a science?' I came near to abandoning psychotherapy in the 1940s because classic Freudian psychobiology, the instinct and oedipal theories, gave me no clues to understand the suffering of patients I later came to recognize as 'schizoid', cases of 'ego-weakness', not of the damming up of so-called id drives. The way forward was opened for me by the more genuinely psychological theories of the American interpersonal relations school (Sullivan, Horney, Fromm) and particularly the British object relations views of Fairbairn, Winnicott and others, the psychoanalytic equivalent of Macmurray's personal relations philosophy. Till the 1960s I felt I watched from the ringside, while physiological and experimental psychologists were shadow-boxing with a subject they could never knock out.

The obligation felt by both J. B. Watson and Freud to be 'scientific' in the physical science sense was forced on them, because, in the pre-Einstein era, no other concept of 'science' existed. All our difficulties over this are a legacy of the scientific materialism of the 'billiard-ball universe' era, eventually exploded by Einstein and quantum physics. Watson pontifically announced that there is no such thing as consciousness, without explaining how he could be aware, or conscious, of that fact. Everything in our richly varied human, personal, creative life was to be 'reduced' to conditioned reflexes, neurological habit patterns, cerebral biochemistry. *Psychology* did not really exist, though as a courteous gestur', it might be called 'physiological psychologye' and then, in an attempt to relate it to our actual living, 'behaviourism'. Despite the vigorous protests of Ward and Stout, and a halfway stand by McDougall, this 'reductionist' psychology became the Establishment Psychology, determined to monopolize academic teaching in university departments of psychology. Now in the last decade the signs of revolt have been multiplying, in the climate of a radically changed philosophy of science which is frankly anti-reductionist. It is becoming apparent that if you start with the dogma that everything 'mental' or 'psychological' can only be explained or known in terms of brain process, then you are bound to end up with nothing but brain process. This so-called 'scientific psychology' based on controlled laboratory experiment and observation has, of course, yielded some valuable results, an array of usable mental tests, behaviour therapy techniques of variable usefulness for suppressing symptoms; they do not profess to do any more, for on Eysenck's authority there is nothing more to do, there is 'nothing behind the symptoms'. Desensitization is the most interesting psychologically (psychoanalysis can be seen as a highly personal process of desensitization of childhood fears of bad parents and/or traumatic situations, liberating personal growth potentials); aversion therapy, the use of fear to suppress a symptom, being the most questionable, though there are cases in which I would not rule it out. A more important result of behaviourism has been to study the large part played by 'habit', by 'repertoires of behaviour patterns' in everyday living, which psychoanalysis has failed to take adequately into account. A patient who was an obsessional and a pianist told me how he sat down to play a Chopin nocturne and after a while, to his surprise, stopped and found he had come to its end. He had played the whole piece entirely unconsciously, while his conscious thought had remained obsessionally stuck on the theme of the opening bars. Here was an elaborate behaviour pattern running its own automatic course, and without the possibility of such habits, we could not carry on our lives at all; but if we had a record of that nocturne, I think we would find it had been played mechanically, devoid of the subtle element of 'artistic interpretation' that is the genius of a real pianist. We see this phenomenon in the hysterical fugue. Burt (1968) quoted Lord Adrian, the neurophysiologist, as saying that he thought most of our daily activity could be behaviouristically explained, but 'one thing does not fit into this neat and tidy scheme, the "I" that does the thinking, feeling and willing'.

At this point we become aware that the overall contribution of the Establishment Psychology to a genuine understanding of our human living as 'persons in relation' has been meagre, leading to charges of irrelevance, and student unrest about overdosage of behaviourism. At a technical college where I lectured on Freud, a male student said to me afterwards: 'I have just finished my course in psychology and got my degree, and it has destroyed my faith in everything. We are nothing but repertoires of behaviour patterns! But I want to thank you for giving me back some hope.' At a university college one student said: 'I chose psychology because I wanted to become a child-care worker and I'm having to study nothing but experimental psychology.' Another said: 'I chose psychology because I want to become an occupational therapist and I'm having to study nothing but statistics and animal psychology.' Both the irrelevance and the authoritarianism of the teaching are important. To get diplomas and degrees you have to give the right answers. This charge of indoctrination can be made against psychoanalysis as well. Both sides have tended to create 'dogma', and now we have raised a question that is being debated on the highest philosophical level between Professor T. S. Kuhn and Sir Karl Popper. In the symposium *Criticism and the Growth of Knowledge* (1970) Kuhn distinguished between what he called 'normal' and 'extraordinary' science. He thinks that nearly all science is 'normal', consisting of 'puzzle-solving within the limits of the theory the scientist has been taught'. The theory is not questioned and if the puzzle is not solved by reference to it, the theory is not invalidated, the scientist has failed in ingenuity. 'Extraordinary' or as Popper prefers to call it 'revolutionary' science, Kuhn thinks is rare, the work of a Galileo, Newton or Einstein. He holds that professionals are educated in 'normal' scientific puzzle-solving without questioning the theories they are taught. That seems an exact account of the psychology teaching and experimentation of this century, along with the theoretical intolerance of the Skinners and Eysencks to what Professor C. Taylor (1964) called genuinely 'psychological psychology'. They would dogmatically debar us from the use of genuine psychological terms at all, and confine us to their 'data language' or 'thing language', and all that developed from its simple beginnings in Pavlov's 'conditioned reflexes'.

Popper's reply to Kuhn is arresting. He writes (1970):

> Normal science in Kuhn's sense does exist. It is the activity of the non-revolutionary, not-too-critical professional: of the science student who accepts the ruling dogma of the day. . . . It does exist and must be taken into account by the historians of science. . . . But it is a phenomenon I dislike (because I regard it as a danger to science). The 'normal' scientist in my view has been taught badly. He is a person one ought to feel sorry for. I believe, and so do many others, that all teaching on the university level should be training and encouragement in critical thinking. The 'normal' scientist has been taught in a dogmatic spirit: he is a victim of indoctrination. He has learned a technique which can be applied without asking the reason why (especially in quantum physics).

I admit to surprise that Popper finds this even in quantum physics, but it makes it so much easier for us to admit its existence in psychology, both physiological and psychoanalytical. My own concern has been with the growth of 'psychodynamic' studies in the light of the needs I met with in psychotherapy, beyond the Establishment theories of classic Freudianism, into the psychodynamics of 'persons developing in personal relationships'; not with behaviour, the study of human beings as objects, nor psychobiology (as illegitimate a mixture as psychophysiology) with its non-psychological 'id' and the monstrosity of the death instinct, but with the psychology of Lord Adrian's 'I' that does the thinking, feeling and willing. This is the viewpoint of the original intuitive, truly psychological genius of Freud, developing through some basic insights of Melanie Klein, into the British object relations theory of Fairbairn, Winnicott and others, and in the American independent interpersonal relations theory of Sullivan and his colleagues. I have already made it clear that I do not simply reject behaviourism, only the monopolistic intolerance of some of its leaders, and regard its study of repertoires of behaviour patterns as important. In our everyday activity, we could hardly move hand or foot without them, and would have to 'stop and think out' every next move. Psychoanalysis has not studied the way such relatively fixed patterns run through the whole of our life, both healthy and pathological: though Dr J. Sandler, editor of *The International Journal of Psycho-Analysis*, has written (Sandler and Joffe, 1969, p. 84) that after emotional determinants have been resolved, a symptom can sometimes persist as a habit for behaviour therapy to deal with. We cannot settle the relationship between general psychology and psychoanalysis solely by the terms 'normal' and 'pathological'. Both fixed habits and disturbed reaction run through both normal and abnormal psychic life. The differences are mostly of degree. The method of 'introspection' is, however, common to both disciplines (q.v. Joynson) and our concern about being 'scientific' includes every type of truly psychological study.

Recent BPS *Bulletins* have shown clear signs of a breakaway from Kuhn's 'normal', dogmatic, orthodox science in psychology, and a growth of critical revolutionary thinking, which Popper holds should be characteristic of science all the time. Thus an occupational psychologist, S. Thorley (1969), writes: 'I cannot stress too strongly the danger of theoretical ideas and laboratory research being propagated which have no connection with the reality of life.' He quotes Lord James, that 'educational research often conceals a pseudo-objectivity. We have got to have the courage to say that some things are not worth discovering.' An educational psychologist, R. Moore (1969), writes of

> the gap between the present state of psychological knowledge and the real problems the educational psychologist has to face. . . . The one-year professional training courses must be so tightly packed with the learning of techniques that only incidental consideration can be given to the quality of understanding that educational psychology demands.

He quotes the Summerfield Report on 'the need to clarify the feelings of a child for other people and his attitudes to them and relations with them. A well-founded knowledge of interpersonal relations and the psychodynamics of families and school groups' is needed. A clinical psychologist, D. Bannister (1969), writes:

> Confrontation by people who are in process of trying to change in a complicated personal context would be a continual reminder to the psychologist of the over-simplifying nature of the psychological por-traits implicit in most standard theories. The demise of trait and S-R theories might well be hastened by a forced recognition of the capacity of people to interpret and reinterpret themselves and their situation. In terms of deriving and testing hypotheses, the psychotherapeutic situa-tion, rather than the experimental laboratory situation, may turn out to be the acid test of the validity and utility of psychological theories.

An experimental psychologist, R. Phillips (1969), writes:

The increasing dependence of experimental psychologists upon complex gadgetry is yet another sign of man's alienation from his fellow man. . . . The machine is erected by the experimenter as a sort of last-ditch defence mechanism. Only the study of psychology can save us: that psychological psychology in which the proper study of mankind is man!

Moreover, the disillusionment of students and field workers has spread to the academics. D. E. Broadbent, an empirical psychologist (1970), admits that his colleague, Miss P. Wright, found that 'among those psychologists of roughly senior lecturer rank and above, about half called themselves behaviourists, but amongst those more junior not one did so.'

The protests cited reflect a notable one in the Presidential Address by R. J. Bartlett (1948):

In common parlance the subject matter of psychology is mind, but there is a serious danger of psychologists becoming so absorbed in the study of organized matter that, as scientists, they become able to deal only with matter and motion, mass and energy. Science has to do with mass and motion, and has no place for mind, except to do its thinking. . . . The concept of mind, which is in danger of being discarded by psychology, lives a strong and healthy life among men. Ought we not to accept this concept, or the supposed reality behind it, as our proper study, instead of being satisfied with the careful recording of the material changes credited by common consent to be the products of its activity. Is not the proper study of the psychologist the psyche. . . . As mind is too often equated with brain, there is grave danger that psychology may become indistinguishable from applied physiology.

This result, foretold by Stout in 1896, is welcomed by Zangwill in 1971: 'One may hope that neurology and psychology will become increasingly integrated into a single scientific discipline', and naturally evokes Joynson's call for 'The Return of Mind'. Bannister writes (1968):

The chances of developing a physiological psychology are about as good (or as bad) as the chances of developing a chemical sociology or a biological astronomy. . . . Psychology needs to be self-referring because the concept of 'self' is essentially a psychological concept. It is no accident that concepts such as consciousness, choice, and teleological models are reiterative in psychology since, in spite of the most gallant attempts, we have failed to get far by adhering to a purely mechanistic model. An unquestioning acceptance of physiological psychology stems from a reductionist approach. Reductionism is a philosophical posture which assumes that physiology is somehow nearer to reality than psychology, and therefore a more 'basic' science.

*No study can claim to be 'scientific' if it refuses to study its field in terms properly relevant to just those phenomena that are in question. To reduce them, or pretend that they are some different kind of phenomena already studied by other sciences, is strictly prejudice, the prejudgement of all the issues at stake,* not as a result of investigation but as a dogma laid down without proof by one of Kuhn's 'normal' orthodox scientists. It is encouraging to find a physicist and biologist, Professor Bronowski, saying: 'Man is both a machine and a self, and there are two qualitatively different kinds of knowledge, knowledge of the machine and knowledge of the self' (1966). The way is now more clear to see that the sophisticated R–f (S,O) formula, where O is the organic internal conditions of the responder, is only an indirect way of acknowledging that behaviour, response, is a manifestation of a 'behaving subject' who has direct access to his 'internal conditions', which are not confined to organic factors, by *introspection*.

   *Does the separation of psychology from biology and physiology then deprive it of the possibility of being a science?* Not if we see science in terms of the post-Einstein philosophy of science, as developed today by Sir Karl Popper and outlined very clearly in Sir Peter Medawar's Jayne Lectures (1969). Science, in the solely physical-science sense, *can only* treat human beings as 'objects of investigation and manipulation', and that is precisely what is most self-defeating, and therefore most unscientific in dealing with psychic phenomena. Behaviourism is an attempt at scientific manipulation, trying to force or manoeuvre the patient into changing; which is only legitimate in certain circumstances and so long as the patient understands and agrees. Psychotherapy is leaving the patient free in a personal relationship of understanding support in which his fears can die down as he explores them, and his inhibited growth-potentials can become active again in developing a real ego or self. How can this kind of experience be conceptualized in a scientific way? It could not be done on the 19th-century physical science model, but the 'billiard-ball universe' of the last century was exploded by quantum physics, and Popper tells us that science has lost its old solid rock-like basis. It 'drives its piles down into the swamp' of the ultimate mysteries, 'only so far as is necessary to support' a theoretical structure for the time being. Its method is no longer the patient collection of facts and induction of 'laws of nature', but rather a somewhat random poking about in various 'areas of interest' to see what turns up. We know that most planned scientific research leads nowhere, or not to the goal it sought, but nearly all great scientific discoveries are the result of 'lucky finds', which suggest imaginative, intuitive hypotheses which might explain them, and then can be tested out: the 'hypothetico-deductive method'. This is the only intellectual process for studying any kind of phenomena. We can know nothing of the ultimate realities that lie behind matter, life, mind, but we can seek to understand *all* the ways in which they *appear to us in our experiencing of our world. All science is a study of phenomena, inorganic, organic, behavioural and social, and psychic, ultimately in the fully personal sense.* Psychological phenomena are as *real* and as inescapably there, demanding understanding, as all other phenomena. This is precisely what is taken into account in Medawar's exposition of the 'hierarchical model of the structure of knowledge'. Knowledge is like a building with a ground floor, physics and chemistry, and rising above them, floor by floor, tier by tier, new levels creating new sciences which study new phenomena in new terms. He firmly rules out 'reductionism'. 'The flow of thought works one way only. Each tier of the natural hierarchy makes use of notions peculiar to itself. The ideas of democracy, credit, crime or political constitution are no part of biology, nor shall we find in physics the concepts of memory, infection, sexuality or fear. In each plane or tier of the hierarchy new ideas emerge that are inexplicable in the language or with the conceptual resources of the tier below. . . . We cannot "interpret" sociology in terms of biology, or biology in terms of physics.' This is the point Bannister made, and we must add: 'nor psychology in terms of physiology or neurology'.

On the topmost tiers we shall find, first, 'social psychology', for human beings react in simpler ways on the crowd level; and finally, 'individual psychology', studying 'the subjective personal experience of human beings creatively developing and relating to one another' in ways that become 'introspectible'. Here Joynson envisages a cooperative dialogue between a new 'introspectionist' general psychology, the 'personalistic' tradition of Kelly, Allport, Bannister, and the later developments of psychoanalysis, in which the ego plays a more central role in theory. This will be helped by the fact that behaviourism has also been undergoing changes, and as, Ralph McGuire (late of Leeds, now of Edinburgh) stated in a recent discussion in Leeds, behaviourists are now prepared to look beyond symptoms for causes and reasons. This brings behaviourism and psychoanalysis on to common ground, and only needs recognition of the further fact that 'causes and reasons' may have to be found in the legacy of a traumatic childhood repressed in the unconscious and emerging disguised in dreams and symptoms. For this reason I feel a cautionary word must be said about 'introspection'. It can lead into deep and disturbing areas of psychopathology and become almost too hot to handle, which may be vaguely sensed by many emotional critics of psychoanalysis. But since a pretty stable person cannot be psychoanalysed (he would not have any reason for letting his ego defenses be breached) we need: (1) a general psychology to make an introspectionist study of repertoires of behaviour patterns on the social psychology level, (2) a more personalistic study of behaviour patterns interwoven with spontaneous and creative functioning on the individual psychology level, and (3) a psychodynamic, psychoanalytic psychology working, not from the normal but from the psychopathology end of the continuum of human experience, while (4) these varying approaches meet in a middle area of human living where the relatively normal and the varyingly psychopathological phenomena are to be found mingled together. Joynson writes (1972): 'Freud's emphasis on the unconscious initially reduced the significance of the conscious, but the conscious ego has gradually acquired a more central role in theory.' This needs some restatement. Initially, the unconscious was the biological 'id', too powerful for the superficial ego to control. Contemporary object relations theory leaves the 'id', the biological 'given', to biology, and studies the 'use' the psychological 'ego' makes of it. The unconscious is part of the ego which is tied to the unresolved anxious problem-relations of the past, an 'inner world' where 'feeling' predominates, while the conscious part of the ego relates to the present-day outer world where 'feeling' must be more governed by 'thinking'; and while it also digests as much of the experiences of its 'unconscious other half' as it can tolerate coming into consciousness. In the emotional unconscious the inspirations of art and the symbolism of dreams arise. Patients are often highly imaginative artists in their dreams. *Psychoanalysis gives us a depth psychology with which to understand the personality as a 'whole'.* Needed behaviour patterns can be consciously studied, and we keep 'half an eye' on our useful 'repertoires' while engaged in spontaneous pursuits. But the 'repertoires' do not explain creativity and spontaneous action, whether in art, personal relations, or the intuitive imaginative hypotheses on which science depends. A final comment from a linguistic philosopher. John Linsie writes (1972): 'Ought we to expect to solve our puzzlement about the meaning of "mind" through a more detailed understanding of brain functioning? I think not.' He says: 'questions of the "meaning" of a word (such as mind) must be solved either by "perceptual reference", pointing to a relevant object (such as brain) or by "conceptual clarification", *clarifying our awareness of a familiar experience (mind)'.* He thinks that most psychologists have put 'the perceptual cart before the conceptual horse. Ordinary language is full of references to "mind" (such as "mind your step", "what's on your mind"). Even psychologists, for whom studying "mind" is professional anathema use the word "mind" in their off-duty moments. No doubt even such an arch-experimentalist as Dr Eysenck advises his students to "mind what they are about" in their exams. As ordinary folk we know what we are talking about when we use the term "mind". We must make explicit what we have always implicitly known about mind. To do this it will be necessary to refer to everyday experience of the market place' (or with Bannister we may say the therapeutic situation) 'not the specialized experience of the psychological laboratory'.

# REFERENCES

Adrian, Lord (1968). Quoted by Sir Cyril Burt in Brain and consciousness. *British Journal of Psychology* 59:56–69.

Bannister, D. (1968). The myth of physiological psychology. *Bulletin of the British Psychological Society* 21:229–231.

_____ (1969). Clinical psychology and psychotherapy. *Bulletin of the British Psychological Society* 22:299–301.

Bartlett, R. J. (1948). Mind. *Bulletin of the British Psychological Society* 1(1):14–24.

Broadbent, D. E. (1970). In defence of empirical psychology. *Bulletin of the British Psychological Society* 23:87–96.

Joynson, R. B. (1970). The breakdown of modern psychology. *Bulletin of the British Psychological Society* 23:261–269.

_____ (1972). The return of mind. *Bulletin of the British Psychological Society* 25:1–10.

Kuhn, T. S. (1970). In *Criticism and the Growth of Knowledge*, ed. I. Lakotos and A. Musgrave. Cambridge University Press.

Linsie, J. (1972). The concept of mind. In *Some Myths in Human Biology*. London: BBC.

Medawar, P. (1969). *Induction and Intuition in Scientific Thought*. London: Methuen.

Moore, R. B. W. (1969). The nature of educational psychology in school psychological and child guidance services. *Bulletin of the British Psychological Society* 22:185–187.

Phillips, R. (1969). Psychological psychology: a new science? *Bulletin of the British Psychological Society* 22:83–87.

Popper, K. (1970). In *Criticism and the Growth of Knowledge*, ed. I. Lakotos and A. Musgrave. Cambridge University Press.

Sandler, J. and Joffe, W. G. (1969). Towards a basic psychoanalytic model. *International Journal of Psycho-Analysis* 50:79–90.

Taylor, C. (1964). *The Explanation of Behaviour*. London: Routledge & Kegan Paul.

Thorley, S. (1969). Psychology: occupation, vocation or profession. *Bulletin of the British Psychological Society* 22:181–183.

Zangwill, O. L. (1971). Correspondence. *Bulletin of the British Psychological Society* 24:88–89.

# 14

# FREUD, RUSSELL AND "THE CORE OF LONELINESS"

IF I WERE ASKED TO QUOTE ONE passage that more than any other expresses the fundamental truth and problem about human nature, I would quote, not any passage from Freud, but one from Bertrand Russell. I must defer for the moment the citing of this passage since, to feel its full force, we must pave the way for it. Yet, in spite of the profundity of that one passage, Russell's life work has contributed little of permanent value for man, in a practical sense, while Freud started what has become the profoundest research into human nature ever yet made. The intriguing problem is why did Russell's profound insight lie sterile and unused in all his later work, while Freud's less profound early observations and tentative theories developed into a systematic "penetration" (to use Russell's own word) into that very region of human experience that Russell might have explored.

Freud and Russell, two of the intellectual giants of the end of last century and the first half of this one, may seem, at first sight, to be an unlikely pair to choose for a comparative study. They reveal, however, not only striking differences but also unexpectedly intriguing parallels. There is a superficial overall parallel in that both of them began with an apparently total dedication to impersonal intellectual work, the one in physical science, the other in philosophy, but in due course both of them moved on to become steeped, in different ways, in most practical human problems. If Freud's early interest was not quite so abstractly intellectual as was Russell's in geometry, his interest in human nature was more intellectual than practical. Ernest Jones tells us that "To medicine itself Freud felt no direct attraction . . . and wished to devote himself to the cultural and historical problems of how man came to be what he is" (Jones 1953, p. 30). After a normal childhood in an unbroken home, Freud was educated as a medical laboratory scientist, working with the methods of objective experiment in the physical sciences. He accepted the dictum of his mentor, Professor Brücke "that there are no energies in the organism other than physical and chemical ones." Brücke "set Freud behind the microscope to work on the histology of nerve cells" (p. 51), and Jones states that in three published papers

Freud "paved the way for the neurone theory. . . . The unitary conception of the nerve cell and processes—the essence of the future neurone theory—seems to have been Freud's own and quite independent of his teachers" (pp. 54–55). He was also the unacknowledged first discoverer of the medical uses of cocaine. This basic intellectual discipline never lost its hold on him, and Jones states that when he brought back into science the concepts of "wish," "intention," "aim," and "purpose," he still "never abandoned determinism for teleology" (p. 50). It is clear that neither Freud nor Jones saw the inherent self-contradiction of this "philosophy of science" in the field of "psychodynamic phenomena," which explains the uneasiness that often made Freud long to get back to the security of his physical science laboratory, where everything was so much less worrying than in the conflict-ridden areas of human motivations.

When Freud was forced out of his laboratory security (by anti-Jewish prejudice, which for once produced a most fortunate result for mankind), and was compelled to earn a living by doing clinical work, seeing patients, coming face to face with human suffering rather than laboratory problems of histological research, it emerged that he possessed genuine genius for intuitive psychological insight into the deep-seated disturbances of human beings as "persons" rather than "organisms." This new field of investigation was not easy to reconcile with his previous scientific training. There were many pitfalls of premature conceptualization, such as his early failure to distinguish between memory and fantasy of early sexual trauma, in the psychodynamic field. He resisted for a long time the need to conceptualize in different terms from those of physical science, and worked hard to cast his early findings in neurological thought forms. Even later in life he expressed the view that psychoanalysis was useful for treating hysteria until such time as neurology could cure it. But steadily, the pressure of hard facts—of stubborn psychodynamic phenomena—compelled him to abandon his "Psychology for Neurologists" because of its uselessness in his clinical work, and he did his best to create a psychological theory that would still be tied to physical science in the form of biology. Classical Freudians, like their master, never got past that position. Heinz Hartmann in 1964, in *Essays in Ego-Psychology*, was still saying that psychoanalysis is one of the biologic sciences, and could not conceive of a "psychology in its own right." Yet Freud's intuitive genius could not be imprisoned, and in spite of his education and the mental habits of his first 40 years, he also gave us "clinical studies" that are profound first-hand observations of human beings in their intimate personal struggles and that provide the data for the purely psychodynamic hypotheses he gave us concerning the unconscious and conscious "motivational" life of humans in their relations with one another from childhood onwards. In his somewhat hybrid theory, the purely theoretical Freud has become dated, the clinical Freud abides as the permanent foundation of all psychodynamic studies of human beings as "persons" not just "organisms." Though he never managed to integrate fully the physical scientist and the psychodynamic therapist in himself, the latter is his imperishable contribution.

There is a curious parallel dualism in Bertrand Russell, but the two sides of him are kept far more completely apart and are not allowed to conflict head on in the way Freud could not prevent in his own case. The two sides of Bertrand Russell are the impersonal, abstract, purely intellectual philosopher (the mathematician, logician, Logical Atomist, and Logical Positivist) and the warm-hearted generous friend, the ardent lover (four times married), and the aggressively campaigning political and social reformer who could lead a "sit down" in Whitehall in protest against nuclear armaments. He agreed with Hume's dictum that "reason is and ought to be the slave of the passions." The philosopher in him could question whether external objects were "logical constructions" or "inferred entities," but that never made him hesitate for a moment in coming to the financial help, un- beknown, of a close friend, or to fall deeply in love four times. Indeed so strong was his capacity to love that it raises a challenging problem, which we shall presently find highly relevant to his understanding, that having fallen strongly in love the first three times and contracted marriages that each lasted an average of ten years, he should gradually have found that he had fallen out of love again. There is a sad but highly important problem here for understanding human nature, especially in contrast to Freud's one marriage, which lasted a lifetime. Freud could feel deeply for one or two other women, but that never for a moment weakened his basic love of his wife. There is a problem here that is absolutely central to the understanding of human nature. On occasion, the two sides of Russell could nod to each other in some of his borderline writings, and to some extent in his rather scanty "philosophy of morals," but in the main there is a gulf between the head and the heart that kept them wider apart than in the case of Freud, a fact from which there is much to learn. There is a gulf between the extreme impersonality of what he regarded as his greatest work, *Principia Mathematica*, and the passionate advocacies of most human causes in some of his later writings. The "intellectual" in Russell became a philosopher, not a scientist as with Freud, and the "humanist" in Russell became a social and political propagandist, not a personal therapist like Freud. This may seem to be a comparison that is sufficiently descriptive and calls for little further comment. The two men might simply offer an interesting variety in human types. But we shall miss very many important and fascinating human problems, if we leave it at that.

Thus, it appears to me that the two sides of Freud's personality maintained a constant tension to the end, and Freud the scientist and Freud the therapist never really settled the issue between them. In one of his late papers, on "Analysis Terminable and Interminable" (1937), he concluded (and I think it must have been sadly) that psychoanalysis would probably in the end prove of greater value as a method of scientific research than as a therapy. I find that astonishing, for if it fails as a therapy, it must be useless as a method of scientific investigation, since on Freud's own theory and experience, human beings will never cooperate in the investigation of their unconscious distresses, unless they can thereby be healed of their emotional pain. The whole point of Freud's discovery of "transference" and "resistance," or "negative transference," is that the traumatic experiences of early childhood, whether they be of sheer fear, or of the ache of unmet needs, or guilt-burdened impulses of aggression, would so seriously interfere with adult living that they must be kept repressed. If they break through our "ego-defences" the result is illness and incapacitation. The only alternative is to "transfer" these disturbing emotions from their infantile situations as preserved in the unconscious to some handy figure in real life and blame that person for the whole disturbance. This is a common phenomenon in everyday life; the only way in which repressed emotional disturbances can emerge into consciousness, other than in the therapeutic situation where they can be understood and lived through, is by working them off on the wrong person. The scientifically investigating psychologist will either not tap the deeper sources of the subject's emotional life, or else will find himself becoming the target of reactions he is not likely to tolerate understandingly, not being concerned with therapy. It seems to me that Freud's conclusion, even at that late date, was unconsciously dictated by his still persisting longing to get out of the difficult psychotherapeutic commitment into the much less disturbing scientific laboratory situation. Only a powerful unconscious motive could have blinded so penetrating a thinker to his own major discoveries, even momentarily. It seems to me evidence that the battle in him between the scientist and the therapist was never really resolved, and that the scientist threatened, without final success, to come out on top at the end, for we must never forget that Freud's last and unfinished contribution to "theory" was his recognition of the fact that the purely psychodynamic phenomenon of "ego splitting" was universal, not confined to psychoses but extending through the entire range of the neuroses. This has been the starting point for the post-Freudian development of "personal ego-psychology," the most momentous development psychoanalysis has made, setting it free from biology and physical science, and enabling it to become a genuine research into our personal "motivations" as we develop our "ego" in "personal relations." Freud's aim, once he was committed to the detailed study of his patients sufferings, was to create a science of the emotional dynamics of our personal living, and in pursuit of this aim he very nearly, if not quite, moved on beyond the physicalistic concept of biological drives or instincts, to the fully *psycho*dynamic concept of "motivational energies of the psychic ego" which, when they conflict with one another, bring about the state of psychic disorder and confusion we call "ego-splitting." But he prepared the way for the discipline he founded to pursue this goal to success in our contemporary "personal" or "object-relational theory."

Russell's development was different. His early philosophical period was imper-

sonal, abstract, purely intellectual, and nonpractical in the extreme. In collabora-
tion with his tutor and close friend, A. N. Whitehead, he buried himself for ten
years in the production of *Principia Mathematica*, of which he wrote the lion's share.
Its aim was to reduce mathematics to logic by reducing "numbers" to "classes." It is
not relevant here to expound that attempt, though I had to wrestle with it as an
undergraduate.

Since my university days, I have kept in touch with philosophy as an interested
reader seeking general information, not as a specialist student, which I did not need
to be. It is sufficient to note that Russell's earlier work led him on to his philosophies
of Logical Atomism and Logical Positivism. This work will have its place in the
history of philosophy, but it did not turn out to be the "final solution" of
epistemological problems I think Russell was seeking. A. J. Ayer (1972) now writes:
"Russell's conception of philosophy is old fashioned . . . in the high tradition of
British empiricism . . . he makes the now unfashionable assumption that all our
beliefs are in need of philosophical justification." Russell failed, as philosophy must
always fail, to isolate and identify the "ultimates" in epistemology and ontology.
The human intellect does not have the capacity to "explain" the ultimate reality or
realities. We may heed the warning of Bion (1962), the psychoanalyst,

> All investigation being ultimately scientific, is limited by human inad-
> equacy to those phenomena that have the characteristics of the inan-
> imate. We assume that the psychotic limitation is due to illness; but
> that that of the scientists is not. . . . Our rudimentary equipment for
> 'thinking' thoughts is adequate when the problems are associated with
> the inanimate, but not when the object for investigation is the phe-
> nomenon of life itself.

In psychotics, grossly disturbed emotion has overwhelmed objective thinking; in
scientists, thinking is, for the time being, simply divorced from feeling. But there
can be no "understanding" of the living and of the ultimate, except by the
cooperation of both aspects of our whole nature, and the difficulty there is in the
concept that "feeling" can grasp and respond to far more than "intellect" can define,
there are "things that lie too deep for words," which still include the profoundest
realities in our lives. I am not thinking at the moment of religion, but for example,
of "human love," the only possible proof of which is for two people to live together
for a lifetime. There is no other way of validating results in this field, and all the
things that are most important to us *are* in the realm of "personal relationships."
The rest is "technology," the invention and use of "machines," varieties of which are
useful for sustaining our physical existence, but, while they can keep us alive, they
do not enable us to "live," in any meaningful sense.

This can be stated another way. The intellect, the philosopher's tool, can only operate with "language" and it is the limitations of this tool that made Ayer and post-Russell British philosophers see Russell as "old-fashioned" in his view that "all our beliefs are in need of philosophical justification." Paul, of Oxford, writing of Wittgenstein in 1956, shows why Wittgenstein and others moved beyond Russell's and the pure empiricist's position. He wrote,

> With Moore, Wittgenstein shared a sympathy for metaphysical philos-
> ophers. [He wrote:] "The problems arising through a misinterpretation
> of our forms of language have the character of *depth*: they are deep
> disquietudes, their roots are as deep in us as the forms of our language."
> These philosophers have when at their best, "run their heads up against
> the limits of language." And Wittgenstein emphasized with Moore, "our
> strange position," that we know what many words and phrases mean
> even though "no philosopher, or anyone else, has succeeded in setting
> out in detail what they mean."

Russell the philosopher worked at an insoluble problem. But, just as Wittgenstein and British philosophy moved beyond Russell, Russell in a different way moved beyond himself, not so much intellectually as practically. He never again devoted all his time and energy to purely abstract impersonal intellectual problems. The dating of his books and their subject matter are instructive. *Principles of Mathe-matics* (1903) and *Principia Mathematica* (1910–1913), represent the early philosoph-ical Russell. He wrote 11 smaller books on problems of logic and epistemology and general philosophy later on, and is probably best known for his both popular and valuable *History of Western Philosophy* (1945), but none of these are on the scale of *Principia Mathematica* (1913). On the other hand, between 1916 and 1954 he wrote 13 books on such subjects as social reconstruction, politics, freedom, Bolshevism, education, religion, marriage, morals, happiness, power, authority and the individ-ual, *New Hopes for a Changing World*, ethics and, as he grew older, five biographical books, ending with *Portraits from Memory* (1958) at the age of 86 and, finally, his monumental *Autobiography* in three volumes, 1967–1969, at the age of 95–97.

His development may be described, in one sense, as akin to that of Freud, who also became ever more interested in broad human concerns, the psychology of art, and religion (*Civilization and its Discontents, Group Psychology, Moses and Monotheism*), though he sought to integrate these studies with his, hopefully, scientific psychology. With Russell, no attempt was made to integrate his intensely human and practical concerns with his early philosophy. With Freud, the intellec-tual scientist kept a dragging hold on his human concerns without contributing anything to their understanding. With Russell, the older he became the abstract philosopher was outstripped by the emotional and intensely personal humanist, once the first ten years were over. One may feel that his final effort, an autobiography, arose out of his own deep need to understand himself as a person, to trace the path of his development to see if he could find out what had really happened to him and what he had become. It is my belief that if only Russell could have addressed himself to this task, equipped with Freud's powers of intuitive psychodynamic understanding, he would have created a psychoanalysis that explored deeper depths than Freud's Oedipus Complex theory. Equally, if Freud would have had Russell's disturbing and lonely childhood, given his remarkable psychodynamic intuition, he also would have given us a psychoanalysis that probed deeper depths than the Oedipal problems he uncovered. Both men moved beyond impersonal and intellectual problems to basic personal and emotional ones, but both were conditioned by the influence of their childhood in the shaping of their personality. Freud's remarkable intuition carried him as deep as he himself needed to go in his self-analysis. Russell, in one astonishing example of intuitive understanding of the suffering of another, but unwittingly in the light of his own personality and early life, saw deeper than Freud's Oedipal or parent–child relations, to the depths of isolation and loneliness that arise from, not positive disturbing parent–child relations, but the failure or nonexistence of such relations, which creates what we have come to call the schizoid problem. Freud had no inner incentive to probe deeper than Oedipal problems and had to wait for the traumatic impact of World War I to drive him to consider the fundamental problem of ego growth. Russell's early life left him profoundly bogged down in the problem of what to do with an ineradicable loneliness and emptiness at the heart of him. He first fled from the problem into the most abstract forms of pure intellectualism, from 1883 to 1913. But the security of his intellectual cloisters was first invaded when he fell in love in 1889 at the age of 17, and he then sought to cure his inner isolation by successive marriages, and by plunging into the social, moral, and political battle for human rights, and finally by delving deeply into his entire life-story, as if his autobiography was his last hopefully therapeutic attempt to understand and make sense of his life. His one astonishing moment of truth came in 1901 at the age of 29, before he had written any of his books, but it will be profitable to defer consideration of that till after we have first examined Freud's childhood, as a standard with which to compare Russell's.

Freud grew up as the eldest son of a second marriage and had an unbroken progress in a united family, in his education from childhood into the medical profession and the scientific laboratory. Jacob Freud, his father, was 41 when Sigmund was born and is described as "a man of gentle disposition, well loved by all his family." There were two sons by the first marriage, Emmanuel, 24 years older than Freud who emigrated to England, and the younger half-brother who was 20 years older than Freud and only one year younger than Freud's mother, who married at age twenty. Freud senior died at the age of 81 — kindly, tolerant, friendly, and intelligent. Sigmund's mother died at the age of 95, a lively personality who would refer to Sigmund as "Mein Goldener Sigi." Freud was breast fed and was his mother's favorite child. Jones says that "a close attachment existed between the two throughout." One would hardly think that any very serious Oedipal problems would arise for Sigmund in such an intelligent and affectionate family. Such problems were certainly not forced on him by inadequate parental behavior. He consciously loved and deservedly respected his father, and in adult life would say that he got his sense of humor and intellectual liberalism from his father and his deeply emotional nature from his mother. The father's influence on Sigmund is there, even in religion. Jacob Freud began as an orthodox Jew and moved quietly and unostentatiously to a more and more liberal theology, at the end being religious rather in the sense in which Ayer described Russell as "a man of religious temper" rather than theological orthodoxy. Freud disavowed religion but developed a lasting friendship with the Reverend Oscar Pfister, the first clerical psychoanalyst, writing to him as "Dear Man of God." (Their letters have been published.) Freud used his psychological theory to explain religion away as the projection of the father image on to the universe, thereby admitting indirectly the enormous importance of the father image in his own mind: it was the prototype of God. He remained fascinated by religion, and by Michaelangelo's "Moses" in Rome (which he visited repeatedly). He could not leave the subject alone; his last book was *Moses and Monotheism*. His mother was more simply emotionally if healthily religious. One may say that there was an emotional, if not an intellectual, continuity between the young Freud, who was the eldest and favorite son in a good family life, and Freud the creative adult thinker.

One might think that Freud's family life would contain little more than the usual jealousies, possessiveness, demands for attention, rivalries among siblings, and resentments of authority that are normal in vigorous growing children. Had that been the case, I do not think Freud would have had the motivation to create his full-blooded Oedipus Complex theory of heterosexual possessiveness and homosexual hate and aggression, deep guilt, and self-punishment that demanded the use of the Oedipus myth for its symbolic expression. He certainly would have created a theory of the unconscious as retaining permanent emotion-loaded traces of parent-child relationships, which are never completely outgrown and which can become pathological if the emotions locked in them are powerful enough. I do not think any experienced person would question the truth of the Oedipus theory in this broadest sense as embodying the ineradicable influence of the parents on the growing child, much as Adler's Family Constellation theory embodies the totality of family influences. We have, however, to account for the fact that when Freud undertook his self-analysis at the age of 41, he was startled to find in his dreams evidence of far more disturbingly intense emotions than that. There was, in fact, a curious reason.

Sigmund was the eldest son of his father's second family, and the younger of his two half-brothers, Phillip, 20 years older than himself and only one year younger than Freud's mother, lived close by and was always in and out. Sigmund was in the curious position of living with two senior males, a half-brother old enough to be his father, and who was very friendly with his mother, and his actual father old enough to be his grandfather. Consciously he felt very strong affection for his actual father, and felt markedly hostile to his half-brother Phillip who seems to have given him no adequate reason for this. At 41 he was more than surprised to find himself dreaming of intense hate of his real father, and remembered an occasion when he had gone as a child into his parents bedroom and his father had angrily ordered him out. Evidently he was saved from the difficulties, at least superficially, of having an ambivalent relationship with his real father, by having a convenient half-brother at hand, old enough to be his father, and close enough to be a rival for mother's attentions, on to whom he could project his hate without much harm. Though I do not agree with E. Jones in all his detailed and literal Oedipal interpretations, and I do not believe in, or I have not myself found, a full-blooded Oedipus Complex in every patient, I am prepared to accept that this unusual family set-up was the source whence arose the powerful emotional conflicts that troubled Freud and puzzled him with neurotic reactions and depressions, which began to abate with his self-analysis. His early nicotine addiction, his highly ambivalent friendship with Dr. Fliess, dependent yet increasingly full of hate, his phobia of traveling and street phobia, his guilt and reparation in having to sacrifice or smash a valuable vase when his daughter's life was spared in an illness, and his preoccupation with death, were all signs of an analyzable emotional disturbance of the order of neurosis. Only by knowing ourselves do we become able to understand others, and Freud's self-analysis was a unique and very great achievement. Fairbairn once said to me, "I can't think what could motivate any of us to become psychotherapists unless we had difficulties of our own," but this is not a welcome fact to many would-be students of human nature, and Freud's courage in facing this extremely difficult fact must remain perhaps his greatest claim on our respect. It was through lack of the capacity (not the courage) to do this, that Russell missed the chance, not only of solving his own personal problem, but also of creating a profounder psychodynamic theory than Freud's Oedipus complex, as we shall see. But Freud probed as deeply as his own unconscious fantasy life called on him to probe. This favorite son being faced with two older rivals, a father and a half-brother, for the exclusive attention of his much-loved and highly attractive mother, seems to have generated a powerful jealousy and hate of them, which he might have resolved in the process of emotional maturing had there been only one rival. As it was, there being two, he could the more easily separate his love and hate for both of them, and thus preserve intact in consciousness his love of his father, while in time repressing also intact his hate of the other rival, only to find in his dreams that that too ultimately had been felt against his real parent. The fact is too obviously important to ignore that the death of his father was the immediate precipitating factor in his starting self-analysis, in the very middle of his highly ambivalent and growingly hostile five-year friendship with Dr. Fliess, the Berlin throat and nose surgeon. For a man of Freud's stature to become emotionally fixated on an intellectually inferior man and make him practically a father-confessor for some five years requires explanation. This emerges in the fact that his self-analysis of his ambivalent love–hate relation to his father, freed him from his fixation on this father substitute. So Freud's psychodynamic theory went no deeper than his own personal problem, as we might expect. His theory of "moral control" embodied in his "superego" concept, grew out of his view of the absolutely fundamental nature of parent–child relations. The "superego" or conscience was the psychically molded, internalized version of the parental authorities. Freud's whole psychology is an exploration of the long-lasting, often permanent, results for good or evil of the relationships between parents and the child, especially in *early* childhood. Two points of critical interest call for comment: the term "relationships" and the term "early" as distinct from "earliest." The concept of "relationship" was not the ultimate one for Freud, at least theoretically. His basic concept was "instinct" and for him relationships were the arena in which "instincts" of sex and aggression played out their roles. Bad parents frustrated the child's instincts and caused the damming up of "instinctual tensions," which could be discharged in psychotherapy. Today, the emphasis has moved off the biologic on to the psychodynamic concept of "personal relationships" as the medium in which the beginnings of a child's ego grow to stability or instability. The move from an instinct psychology to an ego-development psychology in post-Freudian psychoanalysis, on which we have already commented, was prepared by Freud himself in his post-war writings. The point is relevant to my use of the term "early" rather than "earliest" relationships of parents and child. His delving into the unconscious did not go deeper than the *early* relationships of the child to parents, which do so often seem to be experienced in terms of body functions, sexuality, jealously, possessiveness, and aggression: "bad" impulses which are kept in control and under repression by the "parentally moulded superego." Freud did not explore the still earlier, or rather *earliest* psychic levels of the first two years. When Melanie Klein began to probe as deep as that, she was accused of "reading back" Oedipal phenomena into a period when they could not yet have appeared. The point did not emerge clearly, until object-relations theory developed, that the problems of the earliest phases are not problems of "impulse control" such as Freud's Oedipus Complex theory envisaged, but problems of ego development, of the very beginnings of the experience of being a *self* at all. If ego growth fails at the start, because parents cannot or do not genuinely really *relate* to the child, then we get, not classic Freudian Oedipal impulse problems, but schizoid and even schizophrenic and paranoid states of mind. Freud regarded these, as did all psychiatrists at that date, as untreatable, certainly by psychoanalysis, because he held that the patients cannot form a relationship, or experience "transference" with the analyst. Freud's successors have been compelled to reject that view and to discover that "psychotics" can be treated if the therapist understands that what they bring to us in the transference is the terror of their isolation, their own inability to do anything about it, and their desperate hope that we may be able to understand this and get in touch with them. Freud did not penetrate, in his psychoanalysis, to this inner core of hopeless loneliness that is the real basis of all serious mental illness. That must have been because, in his own self-analysis, he did not find that problem emerging; or else because that kind of problem cannot emerge in a self-analysis (at least not till a transference analysis has prepared the way), since the problem of isolation can only be dealt with by the availability of a relationship with a therapeutic person. But his own family history would suggest a marked contrast to Bertrand Russell's at this very point, i.e., Freud did not experience any drastic lack of genuine parental, and especially maternal, relationships at the beginning. Freud did not need to probe deeper than the rather later childhood Oedipal parent–child relationships. He had not experienced the disaster of catastrophic loss or deprivation, the ultimate disaster, of the *failure* of parental relationship that leaves the child in an emotional vacuum which generates the schizoid problem.

It may come as a surprise to anyone not familiar with the life of Bertrand Russell to learn that he discovered this very problem in a "sudden revelation" in 1901, and I venture to say that if his energies and researches had gone into Freud's field of psychopathology, he would, in fact, have gone deeper than Freud did, and created, not a psychology of conflicting impulses and the guilt producing super-ego, but of experiencing *the basic psychodynamic problem, the initial failure or early breakdown of primary experiences of "relationships" in which the beginnings of a coherent developing ego could arise, with the result that no secure "self" exists capable of owning the body, using its appetites, having motives and impulses, or entering into relationships.* Freud took relationships for granted because he had not been failed in that respect as Russell had, and had no personal problem there for his self-analysis to explore. He had his Oedipal and superego problems, as his already mentioned analyzable symptoms show. Since probably some degree of schizoid introversion is universal, we could trace that problem in Freud's personality, but it was, it seems, not severe enough to force its way into his self-analysis. But it is also likely that "schizoid aloneness" is intrinsically incapable of being therapeutically analyzed without a therapeutic relationship to supply what was missing in infancy. Freud recognized diagnostically the existence of that problem in paranoid and psychotic patients, but he never explored it in actual psychoanalysis, regarding it as beyond its scope: a view analysts have now been compelled to abandon. But since we now know that both Oedipal conflicts and abstract intellectual interests (scientific or philosophic) can be used as a defence against an underlying schizoid problem, it seems justifiable to infer that Freud operated both these defences successfully, and paid for it by some loss of faith in psychotherapy at the end. Nevertheless, with his family history, his schizoid problem could not have been so severe as was Russell's, whose family life was utterly different.

Russell's mother and sister died when he was only two years old. His father died before he was four. He had none of Freud's continuity of family life. He was seven years younger than his brother Frank. Their grandfather died at 83 – only three years after they went to live with him and their grandmother. Thus, since his brother had been sent away to school, he was left to a very lonely childhood with his grandmother, who was 60 and hardly an emotionally adequate mother substitute. She was a staunch Presbyterian of rigid moral and religious convictions, known to her husband's political friends as "Deadly Nightshade." Bertrand, endowed with an exceptionally brilliant and original intellectual capacity, rapidly outgrew her moral and theological constraints. Ayer writes:

> In adolescence he began to suffer from loneliness and he was made unhappy by his sense of an intellectual estrangement from his grandmother. The moment of his greatest intellectual awakening was his discovery of the geometry of Euclid . . . at the age of eleven.

an interest in science having already been aroused by an uncle. Mathematics is often the refuge of the schizoid intellectual, just because it is so impersonal and nonemotional. A young schizoid scientist once said to me: "I'm all right at work during the day. I know my stuff and do my calculations accurately. But when that's over, I'm a non-person. I can't make friends. I can't enter into human relationships," though he longed for them as only the desperately lonely can. Russell also deeply needed a fundamentally satisfying emotional relationship, and for years to come, we may say metaphorically, his heart longed for love while his head for a long time sought to do without it.

At seventeen, he met and "fell instantly in love with" Alys Pearsall Smith (Ayer 1972), five years his senior, surely suggesting a deep need for a mother. They married five years later, in 1894, and were very happy till 1902. When Russell was 18, a mathematics scholarship took him to Trinity College, Cambridge, under A. N. Whitehead, a partnership which by 1913 produced *Principia Mathematica*. For the last decade of the nineteenth century mathematics took care of his head and Alys of his heart, at least till 1902. The next nine years were very unhappy and they parted in 1911 with Russell threatening suicide. It was in 1902, when out cycling, that he suddenly realized that he no longer loved Alys, though she loved him to the end. It cannot be without significance that this sudden breakdown of a stable relationship, for no apparent reason other than a sudden and seemingly inexplicable discovery by Russell that he did not love her, followed not so long after the momentous experience in 1901, which I have already referred to as Russell's "moment of truth" and which Ayer calls a "sudden revelation." He and Alys were sharing a house with the Whiteheads, and Mrs. Whitehead was an invalid with heart trouble. Ayer writes:

> Russell describes an occasion when, finding her isolated in pain, he had a sudden revelation of "the loneliness of the human soul." He reflected that 'nothing can penetrate it except the highest intensity of the sort of love that religious teachers have preached. . . . In human relations one should penetrate to *the core of loneliness* in each person and speak to that'. . . . He was a man of a religious temper . . .

even if he rejected organized religion. I find this one of the most profoundly moving and revealing intuitive insights I have ever seen put into words. He discovered "the central fact of human personality" at the age of 29. Had he been able to follow it up with factual investigation, he would have created a profounder psychodynamic theory than Freud's classic Oedipal psychoanalysis. He had discovered what post-Freudian analysts were driven to probe and understand half a century later. It was the discovery of a man who had his own "inner core of loneliness" and it must have weakened his defences against the repressed unmothered loneliness of his childhood, against which Alys, ever since 1889, had been a protective bulwark. Then quite suddenly the secret schizoid isolated core of him, which could neither love nor relate, erupted and destroyed his marriage. Thereafter his emotional history was a sad story of deep and happy attachments breaking down in the tragic discovery that he did not love. With Alys he maintained, for nine years, the typical "schizoid compromise" of a "half in and half out relation." Then after two love affairs (with Lady Ottoline Morrell, in 1911, and Lady Constance Malleson in 1916 – she became for him a "refuge from the world of hate"), he married Dora Black in 1921 and left her in 1932, married Patricia Spence in 1936 and left her in 1949, and finally in 1952, at the age of 80, he married Edith Finch. He died in 1970. This sad story is clearly important. One cannot for a moment think that a man of Bertrand Russell's caliber was fickle. His first three marriages lasted happily for nine, 11, and 13 years, and while they lasted were deeply satisfying to him. But each time, from somewhere deep within him there would erupt the legacy of his unmothered childhood, his deep inner "core of loneliness," to break down the security of the closest of his human relationships. Fortunately, he gave us the clue that he himself could not use, to understand a great man's tragic predicament, and it came to take precedence over his intellectual and philosophical curiosity. He sought to find a solace for it, perhaps even a cure of it, in two ways: marriage and intellectual immersion in "mathematica" until that was complete in 1913. From time to time his analytical intellect continued to probe philosophical problems both in lecturing and in book writing but, beginning with *Principles of Social Reconstruction* in 1916, his interest in righting human wrongs grew steadily over the years to crusading strength, while from the publication of *The Amberley Papers* in 1937, the biographical interest grew, and finally became predominant with the publication of *Portraits from Memory* in 1958 and the three volumes of his autobiography in 1967–1969, completed one year before his death. He shifted over a lifetime, from a lonely childhood, immersion in impersonal philosophical methematics and logic, to a lifelong search for a love that could speak to "the core of loneliness" in his heart, and an increasing awareness of the practical problems of *living*, as distinct from *thinking*, that affect all human beings in economic, social, political, moral, and personal problems in a changing world. Certainly his own unsolved problem of that core of loneliness was the motivating force behind both his search for love in successive marriages and in his public crusading in aid of human happiness. One cannot but regret that so great a man, with such extraordinary intellectual powers and at the same time such powerful emotional needs and sympathies, could not have had his attention diverted to the much closer study of the therapeutic possibilities of "the sort of love that religious teachers have preached," combined with a newly developing psychological knowledge which could have enabled him to use "human relations" as an experimental therapeutic set-up which would have enabled him to "penetrate to the core of loneliness in each person and speak to that." There is every evidence that the women he married genuinely loved him, and for an average of ten years each gave him a basic stable relationship. The sad thing is that each time his "frozen" core of loneliness broke through and he found a part of himself that could not love in return, he was plucked helplessly away from his only hope of a lasting cure. For he lacked Freud's motivation to and training for personal therapy. As it was, I think we must say that Freud has made by far the more lasting contribution to human well-being. Russell's family roots were too deep in liberal politics and utilitarian philosophy and ethics, with John Stuart Mill as his godfather, and a grandfather who was twice Liberal Prime Minister, and a mother who was a daughter of the liberal aristocracy. Probably each of his marriages gave him enough emotional support for a time, to free his energies for social crusading.

It is not accidental that while both Freud and Russell were professedly antireligious, they were both, in another sense, deeply religious men. Freud would address Pastor Pfister as "Dear Man of God" and Ayer describes Russell as a man "of religious temper." I take this to mean, by Russell's own definition, a profound concern for personal relationships as the only real cure for the "core of loneliness" that exists to some degree in all of us. Religion is not about theological metaphysics, but about therapeutic personal relationships, which are given absolute preeminence over problems of science and technology which are purely utilitarian and cannot of themselves give any meaning or value to our personal existence.

Wittgenstein regarded Russell, philosophically, as "a man who had run out of problems." The one profoundest problem for all men is the one to which Russell never began to find any answer, and which could be of any use to other people; it was the one basic problem that Freud's life work has eventually opened up constructively for us. R. Harré (Oxford) writes in *The Philosophies of Science*, "Freud was a great scientist because he looked for the causes of such commonplace occurrences as slips of the tongue, as well as for the causes of such unusual happenings as fits of hysteria." We should add "such commonplace happenings as dreams." Unlike Medawar, who unscientifically and rather airily dismisses this universal phenomenon as "nonsense," Freud saw that they are "the royal road into the unconscious."

One of my schizoid patients recently dreamed "I was at a card party with the family, I had some cards. They all played but I couldn't think or move. I just sat. Then they asked me 'What's your score?' I said 'I haven't played.' " She was in a family where, to use Russell's words, no one knew how to "penetrate to the core of loneliness [in her] and speak to that." I could wish that after his "revelation" in 1901, he could have spent the next ten years seeking to understand how to penetrate to the loneliness in people and in himself—that he might have been able to write a "Principia Psychologica" which would have been of greater service to mankind than showing how mathematics can be reduced to logic. I do not dispute the right of the born philosopher to pursue his own natural interests. I feel sad, however, that such an extraordinary flash of profound insight, which does not often come to the physical scientist or philosopher, and certainly never to the "Behaviourist," was not recognized by Bertrand Russell as more profoundly important than anything else he had ever thought, and was wasted at that time, because he had not the means of following it up. Fortunately, psychoanalytically orientated psychotherapists have, since Freud's death, been able to develop and use his theories and methods in new ways to open up this ultimate region in human personality. It is sad that psychoanalysis had not progressed far enough at an earlier date for Russell to have made use of it, for through the Bloomsbury Circle he had contacts with it in the 1930's.

# REFERENCES

Ayer, A., (1972). *Russell*. London: Fontana/Collins.
Bion, W. (1962). *Learning from Experience*. London: Heinemann.
Jones, E., (1954). *Sigmund Freud: Life and Work* vol. 1. London: Hogarth Press.
Paul, G., (1956). In *The Revolution in Philosophy*. London: Macmillan.

# 15

# PSYCHODYNAMIC
# REALITIES

D EVELOPMENTS IN THIS POST-EINSTEIN era of the philosophy of science, associated with such names as Popper, Kuhn, Polyani, Lakatos and others and popularly expressed in Sir P. Medawar's *Induction and Intuition in Scientific Thought* should compel us to rethink the nature of psychoanalysis as an area of investigation of certain phenomena, which no one else is investigating in what we feel to be terms appropriate to its proper nature. From time to time eminent thinkers including Popper and Medawar tell us that psychoanalysis is not science. Psychoanalysts rarely reply, partly because the evidence is confidential, the study of the very private, personal inner suffering of a human being often disturbed for years, dating back into childhood. Full length case histories cannot be published. Marion Milner's *The Hands of the Living God* (a D. H. Lawrence quotation by the patient), a successful 20-year treatment of a schizophrenic girl, told with her consent, was a tremendous exception, as was Hannah Green's autobiographical account of her treatment by Dr. Frieda Fromm-Reichmann, *I Never Promised You a Rose Garden.* A University graduate wrote to ask me for some psychotherapeutic help: "I am suffering from anxiety with a continually thumping heart and attacks of terror and paralyzing feelings of being a nonexistent person. My troubles go right back as far as I can remember. I believe you could help me." That represents word-for-word scores of such letters. Such people cannot submit themselves to investigation as objects of pure scientific research. They can only cooperate if they feel they will be understood and helped. So if psychoanalysis is a science at all, it can never be a pure science. The nature of its task compels it to be an "applied science." Most analysts are hard-worked "general practitioners" with little time or training for research and writing, which may, unhappily, have fostered a type of theory which can seem esoteric, the dogma of a "closed in-group." Few, if any, of its critics have first-hand experience of psychoanalysis in practice, in the nature of the case. The result is a communications breakdown between the therapists and their critics, medical, scientific or philosophical. Yet it may well now be incumbent on us to rethink our discipline in the changing scene of the philosophy of science today: first, because it is changing and viewing science in ways that were not open to Freud, and could help us to better conceptualize our clinical data; and second, because if we do not make our contribution to contemporary thinking, we are shirking a cultural responsibility, for it is now clear that the question "Is psycho-analysis science?" is only part of an overall question, "Is any kind of psychology science? And if so, in what sense?"

## THE PHILOSOPHY OF SCIENCE

The dilemma which arises over whether any psychology can be a science, concerns psychiatry, general psychology, and psychoanalysis. An article written by Eliot Slater, an eminent psychiatrist, in *World Medicine* (Feb. 1972) was entitled "Is psychiatry a science? Does it want to be?" He wrote: "It is surely only the glamour the name of 'science' exerts which has induced us all to mistake out functions," i.e., by claiming to be scientific. He states the problem:

> The scientific method can only concern itself with the real world, the world outside us, which we can to some extent study objectively. There is also the world within us, for ever the domain of subjectivity, for ever beyond the reach of science, the territory of the arts and humani-ties. . . . Despite its inaccessibility to science, it yet contains the possi-bility of greater understanding. This is a world the psychiatrist cannot ignore and in which the psychoanalyst seeks his understanding.

His problem is that the Positivist philosophy of over 2 centuries only allows him to regard the world outside us as real and open to scientific study, yet he sees the urgency of understanding the "world within us." But this restricted use of the term "real" to mean only what the physical sciences can study, is quite unreal. Hitler's delusions of greatness were not only subjectively real for himself but also terribly objectively real for the rest of us. If someone threatens us, we need to know "Does he really mean it?" The objective reality of the nuclear bomb only worries us because of the possible objective reality of someone's preparedness to use it. It is impossible to accept the restriction of reality to what can be studied by the physical sciences. Science from "scio," to know, means simply knowledge. Consciousness, also from "scio," means self-knowledge, knowledge of the world within, but we are very resistant to self-knowledge and so the knowledge of the so-called outer or material world developed first. Comte's Positivist philosophy excluded psychology from the sciences. Psychology belonged to the humanities, where speculation, fantasy, fiction, even superstition were rife. The pseudo-philosophy of scientific materialism grew in this atmosphere. When at the turn into the 20th Century, specifically psychological studies began to grow apace, they were gravely handicapped by the dogma that they must be scientific in the Positivist sense.

At the turn of the century, it seemed to Pavlov, J. B. Watson, and even McDougall with his early book *Physiological Psychology*, and also to Freud with his *Psychology for Neurologists*, that it was more important to be scientific than to be genuinely psychological. Freud struggled uneasily to yoke together a physicalistic biological theory and truly psychological intuitive understanding, and never succeeded; probably the main reason why the claim of psychoanalysts that their theory is scientific seemed to so many intellectuals equivocal and easy to reject. J. B. Watson was not gifted with Freud's psychologically intuitive genius, so it was easy for him to be a Positivist. He denied the very existence of consciousness; all the phenomena included under it were illusions, but he forgot to explain how he became aware, i.e., conscious, of the nonexistence of consciousness, or what we have illusions with, and how they come to have such terrible destructive reality in many cases. Everything was either fact or fiction, brain or mind, neurological system or consciousness, reality or appearance. It was held not necessary to account for the existence of mind, consciousness, appearance. The Idealist philosophers from Berkeley to F. H. Bradley did not help for they only reversed the other, saying that mind is the reality and matter the appearance. Neither side saw that the distinction between appearance and reality is itself unreal, and only rested on the apparent irreducibility of supposedly solid matter in the billiard-ball universe of that era. All that has now changed, in the relativity atmosphere of post-Einstein thinking, and with quantum physics disillusioning us about the solidity of the atom. As Bertrand Russell (1946) put it: "When an electron and a proton collide, they do not break-up into still smaller things but disappear into a wave of energy. No one knows what that is, but at any rate it is not a 'thing.'" So the ultimate reality of matter has become as mysterious as that of mind, and the distinction between reality and appearance has faded. Appearance can only be the appearance of reality, and we can only study reality in the forms in which it appears to us. What we experience is phenomenal reality, and that enters into our experience in at least three ways—inorganic, organic, and psychic; matter, life, and mind, all equally real and equally ultimately mysterious. Yet we can develop increasing understanding of all three, and do not need to be as wistfully hesitant as Dr. Slater in seeking increasing understanding of the world within us.

Scientific materialism is now renamed "reductionism," and contemporary reductionists, hardline Behaviourists in the Watson tradition such as Skinner and Eysenck, have not absorbed the change in the philosophy of science. They seek to foreclose the issue as to the nature of a science of psychology by dismissing psychic reality as mere fantasy, fiction, imagination, illusion, only to be studied scientifically by reducing it to physical science terms in neurophysiology. All we are left with is molecular biology, genetics, cerebral biochemistry, and neurological conditioning and reconditioning. But once we leave the experimental laboratory to confront real life, as analysts have to do, these sciences do not help us to understand the meaning of the joys and sorrows human beings experience in their struggles to relate constructively or destructively with one another, as the subjects of their own experience. These sciences are indispensable to understand what Sullivan called "the biological substrate" of personality, but when we turn to the psychic reality, the actual stuff of human beings' experience of themselves, we face again the fantasies and imaginative symbolism in which human beings express the emotions that correlate with differing qualities of personal relationships, all of which are inescapably real for their happiness and even existence. They turn up at times as frighteningly powerful determinants of destructive behavior, or again as the inspirational basis of the world's greatest art and literature. Would biochemistry really help us to understand the tragedies of *Macbeth* or *Hamlet*, or Ibsen's *Hedda Gabler*, and their effects on the people round them. There is an area of real facts here which demands study in terms appropriate and intelligible in the light of the nature of the subject matter. The terminology of physical science throws no light at all of understanding in this region of psychic reality. It is significant thus, that a physical scientist, the physicist Professor Bronowski (1965), reflecting the new outlook, says that man is both a machine and a Self, and that there are two qualitatively different kinds of knowledge, of the machine (the organism) which is physical science, and of the Self, which he says is found in literature. But that is only one area in which knowledge of the Self is found. Psychopathology is certainly another. Literature is such an expression because it is the firsthand expression of human experiences in relations with other Selves, and with subhuman life and inorganic nature: of which Thomas Mann's short story *Tobias Mindernickel* is a startling example. Many great artists and writers had deeply disturbed personalities; their psychopathology did not explain their genius, but it was expressed by their gift. Fairbairn told me that he once successfully treated a painter for depression which had become so bad that he could not paint at all. But after his depression was relieved, something vital had gone out of his painting. The emotional tensions of his depression had found direct expression in his art. But this kind of knowledge of the Self, of the private and shared experience we have as subjects meaningfully relating (not just objects observed and experimented with from the outside, but subjects understood from the inside) only exists in literature in spontaneous and wholly unorganized form. Any serious study of the nature of this kind of knowledge of the Self must attempt some systematic conceptualization and organization, for the sake of clarity of understanding and further testing and correcting. We have then arrived at the concept of a possible Science of the Personal Self in Personal Relations, a systematic study of our meaningful subjective experience as psychic reality, a definition emerging in psychoanalysis today after 70 years of critical research.

The fact that the older Positivist view of science cannot accommodate this view, is leading, on the evidence of *The Bulletins of the British Psychological Society*, to increasing disillusionment among British psychologists. Joynson of Nottingham University, in two articles, "The Breakdown of Modern Psychology" (1970) and "The Return of Mind" (1972) spelled out in detail how Stout's 1896 prediction that the laboratory experimentalist approach would lead to the absorption of psychology into physiology, has become fulfilled in Behaviorism, and a return to introspectionist study of the Self that behaves is required. Bannister, a clinical psychologist wrote (1968): "The concept of 'Self' is essentially a psychological concept. Consciousness, choice, and teleological models are reiterative in psychology, since, in spite of the most gallant efforts, we have failed to get far by adhering to the mechanistic model. Reductionism is a philosophic posture which assumes that physiology is somehow nearer to reality than psychology." In line with this, Skinner's *Beyond Freedom and Dignity* has had the most drastically critical reviews, viewing it as 19th Century Utilitarianism, Bentham's pleasure motive (positive reinforcement) and as advocating a technocratic dictatorship. This would highlight the dangerous negative, manipulative aspect of hardline Behaviorism. Similar criticisms were voiced by Witenberg at The W. A. White Institute:

A threat is posed by the rise of Behaviorism as a theory. It represents an idolatry of law and order. Everyone is programmed in his proper place. It goes with the virtual disappearance of courses on personality development from the curricula of graduate schools of psychology. . . . The challenge to the theoretician is an Open-ended view of the human being. Physics has been able to introduce the principle of indeterminacy. Why cannot we? We are daily confronted with clinical material we cannot explain in a deterministic manner. Why then do we try to fit these data into theories based on determinism?

There is clearly a growing call for a nondeterministic, non-Positivistic, teleological theory, what C. Taylor called a "psychological psychology" to aid us in the study of the psychodynamic phenomena of human beings as persons in relationships. The key psychological concept is not just the Self but the Self growing in personal relations. Whatever may be thought about psychoanalytic theories, we have an enormous amount of sheer clinical data about the nature of psychic reality, which demands review in the light of the newer concepts of science today. There seem to be three criteria of what constitutes a science—logical, epistemological, and phenomenological.

*The Logical Criterion* concerns the intellectual method used by science. The

Inductive method of last century is now discredited. Science does not grow by endless experiments piling up collections of particular facts out of which emerge generalizations which are laws of nature. Karl Popper's Hypothetico-Deductive Method is expounded by Peter Medawar as starting with the investigator developing an interest in certain phenomena; for example, A. Fleming's interest in infected war wounds, and we may add Freud's interest in the similarities between certain neurotic symptoms of hysteria and some hypnotic phenomena. The next step is an intuitive or imaginative guess at a possible explanation, which is formulated as a hypothesis, to be tested out by experiments. For Popper these should be designed not to support but to falsify the hypothesis. If the experiment does not falsify the hypothesis, then to that extent it is confirmed till such time as an experiment is made which finds a flaw in it. Then the hypothesis is, to use Medawar's expression, not so much disproved as repaired or mended. So there is a slow steady development of theory under pressure all the time from confrontation with phenomena. It is in exactly this light that I regard psychoanalytical interpretations. They are not authoritarian dicta imposed by the analyst. They are possible explanations of the problem the patient is unfolding, to be tested by reference to his reaction. I personally never announce the meaning of any dream, symptom, fear, or what not. Based on my experience, I will suggest a tentative view of what this or that may mean, and the patient may say: "No, that doesn't ring a bell"; in that case the interpretation is not true for him, or not true for him as yet, and we drop it. But he may say: "Ah! Do you know I thought that only the other day," and his own insight into himself is supported. Exactly by this Hypothetico-Deductive Method I found years ago that with my patients Freud's original classic Instinct Theory of Sexual and Aggressive drives dammed up inside, and needing abreaction or detensioning, did not prove adequate; not that there were no sexual or aggressive phenomena; there nearly always were, but I found them pointing back to deeper problems of sheer Ego-Weakness, arrested development of a basic Self in the earliest years. Precisely this method had led psychoanalysts increasingly to see that what Freud called "Oedipal phenomena" are so often a defence against the far deeper and more serious schizoid problems, fundamental failures of secure, integrated whole-ego experience from earliest infancy. By this method of falsification of the classic psychobiology, psychoanalysis has preserved the factual clinical data Freud observed and steadily developed the Personal Relations Theory out of the work of Melanie Klein, H. S. Sullivan, R. Fairbairn, D. Winnicott, and many others. It is certainly true that psychoanalytic theory has also been too often expounded as an orthodox dogma, but this is also true of behavioral and experimental psychology, and Popper holds it to be true even in quantum physics. Kuhn and Popper both agree that most scientific investigation is in support of orthodox theory, but Popper says plainly that this is very bad science, and that true science should be critical and revolutionary all the time. Psychoanalysis cannot be singled out for criticism on this score and it has its own history of constant critical revision of theory, for which Freud himself set the example. He once wrote in 1914 that anyone whose work starts with transference and resistance (which are psychic phenomena, not theories) "can call his work psychoanalysis, even though he arrives at conclusions different from mine." Psychoanalysis stands up to the logical criterion of scientific method.

*The Epistemological Criterion*, as expounded by Medawar, the "hierarchical model of the structure of knowledge," is of the greatest importance. Knowledge is like a building with a ground floor, and floors rising above it, each floor higher than the one below. The ground floor is the basic sciences of physics and chemistry, and as we go up we come upon the various sciences that have come into being, many of them this century: biology, ethology, anthropology, sociology, to name a few, and from our point of view, arriving at psychology at the top. Medawar is specifically anti-reductionist. He writes: "Each tier of the natural hierarchy makes use of notions peculiar to itself. The ideas of democracy, credit, crime, or political constitution are no part of biology, nor shall we expect to find in physics the concepts of memory, sexuality or fear . . . In each tier or plane of the hierarchy new notions or ideas seem to emerge that are inexplicable in the language or with the conceptual resources of the tier below. The flow of thought works one way only. We cannot 'interpret' sociology in terms of biology, or biology in terms of physics." Nor, we must add, psychology in terms of any lower-level science. Results of research on lower levels may be utilized on higher levels as when drugs are used to control emotions; but higher-level phenomena cannot be reduced to the terms of lower-level phenomena. Psychology must be psychology and not neurophysiology. This is a charter for the investigation of psychodynamic phenomena in their own terms.

*The Phenomenological Criterion*. This concerns the nature of the phenomena that are under investigation, and it follows from Medawar's view that on each tier of the hierarchy of knowledge new ideas representing new phenomena arise, that all the various types of phenomenal reality—inorganic, organic, psychic—must be studied in term that are realistic, appropriate, and relevant to the nature of just those phenomena in question. Thus Skinner's "data or thing" language, forbidding the use of psychological terms in the study of behavior is merely an arbitrary dogma and sins against the whole orientation of the present-day philosophy of science. It is incumbent on us to say what we mean by "psychodynamic reality" for once that is settled, the way is now clear, philosophically, for the creation of a field of genuine psychological studies, in which a progressive Behaviorism, an up-to-date introspectionist general psychology, and the personalist psychology of Allport, Kelly, and Bannister, could maintain a valuable dialogue with the Personal Relations Theories of our contemporary psychoanalysis. Since life is always a mixture of time-saving habit and creative spontaneity, there is room for both a truly psychological

Behaviorism and a psychodynamic depth psychology. The matter has been clearly put by Adrian, the neurophysicist, in saying that while "most of our everyday activities could be behavioristically explained, there is one thing that does not fit into this neat and tidy scheme, the 'I' that does the thinking, feeling, and willing." To illustrate the existence of behavior patterns, a patient who was an obsessional and a pianist told me that one day he was playing a Chopin Nocturne and was suddenly surprised to find he had stopped playing. He discovered he had come to the end, and had actually played the entire piece right through automatically while his consciousness was fixed on the theme of the two opening bars. A different type of example is that of social and cultural conditioning, as studied for instance by Erikson and others. If we had been born in Russia or China all our modes of adapting and relating to one another would be different, though our basic human nature would be the same. All these are matters for genuine psychological study, but in this wide area of personal psychic phenomena, whether considered objectively as behavior, or subjectively as experience (the "I" that does the thinking, feeling, and willing), psychoanalysis has a special concern with depth phenomena. The hierarchical model of knowledge makes it unnecessary to adopt Slater's restricted Positivist view of science, or to view "the world within us, for ever the domain of subjectivity [as] forever beyond the reach of science, in which no possibilities of verification exist." We shall rather hold that for each level of phenomena, there exists an appropriate conceptualization and relevant methods of verification. In particular, prediction and validation as found in the physical sciences are not relevant to psychic reality. As Bronowski says: "If I was predictable I would not be a Self but a machine," and what is to be looked for in a Self is not rigid predictability but constancy, reliability, and consistency. As to methods of validation, Medawar writes: "Matters of validation are important in the experimental sciences, but not as important as they are sometimes made out to be. . . . An obsessional preoccupation with matters to do with ascertainment is part of the heritage of inductivism." Eysenck has called for comparison of cases under psychotherapy with untreated control cases, but he overlooks the fact that all patients are so highly individual with such great differences of both history and present-day environment, that none could serve as genuine controls for comparison with any of the others. I have treated a considerable number of patients who could have been given the same diagnostic label but they were all so individually different that none of them could have served as a genuine control case for comparison with any of the others. Also in cases of the break up of a massive amnesia for a serious traumatic event, no control case would be possible for we do not know at the start what the trouble is for which a possible comparative control case could be sought. Eysenck has also made play with the idea that untreated cases (in the Barron-Leary study of 150 cases for under 9 months) show as much remission of illness as those treated by psychotherapy. But he does not cite the fact that many people have suffered from nervous breakdowns repeatedly at intervals of 3 to 5 years from their teens into advanced age, and the intervening remissions were meaningless in any fundamental sense. Such valueless objections all arise out of the mistake of comparing psychoanalytic psychotherapy with the physical science criteria. We are concerned with the creation of a genuinely psychological science that is a psychodynamic science in its own right dealing in appropriate concepts with its own special field of phenomenal reality. I am not concerned to maintain that psychoanalysis has at this time succeeded in conceptualizing its findings in a way that would satisfy the philosopher of science. Slater may be right when he says: "Psychoanalysis (i.e., at present) is not a science, but a womb in which a science might grow." That concedes the real point, that a psychodynamic science is possible, and we may proceed to consider both the criticisms made and the conceptualizations achieved in the light of that admission, that a genuinely psychological science, not reduced to any physical science model, is a reality.

## A POSSIBLE SCIENCE OF PSYCHODYNAMIC REALITY

I am not claiming scientific status for psychoanalytic theory as it stands today. It is in no sense a unity and many contributions are repetitive and orthodox, but certain things must be said on this point. Medawar (Romanes Lecture 1969) regarded psychoanalysis as a mythology, not a science, and did not wish his criticism to apply to psychotherapy, but rather to Freudian theory. Psychotherapy as we understand it today, is fundamentally psychoanalytic in method, regardless of differences in theory, and is basically Freud's gift to the world. Slater refers to a New York University Institute of Philosophy discussion which rejected the claim of psychoanalysis to be science "because psychoanalysts had not approached their unified and complex theory in an experimental spirit. It should be broken down into part theories and subjected to piecemeal confirmation or refutation." But there is no unified theory as yet, acceptable to all or most psychoanalysts. There are great differences between the views of classic Freudians, Kleinians, Hartmann's "Ego-Psychology," Fairbairn, and British Independents; and outside the official societies, the important Interpersonal Relations Theory of H. S. Sullivan and his followers; also of Adler and Jung in the wider psychotherapeutic field. There are possibilities of a unified theory, and such theory as exists has for a long time been subjected to piecemeal testing resulting in steady far-reaching modifications. That discussion took place in 1958, but Fairbairn's fundamental revision (developed from the work of Melanie Klein, though disagreeing in basic matters from her), was published in 1952. Klein's own work dates back to the late 1920's and 1930's and led to intense controversy and division in the British Psychoanalytical Society, about which

Ernest Jones wrote in 1948: "[S]ome held the opinion that Mrs. Klein's conclusions not only diverged from but were incompatible with Freud's. Not that this should be a decisive consideration, if experience showed that her conclusions were nearer the truth. . . . If psychoanalysis is to remain a science, now that Freud's magnificent impetus has been extinguished, advance beyond the limits he reached is inevitable." The post-Freudian Object-Relations Theory in Britain has been one result. For myself, it was the piecemeal testing of the orthodox theory against the evidence of patients that led me steadily to depart from Freud's physicalistic psychobiology. Fairbairn's (1952) rejection of Instinct Theory and gradual development of a consistently psychological theory of the Development of Persons in the Medium of Personal Relationships, crystallized out on the remark of a patient: "You keep saying I want this or that instinct satisfied, but what I want is a father." The piecemeal breaking down into part theories for confirmation or refutation, called for by New York philosophers in 1958 had been going on for a long time, but critics of psychoanalysis are not usually well informed on its progressive developments either during or since Freud's own day. In the New York discussion Ernest Nagel called for experimental validation but did not discuss the question, "What kind of experimental validation is relevant to the study of psychic reality?" In exploring this matter further I shall consider that the claim of psychoanalysis to be, or to become, a science ("a womb out of which a science could grow") can only be rejected on two grounds: (1) That its Analytical Therapeutic Method is not truly Hypothetico-Deductive and (2) That the psychodynamic phenomena it explores are not truly real. An examination of Medawar's (1969) criticisms in some detail will further this end. Two of his criticisms are different aspects of the same basic misunderstanding. He thinks that (1) Psychoanalytic Theory disallows criticism and (2) that in practice it is authoritarian, and so more a religious cult than a scientific inquiry. He writes: "We obviously cannot accept into science any system (e.g., psychoanalysis) which contains a built-in antidote to disbelief: to discredit psychoanalysis is an aberration of thought that calls for psychoanalytic treatment." This is glaring misunderstanding or equally glaring ignorance of psychoanalytic theory. He simply equates resistance to psychoanalytic treatment with objective criticism of psychoanalytic theory. If Medawar had firsthand experience of psychoanalytic therapy he would know how intensely patients resist being helped to become aware of their own repressed tensions (not our theories about them) because they begin to feel ill, anxious, or violent when these break through into consciousness. Thus, a very able obsessional patient who was constantly blocking his own thought processes, said, after some 3 years of therapy: "Life's taking on a new dimension. I feel I'm breaking through to contact something I've lost contact with in my past: I think its the atmosphere of bickering we lived in at home all my childhood. I'm getting the feel of it coming back. We were pounced on for everything we said or did, and now I pounce on myself and interfere with myself. I can't do anything straightforwardly.

I have to keep stopping and checking myself." Then he stopped and after a pause said: "There, I had something in mind about it just then but its gone. I've lost it." Here is resistance to psychoanalytic therapy, forcibly illustrating Freud's insight into the perpetuation of childhood experience in the unconscious, a fact of psychodynamic reality we have to reckon with. A patient who was an outstanding biology teacher once said: "When I'm very anxious I find myself thinking 'psychoanalysis isn't true. I can explain all this biologically.' But when my anxiety dies down, I know that is not true. I'm making an excuse for not knowing what I'm really anxious about," which turned out to be a truly terrible childhood trauma for which he had a total amnesia. I shall illustrate resistance again when we turn to dreams. But the theories analysts develop in seeking to understand such phenomena are fully open to informed criticism. Our trouble is to find fully informed critics.

Of course, psychoanalysts are as human as other scientists. All thinkers tend to develop an emotional investment in their theory. A psychologist, N. Johnson, said over Radio 3, B.B.C. (Sept. 1971), "Science is a social product. It has a sociology and a psychology. Scientists are often resistant to innovation. Scientific papers are fraudulent in their representation both of the process of scientific thought and of the personal detachment of the scientist." Anna Freud (1936) wrote with courageous candor, "the odium of analytical unorthodoxy attached to the study of the Ego" before Freud's 1920 monographs, a somewhat sinisterly unscientific note to sound. Even the already quoted progressive Dr. Ernest Jones invited criticism when he rejected the theoretical deviations of some of Freud's early critics inside the movement, such as Rank, Adler, Ferenczi, as psychopathologically determined. He (1955) wrote: "When an analyst loses insight he previously had, the recurring wave of resistance that causes the loss is apt to display itself as pseudo-scientific explanations of the data . . . dignified as a new theory." But in those days psychoanalysts were a small group fighting for existence in a very hostile environment. However, if Adler had unconscious motives for preferring a teleological theory of motivation and an Ego theory of personality, why could not Freud have unconscious motives for clinging to biological determinism and not recognizing the centrality of the Ego concept for over 20 years. Psychoanalysts have human frailties, but Medawar's equating of resistance to psychoanalytic therapy with criticism of the theory is just untrue. The other twin aspect of his criticism of psychoanalysis as a method is that it is authoritarian. He would have to reject my own practice of treating every interpretation as a hypothesis to be experimentally tested by the patient's reaction to it, as either falsifying it or confirming it. He writes: "The purpose (of psychoanalytic treatment) is (not cure which analysts repudiate) but rather to give the patient a new and deeper understanding of himself and of the nature of his relationship to his fellow men." So far there is nothing objectionable about that; it does happen in the course of the slow freeing and regrowing of the patient's potentials for being a real person in his own right. But

Medawar adds: "So interpreted, psychoanalysis is best thought of as a secular substitute for prayer. Like prayer, it is conducted in the form of a dualogue, and like prayer (if prayer is to bring comfort and refreshment) it requires an act of personal surrender, though in this case to a professional and stipendiary god." Medawar knew that in the audience he was lecturing to, he could count on a number of listeners seeing that his comparison of psychoanalysis with religion was meant to imply a credulous and willingly dependent patient. If he were ever involved in psychoanalytic treatment some rude shocks would be in store for him. The idea of an act of personal surrender is at once negated by the phenomenon of resistance. The patient in a florid hysteric phase may demand a relationship of dependency and surrender to being supported, but, if one were not prepared for it, it would be disconcerting to find how suddenly this can switch to paranoid hostility and suspicion. Both positive and negative transferences result from persisting child-hood problems and call to be outgrown. Is Medawar so uninformed about psychoanalytic therapy as not to know of this?

What accounts do patients give of their reasons for wanting psychoanalytic therapy? I have a pile of letters averaging one every 3 or 4 weeks, all saying much as follows: "My doctor tells me it is all in my mind and I must pull myself together and get out more. I have had pills, electric shocks, been in hospital several times, told I was better, but I still feel the same. No one has told me what is wrong with me. I am a puzzle to myself and family, and I can't make normal friendships. Where can I get psychotherapy?" But this does not guarantee that every patient will use psycho-therapy to resolve his problems. One man began discussing his problems in a de-tached intellectual way and said: "I shall enjoy this. It will be as good as a course in psychology." I simply said: "In that case you will waste your time getting nowhere." He did not come again. A very much more difficult problem was presented by a deeply depressed woman in the fifties, threatened with premature retirement, who came reluctantly and on the defensive. She made enough use of my help to keep going till she got her pension, while becoming uncomfortably aware of how much her life-long hate of her sarcastic father absorbed her mental energies. Then she brought this dream: "I was walking along and came to a huge wall, too high to get over and too long to get around." I said: "You seem to feel you have come to a dead end." She replied: "I must go on, if you can stand it." From then on her treatment became a repetitive working up of a quarrel with me, ending in her flinging out and slamming the door. Some months later she would write: "I'm so depressed. Can I come back?" Several times I agreed till finally, on returning once more, she reported this dream: "I got on a tram car, walked through to the driver's platform, turned him off and drove myself." I simply said: "Isn't that what you wanted to do with father, and try to do with me?" She never came again. Her running quarrel with her father had become her *modus vivendi* and she only wanted to use me to keep it going, a role I naturally refused. Yet she was not as ill and incapacited as when she first came to see me, a partial result by no means unimportant to her. This may be compared with a similar case of a man who had a standing quarrel with a very dictatorial father, and was referred to me with high blood pressure for which no organic cause was found. As he talked out the details of this quarrel, his tension relaxed, though he was always resistant to me (and in business always quarrelling with authorities). Finally he brought this dream, saying he felt well enough now to end therapy: "I was fighting for life with my father. I defended myself so well that he suddenly stopped fighting and walked away, and I thought: 'Oh! I didn't bargain for that. What shall I do now'?" I said: "Perhaps you are wondering what you'll do now, when you haven't me to argue with." However, since then, he has lived an active life with no recurrence of high blood pressure. We may bear these two dreams in mind as we turn to Medawar's view of dreams. Meanwhile, such examples show his view of the psychoanalytic situation to be totally out of touch with realities. Unwitting and unprejudiced confirmation of this negative-transference problem was provided by an ex-criminal interviewed on B.B.C. Radio 3, who said: "I never used violence except in prison against warders, and then I always felt I was punching up father." I was twice attacked by one patient in a paranoid phase and had to defend myself. After the second incident, I said: "You are trying to force me to hit you as your father did. Now we know there's no need to repeat it and if you do it again, I shall stop seeing you." That was the end of it, and very good progress was made after that. The psychoanalytic therapist is then not a comforting professional and stipendiary god but an understanding and trustworthy person who will stand by the patient and help him to express and resolve usually repressed bitter uncon-scious problems of long standing, so as to free his real, natural personality to develop in the present-day world. I have chosen these examples, at this point, because they show the dangerous and inescapable reality of psychodynamic phenomena, and also reveal the psychoanalytic therapy session as the only experimental laboratory in which such phenomena can be studied, because it is a personal relationship situation. In an impersonal experimental and observational situation, no patient could express his real problem, and it would not be welcomed if he did. As H. S. Sullivan put it, "[T]he psychotherapist is a participant observer and only so can he both study psychodynamic phenomena and help the patient to free himself from his traumatic past."

Medawar's third criticism concerns not the nature and validity of the method used by psychoanalysis, but the nature and reality of the psychodynamic phe-nomena it investigates. These are heavily emotion-loaded memories of unresolved traumatic experiences in bad personal relationship, going often as far back as infancy; yet they are more than memories of past events, for they are kept alive, excluded from ordinary consciousness except in disguised forms, in an unconscious inner psychic world whence they erupt to disturb the waking Self, through the media of irrational transference reactions to other people in the present day, and disguised as symptoms and expressed in dreams. Medawar throws doubt on the reality of all these psychodynamic phenomena when he writes: "Dreams are not messages or communications of any kind" and attributes to them utter nonsensicality. The dreams I have already cited should show that no one who has extensive firsthand knowledge of dreams could make a statement so out of touch with the facts. Dreams often appear irrational, are by no means always easy to understand, and some we never do understand. But anyone who has studied dream sequences in the same patients, over long periods, and in the light of what is known of the patients' histories, can have any doubt that they are phases in the unconscious intelligible growth processes of personality. This fact is implied, even if no interpretations of actual dreams are attempted, in the fact that laboratory experiment has shown that if people are allowed to have adequate deep dreamless sleep (always felt to be the most important kind) but are deprived of light dreaming sleep, they become increasingly mentally disturbed. In our dreaming, we are doing our mental homework on the legacies of our unresolved emotional tensions of the past, sometimes the past as recent as the day or few days before, but in the end the past that goes right down to the foundation experiences of early life. The early idea of fixed dream symbols is not valid. Dream components mean exactly whatever the dreamer wants to express by them, and that has to be found out by free association, the uncriticized spontaneous flow of thoughts that can at last lead to the underlying problem, in spite of the patient's frequent interference with his free flow of thoughts at a conscious level. A dream is the uncritical semiconscious expression of some aspect of the patient's complex unconscious emotional state at that time. It is often immediately repressed on waking to full consciousness. One patient expressed resistance by regular dreaming all of which was instantly blotted out at the moment of waking. A male patient with a hysterical tremor of the right hand and an unusually traumatic childhood at the hands of a drunken father, got rid of his tremor after some 4 years of analysis, but by then had come dangerously near to dreaming out more than he could tolerate. He dreamed furiously but could remember nothing in the morning; so he took paper to write them down at night, and for 4 nights dreamed nothing. Thinking that he had just stopped dreaming, he did not write anything the next night, and dreamed furiously, a dream that he remembered: "I went down into my cellar and found there a man of my own age in the grip of an octopus. I seized a knife to set him free, and then suddenly dropped it and came out, locked the door and came upstairs." He never came again for further sessions, but I heard later he had no recurrence of the right-hand tremor. Nightmares are volcanic eruptions of violently disturbing early experience, as with a man whose psychotic violent mother had terrified him, and in adult life he would start up out of sleep screaming and see his mother's face superimposed on his wife's. In view of such evidence it is Medawar's rhetorical rejection of dreams that is the nonsense. Dreams can be psychodynamic reality with a vengeance, as such patients know to their cost.

## AUTISTIC THINKING

This brings me to the last point: In the long run the possibility of a psychoanalytic or psychodynamic science can only be rejected if the psychodynamic phenomena it investigates are dismissed as unreal. This can only be done by taking the phenomena studied by the physical sciences as the sole standard of the real which I hope I have shown is philosophically arbitrary. Psychic reality has its own kind of reality and must be studied in terms that are appropriate to the understanding of these facts of our personal subjective experiences in living. Perhaps it is most of all in the more extreme forms of psychopathological experience that stubbornly real subjective phenomena cannot be evaded or dismissed, but must be understood. We will look finally, if briefly, at autistic phenomena to illustrate this. A dream is the uncritical semiconscious expression of the dreamer's actual psychodynamic condition (which can be very complex) at that moment, and is experienced as an internal world in which the dreamer is actually living in tension-filled relationships with other persons, undisguised or symbolized. Its immediate repression reveals dramatically the splitting of the total psychic self into two aspects—conscious and unconscious. If the unconscious experience usurps consciousness and floods it totally, we have a hallucination, an experience in which normal adult conscious experience of the outer world is blotted out for the time being. This illustrates how entirely a human being can live in his inner world which has a stubborn reality of its own which has long since ceased to correspond with the externally real world. When a person is in this state all the time he is termed "autistic;" he lives enclosed in his inner subjective reality and simply sees the external world and people as identical with it, without having any knowledge of the unreality of his experience from other people's point of view; it is real to him. Such people are psychotic. Many psychiatrists are satisfied to treat psychosis as a genetic or biochemical disorder, and many of its manifestations can be controlled by drugs which, like Largactil, tranquillize the acute anxiety involved, but only so long as the drug continues to be taken. Perhaps the major factor that has forced psychoanalysts to move beyond Freud's theory of the repression of instincts has been the discovery that, despite Freud's view to the contrary, psychosis can be understood in transference terms, even ultimately by the patient, so paving the way for his growth out of this condition. Stella Chess (1966) writes of "early infantile autism, a term coined by Kanner. These children are non-responsive to persons giving them their early nurture; they neither cuddle nor smile nor show evidence of pleasurable recognition of familiar people—and may persevere in repetitive or rhythmic activity. . . . Cases of childhood schizophrenia have failed to differentiate their own identities from those of their mothers because of a failure in maternal handling. Those giving them their early nurture" were nonresponsive to the children. Though Freud (1911) did not think psychotherapy could reach them, he recognized their strange self-enclosure and inability to form normal personal relations. Autism derives from the Greek "autos" or "self," and stands for a condition in which the human psyche is a prisoner within itself, shut up in pure subjectivity, not capable of any realistic relations to the outer world. The term, though convenient, is somewhat misleading because the individual has not really grown a Self but is shut up in purely subjective and fragmented experience. Because of early environmental failure to meet his needs, he has been unable to relate or differentiate, and a Self cannot develop in a vacuum of personal relations. Thus he is acting out a drama that is exclusively his own subjective psychic life; psychodynamic reality isolated from everything else. As intelligence and sensory perception grow, he can involve other people in his drama, but he is not seeing or relating to them as separate persons, only using them as material for acting out his fantasy life, as if they were parts of his subjective world. He is not even using them as projection screens for his fantasy. He cannot distinguish between them and his own experience which is why Freud thought psychotics were incapable of transference and could not be reached.

I shall quote two authorities: Donald Winnicott of London, on childhood schizophrenia, and Harold Searles of Washington, on adults. Winnicott (1965b), a pediatrician for 40 years seeing over 60, 000 mothers and children at two hospitals, wrote the following concerning babies:

> Is there an ego from the start? The start is when the ego starts. . . . In the very early stages of development of a human child, ego-functioning is inseparable from the existence of the infant as a person. . . . Is the ego weak or strong? The answer depends on the actual mother and her ability to meet the absolute dependence of the actual infant at the beginning, at the stage before the infant has separated out the mother from the Self. . . . There is no value whatever in describing babies in the earliest stages except in relation to the mother's functioning. . . . The baby is an immature being who is always on the brink of unthink-able anxieties . . . specifically the stuff of the psychotic anxieties, and these belong clinically to schizophrenia or to the emergence of a schizoid element hidden in an otherwise nonpsychotic personality. . . . In a proportion of cases (of infantile schizophrenia or autism) there is no evidence of neurological defect or disease. It is a common experience in child psychiatry for the clinician to be unable to decide between a diagnosis of primary defect, mild Little's disease, pure psychological failure of early maturation in a child with brain intact, or a mixture of all these. In some cases there is good evidence of a reaction to failure of Ego support. [pp. 56–57]

He repeatedly stresses: "A baby's Ego is as weak or strong as the mother's Ego support is weak or strong," the starting point of disintegration through failure to differentiate out from the mother, or else stable development.

Harold Searles (1959), with over 30 years experience of long-term treatment of hospitalized adult schizophrenics, writes:

> Schizophrenia can be seen to consist essentially in an impairment of both integration and differentiation. The schizophrenic cannot integrate his life experiences over a span of time as being all part of a continuing unbroken pattern. His past and present experience becomes all jumbled up. His reactions to other persons are an uncoordinated welter of ambivalent feelings which suddenly erupt, or as suddenly become unavailable to him through repression. Memories experienced with hallucinatory vividness and immediacy are sensed as perceptions of present events, and perceptions of present events may be experienced as memories. He has difficulty in differentiating one person from another, and may consciously experience the therapist as being his father, mother, or brother. [pp. 261–262]

(My own mother, senile and dying in her eighties, in the last few days would address me alternately as her son, husband, and father.) Searles agrees that the schizophrenic's condition is "attributable to regression to the level of early infancy, at which developmental phase the infant has not yet become effectively differentiated from the outer world, and feels at one with all the world which came within his kin—a world much too vast for his rudimentary ego to integrate." He described a woman patient "whose mother was particularly poorly organized and changeable in her moods. Her daughter insisted for years that she had not one but many mothers, and once explained to me, 'Whenever you use the word mother I see a whole parade of women, each one representing a different point of view'." The schizophrenic's reactions to the therapist are complicated in the same way. Instead of finding comfort and refreshment in an act of surrender to a professional and stipendiary god as Medawar imagines, the patient would find himself confused by a whole Olympic Pantheon of professional, stipendiary and often very bad gods, if he would be able to use such imagery. He is not psychically free to conform to Medawar's theories, which shows the pitfalls of speculating about psychoanalysis without firsthand experience of it. Searles (1971) wrote: "I have more than once felt, when assaulted by a psychotic patient's ways of responding to me, that both to protect one's own sanity and to help the patient regain his, one must develop an instrument exceeding in power his psychotic thought processes, namely, that represented by a strong, accurate, and well thought out armamentarium of theory concerning these psychotic thought processes." Of one patient Searles (1959) wrote: "She gave me to realize that, in the midst of a furious upbraiding of me, she was misidentifying herself as her mother and me as her mother's son. She thus beautifully revealed her prior introjection of the conflict between her mother and her brother." This psychotherapeutic experiment certainly falsifies Medawar's hypothesis about the nature of psychoanalytic treatment. Of psychoanalytic treatment of such cases, Searles writes:

> What the therapist does which assists the patient's differentiation often consists in his having the courage and honesty to differ with the patient's expressed feelings or with the social role into which the patient's sick behavior tends to fix the therapist. What I am describing is, of course, to only a minor degree a consciously planned therapeutic technique. It is rather a natural flow of events in the transference evolution, with which the therapist must have the spontaneity to go along. [p. 275]

Most intellectual critics of psychoanalysis would not, I suspect, care to test the falsifiability of their views by personal confrontation with this kind of psychodynamic reality. The psychoanalytic session is not primarily intended to be a scientific experiment, but a therapeutic personal relationship which provides an opportunity for regrowing the personality, if the patient wants to use it that way. But *qua*-science, it is the only situation in which hypotheses about this area of psychodynamic reality can be tested out, and the theoretical model of disintegrated psychic functioning repaired and improved. Autistic phenomena doubly underline the fact that the Self in personal relationships is the key psychological concept, and that the psychodynamic processes of the development, disintegration, and reintegration of the Self are the phenomena that both psychology and psychoanalysis, from different points of view, must study.

Psychoanalytic therapy has its strains but also its satisfactions. A man in his middle thirties came to me 20 years ago, exhausted, having screaming nightmares, severe chest pains, and fears of attacking his wife. His near-psychotic mother had been consistently violent, frothing at the mouth, threatening to slit him with a knife if he disobeyed her. He grew up severely schizoid and withdrawn. Slowly over the next 20 years, as he talked out and dreamed out his traumatic childhood, the nightmares, and more slowly the chest pains faded; he never missed a day of work again, and reached the top of his profession. Recently he said to me: "I realize I feel alive in a way I don't remember before. I can run up the office stairs two at a time and have no pains; a thing I've never done. Three days ago I had to explain to a top-level audience the complicated Housing Finance Act, and for the first time did it without pills. I'm seeing things as three-dimensional. I used to say people looked like three-ply cut-outs. I see you as a person and I feel more real myself. For years I've felt a kind of confusion between people and myself. I took it for granted that they felt as I did, and my feelings were theirs." Over the years of psychoanalytic therapy he had slowly become differentiated, integrated, and able to relate as a real person to a world of real persons. A dream he brought me recently was: "It was spring. Everything was growing. I went to my allotment and began to dig, and then noticed a sack on the rubbish heap. I opened it and inside was a baby. I thought it was dead, but as I took it out it breathed. I was delighted and took it home to my wife" (for some years now a much relieved wife). Here was the rebirth of what Winnicott used to call "the true Self, put into cold storage when born into an unnourishing environment." Here are psychodynamic phenomena, more momentous for us and of more ultimate significance; therefore more real than the phenomena of the physical mechanics of living which the physical sciences study. Here lies the urgent need, not just for more understanding of the world within (Slater 1972), but for a reliable psychodynamic science which is always testing and improving its hypotheses in the experimental laboratory of the whole of human living.

## REFERENCES

Bannister, D. (1968). The myth of physiological psychology. *Bulletin of the British Psychological Society* 21:229–231.

Bronowski, J. (1967). *The Identity of Man*. London: Pelican.

Chess, S. (1966). Psychiatry of the first three years of life. *American Handbook of Psychiatry* 3:18–29.

Fairbairn, R. (1952). *Psychoanalytic Studies of the Personality*. London: Tavistock Publications.

Freud, S. (1914). On the history of the psychoanalytic movement. *Collected Papers*, vol. 1. London: Hogarth Press.

Jones, E. (1947). In *Contributions to Psychoanalysis*, ed. M. Klein. London: Hogarth Press.

_____ (1955). *Freud*, vol. 2. London: Hogarth Press.

Joynson, R. B. (1970). The breakdown of modern psychology. *Bulletin of the British Psychological Society* 23:261–269.

_____ (1972). The return of mind. *Bulletin of the British Psychological Society* 25:1–10.

Kuhn, J. (1970). In *Criticism and the Growth of Knowledge*, ed. I. Lakatos and A. Musgrave, Cambridge: Cambridge University Press.

Mann, T. (1961). *Little Herr Friedemann and Other Stories*. London: Penguin Books.

Medawar, Sir P. (1969). *Induction and Intuition in Scientific Thought*. London: Methuen.

Searles, H. (1959). Integration and differentiation in schizophrenia. *British Journal of Medical Psychology* 32:261–281.

_____ (1971). Pathologic symbiosis and autism. In *In The Name of Life*, ed. Landis and Tauber. New York: Holt, Rinehart and Winston.

Slater, E. (1972). Is psychiatry a science? Does it want to be? *World Medicine* (February 1972): 79–81.

Taylor, C. (1964). *The Explanation of Behaviour*. London: Kegan Paul.

Winnicott, D. W. (1965a). *The Family and Individual Development*. London: Tavistock Publications.

_____ (1965b). *The Maturational Processes and the Facilitating Environment*. London: Hogarth Press.

# 16

# ANALYSIS WITH FAIRBAIRN AND WINNICOTT: (HOW COMPLETE A RESULT DOES PSYCHO-ANALYTIC THERAPY ACHIEVE?)

IT DOES NOT SEEM TO ME USEFUL to attempt a purely theoretical answer to the question forming the sub-title. Theory does not seem to me to be the major concern. It is a useful servant but a bad master, liable to produce orthodox defenders of every variety of the faith. We ought always to sit light to theory and be on the look-out for ways of improving it in the light of therapeutic practice. It is therapeutic practice that is the real heart of the matter. In the last resort good therapists are born not trained, and they make the best use of training. Maybe the question 'How complete a result can psycho-analytic therapy produce?' raises the question 'How complete a result did our own training analysis produce?' Analysts are advised to be open to post-analytic improvements, so presumably we do not expect 'an analysis' to do a 'total' once for all job. We must know about post-analytic developments if we are to assess the actual results of the primary analysis. We cannot deal with this question purely on the basis of our patients' records. They must be incomplete for the primary analysis and non-existent afterwards. As this question had unexpected and urgent relevance in my case, I was compelled to grapple with it; so I shall risk offering an account of my own analysis with Fairbairn and Winnicott, and its after-effects: especially as this is the only way I can present a realistic picture of what I take to be the relationship between the respective contributions of these two outstanding analysts, and what I owe to them.

The question 'How complete a result is possible?' had compelling importance for me because it is bound up with an unusual factor; a total amnesia for a severe trauma at the age of three and a half years, over the death of a younger brother. Two analyses failed to break through that amnesia, but it was resolved unexpectedly after they had ended, certainly only because of what they had achieved in 'softening up' the major repression. I hope this may have both a theoretical and a human interest. The long quest for a solution to that problem has been too introverted an interest to be wholly welcomed, but I had no option, could not ignore it, and so turned it into a vocation through which I might help others. Both

Fairbairn and Winnicott thought that but for that trauma, I might not have become a psychotherapist. Fairbairn once said: 'I can't think what could motivate any of us to become psychotherapists, if we hadn't got problems of our own'. He was no super-optimist and once said to me: 'The basic pattern of personality once fixed in early childhood, can't be altered. Emotion can be drained out of the old patterns by new experience, but water can always flow again in the old dried up water courses'. You cannot give anyone a different history. On another occasion he said: 'You can go on analysing for ever and get nowhere. It's the personal relation that is therapeutic. Science has no values except scientific values, the schizoid values of the investigator who stands outside of life and watches. It is purely instrumental, useful for a time but then you have to get back to living.' That was his view of the 'mirror analyst', a non-relating observer simply interpreting. Thus he held that psychoanalytic interpretation is not therapeutic *per se*, but only as it expresses a personal relationship of genuine understanding. My own view is that science is not necessarily schizoid, but is really practically motivated, and often becomes schizoid because it offers such an obvious retreat for schizoid intellectuals. There is no place for this in psychotherapy of any kind.

I already held the view that psychoanalytic therapy is not a purely theoretical but a truly understanding personal relationship, and had published it in my first book before I had heard of Fairbairn; after reading his papers in 1949, I went to him because we stood philosophically on the same ground and no actual intellectual disagreements would interfere with the analysis. But the capacity for forming a relationship does not depend solely on our theory. Not everyone has the same facility for forming personal relationships, and we can all form a relationship more easily with some people than with others. The unpredictable factor of 'natural fit' enters in. Thus, in spite of his conviction Fairbairn did not have the same capacity for natural, spontaneous 'personal relating' that Winnicott had. With me he was more of a 'technical interpreter' than he thought he was, or than I expected: but that needs qualification. I went to him in the 1950s when he was past the peak of his creative powers of the 1940s, and his health was slowly failing. He told me that in the 1930s and 1940s he had treated a number of schizophrenic and regressed patients with success. That lay behind his 'theoretical revision' in the 1940s. He felt he had made a mistake in publishing his theory before the clinical evidence. From 1927 to 1935 he was psychiatrist at The University Psychological Clinic for Children, and did a lot of work for the N.S.P.C.C. One cannot be impersonal with children. He asked one child whose mother thrashed her cruelly: 'Would you like me to find you a new kind Mummy?' She said: 'No. I want my own Mummy', showing the intensity of the libidinal tie to the bad object. The devil you know is better than the devil you do not, and better than no devil at all. Out of such experience with psychotic, regressed and child patients, his theoretical revision grew, based on the *quality* of parent-child relations, rather than the *stages* of biological growth, a 'personality-theory' not an impersonal 'energy-control theory'. He summed it up in saying that 'the cause of trouble is that parents somehow fail to get it across to the child that he is loved for his own sake, as a person in his own right'. By the 1950s when I was with him, he wisely declined to take the strains of severely regressing patients. To my surprise I found him gradually falling back on the 'classical analyst' with an 'interpretative technique', when I felt I needed to regress to the level of that severe infancy trauma.

Stephen Morse (1972), in his study of 'structure' in the writings of Winnicott and Balint, concluded that they discovered new data but did not develop structural theory in a way that could explain them; which, however, he felt could be done by what he called the 'Fairbairn-Guntrip metaphor'. Having had the benefit of analysis with both these outstanding analysts, I feel the position is somewhat more complex than that. The relation between Fairbairn and Winnicott is both theoretically important and very intriguing. Superficially they were quite unlike each other in type of mind and method of working, which prevented their knowing how basically close they were in the end. Both had deep roots in classic Freudian theory and therapy, and both outgrew it in their own different ways. Fairbairn saw that intellectually more clearly than Winnicott. Yet in the 1950s Fairbairn was more orthodox in clinical practice than Winnicott. I had just over 1, 000 sessions with Fairbairn in the 1950s and just over 150 with Winnicott in the 1960s. For my own benefit I kept detailed records of every session with both of them, and all their correspondence. Winnicott said, 'I've never had anyone who could tell me so exactly what I said last time.' Morse's article suggested a restudy of those records last year, and I was intrigued to find the light they cast on why my *two analyses failed to resolve my amnesia for that trauma at three and a half years, and yet each in different ways prepared for its resolution as a post-analytic development.* I had to ask afresh, 'What is the analytic therapeutic process?'

In general I found Fairbairn becoming more *orthodox in practice* than in theory while Winnicott was more *revolutionary in practice* than in theory. They were complementary opposites. Sutherland (1965) in his obituary notice wrote:

> Fairbairn had a slightly formal air about him—notably aristocratic, but in talking to him I found he was not at all formal or remote. Art and religion were for him profound expressions of man's needs, for which he felt a deep respect, but his interests revealed his rather unusual conservatism.

I found him formal in sessions, the intellectually precise interpreting analyst, but after sessions we discussed theory and he would unbend, and I found the human Fairbairn as we talked face to face. Realistically, he was my understanding good father after sessions, and in sessions in the transference he was my dominating bad mother imposing exact interpretations. After his experimental creative 1940s, I feel his conservatism slowly pushed through into his work in the 1950s. The shock of his wife's sudden death in 1952 created obvious domestic problems. Early in the 1950s he had the first attack of viral influenza, and these became more virulent as the decade advanced. For two years after his wife's death he worked hard on his fine paper, 'Observations on the nature of hysterical states' (Fairbairn, 1954) which finalized his original thinking. He clarified his views on 'psycho-analysis and science' in two papers (Fairbairn, 1952b, 1955). But there was a subtle change in his next paper, 'Considerations arising out of the Schreber case' (Fairbairn, 1956). Here he fell back from his 'ego and object relations' psychology, explaining everything as due to 'primal scene' libidinal excitations and fears. Finally, in his last paper, 'On the nature and aims of psycho-analytical treatment' (Fairbairn, 1958) his entire emphasis was on the 'internal closed system' of broadly oedipal analysis, not in terms of instincts, but of internalized libidinized and antilibidinized bad-object relations. I went to him to break through the amnesia for that trauma of my brother's death, to whatever lay behind it in the infancy period. There, I felt, lay the cause of my vague background experiences of schizoid isolation and unreality, and I knew that they had to do with my earliest relations with mother, though only because of information she had given me.

After brother Percy's death I entered on four years of active battle with mother to force her 'to relate', and then gave it up and grew away from her. I will call that, for convenience, the oedipal internalized bad-object relations period: it filled my dreams, but repeatedly sudden, clear schizoid experiences would erupt into this, and Fairbairn steadily interpreted them as 'withdrawal' in the sense of 'escapes' from internalized bad-object relations. He repeatedly brought me back to oedipal three-person libidinal and anti-libidinal conflicts in my 'inner world', Kleinian 'object splits' and Fairbairnian 'ego splits' in the sense of oedipal libidinal excitations. In 1956 I wrote to ask him to say exactly what he thought about the Oedipus complex, and he replied: 'The Oedipus complex is central for therapy but not for theory.' I replied that I could not accept that: for me theory *was* the theory of *therapy*, and what was true for one must be true for both. I developed a double resistance to him consciously, partly feeling he was my bad mother forcing her views on me, and partly openly disagreeing with him on genuine grounds. I began to insist that my real problem was not the bad relationships of the post-Percy period, but mother's basic 'failure to relate at all' right from the start. I said that I felt oedipal analysis kept me marking time on the same spot, making me use bad relations as better than none at all, keeping them operative in my inner world as *a defence against the deeper schizoid problem*. He saw that as a defensive character trait of 'withdrawnness' (Fairbairn, 1952a, chap. 1). I felt it as a problem in its own right, not just a defence against his closed-system 'internal world of bad-object relations'.

But my oedipal analysis with Fairbairn was not a waste of time. Defences have to be analysed and it brought home to me that I had actually repressed the trauma of Percy's death and all that lay behind it, by building over it a complex experience of sustained struggle in bad-object relations with mother, which in turn I had also to repress. It was the basis of my spate of dreams, and intermittent production of conversion symptoms. Fairbairn for long insisted that it was the *real core* of my psychopathology. He was certainly wrong, but it did have to be radically analysed to open the way to the deeper depths. That happened. Steadily regressive and negative schizoid phenomena thrust into the material I brought to him, and at last he began to accept in theory what he no longer had the health to cope with in practice. He generously accepted my concept of a 'regressed ego' split off from his 'libidinal ego' and giving up as hopeless the struggle to get a response from mother. When I published that idea, Winnicott wrote to ask: 'Is your Regressed Ego withdrawn or repressed?' I replied: 'Both. First withdrawn and then kept repressed'. Fairbairn wrote to say:

> This is your own idea, not mine, original, and it explains what I have never been able to account for in my theory, Regression. Your emphasis on ego-weakness yields better therapeutic results than interpretation in terms of libidinal and anti-libidinal tensions.

When in 1960 I wrote 'Ego-weakness, the hard core of the problem of psychotherapy' he wrote to say: 'If I could write now, that is what I would write about'. I knew my theory was broadly right for it conceptualized what I could not yet get analysed. With I think great courage, he accepted that.

I shall complete my account of Fairbairn as analyst and man by illustrating the difference in 'human type' between him and Winnicott, a factor that plays a big part in therapy. The set-up of the consulting room itself creates an atmosphere which has meaning. Fairbairn lived in the country and saw patients in the old Fairbairn family house in Edinburgh. I entered a large drawing room as waiting room, furnished with beautiful valuable antiques, and proceeded to the study as consulting room, also large with a big antique bookcase filling most of one wall. Fairbairn sat behind a large flat-topped desk, I used to think 'in state' in a high-backed plush-covered armchair. The patient's couch had its head to the front of the desk. At times I thought he could reach over the desk and hit me on the head. It struck me as odd for an analyst who did not believe in the 'mirror-analyst' theory. Not for a long time did I realize that I had 'chosen' that couch position, and there was a small settee at the side of his desk at which I could sit if I wished, and ultimately I did. That this imposing situation at once had an unconscious transference meaning for me became clear in a dream in the first month. I must explain that my father had been a Methodist Local Preacher of outstanding eloquence as a public speaker, and from 1885 built up and led a Mission Hall which grew into a

Church which still exists. In all my years of dreaming he never appeared as other than a supportive figure *vis-à-vis* mother, and in actual fact she *never* lost her temper in his presence. I wanted Fairbairn in transference as the protective father, helping me to stand up to my aggressive mother, but unconsciously I felt otherwise, for I dreamed:

> I was in father's Mission Hall. Fairbairn was on the platform but he had mother's hard face. I lay passive on a couch on the floor of the Hall, with the couch head to the front of the platform. He came down and said: 'Do you know the door is open?' I said: 'I didn't leave it open', and was pleased I had stood up to him. He went back to the platform.

It was a thinly disguised version of his consulting room set-up, and showed that I wanted him to be my supportive father, but that wish was overpowered by a clear negative transference from my severe dominating mother. That remained by and large Fairbairn's transference role 'in sessions'. He interpreted it as the 'one up and the other down' bad parent–child 'see-saw' relation. It can only be altered by turning the tables. I found that very illuminating, containing all the ingredients of unmet needs, smothered rage, inhibited spontaneity. It was the dominant transference relationship in sessions. After sessions Fairbairn could unbend in our theory and therapy discussion, the good human father.

This negative transference in sessions was, I feel, fostered by his *very intellectually precise interpretations*. Once he interpreted: 'Something forecloses on the active process in the course of its development'. I would have said: 'Your mother squashed your naturally active self'. But he accurately analysed my emotional struggle to force mother to mother me after Percy died, and showed how I had internalized it. That had to be done first, but he held it to be the central oedipal problem, and could not accept till it was too late that this masked a far deeper and more serious problem. Later Winnicott twice remarked: 'You show no signs of ever having had an Oedipus complex'. My family pattern was not oedipal. It was always the same in dreams and is shown by the most striking one of them.

> I was being besieged and was sitting in a room discussing it with father. It was mother who was besieging me and I said to him: 'You know I'll never give in to her. It doesn't matter what happens. I'll never surrender'. He said, 'Yes. I know that. I'll go and tell her' and he went and said to her, 'You'd better give it up. You'll never make him submit', and she did give up.

Fairbairn's persistence in oedipal interpretations I could not accept as final, cast him in the role of the dominating mother. It came to our ears that Winnicott and

Hoffer thought my adherence to his theory was due to its not allowing him to analyse my aggression in the transference. But they didn't see me knock over his pedestal ashtray, and kick his glass door-stopper, 'accidentally' of course, and we know what that means in sessions, as he was not slow to point out. They did not see me once strew some of his books out of that huge bookcase over the floor, symbolic of 'tearing a response out of mother', and then putting them back tidily to make reparation à la Melanie Klein. But after sessions we could discuss and I could find the natural warm-hearted human being behind the exact interpreting analyst.

I can best make this clear by comparison with Winnicott. His consulting room was simple, restful in colours and furniture, unostentatious, carefully planned, so Mrs Winnicott told me, by both of them, to make the patient feel at ease. I would knock and walk in, and presently Winnicott would stroll in with a cup of tea in his hand and a cheery 'Hallo', and sit on a small wooden chair by the couch. I would sit on the couch sideways or lie down as I felt inclined, and change position freely according to how I felt or what I was saying. Always at the end, as I departed he held out his hand for a friendly handshake. As I was finally leaving Fairbairn after the last session, I suddenly realized that in all that long period we had never once shaken hands, and he was letting me leave without that friendly gesture. I put out my hand and at once he took it, and I suddenly saw a few tears trickle down his face. *I saw the warm heart of this man with a fine mind and a shy nature.* He invited my wife and me to tea whenever we visited her mother in Perthshire.

To make the ending of my analysis with Fairbairn meaningful, I must give a brief sketch of my family history. My mother was an overburdened 'little mother' before she married, the eldest daughter of 11 children and saw four siblings die. Her mother was a feather-brained beauty queen, who left my mother to manage everything even as a schoolgirl. She ran away from home at the age of twelve because she was so unhappy, but was brought back. Her best characteristic was her strong sense of duty and responsibility to her widowed mother and three younger siblings, which impressed my father when they all joined his Mission Hall. They married in 1898 but he did not know that she had had her fill of mothering babies and did not want any more. In my teens she occasionally became confidential and told me the salient facts of family history, including that she breast-fed me because she believed it would prevent another pregnancy; she refused to breast-feed Percy and he died, after which she refused further intimacy. My father was the youngest son of a High-Church and high Tory family, the politically left-wing and religiously Nonconformist rebel; and anti-imperialist who nearly lost his position in the City by refusing to sign his firm's pro-Boer War petition. That passing anxiety gave my mother the chance to wean me suddenly and start a business of her own. We moved when I was one year old. She chose a bad site and lost money steadily for seven years, though everything was more than retrieved by the next move. *That first seven years of my life, six of them at the first shop, was the grossly disturbed period for me.* I was left to the care of an invalid aunt who lived with us. Percy was born when I was two years old and died when I was three and a half. Mother told me father said he would have lived if she had breast-fed him, and she got angry. It was a disturbed time. In her old age, living in our home, she would say some revealing things. 'I ought never to have married and had children. Nature did not make me to be a wife and mother, but a business woman', and 'I don't think I ever understood children. I could never be bothered with them'.

   She told me that at three and a half years I walked into a room and saw Percy lying naked and dead on her lap. I rushed up and grabbed him and said: 'Don't let him go. You'll never get him back!' She sent me out of the room and I fell mysteriously ill and was thought to be dying. Her doctor said: 'He's dying of grief for his brother. If your mother wit can't save him, I can't', so she took me to a maternal aunt who had a family, and there I recovered. Both Fairbairn and Winnicott thought I would have died if she had not sent me away from herself. All memory of that was totally repressed. The amnesia held through all the rest of my life and two analyses, till I was 70, three years ago. But it remained alive in me, to be triggered off unrecognized by widely spaced analogous events. At the age of 26, at the University, I formed a good friendship with a fellow student who was a brother figure to me. When he left and I went home on vacation to mother, I fell ill of a mysterious exhaustion illness which disappeared immediately I left home and returned to College. I had no idea that it was equivalent to that aunt's family. In 1938, aged 37, I became minister of a highly organized Church in Leeds, with a Sunday afternoon meeting of 1,000 men, an evening congregation of 800, and well organized educational, social and recreational activities. It was too large for one minister and I had a colleague who became another Percy-substitute. He left as war clouds loomed up. Again I suddenly fell ill of the same mysterious exhaustion illness. It was put down to overwork, but by then I was psychoanalytically knowledgeable, had studied classical theory under Flugel, knew the stock literature, had an uncompleted M.A. thesis under supervision of Professor John Macmurray, seeking to translate Freud's psychobiology, or rather clinical data, into terms of 'personal relations' philosophy, and had studied my own dreams for two years. So I was alerted when this illness brought a big dream.

> I went down into a tomb and saw a man buried alive. He tried to get out
> but I threatened him with illness, locked him in and got away quick.

Next morning I was better. For the first time I recognized the re-eruption of my illness after Percy's death, and saw that I lived permanently over the top of its repression. I knew then I could not rest till that problem was solved.

   I was drawn into war-time emergency psychotherapy by the Leeds Professor of Medicine, appointed to a lectureship in the Medical School, and went on studying my own dreams. I recently re-read the record and found I had only made forced text-bookish oedipal interpretations. Of more importance was that three dominant types of dream stood out: (1) a savage woman attacking me, (2) a quiet, firm, friendly father-figure supporting me, and (3) a mysterious death-threat dream, the clearest example based on the memory of mother taking me at the age of six into the bedroom of my invalid aunt, thought to be dying of rheumatic fever, lying white and silent. In one dream:

> I was working downstairs at my desk and suddenly an invisible band of ectoplasm tying me to a dying invalid upstairs, was pulling me steadily out of the room. I knew I would be absorbed into her. I fought and suddenly the band snapped and I knew I was free.

I knew enough to guess that the memory of my dying aunt was a screen memory for the repressed dead Percy, which still exercised on me an unconscious pull out of life into collapse and apparent dying. I knew that somehow sometime I must get an analysis. In 1946 Professor Dicks appointed me as the first staff member of the new Department of Psychiatry, and said that with my views I must read Fairbairn. I did so and at the end of 1949 I sought analysis with him.

For the first few years, his broadly oedipal analysis of my 'internalized bad-object relations' world did correspond to an actual period of my childhood. After Percy's death and my return home, from the age of three and a half to five, I fought to coerce mother into mothering me by repeated petty psychosomatic ills, tummy-aches, heat spots, loss of appetite, constipation and dramatic, sudden high temperatures, for which she would make me a tent-bed on the kitchen couch and be in and out from the shop to see me. She told me the doctor said: 'I'll never come to that child again. He frightens the life out of me with these sudden high temperatures and next morning he's perfectly well'. But it was all to no purpose. Around five years I changed tactics. A new bigger school gave me more independence, and mother said: 'You began not to do what I told you'. She would fly into violent rages and beat me, from about the time I was five to the age of seven. When canes got broken I was sent to buy a new one. At the age of seven I went to a still larger school and steadily developed a life of my own outside the home. We moved when I was eight to another shop where mother's business was an outstanding success. She became less depressed, gave me all the money I needed for hobbies and outdoor activities, scouting, sport, and gradually I forgot not quite all the memories of the first seven bad years. It was all the fears, rages, guilts, psychosomatic transient symptoms, disturbed dreams, venting the conflicts of those years from three and a half to seven, that Fairbairn's analysis dealt with. In mother's old age she said: 'When your father and Aunt Mary died and I was alone, I tried keeping a dog but

I had to give it up. I couldn't stop beating it'. That's what happened to me. No wonder I had an inner world of internalized libidinally excited bad-object relations, and I owe much to Fairbairn's radical analysis of it.

But after the first three or four years I became convinced that this was keeping me marking time in a sadomasochistic inner world of *bad-object relations* with mother, as a defence against quite different problems of the period before Percy's death. This deeper material kept pushing through. The crunch came in December 1957 when my old friend whose departure from College caused the first eruption of that Percy-illness in 1927, suddenly died. For the third time exhaustion seized me. I kept going enough to work and travel to Edinburgh for analysis, feeling I would now get to the bottom of it. Then, just as I felt some progress was being made, Fairbairn fell ill with a serious viral influenza of which he nearly died, and was off work six months. I had to reinstate repression, but at once began to 'intellectualize' the problem I could not work through with him in person. It was not pure intellectualization by deliberate thinking. Spontaneous insights kept welling up at all sorts of times, and I jotted them down as they flowed with compelling intensity. Out of all that I wrote three papers; they became the basis of my book *Schizoid Phenomena, Object-Relations and the Self* (1968): 'Ego-weakness, the core of the problem of psycho-therapy' written in 1960 (chapter 6), 'The schizoid problem, regression and the struggle to preserve and ego' (chapter 2) written in 1961, and 'The manic-depressive problem in the light of the schizoid process' (chapter 5) written in 1962. In two years they took me right beyond Fairbairn's halting point. He generously accepted this as a valid and necessary extension of his theory.

When he returned to work in 1959, I discussed my friend's death and Fairbairn's illness and he made a crucial interpretation: 'I think since my illness I am no longer your good father or bad mother, but your brother dying on you'. I suddenly saw the analytical situation in an extraordinary light, and wrote him a letter which I still have, but did not send. I knew it would put a bigger strain on him than he could stand in his precarious health. I suddenly saw that I could never solve my problem *with* an analyst. I wrote: 'I am in a dilemma. I have got to end my analysis to get a chance to finish it, but then I do not have you to help me with it.' Once Fairbairn had become my brother in transference, *losing him* either by ending analysis myself, or by staying with him till he died, would represent the death of Percy, and I would be left with a full scale eruption of that traumatic event, and no one to help me with it. Could Fairbairn have helped me with that in transference analysis? Not in his frail state of health and I phased out my analysis in that year. I have much cause to be grateful to him for staying with me, in his increasingly weak state of health, till I had reached that critical insight. The driving force behind my theory writing in 1959–1962 was the reactivation of the Percy-trauma, causing a compelling spate of spontaneous ideas. I could contain it and use it for constructive research, partly because I was giving Fairbairn up gradually, partly because he accepted the validity of my ideas, and partly because I had resolved to seek analysis with Winnicott before Fairbairn died.

Fairbairn first introduced me to Winnicott in 1954 by asking him to send me a copy of his paper: 'Regression Within the Psycho-Analytical Set-Up' (in Winnicott 1958). He sent it and, rather to my surprise, a letter saying: 'I do invite you to look into the matter of your relation to Freud, so that you may have your own relation and not Fairbairn's. He spoils his good work by wanting to knock down Freud'. We exchanged three long letters on each side. I stated that my relation to Freud had been settled years before I had heard of Fairbairn, when studying under Flugel at University College, London. I rejected Freud's psychobiology of instincts, but saw the great importance of his discoveries in psychopathology. Regarding that correspondence I now find I anticipated Morse's (1972) conclusion almost in his words, 18 years earlier: that Winnicott's 'true self' has no place in Freud's theory. It could only be found in the id, but that is impossible because the id is only impersonal energy. In fact I felt that Winnicott had left Freud as far behind in therapy as Fairbairn had done in theory. In 1961 I sent him a copy of my book *Personality Structure and Human Interaction* (Guntrip 1961) and he replied that he had already purchased a copy. I was reading his papers as they were published, as also was Fairbairn who described him as 'clinically brilliant'. By 1962 I had no doubt that he was the only man I could turn to for further help. I was by then only free to visit London once a month for a couple of sessions, but the analysis I had had made it easier to profit by that. From 1962 to 1968 I had 150 sessions and their value was out of all proportion to their number. Winnicott said he was surprised that so much could be worked through in such widely spaced sessions, due I think in the first place to all the preliminary clearing that had been done by Fairbairn and to the fact that I could keep the analysis alive between visits; but most of all to *Winnicott's profound intuitive insights into the very infancy period I so needed to get down to.* He enabled me to reach extraordinarily clear evidence that my mother had almost certainly had an initial period of natural maternalism with me as her first baby, for perhaps a couple of months, before her personality problems robbed me of that 'good mother'. I had quite forgotten that letter I did not send to Fairbairn about the dilemma of not being able either to end analysis or go on with it, once my analyst became Percy in the transference. Ending it would be equivalent to Percy dying and I would have no one to help me with the aftermath. If I did not end it, I would be using my analyst to prevent the eruption of the trauma and so get no help with it, and risk his dying on me. My amnesia for that early trauma was not broken through with Winnicott either. Only recently have I realized that in fact, unwittingly, he altered the whole nature of the problem by enabling me to reach right back to *an ultimate good mother, and to find her recreated in him in the transference.* I discovered later that he had put me in a position to face what was a double trauma of both Percy's death and mother's failing me.

As I re-read my records I am astonished at the rapidity with which he went to the heart of the matter. At the first session I mentioned the amnesia for the trauma of Percy's death, and felt I had had a radical analysis with Fairbairn of the 'internalized bad-object defences' I had built up against that, but we had not got down to what I felt was my basic problem, not the actively bad-object mother of later childhood, *but the earlier mother who failed to relate at all*. Near the end of the session he said: 'I've nothing particular to say yet, but if I don't say something, you may begin to feel I'm not here'. At the second session he said:

> You know about me but I'm not a person to you yet. You may go away feeling alone and that I'm not real. You must have had an earlier illness before Percy was born, and felt mother left you to look after yourself. You accepted Percy as your infant self that needed looking after. When he died, you had nothing and collapsed.

That was a perfect object relations interpretation, but from Winnicott, not Fairbairn. Much later I said that I occasionally felt a 'static, unchanging, lifeless state somewhere deep in me, feeling I can't move'. Winnicott said:

> If 100% of you felt like that, you probably couldn't move and someone would have to wake you. After Percy died, you collapsed bewildered, but managed to salvage enough of yourself to go on living, very energetically, and put the rest in a cocoon, repressed, unconscious.

I wish there were time to illustrate his penetrating insight in more detail, but I must give another example. I said that people often commented on my ceaseless activity and energy, and that in sessions I did not like gaps of silence and at times talked hard. Fairbairn interpreted that I was trying to take the analysis out of his hands and do his job; steal father's penis, oedipal rivalry. Winnicott threw a dramatic new light on this talking hard. He said:

> Your problem is that that illness of collapse was never resolved. You had to keep yourself alive in spite of it. You can't take your ongoing being for granted. You have to work hard to keep yourself in existence. You're afraid to stop acting, talking or keeping awake. You feel you might die in a gap like Percy, because if you stop acting mother can't do anything. She couldn't save Percy or you. You're bound to fear I can't keep you alive, so you link up monthly sessions for me by your records. No gaps. You can't feel that you are a going concern to me, because mother couldn't save you. You know about 'being active' but not about

'just growing, just breathing' while you sleep, without your having to do anything about it.

I began to be able to allow for some silences, and once, feeling a bit anxious, I was relieved to hear Winnicott move. I said nothing, but with uncanny intuition he said:

> You began to feel afraid I'd abandoned you. You feel silence is abandonment. The gap is not you forgetting mother, but mother forgetting you, and now you've relived it with me. You're finding an earlier trauma which you might never recover without the help of the Percy trauma repeating it. You have to remember mother abandoning you by transference on to me.

I can hardly convey the powerful impression it made on me to find Winnicott coming right into the emptiness of my 'object relations situation' in infancy with a non-relating mother.

Right at the end of my analysis I had a sudden return of hard talking in session. This time he made a different and extraordinary statement. He said:

> It's like you giving birth to a baby with my help. You gave me half an hour of concentrated talk, rich in content. I felt strained in listening and holding the situation for you. You had to know that I could stand your talking hard at me and my not being destroyed. I had to stand it while you were in labour being creative, not destructive, producing something rich in content. You are talking about 'object relating', 'using the object' and finding you don't destroy it. I couldn't have made that interpretation five years ago.

Later he gave his paper on 'The use of an object' (in Winnicott 1971) in America and met, not surprisingly I think, with much criticism. Only an exceptional man could have reached that kind of insight. He became a good breast mother to my infant self in my deep unconscious, at the point where my actual mother had lost her maternalism and could not stand me as a live baby any more. It was not then apparent, as it later became to me, that he had transformed my whole understanding of the trauma of Percy's death, particularly when he added:

> You too have a good breast. You've always been able to give more than take. I'm good for you but you're good for me. Doing your analysis is almost the most reassuring thing that happens to me. The chap before

you makes me feel I'm no good at all. You don't have to be good for me.
I don't need it and can cope without it, but in fact you are good for me.

Here at last I had a mother who could value her child, so that I could cope with
what was to come. It hardly seems worth mentioning that the only point at which
I felt I disagreed with Winnicott was when he talked occasionally about 'getting at
your primitive sadism, the baby's ruthlessness and cruelty, your aggression', in a
way that suggested not my angry fight to extract a response from my cold mother,
but Freud's and Klein's 'instinct theory', the id, innate aggression. For I knew he
rejected the 'death instinct' and had moved far beyond Freud when I went to him.
He once said to me: 'We differ from Freud. He was for curing symptoms. We are
concerned with living persons, whole living and loving'. By 1967 he wrote, and gave
me a copy of his paper, 'The location of cultural experience' (in Winnicott 1971), in
which he said: 'I see that I am in the territory of Fairbairn: "object-seeking" as
opposed to "satisfaction-seeking"'. I felt then that Winnicott and Fairbairn had
joined forces to neutralize my earliest traumatic years.

I must complete this account with the one thing I could not foresee.
Winnicott becoming the good mother, freeing me to be alive and creative,
transformed the significance of Percy's death in a way that was to enable me to
resolve that trauma, and my dilemma about how to end my analysis. Winnicott,
relating to me in my deep unconscious, enabled me to stand seeing that it was not
just the loss of Percy, but being left alone with the mother who could not keep me
alive, that caused my collapse into apparent dying. But thanks to his profound
intuitive insight, I was not now alone with a non-relating mother. I last saw him in
July 1969. In February 1970 I was told medically that I was seriously overworked,
and if I did not retire 'Nature would make me'. I must have felt unconsciously that
that was a threat that 'Mother Nature' would at last crush my active self. Every time
I rested I found myself under a compulsion to go back to the past, in the form of
rehearsing the details of my ministerial 'brother-figure's' leaving in 1938, and my
reacting with an exhaustion illness. I soon saw that this was significant and it led on
to an urge to write up my whole life-story, as if I had to find out all that had
happened to me. By October I developed pneumonia and spent five weeks in
hospital. The consultant said: 'Relax. You're too overactive'. I still did not realize
that I was fighting against an unconscious compulsive regression. I had never linked
the idea of 'retirement' with the deep fear of losing my battle with mother to keep
my active self alive, in the end. After a slow winter recuperation, I heard in the New
Year 1971 that Winnicott had a 'flu attack. Presently I enquired of Masud Khan
how Winnicott was, and he replied that he was about again and liked to hear from
his friends, so I dropped him a line. A little later the phone rang, and the familiar
voice said: 'Hallo. Thanks for your letter' and we chatted a bit. About two weeks
later the phone rang again and *his secretary told me he had passed away. That very*

*night I had a startling dream. I saw my mother*, black, immobilized, staring fixedly into space, *totally ignoring me* as I stood at one side staring at her and feeling myself frozen into immobility: the first time I had ever seen her in a dream like that. Before she had always been attacking me. My first thought was: 'I've lost Winnicott and am left alone with mother, sunk in depression, ignoring me. That's how I felt when Percy died'. I thought I must have taken the loss of Winnicott as a repetition of the Percy trauma. Only recently have I become quite clear that it was not that at all. I did not dream of mother like that when my college friend died or my ministerial colleague left. Then I felt ill, as after Percy's death. This time it was quite different. That dream started a compelling dream-sequence which went on night after night, taking me back in chronological order through every house I had lived in, in Leeds, Ipswich, College, the second Dulwich shop, and finally the first shop and house of the bad first seven years. Family figures, my wife, daughter, Aunt Mary, father and mother kept recurring; father always supportive, mother always hostile, but no sign of Percy. I was trying to stay in the post-Percy period of battles with mother. Then after some two months two dreams at last broke that amnesia for Percy's life and death. I was astonished to see myself in a dream clearly aged about three, recognizably me, holding a pram in which was my brother aged about a year old. I was strained, looking anxiously over to the left at mother, to see if she would take any notice of us. But she was staring fixedly into the distance, ignoring us, as in the first dream of that series. The next night the dream was even more startling.

> I was standing with another man, the double of myself, both reaching out to get hold of a dead object. Suddenly the other man collapsed in a heap. Immediately the dream changed to a lighted room, where I saw Percy again. I knew it was him, sitting on the lap of a woman who had no face, arms or breasts. She was merely a lap to sit on, not a person. He looked deeply depressed, with the corners of his mouth turned down, and I was trying to make him smile.

I had recovered in that dream the memory of collapsing when I saw him as a dead object and reached out to grab him. But I had done more. I had actually gone back in both dreams to the earlier time before he died, to see the 'faceless' depersonalized mother, and the black depressed mother, who totally failed to relate to both of us. Winnicott had said: 'You accepted Percy as your infant self that needed looking after. When he died, you had nothing and collapsed.' Why did I dream of 'collapsing' first, and then of going back to look after Percy? My feeling is that my collapse was my first reaction of terrified hopelessness at the shock of finding Percy dead on mother's lap, but in that aunt's family I quickly seized the chance of staying alive by finding others to live for.

That dream series made me bring out and restudy all my analysis records, till

I realized that, though Winnicott's death had reminded me of Percy's, the situation was entirely different. That process of compelling regression had not started with Winnicott's death, but with the threat of 'retirement' as if mother would undermine me at last. I did not dream of Winnicott's death, but of Percy's death and mother's total failure to relate to us. What better dream-evidence could one have of Winnicott's view that 'There is no such thing as a baby': i.e. there must be a 'mother and baby', and what better evidence for Fairbairn's view that the basic psychic reality is the 'personal object relation'? What gave me strength in my deep unconscious to face again that basic trauma? It must have been because Winnicott was not, and could not be, dead for me, nor certainly for many others. I have never felt that my father was dead, but in a deep way alive in me, enabling me to resist mother's later active paralysing inhibiting influence. Now Winnicott had come into living relation with precisely that earlier lost part of me that fell ill because mother failed me. *He has taken her place and made it possible and safe to remember her in an actual dream-reliving of her paralysing schizoid aloofness.* Slowly that became a firm conviction growing in me, and I recovered from the volcanic upheaval of that autonomously regressing compelling dream-series, feeling that I had at last reaped the gains I had sought in analysis over some twenty years. After all the detailed memories, dreams, symptoms of traumatic events, people and specific emotional tensions had been worked through, one thing remained: *the quality of the overall atmosphere of the personal relations that made up our family life in those first seven years.* It lingers as a mood of sadness for my mother who was so damaged in childhood that she could neither be, nor enable me to be, our 'true selves'. I cannot have a different set of memories. But that is offset by my discovery in analysis of how deeply my father became a secure mental possession in me, supporting my struggle to find and be my 'true self', and by Fairbairn's resolving my negative transference of my dominating mother on to him, till he became another good father who had faith in me, and finally by Winnicott entering into the emptiness left by my non-relating mother, so that I could experience the security of being my self. I must add that without my wife's understanding and support I could not have had those analyses or reached this result. What is psychoanalytic psychotherapy? It is, as I see it, the provision of a reliable and understanding human relationship of a kind that makes contact with the deeply repressed traumatized child in a way that enables one to become steadily more able to live, in the security of a new real relationship, with the traumatic legacy of the earliest formative years, as it seeps through or erupts into consciousness.

Psychoanalytic therapy is not like a 'technique' of the experimental sciences, an objective 'thing-in-itself' working automatically. It is a process of interaction, a function of two variables, the personalities of two people working together towards free spontaneous growth. The analyst grows as well as the analysand. There must be something wrong if an analyst is static when he deals with such dynamic personal experiences. For me, Fairbairn built as a person on what my father did for me, and as an analyst enabled me to discover in great detail how my battles for independence of mother from three and a half to seven years had grown into my personality make-up. Without that I could have deteriorated in old age into as awkward a person as my mother. Winnicott, a totally different type of personality, understood and filled the emptiness my mother left in the first three and a half years. I needed them both and had the supreme good fortune to find both. Their very differences have been a stimulus to different sides of my make-up. Fairbairn's ideas were 'exact logical concepts' which clarified issues. Winnicott's ideas were 'imaginative hypotheses' that challenged one to explore further. As examples, compare Fairbairn's concepts of the libidinal, antilibidinal and central egos as a theory of endopsychic structure, with Winnicott's 'true and false selves' as intuitive insights into the confused psychic reality of actual persons. Perhaps no single analyst can do all that an analysand needs, and we must be content to let patients make as much use of us as they can. We dare not pose as omniscient and omnipotent because we have a theory. Also Fairbairn once said: 'You get out of analysis what you put into it', and I think that is true for both analyst and analysand. I would think that the development of clear conscious insight represents having taken full possession of the gains already made emotionally, putting one in a position to risk further emotional strains to make more emotional growth. It represents not just conscious understanding but a strengthening of the inner core of 'selfhood' and capacity for 'relating'. So far as psychopathological material is concerned, dreaming expresses our endopsychic structure. It is a way of experiencing on the fringes of consciousness, our internalized conflicts, our memories of struggles originally in our outer world and then as memories and fantasies of conflicts that have become our inner reality, to keep 'object relations' alive, even if only 'bad-object relations', because we need them to retain possession of our 'ego'. It was my experience that the deeper that final spate of dreams delved into my unconscious, the more dreaming slowly faded out and was replaced by 'waking up in a mood'. I found I was not fantasying or thinking but simply feeling, consciously in the grip of a state of mind that I began to realize I had been in consciously long ago, and had been in unconsciously deep down ever since: a dull mechanical lifeless mood, no interest in anything, silent, shut in to myself, going through routine motions with a sense of loss of all meaning in existence. I experienced this for a number of consecutive mornings till I began to find that it was fading out into a normal interest in life: which after all seems to be what one would expect.

There is a natural order peculiar to each individual and determined by his history, in which (1) problems can become conscious and (2) interpretations can be relevant and mutative. We cannot decide that but only watch the course of the individual's development. Finally, on the difficult question of the sources of theory, it seems that our theory must be rooted in our psychopathology. That was implied in Freud's courageous self-analysis at a time when all was obscure. The idea that we could think out a theory of the structure and functioning of the personality without its having any relation to the structure and functioning of our own personality, should be a self-evident impossibility. If our theory is too rigid, it is likely to conceptualize our ego defences. If it is flexible and progressive it is possible for it to conceptualize our ongoing growth processes, and throw light on others' problems and on therapeutic possibilities. Balint's 'basic fault' and Winnicott's 'incommunicado core', since they regard these phenomena as universal, must be their ways of 'intuitively sensing' their own basic reality, and therefore other people's. By contrast with Fairbairn's exactly intellectually defined theoretical constructs which state logically progressive developments in existing theory, they open the way to profounder exploration of the infancy period, where, whatever a baby's genetic endowment, the mother's ability or failure to 'relate' is the sine qua non of psychic health for the infant. To find a good parent at the start is the basis of psychic health. In its lack, to find a genuine 'good object' in one's analyst is both a transference experience and a real life experience. In analysis as in real life, all relationships have a subtly dual nature. All through life we take into ourselves both good and bad figures who either strengthen or disturb us, and it is the same in psychoanalytic therapy: it is the meeting and interacting of two real people in all its complex possibilities.

## REFERENCES

Fairbairn, W. R. D. (1952a). *Psychoanalytic Studies of the Personality*. London: Tavistock Publications.

_____ (1952b). Theoretical and experimental aspects of psycho-analysis. *British Journal of Medical Psychology*. 25:122–127.

_____ (1954). Observations of the nature of hysterical states. *British Journal of Medical Psychology*. 27:106–125.

_____ (1955). Observations in defence of the object-relations theory of the personality. *British Journal of Medical Psychology*. 28:144–156.

_____ (1956). Considerations arising out of the Schreber case. *British Journal of Medical Psychology*. 29:113–127.

_____ (1958). On the nature and aims of psychoanalytical treatment. *International Journal of Psycho-Analysis*. 39:374–385.

Guntrip, H. (1960). Ego-weakness, the hard core of the problem of psychotherapy. In Guntrip (1968).

_____ (1961). *Personality Structure and Human Interaction*. London: Hogarth Press.

_____ (1968). *Schizoid Phenomena, Object-Relations and the Self*. London: Hogarth Press.

Morse, S. J. (1972). Structure and reconstruction: a critical comparison of Michael Balint and D. W. Winnicott. *International Journal of Psycho-Analysis*. 53:487–500.

Sutherland, J. (1965). Obituary. W. R. D. Fairbairn. *International Journal of Psycho-Analysis.* 46:245–247.

Winnicott, D. W. (1958). *Collected Papers. Through Paediatrics to Psycho-Analysis.* London: Tavistock Publications.

———— (1971). *Playing and Reality.* London: Tavistock Publications.

# 17

# CONFRONTING THE CRITICS ON THE REALITY OF PSYCHODYNAMIC EXPERIENCE[1]

THROUGHOUT THIS CENTURY a steady change has developed in philosophy away from 19th century positivist empiricist determinism and reductionism. Its 'pseudo-psychologism' of the association of ideas and of sense-data was rejected by such opposite philosophers as Bradley and Bertrand Russell, and superseded by the search of 'analytical philosophy' for the 'meaning of meaning'. But 'the philosophical scent given by the logically conditioned conjunctions petered out and the ultimates of logical atomism (i.e. Russell and Wittgenstein) took sanctuary in Utopia' said Ryle (1956, p. 10). The failure of the logical positivists of Vienna to convince their critics (such as Russell and Moore, and Popper within the circle) paved the way for the development of a new realist philosophy. The publication by Popper of *The Logic of Scientific Discovery* (1959) greatly stimulated the discussion of the nature of scientific knowledge, even by those who do not wholly agree with him, such as Kuhn of Princeton (Lakatos and Musgrave, 1970) and Harré of Oxford (1972, pp. 48–52). Harré writes:

> The positivist position restricts empirical knowledge to the passing show of sense experience. Over against this is the realist point of view which emphasizes the work of the human imagination in leading to conceptions of the realities behind sense-experience, and which admits the content of theories to the status of empirical knowledge. The case against positivism on intellectual, historical and moral grounds, I believe to be overwhelming. [1972, Preface]

---

1. This chapter is a shortened version of the first part of a fresh systematic appraisal of object relations theory which Dr Guntrip was writing just before he died in 1975. He prepared it himself and only a few minor amendments have been made. The quality and independence of Dr Guntrip's thinking in clarifying issues that have bedevilled the status of psychodynamic thought add greatly to our regret that his larger work had not progressed far enough for publication.

Not only psychoanalysts, but all types of psychologist must heed this, because positivist empiricism and reductionism was the philosophy of science in which Freud was educated from 1870–1890, on which he and also Pavlov, Watson and later behaviourists, with their propaganda 'reduction' of psychology to neurology, based all their theories. We shall consider (1) The philosophy of science; (2) Critics of psychoanalysis; and (3) How can we now conceptualize psychodynamic phenomena in a scientific way?

## THE PHILOSOPHY OF SCIENCE

Medawar (1969) gives a concise study of 'the methodology of science' but is more rejective of induction than many contemporary philosophers. Inductionism and reductionism are the two critical issues. The triumphs of physical science have given 'science' an aura of mystical omnipotence, so that all research wishes to claim 'scientific status'. Rapidly developing or new specialities – anthropology, ethology, sociology, archaeology, economics, psychology – all claim to be 'science'. None of them can operate with the precision of physics, chemistry, biochemistry or neurology, for they cannot 'experiment' as exactly as the physical sciences. Ethologists find that animal behaviour patterns cannot be studied in a laboratory; they disappear for they are responses only to natural habitats. So uncertainty arises as to what is 'science'. What is the criterion? We might say 'science' (from Latin *scio*, to know) simply means 'knowledge'. Wherever reliable knowledge is come by, that is science. But what is 'knowledge'? Is real 'objective' knowledge found only in physical sciences, or are there different kinds of knowledge? Bronowski (1967) says there are two kinds of knowledge, of the machine (physical science) and of the self. We face the issue of the 'methodology' of science, the methods of 'real' science to arrive at 'real' knowledge. This seems easily answered in the physical sciences where *experiments* can be made under fully controlled conditions in a way not possible for 'sciences' of man in his social and personal existence. Maybe hypotheses about human beings in sociology, economics, psychology could be experimentally testable if people would submit to the imposed tests. Skinner's dream of universal reconditioning of entire populations by behaviour methods has only been attempted in totalitarian police states where the ordinary spontaneous human behaviour we seek to study disappears. Sometimes 'history' obliges. The 'permissive society' experiment tests Freud's hypothesis that the abandonment of 'civilized sexual morality' would cure 'neurosis'. The result has 'falsified' Freud's theory, though Popper holds that psychoanalytic hypotheses cannot be falsified and so are not 'science'. However, we cannot wait for history to experiment for us, and only use it when it does. We hear of 'exact sciences' implying that there are 'inexact sciences'; but of what use is inexact knowledge? Every study must aim to make whatever knowledge it believes it has as exact as possible. In this uncertainty, psychoanalysis is bound to encounter criticism.

Hence the importance of the new exploration this century of logic or methodology of science, emerging out of the demise of the older philosophy which was Freud's intellectual foundation for conceptualizing psychopathological phenomena.

Freud was taught the *inductive procedure* of science from Bacon to J. S. Mill (one of whose works Freud translated) — scientists collect *observations* of matters of fact, the basis for *generalizations* as to what is true of all those facts, regarded then as *laws of nature*. Even Russell could find no answer to Hume's query that however many samples confirm a theory, there is no way of knowing whether the next one will prove different. All swans were white till Australian swans were found to be black. When after 200 years Einstein showed Newton's theory to be inadequate, Popper was so impressed that he substituted 'falsification' for 'confirmation' as the logic of scientific discovery. Thus, when Popper worked with Adler and knew of the Freudians in Vienna in the 1930s (a long time ago psychoanalytically speaking), he rejected the claim of psychoanalysis to be science, and wrote: 'The Freudian analysts emphasized that their theories were constantly verified by "clinical observations"' (1963, p. 45). However, many philosophers of science who accept that hypotheses are not produced by the 'inductive procedure' but by 'creative imagination' as Einstein, Popper and his disciple Medawar say, retain the 'inductive relation' that *conclusions are supported by evidence*. That is adequate for psychoanalytic purposes. We do not need to believe in absolute confirmation or infallible proof (which does not exist). We only need hypotheses that are sufficiently supported by evidence to be usable, and improved in the process. It has been pointed out that if *all* observations are 'theory-laden', that applies as much to Popper's 'falsification' as to 'confirmation'. If the philosophy Freud has to use no longer holds good, it would seem to be not because of its inductivism, but because of its positivist reductivism. Medawar is strongly anti-inductivist and dismisses psychoanalysis. Slater, however, regards psychoanalysis as 'a womb in which new sciences might grow' (1972). Popper (1963) himself added to his stricture:

> This does not mean that Freud and Adler were not seeing certain things correctly: I personally do not doubt that much of what they say is of considerable importance, and may well play its part one day in a psychological science which is testable. [p. 37]

Medawar, however, accepts Baconian inductivist collection of facts as a starting point 'to enrich the repertoire of information' (1969, p. 35) about what interests the scientist, e.g. Fleming's interest in infected war wounds, and Harré's (1972) comment:

> Freud was a great scientist because he looked for the causes of such commonplace occurrences as slips of the tongue, as well as of such unusual happenings as fits of hysteria. [p. 115]

This *at least* justifies our regarding Freud's work in psychopathology as the necessary first stage of a 'science of the individual human personality'. Medawar holds Popper's view, closely related to Einstein's method of working, that theories, hypotheses, explanatory ideas, are not generated by any logical process but are products of 'creative imagination' brooding over the 'interesting facts', which is still the 'inductive relation' if not the logical 'inductive procedure'. Moreover, Einstein wrote: 'For me it is not dubious that our thinking goes on to a considerable degree unconsciously' (1949). From his hypothesis the scientist proceeds by 'deductive reasoning' to 'experimental testing'. If the hypothesis is true, so-and-so logically follows, and experiments are made to find out if it does. A positive result only relatively supports the hypothesis. Many philosophers think Popper concedes too little value to that. If an experiment falsifies it, it must be replaced, though Medawar holds that hypotheses are more often repaired than rejected. This 'hypothetico-deductive method', foreshadowed by Kent, Whewell and others, is Popper's 'Logic of Scientific Discovery'. *All knowledge is hypothetical*, relatively true till its inadequacies are discovered by experimental testing. Popper's critierion of science is 'falsifiability'. A hypothesis is only scientific if it admits of the deduction of consequences capable in principle of being falsified by experimental tests. He regards that as not possible in psychoanalysis, an opinion I see reason to challenge. Moreover Kuhn, Harré and others regard Popper's view of science as too narrow. It would indeed seem that the rejection of induction as 'a relation of evidence to conclusion', and the denial of all value to 'provisional confirmation' is unrealistic.

In a symposium on the views of Kuhn and Popper (see Lakatos and Musgrave 1970), Popper's view that only ideal absolute critical testing of hypotheses all the time is 'science', was limited by Kuhn to 'revolutionary science', the work of the few geniuses, Newtons and Einsteins. He sees most science as 'normal science', routine practical experimental problem solving, applying existing theory rather than deliberately seeking to falsify it. Popper (1959) admits such science exists and castigates it as

> [t]he activity of the non-revolutionary, not-too-critical professional, who accepts the ruling dogma of the day, a person one ought to be sorry for, he has been badly taught. He has learned a technique which can be

used without asking the reason why (especially in quantum physics).
[pp. 52–53]

I own to some surprise and relief that dogmatism and blind operation of a learned
technique exists 'especially in quantum physics'. Then we need not be too disturbed
to find it in behavioural and psychoanalytic circles. For Popper that disqualifies any
work as 'science'. Kuhn, however, holds that only by ongoing 'normal' scientific
work by people who are not great geniuses, is the ground prepared for new
revolutionary theory. We may ask, 'Is the experimental test falsifying the old theory
or confirming the new one?' In the symposium two discussants agreed with Popper,
two with Kuhn and two were neutral. Harré (1972) rejects the discarding everything but ideal falsification of intuitive hypotheses. He sees two aspects of Popper's
theory: (1) conservative and (2) radical.

> (1) The inductivist picture of 'laws of nature' as general statements of
> correlations among phenomena, and 'evidence' as particular statements
> of correlations among observables.
>
>    (2) Evidence is valuable *only in so far* as it would tend to *falsify*
> general statements. A piece of evidence that would usually be regarded
> as supporting a hypothesis is treated by Popper, at least in some of his
> work, rather as an instance of the failure to falsify the hypothesis under
> test. He uses this radical principle in reverse, to classify hypotheses as
> either empirical, or non-empirical and non-scientific. Those which
> could be falsified by empirical (experimental or observational) evi-
> dence, he regards as empirical or scientific, and those which could not
> be falsified by any kind of test he regards as non-empirical, 'metaphys-
> ical'. I refer to this as the radical demarcation principle because it
> excludes from science a very great deal of what is usually thought to be
> characteristically scientific. [p. 49]

Clearly Harré rejects Popper's view as too narrow, extreme and one-sided, and it
has not met with general acceptance. This disposes of Popper's general criticism of
psychoanalysis. Medawar (1969) implies that Popper's strict logic would considerably depopulate the scientific field. He writes:

> If the purpose of scientific methodology is to prescribe a system of
> inquiry for scientific behaviour, then most scientists seem to get on very
> well without it. Most scientists receive no tuition in scientific method,
> but those who have been instructed perform no better than those who
> have not. [p. 8] Nearly all scientific research leads nowhere — or if it does

lead somewhere, then not in the direction it started off with. The 'scientific method' appears very much more powerful than it really is. For all the use it has been to science about four-fifths of my time has been wasted. [p. 31]

This refreshing realism seems less hard on Kuhn's 'normal science' than on Popper's unrelenting logical idealism. Popper may be right that the *purely logical core of radical growth* of scientific knowledge, lies in exposing inadequacies of theories by finding legitimate deductions from them not borne out by testing and so calling for rethinking of hypotheses. But in practice science is more than pure logic, and there is a logic of induction, of provisional confirmation. In real life and psychotherapy, we need to *use* sufficiently reliable knowledge to tackle practical problems. Falsification must go along with use as in Kuhn's 'problem-solving'. Harré regards Mill's inductivism and Popper's deductivism and falsification as 'unsatisfactory only if they are offered as exclusive and complete accounts of the logical, rational part of scientific method' (p. 57). But *knowledge to satisfy logical criteria and knowledge for practical use* cannot be kept strictly apart. Does scientific technology, e.g. space science, add nothing to science? Harré (1970) examines this closely, and writes:

Science has its origin according to Popper, in a cloud of conjectures about how things go on. This body of hypotheses is whittled down by the work of experimentalists whose results falsify certain of its components. The progress of anatomy on this view, is to be understood not as the development of *correct* ideas about the origins and structures of organisms by dissection and observation but by falsification of incorrect conjectures as to what lies under the skin. The discovery of the capillaries by Malpighi is to be understood not as the confirmation of one of Harvey's hypotheses, but as the falsification of some other contradictory conjecture. A vital consequence is that general existential statements are demoted from scientific status. [p. 50]

He thus regards Popper's exclusive view as wrong per se and out of touch with the realities of actual 'scientific' work. This exempts us from dealing with Popper's criticisms of psychoanalysis as based on 'inductive observations' and 'incapable of falsification', though the latter view is in any case, in my opinion, not correct. But psychotherapy needs close contact with 'living experience', and psychoanalysis must contain Harré's 'general existential statements'.

One other extremely important theory to consider is the anti-reductionist epistemology of the 'hierarchical model of the structure of knowledge' summarized by Medawar (1969) under the heading 'Reducibility: Emergence'. He writes:

If we choose to see a hierarchial structure in nature—if societies are composed of individuals, individuals of cells, and cells of molecules, then it makes sense to ask whether we may not 'interpret' sociology in terms of biology, or reduce biology to physics and chemistry. This living methodological problem does not seem to have been satisfactorily solved. At first sight the idea of *reducibility* seems hopeless of achievement. Each tier of the natural hierarchy makes use of notions peculiar to itself. The ideas of democracy, credit, crime or political constitution are no part of biology, nor shall we expect to find in physics the concepts of memory, infection, sexuality or fear. In each plane or tier of the hierarchy new ideas seem to emerge that are inexplicable in the language or with the conceptual resources of the tier below. But if in fact we cannot 'interpret' sociology in terms of biology or biology in terms of physics, how is it then that so many of the triumphs of modern science seem to have been founded on a repudiation of the doctrine of irreducibility. [p. 15]

Medawar has the courage to accept a fact he could wish were otherwise. The triumphs of modern science are not actually based on repudiation of irreducibility. They simply used knowledge of lower level phenomena on higher levels of aim and purpose, which does not 'falsify' the hypothesis of 'irreducibility', as Medawar (1969) recognizes in adding further:

Many ideas belonging to a sociological level of discourse make no sense in biology, and many biological ideas make no sense in physics. But this restriction on the flow of thought works one way only. Nothing disqualifies the inclusion of physical or chemical propositions in the biological and social sciences. [p. 16]

Hence the triumphs of modern science. Thus also in psychoanalytic therapy a tranquillizer or antidepressant may tide a hard-pressed patient or his family over a dangerous period of stress, while the essential work of *psycho*therapy proceeds not on the organic, but on the higher personal *psycho*logical level. No understanding is gained by confusing different levels and their concepts. 'Cerebral biochemistry' is a correct term, but 'psychoneurology' confuses different disciplines. Fairbairn, who in the 1940s switched psychoanalysis off Freud's psychobiology onto a consistent psychological basis, stated that he was not a dualist but regarded body and mind as different levels of abstraction in research. But Medawar did not complete the hierarchical model of the structure of knowledge. It involves that *we cannot reduce psychology to any lower level science. Psychological phenomena exist in their own right, the top level of the hierarchy.* Bannister (1968), a clinical psychologist, writes:

The chances of developing a physiological psychology are about as good (or as bad) as the chances of developing a chemical sociology or a biological astronomy. The concept of 'self' is essentially a psychological concept. In spite of the most gallant attempts, we have failed to get far by adhering to a purely mechanistic model. An unquestioning acceptance of physiological psychology stems from a reductionist approach. Reductionism is a philosophical posture which assumes that physiology is somehow nearer to reality than psychology, and therefore a more basic science.

Medawar seems nostalgic for 'reductionism' but accepts 'emergence' of new unique phenomena, the absolute basis for conceptualizing the psychodynamics met with in psychotherapy. I repeat here a statement I made in 1972:

No study can claim to be 'scientific' if it refuses to study its field in terms properly relevant to just those phenomena that are in question. To reduce them, or pretend that they are some other different kind of phenomena already studied by other sciences, is strictly prejudice, prejudgment of all the issues at stake, not as a result of investigation, but as a dogma laid down without proof. [p. 278]

We may note three important statements by eminent thinkers in this field.

1. Burt's credo: a phenomenal dualism of matter and mind on the basis of a metaphysical monism, the unprovable assumption that all thinkers, even reductionists in their own way, make that in some sense all reality is 'one'. But it can only be studied in the forms in which it 'appears' in our experience on the hierarchy of different levels, each with their own relevant concepts (Burt 1968).
2. The protest of Bartlett (1948) in the first Presidential Address to the British Psychological Society, against ignoring this in psychology:

Science has to do with mass and motion and has no place for mind, except to do its thinking. As mind is too often equated with brain, there is grave danger that psychology may become indistinguishable from applied physiology. [pp. 14–24]

3. Adrian, the neurophysiologist quoted by Burt, held that much of our public behavior could be behaviouristically explained but: 'One thing seems to lie outside this tidy and familiar framework—the "I" who does the perceiving, the thinking and the acting'.

Before we discuss how we can conceptualize the 'psychodynamic phenomena' that confront psychoanalytic therapy on the highest level of the 'hierarchical model of the structure of knowledge' so as to meet the legitimate demands of the logic and methodology of science—in so far as there is reasonable agreement among philosophers of science as to what these are—we will examine some criticisms of psychoanalysis.

## CRITICS OF PSYCHOANALYSIS

I must confine myself to three critics, Slater, Medawar and Popper. In an article on 'Is psychiatry a science? Does it want to be?' Slater (1972) classes psychoanalysis with the arts and humanities, and writes:

> Popper's criterion (i.e. falsifiability) covers the empirical sciences and excludes the arts and humanities. Theories are useless unless they are refutable, so even incorrect theories can help us towards the truth.

This implies the surprising view that science is not 'knowledge' but only the interim method of seeking it. A true theory must be a possibility in principle even though only relative truth is possible in fact! But if a finally true theory were reached, it would not be refutable. For Popper and Slater science would then have ceased to exist; only technology would remain, the absurd result of excluding Harré's 'existential statements of fact' supported by the 'inductive relation' to observations. Slater regards doctors and psychiatrists as not scientists but only technicians, 'a caring profession', though in fact all medical treatment must be a 'testing' of medical science. Psychoanalysts also, he says, belong to the caring professions only. Slater writes:

> The doctor cannot carry out any experiment on a controlled basis. However he can accumulate observations which can be passed on to the medical scientist for rigorous examination. Scientific medicine is a technology derived from medical science (used) in the non-scientific work of helping people. In the experimental or control series the individual human being loses his individuality and is treated only as a member of a class.

This distinction between 'knowledge for testing' and 'knowledge for use' seems quite artificial. A surgical operation is a scientific controlled experiment testing 'usable knowledge' on an anaesthetized patient who is only a 'thing' for a time. But when 'helping people' involves, not operating on an unconscious body but understanding an individual personality by 'intuitive insight' and 'knowledge for use', it is irrelevant to say with Slater:

> It is no part of the psycho-analyst's duty, any more than of the psychiatrist's, to develop his field along scientific lines. They all in their own field accumulate experience and try to formulate guesses which might then be put to the test.

What test? In the psychotherapeutic situation, the analyst-patient relation is the only possible 'experimental situation' in which guesses, hypotheses, about 'individuality' can be tested, for as Slater sees, in any other situation 'the individual human being loses his individuality'. What Slater calls 'applied technology' is Medawar's 'inductive experiments to enrich the repertoire of knowledge', and Kuhn's 'normal science of problem-solving', and Harré's 'development of correct ideas as general existential statements'. *The 'emergence' of 'individuality' is what constitutes the uniqueness of the psychological level of phenomenal reality.* Psychiatry is concerned with 'organic malfunctioning' which disturbs the individual personality. Psychoanalysis is concerned with the opposite problem, 'personal psychic malfunctioning' which can disturb organic functions, as in conversion hysteria, but here the experimental control series must retain 'individuality'. Though science must include logically testable hypotheses, it cannot be limited only to them, for it is our major trustworthy source of usable knowledge. *Psychoanalytic psychotherapy is at the same time research into the psychological realities of the human being qua individual person, who cannot be studied in impersonal ways. The psychoanalyst cannot hand over his problems to other scientists.* Not all analysts need be scientists but the only scientists in this field must be therapists. Since Slater calls urgently for 'greater understanding of the domain of subjectivity', and sees psychoanalysis as 'a source of ideas for translation into testable terms', we must show that such testing does actually take place. Slater's positivist philosophy prevents him from seeing this. He writes:

> The scientific method can only concern itself with the real world, the world outside us, which we can study objectively. There is also the world within us, forever the domain of subjectivity, forever beyond the reach of science, in which no possibilities of verification exist. It is this world which is the territory of the arts and humanities, of philosophy and religion. Despite inaccessibility to science, to the use of any self-correcting process, *it yet contains the possibilities of greater understanding*. This is the world which the psychiatrist cannot ignore and in which the psycho-analyst seeks his understanding.

This is logical positivism, limiting knowledge to mathematics and physical science. Everything else is meaningless. Slater does not accept that, but is a positivist, empiricist, reductionist in saying that only the external world outside us is 'real' and open to 'objective study'. He is an early Wittgensteinian in distinguishing between 'factual propositions' of science, and phenomena of the inner world as the 'domain of subjectivity' beyond the reach of verification. Wittgenstein held that religion, morality and philosophy contain deep truths which cannot be expressed in factual language. In reality, Slater has overlooked the basic distinction between the existential 'fact' of the reality, nature and manner of working of our subjective inner world, and the quite different fact of its cultural products; as if psychology were the same thing as 'the humanities, philosophy and religion'. Psychodynamic theory is not concerned with the 'humanities, philosophy and religion'. They are not 'the world in which the psycho-analyst seeks his understanding'. In an unsystematized way they illustrate it, and psychodynamic studies may throw light on the humanities. But 'psychological science' seeks to express in factual propositions, which can be tested and, if in error, falsified, the actual processes experienced in our psychodynamic personal 'self', the realities of our psychic nature and its modes of operation; the ways infants grow from birth onwards to be either stable or unstable in the family and social personal-relationships medium of which they develop a psychic duplicate as a built-in complex pattern of functioning which makes for psychic security and health, or else insecurity, neurosis or psychosis. It is not the function of psychoanalysis to seek 'understanding' of the 'truth-value' of the humanities, though they provide secondhand illustrations of human psychic functioning. Only in that sense is Bronowski's 'knowledge of the self' found in 'literature'. *Psychoanalytic therapy studies at first hand the way the psychic self 'works' in sickness and health, the phenomenal reality on the top tier of the hierarchy of existence.*

In real life there is artificial distinction between the 'objective external world' as real, and the 'subjective world inside us' as unreal in the scientific sense, incapable of prediction and verification. The megalomania of Hitler and the paranoia of Stalin were 'subjective' to them, but desperately objectively real to millions of other people. As to prediction, none of us would like to test the matter by 'predicting' what a Hitler or Stalin would do if he came to power here, and test the prediction by letting him do so. We would find our predictions all too uncomfortably reliable. If someone threatens us, we want to know if he *really* means it. Slater with Mayer-Gross and Roth (1954) recognized the 'fact-seeking objective knowledge' nature of Freud's basic work, for while they dismissed his overall theory as 'crazy in structure', they gave an impressive list of his 'factual contribution'.

> Freud's concepts of the unconscious, repression, emotion attached to repressed memories affecting the individual's responses to events in the present, all revolutionary ideas, represented a great advance and are

generally accepted. Much of what Freud said of the Oedipus Complex
stands. Until his day, the emotional attitudes of the infant and child
were unexplored territory submerged in sentiment. People were not
prepared to see that the relations of parents and children could be
governed by emotions of a most primitive kind. The magnitude of
Freud's achievement should not be minimized. Where there had been
humbug and wilful self-deception, he brought realism and clarity.

That is the area of objectively real psychodynamic phenomena presented for our
understanding. Slater quotes Medawar's Romanes Lecture (1969) stating that
psychoanalysis is a mythology not a science, a view derived from Popper which we
shall examine. Slater writes:

> The concept of truth in Freudian and other quasi-scientific psycholo-
> gies is that of imaginative literature. But he [i.e. Medawar] did not wish
> his criticism to apply to psychotherapy, but only to that 'special
> pedigree of psychological doctrine and treatment which can be traced
> back to the work and writings of Sigmund Freud.

Here is the same confusion of cultural products and psychological facts. The actual
relation is that psychic facts lie behind cultural products; as when Winnicott states
that a child's cuddly toy representing mother and its need of secure personal
relations, is the first *symbol* of the object, the 'first *cultural product*' (1971). Both
Slater and Medawar overlook the fact that 'psychotherapy' in any meaningful
modern sense was the creation of Freud. That does not imply that all his theories
were right but it does mean that he should not be misrepresented.

Slater refers inter alia to a different kind of criticism made at a New York
University Institute of Philosophy symposium in 1958, which rejected the claim of
psychoanalysis to be science because: 'Psycho-analysts had not approached their
complex and unified theory in an experimental spirit. Psycho-analysis should be
broken down into part theories and subjected to piecemeal confirmation or
refutation.' The discussion must have been with particularly orthodox analysts.
There are, naturally, expository attempts to gather our findings together into as
systematic a whole as proves possible or illuminating, but there is nothing sacro-
sanct about this 'unified theory'. It is an invitation to further psychotherapeutic
testing. Critics appear to be ignorant of the important 'piecemeal' changes in
post-Freudian theory made by such analysists as Klein, Fairbairn, Erikson, Balint,
Bowlby, Winnicott. Morse of Harvard wrote in 1972:

> Thus it seems to me that the Fairbairn-Guntrip metaphor 'descriptively
> explains' the data presented by Balint and Winnicott, and that as a

structural theory, it fits the clinical data better. Balint and Winnicott have discovered data calling for some fundamental reconstruction of theory, without fully carrying out that reconstruction themselves. [p. 500]

There is 'piecemeal confirmation or refutation' going on in the official literature, a progressive development of ideas arising out of clinical experience. In teaching in the Leeds Department of Psychiatry, I made a practice of beginning a course by saying: 'Set light to theory. It is a good servant but a bad master, and is only the best we can do to date to conceptualize what patients show us.' Winnicott held that no analyst can be original 'because what we write today, we learned from a patient yesterday', the very point made in that symposium by the philosopher Ernest Nagel, that 'theoretical notions must be tied down to specific observational material', inductive piecemeal 'confirmation' or 'supporting evidence'. *The result of this survey is that 'our subjective experience of our inner world' has its own kind of 'psychic reality' on the highest level of the hierarchical structure of the phenomenally 'real'. 'Existential statements of facts' can be made about it, and the 'inductive relation' that evidence supports conclusions is valid for psychodynamic research: subject to such 'knowledge' being always open to testing, by confronting our hypotheses with the reality of patients' experiences. Whenever the theory is 'falsified', proves inadequate, as does happen, we brood over the new phenomena to produce a new theory for testing.*

Medawar's criticisms are not intellectual examination but mildly frivolous depreciation; although they create a useful way to confront them with 'clinical facts'. In the Preface to The Jayne Lecture (1969) he writes: 'I never write on subjects outside my own' but breaks his own rule by giving a description of a psychoanalytic session, an explicit statement on the nature of dreams and a mistaken view of psychoanalysis as 'a system of thought'. He thinks that a Galton-like

[s]tatistical enquiry into the efficacy of psycho-analysis treatment might show that the therapeutic pretensions of psycho-analysis were not borne out. . . . Analysts dismiss as somewhat vulgar the idea that the chief purpose of psycho-analytic treatment is to effect a cure. No: its purpose is rather to give the patient a new and deeper understanding of himself and of the nature of his relationship to his fellow men. So interpreted, psycho-analysis is best thought of as a secular substitute for prayer. Like prayer it is conducted in the form of a duologue and like prayer (if prayer is to bring comfort and refreshment) it requires an act of personal surrender, though in this case to a professional and stipendiary god.

No doubt Medawar was rewarded for this clever skit by audience smiles. If he ever attempted to treat an obsessional, or a patient oscillating between severe hysteric and paranoid phases, or a markedly schizoid, withdrawn, derealized patient or even the 'resistances' that occur in every patient he would get a shock. Let us subject his hypothesis of 'a personal surrender' to 'observational falsification'. One schizoid young scientist walked in like a mechanical figure, stared in silence and then said: 'I'm a non-person. I'm a good scientist. All day I do my calculations correctly, but when work is finished I'm a non-person. I can't make friends. I don't know what you mean by personal relations. I'm a nobody.' A successful businessman severely hampered by obsessions, regularly came late for sessions, disagreed with anything I suggested (I never make dogmatic interpretations), and would at times ring five minutes before he was due to say he was detained. Then I gathered all this together and did interpret, that people with obsessional symptoms are often strong natures over-dominated as children, as he was, and his main aim at this time was to see that nobody, including me, ever got any hold over him again. He would control the treatment, not come at my times nor ponder anything I said. He hoped to ease up on himself by controlling me instead, which I felt would mean denying himself any worthwhile result. This behaviour slowly faded out and he made progress. Even the hysteric who may develop an overt dependent attitude, is not making a 'personal surrender' but secretly exploiting the therapist to get the needs of a seriously deprived inner child-self met. Medawar's fantasy of a psychoanalytic session is out of touch with the realities of 'transference and resistance', both visible in dreams. Medawar's (1969) hypothesis is that 'dreams are not messages or communications of any kind. The utter non-sensicality of dreams is probably the most significant thing about them'.

From his hypothesis we can deduce a testable consequence, that no dream ever has a real meaning in relation to the dreamer's actual life-situation. Let us test this by three dreams that also throw light on the 'nature of sessions' and on 'transference and resistance'. A spinster in the late 50s was deeply depressed. Her doctor said she would never work again which would mean retiring on less than her full pension. She had good reason for wanting to be helped. Her depression was rooted in vehement hate of an autocratic father, now dead, with whom she had quarrelled and left home. She was argumentative and resistant, but let me help her to relate her depression to her hate of father and to find some relief by being open about it – to an extent that allowed her to work till she retired on full pension. Then I saw the end was coming. She dreamed: 'I was walking along a road and came to a wall, too high to get over and too long to go round'. I said: 'You seem to feel you are at a dead end'. She said: 'I must go on *if you can stand it*'. For a couple of months she would work up a quarrelsome argument and finally fling out, slamming the door. Presently I would get a letter: 'I'm so depressed. Can I come back?' For a third time I agreed, intending to tell her that I thought she was keeping up a running fight with me to make her quarrel with father her *modus vivendi*. But she brought a dream: 'I got on a tram, walked through to the driver's platform, turned him off and drove myself'. I simply said: 'The tram is your therapy, the driver is me and father. You are determined to carry on your battle to get the better of us.' She left finally but had got her pension out of the initial period of therapy.

A similar situation ended more happily and shows the real nature of the psychoanalytic session. A man, also with an autocratic father, was forced against his will into the family business. The father died and he had to carry on which he did successfully. He was constantly quarrelling, however, with males in any positions of influence, developed high blood pressure and tried to argue with me. As he found that I accepted the validity of his feelings about father so that he could talk about them freely for the first time, his blood pressure became normal. Then suddenly one day he said: 'I'll stop coming after two more sessions'. I felt it was somewhat premature but merely said: 'That's up to you'. Next time he brought a dream: 'I was fighting my father. It was a deadly life and death battle, but I defended myself so well that he suddenly stopped fighting and walked away. I felt lost and thought: "Oh! What shall I do now".' I commented: 'I think you must have felt I walked away and refused to give you a fight, when I accepted without comment your saying you would end in two more sessions. But I don't think you really need to go on with this battle any longer, or use me as a stand in for father.' He ended and to my knowledge is well and active after 15 years. These dreams which 'falsify' the nonsense hypothesis, enable us to make Harré's 'general existential statements' conveying 'knowledge' about the dreaming process, repression, transference and resistance which are basic to psychoanalysis as science.

Medawar's third criticism is based on a simple mistake. He writes:

> If we accept falsifiability as a line of demarcation, we cannot accept into science any system of thought (for example psycho-analysis) which contains a built in antidote to disbelief: to discredit psycho-analysis is an aberration of thought which calls for psycho-analytical treatment.

Medawar simply confuses 'resistance to analytic therapy' with 'criticism of theory'. I had a patient who was a biology lecturer, an obsessionally hard worker in his struggle to keep a serious depression at bay. He once said: 'When I'm very anxious, I start thinking "Psycho-analysis isn't true. I can explain all this biologically. But when my anxiety lessens I know that isn't true. It's that I don't want to face my problems".' Psychoanalysts are human and I do not think anyone holds that a training analysis solves all emotional problems. If an analyst becomes too rigidly orthodox, one would feel that a too blind acceptance of a too palaeo-Freudian theory called for psychoanalytical treatment. Any theory (apparently even in quantum physics) can be blindly adhered to as a source of security, instead of as a basis for expanding knowledge. The same would hold true for equally dogmatic critics of any theory. But nothing in psychoanalytic theory forbids critical examination of the theory objectively. Such criticism goes on in psychoanalytic circles, and much current theory has moved a long way beyond Freud's original formulations, especially his psychobiology and wholly inadequate 'system-ego' theory. He once wrote: 'instincts are our mythology', and his later reification of the impossible Death Instinct theory has been rejected by very many analysts, from the orthodox Fenichel to the progressive Fairbairn and Winnicott. Even Freud's model of the 'session', and impersonal 'mirror' analyst out of sight, detached like a surgeon, using a 'technique of interpretation', is today increasingly humanized because 'experimentally falsified' by patients. Analytic 'interpretation' is not a 'technique' but an 'intuitive understanding' guided by the best theory we have up to date, a 'hypothesis' to be confirmed or falsified by the patient's reaction. In the end every patient knows more about himself than we can ever do, even though he is unconscious of so much of it. Freud said that the time to make an interpretation is when you see the patient is on the point of seeing something and needs help over some resistance. The psychoanalytic session is thus turned into an experimental situation without being depersonalized. One patient of mine suddenly falsified Freud's theory that the 'sex instinct', libido, is the source of all energy for living. He had long suffered from compulsive sexual urges which drove him to prostitutes and which he hated. Gradually the strength of these compulsions waned till suddenly in one session he burst out with: 'I don't want to be just a penis. I want to be a person', i.e. the basic psychological reality is the need to develop stable selfhood, not to satisfy biochemical appetites, however much they may be exploited by our 'personality problems'.

## HOW CAN WE CONCEPTUALIZE PSYCHODYNAMIC REALITY IN A SCIENTIFIC WAY?

Slater asks: 'Is psychoanalysis a science? Does it want to be?' Yes, not because of any prestige value science may have, but because we need the most accurate sifted tested knowledge we can formulate, to give genuine help to the tortured 'self' patients bring to us. The basic psychoanalytic assumption today tends ever more to the view that every patient, no matter what his symptoms or diagnostic label, is struggling to preserve and develop a genuine 'personal self', the secure growth of which has been impeded by serious traumatic events and/or human relationships. Any false starts and partial truths have been worked through en route to a satisfactory 'ego' psychology. The earlier the trauma, the more serious the results – and the longer it takes to outgrow them. The therapeutic session is the analyst's way of offering the patient a genuine recognition of his right to be a human being, a 'personal self', an ego developed with inner freedom and unimpeded creativity, and an ability to make meaningful personal relationships. *The humanities are concerned with 'cultural products' that are the 'creations' of the psyche. Psychoanalysis is concerned with the 'factual modes of operation' of the psyche which produces the humanities and science and every meaningful human activity, and reveals psychic health and wholeness and also psychic disorder and conflict.*

How can we best conceptualize the results of this growing study of this area of phenomenal reality. We have surveyed three stages of the scientific process.

(1) Medawar's *Baconian collection of facts* 'to enrich the repertoire of information' about something that interests the investigator: Harré's 'existential statements' which are a part of science. Freud, as the first to explore the area of *psychodynamic* psychopathology found it disturbing and quoted *movebo acheronta* – I will stir up the underworld. It has involved psychoanalysts in a lot of Kuhn's routine 'normal science' of applying theories accepted at least for the time being, while the few original minds were sensing Kant's 'species of knowledge which involves understanding' which is embedded in experience.

Out of this grew stage (2) *an ongoing invention of hypotheses, theories*, that aimed to explain the facts. Can psychoanalysis go from there to stage (3) *where inadequate theories are 'falsified' and improved?*

I have claimed that the psychotherapeutic session is the 'laboratory', the 'experimental situation' in which our hypotheses are under unremitting testing all the time in the light of the reactions of patients who are nothing like as docile as Medawar fancies. We must then look at Popper's rejection of this claim, at least as he met it in the Vienna analysts of the 1930s. He (1969) writes:

> The 'clinical observations' which analysts naively believe confirm their theory, cannot do this. . . . And as for Freud's epic of the ego, super-ego and id, no substantially stronger claim for scientific status can be made for it than for Homer's collected stories from Olympus. These stories describe some facts, but in the manner of myths. They contain most interesting psychological suggestions but not in testable form. At the same time I realized that such myths may be developed and become testable: that historically speaking – all or very nearly all scientific theories originate in myths, and that a myth may contain important anticipations of scientific theories. [p. 37]

Harré is not as negative about 'confirmation' as Popper. In so far as observations do not 'falsify' a theory, they *provisionally confirm* it and we go on working with it till we discover phenomena concerning which it fails. My experience is that 'clinical observations' sometimes confirm and sometimes falsify a theoretical expectation, so that earlier theory comes to be seen as more partial than one at first thought, and theory goes on developing greater accuracy. Thus Freud's 'oedipus complex' was laid down as universal but I early began to doubt that. The nearest to an oedipal dream that any patient has brought to me in over 35 years, was that of a very disturbed spinster of over 40, most of whose dreams were nightmares of being thrashed by mother, which were true to life. She had a quiet friendly father who protected her when he could. She came very embarrassed to one session and said: 'I've dreamed that I was married to father and was just getting into bed with him, when mother burst in in a rage and dragged me out'. It seemed to me that that did not necessarily confirm Freud's theory of 'instincts', but it showed how literally an actually existing pathogenic triangular 'family-relationships' pattern is forced on the mentality of the child. I found that broadly oedipal patterns did dominate in some cases, but in others quite different 'family-relations patterns' held sway. During my second training analysis with Winnicott, he twice observed 'You show no signs of ever having had an oedipus complex' and he was certainly right. The most typical family-triangle dream I ever had was

> A great siege was in progress and I was being besieged. Father and I were sitting talking in a room and mother was carrying on the siege. I said to him: 'You know it's no good. I shall never give in to her.' He said with a smile: 'Yes, I know you won't. I'll go and tell her she'd better give it up. You'll never submit.' He did and the siege was called off.

The falsification of the theory of the universality of the oedipus complex cannot be evaded by calling this an 'inverted oedipus complex'. I produced no evidence of any sexual fixation on father, and my struggle to break my mother's domination over me was a hard fact of life in the family pattern. Such 'clinical observations' convinced me that there could exist an Oedipus complex in some cases, but that *the important basic reality was not 'instincts'—it was the great variety of different 'patterns of family relationships' forced on children to grow into their mental make-up*. I later made a further important discovery, that patients could actually 'keep on operating' in dreams and symptoms a broadly oedipal, in the sense of triangular, pattern of bad family relationships as a defence against the emergence of the far more frightening earlier 'schizoid' problems of '*failure* of real relationships'. Such failures generate the undermining experiences of derealization, extreme introversion, and feelings of unreality. They have their origin in the pre-oedipal two-person mother–child relationship. Yet Freud's original theory of the oedipus complex was a highly imaginative, provocative, original and challenging hypothesis, and though it is easy to falsify if taken literally, it has led to an enormous amount of fruitful research into the relations of parents and children. What more need we ask of the first intrepid explorer in a new field? It offers no basis for Popper's unrealistic comparison with Homer's myths of Olympus.

It has been suggested to me that Popper would say that my 'great variety of different "patterns of family relationships" forced on children', is too imprecise and general to be capable of falsification. I stated it, however, as a factual observation that falsifies the *universality* of Freud's original theory of an oedipus complex based on two instincts of sex and aggression. Taken as a general statement of hypothesis, it would be falsified by one observation of a case where parents had brought up a child who had no organic defect, without any effect at all on the quality and pattern of its characterological development. But since Popper's view of 'falsification' as the sole criterion of 'scientific empirical knowledge' has not found general acceptance, and due weight is given by most philosophers to the 'inductive relation' of evidence supporting conclusions, i.e. the value of 'provisional confirmation', it is relevant to say that in 35 years of psychoanalytic therapy, I have found no observations that would falsify the hypothesis that the 'qualitative pattern of parent–child relations', whatever it is, is the environment in which the child grows, and which he psychically internalizes as the structure of his personality. The way he develops is determined by 'ego-development in the personal relationships medium' of his basic dependence on parents; and their influence is most fundamental in his most impressionable years, starting with the initial 'mother–infant relations', i.e. the quality of mothering. The possible variations of pattern are infinite in detail yet the basic principle is the same; and it falsifies Freud's view that development is determined by the need to control sexual possessiveness towards the parent of the opposite sex and aggression, fear and guilt towards the parent of the same sex. If that pattern is found, it is traceable to the quality of parental handling.

Popper's comparison of Freud's 'ego, super-ego and id' theory to pre-scientific myths is even more unrealistic. This was Freud's final form of expression for his 'theory of endopsychic structure', and the use of the terms 'epic' and 'myth' here strike me as irrelevant. An epic is 'a poem narrating the achievements of heroes, as the *Iliad* or *Odyssey*' (OED). I doubt whether the myths of Zeus the thunder god, Apollo the sun god, etc., contributed much to the beginnings of astronomy, or qualify for comparison with Freud's ego, super-ego and id, which constituted an attempt to identify clinically observable aspects of our psychic functioning in states of inner mental conflict, the first theory of 'endopsychic structure'. Freud's terms ego and super-ego are not 'theories' but names given to certain recognizable psychic phenomena so that we may identify and discuss them. So far from being mytho-logical, Popper used the same term when he wrote: '*I* do not doubt, etc.' The term ego registers the fact that every one of us recognizes himself as an 'I', a subject of experience, what Lord Adrian referred to as 'the "I" who does the perceiving, thinking and acting'. At the age of 70 I had two dreams in which I saw myself clearly as a small boy of 3½ in a traumatic situation that I was actually in at that age. I recognized myself as the same 'I' then and now, and know that no one else possesses that memory but me, my ego as an unbroken continuity over 70 years. 'Ego' is not myth, not even theory, but the naming of an experience we all have of our own personal reality and continuity, or rather of one aspect of it, for there are others. It is not even Freud's invention but a common possession of all times and languages.

Similarly the term 'super-ego' is neither theory nor myth but a name, this time invented by Freud to identify another aspect of our experience of ourselves, often observable in dreams, and in conscious self-accusations. Its popular name is 'conscience'. For psychoanalysts the term super-ego registers the fact that our conscience begins to develop in us as children as a product of the influence of parents, as if the parent were 'super-imposed' on our developing ego in our psychic make-up, and remains an identifiable aspect of our psychic make-up or 'endopsychic structure'. Thus a woman who had been married ten years with a child of her own, and living away from her mother all that time, dreamed that everywhere she went she was followed by a tall, dark, stern-faced woman, in fact her mother, keeping an eye on her. That mother's influence, so vividly pictured in that dream as part of her own psychic make-up, was recognizable in her waking reactions also. Freud's term 'super-ego' is not theory but an appropriate term (another ego standing over the dreamer's ego), to identify a psychological phenomenon that occurs in varying degrees in everyone.

With the term 'id' however, we do come upon 'theory', yet hardly a myth comparable to Homer's stories. It is an appropriate name for the theory Freud's medical scientific education forced on him, that our basic psychological energy is impersonal biological energy. Many now reject this illegitimate mixing of different disciplines, biology and psychology. 'Id' is not a useful myth but an epistemological confusion. Freud borrowed it from Groddeck who said: 'We ought not to say "I live" but "I am lived by the It" '—the organic body functioning impersonally with no reference to our intelligible values and purposes. That view forced 'instinct theory' on Freud, the source of all the later theoretical difficulties. Bowlby (1969) rejects Freud's 'psychic energy' because it is not psychic, only physical. Fairbairn (1952) rejected Freud's hybrid psychobiology and suggested a more consistently psychological 'ego-theory' of endopsychic structure, based on observable evidence of ego-splitting' which Freud in his last book accepted as universal. Ego and super-ego are data. Ego-splitting is a hypothesis of Freud's which Fairbairn related to Melanie Klein's (1957) observations of 'object-splitting', as its logical consequence. This is shown by a patient who, at her first session said: 'I have the most wonderful mother on earth'. I realized at once that mother was the source of all her problems—subsequently proved by the mother's active interference in her treatment till I personally warned her off. I asked the patient: 'Is there anyone you hate?' She said at once: 'Yes. My aunt.' It emerged that this aunt lived several hundred miles away and the patient only saw her for a few days each year. She was using her as the 'split-off bad mother' she hated, while she meekly submitted to, and felt guilty towards, the ruthless mother at home, the 'super-ego' mother. Fairbairn developed a different theory of 'endopsychic structure' based on these 'splitting phenomena'; in non-technical terms, the needy ego relates to what is maternal in mother, the angry ego relates to the frustrating mother, and the moral ego relates to the disapproving mother. Fairbairn's actual technical terms call now I think for further revision, but an enormous number of dreams of patients who know nothing of the theory, show the broad accuracy of this 'technical description' of the pattern of disturbed ego-disintegration. Psychic energy is not the biochemical drives of organic 'appetites'. The ego uses and exploits bodily appetites for its personal purposes. Compulsive sexuality and eating, or impotence and anorexia nervosa, represent the need to be a 'person' or a hopeless denial of it. Psychic energy is 'motivational energy' the intelligible drive to secure the good personal relations which make individual development free of crippling inner conflicts possible.

I believe Popper to be wrong in holding that psychoanalytical terms are untestable theories, like myths. Since observation is 'theory-laden', even if at first unconsciously, identifying and naming psychic phenomena evolved into the first theories. *The unconscious, transference, resistance, repression, etc., both name psychodynamic phenomena and add up to a theory of mental functioning, all aspects of which are tested, provisionally confirmed or falsified piecemeal by the evidence patients bring of what is going on in their disturbed mental experience.* But falsification only gives negative information about what is not true. It can't tell us what is provisionally true enough to go on being used, and *'use' is the experimental test which in time exposes errors.* The psychoanalytic theory of psychic structure and functioning is tested and developed against the evidence produced by every patient treated. Freud, of course, had his own legitimate psychological interests in myths as myths. The great mythologies of the race must contain not only pre-scientific notions about the mysterious universe, but also projections of the fantasies of the deep unconscious: but as myths they are 'cultural products', not 'psychodynamic phenomena' per se. Freud even once said: 'Instincts are our mythology'; but he still treated them as biological factual phenomena having exact psychological correlates rooted in them, a confusing and unnecessary dualism. Fairbairn provided an example of testing and falsification of theory on this very point. He began as an orthodox Freudian with an independent questioning mind. He reported one patient as saying: 'You keep saying that I want this or that "instinct" satisfied but what I want is a father', a reaction from the patient that was a catalyst promoting the crystallizing out of his entire 'Revised Theory of the Psychoses and Psychoneuroses', which switched psychoanalytic theory from its biological basis onto a genuine psychological 'personal relations' basis. If, so Medawar says, hypotheses are more often repaired than scrapped, then in a young science we must be particularly careful to treat all theories as approximations to the non-existent final truth, to be used always critically, in psychoanalysis as in every other field.

In the meantime we have practical needs to meet and must use such knowledge as we have. If we wait for final knowledge, we shall never act in any situation let alone psychotherapy. The position of psychoanalysis in this is no different in principle from any other science or activity, but in psychotherapy there are peculiar difficulties not met with elsewhere. We study persons, free agents, on whose cooperation we cannot always depend; not impersonal objects which cannot 'resist' experiment. We have to study a phenomenon which is at once both subjective and objective. In studying the disturbed 'psychic reality' of 'persons', both their cooperation and their resistance is equally important for understanding their functioning. This was one of Freud's earliest and most important discoveries, and as early as 1904 he wrote:

> The theory of psycho-analysis is an attempt to account for two ob-
> served facts that strike one conspicuously and unexpectedly whenever
> an attempt is made to trace the symptoms of a neurotic back to their
> sources in his past life: the facts of transference and resistance. Any line
> of investigation, no matter what its direction, which recognizes these
> two facts and takes them as the starting-point of its work may call itself
> psycho-analysis, though it arrives at results other than my own.

Freud here unwittingly actually implies Popper's 'hypothesis-testing,' which is deeply relevant here, for psychoanalysis must study the development of the individual from birth onwards through every phase of life, simply because patients willy-nilly present us with all that material embedded in the complex structure of their personality disturbances. We must take account of the new epistemology where knowledge gained on lower levels of phenomena may be usable on higher levels, although the opposite is not true.

So far we have considered seriatim a variety of criticisms of psychoanalysis made by three eminent thinkers. This has involved a somewhat disjointed and unintegrated treatment of the basic problem, and the results must now be gathered into as logical a whole as proves possible in small space. As a preliminary observation, critics reveal a serious lack of first-hand knowledge of psychoanalysis in practice. It is hard to see how this can be avoided, for no patient can respond in the presence of a disinterested third person, as he would do alone with his therapist. For teaching purposes tape-recordings, one-way screen interviews, televised sessions, have all been tried, but as Bion (1962) wrote, the apparatus muddies the stream of the patient's spontaneous mental processes. At least, however, critics could discuss thoroughly the nature and experience of the 'therapeutic encounter' with experienced analysts of a variety of theoretical viewpoints, for psychoanalysis is definitely not a unified theoretical system; as the theory of therapy it must reflect the diverse ways in which human beings can cooperate in the therapeutic aim. A good description of this diversity is to be found in *True and False Experience* by

Lomas (1973), which will dispel the illusion of psychoanalysis as a tight-knit unified, dogmatic orthodox theory. Secondly, Popper's view that psychoanalysis corresponds to the mythological pre-scientific stage of the established sciences, does not, in my judgement correspond with the facts. It entirely overlooks the very great amounts of observation, recording, correcting, critical discussion, that constitutes the first Baconian stage of data-collection for all sciences, and the establishment of 'general existential statements' which Harré does not agree to have demoted from scientific status. This constitutes a great deal of 'knowledge for use' that the trained therapist must have and keep under constant critical checking. It includes a great deal of information about symptoms and their modes of formation and the complex states of mind that find either clear or disguised expression in them. This is found to imply the development of *imaginative hypotheses*, as to how the individual human being grows and develops into a sufficiently secure, stable person who does not break down into mental 'illness' but is normally spontaneous, active, creative, capable of forming sound and durable personal relationships, or else at some stage of life meets with pressures and problems that he has not the inner 'wholeness of personality' and absence of a legacy of anxiety from the past to enable him to cope with, without breakdown.

    We accept as a starting-point the genetic endowment of the individual. Not that we have much exact knowledge of it, but it is obvious that not all people are basically alike, that they differ widely in gifts, and practical and intellectual capacities, and general emotional type, and if they fall ill, it will be broadly within their constitutional type. It doesn't help much in treatment but it warns us not to expect that every patient will get well in the same way, or to think that we can know what any given patient should be like when he does get well. *Our task is to help him to get free to be whatever it is in his nature to be.* Winnicott (1965) summed this up in the title of one of his books – genetic endowment needs a facilitating environment for its healthy development, and the basic aim of the psychoanalytic therapist must be to provide the kind of respecting, understanding, reliable 'environment' that the patient has never had, and needs if he is to redevelop out of inner conflicts and inhibitions, and find out for himself what it is natural for him to be. This must in large part be done by enabling him to discover just what it was in his past life, perhaps going right back to infancy, that blocked the growth of his true ego-potentials, and filled him instead with stored up suppressed fears, hates, unmet needs, guilty feelings, and ingrown compulsive patterns of bad persecutory personal human relationships which he unwittingly reproduces in his disturbed present-day living. His genetic type lays down what it is possible for him to become, if we knew what it is, but it does not explain what it was that prevents him from becoming that. For that, we need to know all that he can tell us about his post-natal history. But much of that is usually taboo because of guilty feelings towards parents, profoundly repressed and so anxiety-loaded that its eruption sabotages conscious living. Here our problems begin. *We need not only to collect data but to invent imaginative hypotheses to make them intelligible.* Data are provided by patients' symptoms, dreams, memories, patterns of personal relating, moods, needs, guilts, fears, transferences, resistances, etc. To make all this intelligible, we need a hypothesis about the basic nature of 'ego-development' in health and sickness from birth on, leading to a theory of 'endopsychic structure' that describes the nature of the patient's capacity for 'ego-relatedness' or suffering of 'ego-isolation'. This hypothesis should clarify the meaning of the various diagnostic labels long used by psychiatry. This fundamental psychodynamic hypothesis must never be a fixed, completed theoretical entity but must cover all the complexity of human life along with what we have in common that makes us share a common humanity. *Psychoanalytic theory is our attempt to clarify our growing understanding of how a baby develops and functions as a 'person', 'ego' or 'self' in health and sickness in the media of the personal relationships provided by his 'facilitating' or 'non-facilitating' environment.* Descriptively, 'health' is wholeness, harmony, unimpeded creative self-expression, capacity for constructive human relationships, and sickness is internal disintegration of personality, at cross purposes in oneself and with others, the thwarting of innate potentialities for stable growth and functioning. It would be *theoretically possible* (if the infinite complexity of human life allowed it in practice) to *predict* how any individual person would react to any specific situation, *if* we knew enough about his total complex personality including his unconscious, as well as complete knowledge of the external situation as he sees it, to which he must react. Of course we cannot know enough, so that no analyst would predict a 'cure' (whatever that might mean). Nevertheless we know that many patients do obtain substantial gains from losing symptoms to developing a more free and confident personality and begin to 'live' in a more real way as a result of cooperative exploration of their problems and history. That is what we seek a growingly accurate theory to explain. In psychodynamics *freewill* and *determinism* have special meanings. 'Freewill' is the ability to choose what we really want to do in given circumstances without prevention by unconscious inner processes in our total self. 'Psychic determinism' is sabotage of our conscious realistic choices by conflicts of unconscious origin, as when an obsessional patient missed an important train because of an overmastering compulsion to keep going back to check on the exact position of a lamp post, irrational but irresistible. *All depends on how much we can know 'in depth' about the motivational energies of 'persons'. The task of psychoanalysis is to correct and extend our hypothetical knowledge in this area:* an inquiry in its own way even more complex if possible, than inquiries at the other end of the scale of 'phenomenal reality', the physical universe and what we call 'matter'.

Are hypotheses in this area falsifiable? Though not accepted by all as the only ultimate criterion of 'science', it has its uses. Freud's most comprehensive hypothesis, the 'hydraulic model' of a system-ego controlling (under social pressures) biochemical energies of sex and aggressive instincts has been long falsified for all but ultra-orthodox analysts and replaced by the 'person-ego hypothesis', the gradual differentiation of the infant out of the state of 'primary identification' with mother at birth through adequate mothering in the first two years. Failure then by the 'facilitating environment' leaves the infant a prey to 'ego disintegration' and schizoid derealization, at best only masked by the conscious development of what Winnicott called a 'false self on a conformity basis' (or a rebellious, or an abstract intellectual, or any other social persona basis). If, however, that first phase goes well, the child enters the second important phase of childhood, latency and adolescence, when his growing personality must expand to cope with various good, bad and indifferent kinds of personal relations both in the family and beyond it. In these years the basic triangular 'parents and child' relationship patterns steadily complicated by ever more varied experiences beyond the family circle, become 'built-in' as the 'endopsychic structure' of the developing personality. This period of Freud's oedipus complex is too narrow a formula to cope with all the facts. It is the period when the hard core of the 'psychoneuroses' develops, just as 'schizoid' problems have their deepest roots in the infancy period, which has only been deeply studied in the post-Freudian era. Even in the third main phase, adulthood, from say 18 onwards, too hard pressures in real life may produce emotional stress of the intensity of illness, but this is less likely in proportion as the earlier years gave a facilitating environment for the growth of a basically stable ego.

We have roughly three levels of therapy:

1. Short-term therapy in which stress in adult life has not necessarily played on deeper hidden discords in the personality.

2. Complex problems in basic personal relationships, so severe as to break down a veneer of adult stability and trigger off diagnosable neurosis. Here the causes will be found at least as deep as the 3 to 18 years period.

3. Drastic inner collapse of the personality, with apparently complete inability to cope with life, and regression to states of 'infantile dependence', schizoid characters of psychotic illness in so far as these are psychogenic. That such cases can be psychogenic has now been shown by successful treatments of some cases of schizophrenia.

Is the existence of an 'unconscious' area of our personality implied in this scheme as the hidden storehouse of our legacy of the early past, a statement of 'fact' or a 'falsifiable hypothesis'? A brief word on this must serve as illustration for many other similar questions about psychoanalysis. Two of the most important psycho-analytic hypotheses are

1. the quality of mother-infant relationship, especially as mediated in breast feeding, creates the basic character-formation in the infant:

2. early infant and childhood experience persists as the *psychically alive but unconscious* basis of the whole personality.

Are these hypotheses testable? It has been suggested to me that what is 'unconscious' must be 'unfalsifiable in principle'. If the 'unconscious' simply remained always unconscious that would be so, but in fact it repeatedly erupts and subsides.

It is worth citing the most dramatic example of this I have witnessed. An extremely schizoid young mother who had failed in a suicide attempt, responded slowly over several years of uneventful therapy. It was clear that her mother, a grossly abnormal woman, whom I once saw, had been exceptionally cruel to her as a child, though she could give no details. She once dreamed that she had to pass a dark wood in which was a terrible witch, but she was not afraid because I was with her. Slowly she was feeling that with my protection she could face whatever was there. One night her husband rang at 2:00 a.m. and I motored to their house. She was fast asleep, sitting on the bedroom floor, writhing in pain and moaning, 'Don't, Mummy. I will be good.' I said, 'It looks as if her mother is doing something to her back. Have a look.' Her husband looked and found faint scars there, and one larger one. In the morning she remembered nothing, but went on 'acting out' in sleep the terrifying scenes of childhood, till one day her husband lost his job through a merger. They were a young couple and very anxious now over economics. Her midnight 'acting out' stopped at once, though she was quite unaware of the fact. Two weeks later he got another good job and that very night she again began to 'act out' in sleep her childhood terrors. I witnessed these several times and saw her next morning and very slowly she began to remember, little by little, what had happened in the night. Then suddenly her total amnesia for those traumatic events broke up; memories flooded back. Her mother had burned her with a red hot poker, and once with a heated flat iron which had caused a bad burn that went septic, leaving the large scar. The breakdown of her total amnesia and the security gained by reliving it all with me and her husband initiated an enormous improvement through which she was ultimately able to end her treatment.

I have had two other cases of the eruption in therapy of deeply repressed traumata with most beneficial results. In one of these cases a long period of deep depression ended with the recovery of the buried memory of the patient's mother cursing him on her death bed after he had nursed her in her terminal illness. In the case of the first patient I actually witnessed the verbal and emotional expression of her unconscious while it was totally dissociated from her conscious self, which was wrapped in a trance-like sleep: and I then saw these terrible memories slowly work through into normal memory. If anything can be absolute, that experience was for me absolute confirmation of the reality of the unconscious.

As for the first hypothesis, the relationship between breast-feeding and character-formation, Margaret Mead (1935) found excellent breast-feeding in the friendly Arapesh tribe, and drastically rejective breast-feeding in the paranoid, aggressive Mundugumor tribe.

No adequate study of so large a subject can be made in a single paper. That would take several volumes, and would have to involve very detailed study of actual case material. The biggest difficulty here is that in general it is too confidential to be published at full length, but the scientist or philosopher who wants to make a genuine critical study of psychoanalysis must be prepared to go beyond merely 'intellectual criticism' of theory. He must be prepared to collaborate with analysts in critical study, confidentially, of actual case-material, however difficult that may be. My aim here has been simply to show reason for staking a serious claim for psychoanalysis to be recognized as a growing if young science, that is seeking therapeutically usable tested knowledge of human beings as 'persons in relationships', whether ill or well.

## REFERENCES

Adrian, Lord. (1968). Quoted by Sir C. Burt in Brain and consciousness. *British Journal of Psychology* 59:56–69.

Bannister, D. (1968). The myth of physiological psychology. *Bulletin of the British Psychological Society* 21:229–231.

Bartlett, R. J. (1948). Mind. *Bulletin of the British Psychological Society* 1:14–24.

Bion, W. R. (1962). *Learning from Experience.* London: Heinemann.

Bowlby, J (1969). *Attachment and Loss.* London: Pelican.

Bronowski, J. (1967). *The Identity of Man.* London: Pelican.

Burt, Sir C. (1968). Brain and consciousness. *British Journal of Psychology* 59:56–69.

Einstein, A. (1949). *Philosopher Scientist,* ed. Schilff and Friedman. Cambridge: Cambridge University Press.

Fairbairn, W. R. D. (1952). *Psychoanalytic Studies of the Personality.* London: Kegan Paul.

Guntrip, H. (1961). *Personality, Structure and Human Interaction,* chapters 7 and 14. London: Hogarth Press.

_____ (1972). Orthodoxy and revolution in psychology. *Bulletin of the British Psychological Society* 25:275–280.

Harré R. (1972). *The Philosophies of Science.* Oxford: Oxford University Press.

Klein, M. (1957). *Envy and Gratitude.* London: Tavistock Publications.

Lakatos and Musgrave. (1970). *Criticism and the Growth of Knowledge.* Cambridge: Cambridge University Press.

Lomas, P. (1973). *True and False Experience.* London: Allen Lane.

Mayer-Gross, Slater, and Roth (1954). *Clinical Psychiatry,* 1st ed. London: Cassell.

Mead, M. (1935). *Sex and Temperament in Three Primitive Societies.* New York: Morrow.

Medawar, Sir P. (1969). *Introduction and Intuition in Scientific Thought.* London: Methuen.

Morse, S. (1972). Structure and reconstruction: a critical comparison of M. Balint and D. W. Winnicott. *International Journal of Psycho-Analysis* 53:487–500.

Popper, Sir K. (1959). *The Logic of Scientific Discovery*. London: Hutchinson.

_____ (1963). *Conjectures and Refutations*. London: Routledge and Kegan Paul.

Ryle, G. (ed.) (1956). *The Revolution in Philosophy*. London: Macmillan.

Slater, E. (1972). Is psychiatry a science? Does it want to be? *Journal of World Medicine* February, 79–81.

Winnicott, D. (1965). *The Maturational Processes and the Facilitating Environment*. London: Hogarth Press.

_____ (1971). *Playing and Reality*. London: Tavistock Publications.

# Appendix 1

# CAN THE THERAPIST LOVE THE PATIENT?

I HAVE READ PROFESSOR J. C. MCKENZIE'S article "Limitations of Psychotherapy" in the *British Weekly* of March 6, 1958. Having enjoyed and profited by Professor McKenzie's books, it is with sorrow that I have now to record my strongest possible disagreement with his conclusions in this article. I must quote at length the passage that surprises, indeed astonishes me.

> Every psychiatrist acknowledges that we have *A Need to Love and be Loved, a Need to belong, a Need for a Moral Standard, and a Need to Believe.* But these are needs which the psychotherapist, as such, cannot satisfy. All that the psychotherapist can do is to lay bare what is hindering these needs to be fulfilled. There are psychiatrists who contend that we must "love the patient better". They cannot, however, supply the love the patient needs or accept the love he wants to give. . . . They know that love is the greatest therapeutic agent; but they can neither give nor receive, as Freud knew. Hence his condemnation of Ferenczi's methods. It is here the minister can turn the patient to Christ's love which can come through the action of the Holy Spirit.
>
> So when we come to the dissipation of guilt feelings, all the psychotherapist can do is to help the patient to repress the guilt; and for a time the patient may seem "cured". Alas! the guilt returns, and we get a cyclic condition — for a period on top of the world, then down in the depths of misery. *The only thing that can dissolve guilt feelings is the forgiveness of God.*

This is a seriously erroneous description of psychotherapy. Professor McKenzie is saying in fact that love is the therapeutic factor, and the psychotherapist cannot love his patient, so that psychotherapy is not therapeutic. It is not a case of the "Limitations" of psychotherapy. In Professor McKenzie's sense it is a case of the impossibility of professional psychotherapy. Psychotherapy is mere diagnosis: only religion cures.

That is a false way of opposing, rather than relating, psychotherapy and religion. The only thing that could make a psychotherapist adopt such views is a defensive fear of the patient's need towards himself. When Dr McKenzie writes: "All that the psychotherapist can do is to lay bare what is hindering (the patient's) needs from being fulfilled", he is putting psychotherapy back into the position characteristic of the most arid days of Freudian orthodox and scientifically impersonal technique. Freud wished to make psycho-analysis a "natural science" and to create psycho-analytic treatment as a purely scientific 'method of investigation'. It is well known that Freud's experience led him, as he grew older, to become more and more pessimistic of psycho-analysis as treatment, as "curative", and to value it more and more as a method of scientific research. Psycho-analysis has, as Dr Clara Thompson states ("Psycho-Analysis: Evolution and Development"), suffered from recurring periods of therapeutic pessimism. It was not then recognised that this was due to the fact that a purely scientific investigation cures no one of anything. The method of investigation is essential to the discovery of what is buried in the patient's mental make-up that needs to be cured.

But the curious and startling thing is that this method of investigation proves to be unworkable, unusable, in any deep-going sense, if it is merely a scientific investigation. No one lays bare the most disturbed and painful areas of their inner life, which for a lifetime they have been doing their utmost to hide even from themselves, to the impersonal gaze of a mere scientific investigator. Only the psychotherapist who can approach these "wounded areas" of the human spirit with deep and loving sympathy will be allowed to see them.

I have had to treat two patients who had previously been treated by psychotherapists who were cold, detached and intellectually remote on principle, believing that to be, as Professor McKenzie apparently holds, the proper attitude for the therapist. The results were disastrous. In both cases, the patients became steadily more and more frustrated and disturbed until at length they could not stand the situation any longer and left the therapist, the one in a despairingly depressed condition and the other afraid of an accumulation of pent up frustration-rage which was becoming incredibly difficult to manage.

Freud's technique was not at first so impersonal as it later became. A number of his earlier therapeutic successes were obtained with friends whom he analysed as they went for walks. But his predilection for a strictly scientific technique, and also, as he himself said, his dislike of being directly stared at by patients for eight hours a day, that made him adopt the highly impersonal technique that became the classic psycho-analytic method. It is becoming increasingly recognised today that to make a patient lie on a couch while the analyst sits out of sight behind, saying nothing except to put in an occasional word of "interpretation", is, with the more disturbed and ill patients, especially if they suffer from hysteria, to repeat on them all the traumatic deprivations they suffered at the hands of inadequate parents in childhood. The only result is to drive the patient deeper and deeper into a regression to emotional infantilism. Dr Fairbairn of Edinburgh and Dr Frieda Fromm-Reichmann of America have expressly stated in their writings that this impersonal set-up is undesirable and many psychotherapists have abandoned it in practice.

Dr McKenzie says: "Love is the greatest therapeutic agent; but (psychotherapists) can neither give nor receive, as Freud knew. Hence his condemnation of Ferenczi's methods". But the controversy over psychotherapeutic method as between Freud and Ferenczi is not settled. Today, a new point of view is gathering force in the psycho-analytic world. The followers of Mrs Melanie Klein hold that in order to get well a patient must be able to "introject" (i.e. to possess mentally) the analyst as a "good object". Dr Fairbairn has stated that the therapeutic factor is not simply insight, but the personal relationship between the analyst and the patient. This point of view is growing rapidly.

I do not agree that the psychotherapist cannot either give to or receive love from the patient. Everything turns on the meaning of the elusive word "love". One patient of mine substituted for it the word "cherishing" to express what she felt my attitude to her was. In fact, the therapist's attitude to the patient should be a maturely parental one, otherwise that patient cannot come by those experiences by means of which alone it is possible to outgrow the disastrous effects of early bad human relationships. If it is bad human relationships that make people emotionally ill, it can only be a good human relationship that can make them well again. It is the psychotherapist's responsibility to discover what kind of good parental relationship each patient needs in order to get well. Moreover, as the patient gets better, he or she usually feels perfectly genuine emotions of gratitude and regard for the psychotherapist.

This itself represents one aspect of the cure, that the patient whose capacity to love has hitherto been choked by hates and fears is now becoming free to feel in more natural human ways. If the therapist were to reject the patient's love at that point he would inflict most serious damage to growing normality and confidence, and repeat the original trauma that caused the illness. It is simply not true to say that "the psychotherapist cannot supply the love the patient needs or accept the love he wants to give". No doubt there are psychiatrists who are unable to love their patients constructively and can only investigate them scientifically; and there are ministers who cannot love their people but can only preach at them. But no real "therapy" takes place in either case.

It is essential that, if the patient is to be "cured" of personality disturbances, the psychotherapist should be capable of giving him that kind of constructive love the components of which constitute the "vitamins of personality growth". The child grows up to be a disturbed person because he is not loved for his own sake as a person in his own right, and as an ill adult he comes to the psychotherapist convinced beforehand that this "professional man" has no real interest or concern for him. The kind of love the patient needs is the kind of love that he may well feel in due course that the psychotherapist is the first person ever to give to him. It involves taking him seriously as a person in his difficulties, respecting him as an individual in his own right even in his anxieties, treating him as someone with a right to be understood and not merely blamed, put off, pressed and moulded to suit other people's convenience, regarding him as a valuable human being with a nature of his own that needs a good human environment to grow in, showing him genuine human interest, real sympathy, believing in him so that in course of time he can become capable of believing in himself. All these are the ingredients of true parental love (agape not eros), and if the psychiatrist cannot love his patients in that way he had better give up psychotherapy.

Professor L. W. Crenstead, D. D., in his foreword to my book *Mental Pain and the Cure of Souls*, says that the "gravest issue that psychiatry has to face is the fear of patients that they are being treated as less than persons of full and individual human worth. To depersonalise them at the very heart of their being and to treat them as cases and nothing more is the final dishonour". If Professor McKenzie had said that in the hands of some "scientific psychotherapists" psychotherapy can only diagnose and not cure because there is no love there, I could agree. But his view is that the psychotherapist *cannot* give the patient the love he needs, which is a denial of everything that true psychotherapy is. I would like to refer readers to *The Leaven of Love* by Mrs Isette de Forrest for a profoundly true account of psychotherapy.

One analyst of my acquaintance, in a private communication, expressed the view that to get real therapeutic results we need to add to psycho-analysis another factor, namely, "Suffer the little children to come unto Me", for all patients are hurt children at heart. Very slowly, perhaps over a period of years, as patient and psychotherapist work together, the patient grows by little and little out of the legacy of an unhappy childhood, in and through the medium of his relationship with the therapist, until at last the mature human being can emerge into healthy and active self-expression and self-fulfilment.

When finally Dr McKenzie says about guilt feelings: "All the psychotherapist can do is to help the patient to repress the guilt", it is necessary to say plainly that this is an utter distortion of the facts. The psychotherapist is confronted with the patient's pathological guilt, a morbid factor in his personality which cripples and crushes him. The therapist seeks to bring this diseased pseudo-moral guilt into the fullest consciousness, not that the patient may seek forgiveness for it, but that he may get rid of it, grow out of it. The mental field is now clear for the development of a healthy moral sense, which will only arouse guilt that is realistic. We do no service to either psychotherapy or religion if we try to make out that psychotherapy can only diagnose and then hand the patient on to the Church that he may be directed to seek the forgiveness of God. Such an account of the situation is seriously wrong both in fact and in principle.

Sir, —I would like to thank Dr. McKenzie for the time he has devoted to such a lengthy reply to the two points I raised. No doubt this was due to his recognition of the very great importance of the whole subject of the relationship of psychotherapy to religion. His two articles raise so many and such large issues, and rightly so, that I shall not attempt to deal with them now.

I would say that I originally joined issue with Dr. McKenzie on two specific points only. They were his explicit statements:

(1) That the psychotherapist cannot give love to the patient and (2) That all that the psychotherapist can do about guilt is to help the patient to repress it. So far as I can see his first article in reply concedes my point. He writes: "What the psychotherapist can give is loving understanding! It is this which breaks down the barriers of repression and resistance". So far as I am concerned "loving understanding" *is* "love": if it is not, then the understanding is not "loving". It is, in fact, exactly the type of love that the patient has never hitherto received in adequate measure. The psychotherapist can love his patient in as fully real a way as the minister can love his people. Today that would amount to denying that the Holy Spirit can work through the psychotherapist, which I am sure Dr McKenzie does not wish to imply.

On the question of guilt feelings, I remain less satisfied with Dr. McKenzie's reply, to the effect "that the psychotherapist cannot dissolve *real* guilt". If that had been his original statement I would have seen no reason to challenge it. What I disliked was the very definite statement that the psychotherapist can only seek to *repress* guilt.

That statement ignored the difference between pathological and real guilt. Furthermore, an experienced psychotherapist does not help the patient to repress anything at all, whether pathological or real, but rather helps him to remain conscious of as much as he can of his mental life and deal with it with full awareness: only so can genuine maturing of personality occur. No doubt, there are untrained and inexperienced people practising psychotherapy, some of whom make the disastrous mistake of making light of "guilt feelings" but the shortcomings of some individual psychotherapists are not part of the limitations of psychotherapy, per se, as practised by its acknowledged authorities. I do not see why, unless it is a protest against bad psychotherapy, the point needs to be made that the psychotherapist cannot dissolve *real* guilt. I do not think any really competent psychotherapist would attempt to do what could only damage the patient's realistic moral values. The psychotherapist's whole aim is to help the patient to grow to a mature capacity for responsible and loving relationships with people.

Dr McKenzie quotes Professor Allport as saying: "Mental disease has not diminished, rather it has increased . . . statistically viewed, the success of modern psychotherapy has been up to now not merely negligible but negative".

What truth there is in this amounts to the fact that individual psychotherapy, while supremely important for the lucky few who can obtain it in adequate form, is a drop in the bucket. The Churches are as little successful as psychiatry and psychotherapy in arresting mass mental disease, in a world so disturbed that neurosis is created faster than it can be cured. Prevention is our great need.

I am sure that Dr. McKenzie joins with me in thanking you as Editor, for making possible this discussion of matters that are of ever-growing importance in our modern life.

# Appendix 2

# REPLY TO HAMMERTON[1]

$S$OME TIME AGO A TALK WAS GIVEN on the Third Programme by Dr.
Max Hammerton of Cambridge, entitled: 'Freud: The Status of an Illusion'. He
held that psychoanalysis was not a science and that Freud's work had only
entertainment value, providing the amusement of trying to psychoanalyse famous
men. Opponents of Freud often attack him with ridicule. He is a disturbing thinker
to take seriously. The very stature of Freud has been of some disadvantage to
psychoanalysis. He so dominated the scene, that it was difficult for analysts to take
his hypotheses as stimulating starting-points, and move on to newer developments.
It is no service to Freud to turn his theories into an orthodoxy, when he said to one
of his translators: 'The book will be out of date in thirty years'. In due time, quoting
Freud will be like a physicist quoting Newton, and that is how Freud would have
liked it. Yet, in truth, psychoanalysis is far more identified with Freud's early work
by those who are *outside* the psychoanalytic movement, in the general cultural field,
than by those inside it. Many literary avant-garde idealisers of sex and aggression
appeal to the Freud of 1910, and are quite unaware of the tremendous developments in psychoanalysis since Freud in the 1920s turned his attention from
'instincts' to the 'ego', thereby focussing attention on the very centre of our human
nature as 'persons'. Dr. Hammerton spoke repeatedly of 'Freudians' as if all analysts
were stuck fast in a closed body of theory.

I want to put the question 'What did Freud really do?' I ought to say that I am not
a member of the British Psychoanalytical Society, but an independent thinker, for
twenty four years research worker in long-term psychotherapy in the Leeds
University Department of Psychiatry. I was never expected to plug any particular
theory or method and have been left completely free by successive heads of
Department to use any theory or method that seemed useful. After an initial

---

1. A reply published in *The Listener* magazine, August 29, 1968, to a talk by Dr. Max
Hammerton of Cambridge, on 'Freud, the Status of an Illusion.'

academic training in philosophy and psychology, and an exploration of Freud, Jung, Adler, and other later explorers in this field, I found myself arriving at a fairly well-defined position. This was due more to the pressures of clinical work than anything else, a matter of what helped most to understand the problems of very disturbed people. I came to the conclusion that Freud's work was the most important in this field, that I rejected some of it, particularly his dual-instinct theory, but that his stress on the extreme importance of personal relations in family life for shaping either stable or very disturbed personalities in children, loomed ever larger in my work. I owe a great deal to a number of leading psychoanalysts for criticising and furthering my research, but I remain an independent thinker with no axe to grind other than my own freely developed conclusions, in attempting to assess 'What did Freud really do?'

I will give a provisional answer at once. Freud was the real creator of that whole complex of activities known as 'Psychotherapy', in every modern sense of that term. That at once raises the first big issue. Dr. Hammerton and similar critics falsify the issue by setting analytic therapy and psychiatry in opposition as rivals for the treatment of mental ill health. They say modern developments in psychiatry and biochemistry have outdated psychotherapy. Not by any means all psychiatrists take this view. It ought to be ruled out on principle, for it implies that 'persons' cannot have any true healing influence, on each other as 'persons', which simply flies in the face of all our own experience of living. That persons can have a bad, disturbing influence on each other is too obvious to be argued. A human being is a Self, a 'Person' with a subjective mental experience of life that has deep meanings, values, and purposes; and he lives this life in and through his body with all its organic processes. He must be understood from both sides of his complex nature. A purely physical disturbance can upset his state of mind. Far more frequently, emotional upsets disturb his biochemistry. The study of body and mind must be partners and allies. I have had patients who, through a long psychoanalytically directed therapy, have grown far-reaching changes of personality in the reduction of nervousness and fear, greater ease in getting on with people, increased spontaneity and enjoyment in living, who never had a single pill. But some other patients would have been unable to carry on their work, or even at times to carry on with psychotherapy, without the help of psychiatric drugs, or in a few cases, hospitalisation. I am stressing this two-sided approach.

Psychiatric treatments aim at controlling the *symptoms* of mental disturbance through the body, hoping to cut the illness short altogether. Sometimes this occurs, but very often not. When it succeeds the personality may stagnate at that point. An able graduate patient, whose job was saved in a crisis period by wise medication, said later: 'I must stop taking these pills. They have done me a very good turn, but now they are making me an artificial person. I'm more honestly me when I'm more anxious than this, and they are stopping me making use of psychotherapy.' The end result was excellent. The patient benefited from both the psychiatric and psychotherapeutic methods. If psychotherapy were *always* available, there would be far fewer re-admissions to hospital. Alas, there are few fully trained psychotherapists outside London, and in general psychotherapists are more ready to see the need for psychiatry, than many psychiatrists are to understand the value of psychotherapy. Most psychiatrists have no chance of first-hand acquaintance with expert psychotherapy. Letters come to me on average about one per fortnight, saying 'I have been in hospital several times, taken a number of different pills or had E.C.T. (electro-convulsive therapy), and been told I'm better, but I still have all my old difficulties in living. Where can I get psychotherapy to help me understand and get over my problems?' I cannot tell them where. We are told that psychoanalytic therapy is too long and expensive for all but the fortunate few. In fact, there are many cases where psychiatric treatment has gone on for years and been just as expensive in time and money, and some of these are cases where re-admissions to hospital would have been unnecessary if psychotherapy had been available. Some of my own patients would have been hospitalised without it. Trained experienced psychoanalytic therapy is so rare that there is a great deal of ignorance of what really goes on in it. It is impossible to publish detailed case histories; they are too confidential. In fact, excellent results that stand the test of time, are more frequent than is realised. Only by psychiatrists and therapists working together can such knowledge be shared. I speak out of the experience of many years of exchanging patients with a very experienced hospital Superintendent.

All I can do here is to describe what psychotherapy is. I use this term, in asking 'What did Freud really do?' because his influence has spread much farther than his own psychoanalytic movement. My view is that psychoanalysis has contributed more than any other school to psychotherapeutic research, and its effects are felt far beyond its borders. Every school of psychotherapy today owes a big debt to Freud, including all the trained social-work professions, which are increasingly given at least introductory knowledge of psychoanalytic concepts. By psychotherapy then I mean all the trained 'helping professions' but particularly those directly concerned with individual treatment, which have been influenced.

Psychotherapy belongs to and is part of a much bigger thing, *the whole field of human relationships*, including parenthood, friendship, marriage, all partnerships in human enterprise, and all the social and 'helping' professions. To say that psychotherapy is not science is as irrelevant as to say that parenthood is not science. In fact parenthood and psychotherapy are the two most closely related parts of this field of human relationships. What the therapist is having to do is in part what the patient's parents were too disturbed to be able to for him at first, that is give him a secure personal relationship that both supports him and leaves him free to develop his own individuality. Thus the therapist must be able to accept, understand and help the patient, to see through and grow out of the insecurities, suspicions, incapacity to trust, resentments, and hates, morbid guilts, and sheer lack of inner freedom due to the deep fears of life that inhibit all spontaneous growth of personality. Naturally, in this work we sift our experience and form general concepts to explain better what 'human nature' is. Dr. Winnicott says: 'A psychoanalyst cannot be original, for what he writes today he learned from a patient yesterday'. A body of theory has grown which we call psychodynamic science, entirely different from physical science. When critics say psychoanalysis is not science, they mean it is not 'physical science'. That is obvious but, as a criticism, irrelevant. I call to witness, not a psychoanalyst but a physical scientist, who has thought deeply about the 'wholeness' of human living. Dr. Bronowski, in *The Identity of Man*, says that man has a dual nature, he is both a machine and a Self, and there are two kinds of knowledge, knowledge of the machine and knowledge of the Self. The example he selects for expression of knowledge of the Self is literature. He regards physical science as knowledge of the machine, which we only have from the 'outside'. Literature gives us knowledge which we can only have from the 'inside'. Actually the only Self we know directly is our own Self. We know our own experience 'on the inside', but we communicate with one another on the basis of this self-knowledge. By identification we share in and know each other's experience. This is the kind of 'knowledge' used in psychoanalytic therapy. The therapist 'lives it', if he cannot always turn it into literature. If anyone doubts this, he should get access to the *British Journal of Medical Psychology*, June 1968, and read 'Psychotherapy with the More Disturbed Patient' by Yvonne Blake of South Africa. She records part of her first session with an aggressive psychopath who had been before the Courts more than once for assaulting girls. Her intuition and personal courage in dealing directly with this extremely difficult man, and the way in which she so soon disarmed his aggression and won his trust, makes as absorbing reading as any Shakespeare drama. Moreover, seven years of such therapy enabled this very ill man to live through his 'fear of madness', accept a period of extreme 'dependency'; discard his completely unscrupulous behaviour and end up by running a useful and successful business of his own. Dr. Hammerton might note that this kind of psychotherapy is no 'entertainment' for either patient or therapist. She acknowledges her debt to Dr. Winnicott, a psychoanalyst. Psychoanalytic or psychotherapeutic theory must constantly develop under pressure of clinical experience, if our understanding of human beings as 'persons' is to grow. This knowledge is generalised and presented abstractly in concepts and hypotheses quite unlike those of physical science. This 'psychodynamic science' cannot make a good therapist, any more than a good parent or friend, but it can guide the understanding of those who already have the capacity to make good human relationships, to be therapeutic. Psychoanalysts undergo a training analysis, but not to learn theory which they can get from textbooks. They undergo analysis because we only have the right to offer help by deep emotional exploration of anyone's personal problems, if we have already faced our own. A psychotherapist is not a doctor carrying out an impersonal scientific treatment, but an experienced person offering a disturbed human being a certain kind of human relationship. He must be the kind of person with whom this particular undermined and hurt individual can win his way back out of the fear, hate, guilt and despair, to a capacity to trust and relate to people. The real qualification for the therapist is to be the kind of person, partly by natural temperament, partly by having this training which consists in being helped by just such an experienced therapeutic person, to face and resolve in himself just the kind of problems he will find his patients struggling with.

Modern psychotherapy, of which Freud and the psychoanalytic movement was the true founder, treats, not the symptom nor the illness but the person who has it. When it is not primarily an organic but a personality disturbance, if we can help that person to feel secure and real in personal relationships, the illness and the symptoms fade out. Whether we can do this depends partly on the patient's present day environment, partly on how deep-seated the disturbance is, but mainly on how genuine our care for the patient is, and whether our own experience is adequate, but there are many gratifying successes. That for most people psychotherapy is unavailable, is a reproach against us all. We must make it available. It is not relevant that psychotherapy does not help everybody. No treatment is equally successful in all cases. Patient and treatment must be carefully matched. What is relevant is that very many able and intelligent people know well what is the real cause of their disturbed personality, and do not want its symptoms drugged into quiescence by indefinite dependence on tranquillisers. They want to get to the bottom of their problems and are asking for psychotherapy. The demand is far more widespread than I have seen admitted. Psychotherapy must become a 'Speciality' in its own right. Freud, its true founder, did not want to see it confined to any one profession, medical or otherwise, or to see it treated as an appendix to textbooks on psychiatry. The expertise built up in the psychoanalytic movement must become available to training centres in all parts of the country, where all concerned with helping human beings in their personal lives can learn from one another. Dr. Balint's seminars for G.P.s at the Tavistock Clinic are a fine example of how this knowledge can be spread. Dr. Sutherland, for 30 years Director of the Tavistock Clinic, writes in *The British Journal of Medical Psychiatry*, about 'The Consultant Psychotherapist in the National Health Service'. In fact there are very few of them. He calls for Psychotherapeutic Centres where 'All the professional sources of help must *share the framework* on which their therapeutic work is based . . . and formulate and communicate their working hypotheses in terms of the data of human relationships'. He adds:

> The stimulus which psychoanalysis gave to the social sciences, has led
> to an enormous amount of research into the social development of the

child, and the ways in which adult behaviour is governed by social
relationships. . . . The importance of the study of the self and its
identity. . . . its intimate relatedness to social transactions . . . makes it
increasingly likely that detailed psychoanalytic work with individuals
will have to be matched with equally intensive work into those social
transactions that are essential to being a person. . . . We must marry
psychodynamic knowledge of the inner world with a sociological
sensitivity to the outer.

The answer, therefore, to the question 'What did Freud really do?' is that he
opened our eyes to what we prefer to be blind to. He was the effective starting-point
of this entire, far-flung, steadily expanding development of the many-sided problem
of understanding and helping the very many people, young and old, who need to
be understood and stood by when life overwhelms them. Once we have understood
Freud, we cannot just criticise and blame them, if we are to retain our self-respect.
The foundations of security and self-confidence are laid in childhood and infancy.
It is now known that a baby's heart beats faster in response to noise, light and
movement, even before birth. So early do we begin to react to, and can be disturbed
by, our environment. Such influences are at their maximum in the early impressionable years. If things go wrong then, a child can grow into an adult who is like
a superstructure of a house with no foundations. A young married man said to me:
'I need the support of someone who cares for me, to enable me to feel real. By
myself, I can't feel substantial, can't feel I am anybody. With someone, I don't worry
about my existence. Alone I become afraid I'll die. I feel I've got a hollow centre to
my personality. I lack self-reliance because I feel empty.' He was saying in adult
terms what a little girl said simply: 'What's the use of being me, if nobody cares?'
The secret tragedy of those who struggle on day by day with this inner feeling of
deep mental inadequacy, inability to cope with life, is often expressed in dreams of
struggling in a flood tide and only just managing to keep one's head above water.
One patient, after a period of expressing bitter hates and resentments, began to
experience a mounting sense of fear and said: 'I'd go under, or have to go to
hospital, but for you.' Not till we recognise that hostile and destructive behaviour
is a defence against inner fears, will we deal constructively with the problem of
aggression.
        Such mental sufferers do not necessarily lack ability, experience or physical
health. People can have all these and still feel this basic nonentity in their
personality. They may or may not produce physical symptoms of tension. Their
real symptom is that they feel mentally unable to relate vitally to their environment
and feel alive, interested and adequate. They are driven to shrink into themselves
from a world that seems hostile, because they feel they cannot cope with it. They
have all they need for coping, except a sense of reality and confidence in them-

selves. This is the fundamental problem, hidden behind all sorts of defences and symptoms. Recently a woman said to me, 'I've come out of hospital. I'm told "All the possible tests have been taken, the results are all negative. There is nothing at all wrong with you". But I feel in despair. I'm just no good as a wife or mother.' To such, the psychotherapist has to give a kind of relationship the patient can use to discover his own proper selfhood. Let us face it. This is far harder than prescribing pills.

The problem of psychotherapy is not that it is not scientific; it has its own kind of science. The difficulty is that we ourselves may not be equal to its demands. We may not have the depth of understanding, sympathy, tolerance, and capacity to take the strain, that is required to help a suffering human being to drop his defences and lay bare his crippling fears, in the confidence that we can understand and stand by him till he has grown out of them. But the therapist grows with his patients. If he did not, I do not think we could do this work. Yet in the end it is the most rewarding experience of all. It has always played a part in life. It has always been present in religion. The old-fashioned family doctor was a psychotherapist without being called one. No advances in purely physical medical science can solve the problems of the 'person' as distinct from the 'organism'. But we owe it above all to Freud that this most important of all healing arts, the healing of 'personal Self', has become a field of systematic research, yielding results capable of being applied in practice by those who are sufficiently motivated to tackle human problems on this basic level. The name of Freud will certainly stand permanently among the great ones in the history of discovery.

# Appendix 3

# RESPONSE TO EYSENCK

$P$SYCHOANALYSTS DO NOT SPEND TIME attacking behaviour therapy. Charles Rycroft (a psychoanalyst) reviewing one of H. J. Eysenck's books gave a very favourable account of his experimental work but castigated him for out of date ideas of analysis. Many behaviourists, and Eysenck in particular, do not reciprocate this attitude. He is for "Behaviour therapy versus psychotherapy" (the title of this article last week). Behaviour therapy, he writes is an "alternative to psycho-analysis and psychotherapy," and is "much more effective." Again, "behaviour therapy not only has been shown to work but is the *only* method of therapy for which this can be claimed."

Attacking psychotherapy is an obsession with Eysenck—a "behaviour pattern" which might do with reconditioning. He writes: "Research psychologists and clinical psychiatrists do not necessarily share the same aims and concerns." But they can respect each other.

I was genuinely interested in Eysenck's account of Wolpe's "gradual desensitisation" treatment of phobias. I do not accept Wolpe's own naively over-simplified definition of neurosis: "Most neuroses are essentially persistent habits of reacting with anxiety to stimulus situations that objectively are not dangerous." His illustration is that a child who burns his hand on the big black stove in the kitchen, then develops a fear of a big black box in the bedroom, and this reappears in later life as a neurotic phobia. If only it were so simple. That is an ideal case for desensitisation therapy, and I do not doubt such cases can be found. But Eysenck agrees that, "the value of desensitisation was found to be inversely proportional to the amount of severe free floating anxiety." In over 30 years, I have found that most of the cases referred to me revealed increasingly severe anxiety, the more one knew about them; and it was not "free floating" but directly related to tragic family histories often over several generations.

There is a place for behaviour therapy. Habit plays an enormous part in life as the great time saver. And while there are useful healthy habits, or behaviour patterns, so there are maladaptive, pathological patterns which become symptoms preventing the personality from functioning freely. Some bad patterns originate accidentally or incidentally, but I have abundant evidence that they can originate in the profoundly disturbed history of a lifetime. Sometimes if an emotional problem is resolved, a symptomatic habit that it created fades out. I have seen transient phobias come and go (fears of snakes, spiders, heights, open or closed spaces) as complex anxieties were unravelled. But there are, I doubt not, cases where the originating emotional causes die down under psychotherapy, and the symptom persists by force of habit. Dr. J. Sandler (editor of the *International Journal of Psycho-Analysis*) accepts behaviour therapy for such symptoms. In such a case I would have no hesitation about "the gradual introduction of the feared object while the patient is in a state of relaxation." But would one dare risk "actually placing the subject in the situation" which evokes anxiety, if it is suicidal anxiety which is usually evoked by mental isolation? In such a case only a security-giving personal relationship has any value. This is the reason for the failure of "desensitisation" with severe agoraphobics, who, like schizoid personalities, have at heart a core of utter depersonalisation, terror of which is the deepest and hardest problem for every kind of therapy.

Critics of psychoanalysis and psychotherapy rarely shows signs of knowing anything about psychoanalysis later than the Freud of about 1910–1915. They betray little sign of understanding the enormous change from basic emphasis on instincts to that on personal relationships, from emphasis on the later Oedipal (or family group) rivalries and jealousies to the early fundamental mother-infant relation where the foundations of a secure stable personality are, or are not, laid. They seem to know little of Balint, Fairbairn, Bowlby, Winnicott. Quoting Freud in psychoanalysis is beginning now to become rather like quoting Newton in physics.

In his recent book, *Attachment and Loss* (Hogarth) John Bowlby writes: "What is believed to be essential for mental health is that the infant and young child should experience a warm, intimate and continuous relationship with his mother, in which both find satisfaction and enjoyment . . . The young child's hunger for his mother's love and presence is as great as his hunger for food, and in consequence her absence inevitably generates a powerful sense of loss and anger." I would add fear.

Extensive observation of children, by Bowlby and James Robertson, before, during and after separation from mother (as in hospital), revealed that on return they showed, "on the one hand an intense clinging to mother which can continue for weeks, months or years, and on the other a rejection of mother as a love-object, which may be temporary or permanent (i.e. detachment). These responses and processes are the very same as are known to be active in older individuals who are still disturbed by separations suffered in early life." Moreover physical separation is not the only separation. Parents can be physically present and yet emotionally either absent or actively hostile. Most people who seek psychotherapy were rejected or hated by their parents, often in extremely subtle ways, and their entire personality undermined in growth. These are the preoccupations of present-day psychoanalytic therapy.

An eminent analyst said to me recently: "Freud was interested in symptoms. We have become interested in persons." Eysenck is still interested in symptoms not whole persons. Indeed for his theory "the self" does not exist. He has told us, "There is nothing behind the symptoms. The symptoms are the neurosis."

Eysenck writes: "For Freud and his followers even mild errors and minor misspellings were evidence of deep-seated complexes, and snake phobias in particular were explained along symbolic lines which linked them securely with his theoretic system." Evidently Eysenck sees the snake as the grand Freudian sex symbol and if only behaviour therapy can dissipate a snake phobia and show it to be accidental and having no sex significance, then the entire structure of psychoanalysis collapses. In over 30 years I have never met a full-blown snake phobia. I have known patients produce transient ones, and also have dreams about snakes, which sometimes did seem to have a sexual significance, but not always. Sex is a part of life and people do dream about it, but as Ronald Fairbairn wrote in *Psycho-Analytical Studies of the Personality:* "Sex is simply one area of biological functioning in which personality problems are played out."

Problems of the philosophy of science are raised by Eysenck and other behaviourists when they try to claim that they alone are scientific psychologists. In an international conference of neurophysiologists in 1966 Lord Adrian, in a paper on consciousness, said: "In our 'public' behaviour there is little or nothing which cannot be brought within the framework of physical science; and to this extent the behaviourist's hypothesis seems adequate. Yet for many of us there is still one thing which seems to lie outside this tidy and familiar framework—the 'I' who does the perceiving, thinking and acting."

The "I" is far more in evidence in our "public" behaviour than Lord Adrian recognised, and the psychoanalytic therapist is compelled to be directly concerned with the patient's "I" which lies at the heart of his "behaviour." It is precisely his subjective experience of himself, at worst his deep doubts as to whether he is a real "self" or just a nonentity, that for him is his illness. Dr. J. Bronowski in *The Identity of Man* (Pelican) holds that man is both a machine (a biochemical organism) and a self, and that there are two qualitatively different kinds of knowledge, knowledge of the behaviour of the machine, any machine, from the outside, which is physical science; and knowledge of the self from the inside, which he finds expressed in literature (and also in dreams). It is this subjective knowledge of the self that the new science of psychodynamics explores.

Early this century, following Pavlov's conditioned reflex concept, J. B. Watson developed behaviourism in America, leaving, according to Pillsbury in his *History of Psychology*, "nothing of psychology but conditioned reflexes and tongue movements. He denied that consciousness had any existence at all." Today the American Skinner disallows the use of psychological terms, such as feeling, intending, purposing, desiring, aggression, guilt; all these must be translated into "physical thing language," description of "patterns of behaviour." There can be no objection to the study of behaviour as such, but there is every objection to the view that this alone covers the entire truth about the whole reality of man.

I shall go on studying man's subjective experience of himself in both healthy and suffering relations with his fellows, because this psychic experience is actually there to be studied, and I see results not obtained by behaviour theory, but purely by what has gone on in mutual personal interchange.

Proof? A young mother with a bed-wetting child and no symptoms but coldness and apathy towards her family. She had a violent mother and quarrelling parents, and suddenly began to act out in sleep terrible scenes of her mother burning her on the back and her self screaming. Her husband discovered the scars, would ring me in the night, and I witnessed several scenes of which she remembered nothing next day. Suddenly he lost his job and for two anxious weeks the nightmares stopped. Then he got a good job and the acting out began again. Slowly she remembered it in the morning and discussed it in sessions, and began to thaw out emotionally. Afterwards she told me: "My husband says I don't freeze him off now, and my little girl has stopped bed-wetting." Another man was referred to me for serious depression, but he also had had for years severe attacks of sinusitis which always required surgical intervention. He unfolded a tragic story of his relationship with his mother but always there was total amnesia for the day of her death. Then came another severe sinusitis, and next day he rushed into my room saying: "It's come back to me. I woke in the night and I could see my mother on her death bed. She died cursing me, when I was the only one who looked after her. As it came back to me, too horrible to be remembered, my sinuses opened, the pus poured out and for the first time I have got rid of it without the doctor." Both sinusitis and depression have gone.

Behaviour is there to be studied and many useful things can be found out by its scientific experimental investigation, but the tide has begun to turn against its attempted take-over bid for all psychology. In the *Bulletin of the British Psychological Society* (no. 73, 1968) D. Bannister has written:

> Psychological and physiological concepts stem from such different semantic networks that they cannot be meaningfully related. Ryle's criticism of the "ghost in the machine" concept did not recognise the usefulness of this concept in drawing attention to the differences between the language in which we discuss the "ghost" and the unrelated

language in which we discuss the "machine." The chances of developing a physiological psychology are about as good (or as bad) as of developing a chemical sociology or a biological astronomy.

Eysenck says that "impersonal methods (computer) work as well as personal methods." But he cites Truax and Carkhuff who

> describe the personality qualities and "therapy styles" of the two contrasted groups of therapists. They find empathy, warmth, and genuineness characteristic of successful therapists; absence of these qualities, and in particular presence of their opposites, is found in therapists who actually harm their patients. . . . Cold, "interpretive" and purist behaviour on the part of the therapist . . . prevents relaxation and increases anxiety.

So "impersonal methods (computer)" are not therapeutic after all. Eysenck perversely writes: "It is in line with my view of successful psychotherapy as embodying behaviourist principles; empathy, warmth and genuineness generate an easy relaxed atmosphere in which to develop the hierarchies which carry so much of the burden of successful therapy."

This is disguised capitulation. Plainly, only in a genuine personally therapeutic relationship does real personality growth out of anxiety take place—the *quality* of the person of the therapist is always more important than his technique.

One last word. The "scientific" status of psychoanalysis is usually criticised on the ground that analysts do not study cases against "control cases," and do not frame hypotheses that enable "predictions" to be made. Since no two human beings are ever as exactly alike as two bits of the same chemical, only roughly similar "controls" can be found and no absolute conclusions can be drawn, though useful attempts have been made as by Bowlby here and Carl Rogers in America. But it would be utterly impossible to find any true "control case" for the stark uniqueness of the two cases I have cited here. As to "prediction," Bronowski, a biologist, has I hope settled that question by pointing out that prediction is impossible for a "self," for if it were predictable it would be a machine and not a self. What is required of a self is not predictability but consistency.

# CREDITS

THE AUTHOR GRATEFULLY ACKNOWLEDGES the cooperation of the following professional bodies in releasing the relevant material for publication in this volume:

*British Journal of Medical Psychology:* Chapter 1: (originally entitled "A Study of Fairbairn's Schizoid Reactions") 1952, vol. 25, pp. 86–103; Chapter 2: (originally entitled "The Therapeutic Factor in Psychotherapy") 1953, vol. 26, pp. 115–132; Chapter 3: (originally entitled "Recent Developments in Psychoanalytical Theory") 1956, vol. 29, pp. 82–99; Chapter 5: (originally entitled "Ego-Weakness and the Hard Core of the Problem of Psychotherapy") 1960, vol. 33, pp. 163–184; Chapter 6: (originally entitled "The Schizoid Problem, Regression, and the Struggle to Preserve an Ego") 1961, vol. 34, pp. 223–244; Chapter 8: (originally entitled "The Schizoid Compromise and Psychotherapeutic Stalemate") 1962, vol. 35, pp. 273–287; Chapter 9: (originally entitled "Psychodynamic Theory and the Problem of Psychotherapy") 1963, vol. 36, pp. 161–172; Chapter 11: (originally entitled "Religion in Relation to Personal Integration") 1969, vol. 42, pp. 323–333; Chapter 12: (originally entitled "The Ego Psychology of Freud and Adler Re-examined in the 1970s") 1971, vol. 44, pp. 305–318; Chapter 17: (originally entitled "Psychoanalysis and Some Scientific and Philosophical Critics") 1978, vol. 51, pp. 207–224.

*Leeds University Medical Journal:* Chapter 4: (originally entitled "Centenary Reflections on the Work of Freud") 1956, vol. 5, pp. 162–166.

The Institute of Psycho-Analysis: *International Journal of Psycho-Analysis:* Chapter 7: (originally entitled "The Manic-Depressive Problem in the Light of the Schizoid Process") 1962, vol. 43, pp. 98–112; Chapter 10: (originally entitled "The Concept of Psychodynamic Science") 1967, vol. 48, pp. 32–43.

*International Review of Psycho-Analysis:* Chapter 16: 1975, vol. 2, pp. 145–156.

*Bulletin of the British Psychological Society:* Chapter 13: (originally entitled "Orthodoxy and Revolution in Psychology") 1972, vol. 25, pp. 275–280.

*Contemporary Psychoanalysis:* Chapter 14: (originally entitled "Sigmund Freud and Bertrand Russell") 1973, vol. 9(3), pp. 263–281.

*Journal of the American Academy of Psychoanalysis:* Chapter 15: (originally entitled "Science, Psychodynamic Reality and Autistic Thinking") 1973, vol. 1(1), pp. 3–22 (with permission of The Guilford Press).

The author is particularly grateful to Gwen Greenald and Bertha Guntrip, the daughter and widow of Harry Guntrip, for their kind permission to reprint material from his writings.

# INDEX